MW00815202

Global Perspectives on the Bible

Editors

Mark Roncace
Wingate University

Joseph Weaver
Wingate University

PEARSON

Boston Columbus Indianapolis New York San Francisco Upper Saddle River
Amsterdam Cape Town Dubai London Madrid Milan Munich Paris Montréal Toronto
Delhi Mexico City São Paulo Sydney Hong Kong Seoul Singapore Taipei Tokyo

Editorial Director: Craig Campanella
Editor in Chief: Ashley Dodge
Publisher: Nancy Roberts
Editorial Assistant: Molly White
Executive Marketing Manager: Kelly May
Marketing Coordinator: Jessica Warren
Marketing Assistant: Paige Patunas
Digital Media Editor: Tom Scalzo
Production Manager: Meghan DeMaio
Creative Director: Jayne Conte
Cover designer: Suzanne Behnke
Cover Image: Shutterstock, Inc.
Full-Service Project Management and Composition: Integra Software Services
Printer/Binder/Cover Printer: R.R. Donnelley & Sons

Library of Congress Cataloging-in-Publication Data
Global perspectives on the Bible / Mark Roncace, Wingate University, Joseph Weaver, Wingate University. —1 [edition].
pages cm
ISBN-13: 978-0-205-86538-3
ISBN-10: 0-205-86538-0
1. Bible—Criticism, interpretation, etc. I. Roncace, Mark, editor of compilation.
BS511.3.G56 2013
220.6—dc23

2012045531

Library of Congress Control Number: 2013930151

15 2020

PEARSON

ISBN 13: 978-0-205-86538-3
ISBN 10: 0-205-86538-0

GLOBAL PERSPECTIVES ON THE BIBLE

BRIEF CONTENTS

CONTENTS

PREFACE

This book is a lot like the Bible itself in that it is a diverse collection of writings emanating from a variety of geographic, social, cultural, political, economic, and religious contexts. But wait—that first sentence has already indicated a great deal about us (the editors) and about our views of the Bible. Maybe we've already revealed more about us—our background, education, life experiences, and so on—than about the Bible itself. To us, the Bible is indeed an eclectic anthology, much like this book. However, if someone else were to have written that first sentence, they might have started by introducing the Bible as the infallible Word of God, a book that provides moral and ethical guidelines for everyday life and God's plan of salvation. Another person might have opened with the claim that the Bible is one of the most toxic texts ever produced and that its continuing influence in our world is one of the great mysteries and tragedies of our day. Incidentally, neither of these two potential perspectives is incompatible with our statement that the Bible is an eclectic anthology.

The point is this: It's all about perspective. People are different. They approach the Bible with their own various ideas, beliefs, and assumptions, which means there are a myriad of possible ways to write that first sentence. Nobody can say anything without saying something about themselves.

But you may have already known that. Most people living in our postmodern world—or whatever we are supposed to call it now (that's also a matter of perspective)—realize that there is no neutral, objective perspective from which to assess things, no position that is unencumbered by a specific life setting. Everyone comes from somewhere. Everyone is born in a certain time and place to certain parents and has had certain experiences that shape how we see the world. All those "certainties," to which many more could be added, make up who you are; they define your specific context and perspective. They also mean that you can be certain that your interpretation of a given biblical text is not the only way that it can be interpreted. While the idea of varied perspectives is hardly new, you may not be aware of the extent and nature of some of those different readings. Hence this book.

FORMAT OF THE BOOK

Herein we have gathered four essays around 40 biblical texts. Our intention is for you to read the given portion of the Bible and then to consider what four people from various contexts and backgrounds have written about it. In doing so, you will see the biblical text in a new light; you will learn something about the various interpreters and their particular location; and you will discover something about yourself. Put differently, when we encounter views that are different from our own, we have the wonderfully enriching experience of learning about (1) the Bible and (2) other interpreters and the places from which they come, which in turn (3) helps us see our own lives and views in a new way. We are thus engaging the Bible, each other, and ourselves. It's a dynamic, interactive triangle.

But all three corners of the triangle must be present. The importance of your corner bears emphasizing: You must read the Bible for yourself. This is absolutely indispensible. You must read carefully and develop your own insights and analyses. This will not only help you "hear" the biblical voice (filtered through your own context, of course), but it will also enable you to appreciate the four different perspectives. We instructed the authors of the essays not to summarize the biblical passage; there is no sense in using valuable space on something that you can do for yourself. So, you must uphold your end of the deal: You must read the Bible! Yes, you are reading a translation of the Bible and a translation is already an interpretation; but, still, it's crucial that you experience the text on your own.

To encourage you to do this, we have not included any of our own introductory material to each biblical passage, as it would inevitably reflect our own perspective, which would defeat the book's purpose of including as many different points of view as possible. Furthermore, you should read the essays with a Bible in hand; many times the authors include only the biblical reference (not the full quotation), which you would do well to look up in order to help you interact thoughtfully with the essay.

To facilitate further your engagement with all three corners of the triangle, we have included four questions at the end of each set of essays. Use the questions to prompt your critical interaction with the various essays. If the question could occasionally be answered "yes" or "no," don't simply leave it at that. Assume that "Why or why not?" or "Explain your answer" follows—we just thought it unnecessary to write it out for you. Yes, our questions inevitably reveal our own interests and ideas, so please feel free to add your own questions and to question our questions. In fact, if you don't, you probably aren't thinking hard enough.

There are a mere 160 essays in this book; this, needless to say, is a pittance of the possible number. A book titled *Global Perspectives on the Bible* should not be a book at all, but rather a multivolume encyclopedia. But if that were the case, you would have had a much harder time buying it and carrying it around—or at least it would be much more arduous to use. Think for a moment about how this book barely scratches the proverbial surface of global perspectives on the Bible. If there are approximately 7 billion people in the world and if only 1 in every 1,000 has something to say about the Bible, then our 125 authors represent only about 0.000017 percent of perspectives on the Bible. We make this point—odd as it may seem—because we hope this collection of essays encourages you to seek out many more interpretations of the Bible, whether they be from scholarly books and commentaries or friends and family over lunch. These essays are intended to start conversations, not end them. It's a big world, and this book is terribly small. We are hoping you will create the rest of the encyclopedia.

We have done our best to assemble a wide range of views. Nevertheless, the book should probably be titled *Global* Perspectives* on the Bible**. With the first asterisk we call attention to the fact that as English speakers we could only accept essays written in English. We also solicited submissions via e-mail. As such, by requiring contributors to write in our native language and to have Internet access, we have by necessity precluded a majority of the world's population. Furthermore, we live and work in the United States. Most of our personal and professional connections are here; therefore, there are far more contributors from the United States than any other single country. Because of this, we feel as though we should iterate that we mean "global" in more than simply the geographic sense. There is religious, ethnic, ideological, political, and socioeconomic diversity in the essays, and those elements, of course, are not bound by particular geographic location. We also assembled contributors from various walks of life; this book is much more "global" than a typical collection of professional academic papers.

The second asterisk shows that, while limiting our fingerprints as much as possible, the essays were proofread and minimally edited. We made the decision to standardize spelling and punctuation, and even to capitalize the word "Bible." Beyond that, we did little else. We did not standardize, for example, the style of referring to eras (B.C.E., C.E., B.C., A.D.); we did not change inclusive or non inclusive language or capitalization for pronouns referring to deity. The third asterisk denotes that there are a variety of Bibles featuring different numbers and arrangements of books. We decided to follow the order of the Hebrew Bible (rather than the Christian Old Testament) and not to include any deuterocanonical or apocryphal books. Furthermore, although we did not begin with a prescribed list of 40 biblical texts for which to solicit essays, we did, of course, ultimately determine which texts the book would address.

Let's mention one more asterisk-worthy matter. You will notice that each set of essays opens with a page featuring a map locating each of the four authors in that set. But where on the map should we put each author's dot? Where the author was born? Where they have spent most of their life? Where they went to school? Where they were when they wrote the essay? Where they reside now? The place about which they write? It's not that easy. We live in a transient world. We have, somewhat arbitrarily, decided to put the dot in the place, or places, about which they are writing. Or if geographic location or context is not central to their essay, then the dot is located in the place of their primary current residence. Hence all the dots should have an asterisk to that effect too.

In short, this is only one of many possible ways to assemble a book called *Global Perspectives on the Bible*. Despite its limitations and the inherent difficulty of producing a book of this nature, we are confident that you will find these perspectives to be enlightening and engaging.

There are many additional introductory and hermeneutical issues that we could explore at the outset, but we won't. So let us limit ourselves to two final thoughts. First, the Bible is the sacred literature of the Jewish and Christian traditions, but the influence and impact of the Bible have extended beyond those two religions. People who are not Christian or Jewish read the Bible. In our effort to offer as many global perspectives as possible, we have included views by those who do not treat the Bible as Scripture. We fully understand that some people with a faith commitment to the text may feel that those outside the tradition do not have anything to offer. We respectfully disagree, and both of us—for the record—are in the Christian tradition. Our world is too big and complex to ignore thoughtful and intelligent readers simply because they approach the text without a set of traditional religious lenses—or because they come from a tradition other than Judaism or Christianity. We sincerely appreciate all of the authors of these essays for allowing their work to be published in a book that includes approaches with which they may strongly disagree.

Second, if the essays are eclectic, then so too are the biblical texts that they interpret. You will notice that some sets of four essays deal with only one chapter from the Bible (Genesis 22, Acts 2), some with part of a book (Genesis 37–50, Exodus 1–15), others with a whole book (Ruth, Revelation), and still others with types of stories (Parables of Jesus). Much of this has to do with the nature of the Bible—it's not a tidy collection, and some parts have garnered more attention than others. As a result, sometimes the essays in a chapter are in direct dialogue over the same specific text or topic, while other times they address different portions of the passage. Hopefully, every set of essays will draw you into the discussion.

The Bible has a sort of "unevenness" to it, and so do the various sets of essays that follow, which in turn reflects the complex nature of the world in which we live. And thus, we end this short Introduction where it began: If the perspectives herein feel somewhat scattered—all over the place—then we say, "Yes, exactly, and so is both our global world and the Bible." Hence a book with our title will inevitably be a bit messy. And yes, this view again reflects our particular perspective as white, Western-educated, middle-class, married men in our thirties in the Christian tradition. From where we stand, the following essays offer fresh, compelling readings of the Bible from a variety of perspectives. Tell us what you think from where you stand.

STUDENT AND TEACHER RESOURCES

MySearchLab with eText

A passcode-protected website that provides engaging experiences that personalize learning, MySearchLab contains an eText that is just like the printed text. Students can highlight and add notes to the eText online or download it to an iPad. MySearchLab also provides a wide range of writing, grammar, and research tools plus access to a variety of academic journals, census data, Associated Press news feeds, and discipline-specific readings to help hone writing and research skills.

Instructor's Resource Manual and Test Bank (0-205-86540-2)

For each chapter in the text, this valuable resource provides a chapter outline, preview questions, lecture topics, research topics, and questions for classroom discussion. In addition, test questions in short essay formats are available for each chapter.

MyTest (0-205-86539-9)

This computerized software allows instructors to create their own personalized exams, to edit any or all of the existing test questions, and to add new questions. Other special features of this program include the random generation of test questions, the creation of alternative versions of the same test, scrambling question sequences, and test previews before printing.

ACKNOWLEDGMENTS

As the editors, not the authors, of this book, the list of people we gratefully acknowledge can be found in the Table of Contents. Indeed, the 125 contributors deserve more thanks than we can offer. Their timely and insightful work made this project a reality. We offer our sincerest gratitude to each and every one of them.

We also express appreciation to our wonderful colleagues at Wingate University for designing and implementing a new core curriculum, which was the impetus for this textbook. Without their vision and support, this book never would have happened. We are so grateful to the reviewers who took the time to assess this text prior to its publication: Wayne Brouwer, Hope College; Steven Godby, Broward College-South Campus; Warren Johnson, East Texas Baptist University; and Jeff Tillman, Wayland Baptist University. We also thank Maggie Barbieri for expert editorial guidance and Nancy Roberts for her willingness to take on such an unwieldy project.

Mark Roncace

Joseph Weaver

Global Perspectives on the Bible

CHAPTER 1

GENESIS 1–3 (PART I)

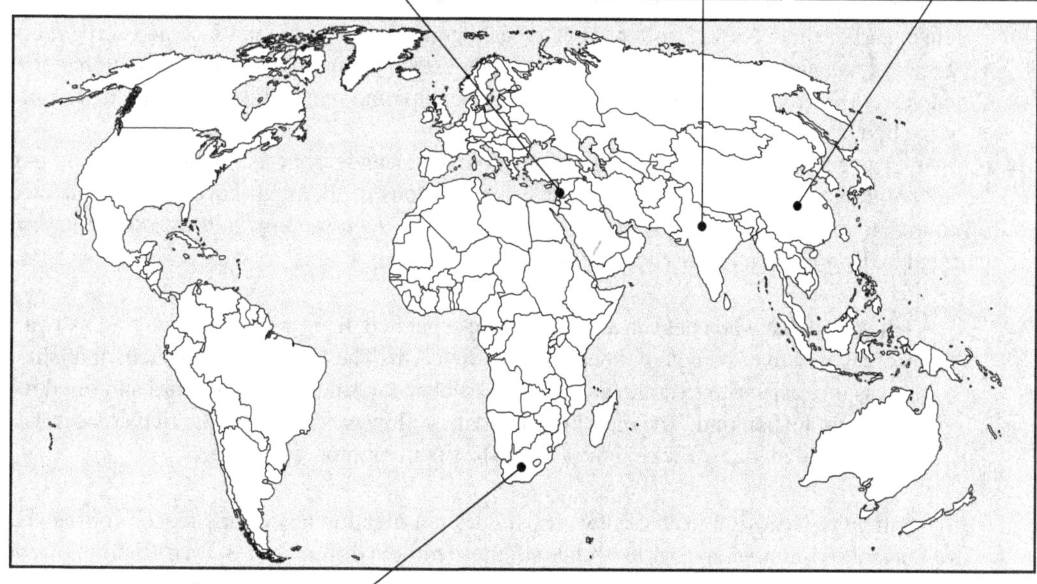
Meir Bar-Ilan outlines six differences between the two creation stories in Genesis, beyond the ones that are typically noted.
M. Aravind Jeyakumar compares the interpretation of the Hindu *Purusa-Sukta* creation accounts with traditional readings of the biblical text.
Sonia Kwok Wong compares the biblical text to Chinese creation myths, with attention to how one accounts for the similarities found in various creation myths.
David T. Williams explains the challenges of reading the biblical creation stories in African cultures and the greater appreciation of human community that it brings.

READINGS

A Comparison of Chinese Creation Myths and Biblical Texts
Sonia Kwok Wong

The Hindu *Purusa-Sukta* Compared to Biblical Texts
M. Aravind Jeyakumar

The Concept of Human Community in African Creation Stories
David T. Williams

Six Differences between Two Creation Stories in Genesis
Meir Bar-Ilan

A Comparison of Chinese Creation Myths and Biblical Texts

Sonia Kwok Wong (China)

Creation is a common theme in mythologies worldwide. In China alone, there are six separate creation myths. In spite of geographical distance and cultural divergence of the countries in which they are attested, creation myths display striking resemblances. As a Chinese biblical scholar, I am intrigued by the similarities that I find between the biblical and the Chinese creation myths. In this essay, I will compare one of the earliest versions of the Nüwa creation myth of China with the biblical one (Gen. 1–3), demonstrating that the methodological lens in reading Chinese myths could be applied to the biblical creation story.

The earliest versions of the Nüwa myth are found scattered fragmentarily in the Chinese literature of the Warring States era (c. fourth century B.C.E.), although the myth is dated to a much earlier time. Nüwa is often depicted as a goddess with a human face and serpent body in ancient texts and grave paintings. She has been esteemed and worshipped as the creator of the universe, the great progenitor of humankind, the supreme matchmaker, and the patron of marriage by many people in China.

The Nüwa myth is nonstatic and malleable. It has undergone a complex process of oral and textual transmission. Consequently, numerous versions of the myth have been engendered. To quote (my translation) an early Han-dynasty version in *Fengsu tongyi* (*Penetrating Customs*), as cited in *Taiping yulan* (*The Imperial Readings of Taiping Era*):

> It is said that when heaven and earth were separated, there was no humankind. Nüwa created human beings by kneading yellow earth. The task was so arduous that she was too exhausted to complete it. So she flicked the sludge with her cord and lifted it to form humankind. The ones kneaded with yellow earth became the rich aristocrats and those made by flicking the sludge the poor commoners.

In contrast to Genesis 1–3, the Nüwa myth does not mention any divine reason for the creation of humankind, and, of course, the gender of the creator is different. It is not difficult, however, to notice the striking similarities, such as the motifs of the separation of heaven and earth and molding humankind from earth. These motifs are by no means limited to Chinese and biblical creation myths. In fact, they also appear, for instance, in the folk literature of Ireland, Greece, Babylonia, Siberia, Indonesia, Australia, and India.

If I expand my comparison to other Chinese creation myths, more parallels to Genesis 1–3 emerge. For instance, it is said that the mythological figure Pangu created the universe out of chaos (cf. Gen. 1:2) and that Yilou enlivens humans by blowing air into them (cf. Gen. 2:7). How do we account for the similarities found in the creation myths of cultures that are so different and so far apart geographically?

One way to account for them is by conjecturing a common ancestry. In the mid-nineteenth century, some scholars, such as Max Müller, who believed in the common ancestry of Indo-European languages, postulated a protomythology of Indo-European folktales. The monogenetic theory has now been dismissed and regarded as a "myth" itself, because it fails to explain the similar and even identical motifs found in folktales of non-Indo-European languages. It is possible that similar myths found in geographical proximity might have developed from a "protomyth"; however, it is extremely hard to prove genealogical link of those found in remote places with independent language systems.

Another possible explanation is to attribute the similarities to the parallel development of cultures. Anthropologists once had assumed that all human cultures undergo the identical process of cultural evolution. Cultures in the same developmental stage, irrespective of their geographical distance, would produce folklores that converge in thematic elements because of the commonality in the way that the "primitive" people perceive the world and express themselves. Myths, in this sense, are polygenetic and regarded as remnants of the "primitive" culture in the contemporary world. This view presupposes that all human societies progress in the same sequence and number of stages, and thus it fails to acknowledge that cultures evolve and develop differently based on contextual constraints.

Societies need not follow the same developmental path. Similarities in myths could be attributed to similar concerns, customs, beliefs, values, and circumstances shared by cultures, even if they do not follow a programmed path of development. Similar, or even identical, ideas could be genealogically related or have originated separately (each case must be assessed independently). Also, independent myths could subsequently exert influence on each other through the process of dissemination. In the case of the similarities in the Chinese and the biblical creation myths, it would be far-fetched to postulate a common ancestry because of the geographical distance and cultural divergence between ancient China and Palestine.

The construction of many myths reflects an urge to find explanations on how the world came to be in its present form (an etiology). While the urge might be a spiritual concern, its ideological dimension cannot be overlooked. The Nüwa myth quoted above is conspicuously a product of a stratified society. The last line, likely a later addition to the original version, is an etiology of social stratification. The distinction between the rich and the poor is said to have been preestablished by the goddess Nüwa in primeval time. The implication is that social stratification is a divine mandate, predestinated and unalterable. The myth serves to perpetuate social inequality through the rhetoric of divine legitimation. Ancient myths were often produced or reappropriated by ruling elite for their own interest and agenda, be it for the purpose of maintaining social status quo, inducing social transformation, or forging a sense of group identity.

This methodological lens can also be applied to the stories in Genesis 1–3. What are the ideologies embedded in the biblical creation story? Who benefits from these ideologies? Is it a rewritten version of an earlier myth for ideological purposes? Has it been reappropriated subsequently as a means to legitimate certain social structures? By reading the biblical text as an ideologically charged myth, new insights will be gleaned.

Sonia Kwok Wong (M.Div., Chinese University of Hong Kong) is a Ph.D. candidate in Hebrew Bible at Vanderbilt University, Nashville, Tennessee, United States.

The Hindu *Purusa-Sukta* Compared to Biblical Texts

M. Aravind Jeyakumar (India)

Every culture of the world has creation stories which attempt to trace the origin of the universe and its components with special reference to human beings. These stories are conditioned by the religious, cultural, social, and political context from which they originate. The same is true of the interpretations of these narratives: they derive from a particular location. As such, creation stories may be used to explain and justify certain political, religious, and social realities that are oppressive and discriminatory. Such is the case with the Genesis creation narratives and the Hindu *Purusa-Sukta* creation accounts. Here I will first explain the traditional reading of each text which has fostered inequity and repression through the centuries. Then I will explore an egalitarian rereading of both accounts.

There is not one Hindu creation story. Numerous cosmogonies can be found in almost all of the important Hindu scriptures and there are many interpretations for those creation myths. They are all representations of the main principle of Brahman, which is described as being "everywhere and nowhere, everything and nothing." Creation came from Brahman's thought, or the actions of the god Brahma, who is the representation of Brahman as a man.

According to the *Purusa-Sukta* creation hymn (*Rig-Veda* Book: X. Hymn: 90), creation is the result of the sacrifice of *Purusha* (Man), the primeval being, who is all that exists, including "whatever has been and whatever is to be." When *Purusha*, who had "a thousand heads, a thousand eyes, and a thousand feet," was sacrificed, the clarified butter that resulted was made into the beasts which inhabit the earth. From the dismemberment came also the animals, plants, rituals, sacred words, and the Vedas. This same sacrifice produced the gods, *Indra* (the menacing king of gods), *Agni* (Fire), *Vayu* (Wind), as well as the Sun and Moon. From *Purusha's* navel the atmosphere was born; his head produced the heaven, his feet produced the earth, his ear the sky, his mind the moon, his eye the sun, his breath the wind, his feet the earth, and his belly button the atmosphere. The four *varnas* were also born from *Purusha*: the mouth was the Brahman (priest), the arms the *Kshatriya* (warrior), the thigh the *Vaishya* (general populace), and the feet the *Sudra* (servant). For centuries the *sudras* and the outcastes (Dalits) have been treated as lesser humans by the so-called upper dominant castes. This creation hymn is understood in all later Hindu scriptures to sanction the caste system as divine ordination. Thus India follows a social caste structure based on this ancient narrative.

Traditional interpretations of the Genesis narratives have also been used to support hierarchical social structures. Here God is seen as the ruler over the whole creation; God alone commands and controls. God is over the whole creation and the creatures have to submit to the creator. Man is created first and then woman is formed from the rib of the man; therefore woman is subordinate to man. This interpretation, then, establishes God as superior to human beings, and man as superior to woman. It has been used to oppress women folk and to propagate man's superiority over woman.

But different, egalitarian readings of both Genesis and *Purusa-Sukta* can be offered. A liberating reading of the Genesis creation account presents the following insights: God is the source of all creation. God is creator, but at the same time God's re-active and re-creative aspects in the process of creation are emphasized. While the image of the deity as transcendent in Genesis 1 detaches God from humanity and nature, the anthropomorphic picture of God in Genesis 2–3 emphasizes God's activity in the creative process and humankind's active role along with God. Creatures participate with God in creation by separating, ruling, developing, and reproducing; this emphasizes their involvement as cocreators along with God. God does not place Himself above all else but rather works alongside the rest of creation. This reading dismantles the traditional and colonial idea of God as king or ruler and establishes a smooth nexus between God, humans, and the natural world.

Moreover, both male and female are created in the image and likeness of God. Here, both man and woman have the freedom to think and express themselves without fear; both have self-dignity and self-respect. The creation of woman after man from his rib does not imply hierarchy, but rather it brings completion and wholeness. Their physical oneness, commonality of concern, and loyalty and responsibility to one another are emphasized. The spirit of God breathed into human beings highlights that both man and woman share divine life and breath.

An egalitarian rereading of *Purusa-Sukta* focuses on the fact that every human being is from the cosmic person, Brahma, the Supreme Being, so there should not be any inequality among human beings in the name of caste. Brahma is the source of all creation. Everything originates from Him and into Him all is absorbed. Since all the four groups of people originated from the same flesh, there are no hierarchical differences. All groups originated from parts of the body that are divine and thus there is no issue of pure and impure or purity and pollution in the name of caste. The diversity of all creatures—humans, plants, and animals—originated from the same substance, indicating their ultimate unity within the diversity of God's creation.

The heterogeneous creation concept highlights differences in creatures created by Brahma, but rejects hierarchical social structures in which one group dominates and oppresses another. Different people with different skills are necessary for the smooth functioning of society. But superiority or inferiority is not the purpose here; every human being must be given equal respect irrespective of his or her occupation. Occupational skills should not be designated in terms of caste. The idea is that all *varnas* are contained in every individual instead of every individual being comprised within one of the four *varnas*; no one should be humiliated at any cost because everyone is created from the same Brahma (same substance).

Furthermore, the anthropomorphic account of *Purusa-Sukta* exposes God in human form and God sacrificing His own body to create the human and natural world. It is thus a creation story of love and peace. Through the sacrificial love of Brahma, the whole world and humanity was formed. This narration proclaims a message of peace between diverse creatures and humankind created from the "same substance" of Brahman.

In sum, our rereading the Genesis and *Purusa-Sukta* creation stories has undermined the traditional understanding of them as sanctioning hierarchical structures. Creation means differences, plurality in creatures, and diversity in skills or tasks assigned to the creatures. But no one is inferior or superior to another because all are created by God and from God. Even God is not superior since he is cocreator (Gen. 2–3) and sacrificially offers his own body (*Purusa-Sukta*). The created order demands the plurality of creatures with interdependence; it requires participation without dominance or hierarchical structures for peaceful coexistence. Thus discrimination in the name of gender, caste, class, or any such form is against the created order.

M. Aravind Jeyakumar (B.D., M.Th., Gurukul Lutheran Theological College and Research Institute, Chennai, South India) is Lecturer in the Department of Biblical Studies at Leonard Theological College, Jabalpur, Madhya Pradesh, India.

The Concept of Human Community in African Creation Stories

David T. Williams (South Africa)

Europe and its offspring in other parts of the world have had a tradition of treating Genesis 1–3 as literally true, an historical account of primal events which set the scene for the development of all human history. Although this view has begun to change somewhat in recent years—for example, the belief that God created the world in six 24 hour days has waned—the tradition still persists among many Christians around the world.

African Christians, however, are much less likely than those in the United States and other places to accept a literal explanation of Genesis. There are a number of reasons. First, Africa has a far shorter history of writing, and therefore much less respect for the authority of the written word. While a written signed document is treated as authoritative among Europeans, this is not the case in Africa. Second, whereas European religious and literary history did have a variety of stories to explain the origin of the world, these have long since generally been forgotten, partly because they were regarded as just stories. In contrast, while the old stories of origins in Africa, explaining such things as why palms of black people are not pigmented, may not be believed, they are still widely known. The natural reaction for African Christians, then, is to treat the Genesis accounts in the same way, namely, as "white" myths. Indeed, the Bible itself is still commonly regarded as a "white" book, so not really a part of Africa; therefore it can readily be rejected, which it is in many cases.

Africa is pervaded by spirituality. Indeed, Africa tends to be much more religious than the modern West. But this spirituality is not in relation to God, which is yet another reason that it is difficult to identify with the creation stories in Genesis. It is common in Africa to stress the separation of God from the world rather than a connection between the two. This is so strong that many early missionaries did not see any belief in God at all. The belief was always there, but it was in a God who is clearly transcendent—a God who made the world, but has minimal involvement with it thereafter (much like European deism and the "absent watchmaker" God). In Africa, people do not relate to God directly, leading to what is perhaps the most characteristic religious belief in Africa, namely, that people can interact with the dead and with their ancestors, and that only through their mediation is any approach to God possible. It is in this belief that African spirituality resides. The absence of this crucial element from the Genesis stories contributes to its lack of relevance for many Africans.

Interaction with ancestors is part of a view of humanity which complements the belief in the absence of God. Without a direct individual relationship with God, interpersonal human relationships are more important. In contrast to the excessive individualism in the West is what we might call "communitarianism" in Africa. This, again, makes the Genesis stories—at least as they have been presented to Africans—not particularly meaningful. For example in the story of the Fall, the human couple are portrayed as individually responsible and individually guilty. But in a culture where the emphasis is on the community, there is little sense of personal guilt. This means that there is little felt need for individual salvation—certainly not salvation in the afterlife. Indeed, the African view is that people will naturally survive after death as ancestors. The whole notion of the separation of righteous people from wicked people is difficult to accept where the unity of the community is paramount.

There are, however, a couple of ways in which an African context does connect nicely with Genesis 1–3. First, the phrase "these are the generations" in 2:4 does put individuals firmly into the context of the group. More important, though, is that the story of the Fall indicates the effect of sin not just on individuals but on the group as well. Paul develops this in Romans 5, where he explains his notion of "original sin," which applies to all of humanity, the human community we might say. Here the unity of humanity is significant in an Africa that has felt the brunt of racism, where people have sometimes been treated as subhuman. For Paul and Christian theology, all humans are affected by events in the Garden. Furthermore, the African emphasis on community finds a point of contact with Genesis in that humans are created in the image of God (1:26–27). Although exactly what it means to be created in the image of God has been much debated, it seems clear enough that all people—regardless of gender, race, ethnicity, or any other factor—have a special significance which separates them from the animals and bonds together all of humanity.

Notably, however, an African reading of the text does not resonate with the fact that the passage describes the creation of a single couple—one man and one woman. That is, in the biblical story the richness of community does not extend beyond the model of a monogamous, nuclear family—husband, wife, and children. In African culture, the extended family is much more important, not to mention the practice of polygamy—neither of which are in the purview of Genesis 1–3.

Here we might argue that if the God-given monogamy of the Genesis account were practiced more diligently in Africa, our continent might not have the highest prevalence of HIV/AIDS in the world—a problem which is not disconnected from a celebration of community. Indeed, Genesis flows quickly from the description of the creation of humanity to its perversion. The story of the Fall is a reminder that the ideal for human behavior is not humanity, but God's norms. Indeed, the essence of the serpent's primal temptation is the elevation of humanity as a norm. Where this is done, disaster follows. The one thing that comes over so strongly in the story of the Fall is that there are norms set by God, and disobedience to them has serious consequences.

An African reading of Genesis 1–3—and of Scripture in general—brings greater appreciation of human community, an emphasis that has tended to be overshadowed elsewhere. It also makes a valuable contribution to the key questions concerning the nature of humanity and how humans should behave toward each other. This fits beautifully with the uniquely African philosophical concept of *ubuntu*. Literally translated as "humanity," Archbishop Desmond Tutu explained *ubuntu* this way in his book *No Future Without Forgiveness*: "A person with Ubuntu is open and available to others, affirming of others, does not feel threatened that others are able and good, for he or she has a proper self-assurance that comes from knowing that he or she belongs in a greater whole and is diminished when others are humiliated or diminished, when others are tortured or oppressed." There is no doubt that the world stands in great need of this ethic, as long as it is seen in the context in which Genesis puts it: as something given through God and in relationship to him.

David T. Williams, originally from the United Kingdom, has served as a missionary in Southern Africa since 1971; he is currently Professor of Systematic Theology at the University of Fort Hare, South Africa.

Six Differences between Two Creation Stories in Genesis

Meir Bar-Ilan (Israel)

It has been well known for centuries that Genesis 1–3 contains two different stories: one in 1:1–2:3 and a second in 2:4–3:24. Originally scholars stressed the fact that in the first story the deity is named Elohim (God), while in the second story he is called Yahweh-Elohim (Lord God). While there is no need to underestimate this difference, it should be noted that the change of the divine name is not essential, but rather technical (just like the difference in the number of

Hebrew words: 469 in the first story and 640 in the second). The aim of this paper, therefore, is to analyze the essential differences between the two stories. There are six such differences:

The Aim of the Stories In the first account there is only one protagonist: God. Given that His deeds are so tremendous, with no precedent, it is clear that the aim of the first story is to glorify God (as creator). However, in the second story there are several protagonists, each of them is doing or saying something in his or her turn. The bottom line of this second story is that man has to toil hard for his living, woman has to suffer, and wild animals will threaten man's existence. That is, it is an etiological story, explaining the destiny of human beings, why the world is the way that it is. The differences between the stories become evident by looking at statistics of words and their dispersion. In the first story, man appears after 317 words (63 percent of the text), and he is mentioned in 102 words, that is 20 percent only. However, in the second story, man is mentioned after 29 words (4 percent of the text) and he takes up more than 80 percent of the text. In short, one story is God oriented while the other is man oriented.

Time versus Space Time governs the first story (day one, day two, and so forth). Moreover, the luminaries were created to enable man to reckon times (not for warming or ripening fruits, for example). There are different types of times: linear (1:1–7), cyclical (evening, morning), and secular time of the working days and the holy time (day seven), a "quality-time" according to religious perspective, not a social one. Other than God himself, time governs the world, and there is no specific space. The second story is by contrast space oriented. The narrator depicts the Garden of Eden, the venue of the story, by giving it geographical dimension aided by four rivers (and lands). Moreover, the importance of the location is augmented by the fact that man is expelled from his congenital territory, marking the importance of realm in one's life. While holy times mark the life of religious persons, territory marks the more mundane man (who ignore God's ruling).

The Power of the Word In the first story, the word of God is His tool to create the world. The power of speech is evident. Speech is a divine tool that preexisted the world. Names that were given by God to His deeds, such as "day" or "sky," marked the end of their creation. With this power of the word, God blessed His creatures—fish, fowl, man, and the seventh day—showing that the existence of the world is word dependent. And only God speaks. Unlike the first story, in the second God does not use His speech ability as a tool of creation; rather man uses it to impose his own supremacy. The word has no divine merit and God brings forward the animals to man waiting for man to name them. In other words, the first story implies that language is divine, denoting it is part of the creation, while in the second story language is a man-created phenomenon.

Order and Law The first story is marked by the order of numbers (one, two, three) and comes to its culmination in the seventh day. Order is also implied in the creation of the luminaries and stars, as in the "rules of Heaven" (cf. Jeremiah 33:25; Job 38:33), and in the "laws" necessary for creation (cf. Proverbs 8:27–29). So although the terms "law" and "order" do not appear in the first story, it is clear they were there from the very beginning. Stars have laws and order, and God, their Creator, is not only the Lord of time but also the Lord of order. However, in the second story there is no order (even not implied) and there is no law. As a matter of fact, God decreed a law (not to eat from the Tree) but after a short while this law is transgressed and chaos seems to dominate the world. In brief, God goes together with time and order, while man goes together with space and disorder.

The Role of Numbers In the first story, numbers are the spine of the story and their appearance at the end of each passage denotes the tempo, or dynamics, of the story. In the first story there are 469 words and among them there are 10 number-words, in this order: *one*, *two*, *three*, *two*, *four*, *five*, *six*, *seven*, *seven*, and *seven*. The percentage of number-words is 2.016. In the second story, there are 640 words and only six are number-words (*four*, *one*, *two*, *three*, *four*, *one*), which means a percentage of 0.937. This difference in the use of numbers, part of what is called "stylometry," reflects attitude toward science (and order). While God did not create numbers, He did something to them: He bestowed quality on quantity. The number seven is related to God as well as to blessing and nonactivity, which exemplifies holiness. Thus the number seven was transferred from being quantity only to become a symbol of quality. The number seven accompanies God from primordial till the end of times; seven means divine.

Sermon versus Story The structure of the two stories is very different. The first story is full of formulas. Each and every passage begins and ends with a formula (and God said, let there be, and God saw that it was good, etc.). As a matter of fact, roughly 20 percent of the text is formulaic. Thus it has a clear, special, and "tight" structure. The second story, by contrast, is "loose"—it has no specific structure (but like any story there is an exposition, a change, and an end). Therefore, it is assumed that the first story originally began as a sermon, probably to mark a new year, while the second story was nothing but a story. The second story is the craft of a narrator, but the first one is a speech made by a speaker, a preacher (a priest and a prophet).

Meir Bar-Ilan is Professor of Jewish History and Talmud at the Bar-Ilan University, Israel; he is the author of more than 100 learned papers and five books.

QUESTIONS

1. What if, for the sake of discussion, it could be proven that the biblical tradition was in fact influenced by the Chinese stories or vice-versa? How, if at all, would that influence your understanding and interpretation of the texts?
2. Jeyakumar notes how both Genesis 1–3 and the *Purusa-Sukta* have been used to sanction hierarchical social structures. Are such interpretations distortions of the text? Or does the text lend itself to such interpretations?
3. In addition to the ways that African "communitarianism" resonates with Genesis 1–3, identify several additional aspects of the text that might also lend themselves to a "group-oriented" perspective.
4. In addition to the ones that Bar-Ilan mentions, identify some reasons for viewing Genesis 1–3 as two separate stories.

CHAPTER 2

GENESIS 1–3 (PART II)

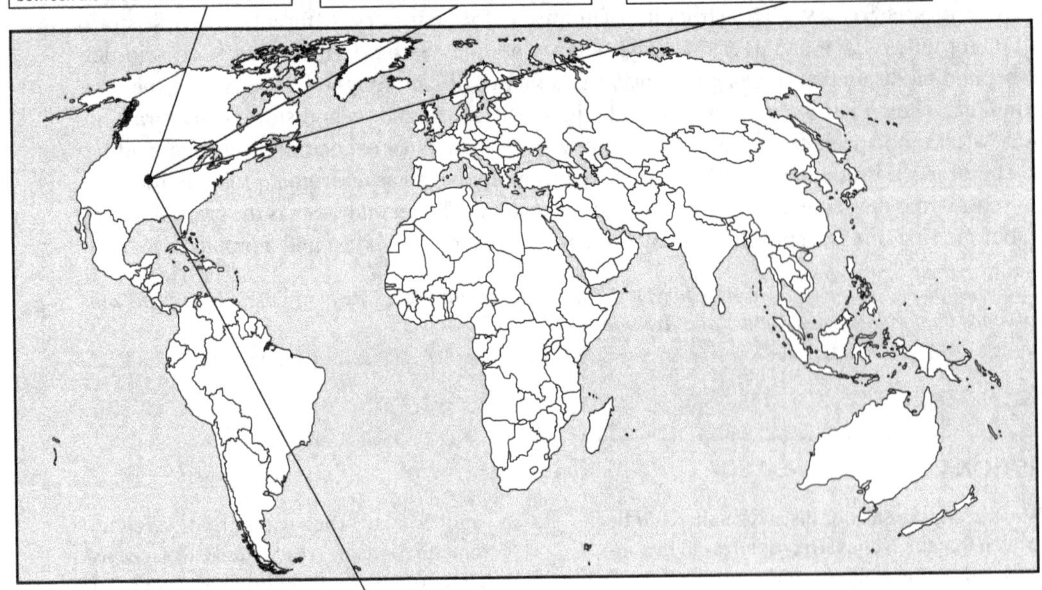

Patrick Gray presents a theistic evolutionist perspective, with a list of questions that surface in the encounter between the Bible and modern science.
Keith Megilligan argues for a literal reading of Genesis 1—God created the world in six 24-hour days—based on an acceptance of divine revelation.
Jonathan Merritt proposes that a proper reading of Genesis 1:28 and 2:15 requires that humans treat the natural world with care and benevolence.
Phillip Sherman considers how biblical texts, specifically Genesis 1:26–28 and the Garden of Eden story, understand animals and our relationship to them.

READINGS

A Theistic Evolutionist Perspective on the Bible and Modern Science

Patrick Gray (United States)

Jews and Christians have studied the opening chapters of Genesis for centuries without pausing to think about Charles Darwin, but it is increasingly difficult for many Western readers to do so at the turn of the twenty-first century. Many readers assent to the idea that evolution in some form has in fact taken place over the course of the history of plant and animal life. Of this group of readers, many also believe in God. It is therefore not inaccurate to label them proponents of theistic evolution.

For some of these readers, the Bible and biology are apples and oranges. Contradictions between the account in Genesis 1–3 and the findings of biologists, geologists, and astronomers do not bother them because they see them as belonging to two very different literary genres. In this approach, it is misguided to try to harmonize the biblical account with the theory of evolution because the author(s) had neither the intention nor the capacity to provide a scientifically accurate explanation of the origin and development of life on earth. It is important to note that this position has ancient roots. Philo, a first-century Alexandrian Jew, and Origen, the most learned Christian scholar of the third century, believed that it was a mistake to read the Bible only literally and never allegorically or symbolically. Augustine in the fourth century agreed, remarking (in *The Literal Meaning of Genesis* 1.19.38–39) that Christians sometimes make fools of themselves by insisting on specific scientific explanations of statements such as "And God said, 'Let there be light' " (Gen. 1:3).

Other proponents of theistic evolution hold that Genesis and modern science are compatible, or at least not incompatible. Read in a certain way, a number of texts provide a basis for this position. For example, the sequence of events in the first chapter of Genesis—though not the second chapter—more or less corresponds to the scientific understanding of the order in which life on earth developed, beginning with aquatic animals and proceeding to land-based mammals and, finally, human beings. Different species emerge at different stages of creation.

More than offering positive, specific evidence for compatibility with evolutionary theory, however, it is more accurate to say that certain aspects of Genesis are sufficiently vague as to leave the door open for such a reading. Whereas the six-day creation would seem to rule out the timeline proposed by biologists for the first appearance of living organisms, the Hebrew term *yom*, like its English equivalent "day," can denote an "age" and not simply a period of 24 hours. The verbs translated "make," "create," and "form," likewise, do not imply any specific duration. Biblical narrative can be notoriously uneven and imprecise when it comes to chronology, and some readers have proposed a "gap" between Genesis 1:1 and 1:2 into which one might fit the millions or billions of years required for natural selection to produce the biodiversity witnessed today.

Apart from the story of Eve's creation from Adam's rib, the Bible is mostly silent about the precise mechanism by which God created. Exactly how or when God intervened to produce various species is not stated. (This leads Gary Larson, in his *Far Side* comic strip, to imagine the possibilities. One strip depicts God telling an assembly of animals, "Well, now I guess I'd better make some things to eat you guys.") Proponents of theistic evolution argue that the laws of nature described by Darwin and his descendants are the unstated means by which God brought the various species into existence. There are differences of opinion as to the extent and frequency of any divine intervention this required, and it is too simplistic to try to fit everyone into a few neatly defined categories. To be sure, Basil of Caesarea speaks for many when he says in the fourth century that "those who think that all that exists is without government or direction, but borne about by chance, are... infected by the deceit of atheism" (*Hexaemeron* 1.2). Yet Alfred Russel Wallace, Darwin's contemporary who independently formulated a theory of natural selection, still saw a "directive mind" and a sense of purpose manifested in evolutionary processes even as he rejected Christianity.

It is undeniable that one's presuppositions about creation and evolution can have a distorting effect when reading. At the same time, certain theological and scientific biases can frequently promote close, careful interpretation as readers are keenly attuned to what, exactly, the text of Genesis says and does not say, as well as to what Darwinian theory entails and does not entail. Attentive, invested reading can bring to the surface critical questions which are only implicit in the encounter between the Bible and modern science. Such questions include the following:

Has the history of the human race consisted of "rising" from more primitive life forms or "falling" from an original state of grace, as the traditional interpretation of Genesis 3:1–19 suggests? Or perhaps both?

Can the human mind or soul evolve in the same way that anatomical and physiological structures evolve? Or is any talk of nonphysical "evolution" (as in social Darwinism or evolutionary psychology) fundamentally different in kind from what biologists study?

If God "creates" by means of natural selection, should he be seen as a "sloppy" creator for tolerating all the death and extinction that is a natural part of this lengthy process? By contrast, is he a "deadbeat" creator for calling the universe into existence and then abandoning it, stepping back and allowing it to unfold without intervening to guide it with his providential hand?

What is a human being? And how does it differ from other humanoid forms? Is it a matter of genetics or anatomy or is it something intangible? Can something like the soul or "the image of God" (1:27) emerge via chance mutations or does it require a supernatural touch? Does the dignity accorded to humans in Genesis 1–3 depend on a particular understanding of their emergence?

Does Genesis support the idea of creation *ex nihilo*, "out of nothing"? This is technically a matter of astronomy or physics or metaphysics, but it is a useful reminder that Darwin wrote *On the Origin of Species* and not on the origin of whatever raw materials gave rise to living organisms that grew into various species. Evolution is about development and change, not about ultimate origins.

Patrick Gray (Ph.D., Emory University) is the Albert Bruce Curry Professor of Religious Studies at Rhodes College, Memphis, Tennessee, United States.

A Literal Reading of Genesis 1

Keith Megilligan (United States)

The Hebrew of the Old Testament has an emphasis upon form and function, not necessarily flowery prose. That is, the language is concise and purposeful. Its expressions attempt little by way of "logic" or sophisticated argumentation. The prose portion of the Old Testament is pretty straightforward. So when the text starts with a somewhat flat, yet very profound, interjection, "In the beginning, God created...," it is not laying the basis for an argument. The Bible *assumes*, even presupposes, the existence of God; it is not interested in trying to prove such a claim. That being said, anything that God does is therefore not only noteworthy, but it is also considered fact. And so this language of form and function gives the creation event to us straightforwardly, with an emphasis upon action: God created.

Further, the Bible also assumes that God's existence is eternal because it is He that is responsible for chronological events. He is, in fact, responsible for time. Once again, the text is pretty simple in its assertion, "In the beginning...." Such a declaration about time and its *genesis* (pardon the pun) shows us that whenever the beginning was, God was already there, and that we, humanity, needed some help with time–space continuum, not God. So, God is presented not only as being present when "time" began, but He also was/is responsible for its construction for our benefit.

The evidence for this in the text is fairly clear. Using the Hebrew/Jewish historical notation of what constitutes a "day," the text then states what God did within each day. In order for God to give us such "timing," He establishes a light source in the heavens as a verification point for measuring evening and morning. Without any fanfare or explanation, God weaves creation (of a light source) together with "time" so that the two become inseparable for mankind. His means for accomplishing such a feat is simply His powerful spoken word (cf. Psalm 33:6, 9).

An additional notation about time is critical to the acceptance of the biblical account of creation. The descriptive phrase about evening and morning is presented as a modifier of the daily events of creation, and the numeric notation associated with each day is likewise critical. For example, "And there was evening and there was morning, a third day" (1:13). While some have argued for extremely lengthened periods of time in order to help coordinate the biblical account of creation with "modern scientific data," the question of time related to creation is an exegetical one, not a scientific one. Quite simply, and I realize that I set myself up for target practice at this point, one either accepts the Word of God's presentation about creation or one does not.

The Hebrew word for "day" as it is used in Genesis 1 is *yom*. The normal understanding for the translation of this word is "day," as in one 24-hour period. Not only does the previous reference to a light source and planetary rotation validate and support this view but so too does the use of a numeric adjective (first, second, etc.). Thus, the normal, natural way of understanding "day" in Genesis 1 is the 24-hour period. But lest such a normal/natural understanding escape our grasp, the Lord provides additional support for such an understanding when He gave the Ten Commandments: "For in six days the Lord made the heavens and the earth, the sea and all that is in them, and rested on the seventh day; therefore the Lord blessed the Sabbath day and made it holy" (Exodus 20:11). This passage illustrates in a couple of ways that "day"/*yom* in Genesis should be understood as a 24-hour period. First, the adjectives "six" and "seventh" declare a simple/normal way of viewing a "day" in the Genesis account. Second, since the Lord blessed the seventh/Sabbath day by making it holy, it defies exegetical logic to understand that God (and thus man) should be resting for more than a 24-hour period. Much less should we be expected to understand it as, for example, an extended geological age of any significant duration.

Correspondingly, it would follow that if the "days" of Genesis are 24 hours in length, then the cumulative effect upon time (following creation) would be similarly impacted. That is, the days that accumulate into weeks which accumulate into months and then years would mean that the total time since creation would be much less than the eons of time proposed by evolutionary models. By "much less" is meant a universe and world that has been in existence for only thousands (possibly tens of thousands) of years rather than millions or billions. The Bible helps demonstrate this by providing two genealogies later in Genesis 5 and 11, which provide for a briefer time continuum of historical portions.

The coordination of God establishing "time" with the event of creation becomes a theological and practical necessity for man. The theological/exegetical evidences presented above speak to the first necessity. The practical necessity is evidenced each "day" of our lives. Mankind has been created as creatures of time. Time to us has become necessary for so many things—from baking a cake to running a race to the duration of holding an elected office. The focus of such necessity is further confirmed by our emphasis upon validating our individual existence: with a birth certificate and a death certificate. It is hard to imagine that either one of those items would be important if time were not created by God as a "birthright" to humanity. Our struggle with understanding creation and cosmogony is not as much a scientific one as it is a spiritual one. By God's Spirit we are either graced with the ability to accept the biblical record of creation or we are not (see 1 Corinthians 2:12–16).

When one attempts to understand the meaning of the Old Testament, one either has the humility and grace to accept the revelation of Scripture or one does not. Natural minds, those who are bereft of the presence of the Spirit of God, cannot understand such revelation. Scientists attempt to explain creation in rational terms, whereas God has given it to us by divine revelation. Principally, from the time of Darwin onward, disciplines of science have impacted "modern" thinking to the extent that we have been left with only one perspective on history, an evolutionary one. By definition and implication, evolution must have huge measures of time. If it does not, then the theory is weakened if not completely compromised. But God does not have that "problem" for at least a couple of reasons. First, if we accept that creation is a biblical issue and not exclusively a scientific one, our answers rest with the Creator, not scientists. And second, in order to accept and even value the biblical viewpoint, we need the author's (Creator's) assistance to comprehend the evidence that He has presented. To do that, we need His Spirit to bear witness with our spirit (Romans 8:9–17) that we are children of God and have the ability to understand what our Heavenly Father would teach us about His creation.

Keith Megilligan (B.A., John Brown University; Th.M., Grace Theological Seminary; D.Min., Westminster Theological Seminary) has served as pastor and teacher for more than 30 years.

Genesis and the Treatment of the Natural World

Jonathan Merritt (United States)

In 1843, Ludwig Feuerbach proclaimed, "Nature, the world, has no value, no interest for Christians. The Christian thinks only of himself and the salvation of his soul" (*The Essence of Christianity* [New York: Harper and Row, 1957], 287). Feuerbach wasn't the only one to claim such a thing. In the 1967 issue of *Science*, Lynne White Jr. released his now-infamous paper "The Historical Roots of Our Ecological Crisis." In it, he labels Western Christianity "the most anthropocentric [human-centered] religion the world has ever seen."

It's hard to dispute that Feuerbach's and White's claims are at least partially grounded in reality. Many pastors and congregants today don't understand the importance of a biblically grounded, historically informed theology of nature. According to a 2009 study by LifeWay Research, about half of all Protestant pastors in the United States say they speak to their church about creation care "rarely" or "never." Most seem to grasp the importance of soul salvation, but far fewer—especially those in fundamentalist circles—express sincere interest in nature and environmental issues.

Why is this? To what can we ascribe this discrepancy? It seems that at least part of the blame lies with our misunderstandings, misinterpretations, and misapplications of critical passages in the opening chapters of Genesis. We are able to properly frame our theology of nature and role as creation's stewards when we understand critical passages in the opening book of our sacred text.

The creation account in Genesis 1 is one of the most widely known passages in the entire Bible. Unfortunately, this passage has become so embroiled in scientific debates about the origin of life that few are mining the theological truths hidden within the text. In the poetic rhythm of this 31-verse chapter, we find several repeated actions that greatly inform a theological conversation about creation and stewardship. Both actions come from God and both actions speak volumes about nature.

First, we encounter the act of creation. Over and over God creates and forms matter into land and water and life. And each time God purposes to create, the text simply says, "It was so." This teaches us that God has a powerful purpose for his creation. Indeed, the very fact that God created it tells us that it is meaningful and purposeful. Additionally, we encounter the act of commentary. God doesn't see fit to merely create; God shares his perspective about his creation: "God saw…it was good." Notice that God didn't call it useful or beautiful. He called it good, ascribing to creation intrinsic value and worth. And the writer includes the phrase repeatedly. Why? Because he is emphasizing and underscoring the pleasure God feels. It is an expression of delight or, one might say, the seal of divine approval. But it is also more than that. For modern readers, it is a warning that we dare not treat the object of God's pleasure with wanton disregard. Properly read and understood, the creation narrative teaches us about a God who made all things, imbued these things with value, and takes great pleasure in the natural world. This passage bolsters the idea that creation is a special treasure of God, and one worthy of our attention and care.

Although the creation narrative itself sets us in the right direction, many great Christian thinkers throughout history have stumbled when they interpret "the dominion passages" (1:28; 2:15). These verses are perhaps the biggest textual influencers driving Feuerbach's and White's conclusions. The idea that humans have dominion over creation has shaped the so-called "instrumentalist" view of nature: that the natural world exists solely to meet human needs.

The immediate problem we encounter is the seeming contradiction between 1:28 and 2:15. In the former, we find the seemingly harsh command to "subdue" the earth and "have dominion" over it. In the latter, we find a softer command to "keep" and "care for" the earth. When used selectively and in isolation, either of these passages can be effective in debate. But a proper understanding of the divine plan must bring these passages into harmony to synthesize a biblically informed definition of "stewardship" or "dominion."

The Hebrew word for "subdue" in 1:28 literally means to take control of something. It is usually found in a political context in scripture. Genesis 1 is the only place in the entire Old Testament where the object of this verb is the earth. The Hebrew word for "rule over" or "dominion" literally means to exercise a given authority over something. Unfortunately, many Christians perceive the word "dominion" to mean "domination." But a closer look reveals a different understanding. This word can be used to describe priests executing their duties or shepherds taking care of their sheep, but it is most often used to refer to the power of kings over their subjects. We can infer, then, that 1:28 gives humans a monarch-like role over nature.

What was the role of a monarch in the Old Testament context? An Israelite king was unique. He was not to be a ruler like those the other nations had. In 1 Samuel 8:6, the Israelites ask for a "king to judge us like all the nations." This apparently disappointed God and Samuel because Israel wasn't like all the other nations. Their ultimate ruler was God, and their earthly rulers weren't given carte blanche authority. An Israelite king was not to rule oppressively or be greedy. He was to remain a servant and subject of Almighty God (see Deuteronomy 17:16–20). When an Israelite king abused his dominion—when he got greedy, oppressed the people, or enslaved his subjects—God would judge and punish him.

As God gave "dominion" to Israelite kings, we have been given limited authority over the natural world. After all, "the earth is the Lord's and everything in it" (Psalm 24:1). We do not have license to treat animals cruelly and use the earth however we wish so long as humans benefit from it. We do not have carte blanche power, but rather the privilege of responsibly managing the earth's many benefits and resources as servants of the Lord.

In Genesis 2, God has just placed the first human in a garden that God himself has planted and cultivated. In verse 15, we learn why God placed him there: "to work it and take care of it" (translations vary on the two verbs, but all contain the idea of showing concern for the earth). The command to Adam—as a representative for all mankind—is really a charge for us all to care for the world. And nowhere in scripture is it ever revoked. The passage is clear and is reiterated in the chapter that follows (3:23): Humans are commanded by the Creator to care for His creation.

In this way, then, we can synthesize God's command to Adam to take care of the earth (2:15) with the instruction to subdue and have dominion over it (1:28) into a single understanding of biblical stewardship. We can conclude that humans are given the task of ruling the earth as "benevolent kings."

The words of Feuerbach and White haunt contemporary Christians with the same ferocity they did when they were first spoken. In fact, one might argue that they are even more damning today in light of contemporary ecological developments. But where Feuerbach and White get it wrong is in the true witness of the scriptures. The Bible is not the enemy of ecological responsibility, but one of its greatest assets. If we rediscover what the text actually teaches about nature, we will see the world as God sees it and care for it as he has commanded.

Jonathan Merritt (M.Div., Southeastern Baptist Theological Seminary; Th.M., Emory University) is author of Green Like God: Unlocking the Divine Plan for Our Planet; *his work has appeared in* USA Today, The Atlanta Journal-Constitution, Christianity Today, *and* The Washington Post.

Animals and Our Relationship to Them as Outlined in Genesis

Phillip Sherman (United States)

Several years ago I read the book *Animal Liberation* by the moral philosopher Peter Singer. In this (now-famous) work, Singer argues that the majority of human beings fail to treat animals in an ethical fashion and that humanity ought no longer to act as though the pain and suffering of animals is morally inconsequential. He advocates for a vegetarian diet and strict limitations on animal-based experimentation. Many who agree with Singer hold that human antipathy toward animals flows naturally from a profound cultural misunderstanding of the relationship between human beings and other forms of animal life. I have remained somewhat ambivalent with regard to Singer's argument. I do not, for example, eschew the eating of meat. But I was troubled. There is a tendency for many advocates of animal rights to claim that biblical texts were partly responsible for current attitudes toward the lives of animals. I realized, however, that I had never thought systematically about the presence of animals in the Hebrew Bible. "Biblical" animals were largely invisible to me. I was also troubled by the truth I perceived in Singer's work. The modern food industry has reduced animals to objects. Their pain and suffering is less important than the financial bottom line and the need to supply meat to a voracious public at a low cost. We bring countless millions into existence only to slaughter them. As someone who studies ancient Israelite texts, I found myself increasingly asking this question: "How do biblical texts understand animals and our relationship to them?"

The Hebrew Bible has a great deal to say about the lives of animals. There is scarcely a book in the Hebrew canon which does not make at least a passing reference to animals. It has even been suggested that upwards of 120 species of animals populate the pages of the Hebrew Bible. It is curious, therefore, that contemporary readers of the Bible, broadly speaking, often seem oblivious to this ubiquitous animal presence. This is curious as animals and their lives were clearly important, indeed essential, to the lives and well-being of the peoples responsible for the production and transmission of biblical texts. The marginalization of animals amongst readers of the Bible—both critical and devotional—can arguably be connected to a foundational passage from Genesis 1.

Genesis 1:26–28 (in)famously contains a divine blessing on *homo sapiens* and commands only one type of animal to exert dominion and rule over the created order and over all other forms of life. This passage has encouraged and continues to encourage countless readers to view animal life as subordinate to the lives of human beings. Accordingly, the lives of animals carry less moral and ethical value. Various advocates for the ethical treatment of animals have adopted the term "speciesism" to describe a common human tendency to marginalize or fail to recognize the moral considerations owed to animals. (Singer himself makes ample use of the term.)

Such an ideology is not without its attractions. Human beings, male and female, are said to be created in the divine image and, according to one dominant interpretation of that phrase, are to function as the divine's coregent on earth. Many interpreters have seized on the claim that humanity is created in the divine image to assert a biblical foundation for the "rights" of human beings or to claim human dignity as a biblically grounded concept. Such dignity, however, is purchased at a price. The special status accorded human beings is inseparable from their superiority to all other classes of living beings. Indeed, their vocation is fulfilled in their rule over the other creatures. The very idea of "humanity" is dependent upon the control and suppression of the "animal." The distinctive, semidivine status of human beings and (therefore) the nondivine, subhuman status of other forms of life are presented as a function of creation itself, built into the very structure of the created world and closely linked to the divine, primal blessing. That this ideological program remains largely invisible to modern readers of the Bible who relate to animals (wild and domestic) in radically different ways from the producers of biblical literature is a testament to its persuasiveness. An effective ideology is an invisible ideology.

To name an ideology is not to dismiss it outright. Every ideology served a purpose for the culture that created it. It is not my goal to claim that such an ideology was without use to the earliest readers of the Hebrew Bible who lived, simultaneously, in greater community and in heightened tension with the animal world. Perhaps such an ideology was even necessary. My goal, rather, is to suggest that readers of biblical texts ought to attend to the full range of views concerning animals and their lives contained within the pages of the Hebrew Bible. Most biblical scholars would hold that 1:26–28 was produced by elite, Priestly scribes writing during or shortly after the Babylonian exile of the people of Judah—that is, Genesis 1 may have been one of the last written texts in the Hebrew Bible, even though it appears first in the Bible. Some scholars would also assert that the work of these Priestly scribes included a reevaluation of many of the sacred traditions of the people of Israel. Such reevaluation was the result of life in a radically new social and political context. In addition, much biblical scholarship is devoted to tracing the chronological development of central ideas throughout the literary history of ancient Israel. We should, accordingly, be more critical in our reading of this ideology of human dominion and seek to contextualize the emergence of such a viewpoint in Israel's long history with animals. Readers have too often allowed what is admittedly a rather chronologically late and theologically sophisticated reflection on the nature of the relationship between human beings and the rest of the animal world (i.e., 1:26–28) to serve as the dominant model by which all other biblical texts concerning animals ought to be read.

But where else might we look to determine ancient Israelite views concerning animals and their lives? What other models for the human/animal relationship might we find? A major counterbalance to the ideology of 1:26–28 can be found close at hand in the creation story located in Genesis 2–3, which most scholars would assert was written prior to Genesis 1. In this account, the human male is created before the animals. The Israelite deity, noting Adam's isolation, brings all of the animals before Adam to see what he will name them (2:19). While this passage has traditionally been read as an example of human domination—Adam imposing various names upon the animal kingdom—a less anthropocentric reading is possible. The deity seems to believe that a suitable companion for the first human being might be found among the animals. The fact that none of the animals are found to be an appropriate associate for Adam does not place humanity in a superior position to them. A gulf of some sort certainly separates them. As the serpent will prove, however, the gulf is not unbridgeable and is not defined by hierarchy. Commentators have noted that both Adam and the animals are created from the same substance (the ground/*adamah*) and are infused with the same animating presence (life-breath/*nephesh*). Human animals and nonhuman animals are not two kinds of beings, demarcated by reason or linguistic ability, but rather very similar kinds of being. There is no sharp break between the two. Alienation and animosity do eventually threaten the relationship between human beings and animals outside of Eden. The second creation account, however, recalls a time before the origin of such animosity and alienation, a time before the origin of speciesism.

That modern readers seldom attend to the animals that populate the pages of the Hebrew Bible is an indication of the little respect we grant animals in our own collective lives. Reading the Hebrew Bible looking for the lives of animals is one way to ensure that we are attending to the animals in our own culture.

Phillip Sherman is Assistant Professor of Religion at Maryville College, United States.

QUESTIONS

1. What is the importance for Gray of referring to early commentators on the Bible such as Philo and Augustine?
2. Assess Megilligan's last paragraph. Is he essentially rejecting science and reason? If so, what are the implications of such a move?
3. What would one have to do or know in order to assess Merritt's arguments about the proper understanding of the word "dominion" in Genesis 1:28? What are the potential benefits and pitfalls of looking at how a specific word is used in other contexts?
4. Reflect more fully—Sherman only makes one passing comment—on the role and portrayal of the serpent (the most prominent animal in the text). Does the serpent help or hinder Sherman's argument?

CHAPTER 3

GENESIS 12–21

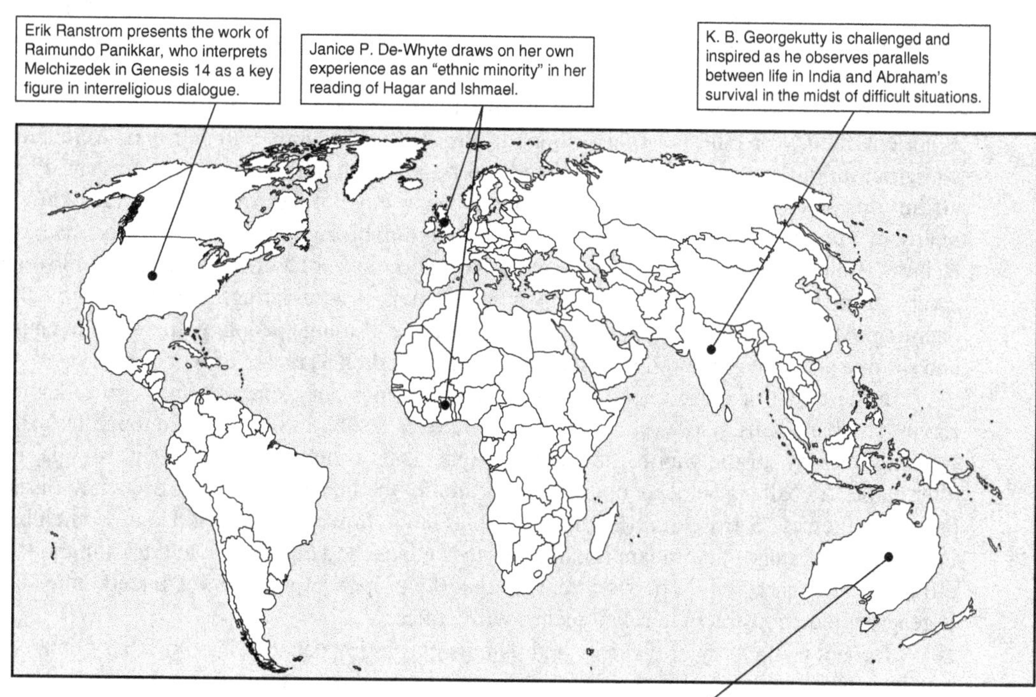
Erik Ranstrom presents the work of Raimundo Panikkar, who interprets Melchizedek in Genesis 14 as a key figure in interreligious dialogue.
Janice P. De-Whyte draws on her own experience as an "ethnic minority" in her reading of Hagar and Ishmael.
K. B. Georgekutty is challenged and inspired as he observes parallels between life in India and Abraham's survival in the midst of difficult situations.
Roland Boer reads the story of Sodom and Gomorrah in Genesis 18–19 in light of the world-famous Sydney (Australia) Gay and Lesbian Mardi Gras.

READINGS

Parallels between Life in India and Abraham's Trials

K. B. Georgekutty (India)

When I was a young child attending Sunday classes, I held the idea that Abraham was a man who had everything together. I considered Abraham to be a great man who enjoyed God's never-ending provision. The trouble, however, is that we tend to overlook the details in the Abraham stories. There is a tendency to dwell on the mountain-peak experiences of the lives of great men and miss many great lessons that need to be learned from other aspects of their lives. The praiseworthy experiences must be observed in the context of their entire lives. Now when I look at the stories in Genesis 12–21 as an Indian who lives among uncertainties and diversities, it challenges me.

First of all, the life under the divine mission is not easy, but uncertain. Abraham's story is not one mainly of faith but of a struggle in the midst of poverty and survival. Abraham was a migrant to Palestine, a sparsely populated and poor region. His descent to Egypt and Philistia affirms this perception of Palestine. The general background of the Ancient Near East knows the reality of migration all too well. The Code of Hammurabi, Egyptian laws, and the laws of the Hebrew Bible acknowledged the existence of migration in search of food. Abraham moves into a very strange country. Moving into new areas is always intimidating. New territory is always daunting. Abraham settled in Moreh at Shechem among a strange people with a strange language and strange gods who required the sacrifice of their children as an act of worship.

In the midst of those uncertainties, a famine comes and Abraham must go to Egypt. In Egypt Abraham's struggle was a struggle for life over death. So he starts the tough task of networking his way all the way to Pharaoh's throne. Then follows struggle after struggle, battle after battle. It challenges me as one who lives among the uncertainties of life: natural disasters, poverty, illiteracy, corruption, black money, child labor, dowry, prostitution, and women battering. To me, the story of Abraham is calling us to boldness and confidence and trust in the face of difficulty and uncertainty. The story teaches that the proper response to the uncertainties of life is generosity demonstrated in relationships with others.

Second, it is a story of diversity and pluralism as in my country. It is amazing to notice that Abraham lived among and interacted with people of diverse cultures and religious traditions—Babylonians, Canaanites, Philistines, and Egyptians. It is astonishing to see how a man of Abraham's stature would move (back) to a place where people did not share his religious beliefs. Indeed, if Abraham's neighbors had no respect for Abraham's God, then he was in danger. He lived in the heart of a hostile country. Likewise, India is among the most diverse societies in the world. It has people from all the major world religions—Hindus, Muslims, Christians, Sikhs, Buddhists, Jains, and Zoroastrians (Parsis). Religious diversity is coupled with enormous linguistic and cultural diversity. Although India has no official or established state religion, Hindus are the majority. In such a context, it is always a big challenge for a Christian to live as a member of a minority group where one feels alienated and insecure.

Third, the story continues with the traditions of Hagar and Ishmael. Hagar has been driven out from her home to safeguard the interest of her oppressor Sarah. Hagar does not have her own independent voice. More precisely, Hagar represents the women of India, many of whom suffer from poverty and social exclusion. They are often the target of family violence, which is a particularly acute problem in India. Both Hagar and Ishmael faced the same circumstances as Indian lower-caste people and communities that were excluded from the rest of society and denied access to social and economic goods. They both remain as the model of resistance and rebellion in the midst of unjust circumstances. Thus we have the responsibility to support the weak and silent voices of the text in order to make them audible.

Fourth, I am forced to confront one of the most difficult questions: How do we evaluate the views of the writers of the Abraham story? Their attitudes were exclusive and hostile to poor people. This was articulated clearly in the affliction and expulsion of Hagar in Genesis 16 and 21. And still, the writers also represented the positive understanding that God is the one who helps those who are in trouble and who are oppressed. If these ideas are brought together they create an obvious tension between exclusive social actions and an inclusive theological understanding of God. How is it possible that the same deity contains such a strong contradiction? God is the one who takes care of those who are excluded by the people guided by the very same God. In the story, the deity is on both the side of the oppressed and the oppressors.

In sum, Genesis 12–21 reflects the life situation of the majority of Indians. It is a story of resistance and survival in the midst of diverse and hostile situations. Although the stories are written from the perspective of the rulers/oppressors, the story offers inspiration and challenges in new contexts where people are still in danger of poverty, being (ab) used, and being dealt with harshly and unjustly.

K. B. Georgekutty is Lecturer in Old Testament at Faith Theological Seminary, under Senate of Serampore College, Kerala, India.

Raimundo Panikkar's Interpretation of Melchizedek in Genesis 14

Erik Ranstrom (United States)

Raimundo Panikkar (1918–2010) was one of the leading theological proponents of Christian interreligious dialogue in the twentieth and early twenty-first century. From an early age, Raimundo wondered about the relationship between Christianity and Hinduism, not from a detached, academic perspective but from within the very crucible of identity formation. Born to a Spanish Catholic mother and Indian Hindu father, Panikkar was ordained into the Catholic priesthood in 1946 and traveled throughout India in the 1950s. Panikkar returned to Europe almost a decade later, and famously quipped: "I 'left' Europe a Christian, 'found' myself a Hindu, and I 'return' a Buddhist, without having ceased to be a Christian" (*The Intrareligious Dialogue* [New York: Mahwah/Paulist Press, 1978], 2). For the remainder of his career Panikkar extolled the virtues of interreligious encounter to the point where some called him the "apostle of interreligious dialogue." Panikkar believed that being a Hindu made sense within his Catholic Christian identity and even contributed to its depth. Here, I will examine these themes in just one of Panikkar's many scholarly works, "Meditacion sobre Melquisedec" (*Nuestro Tiempo*. Pamplona IX 102 [1962]: 575–595; all translations are mine). Here Panikkar offers a way of viewing the convergence of the world's religions, including Hinduism, in the person of Jesus Christ and Christian faith.

The main biblical character in Panikkar's theology of world religions is the mysterious, enigmatic Melchizedek. Melchizedek appears only three times in the entire Bible, including

Genesis 14:18–24. In this story, Abram is moving into the land God had promised him and encountering the destabilizing conditions of territories divided by factions of all kinds. After rescuing Lot from the hands of one of these forces, Abram is approached by a Melchizedek, King of Salem. Melchizedek, a Canaanite priest-king, blesses Abram and praises God for his protection of Abram and his kin. Abram in turn gives to Melchizedek the tithe, a tenth of everything. In many apocryphal stories about Abraham in Judaism, Christianity, and Islam, he is imagined as rejecting his "pagan" past so as to prepare himself for the revelation of the one God. Genesis 14:18–24, however, paints a much different picture. Here a "pagan" priest thanks God on behalf of Abram, who acknowledges the priestly status of Melchizedek and defers to him. And Melchizedek's story does not end in Genesis 14. In Psalm 110, Melchizedek is proclaimed an eternal priest, and Hebrews 7 sees Melchizedek as foreshadowing Christ. Panikkar works with all these elements to construct a Christian theology of world religions and to point the way to an interreligious vocation in the Church.

Christians typically read the Old Testament in light of Jesus Christ. The story of salvation moves toward Christ as the fulfillment of God's promises to the world and the hope of its peoples. Panikkar contributes something significant to this christocentric hermeneutic. He stresses that not only Israel but also the world's religions find completion in Jesus Christ. Christ did not come to destroy the Law and the Prophets, nor the world's religions, but to fulfill them. God promised the world a Savior through the covenantal promise God made with the entire creation. This cosmic covenant, oriented toward Christ, is for Panikkar the true spiritual meaning of the world's ancient religions. Insofar as the people of various religions of the world through their prayers and spiritual desires are implicitly awaiting the fulfillment of their hopes for God in the world, that is, the manifestation of Jesus Christ ("God-with-us"), Panikkar says, "in a certain sense, Christianity has existed since the beginning of creation" (589). Therefore, Panikkar's Christian faith does not alienate him from Hinduism, but unites him with it at its very core, its deepest longings and intentionality.

Panikkar continues to tease out the implications of this fulfillment theology by introducing the idea of a "physical continuity" between Christ and the religions of the world. The meaning of this phrase is very suggestive. Christ's very person exists in deep solidarity with the bodiliness and history of the world's religious traditions. Though Jesus Christ represents "something new and unknown," it must also be affirmed that "history never commences newly and absolutely" but is always marked by an intimate relatedness with what has gone on before (590). God entering into history in the person of Christ consummates this relatedness and fulfills the religions, according to Panikkar, by assuming the priestly order of Melchizedek (Hebrews 5:6). Melchizedek, who represents the priesthood of the religions of the world, anticipates the hope of the God who would come into their midst by offering the eucharistic elements of bread and wine.

Panikkar was unique in his articulation of this fulfillment theology not because he demonstrated how Christ's redemption fulfilled the histories of the world's religions and Israel, as other Catholic Christian theologians in the mid-twentieth century were also advancing similar theses. But what sets Panikkar apart from these thinkers was how he inverted the fulfillment thesis in a way that opened Christianity up to dialogue. Usually this theology emphasizes how much the religions need Christ. Panikkar does not deny this. But he also avoids what could be a stance of arrogant superiority by emphasizing how much Christians need the religions to understand Christ. If Christ is the fulfillment of the religions, then the religions have much to tell us about who this Christ is. As relative newcomers to God's story of salvation, Christians have much to learn from these traditions about this Christ.

Another way in which Panikkar went beyond the simple appreciation of the world's religions was by eschewing a gradualist approach to the order of salvation history. Such an approach usually explains God's involvement in the world as comprising three increasingly intensifying movements from lesser to greater divine presence and manifestation: cosmos, Israel, and Christ. The upshot of this is usually to overlook the world religions of the cosmic covenant because the entire movement is toward a greater intensity and fullness of what the previous epoch lacked (i.e., the third and final movement is all that matters, Christ). Panikkar's thinking essentially rearranges this order by presenting Christians with a mandate to learn from and honor the religions of the cosmic covenant. Panikkar points to Melchizedek's superiority over Abraham and the Jewish levitical priesthood as a way of giving more weight to the religions. Thus, he opens a space for reconsidering the world religions as holding a privileged place in God's salvation history—though in the process he is unfortunately influenced by a strain of anti-Judaism. Panikkar interprets Melchizedek's blessing of Abram in Genesis 14:17, following Hebrews 7:7, as a sign of "the greater blessing the lesser" (581). Christ's priesthood is better understood in reference to the world's religions than to Israel, for Melchizedek's priesthood is "a fruit of the Word and not of the Jews" (579).

Not all of Panikkar's early reflections on Christ and Melchizedek work for us anymore. We are more sensitive to the fact that the world's religions are not primarily about the promise and expectation of a foreseen Savior. We know that the New Testament's interpretation of the Old Testament, which Panikkar took for granted, is both dangerous in light of anti-Semitism as well as ignorant of the fundamental Jewishness of Christianity in general. Yet, there is much to learn from Panikkar's journey into the scriptures, into the world's religions, and into his very identity, for he found the Christ in all those places. Panikkar disrupted the way Christians normally think about revelation, encouraging Christians to contemplate Melchizedek and the world's religions in order to understand who the God of Jesus Christ really is. Once one internalizes this contemplation, the distinctions between "Christians" and "non-Christians" begin to blur. Hindu and Christian are no longer two separate realities, but cohere together, even within one's very self.

Erik Ranstrom is a Teaching Fellow in the Department of Theology at Boston College, United States.

An "Ethnic Minority" Interpretation of Hagar and Ishmael

Janice P. De-Whyte (Ghana, England)

I am a Ghanaian woman. My people are matrilineal; thus I belong to my mother's family and to her tribe, the Ashanti. I am also a British woman. Once, I won an academic award called "The Ethnic Minority Excellence Award," given by the government to a few secondary school students in London, England. I have lived under the designation of "ethnic minority" for most of my life.

I read cultural and religious practices in the Old Testament and I resonate with them because of they are similar to practices of my heritage. I read Scripture with an intuitive sensitivity toward the "minority"—those women and men whose stories are far less told in sermons and popular religious literature. I've heard numerous sermons on the faith of Sarah and Abraham, in which Hagar is a byword, an incidental character to be passed over. Yet, Hagar's story reveals to contemporary society the God who is able to engender spirituality despite social disadvantage and dysfunction. Such a cultural reading flows out of a deep respect for Scripture and a belief that the Holy Spirit must be the guide of all interpretation, whether Western or African. Scripture interpretation for the "minority" is in focus here.

The Ashanti of Ghana prize the gift of children. Traditionally a woman does not inherit the property or material wealth of her family; thus children are the means through which she may build her own legacy. The matrilineal nature of the Akan and the importance placed on the bond between mother and child is highlighted through the proverb *wo na awu a, wo abusua asa* (when your mother dies, you have no relatives left). Sarah knew that to be considered a true wife in the Ancient Near East was to have children who would carry on her legacy. It is understandable then that Sarah would go to any lengths in order to be "built up" (Gen. 16:2).

Ultimately, Sarah's surrogacy plan turns sour. Instead, the mistress' desire to be "built up" by her maidservant results in her "being small" in Hagar's eyes (16:4). The dynamics of honor and shame are as central to Ghanaian culture as they were to the Ancient Near East. An Ashanti woman or man strives to bring *animonyam* (honor) and not *animguase* (shame) to their family name. What Sarah and Abraham did with their authority challenges us; do we use our authority in line with the promises and revelation of God or do we go our own way? In due course, it is God's plan, not our own schemes, which will bring honor.

Yahweh's encounters with Hagar communicate his interest in those labeled as "ethnic minority" or any other minority group. After she has seen the angel of the Lord, Hagar is surprised that she has seen God in angelic form and lived. The young Egyptian maid is the first to name God, as she calls him *El Ro'i*, "the God who sees me" (16:13). As a young woman who often finds herself in religious and professional contexts in which I am the minority, I can sometimes identify with the feeling of being unseen and unheard. Hagar's comfort came in her realization she was neither irrelevant nor disposable to God.

Throughout the biblical tradition, God gives promises of many offspring only to the males, the Patriarchs. Interestingly the African Hagar is the only woman to whom Yahweh directly promises many descendents (16:10). Furthermore, the same promise which Yahweh gives to Hagar is that which the Angel Gabriel gives to Mary hundreds of years later, "You will bear a son and you shall call him..." (Gen. 16:11; Matthew 1:23).

Through Hagar's son a great nation will emerge (Gen. 21:18). We are told concerning Ishmael that "God was with the lad and he grew" (21:20). Significantly, this same notice of divine presence and favor during childhood is given in the stories of Samson, Samuel, John the Baptist, and Jesus (Judges 13:24; 1 Samuel 2:21, 26; 3:19; Luke 1:80; 2:40, 52). Ishmael is placed in the same company with these other special children and even the Messiah himself.

Notably, even before there were the twelve sons of Jacob, there were the twelve princes of Ishmael (Gen. 17:20; 25:16). Ishmael had favor and blessing in his life as he died at the ripe old age of 137. In the Ashanti worldview, growing old to meet one's grandchildren and great-grandchildren is the ultimate blessing from God.

As I read the narrative, I cannot help but think of the many children who grow up in single-parent families, as Ishmael did. Often, such children are made to bear the brunt of their parents' decisions by the religious community. Whether a child of a divorcee or an unwed teenager, children of single-parent homes are sometimes ignored and neglected by the faith community. Through Hagar's narrative we see that God cares as much for Ishmael as he does for Isaac, the heir of a nuclear family. Furthermore, while the decisions of the parents made it impossible for all to live under the same roof, God made provisions for Ishmael just as he did for Isaac. Our faith communities must embrace and provide for the Ishmaels and not just the Isaacs of our time.

I am a British woman. I am a Ghanaian woman. Living in two worlds results in constant dialogue between my Western education and Ghanaian heritage. Such dialogue sensitizes me to the actions of God on behalf of the young and voiceless, thus encouraging readings which highlight the "minor" as well as "major" characters of the Bible.

Janice P. De-Whyte is a Ph.D. candidate at McMaster Divinity College, Canada; she also serves as a Youth Pastor.

Sodom and Gomorrah in Light of the Sydney Gay and Lesbian Mardi Gras

Roland Boer (Australia)

The twin cities of Sodom and Gomorrah (Gen. 18–19) have become watchwords for the "sins of the flesh," for sex between men and between women, and for every other wanton sexual vice imaginable and indeed unimaginable. Arguably, the infamy of Sodom and Gomorrah has grown with the retellings over millennia. But I wish to read this text in light of the world-famous Sydney (Australia) Gay and Lesbian Mardi Gras. Why? On more than one occasion, opponents of the Mardi Gras have described it as the Sodom and Gomorrah of our day.

But what is the Gay and Lesbian Mardi Gras? Today it is the largest event of its kind in the world, with hundreds of thousands of people attending and participating. Running over two weeks in late February and early March, it includes intellectual events, films, plays, art displays, cabarets, comedy, literary readings, concerts, a fair day, the pool party, the grand parade, and then the postparade party (for which 20,000 tickets are often sold). Needless to say, the Mardi Gras is one of the largest annual tourist boosts for Sydney.

Is Sydney, then, a sin city to rival Sodom and Gomorrah, or perhaps San Francisco? This might be the initial impression, especially if one were to visit during the Mardi Gras. But two items suggest it is not so. First, the Mardi Gras was not always this way. At the first event, on June 24, 1978, the police revoked permission for the celebration, which was then a protest march in commemoration of the Stonewall Riots (in Greenwich Village, New York, 1969). The march of about 1,000 people was broken up by police, with 53 of the marchers arrested. Those arrested were later named publically in the *Sydney Morning Herald*. Given that homosexuality was still a crime in the state of New South Wales (until 1984), and given that many had not come out as homosexuals to employers and friends, the publication of names led to many losing their jobs.

Second, Sydney is generally a conservative city, with arguably the largest conservative religious groups in Australia. It is a stronghold of the conservative evangelical wing of the Anglican Church; the right-wing Cardinal Pell of the Roman Catholic Church is based in Sydney; the Pentecostal mega-church "Hillsong," now a transnational ecclesial corporation, has its base in Sydney; many smaller conservative religious groups (including Muslims and Jews) find fertile ground in that city. Each of them is opposed to the Mardi Gras, although they express that opposition in different ways. Indeed, one might argue that the strength of the Mardi Gras operates in an inverse ratio to the strength of conservative religion in Sydney.

Perhaps the most consistent and well-known opponent is Reverend Fred Nile, known variously as Uniting Church minister, leader of the Sydney City Mission, radio-show host, founder of political organizations known as the Festival of Light, the Christian Democratic Party, and the Fred Nile Group, and long-standing member of the Upper House in the New South Wales Parliament.

From the beginning, Nile has consistently declared the Gay and Lesbian Mardi Gras a blight on Sydney. Indeed, Sydney is the Sodom of his imagination. Not only does filth reign on television, not only do brothels and casinos boom, not only do children avidly pursue pornography on the Internet, not only does abortion flourish, but the Mardi Gras goes from strength to strength.

Each year Nile and his fellow Christian Democrats organize a protest march against the Mardi Gras parade. They begin with a prayer for rain on the parade and, when the heavens invariably fail to open, they hand out leaflets to any Mardi Gras reveler willing to take one. Many leaflets usually make it from one year to the next. In contrast to the hundreds of thousands at the Mardi Gras, usually no more than 100 turn out for Nile's protest—this in response to a call for "10,000 warriors" to bring the Mardi Gras to a halt. Ultimately, of course, it is in God's hands. And that is what Nile fears: Should Sydney continue on its wanton path, it too may be destroyed for "homosexual immorality," just like Sodom and Gomorrah. For Nile, Sydney and its Mardi Gras directly provoke God, since the parade blatantly celebrates homosexuality, which is worse than sex shops, brothels, and strip shows.

At one such protest (in 2010), Nile and his supporters handed out "pieces of brimstone" from Sodom and Gomorrah to warn against what may happen: "Hold them in your hands just for a minute and let the reality of the curse that comes upon the land because of sexual immorality... We do not want Sydney to be another Sodom and Gomorrah," they said.

But let us see how well this effort to read the Mardi Gras in terms of Genesis 19 holds up. The men of the city, young and old, who gather at Lot's house and demand sex with the visitors, may easily be connected with the multitudes of gay men (and presumably women) who both live in Sydney and gather at the Mardi Gras. Further, the destruction meted out by God on Sodom and Gomorrah—the fire and brimstone, or burning sulfur and dense smoke (depending upon one's translation)—is just as easily connected with God's anger against the "wickedness" and "grievous sin" of any other place.

After this, the parallels begin to break down. What role, for instance, does Fred Nile play? Is he one of the "messengers" who arrive in Sodom to warn Lot and his family to flee? Given the elision between these "messengers" and God, that would bring Nile dangerously close to an identity with God. Or is he Lot, bidden to leave the city at the last minute? That would render Nile less as a messenger of warning and doom than as a potentially innocent bystander. Perhaps Lot and his immediate family stand in for Sydney's 5 million residents. If so, then the majority of Sydney is not given over to the pleasures of the flesh and thereby the comparison with Sodom loses its effect.

And what about me as an erstwhile resident of Sydney? Am I one of the residents engaged in all manner of fleshly pursuits, blithely ignoring the warnings of the raining sulfur? Or am I a Lot, a relatively innocent bystander about to be caught in the mayhem? I am certainly not a self-appointed angel of the Lord, or even God himself, about to destroy an evil city.

In closing, it is worth pointing out that the Gay and Lesbian Mardi Gras has taken Fred Nile and other opponents to heart. He is often featured—in parody—in at least one float in the Mardi Gras parade. For instance, one year the Sisters of Perpetual Indulgence carried Nile's head—as a massive roast surrounded by vegetables—on a platter like that of John the Baptist's. Nile threatened prosecution. And while Nile rages against a parade with men dressed as Catholic nuns, or men dressed as church bishops wearing large crosses on their dresses, or other men almost naked wearing only leather straps and other "unfavorable material," he is often depicted as a member of precisely one of these groups.

Roland Boer is a cyclist, ship-voyager, and research professor at the University of Newcastle, Australia.

QUESTIONS

1. Identify all the places in the biblical text where Abraham has "nonpeak experiences."
2. Does Melchizedek demonstrate that other people were in fact worshipping the God of Abraham before Abraham? Does Panikkar draw a legitimate interpretation of Melchizedek?
3. What cultural practices in Genesis 12–21 do you resonate with, if any? Which ones are strikingly hard to connect with? How does the Ashanti's view of children compare to the views of your cultural tradition?
4. Based on a careful reading of the text, is the story of Sodom and Gomorrah about God's disapproval of homosexuality? How would you personally respond to Fred Nile?

CHAPTER 4

GENESIS 22

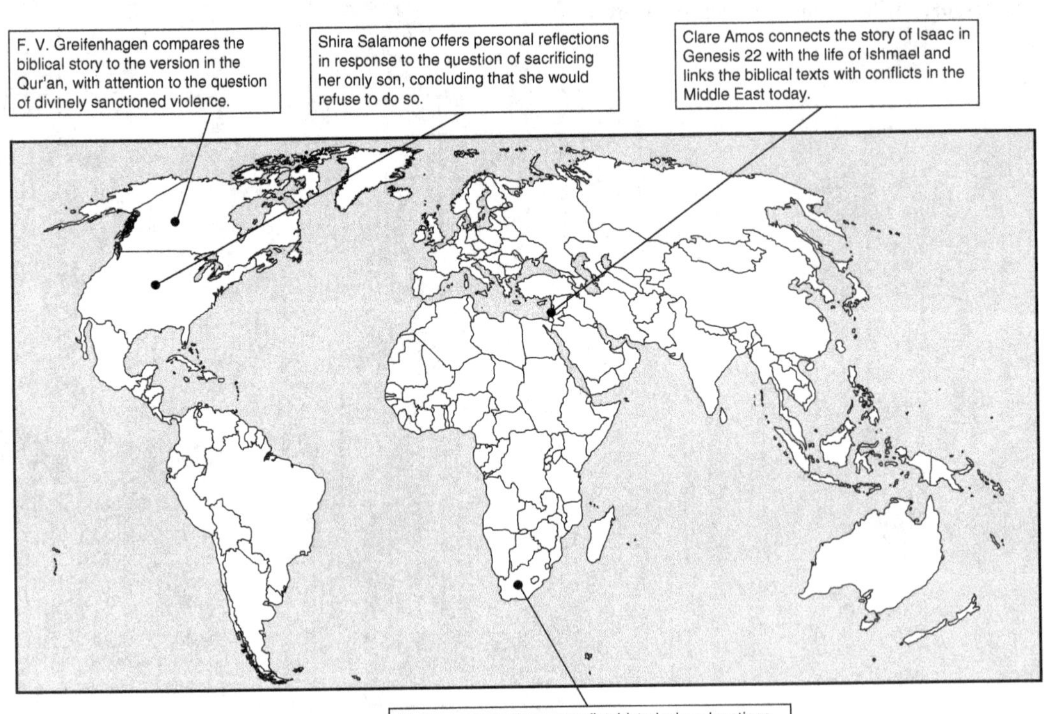

F. V. Greifenhagen compares the biblical story to the version in the Qur'an, with attention to the question of divinely sanctioned violence.
Shira Salamone offers personal reflections in response to the question of sacrificing her only son, concluding that she would refuse to do so.
Clare Amos connects the story of Isaac in Genesis 22 with the life of Ishmael and links the biblical texts with conflicts in the Middle East today.
Christo Lombaard presents five historical explanations for how such a difficult story ended up in Scripture, noting the link between history and theology.

READINGS

Genesis 22 and Conflict in the Modern-Day Middle East
Clare Amos

A Comparison of Genesis 22 to the Qur'an
F. V. Greifenhagen

A Personal Reflection on the Sacrifice of a Son
Shira Salamone

Five Historical Explanations for Genesis 22 and Its Inclusion in the Scripture
Christo Lombaard

Genesis 22 and Conflict in the Modern-Day Middle East

Clare Amos (Lebanon)

In the early years of our marriage my husband and I lived and worked in Beirut and Damascus, where he was the Anglican chaplain. On the walls of our apartment was a cloth print we had bought in the *suq* (marketplace) in Damascus. It depicted a rather grisly looking scene—a man about to sacrifice a young boy is being prevented by the last-minute intervention of a fierce angel. Visitors to our apartment naturally assumed it was a depiction of the biblical story of the near-sacrifice of Isaac. We enjoyed correcting them: It was in fact the sacrifice of Ishmael, for in many Muslim sources it is Ishmael rather than Isaac who is the son that Abraham is apparently instructed to slaughter.

Whenever I read Genesis 22 I remember that confusion between Isaac and Ishmael. Why do the Judaeo-Christian tradition and the Muslim tradition differ regarding who is the intended sacrifice? And does this confusion perhaps offer a hint that is worth exploring in Genesis itself, a hint that perhaps might have something important to offer in the context of the modern Middle East?

Genesis 22 has been described as a text which is "central to the nervous system of Judaism and Christianity." It resonates with Jewish theologies of the Holocaust and Christian understandings of the death of Christ. Its sparse and understated telling, yet one that, as Erich Auerbach put it, is "fraught with background," leaves the reader with a sense of horror mingled with frisson.

But Genesis 22 needs to be read in the context of Genesis 21. This is the account of the expulsion by Abraham of Ishmael and his mother Hagar into the wilderness, apparently with the expectation that they would perish. That the two stories are connected is indicated by several parallels which are central to both: the expression "early in the morning"; the motifs of the delivering angel; the bush; the importance of seeing; two sons of Abraham, one apparently sentenced to death because of internal family strife, the other suffering a similar sentence at God's demand; and two brothers, both rescued from their respective fates by divine intervention at the last minute. Notice too how the narrative of Genesis 22 is introduced by the phrase "After these things," which encourages the reader to see the interconnections between the two chapters. Indeed Abraham's actions in Genesis 21 toward Ishmael and his mother could be said to offer a sort of "rationale" for the seemingly monstrous demand in Genesis 22 that he should sacrifice his other son Isaac. Although the expulsion of Hagar and Ishmael is sanctioned by God even if at Sarah's behest (21:12), we can wonder whether Abraham was perhaps using God simply as a convenient way of sorting out a family quarrel. We can all hear God speaking to us when it is opportune to do so, and Abraham's loyalty to God goes through many twists and turns. So now in turn with the demand for Isaac God seeks to discover just how pure Abraham's faith really is. The "sacrifice" of one son has led to the demand for the sacrifice of the second.

There is one other motif that circles these chapters and entwines them together. It is the theme of the *ger*, which has a major place in the Abraham stories. The Hebrew word *ger* is difficult exactly to capture in translation; it is variously rendered as "alien," "resident alien," "migrant," and "sojourner." It normally spoke of someone without land rights, who in a real sense did not belong in a particular land or country, who was therefore vulnerable and whose existence and well-being depended on the generosity of the settled people of that land. In the law codes of Exodus, justice for the *ger* is one of the touchstones that God requires of his people. Note how the root *ger* as both a noun and a verb occurs several times in Genesis 20, 21, and 23 (20:1; 21:34; 23:4). But the verbal root seems also to be used in the form of a pun on the name of the Philistine city "Gerar" (20:1). Even more significantly, it is also there in the name "Hagar"—the consonants of whose name in Hebrew could simply mean "the alien." Perhaps it is as though she is being pictured as the archetypal *ger.*

Thus, one way of reading these chapters is to suggest that they explore what it means for Abraham and Sarah to be *gerim*—dependent upon the hospitality of people such as Abimelech, who treats them with generosity and good will. But in turn it also raises questions about the treatment by Abraham and Sarah of others such as Hagar. Is the way they behaved toward her in accord with how God's people should treat others who are vulnerable? The writers of Genesis do not provide an easy answer, but they do at least seem to raise the question.

Whether it is through the Muslim tradition that the sacrificial son was Ishmael rather than Isaac or through the way that Genesis entwines the stories of Isaac and Ishmael, it is clear that somehow the fates of the two brothers are "bound" together. Is not this of possible significance for the destiny of the current Middle East, where the spiritual heirs of both Isaac and Ishmael live with hostility between them? It is fascinating that the author of Genesis refuses to write Ishmael out of the biblical story, even though Isaac is seen as the more favored brother. For example, there is a genealogy given for Ishmael in 25:12–18. The way that the two brothers stand together to bury their father near Hebron (25:9) offers a poignant contrast to the way that the site of Abraham's tomb has become a modern flashpoint of hostility and hatred.

Writing with an awareness of the significance of these stories for the life and well-being of the modern Middle East, it is relevant to note that respect for the *ger* is a model that could also have modern-day applications. When the birth of Ishmael is announced to Hagar by the divine messenger in 16:12, the comment is made that he "shall live at odds with all his kin." However, the underlying Hebrew could also be translated another way to read, "He shall live alongside all his kin." The destiny of the Middle East, and perhaps of our world, lies between those two possible meanings.

There is a well-known poem by the Israeli poet Shin Shalom, with verses spoken as from the mouth of Isaac, which is used in some Jewish traditions during the celebration of the New Year, and which reflects on the biblical interweaving of the figures of Isaac and Ishmael. Isaac asks poignantly, "Ishmael, my brother, How long shall we fight each other?" The final lines of the poem stand as aspiration and goal for all who care for the destiny of the Middle East today: "Time is running out, put hatred to sleep. Shoulder to shoulder, let's water our sheep."

Clare Amos served as Director of Theological Studies in the Anglican Communion Office before recently joining the World Council of Churches in Geneva, where she is responsible for Christian–Muslim and Christian–Jewish relations.

A Comparison of Genesis 22 to the Qur'an

F. V. Greifenhagen (Canada)

Would you kill for God? This question is raised by one of the paradigmatic stories for Jews and Christians: the poignant narrative of Abraham's near sacrifice of his son, found in Genesis 22:1–19. The same story also occupies a paradigmatic place for Muslims, and a version of the story appears in Qur'an:

Surah 37 *Al-Saffat* ("Those Ranged in Ranks") 99–113.

> [99]He (Abraham) said: "I will go to my Lord! He will surely guide me!" [100]"O my Lord! Grant me a righteous (son)!" [101]So we gave him the good news of a boy ready to suffer and forbear. [102]Then, when (the son) reached (the age of) (serious) work with him, he said: "O my son! I see in a vision that I offer you in sacrifice. Now see what is your view!" (The son) said: "O my father! Do as you are commanded; you will find me, if Allah so wills, one practicing patience and constancy!" [103] So when they had both submitted their wills (to Allah), and he had laid him prostrate on his forehead (for sacrifice), [104]We called out to him, "O Abraham!" [105]"You have already fulfilled the vision!" And thus indeed We reward those who do right. [106]For this was obviously a trial. [107]And We ransomed him with a momentous sacrifice. [108]And We left (this blessing) for him among generations (to come) in later times: [109]"Peace and salutation to Abraham!" [110]Thus indeed do We reward those who do right. [111]For he was one of Our believing servants. [112]And We gave him the good news of Isaac, a prophet, one of the righteous. [113]We blessed him and Isaac, but of their progeny are (some) that do right and (some) that obviously do wrong, to their own souls. (Translation by 'Abdullah Yusuf 'Ali, 2001)

The Qur'an here generally follows the biblical account: the command to Abraham to sacrifice his son, the aborting of the sacrifice at the last minute, the characterization of the event as a trial, and the commendation of Abraham's faith and obedience. However, the qur'anic version presents a unique perspective on the story. It does not mention many of the details of the biblical account, such as the place of sacrifice; the journey to and from it; or the knife, the wood, the servants, the donkey, the altar, or the binding of the son. The Qur'an seems to assume that its hearers are already familiar with the story, and so it focuses on the particular meaning of the story rather than its details.

Noticeably, the son is not identified in the qur'anic version, and yet he plays a much more active role in the story than he does in the biblical version. In the biblical account, besides carrying the wood and initiating a short conversation with his father, Isaac plays a rather passive role. It is unclear whether he is a willing participant; the fact that his father binds him (22:9) seems to suggest that he was not. And yet postbiblical Jewish and Christian literature transformed Isaac into a willing victim (e.g., Judith 8:26–27; 4 Maccabees 13:12).

The Qur'an continues this interpretive trajectory, portraying the father as consulting with the unnamed son, who is made aware of what God has commanded his father to do. In fact, the son urges his father to obey the command. Father and son are both depicted as willingly submitting to the divine will (37:103). The test in the qur'anic account applies not just to the father but also to the son, and both pass with flying colors.

By omitting the son's name, the qur'anic version has released the story from its context within the sibling rivalry between Ishmael and Isaac as depicted in the Bible, and enabled it to become a general paradigm of faithful obedience to God for believers. While the Bible presents a sacred history in which a choice must be made as to which son will continue the covenantal relationship that leads to the creation of the people Israel, the Qur'an focuses on abstracted models of morality and piety. Both Ishmael and Isaac can be a model of faith and so it is inconsequential which son was almost killed by his father.

Although the identity of the son is not the Qur'an's concern, Muslim and non-Muslim interpreters have argued over whether it was Ishmael or Isaac. At stake in this debate is which religious community can lay legitimate claim to the heritage of Abraham. Isaac appears by name in the qur'anic version only after the sacrifice, seeming to imply that he could not have been the intended sacrificial victim; rather, the victim was his older brother Ishmael. However, the reference to Isaac at the end of the story (37:112) could be a summary statement linked with Abraham's plea for a righteous son at the beginning of the story (37:100), thus implying that Isaac was the intended sacrificial victim. And so the qur'anic version of the story is dragged back into the sibling rivalries, from which it had originally extricated itself.

This religiously sanctioned and revered story of a father's intended violence against his own child raises acute questions for us today about divinely sanctioned violence, child abuse, and patriarchy, questions that are obscured by religious rivalries or mitigated by portrayals of the son as a willing victim. Bruce Feiler, tellingly a journalist and not a professional biblical or qur'anic scholar, writes in his popular book *Abraham: A Journey to the Heart of Three Faiths* (New York: William Morrow, 2002, 108, 110):

> Abraham, I was discovering, is not just a gentle man of peace. He's as much a model for fanaticism as he is for moderation. He nurtured in his very behavior—in his conviction to break from his father, in his willingness to terrorize *both* of his sons—the intimate connection between faith and violence. And then, by elevating such conduct to the standard of piety, he stirred in his descendents a similar desire to lash out, to view pain as an arm of belief, and to use brutality to advance their vision of a divine-centered world...No wonder the story of the binding is so central to Jews, Christians, and Muslims, I thought. It's the part of Abraham's life that cuts closest to our veins and poses the question we hope never to face: Would I kill for God? For many of Abraham's descendents, of course, the answer throughout history has been yes.

This is the question that Jews, Christians, and Muslims would do well to struggle with together as they read this story of Abraham. For the story easily evokes the ancient patriarchal framework, in which fathers, or male authority figures, have the right to sacrifice their offspring on the altar of war. Noticeably absent in both versions of the story is the boy's mother; whether Sarah or Hagar, she is invisible. What would she say or do if given voice and agency? Perhaps she would echo Julia Ward Howe's Mothers Day Proclamation of 1870:

> Our sons will not be taken from us to unlearn
> All that we have been able to teach them of charity, mercy and patience.
> We, the women of one country,
> Will be too tender of those of another country
> To allow our sons to be trained to injure theirs.

Certainly, Muslims, Christians, and Jews, while standing in awe of Abraham's submission to God, in general, do not feel called to emulate him specifically by literally sacrificing their children. Perhaps, just as the ram was substituted for the human sacrifice, the story also powerfully sublimates the terrifying willingness to sacrifice one's own kind by transforming it into a recital of that act as necessarily or divinely unfulfilled. The awesome energy of the impetus to kill is thus not dissipated but rather channeled into self-giving piety.

F. V. Greifenhagen is Associate Professor of Religious Studies at Luther College, University of Regina, Canada.

A Personal Reflection on the Sacrifice of a Son

Shira Salamone (United States)

I've heard the story of the *Akédah*, the Binding of Isaac (and of his near-sacrifice), read in synagogue twice every year for 32 years. It's read on the second day of *Rosh Hashanah* (Jewish New Year) and during the regular cycle of weekly *Torah* (Bible) readings. My husband and I have discussed it many times. We've concluded that G-d (we avoid writing the word *G-o-d* lest we accidentally take G-d's name in vain, which is forbidden) wanted to see whether *Avraham Avinu* (Abraham our Patriarch) would show as much devotion to Him as a pagan would have shown to a pagan god, who, in that era, would have demanded child sacrifice. The difference, of course—and it's a huge one—is that G-d didn't allow *Avraham* to go through with the sacrifice of his child.

To speak of this on an intellectual level is one thing. But to speak of it on a personal level is another. For so many years, I've tried to ignore this question, but, somehow, when it's put to music, it reaches out past my defenses and goes straight to my heart:

> Would you take your only son?
> Would you lay your answer down?
> Would you bind him to the stone?
> Would you take your only son?

The first time I heard Blue Fringe's song *Hineni* ("Here I am") I almost turned it off. The second time, I listened closely, because, given the way the song had affected me the first time, I knew that I would *have* to write about it. The third time was this morning. I listened so that I could write down the lyrics. I'm not sure I'll ever be able to listen to it again. It's a beautiful song, but I can't bear to hear the words.

> Because I have an only son.
> And the answer is "No."

Ani maamin, be-emuna sh'léma (I believe with perfect faith). I sing these words to honor my ancestors, factual or metaphorical, who died with the *Sh'ma* (biblical quotations affirming that we have only one G-d) on their lips. I sing these words for the martyrs who died *al k'dushat haShem* (for the sanctification of G-d's name) during the wars in which the Temples, first and second, were destroyed. For those who died during the revolts of the Maccabees and Bar Kochba. For the Ten Sages, whose terrible deaths we commemorate during the Martyrology on *Yom Kippur* (Day of Atonement). For the victims of the Crusades, the pogroms, and the *Shoah*/Holocaust. For all those who have died because they were Jews. I sing those words to honor my ancestors. Not because I believe in those words. Like Adam and Eve in the Garden of Eden, I'm hiding, but it's my faith that's naked.

Either you believe that life's misfortunes are random or you believe that G-d has His reasons. Neither can I accept the idea, promulgated by some, that misfortune is a punishment for sin nor can I agree with the idea, supported by others, that we must simply accept misfortune and not question why because G-d's ways are beyond human comprehension.

Avinu haAv haRachamun haM'Rachem (Our Father, Compassionate Father Who has compassion). Does He? If so, why did He deem it necessary to put *Avraham* (and, for that matter, *Iyov*/Job) through such a trial?

Eish u'varad, sheleg v'kitor, ruach s'arah osah d'varo (Fire and hail, snow and mist, stormy wind fulfilling His word) (Psalm 148). Why should I trust a G-d who stands by while thousands die in tsunamis and hurricanes to stay my hand and put a ram in my son's place? *Hineni*? Here I am?

No.

I cannot understand how *Avraham* could have argued repeatedly with G-d not to destroy *Tz'dom* and *Amorah* (Sodom and Gomorrah), but did not say a word of protest when G-d told him to sacrifice his own child. Why is *Avraham* nicer to strangers than to his own family? And this is not the first time. He had already sent his son *Yishmael* packing with nothing but bread and water (Genesis 21:8–21). All G-d said was *Sh'ma b'kolah*, listen to her (Sarah's) voice. G-d never suggested that *Yishmael* and his mother Hagar should be sent off into the desert with limited means of short-term survival and no means of long-term support. Judging by the text, *Yishmael* had to have been over 14 years old at the time of his expulsion. *Avraham* could have given him a parting gift of, for example, a small flock of goats. Why didn't he? So, in one sense, is it any surprise that *Avraham* passively accepts the command to sacrifice Isaac?

It appears that G-d wasn't so thrilled with the fact that *Avraham* assented without protest. For afterward, G-d never spoke to him again. Maybe G-d wanted *Avraham* to protest. At any rate, if the choice were imposed upon me, I would die *al k'dushat haShem* (for the sanctification of G-d's name). But I would not take my only son.

Shira Salamone is a Jewish blogger (http://onthefringe_jewishblog.blogspot.com/) who takes Judaism seriously, but not necessarily literally.

Five Historical Explanations for Genesis 22 and Its Inclusion in the Scripture

Christo Lombaard (South Africa)

Genesis 22:1–19 is a tall tale, in a different sense. Though told in a few verses, it is an account with huge implications. The idea of God ordering human sacrifice is utterly disturbing to our moral sensibilities and to our religious sense of God as author of life and love. In this immoral drama, Abraham—father of three world religions—actively colludes by deceiving his son when Isaac asks some penetrating questions (22:7–8). Yet, Abraham eventually emerges as a hero of faithful obedience, an example to all believers. The story told in these few verses reads almost like the script of a third-rate psychothriller movie, for late-night television viewing only.

No surprise, then, that throughout its existence this account has been the subject of debate and speculation. How could such a story find a place in the *Good* Book? For...*good* people!? *Good* God!?

A popular recent way of dealing with these difficulties has been circumvention. Focusing on how the parts of the text stick together (structuralism) or on its storytelling techniques (narratological readings) skirts two kinds of questions: the moral problems, summarized in the first paragraph above, and the matter hinted at in the second paragraph: Why on earth would such an account become Scripture? These questions must never be dodged, simply because people keep asking them. Only one kind of answer *can* address these questions: historical explanations. Five such historical proposals have been made.

The oldest historical understanding of Genesis 22 reads it as a rallying cry opposing child sacrifice in ancient Israel. Scholars debate whether sacrificing children as an act of loyalty to God was ever a part of Israel's faith. Some doubt whether it was part of the cultures surrounding Israel. But the fact remains: The people of Israel recognized the *possibility* of killing children to prove religious commitment—the ultimate "giving till it hurts"! Clearly, at some stage, this possibility came up for serious consideration. To counter this possibility, which would be a difficult fit with Israel's religious make-up, action was needed: Something *had* to be said. So a story—Genesis 22—was told which made the point clear: God desires animal sacrifice, not human. The lesson? From the beginning of Israel's faith, with father Abraham, human sacrifice was anathema. God does not want it; Abraham did not do it; for "us" (the later generations) it is a no-no too!

The second of the historical understandings seeks to grasp very small parts of 22:1–19. Now where did *this* snippet of the story come from, they ask? Once we know the answer, we can respond: Ah, so *that*'s how it came to be. That's how the story ended up in Holy Writ, as an explanation for the origin of something, that is, an etiology. Verse 14 offers one such example. Here we see an explanation of the origin of the name of a certain place. The thinking is that there was a place called—following some English Bibles' renderings—"The LORD Will Provide" (New International Version), or "Yahweh provides" (New Jerusalem Bible), or "Jehovahjireh" (King James Version's direct transliteration of the Hebrew). So people asked: Where does this name come from? Then, the story of Abraham's sacrifice was related to this site. "Ah, so *that*'s how it came to be..."

A second snippet which calls forth etiological explanation is in verse 2. The implicit ancient question here was: Why is it specifically *in the Moriah area* that we regularly sacrifice to God? That matter would then be resolved by Abraham's sacrifice story: that is where God sent Abraham, and some very special events happened there, so that is why we (later generations) continue to offer sacrifices in Moriah.

None of the etiological explanations cover all aspects of the text. These cultural-historical questions are just too specific. Yet, none of the other forms of explanation can do without these etiological elements. Without etiology, certain snippets of the story remain inexplicable.

Third, in many religions, initiation ceremonies allow entrance into membership and advancement through various levels. Christianity, for instance, has baptism, which is an "entry ceremony," as well as other rites which induct one into full church membership or leadership positions. In Genesis 22 we see three different levels of cultic initiation. The "two young men" in verse 3 (literally) go on a first religious excursion, but as novices they may only progress halfway. Isaac, somewhat older, is taken to the point of almost dying in his initiation ritual, which means he has now passed into religious adulthood. Abraham, lastly, passes muster as a priest, willing to sacrifice all for God. In this interpretation, the three strands of narrative are ancient initiation myths. Centuries later, these cultural memories became entwined, to form a new story demonstrating obedience.

A fourth approach reads the text in light of the problem of human suffering, which lies at the heart of many religions and philosophies. It remains foundational: Why do we endure hardship? More religiously: Why does God allow, perhaps even cause, heartache? Job is the most renowned Old Testament book dealing with such *theodicy*. Yet, the fourth historical approach holds that Genesis 22's crude, unrefined vision of suffering actually inspired the book of Job as a response. Whereas Job holds that suffering remains a mystery before God, Genesis 22 states that God *causes* misery. Isaac represents the suffering Israel in exile, with Abraham as Babylonian oppressor. Fortunately, just before extinction, that same God saves Isaac/Israel—still, though, without giving reasons.

The last, most recent, of the historical interpretations places Genesis 22 within the conflict between patriarchal supporter groups. Old Testament scholarship has long accepted that Abraham, Isaac, and Jacob were initially independent clan elders. In time, the clans grew closer. To cement such ties their tribal origin stories were intermingled; these three patriarchs thus *became* related. Inharmoniously, the adherents to the different patriarchal groups were vying for power. This is seen in the famous doublets/triplets in the Pentateuch: stories from one group retold to favor another. In Genesis 22:2–14 and 19, we see the final showdown between Abraham's supporters and Isaac's adherents. The Abrahamites have the upper hand. Evidently, the Isaacites should know their place: They have been finally surpassed in the social competition stakes. The Abrahamites would have eliminated the Isaacites were it not for divine intervention.

The theological subservience of the Isaacites is soon emphasized. In the frame-verses 1 and 15–18, the Isaacites should now accept that they will be blessed only *through* Abraham. The initially dominant Isaacites of early scriptural prophetism are vanquished in the late Persian period. Genesis 22:19 clinches the game: Isaac is not even mentioned; Abraham takes over Beersheba, the Isaacites' home field.

In sum, Genesis 22:1–19 remains without final solution. These five attempts have been made, and more should. Already amply clear, though, is this: Only *in* the history of the text can we follow its faith. Or put differently, once we know the history, we can grasp the theology.

Christo Lombaard (Ph.D., Communications; D.D., Old Testament) teaches Christian Spirituality at the University of South Africa.

QUESTIONS

1. Based on a close reading of the biblical text, consider the merits of Amos' suggestion that Genesis 22 is God's punishment on Abraham for his treatment of Ishmael.
2. Greifenhagen quotes Feiler as saying that Abraham was a religious fanatic. Is this a fair assessment of Abraham? Can Abraham rightly be compared to people "who are willing to kill for God"?
3. Who has the stronger/better faith: Salamone or Abraham? Who deserves more admiration and respect?
4. Lombaard observes that Genesis 22 flies in the face of "our religious sense of God as author of life and love." From where do people get that "religious sensibility"—society, religious leaders, the Bible, or an intuitive morality?

CHAPTER 5

GENESIS 25–33

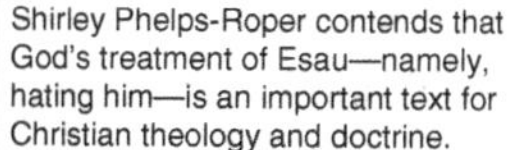
Shirley Phelps-Roper contends that God's treatment of Esau—namely, hating him—is an important text for Christian theology and doctrine.

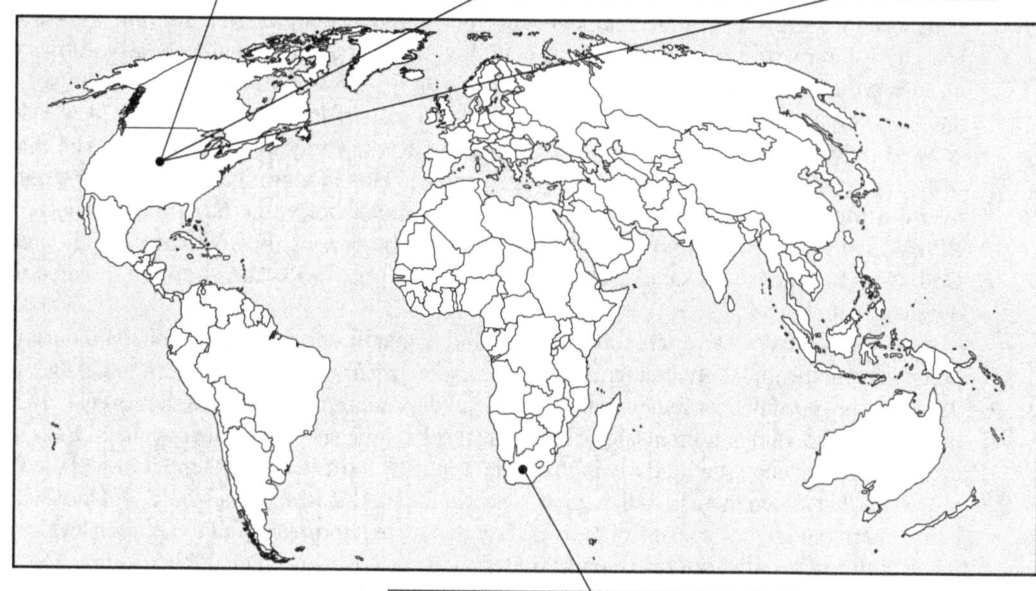
Arlette Poland, reading as a Jewish feminist, argues that Rebekah is a person of exemplary character, whose actions are based on love, not deception.
Clarence Mitchell shares how the story of Jacob facilitated his own reconciliation with his father, which shows the continuing power of the Bible.
Madipoane Masenya focuses on Leah and the challenges of women in a polygynous partnership, specifically their struggle to enjoy their sexuality.

READINGS

A Jewish Feminist Reflection on Rebekah
Arlette Poland

God's Treatment of Esau as It Relates to Theology and Doctrine
Shirley Phelps-Roper

Leah and the Challenges of Women in Polygynous Partnership
Madipoane Masenya

Jacob's Reconciliation with His Father and the Continuing Power of the Bible
Clarence Mitchell

A Jewish Feminist Reflection on Rebekah

Arlette Poland (United States)

I approach the women of Genesis as a feminist, a Jew, and a scholar. Here I will show that Rebekah/Rivka is a person of exemplary character and that she acted out of her love for and obedience to God when she supposedly tricked Isaac into blessing Jacob rather than Esau.

We first discover Rivka's model character in Genesis 24, where Abraham's servant has been sent to find a wife for Isaac. In this scene, Rivka acts virtuously by giving water to both the servant and all his camels until they are filled (25:19). In doing so, she goes beyond the expectation of the servant without thought of herself or a reward, and without knowing who the servant was. Some traditional (male) interpretations argue that Rivka acted selfishly because—through some magical intuition—she knew it was the servant of Abraham searching for a wife for Isaac, but there is nothing in the narrative that logically allows such an interpretation. Later we learn that Isaac truly loves Rivka from the moment he sees her and that she immediately assuages the pain of the loss of his mother, Sarah (24:67). Isaac shows his love by acting proactively on behalf of Rivka, praying for her when she did not conceive some 20 years into their marriage (25:21). This is more than his father, Abraham, ever did for Sarah. Notably, God answers Isaac's prayer before he has finished the prayer. Rivka's value as a wife, lover, and future mother who carries the covenant is validated by God's quick response to Isaac's loving prayer. God's trust in Rivka is now established without question.

Rivka's own positive relationship with God is manifested when she feels pain during her pregnancy. In the midst of her anguish and confusion, her first thought is to turn to God. Genesis 25:22 can be translated variously, but the key to understanding her utterance lies in realizing that this is a woman who is fully aware of her critical role in the success of the covenant. Pain in the course of a pregnancy (particularly in that time) typically indicated the potential loss of the fetus/infant. Further, when there is such pain, it is nearly impossible to speak a whole sentence without being interrupted by the spasms of pain—a fact that male interpreters fail to appreciate. Concern for the life and significance of the child (in terms of the covenant) fueled Rivka's cry. Motherly concern is universal to all women who want to be pregnant and especially where continuation of the family/tribal unit rests on the success of the pregnancy.

God responds instantaneously to Rivka's cry, providing an explanation for the pain—she is having twins—and a prediction of what will become of the twins after their birth (25:23). Interestingly, Rivka alone receives the prophecy concerning the future relationship of the twins. God responds privately to her; Isaac is not included in God's communication. One can speculate why that is so; however, the narrative has established a true love story that must logically lead one to presume that she informed Isaac at some point during the life of the twins. After all, theirs was the first true love story in Genesis and true lovers do not keep secrets. Isaac knows her character and knows of her dedication and love for God. Whatever action is necessary to carry out God's prophecy or command must be done. While it is Rivka who is most active in the so-called trick to gain the blessing of the covenant for Jacob rather than Esau, it is reasonable to assume that Isaac knew of the trick and went along (see below for more on this) with Rivka's plan to keep the secret command/prophecy for the sake of the children and their relationship, and for the sake of the covenant. Further, there was nothing in the command from God to Rivka that required her to keep it a secret from Isaac, only to carry it out and make it a reality.

After the birth of the twin boys, we read that "Isaac loved Esau, because he was fond of game; but Rivka loved Jacob" (25:28). Some commentators assert that Rivka is cunning and manipulative in her apparent favoring of Jacob. It is important to note, however, that there is no clear declaration that Rivka did not also love or favor Esau. Such a conclusion can be drawn because there is no reason stated in the narrative as to *why* Rivka favors or loves Jacob (25:28). Indeed, love of a mother such as Rivka, who is of an exemplary character, as has been firmly established, could not favor one son over another in any way that the relationship between the boys would be damaged or the family unit be torn apart. The love of Rivka for the boys might be expressed differently because they were such different people, but such difference in her expression of love is not tantamount to ignoring or harming one son over the other.

Here, to my Jewish feminist eyes, Rivka was doing three things—and doing them well. First, she was providing some balance to the household since Esau *was* favored by the father and for a certain stated (and self-gratifying) reason. Second, she was keeping secret from the boys the word from God about the future of her two sons. Third, and most importantly, she was preparing her younger son for the task of carrying the critical covenant. She had to know that he must be of a certain character: obedient, devoted to God, and deeply compassionate. How better can a child learn such qualities than by living with a mother who models them? I posit that Rivka understood her responsibilities as a mother to twins, as a critical lynchpin to the future of the covenant, and as an obedient and devoted servant of God. The simple line that she favored (loved) Jacob fulfills those responsibilities; thus, there are no negative connotations associated with her favoring or special affection.

We now turn our attention to the so-called "trickster" scene, where Rivka arranges for Jacob (the second born) to receive the covenantal blessing, a blessing that normally and automatically would go to the firstborn son. In the course of the scene, there are at least three instances where one could logically deduce that Isaac was quite aware that it was Jacob and not Esau. One is where Jacob presented his father with food (27:18). While this was the food that Isaac loved, the food alone was insufficient to lead Isaac to conclude this was Esau. Next, Isaac noticed that it was indeed the voice of Jacob, not Esau, even though their hands felt the same. Isaac was even prompted to ask one last time if this was indeed Esau (27:24). Jacob responded in the positive, lying to his father as instructed by his mother (who also assured him that any curse from these lies would befall her and not him). Meanwhile, the audience knows that she has been commanded by God to assure this result. And Isaac did not confront Jacob any further.

None of these actions by Rivka were designed for her own self-gratification or the imagined manipulation of her husband for Jacob or against Esau. In fact, it is more likely and more logical that Rivka and Isaac were complicit in this "ruse" and that it was Jacob who was tricked, just as he was later in the narrative by Laban (Gen. 30). Too many interpreters ignore the import of the order or command from God that the younger shall gain the covenant rather than the tradition of the elder son gaining it. Such was not the norm and so it was necessary for Rivka (and Isaac) to trick Jacob in order to comply with God's command. The narrative makes it clear that the scheme is devised by Rivka, but that is to be expected since she is the one who heard the command from God. While Isaac was indeed relatively passive, as many interpreters have argued, he was not tricked. Rather, out of love for Rivka and perhaps fear of God, he complied with her scheme and God's command as he willingly ate the food and drank the wine and then bestowed the sacred covenantal blessing on the younger son.

Arlette Poland (Ph.D., Philosophy of Religion, Claremont Graduate University) practiced law for 20 years before becoming an adjunct lecturer in Judaism, Buddhism, Ethics, and Science and Religion.

God's Treatment of Esau as It Relates to Theology and Doctrine

Shirley Phelps-Roper (United States)

The story of Jacob and Esau is a simple but amazing story. From this one story God teaches of heaven and hell, obedience and sin, the earthly man and the spiritual man, the hatred of God and the love of God, and the sovereignty and preeminence of God's will. The story is mentioned several times in the New Testament to make key points. It is the very heart of the excellent doctrines of Election (God elects some for eternal salvation) and Reprobation (God condemns others to hell). You cannot have one without the other!

Jacob and Esau were fraternal twin boys born to Isaac and Rebekah. They both have an impeccable bloodline. Their father Isaac and their grandfather Abraham were both Jewish patriarchs and beloved of God. They were both active participants of the covenant of God! From a DNA perspective it is hard to beat a combination like this. If Godly favor was simply a matter of bloodline, both boys would be entitled to it based solely on their gene pool. However, just being related to Godly people is not enough to earn the favor of the Almighty God.

God told their mother Rebekah even before the boys were born that there were two nations and two manner of people in her womb and that the elder, Esau, would serve the younger, Jacob (25:23). And here is the amazing part of this story: God Almighty predetermined and predestinated before they were born and before they had done any good or evil to love Jacob and get this... to *hate* Esau. Yes, you read right. Even though the false prophets of today preach on every corner that God does not hate, his plain revealed word says otherwise. Indeed, those who say that "God loves everyone" ignore this simple fact straight from the Bible.

And moreover, the fact that God hates Esau is repeated not only in several more places in the Old Testament (Malachi 1:2–3 and Jeremiah 49:10) but also in multiple places in the New Testament. In Romans 9:11–15, Paul writes concerning Jacob and Esau:

> For the children being not yet born, neither having done any good or evil, that the purpose of God according to election might stand, not of works, but of him that calleth. It was said unto her, The elder shall serve the younger. As it is written, Jacob have I loved, but Esau have I hated. What shall we say then? Is there unrighteousness with God? God forbid. For he saith to Moses, "I will have mercy on whom I will have mercy, and I will have compassion on whom I will have compassion."

You can spend your whole life arguing about these passages but it does not change them. There is no interpretation required here. The verses are crystal clear. This story blows to pieces the notion that God loves everyone and that he does not hate. God's hatred is not an evil passion as you find in men. It is God's perfect, righteous, and everlasting determination to send the unrepentant sinner to hell for eternity.

That is the right of the Creator. From the council halls of eternity, God created Jacob according to the election of grace and Esau according to the election of damnation. Welcome to election, friends and neighbors! Remember, two nations are represented in Jacob and Esau; one destined for heaven, and one destined for hell. I can already hear the rabble complaining and the attempts to explain away this story. Paul is ahead of you. He anticipates the complaint and asks a rhetorical question: "What shall we say then? Is there unrighteousness with God? God forbid." Every time this generation says that God does not hate, in the same breath they take away the love of God. They are related—you cannot have one without the other. As it is written, Jacob have I loved but Esau have I hated.

Do you want to complain about that, cry and whine about how unfair it is? Paul anticipates that as well in Romans 9:19–22, where he says, among other important things, that we have no right to question God. God created this world as He wanted. He in His infinite wisdom made Jacob to be a vessel of honor. Likewise, He in His wisdom made Esau, before he was born and before Esau had done good or evil, to be a vessel of dishonor to show His wrath. There is no free will here. Esau had zero free will. Esau sold his spiritual birthright for some soup because his tummy was hungry. Esau is the man of the flesh, who despised his birthright (Gen. 25:34). Paul calls Esau a "profane person... who for one morsel of meat sold his birthright" (Hebrews 12:6). Esau despised the spiritual things of God in favor of the devilish and earthly things of this world, just like this generation does. Esau caused his parents great disappointment by marrying the filthy daughters of Canaan, and when he saw it displeased his parents he married another one (Gen. 28:8–9). Esau had murder in his heart for his brother (Gen. 27:41). At all the critical points of life, Esau did wrong.

Here is the essence of this story: Obey God, keep his commandments, and seek after the righteousness of God and you demonstrate yourself to be as Jacob. Seek earthly things, go after strange women, sell your spiritual soul for a morsel of bread, and live a profane life and you demonstrate yourself to be as Esau and receive the fate of Esau.

But if you are Esau, you are damned. Period. Hebrews 12:17 says Esau "found no place of repentance, though he sought it carefully with tears." This verse again destroys the notion that God loves everyone. Not so, Esau even sought repentance from God and never was granted it. Again, Esau had no free will. God hated him from all eternity past and nothing was going to change that. Not his bloodline, not his begging, nothing. You say, again, this is not fair. But who are you, mortal human, to speak against God?

Jacob and Esau represent the two types of people that are born into this earth. You are either one or the other. If you have understanding of these things, lay it to heart, time is running out! The King is at the door! It is the time of the restitution of all things. He that hath an ear, let him hear!

Shirley Phelps-Roper is an attorney and servant of the God of all creation in the last minutes of the last days.

Leah and the Challenges of Women in Polygynous Partnership

Madipoane Masenya (South Africa)

Here I will use African love songs to engage the narrative of Leah in Genesis 29–30 with a view to foregrounding the struggles and experiences of women in a polygynous partnership. Specifically, the focus will be on these women's struggles to affirm their sexuality and their right to the enjoyment of fulfilling sexual lives.

In any patriarchal culture—including the ancient Israelite and current African cultures—the sexuality of married women is perceived to be the property of their husbands. Thus a sexually passionate woman is never celebrated. In fact, she might be viewed as either a deviant or an anomaly. Furthermore, there seems to be a general perception among scholars that biblical women did not bother much about their rights to fulfilling sexual rights. However, a gender-sensitive, woman-friendly rehearing of the story of Leah, aided by an African-South African song, will hopefully reveal the fact that married women, particularly those who are part of polygynous marriage relationships, do demand their right to a sexually fulfilling life.

Leah, like many daughters or women who are used by men (fathers and brothers) to achieve male agendas in the book of Genesis, was apparently thrown into marriage unprepared. Getting our cue from the text, no connections between Jacob and Leah were made before the night of their marriage. In the case of Rachel, Leah's younger sister, Jacob's affection is clearly revealed (29:11, 18, 21). The intensity of Jacob's affection for the younger wife compared to that of the older wife (if any) is clearly revealed in 29:30: "So Jacob went in to Rachel also, and he loved Rachel more than Leah." Although Jacob is depicted as having sexual encounters with both wives, there is no mention of his love for Leah after his encounter with her, an omission which would have repercussions on the Jacob–Leah relationship because it marked the onset of Leah's struggle for love and sex.

Could it be that Leah provides one example of a woman who refused to fit into prescribed female sexual roles? A couple of elements in the text suggest so. Leah's demand for love (and sex) from her husband is revealed from her conviction that she *owned* her husband. It is no wonder that Leah uses the possessive phrase "my husband" five times within a span of 29 verses! In 29:32, as Leah named her son *Reuben*, she thought that Jacob her husband would love her ("...surely now my husband will love me"). In naming her second-born son *Simeon* in 29:34, she had hoped to be *joined* to her husband ("now this time my husband will be joined to me..."). The expression "my husband" pointedly and painfully occurs again in 30:15 in the context of cowifely hostility and jealousy as Leah protests against the giving of her son's mandrakes to her sister and cowife, Rachel. The reader is not sure if it was a pattern for Leah to show certain favors toward Rachel in order to "buy" her marital right to sexual pleasure and intimacy to her husband. It is clear, however, that Leah's sexual life was malnourished. Her concerted effort at bearing many sons for Jacob was not helpful in winning her husband's love and intimacy.

As concerned readers of this text, we may rush to put blame on the "possessiveness" of Rachel for Jacob. Should not our critique be leveled against the patriarch Jacob, who in essence agreed to have two wives? Should it not be the responsibility of all marital partners (irrespective of how many such they choose to have) to make sure that all their partners' conjugal needs are catered for satisfactorily? What one finds disturbing, though, is that nowhere in the text do we find Leah addressing her concerns about conjugal deprivation to the right person, that is, to Jacob. The narrator mostly presents her as either speaking to herself or the midwives (cf. the context of the birthing and naming of her sons) or to Rachel, her cowife.

Leah does not hide her sexual craving for Jacob. Her reaction to her sister's request for a fertility "drug?" (mandrakes) in Genesis 30:15 gives the readers a glimpse not only of her sexual craving for her husband but also of her perceived right to sexual pleasure and intimacy. Fittingly, in 30:16 she demands a sexual encounter with her husband. This sexually passionate yet unloved wife's motive for using her reproductive powers to the fullest appears to be inspired more by her sexual desire for Jacob (30:5–16) than her commitment toward the fulfillment of her marital role as mother in a patriarchal society.

One may very well argue that Leah represents one of the neglected, invisible, and perhaps intimidating qualities of womanhood (*bosadi*), namely, a woman's legitimate desire to have her sexual needs met. This quality is also endorsed by the following African-South African

(Northern Sotho) song. The lead male singer of the song is joined by a group of women with the main respondent being his wife (Mokgadi), who responds by singing with a group of women. Here are the lyrics:

(Sepedi)	**(English translation)**
A re ye nokeng	Let us go to the river (Man and Women)
Wa mpona nala di a rotha (Mokgadi)	Look at me, my nails are falling away (Mokgadi)
A re ye kgonyeng	Let us go to the grinding stone (Man and Women)
Wa mpona nala di a rotha (Mokgadi)	Look at me, my nails are falling away (Mokgadi)
A re ye go šila	Let us go and fetch wood (Man and Women)
Wa mpona nala di a rotha (Mokgadi)	Look at me, my nails are falling away (Mokgadi)
A re ye ntlong	Let us go to the hut (Man and Women)
Ha ha ha, hi, hi, (laughing loudly)	Ha..ha..ha..hi..hi..(laughing) (Mokgadi)
...as the drum goes up higher! (Mokgadi)	

The male singer who is accompanied by female voices exhorts his wife Mokgadi to go to the river to draw water, to go and grind maize, and to go and fetch wood. All three represent ordinary household chores. Mokgadi responds by flatly refusing: "Look at me, my nails are falling away" means that she is lazy, and consequently, she will not engage in those chores. A sharp turn of events, however, occurs in the fourth line when she is invited to the "hut" for a sexual encounter with her husband. She responds positively, with loud laughter supported by the high volume of the drums. Mokgadi, like the biblical Leah, is thus not embarrassed by her legitimate right to a fulfilling sexual encounter with her husband. It is no wonder that Mokgadi's passionate response to the opportunity to engage in sex rather than in ordinary household chores is viewed with distaste by many traditional African listeners of the song.

The response of the woman in the song as well as Leah's craving to be fully loved by her husband throw light on some of the neglected aspects of women's lives either in sacred texts or secular texts. In my view, such negligence continues to render the full humanness of women invisible. It also renders the marginalization of women as irredeemable even as it undermines the fact that women in our patriarchal contexts are not devoid of power. Although women have power, their power is not legitimated. Indeed, Mokgadi and Leah challenge the status quo and its ideology that sexual pleasure in marriage, both monogamous and polygynous, is the luxury of men only.

It is important that marginalized persons should raise *prophetic* voices toward the injustices which they experience. Leah's persistence in exposing her husband's deprivation of his sexual duties toward her serves as an example of women's capacity to protect their sexual needs. Her tendency to address her concerns to the "wrong" people should be challenged, though. Although

Rachel should not be wholly exonerated from the plight in which her sister was thrown, the right person to address was Jacob and the patriarchal structure which privileged men over women. Mokgadi and Leah remind us that women also, even those within polygynous marriage settings, have the right to sexual pleasure. Women as sexual beings thus need to take pride in their sexuality and sex lives.

Madipoane Masenya (ngwan'a Mphahlele) (Ph.D.) teaches in the Department of Old Testament and Ancient Near Eastern Studies at the University of South Africa.

Jacob's Reconciliation with His Father and the Continuing Power of the Bible

Clarence Mitchell (United States)

The story of Jacob and Esau is one of the Bible stories I remember most from my childhood. Jacob running away after tricking his brother only to end up tricked himself was used to encourage me to always be honest and to never run from my problems. I understood it in theory, but it was not until I had to face a real issue in my own life that this story took on a whole new meaning for me: reconciling with my father.

My dad is a loving but rigid and principled man. If you live under his roof, you follow his rules. When I look back at my childhood there was nothing unfair about his rules; but at the time I felt stifled by them. I didn't feel it was fair that I had to live up to his standards. I didn't understand why he wouldn't consider my desires and my perspective. This all came to a head my freshman year of college.

After several weeks at school I still hadn't heard from him. When I finally called, he didn't sound happy to hear from me, but rather, he gave me a hard time about not calling him. He told me that it was my responsibility and my fault for the lack of communication. Again, I was being told that I had to play by his rules. And even worse, I felt that he expected something of me that he didn't expect of himself. I'd had enough. I was determined not to be the one to reach out. If he wanted to talk to me, he could call me.

Thanksgiving break came and we had not talked for many weeks. Even so, I decided that it was only right that I stop by for Thanksgiving dinner. After all, my stubbornness was pretty immature. I wasn't going to miss out on Thanksgiving at my dad's house because I was annoyed with him. When I got there, I knocked on the door. No answer. I looked in the windows to see if anyone was inside but all of the lights were out. Perplexed, I finally picked up the phone to call him; I learned from my stepmom that they were at my stepsister's house in Fresno for the holiday.

They left town for Thanksgiving and hadn't told me. I felt like a fool for having driven over there, but most of all I felt hurt that no one told me about the plan. Once again he hadn't called, and this time I was excluded from a family gathering.

Needless to say I was upset. For years there was an unspoken animosity that I tried to pretend was not there. The more I pretended there wasn't an issue the more resentful I became, and the more estranged our relationship. I ran away, emotionally. I totally disconnected. I lived life on my own, leaving the safety and comforts of Isaac for the uncharted waters of Laban.

Like Jacob, I was emotionally in a foreign land, indentured to my fears, trying to find my way through life without my father. During that time I fell away from my faith in God, other people, pretty much everything. It seemed like I was running as hard as I could but not getting anywhere. It felt similar to how I imagine Jacob felt when he woke up the next morning to discover Leah in his bed instead of Rachel. Several years passed and I was still at square one. I was still in the same job and the same frustrating places in life. I knew that something had to change, but I wasn't exactly sure what it was. Things may have continued this way were it not for a major event that forced us to reconnect. My grandfather died.

During the week of the funeral and for the next several months my Dad and I finally decided to talk openly and honestly. Then, something amazing happened. He told me about what kind of father my grandfather was to him and the things that he tried to do differently with me. He told me how he thought he succeeded and the ways that he felt he fell short. He didn't make excuses, but rather he gave me perspective. For the first time we talked to each other like men, as father and son.

Then my dad apologized. This was the first time that I had ever seen this side of him. Like Jacob, I had to face the fear of coming home to truly see my father as a person instead of this figure that I had created in my mind as a child. I too apologized for my stubbornness. I told him about all of the things that I would have done differently and for the first time in as long as I could remember I told him that I loved him. It was powerful. In that moment we both felt like Jacob as he anticipated his day of reckoning with Esau. We were afraid. But we could no longer let that fear stop us from coming home, from reconnecting, from being free to open ourselves up to the love that we both held dear in our hearts. We were happy to be close again.

Now when I read this story of Jacob and Esau, the words jump off the page in a totally different way. When I see the foolishness of Jacob, I see the foolishness of my youth. When I read how Jacob was stuck for 20 years working for what Laban promised to give him after seven, I see the years that I spent in my own emotional bondage. I was stuck running in place because I refused to receive the guidance that my father was ready and willing to provide. And when I read about how Jacob prepared to come back home, how he sent gifts of livestock ahead of him, how he knelt before Esau with humility, praying for his forgiveness, I see both me and my father during that fateful time. I see how we offered each other gifts of forgiveness and loving communication, and I thank God that those gifts were a strong enough foundation to start a new chapter in our relationship not only as father and son but also as men. Experience has shown me that the words in the Bible truly have a powerful life of their own; we just have to experience life for ourselves in order to hear them speak their truth.

Clarence Mitchell (B.A., Politics, Philosophy, and Economics, Pomona College) is a Christian blogger (www.aconvowithgod.com) and prayer leader at the Pasadena International House of Prayer.

QUESTIONS

1. Assess the strengths and weaknesses of Poland's view of Rivka/Rebekah. How might one offer a counter reading?
2. How does Phelps-Roper use biblical passages outside of Genesis to bolster her argument? Could one agree with her interpretation of the text, but yet not assent to her theological conclusions?
3. Analyze Masenya's interpretation of Leah. Read the text carefully and raise some challenging questions for Masenya.
4. In what ways do Mitchell's reflections help him understand his own life experiences? Do you see any connections between these biblical stories and your own life?

CHAPTER 6

GENESIS 37–50

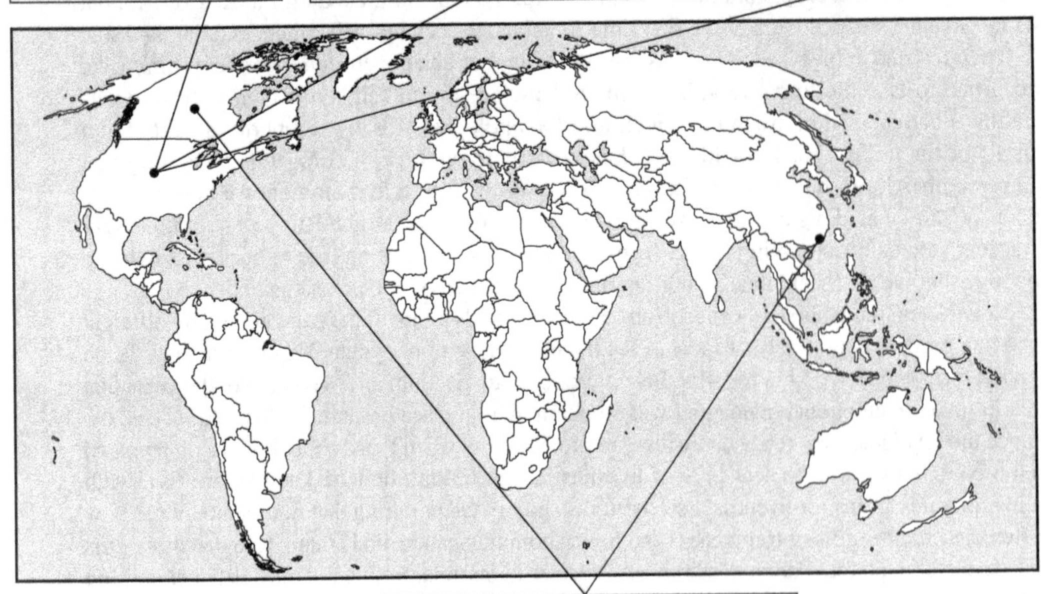
Eric A. Seibert highlights the theme of forgiveness as central to the Joseph narrative, with special attention to the scenes in 45:1–15 and 50:15–21.
Wayne Tarrant employs an economic lens to analyze Joseph's action of saving grain during the years of plenty, which contrasts with policy makers today.
Mona West offers an LGBT reading of the story which shows how garments are used to represent crossing boundaries and to destabilize binary thinking.
Francis G. H. Pang imagines a personal conversation with Joseph about the challenges of moving to a new land and of meeting his family after years of absence.

READINGS

Forgiveness as a Central Theme of the Joseph Narrative
Eric A. Seibert

Joseph's Actions through a Modern Economic Lens
Wayne Tarrant

An LGBT Reading of Genesis 37–50
Mona West

A Personal Conversation with Joseph
Francis G. H. Pang

Forgiveness as a Central Theme of the Joseph Narrative

Eric A. Seibert (United States)

Although the story of Joseph can be read in many different ways, at its core, it is a story about a man who forgave his brothers. The theme of forgiveness, so central to the Joseph narrative, is expressed most vividly in two passages: Genesis 45:1–15 and 50:15–21. This story, with its emphasis on forgiveness rather than retaliation, serves as an especially good example of peacemaking and the nonviolent resolution of conflict in the Old Testament.

Early in the narrative, Joseph has a pair of dreams about ruling over his brothers. When he divulges these dreams to his brothers, they are indignant. At an opportune moment, they devise a plan to kill Joseph, though end up selling him instead. Although nothing is initially said about Joseph's reaction to their abuse and hostility, we later learn that Joseph was in "anguish" and plead with his brothers throughout the ordeal, while they turned a deaf ear (42:21).

Two decades later, Joseph sees his brothers again. But now the tables are turned. Joseph is second in command of all Egypt. He has been stockpiling grain for years because God revealed that seven years of famine were coming. When Joseph's brothers come down to Egypt to buy grain, they unknowingly come face-to-face with the brother they had nearly killed. It is only at the end of their second visit that Joseph reveals his identity to them. This dramatic self-disclosure marks the first of two conciliatory scenes between Joseph and his brothers (45:1–15) with the other occurring years later, just after the death of their father Jacob (50:15–21). These two passages contain a number of thematic similarities that emphasize the centrality and importance of forgiveness in the Joseph narrative.

First, both scenes emphasize how Joseph's theological interpretation of events enables him to forgive. When Joseph reveals his true identity to his brothers, he repeatedly claims that his arrival in Egypt was an act of divine providence (cf. 50:20). Although he acknowledges that his brothers *sold* him there, he simultaneously affirms that God *sent* him there. Specifically, Joseph believes he has been divinely dispatched to Egypt "to preserve life" (45:5). Were he to harbor unforgiveness or retaliate against his brothers at this juncture, Joseph might run the risk of being at cross-purposes with God. By framing his circumstances theologically, Joseph is able to forgive his brothers for their outrageous behavior many years prior.

Second, in both passages, Joseph promises to provide food for his brothers and their families on an ongoing basis. This act of kindness demonstrates the depth of Joseph's forgiveness and his determination to care for his brothers despite what they had done to him. After Joseph reveals his identity, he sends a message to his father telling him to resettle the family in Goshen. Joseph says he will provide for their needs and is true to his word (45:10–11; 47:12). Seventeen years later, after his father dies, Joseph's brothers worry that he might finally take his revenge. But Joseph allays their fears by once again promising to provide for them. This makes his forgiveness tangible. It is concrete evidence that his intentions toward his brothers are good. Rather than returning hostility, Joseph extends hospitality. Rather than punishing, Joseph is providing. It seems a striking example of overcoming evil with good (see Romans 12:21).

Third, both passages end with physical and/or verbal assurances that make Joseph's forgiveness visible and personal. While Joseph's emotions are on display at various points throughout the narrative, they are expressed most dramatically when he reveals his identity in 45:14–15. After embracing Benjamin and weeping with him, we are told that Joseph "kissed all his brothers and wept upon them." Joseph also weeps in the final conciliatory scene after which he offers verbal reassurances to his brothers that they need not be afraid. Apparently, Joseph has no intention of retaliating. In both instances, Joseph's behavior reveals the sincerity of his forgiveness as he attempts to assure his brothers that everything is alright between them.

In addition to these two conciliatory scenes, the virtue of forgiving is also apparent when the Joseph narrative is viewed in its broader literary context. It is instructive to note that this narrative is immediately preceded by another story about fraternal strife and forgiveness. Scholars have noted a number of striking similarities between the story of Jacob and Esau in Genesis 25–36 and the story of Joseph and his brothers in Genesis 37–50. Both of these stories include conflict between brothers, the possibility of fratricide, and estrangement leading to decades of separation. Yet both narratives also emphasize the power of forgiveness to resolve fraternal strife, to remove the threat of fratricide, and to reestablish fractured relationships. Stories like these illustrate the enormous value of forgiveness as a way forward.

The importance of forgiveness is further highlighted when the story of Joseph and his brothers at the end of Genesis is compared to the story of Cain and Abel at the beginning. Once again, both stories describe conflict between brothers. But these two stories have very different endings. Cain kills Abel, while Joseph forgives his brothers. Although Joseph easily could have followed the path of Cain, he chooses to forgive instead. By doing so, Joseph's actions demonstrate that violence is neither an inevitable nor unavoidable outcome when dealing with fraternal strife. Other options exist. Reading the Joseph narrative in light of the story of Cain and Abel reminds us that things could have ended very differently for Joseph's brothers. This once again underscores the desirability of forgiveness.

In a sense, Joseph's actions break the cycle of hostility, mistreatment, and violence that appears early in Genesis and continues through much of the book. Joseph's willingness to forgive wrongs committed against him demonstrates how forgiveness functions as an antidote to violence. Forgiveness effectively ends the otherwise endless cycle of violence.

While not everything Joseph does throughout the narrative may be regarded as praiseworthy, his behavior in 45:1–15 and 50:15–21, the two conciliatory scenes discussed here, certainly seems exemplary. These passages represent the kind of texts that can be used to read the Old Testament nonviolently, in ways that do not encourage or endorse contemporary acts of violence. Given the Old Testament's troubling legacy in this regard, as a text that has been used to legitimate various kinds of violence, it seems particularly important to pay special attention to passages like these, passages that emphasize peacemaking, nonretaliation, and forgiveness.

Eric A. Seibert is Associate Professor of Old Testament at Messiah College, Grantham, Pennsylvania, United States; he is the author of Disturbing Divine Behavior: Troubling Old Testament Images of God *and* The Violence of Scripture: Overcoming the Old Testament's Troubling Legacy.

Joseph's Actions through a Modern Economic Lens

Wayne Tarrant (United States)

The life of the biblical Joseph could certainly be seen as a series of boom and bust cycles. From being a favored son with all the dreams of a splendid future to being thrown into a pit and sold as a slave, he rose to a position of trust in the house of Potiphar only to be thrown into prison by false testimony. From the depths of prison, Joseph rose to be the overseer of all the inmates, where he used his ability to interpret dreams. Although originally forgotten by the cupbearer for two years, he eventually found a place in the house of Pharaoh. Through the interpretation of Pharaoh's dream, Joseph was able to save an entire country and also his own family. It is this last episode on which I wish to lay an economic viewpoint.

As a reminder, Pharaoh's first dream involves seven fat cows grazing beside the Nile. Seven skinny cows come up to the seven fat cows and devour them. The second dream has seven full heads of grain growing from one stalk. Then seven withered heads of grain grow and swallow the seven good heads. Joseph correctly foretells that this will mean seven years of plenty for Egypt and then seven years of famine.

Joseph takes a series of real economic steps beginning in 41:33. I do not find anything in Pharaoh's dreams that would lead to such an ingenious solution as the one that Joseph proposes. Up to this point in Genesis, I also cannot find a place where someone is asked to save for a rainy day, unless one makes an argument about Noah's plan for the ultimate of rainy days.

Joseph knows that there is going to be an agricultural boom for Egypt for the next seven years. He knows that there will be an abundance of grain during these seven years—even more than the people of Egypt could possible consume will be produced. So Egypt will be left with two choices. The most obvious choice is that Egypt could decide to export the grain to other countries in exchange for some other commodity. Maybe the Egyptians would like grapes and olives from other parts of the world, and so they could exchange their excess grain for the products of another country. In this case the Egyptians could not only consume their fill of grain, but they could also have a variety of items to consume. Or maybe they could choose to exchange for gold, silver, or bronze. There is a great temptation to do just this when you have an excess of an item. But an excess of supply often leads to the realization of lower prices. All the trading partners would have to realize that Egypt has too much grain and needs to dispose of it. Each trading partner could offer less for this grain than during regular production times.

But Joseph knows one additional piece of information. The good years will not last. Although they will have an excess of grain for seven years, there will be a dearth of grain in the seven years that follow. So Joseph devises another plan. We must assume that Joseph undertakes a massive project of building storehouses for grain, as we are told that the grain is stored near the fields that produced it (41:48). He knows that the Egyptians can survive on a fraction of the grain that they will produce in the years of plenty. So he decides to squirrel away 20 percent of the grain each year. In this way they will have grain when the times of famine come. This turns out to be the right solution, because we are told that the entire known world experiences famine. The nice gold, silver, and bronze trinkets they might have had for the grain from the years of plenty would now have to be bartered for grain, likely at a higher price than what they had sold it for during the years of plenty, if grain could even be found.

Further, we are told that Joseph's plan gives Egypt so much grain that he stops keeping a record of what Egypt has stored (41:49). Although some in Egypt might have been discouraged to see grain just piling up, unused, it proves to be a very wise move. In 41:55, we are told that the people of Egypt come to the Pharaoh complaining of hunger and that Joseph's storing of grain allows all of the Egyptians to buy food (41:56). Further, Joseph has stored enough so that he is able to sell to the entire known world (41:57). We do not know if Joseph was a shrewd businessman or not, but the scarcity of food throughout the world could have led to higher prices and greater wealth for Egypt. Or Joseph could have chosen to sell at regular prices and retain allies or allay enemies. In any case, the storing during times of plenty must have made Egypt into a more powerful nation for quite some time. It is notable that this wise solution also leads to Joseph being reunited with his family.

In my mind this is a beginning of Keynesian economics. Keynes's theory says that a government should tax more during times of economic boom. This will alleviate the excess supply of money in the system. During times of economic contraction, the government must step in to supply liquidity, for instance, by fiscal stimulus, so that there is not great suffering. If we can view grain as a form of currency for the Egyptians, then we can apply Keynes's ideas. During the time when there was too much grain, Joseph levied a tax on the produce. One-fifth of the production was to go to the storehouses. During the time of famine, Egypt provided the needed produce so that suffering was alleviated.

Many have claimed that the ongoing destruction of Western economies, particularly the European Union and the United States, is a scathing indictment against Keynesian economics. In truth, if the method of Joseph were used today as then, it is likely that there would be little, if any, problem. The problem seems to be more one of character or of will. During times of recession, governments have been willing to step in to bridge the gap, just as Joseph did and just as Keynes would suggest. However, none of the economic authorities have had the wisdom of Joseph during the times of plenty. Politicians get reelected by promising and delivering to their constituents. This leads to spending more than is collected during times of little but also during times of plenty. The saving that Joseph required of the people during the years of great success is absent. Rather than having a surplus "rainy day fund" from the times of plenty, current governments accrue more debt without regard to the present state of the economy. And this does not lead to saving a country from famine, to being able to sell excess to others at a higher price, or to happy family reunions. While Joseph's position was used responsibly as an opportunity to save lives and appropriate good to his family and among the nations, modern authorities have found themselves in quite another situation altogether.

Wayne Tarrant is a mathematician who has written extensively on risk management as it intersects with economic theory.

An LGBT Reading of Genesis 37–50

Mona West (United States)

The thing most people remember about Joseph is his "coat of many colors" made popular by Andrew Lloyd Webber's *Joseph and the Amazing Technicolor Dream Coat.* Clothing figures prominently in Genesis 37–50. Joseph's coat in Genesis 37—a long robe with special sleeves—angers his brothers because it was actually a woman's garment (2 Samuel 13:18) and is a sign of favoritism from his father Jacob. In Genesis 38 Tamar will take off her widow's garments and put on a prostitute's veil in order to seduce her father-in-law Judah, who later is incriminated by the identifying "clothing" of his signet and cord. Potiphar's wife will use Joseph's garment in Genesis 39 to have him imprisoned because of some perceived impropriety. The Pharaoh makes Joseph an Egyptian in Genesis 41 by giving him his signet and a royal garment. Dressed this way Joseph's brothers do not recognize him when they go to Egypt for food in

42–44. When Joseph reveals his true identity to his brothers, he offers them each a set of garments, and his youngest brother Benjamin gets five sets.

In each of these instances clothing is used to cross rigid boundaries of identity which include gender, ethnicity, and class. The term for this in the Lesbian, Gay, Bisexual, and Transgender (LGBT) community is "cross-dressing." In LGBT culture cross-dressing has been used in powerful ways to disrupt categories of gender. Some gay men, known as "drag queens," will dress and perform as women while still using their male voice. Some lesbians, who are often called "butch," will dress in men's clothes but can still be identified as female because of their breasts. Religious categories have also been disrupted by LGBT people who are "out" as ordained clergy and wear clerical collars and liturgical vestments such as robes, stoles, and chasubles. Of course, not all LGBT people are cross-dressers and we are reminded by the singer Madonna in her performance of "Express Yourself" and the actor Dustin Hoffman who played "Tootsie" that not all cross-dressers are homosexual.

Marjorie Gerber (*Vested Interests: Cross-dressing and Cultural Anxiety* [Routledge: New York, 1992], 10–17) states that cross-dressing is a necessary critique of any kind of binary thinking when it comes to identity: male/female; black/white; Jew/Christian; noble/bourgeois. The cross-dresser or transvestite creates a "third term" which is a "mode of articulation," a space of possibility beyond the either/or of the binary. The function of the cross-dresser in culture is to point to a "category crisis" by being able to cross or make permeable the boundaries of such categories of gender, race, and class, thereby destabilizing the binary.

In the Joseph narrative cross-dressing destabilizes the binaries of youngest/oldest, widow/prostitute, and Hebrew/Egyptian in order to create spaces of possibility for Joseph and his brothers, Tamar and Judah, and the descendants of Jacob as the book of Genesis comes to an end and anticipates the Exodus story.

The theme of the triumph of the youngest son over the oldest weaves throughout the patriarchal and matriarchal narratives of Genesis and we find it in the opening chapters of the Joseph narrative. Jacob, Joseph's father, is one of those who, by cross-dressing as his older brother Esau, steals the birthright (Gen. 27). Now in Genesis 37 Jacob gives a special robe with sleeves to Joseph, one of his youngest sons, as a sign of favor. This coat, especially when Joseph wears it, makes his brothers jealous (not to mention all those grandiose dreams of Joseph's). It will become the sign by which the older brothers declare to their father that Joseph is dead, when in reality he has been sold into slavery.

In this special robe Joseph cross-dresses as a favored son, which destabilizes the binary of youngest/oldest and opens a space of possibility for the brothers to create their identities beyond the rigid boundaries of birthright. We see this at the end of the story when the brothers—especially Judah who is the oldest—attempt to protect Benjamin, who is their father's youngest and favored now that he thinks Joseph is gone.

Tamar cross-dresses as a prostitute in Genesis 38 and seduces her father-in-law, Judah, because he has not fulfilled the law of Levirate Marriage by giving his youngest son to her as a husband in order to raise up male offspring that will insure her place in society as a widow. Her cross-dressing destabilizes the binary of widow/prostitute in order to create a space of possibility in which she becomes the agent of her own destiny. This agency is affirmed by Judah himself, who renders her more righteous than he. He is identified through articles of his own clothing (his signet worn around his neck with a cord) as the one who inseminated Tamar. Interestingly enough when she gives birth to twins, a piece of clothing, a crimson chord, is tied around the wrist of the one who came out first!

The remainder of the Joseph narrative uses cross-dressing to destabilize the binary of Hebrew/Egyptian. There is a tension between Joseph's Hebrew identity and his Egyptian identity once he gets to the house of Potiphar that is sustained until the very end of Genesis and continues on into the Exodus story when Moses struggles with his Hebrew/Egyptian identity.

It is Joseph's "Hebrew garment" that Potiphar's wife uses to accuse him of some impropriety which gets him thrown in prison. But prison winds up being Joseph's passage way into Pharaoh's house and his favor. Because Joseph is able to interpret the Pharaoh's dream and thus prepare the land for a great famine, the Pharaoh sets him over the entire land of Egypt. Moreover, Pharaoh makes Joseph an Egyptian by giving him his signet ring, clothing him in garments of fine linen, and giving Joseph the Egyptian name Zaphenath-paneah and an Egyptian wife, Asenath (41:37–45).

Joseph is really an Egyptian "in drag" and his cross-dressing calls into question these seemingly stable identities. His own brothers do not recognize him when they come before him in Egypt to buy grain, and the blurring of identities continues when Joseph is able to overhear their conversation in Hebrew after accusing them of being spies (42:23). Eventually Joseph "comes out" to his brothers and attempts to cross-dress them as Egyptians when he gives each brother a set of garments while Benjamin, the youngest, gets five sets of garments.

Joseph's cross-dressing as an Egyptian creates a "category crisis" for the larger ancestor narratives that extend into the Exodus story. The boundaries between Hebrew/Egyptian are blurred—Egyptians and Hebrews eat together even though it is an abomination (43:32); the Egyptians sell themselves into slavery to the Hebrew (Joseph) who is an Egyptian in drag (Gen. 47), only to have the Hebrews become the slaves of the Egyptians when a new Pharaoh who did not know Joseph begins to rule (Exodus 1). Joseph's Egyptian sons, Ephraim and Manasseh, are adopted as Hebrews by God in Genesis 48. Cross-dressing Joseph destabilizes the binary of Hebrew/Egyptian in order to open a space of possibility for a *mixed group* to come out of Egypt at the Exodus.

In the same way that Joseph's cross-dressing and "passing" as an Egyptian disrupts the binary of Hebrew/Egyptian, crossing dressing is used in the LGBT community to disrupt the binaries of heterosexual/homosexual and male/female. Effeminate gay men may dress more masculine in order to "pass" as heterosexual—often for their very survival in a sexist, heterosexist culture that is violent toward men who do not look and act like "real men." Lesbians who wear lipstick and dress in feminine ways call into question the heterosexist assumption that all lesbians want to be men. Transgender people cross-dress to identify with the gender they were meant to be when their biological sex is different from that gender identity.

Just like Joseph was able to leverage Egyptian privilege in order for his brothers to survive during a time of great famine, so too LGBT people who pass as heterosexuals are able to leverage heterosexual privilege for their own survival. Even after Joseph "comes out" to his brothers, he remains "Egyptian" to the very end of the story by being buried in Egypt (unlike his father Jacob, who requests to be buried in the land of his ancestors). LGBT people who come out also remain in a heterosexist culture. Just as Joseph's coming out creates a mode of possibility for identities to "blend" as the narrative moves toward the Exodus event, LGBT people who come out also create a mode of possibility for all people to claim the good gift of their sexuality without the need for binary categories—and that is a true Exodus indeed.

Mona West (Ph.D.) is a lesbian, formerly ordained as a Southern Baptist minister, who now serves as Director of Formation and Leadership Development for Metropolitan Community Churches; she is coeditor of Take Back the Word: A Queer Reading of the Bible *and* The Queer Bible Commentary.

A Personal Conversation with Joseph

Francis G. H. Pang (Hong Kong, Canada)

Twenty years ago I had to leave home for Canada. I asked my mother, "Why do I need to study abroad? Why do I have to leave? Don't we have good schools here?" My mom said, "It's complicated."

"How complicated?" I contested. "After all, you don't want me to live with you; you want me to leave because you want to live with your new husband and new family."

"No! I want you to have a better education and who knows what's going to happen when the government of China takes over us in a few years."

So there I was, sitting in the darkness, alone, couldn't quite speak the language, downright lonely and sacred. Along came this guy who came to me and said, "I know how you feel, my friend."

"You know?" I said, "What do you know? I am forced to come here. My family doesn't want me to be part of them anymore. And they gave me some lame political reason. It is so unfair! I want to go home. I want to go back to my friends and the people I love."

"Yes, it is unfair, I know," he said. "I was sold to be a slave in a foreign country far away from home by my half brothers. I felt betrayed and, of course, very bitter, at the time. I even blamed my dad for not coming to save me. There I was, like you now, a resident alien in a foreign country with a language that I hardly understood. I was pretty lost."

"Oh so it's you, I know you, I've heard the story about you and your eleven brothers. You are Joseph." I said.

"Yes, that's me," he said. "There are always two sides of the coin. On the brighter side, the language barrier actually helped me to improve my communication skills. You see, when you are learning a new language you think twice before you say anything. It is like doing a quick translation in your head before every sentence you say. I used to be a brash kid, badmouthing my brothers and bragging about my dreams, but I learned to be much tactful by the time I stood before Pharaoh. Indeed, I had plenty of time in prison to reflect on my character issues."

"I guess you are right," I nodded, "but I still think it is easy for you to say this in retrospect, cause even you took a long time to finally make peace with your past. Just look at the names of your sons."

"What about it?" he protested.

"You named your firstborn son Manasseh ("forget"), claiming that God had made you forget about your hardship and your family. But by calling him that, every time you utter his name you are actually reminding yourself about your past! In a sense," I continued my little speech, "you are constantly asking yourself to put the past behind you. So that's why I said it takes time to heal. See, even after you have ascended to the top, even after you have settled down and have a family of your own, even a very luxurious lifestyle cannot rescue you from the demons of your past, at least not until after your second son was born. If naming means anything, the name Ephraim ("twice fruitful") tells us that you are looking at the brighter side of things. Even though your past suffering still lingers in your mind, at least you can turn around and focus on the blessings in your life."

"Yes, you are right, it takes time," he said with a smile on his face, "but time is not the antidote to my bitterness toward my past and my family. Time may take the edge off the pain, but the real remedy is from God. You have to look past the surface and see things God's way."

"But how?" I asked.

"It is hard to describe, but to borrow a term from psychology, it is a matter of 'reframing.' "

"Reframing?" I was puzzled. "What is that?"

"Simply put, you have to put things into another perspective, trying to look at the same situation from another angle. I will say it is also an act of divine grace. You see, during my time in Egypt, I was always bothered by the thought that it was my brothers' evil intent that took me to Egypt to suffer, so I always felt bitter, even after I became the vizier of Egypt. But when my brothers came kneeling down before me and begging for food during the famine, it all became clear to me. It gave everything a new meaning—the dream, the famine, everything started to make sense to me. Of course, the revelation of divine intervention and providence did not instantly take away my bitterness. But it provided an impetus for what came after."

"So you are telling me that I will find out in the future why I am here?" I asked.

"Be patient, my friend, it will either come to you or it will become unimportant. Be patient and trust in the Lord."

So we went on and talked about his life in Egypt. I asked him all kinds of questions—what he thought about the comparison between him and the prophet Daniel, and so on.

Time always goes faster than it seems when you look back. And he was right; my perspective on my family and my life in general has changed. After almost a decade, this once very foreign land has turned into familiar territory. I became a diehard Maple Leafs fan and called myself Canadian Chinese. And at the same time I almost forgot about the problem I had with my family. In fact, the idea of going home seems less and less attractive. Thus when I had to go home after my work permit expired, I was devastated and could not shake away the feelings of déjà vu. It was cultural identity crisis all over again. But I had no choice.

So I went back to this crowded city I once called home. My world turned upside down. The language I once spoke with ease all of a sudden seemed so foreign; the friends that were once very close seemed so distant. I was lost, again. Then Joseph came to me.

"So, how are you there? You are finally home," he said with a grin on his face.

"Home? Honestly I am quite confused: Where is home?" I muttered, pondering the question.

"Oh, I see. Having a hard time adjusting to a 'new' place all over again, right?" he asked.

"Yes, it is as if people don't know me anymore. When I talk to them, it seems as if they don't understand me at all. Even though I try to tell people what I have been through in the past ten years, it still seems very hard for them to accept the new me," I said.

"It is hard," he answered, "especially after all these years people can only remember bits and pieces about you from the past. Between now and then, there is a huge gap which needs to be filled. People seem unable to shake away their perception of the old you. The same also happened to me. After I finally made peace with my brothers, they doubted that I'd changed. They did not believe that I was not their brash little brother anymore. They even lied to me about my father, telling me that he asked me to forgive them from his deathbed."

"Yes, I remembered that part." I said. "But you forgave them nonetheless, even took an extra step and reassured them that you would never harm them. God must have really changed your perspective on your past."

"Take heart, my friend, it may take a bit longer for other people to discover this 'new' you, but the most important thing is that God is always with you, no matter where you call home. He is your family and wherever he is, there too is your home."

Francis G. H. Pang, originally from Hong Kong, is a Ph.D. candidate at McMaster Divinity College, Canada.

QUESTIONS

1. Seibert claims that "at its core" the story is about a man who forgave his brothers. What other "cores," that is, central themes, might one identify?
2. Tarrant praises Joseph's economic decisions in Genesis 41. How might Tarrant evaluate Joseph's policies in Genesis 47? What do you think of Joseph's later tactics?
3. Explain the significance of "cross-dressing" for West. What questions might one raise about her general approach and careful textual analysis?
4. Is Pang's presentation of Joseph faithful to the biblical image? Could one imagine Joseph having a different sort of conversation with Pang?

CHAPTER 7

EXODUS 1–15

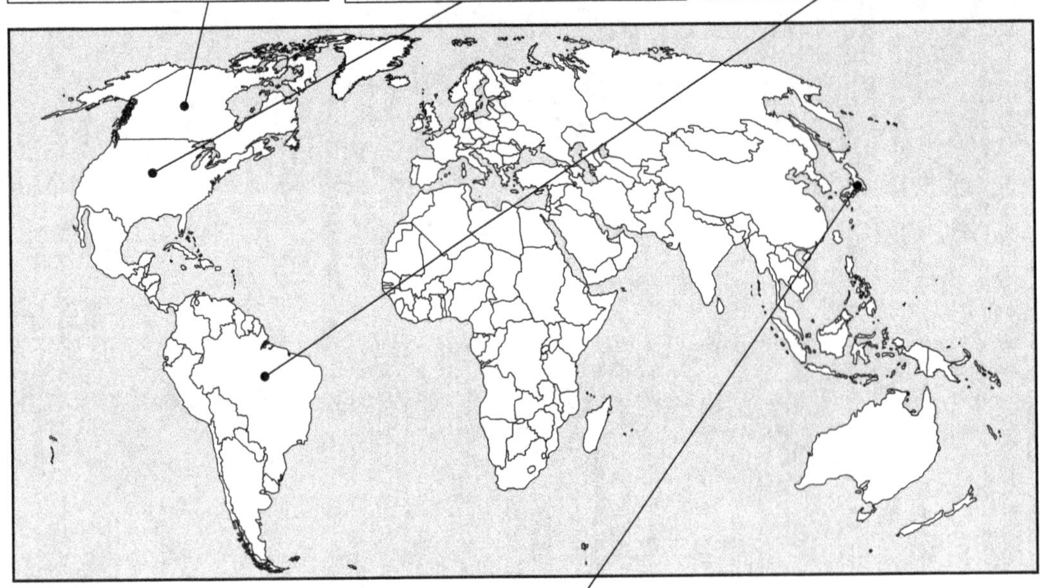

Vanessa R. Sasson reads two aspects of the text through a Buddhist lens: Moses and the Egyptian taskmaster (2:11–15) and the hardening of the Pharaoh's heart.
Megan Bishop Moore reveals the problems of reading the story as accurate history, which leads her to propose that it is better understood as historical fiction.
Gilbert Lozano discusses the policies of the conquistadores and current conditions in Brazil, suggesting the need for a liberationist reading of the biblical story.
Eiko Hanaoka(-Kawamura) compares the revelation of the divine name in 3:14—"I am"—with Japanese philosopher Kitaro Nishida's concept of God.

READINGS

Two Aspects of Exodus through a Buddhist Lens
Vanessa R. Sasson

A Comparison of the Divine Name with Kitaro Nishida's Concept of God
Eiko Hanaoka(-Kawamura)

The Exodus Story as Historical Fiction
Megan Bishop Moore

A Liberationist Reading of the Exodus Story
Gilbert Lozano

Two Aspects of Exodus through a Buddhist Lens

Vanessa R. Sasson (Canada)

Two aspects of the story of Moses and the Exodus can be fruitfully read through a Buddhist lens. The first concerns the scene with Moses and the taskmaster (2:11–15). The Bible tells us virtually nothing about how Moses was raised. His birth story is one of the most famous of the biblical tradition, but beyond that narrative, little is revealed about his early years. He is born an Israelite, but raised as an Egyptian. The question is then, When exactly did Moses discover that he was an Israelite? The text is not clear.

The first time we encounter Moses after his birth is as a young man. According to 2:11, Moses "went out to his people and saw their forced labor. He saw an Egyptian beating a Hebrew, one of his kinfolk." Here it sounds as though Moses is suddenly identifying with the Hebrew slaves, relating to them as his family members. Indeed, he is so overwhelmed by their situation, and by this slave being hit in front of him in particular, that he responds by killing the Egyptian taskmaster (2:12). It is no surprise that so many interpreters assume Moses knew he was a Hebrew before this scene. The story leads the reader in that direction: Moses must have discovered that he was a Hebrew and only then identified with the slaves at his doorstep. He is, moreover, crazed by their suffering and reacts violently—the response of a man who is overwhelmed by new information and has not managed to process it yet.

But what if we were to read the text differently? I have long believed that this is the story not of a man who reacts emotionally to his own people's suffering but rather of a much more universal awakening—a moment that is so powerful, it catapults Moses from one state of being to another and shatters whatever normalcy he had hitherto sheltered himself with. If Moses reacts to the slave only once he knows that he too is an Israelite, then what we have is a man who is moved to action only when his own community is affected. While that may make sense historically and in the context of the Ancient Near East, in which tribal affiliation was paramount, in the realm of mythical heroes and adventures, such a self-centered response would not be very inspiring. Moses must have been greater than that.

The story of the Buddha's awakening may be traced to a number of factors, but one of them is particularly pertinent to this discussion. According to many of the early sources, when the Buddha was a young man, he came across some laborers working in the fields. He watched the beasts of burden toiling the earth; saw the laborers darkened by the sun and covered with sweat; and witnessed innumerable insects, frogs, and snakes being overturned by the plows. His heart was overwhelmed with all of the suffering produced by an ordinary fact of life, and this eventually moved him to leave home to find an answer to the suffering he felt incapable of surmounting. It was a small moment—a picture he must have come across a thousand times before—but for some reason, on that day, the image of labor, suffering, and death pierced his heart and transformed him irrevocably.

I see Moses' story in a similar light. Moses must have come across the slaves on a regular basis. They were surely a fact of his life, something to be expected and ignored much like the homeless people many of us pass on the street. We know they are there, we see them on a daily basis, but we don't really look at them. They are just part of the landscape. But one day, Moses woke up and looked outside and saw the slaves as though for the first time. He saw his "brethren," his fellow human beings, and he could not walk past them blindly again. He looked at them with clear sight and recognized their humanity.

To assume that Moses knew he was an Israelite before this scene limits Moses as a hero. It renders him too self-centered for my Buddhist reading to accommodate. As a universal hero, Moses must have seen the slaves as his fellow human beings, and not simply as his fellow tribesmen. The challenge presented by the Buddhist parallel, however, has to do with his relationship to the oppressors. The Buddha watched men plowing the fields and was overwhelmed with compassion for all the creatures affected: the animals, the men, and the insects. The Buddha did not distinguish one group from another in his emotive response; he did not strike down the men for the suffering they were causing the animals and insects, but appears to have felt compassion for everyone's suffering equally. Moses may have woken to a common humanity when he looked at the slaves, but the taskmaster he killed remained outside his purview. His compassion flowed in only one direction. The question I am therefore left with is whether Moses ever came to see the taskmasters as his brothers too.

The second issue in the Exodus story that can be read through a Buddhist lens concerns one of the most difficult themes of the Hebrew Bible: the hardening of the Pharaoh's heart (7:5, 22; 8:11, 15, etc.). When Moses receives his instructions at the burning bush, God tells him (long before he even returns to Egypt), that he (God) will "harden Pharaoh's heart, and he will not let the people go" (4:21).

What are we to make of this? The text seems to be suggesting that the entire story of the plagues and the exodus was a set-up, predetermined long before any of the characters have a chance to make their own decisions. God will harden the Pharaoh's heart—make him stubborn as some translations have it—and will not let the people go. He will therefore battle with the Pharaoh and demonstrate his many wonders, so that the Egyptians may finally know that he is God (7:5).

Does the Pharaoh not have free will then? And what about Moses? Does he have free will? Moses clearly was reticent to take the job. He struggles with a bramble of excuses to be let off the hook, but God will not hear any of it. Moses is required to speak on his behalf, and the Pharaoh is required to say no. The only real actor in the narrative appears to be God, with everyone else connected to puppet strings from above.

I see in this story a problem that all religions struggle with: How much do we control and how much belongs to a power beyond us? There is no easy answer to this question. We would like to believe we have control, and yet at the same time there is something comforting in the idea that we are not responsible, not in control, and possibly even deeply irrelevant in some way. A burden is removed from our shoulders when we place it all on an otherworldly system instead.

Buddhism struggles with this same question, but the language is one of karma. There are certain inescapable realities that are determined by the karma accumulated in previous lifetimes. The Buddha's awakening is an example of this: His accumulated karma leads him to Buddhahood, rendering all potential attempts at obstruction doomed to failure. Whether Mara (a kind of devil) or anyone else tried to get in his way, the fact remained that Siddhartha was destined to achieve Buddhahood in that lifetime. Even if he himself wanted to do otherwise, he could not escape the footprints awaiting his feet. The powers of the universe conspired together to ensure that he made his way to an awakening that would change the world.

The story of the Pharaoh's hardened heart seems to me a kind of inescapable karma. The outcome is already written and it is just a question of time before the Pharaoh and Moses fulfill their roles accordingly. I don't think this story can be made comfortable though. Neither predetermination nor karma is an ultimately comfortable idea. The rabbis traditionally saw in this story a kind of justice in which the Pharaoh becomes the symbol of Egyptian wrongs, required to pay for the hundreds of years of enslavement the Israelites were forced to endure. But from a modern perspective, such a reading is unsatisfactory: Why would one Pharaoh along with one generation of Egyptians be forced to pay for the mistakes of the past? How would we feel if we were suddenly forced to pay for the mistakes we inherited from our own ancestors? Would justice not at least require that the Supreme Judge offer the Pharaoh a genuine opportunity to change his ways first?

We want to be in control of our lives, to believe that somehow our actions will be reflected in the makeup of our life's outcomes. But deep down inside, we wonder if we really are in charge of anything. When God declares that he will harden the Pharaoh's heart, it is to me a window into the question of human significance. It is akin to the Buddha not having a choice about which path to take as a young man: He is bound to Buddhahood just as the Pharaoh is bound to destruction (and Moses is bound to the pains of prophethood). The hardening of the Pharaoh's heart is meant to be uncomfortable, and that is precisely its most subtle wisdom.

Vanessa R. Sasson is Professor of Religious Studies in the Liberal Arts Department of Marianopolis College, Canada; she has authored several books, including The Birth of Moses and the Buddha: A Paradigm for the Comparative Study of Religions.

A Comparison of the Divine Name with Kitaro Nishida's Concept of God

Eiko Hanaoka(-Kawamura) (Japan)

The first original philosopher in Japan, Kitaro Nishida (1870–1945), understood God as the "Absolute Nothingness," which means the negation of the substantialization and the absolutization of all things and standpoints. A similar way of thinking about God is found in Exodus 3:14, where God is named with the Hebrew verb *hayah*, meaning "to be," "to exist," "to become," and is typically translated "I am." Here God is not an onto-theological substantial God. That is to say, God is not substance or essence or being (person). Rather God is the Acting One, who works as one with the events in our daily life.

Likewise for Nishida, God is also not a substantial onto-theological God. Rather God is one who always works to be able to support each of us with *agape* (perfect love). God, then, is better thought of as acting or functioning, rather than as a separate being. This is precisely the understanding of God that the contemporary world needs.

History shows that postulating a substantial onto-theological God has led to nihilism, as Nietzsche predicted. Nihilism argues that life is without any meaning, purpose, or intrinsic value. The Jewish and Christian traditions hold to a concept of God as being. This God is the basis for all morals and values. God provides the objective truth, the objective standard by which all else can be evaluated. But once it is realized that the Judeo-Christian God is a human construction, then that God ceases to be able to offer any objective meaning, purpose, and value to life. Thus, belief in such a God falls apart and nihilism emerges. Hence, Nietzsche's famous aphorism that "God is dead."

But if we follow the lead of Exodus 3 and Nishida, then other ways of thinking about the nature of God open up. It is true that Nishida's term of "absolute nothingness" and the phrase

"I am that I am" as the name of God are not exactly the same idea. However, in both cases, God is understood as an Action. The Hebrew verb *hayah* means not only "to be" but also "to cause to be," "to become," or "to give rise to." For Nishida, God as "absolute nothingness" is God as action or working—and simultaneously as *agape*. The idea is that the self who tries to live out love as *agape* or compassion negates absolutizing his or her own standpoint. That is, the self-less sacrificing of *agape* necessarily negates the will and desires of the self, the ego—becoming absolute nothingness.

In this way, Nishida helps us link the God of Exodus 3 with the New Testament notion that "God is love." If God is not a being, but rather the action of love, then nihilism can be avoided. God is not a being who creates or is the source of objective moral standards and values which give life meaning and purpose. Rather God is the "absolute nothingness" which negates the self (and all else), allowing one to exercise *agape*. This indeed is a concept of God that our world dearly needs to embrace.

Eiko Hanaoka(-Kawamura) is Professor Emeritus at the Graduate School of Osaka Prefecture University, Japan; he is Vice-President and the chief editor of The Japan Society for Process Studies.

The Exodus Story as Historical Fiction

Megan Bishop Moore (United States)

The exodus from Egypt and the wilderness wanderings, which are described in Exodus 1–19 and in parts of Numbers and Deuteronomy and which comprise the background for the books of Exodus–Deuteronomy, are the first events in the biblical story where Israel is portrayed as, and acts as, a large, unified group. These descendants of the 12 sons of Jacob, the story reports, were enslaved in Egypt but were freed by God acting through Moses. Their escape from Egypt was a dramatic event, but their lives quickly became more mundane as they camped in the wilderness (or desert) for 40 years. During this time, however, God revealed to them important laws of conduct and social organization. Finally, the Israelites invaded the land of Canaan and conquered it for their own settlement.

Since the eighteenth century C.E., scholars of the Bible have been interested in the historical truth of the Hebrew Bible/Old Testament stories, and the exodus and wandering stories were no exceptions. For the most part, the biblical stories of the Israelites' or Hebrews' presence in Egypt, including their slavery, as well as their escape and wanderings, were believed to be historical fact. Following the decipherment of hieroglyphs in the early nineteenth century (made possible by the discovery of the Rosetta Stone by Napoleon's troops in 1799 and the work of Jean Champillon), historians felt they surely had the tools to confirm these events. However, over two subsequent centuries of research, including advanced Egyptology and archaeology, have failed to provide any proof that the stories accurately reflect events and conditions in Egypt and the desert prior to Israel's emergence in Palestine (between 1100 and 900 B.C.E.). Rather, the stories appear to be plausible historical fiction, written at least a half-century after the events they describe, with their intent having been to tell of Israel's salvation by Yahweh and debt to him, rather than to report history as we moderns understand it.

Applying normal historical analysis to the stories of the exodus and wanderings exposes a number of uncertainties and problems. First, the Bible gives different dates for the exodus, and each of these dates is a relative date; that is, it locates the exodus in relation to another biblical event for which an absolute date is also unknown. The exodus is said to have occurred 480 years before Solomon's fourth year (1 Kings 6:1), but this figure (12 × 40) seems to do more with dating the temple's construction than the exodus (and in another ancient version, 1 Kings 6:1 has 440 years). In any case, with no firm chronological marker for either the temple's construction or Solomon's ascendancy (in fact, we have no evidence of Solomon or his building of the temple outside of the Bible), this information can be interpreted as suggesting a mid-fifteenth-century B.C.E. date for the exodus. Another set of dates describes the exodus in relation to Jacob's family's arrival in Egypt: 430 years (Exod. 12:40), 400 years (Genesis 15:13), or three generations (Genesis 15:16). These claims are not only contradictory, but entirely unhelpful historically, as no historical information about Joseph exists. Interestingly, even conservative biblical historians of the mid-twentieth century were willing to ignore the implications of these biblical dates and press for a thirteenth-century B.C.E. date for the exodus, based on their interpretation of archaeological evidence (that was later debunked).

Another difficulty for scholars attempting to use sound historical methodology to examine the exodus stories is that the relevant biblical stories appear to be a compilation of various sources whose dates and provenance are impossible to know, and whose reports can be contradictory. For instance, the documentary hypothesis recognizes three sources at work in the exodus story, but none of the 10 plagues appears in every one. Recognizing this, scholars of the early and mid-twentieth century searched for the oldest, and therefore, they assumed, most reliable pieces of the exodus story. Some concluded that the poetry was the oldest and therefore potentially the most accurate, including the "Song of Moses" (Exod. 15:1–19) and the "Song of Miriam" (Exod. 15:21b). Of course, there is no way to prove that these particular pieces should be singled out as old and reliable. Other related theories that posited that the exodus stories were written in the second millennium B.C.E. were more soundly refuted, such as the idea that the book of Exodus was based on a treaty form known from around 1200 B.C.E.

Additional problems for historians relate to the lack of connections with the great deal that is known about ancient Egypt. For instance, the Pharaoh of the story is not named (though Rameses II has been a popular candidate for decades, since one of the cities named in the story is "Rameses"). No single Pharaoh fits the bill for this character. Even more tellingly, no evidence of the plagues can be found in Egyptian records. It is highly unlikely that any of them, most especially a tragedy so unique and widespread as the death of all the firstborn sons in Egypt, that would dramatically impact not only Egypt but the entire civilized world at that time would go unmentioned and unanalyzed by Egyptian chroniclers. Moses' relationship to and battle with the unnamed Pharaoh is a great story with compelling characters and a riveting plot, but not one that can be taken at face value as a report of real events that occurred in an advanced civilization that left copious records of its existence.

By normal methods of history, then, no history of the exodus or wilderness period can be written. Nevertheless, some scholars maintain that the biblical stories about them are at least plausible in a thirteenth-century B.C.E. Egyptian context. They point to the Egyptian flavor of the stories, including personal and place names (e.g., Moses, Asenath, and Rameses), the known presence of Semites in Egypt in the Late Bronze Age, and the forms of some of the laws given in the wilderness, which they say have thirteenth-century parallels in form and content. These scholars have been challenged by others who claim that the stories have few details about Egypt, many anachronisms, and such a general portrayal that they could have been written in, or set in, almost any ancient time period. There is also a growing opinion that certain clues point definitively to a Persian Period date of composition (late seventh to mid-fourth century B.C.E.), the time when many scholars now believe a substantial part of the Hebrew Bible/Old Testament was written.

Despite popular interest in the exodus events, and the importance of these stories to Israel's identity, they, like many of the other biblical narratives, cannot be definitively located in any time period. The biblical evidence is problematic, vague, and sometimes contradictory, and no extrabiblical evidence affirms any aspect of the stories. As a literary composition, then, the exodus narrative is a compelling historical fiction that originally told the story of God's power and salvation for Israelites trapped in a foreign land, and has lent itself to reinterpretations and retellings over more than 2,000 years.

Megan Bishop Moore is the author of Philosophy and Practice in Writing a History of Ancient Israel *and coauthor of* Biblical History and Israel's Past: The Changing Study of the Bible and History; *she is affiliated with Wake Forest University.*

A Liberationist Reading of the Exodus Story

Gilbert Lozano (Brazil)

The book of Exodus derives its name from a Greek word that means *exit*. It refers to the exit or departure of the Israelites from the land of Egypt. Before that story, however, the book tells the story of how the Israelites had grown in number from the first 70 of Jacob's descendants who had gone to Egypt. The family had grown enormously until it had reached a point when their numbers were seen as a threat by the Egyptian king, who then embarked on several unjust policies. Exodus 1 tells how pharaoh had imposed slavery on the Israelites, and also how he had ordered the destruction of male infants as a way of preventing the possibility of rebellion.

This type of genocidal policy is all too well-known throughout the world, and especially in Latin America. The pharaoh of the story of Exodus was not the first, nor will he be the last, ruler to impose it upon a people. In Brazil, as throughout all of Latin America, the European conquistadores upon their arrival imposed harsh slavery on the native inhabitants. So harsh was the treatment of the Indians (as they came to be known by the European conquerors) that just within a few decades, a population of several million had been decimated. In the context of Latin America, the fate of millions of people was often decided thousands of miles away in the royal palaces of Spain and Portugal. In fact, it was often discussed whether the Indians were truly humans, and whether they had souls. There is probably a connection between the way the Europeans treated the natives and what they thought regarding their lack of humanity. In other words, because the Indians were considered mere creatures of nature, they did not enjoy the same treatment given to those considered to be full human beings. When the Indian populations had been reduced by exploitation, overwork, and death, the Europeans resorted to African slaves in order to provide the labor necessary for the maintenance of the enormous sugarcane estates that supplied the sugar consumed in the European metropolis. Slavery was officially abolished in Brazil in 1888, but not before millions of Indians had been worked to death and millions of Africans had been forcibly removed from their lands and taken to a new continent thousands of miles from their ancestral homes.

Sadly, today we still speak of slave-like working conditions in many parts of Brazil. Just in the year 2010 more than 3,000 persons were found living in such conditions in Brazil. The situation is aggravated by the high concentration of land in the country—the second highest in the world. Latin America, in fact, wins the unfortunate title of being the continent with the largest concentration of land in the hands of the fewest people. The masses do not have access to arable land because it is concentrated in huge estates owned by corporations or rich businessmen, who often live in cities. The working conditions in many of those estates are comparable to slavery. People work for meager wages—if they are paid at all—or for the food they eat and the clothes they wear, and they incur debts which they can never pay back.

The book of Exodus tells that when the pharaoh ordered the annihilation of the male infants, his orders were challenged by the midwives who delivered the Hebrew babies. Moreover, Hebrew mothers also engaged in similar acts of civil disobedience. One of them, Jochebed, refused to obey the law to kill her baby. Probably like many other mothers, she saved her baby, who, by a curious and ironic twist, was raised in the imperial palace, and eventually became the leader of the Israelites. This slave population cried to their God (2:23–25), Yahweh (the Lord), who heard their cries and sent Moses to deliver them. It was the suffering of the Israelites which had moved Yahweh to action in the first place. Though Moses was raised within the Egyptian court and enjoyed a life of privilege, the text points out that Moses is incensed by injustice (2:11–13, 17). The pharaoh, however, stubbornly refused to allow the people to leave, facing, then, God's punishment upon him and his nation.

The story of the liberation of the Israelites from their slavery in Egypt served as one of the most important stories in Latin American liberation theology. For more than three decades (from the mid-1960s to the mid-1990s), the story of the Exodus was used in popular church communities organized in many parishes, especially in northeastern Brazil. This story served to animate the peasants, many of whom identified with the characters in the story because they too were oppressed and cried out for help to the same God who had freed the Israelites many centuries ago. The story was then a favorite among the people, but it was also used by those theologians who were working within this context. Thus, names like Gustavo Gutiérrez, Juan Luis Segundo, Leonardo Boff, and others used the story of the Exodus of the Israelites from Egypt to show that the basic thrust of the Bible is the liberation of the oppressed and that throughout history God has made a preferential option for the poor. Seeing that the God of the Exodus hears the cry of the oppressed, appoints a leader to lead the people out of their conditions, and punishes the system that had oppressed his people, liberation theologians pointed out that the whole thrust of the Bible moved in a similar direction. Thus, in their reading, history inexorably advances toward the liberation of all oppressed people and the removal of oppressive structures.

It is somewhat unfortunate that liberation theology, at least in this part of the world, has lost a great deal of its appeal. The main articulators of that theology have grown old, most have retired, and others have died. The newer theologians here don't have the same interests as previous generations—not that the pressing concerns that plague this continent have gone away. On the contrary, the story of liberation, as told in the book of Exodus, still resonates powerfully in our context, especially since the issues of slavery, economic oppression, inequality, human rights abuses, government corruption, and similar troubles continue to afflict millions of people in this vast continent. The story of a God who hears the cry of the poor and sides with them bringing about their freedom is one that Latin Americans and people everywhere still need to hear.

Gilbert Lozano (Ph.D.) taught at Fidelis, the Mennonite School of Theology, Curitiba, Brazil, and is currently Associate Professor of Biblical Studies at Anderson University, United States.

QUESTIONS

1. Based on the biblical text, make a case both for and against Moses coming to see the taskmasters as his brothers.
2. Explain how Hanaoka connects the revelation of the divine name in Exodus 3:14 with the New Testament concept of God as love.
3. Hypothesize as to why people, prior to important discoveries, assumed that the stories were historical fact. In your experience, does this belief persist among many people? If so, why?
4. Compare and contrast the situation of the Israelites in Egypt and the "Indians" with the conquistadores. Are the differences important?

CHAPTER 8

EXODUS 20

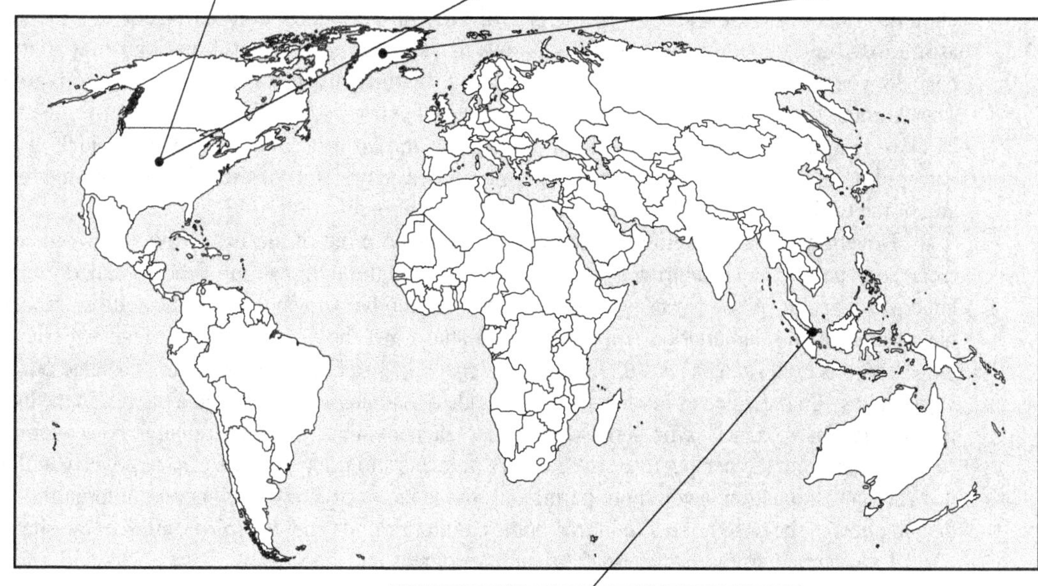
Febbie C. Dickerson explains how the Ten Commandments are understood by her African-American community as a means for establishing right relationships.
Jonathan Redding argues that the Ten Commandments are not applicable in the United States today in light of separation of church and state.
Flemming A. J. Nielsen details the challenges of European missionaries who translated the Ten Commandments into the native language of Greenland.
Maggie Low explains the challenges of honoring God and honoring parents in a Confucian context, where honoring parents supersedes all other duties.

READINGS

THE TEN COMMANDMENTS IN AN AFRICAN-AMERICAN COMMUNITY

Febbie C. Dickerson (United States)

The Ten Commandments are the words of God spoken directly to the mixed multitude liberated from slavery in Egypt. These commandments provided directions for right relationship with God and neighbor, and they also provided order and stability to a group attempting to find its new identity as free people on the way to the Promised Land. For many African-Americans living with the legacy of slavery, the Ten Commandments were not only moral and theological mandates, they were also assurances of a liberation from social and economic discrimination.

Both the gateway to the South and a notch in the Bible belt, Atlanta distinguishes itself by its welcoming of African-American communities. Along with its vibrant African-American churches, this cosmopolitan city is a center of African-American political success, educational aspirations, and economic prosperity. Atlanta has elected an African-American mayor for the past 38 years. It is the only U.S. city with five historically black colleges and universities. The Atlanta Thrashers has the largest percentage of African-American players in the National Hockey League. Economically, Atlanta has one of the largest concentrations of black affluent and middle-class populations. Atlanta also remains a major hub of the Civil Rights movement and home to the Southern Christian Leadership Conference.

Nevertheless, this shining legacy of Atlanta was born out of the Jim Crow south—the era of racial segregation. My grandparents and parents suffered the indignation of the so-called "separate but equal" system. When I was a young girl, my grandmother showed me the separate entrances for blacks at Atlanta's landmarks. Although bolted shut now, the entrance for African-Americans at the "Fabulous Fox Theater" is still visible. The legacy of Jim Crow continues to permeate our lived experiences—in the voice of my then seventh-grade classmate who called me a nigger, in the eyes of my now 10-year-old niece who perceived that her teacher wanted a white student to be academically superior, and from the perspective of African-Americans still trapped in the grip of poverty with limited access to education. Even more pernicious, the legacies of Jim Crow become internalized; like the Israelites in the desert, we live in free bodies, but our minds and our spirits still feel the shackles.

I am an heir to the histories of Atlanta's progress and oppression. I was born and raised in Atlanta and I grew up in a suburban neighborhood with a mixture of black and white families. Eventually the phenomenon of "white flight" gripped some of our neighbors and the neighborhood became an African-American community. Along with seeking diversity in our living space, my parents endeavored to provide me with diversity in my education. Consequently, in my primary school years I was a part of a group of minority students who integrated more fully one of the public schools. Given the complexity of living in a thriving African-American culture but in some instances still viewed as second class, my church was the place that helped me to live within my racially and culturally mixed society. The Bible and the church were necessary foundations for peaceful living.

The Bible, specifically the Old Testament, is central to many African-American religious communities. African-Americans have historically viewed Israel's Exodus from Egypt as a model for African-American liberation. As the enslaved Africans and their descendents read themselves into the stories of Exodus, they laid claim to an identity as Israel, God's people. Pharaoh was the slave master and Moses was the title given to anyone deemed a freedom fighter. Because we identified with Israel, a main understanding from my context was that the Ten Commandments were a sacred reminder of God's presence in our lives. The older folks in my church understood the commandments to be God's requirements for us to "Remember the Sabbath and keep it holy." Complete the housework and schoolwork by Saturday evenings because Sundays were the time to rest just as God rested. Honor your mom and dad, don't murder, don't steal, and don't tell lies against your neighbor were viewed less as prohibitions than as the way in which the divine presence was experienced. If one followed the commandments, one's life was in order. Therefore, we tried our best to adhere to the commandments. In doing so, we viewed the success of our city, our church, and our families as blessings and rewards for the faithful adherence to God's words.

The Ten Commandments were more than just moral guidelines: They offered theological hope. The opening of the Decalogue cannot be separated from its requirements. The mighty works of God provided for our needs. "I am the Lord your God who brought you out of the land of Egypt; out of the house of slavery." We internalized the text, and so we heard, "I am the Lord your God who brought your ancestors out of Jim Crow. I am the Lord your God who has provided you quality jobs so that your families may prosper. I am the Lord your God who has sustained your health. I am the Lord your God who has watched over your children. I am the Lord your God who has spared you from danger. Therefore, you shall have no other gods before me. You shall not make for yourself idols, for I the Lord your God am a jealous God." We understood those idols to be any material possession that took precedence over our reverence for God.

While the accounts of the Exodus and the Decalogue are about a people liberated less because of the evils of slavery than because God remembered the covenant with Abraham, we chose to see that story as our story and we chose to read it as proclaiming a God who liberated as an act of justice. One may point to other factors impacting the success of African-Americans in Atlanta, but we choose to see our success as related to our biblical values, our concern for right relationships between ourselves and our neighbors, and ourselves and God. We kept the Ten Commandments because we wanted to keep them. The commandments allowed us to live in hope and to see God as our eternal equalizer.

Febbie C. Dickerson is a Ph.D. candidate at Vanderbilt University, Nashville, Tennessee, United States.

The Ten Commandments and the Separation of Church and State

Jonathan Redding (United States)

Having been raised in the American South, I experienced a plethora of children's sermons, Vacation Bible School stories, and Sunday school lessons on the Ten Commandments. But what has surprised me as I have grown up is the arguments and legal battles over the legality of displaying the Ten Commandments on public buildings. Such controversy still seems to arise every few years with varied results and resolutions. But the continual presence of these fights testifies to the fact that many people, especially in the American South, still think that the Ten Commandments are a suitable set of laws for us in the United States today. They seem to think that if only people followed the Ten Commandments, everything would be so much better. To my mind, this reflects the deeply misguided belief that the Bible and/or Protestant Christianity is the panacea for what ails the world.

These 17 verses are etched into the psyche of many Southerners, most of whom could name more commandments than local past state senators. Yet few of these very same people go a single day, or perhaps a week, without breaking a commandment—and they do so with no remorse or compunction. The most obvious such example is the fourth commandment: To do no work on the Sabbath day. Never mind that the Sabbath is the seventh day of the week (Saturday), and not the first day of the week (Sunday), few Christians set aside a whole entire day (Sunday) of rest dedicated to God. Sure, they may not actually go to their place of employment, but they prepare meals, take care of household duties, and participate in other activities which constitute work. (The Jewish tradition has developed a complex set of regulations that outlines what constitutes "work" on the Sabbath.) There are other commandments, too, which many Christians seem to violate. For example, I've been taught that Jesus is God and yet I've seen many images of Jesus—pictures of him with little children, paintings of him on the cross, and so forth. Isn't this a violation of the second command: You shall not make any graven images? Or what about, "Thou shall not murder." Is capital punishment or going to war not a form of murder? Indeed, there is a deep irony in someone who cuts their grass on Sunday, wears a crucifix, and supports the death penalty and, at the same time, wants the Ten Commandments displayed in courthouses and school buildings.

Would anyone, then, seriously advocate an implementation of the Ten Commandments in America today. I think not, for several reasons. First, the verses have a clear audience: ancient Israelites and not current societies. Their ancient intended addressees undercut any argument for using the commandments in modern legal issues, much less positioning them as the foundation for every regulation and decree. Second, 20:2–3 says that the Israelites should follow the Lord God because God brought them out of Egypt. Though Christians utilize this text in modern practice, to claim a connection to the Israelites freed from Egyptian bondage is a stretch for any faith group except contemporary Jews. Therefore, the justification for worshipping God within these verses is irrelevant to American Christians. Removing the commandments from their original specific context discredits and relegates their intended purpose while it accommodates American agendas.

Conservative political pundits often lambast Muslim states that utilize Sharia Law. American Republicans and Democrats alike demonize the Islamic practice, saying that it destroys the wall between Church and State or that powerful corrupt leaders misconstrue and abuse the Islamic law code's statutes. Yet the very same people fail to see the striking similarities between criticisms of Sharia Law and unavoidable dangers of implementing biblical Law. Religious and social freedom become jeopardized when one religion gains legalized superiority, and deifying the Ten Commandments only threatens the fickle stability binding the United States together. Indeed, blending politics and religion risks massive loss of life, as history shows us. Nazi Germany had an "official" state church and all others were outlawed upon penalty of imprisonment and death. Corrupt Muslim extremist countries legalize beating and mutilating women. Isn't the separation of church and state one of America's wonderful redeeming merits?

Though it may appear otherwise, I respect and admire the Ten Commandments within their context. These laws were the first strides the Israelites made as they attempted to separate themselves from their enslaved past. The intentions of the commandments were never to oppress or subjugate anyone; in fact, the opposite is true. The Ten Commandments, in short, are an appropriate, admirable even, set of laws for the ancient Israelites. Not for us as Americans. The Bible has an appropriate place in our world, but it cannot simply be transported wholesale from one place to another. Removing Exodus 20 from its biblical context is a dangerous practice that threatens the Bible's place in contemporary society.

Jonathan Redding is a student at Wake Forest School of Divinity and a parttime Minister with Youth and Families at Peace Haven Baptist Church in Winston-Salem, North Carolina, United States.

The Confucian Ideal of Honoring Parents While Also Honoring God

Maggie Low (Singapore)

Obeying the Fifth Commandment in a Confucianist context can be a dilemma. Conversion to Christianity or to any other religion may be seen as a breach of filial piety because loyalty to one's parents is being challenged by allegiance to Another. Confucius taught in his *Analects* (or Sayings) that duty to the family supersedes all other duties because filial piety and fraternal duty are the roots of humaneness (13:18; 1:2, *Analects*). In fact, the veneration of ancestors occupies a more important place in Chinese life than do the gods, for one may choose one's gods but not one's ancestors. How, then, can the Christian in a Confucianist society keep both the First and Fifth Commandments?

For a start, it must be highlighted that there are many similarities between the biblical concept of honoring parents and the Confucianist principle of filial piety. The Hebrew word for honor (*kabed*) means, literally, to treat someone as weighty, and a word study reveals that honor is shown in three ways that are also consistent with Confucianist teachings: through pecuniary (financial), practical, and public expressions.

In Matthew 15:4, Jesus rebuked the Pharisees for breaking the commandment to honor parents by declaring that the support due to father or mother is "corban," that is, designated for God. One of the primary meanings of honor, therefore, has to do with giving pecuniary support to one's parents. In fact, the Chinese pictogram for filial piety is *xiao,* which consists of the element of *lao* (old person) above and *zhi* (child) below, depicting that the child supports the elderly. Giving tithes to God should never be used by the Christian as an excuse to give less to parents. For dependent parents, this is a matter of grave concern, and even if they are financially independent, Chinese parents would consider even a token sum of money (usually enclosed in an auspicious red packet) as an act of honoring them. This is especially meaningful during special occasions such as Lunar New Year celebrations and birthdays.

Second, honor also carries nuances of caring for others in practical ways. Psalm 91:15 says that God honors his people by rescuing them, and one of the last things that Jesus did at the cross was to entrust the care of his mother to his beloved disciple (John 19:26–27). Confucius urged children not to be ignorant of their parents' ages because it is a cause both for rejoicing and for anxiety (4:21, *Analects*). Thus, to honor parents is to care for them in times of physical or emotional needs. This can take many forms such as attending to them when they are sick or doing household chores, especially for single or married children who are living with their parents, as is common in Asian communities.

Third, cultural anthropologists have pointed out that honor also has a public dimension, or in Chinese terms, to honor someone is to "give face," that is, to let that person be able to show his face in public without shame, or better still, with pride. Respect is to be shown both privately and publicly so that children do not cause parents to "lose face." An important aspect of public esteem is posthumous honor. In 2 Samuel 10:3, David sent a message of condolence to a foreign king upon the death of his father, and this is described as an act of honoring the dead, no doubt eulogizing the former king. Filial piety is defined as serving one's parents when they are alive as well as sacrificing to them when they are dead (2:5, *Analects*). The issue of Chinese funeral rites and ancestral veneration is too complex to discuss in detail, but instead of an outright rejection of all such rituals, Chinese Christians seek acceptable ways to demonstrate honor for deceased ancestors.

Having noted the similarities between the Fifth Commandment and the Confucianist rule of filial piety, it is undeniable that there is fundamental difference between the two. From the scriptural perspective, although honoring parents is a sacred duty, the first and highest commitment is to the Lord, as expressed in the first four commandments. It might be said that the biblical view of filial piety is essentially theocentric (God-centered), while the Chinese view is anthropocentric (human-centered). Conversion to Christianity, therefore, involves an unavoidable clash of worldviews and loyalties.

Interestingly, the Fifth Commandment does not enjoin obedience (Hebrew, *shema*) but rather, honor (*kabed*) to parents. The promulgation of the Ten Commandments was addressed, first of all, to adults and particularly, to the male heads of households. Therefore, the commandment is not meant primarily for keeping young children in line; rather it is directed toward the care of elderly parents. In fact, the narrative of Ruth shows that honoring parents may require one to disobey their expressed wishes, just as Ruth refused her mother's-in-law advice to return to Moab and insisted on following her to Israel in order to take care of her (Ruth 1).

Obedience to parents is certainly commanded in the book of Proverbs, but such instructions are based on the presumption that parents are giving godly training in accordance with the fear of the Lord (Proverbs 9:10). What of parents who fail to demonstrate or impart moral teachings and behavior? While Confucius allows a child to gently dissuade his parents from doing wrong, he tells the child to obey even if his advice is ignored (4:18, *Analects*). Though the Ten Commandments make it clear that obedience to God comes first, the Fifth Commandment is not conditional, that is, children are to honor parents irrespective of parental flaws, in obedience to God. At the same time, within the context of the Ten Commandments, parents are also held accountable to God for what they teach and do. Thus, the theocentric view of filial piety safeguards the well-being of both parents and children, while the anthropocentric framework of filial piety poses the danger of becoming oppressive (as children are enjoined to obey their parents regardless).

Furthermore, the concept of filial piety could be used to explain the priority of loyalty to God. Although Confucius has little to say about the spiritual realm, he does make reference to the ancient belief in one sovereign Being addressed as *Shangdi* (Heavenly Emperor). Like the biblical God, *Shangdi* is not represented by any images and is worshipped as the creator and judge of humanity. The idea, therefore, that one should be filial to the Supreme Being as the divine father may be better accepted by the Confucianist mind-set.

In conclusion, though conversion from Confucianism to Christianity may seem like a betrayal of filial piety, it would be better thought of as a willingness to suffer for the sake of one's family, just as Jesus suffered rejection and crucifixion for those whom he loved. Mary Yeo Carpenter ("Familism and Ancestor Veneration: A Look at Chinese Funeral Rites," *Missiology* 24 [October 1996]: 516) cites the example of Buddhism, which entered China initially as a foreign religion from India but became widely assimilated by the Chinese populace: "The Buddhists teach that the highest form of filial piety is to become a Buddhist monk or nun and so earn merit for the parents. The Christian should teach that the highest form of filial piety is to reach parents for Christ." Buddhism believes that merit accumulated by good deeds gives one a better existence in this or the next life, and such merit may also be transferred to a deceased loved one, such as one's parents. Becoming a monk or nun is considered to be the highest form of good deed, and thus, this renunciation of family ties is reframed as an act of filial piety. In the same way, while conversion to Christianity means a change in loyalty, Christians should see their faith and testimony as the means by which God's gracious salvation can reach their parents.

Maggie Low is Lecturer in Old Testament at Trinity Theological College, Singapore.

Translating the Ten Commandments into the Native Language of Greenland

Flemming A. J. Nielsen (Greenland)

Greenland is geographically situated in North America, but historically, politically, economically, and culturally this huge and sparsely populated island is closely connected to Europe. Christianity came to Greenland in 1721 when the Norwegian missionary Hans Egede arrived. Nobody in Europe knew that the Norsemen had disappeared from Greenland and that the Inuit were the sole people there when Hans Egede set out in search of the lost Scandinavian tribe. Instead of finding his kinsmen, he was confronted with a language and a purely oral Inuit culture that were utterly foreign to him. But he stayed for 15 years as representative of the Danish king, learnt an exotic language that had not been described before, developed a written language, invented words for the foreign religious concepts that he wanted to introduce into the native tongue, and taught his audience to read. And he began to produce a number of Greenlandic religious texts for use by his fellow missionaries and the converts. Those texts, the first of which were produced in very broken Greenlandic in 1723, are the earliest texts written in any Eskaleut language.

Although the first Greenlandic translation of the book of Exodus was not printed until 1832, the Decalogue (Ten Commandments) became well known in Greenland from the very outset of Christian presence in the country. But there were many translational problems.

Prior to the coming of the Europeans and their Christianity, the Inuit world—encompassing coastal areas of Chukotka, Alaska, Canada, and Greenland—knew of no god resembling the Christian one. Vast differences between a European religion emanating from the well-established agricultural societies of the ancient Near East and the shamanism of a nomadic Inuit subsistence economy based on sealing, whaling, and hunting hampered the communication of central Christian concepts. In the pre-Christian Greenlandic religion there was behind the visible world an unseen one that could be approached by the shamans, the so-called *angakkut*. Everything visible had its own spirit, *inua*. Important *inui* ("possessed" plural) were the Man in the Moon, Sila—the unpredictable *inua* of the weather—and the Woman of the Sea. But none of them were supreme gods or the leader of a pantheon. In the language of his day, Hans Egede even called his Greenlandic audience "a people without religion and worship" whose language did not "possess words that are applicable to our religion and worship."

Thus, such words and expressions had to be invented, or as Egede said, it was "necessary to borrow words from our own language and naturalize them in theirs." This strategy can be seen in the rendering of the first commandment where "God" was "translated" by the Danish word *Gud*, which Hans Egede had introduced into Greenlandic very early. This word is still used today, though partly Greenlandized: *Guuti*. Once the word "God" had been naturalized in Greenlandic, it was not difficult to insist that this God should be held in respect according to the second commandment and to forbid every kind of traditional sorcery, magic, and necromancy.

Every shaman had his (or—rarely—her) own favorite helping spirit, *toornaarsuk*. Two Greenlandic word lists had been published in Denmark in the seventeenth century, and from one of those lists Egede had learnt that *toornaarsuk* meant the Devil. When he heard the shamans refer to their *toornaarsuk*, he therefore misinterpreted the concept and believed that there was only one *toornaarsuk* and that the Greenlanders were worshippers of the Devil. However, he did not believe that the shamans themselves were really in contact with the Devil. He rather regarded them as con men who were able to seduce their audience and make *them* believe in the Devil. The shamans were his main rivals, and he fought them by all possible means out of pity for a people led astray, as he saw it. If the Greenlanders would not cease practicing their sorcery, Egede even said that they would be killed and exterminated from the earth, for God has commanded "us" to kill shamans and liars. His threats, fortunately, were empty and mostly testify to his desperation.

It was more difficult to explain the concept of Sabbath, let alone weeks. In the pre-Christian Inuit society, the days had no names and thus there were no weeks. Even in our time the days are designated by numbers only in Greenland, except for Sunday, which is called *sapaat*, from Hebrew *šabbāt*, and a week is *sapaatip akunnera*, "the Sunday's interval." Moreover, it proved difficult to explain why in a subsistence economy work should be forbidden every seventh day even if the weather was perfect for hunting and the country was teeming with prey. If the Almighty God wanted his people to stay home and listen to the missionaries on a Sunday, why would he let the sun shine so alluringly?

Cultural differences led to other problems in translation. For instance, the traditional Inuit society was polygamous, which was practical if only because men were in a minority since their work was dangerous and caused many fatal accidents. Nobody can survive on their own in traditional Arctic societies, and widowed women had no choice but to become members of new extended families that would appreciate their working skills.

Another problem was the concept of private property in the ninth and tenth commandments implying that man can own house, wife, servants, and livestock. Traditional Arctic societies are nomadic. In Greenland people lived in half-buried houses built of stone and roofed with driftwood, whale bones, and sod during the winter. In the summer half they were nomads living in tents. In early spring, the roofs were removed from the houses to leave only the walls upright, and when the time came again to overwinter, new constellations of extended families were formed and the houses were reroofed and reused by the first groups to arrive at them. The next groups had to search for other houses or build for themselves. Nobody owned such houses permanently. Likewise, nobody owned his own bag or catch. Every hunter had to share what he had according to detailed customary rules. If he refused to do so, his kinsmen would exclude him or ridicule him by satirical songs.

However, in spite of all the problems and immediate setbacks to the missionaries, the traditional society and beliefs faded away fairly quickly as the indigenous people embraced Christianity and its rites, scriptures, and pictures. In the course of time, a Greenlandic nation was built and an imagined Christian community established. Today Greenland is a proud autonomous Christian nation within the Danish national community. The Danish and Norwegian missionaries' insistence that the Gospel should be preached in the vernacular—though it caused all but insurmountable difficulties to themselves—saved the Greenlandic language for posterity, unlike so many other languages in the American hemisphere.

Flemming A. J. Nielsen (Ph.D.) is Associate Professor in the Department of Theology and Religion at University of Greenland.

QUESTIONS

1. Dickerson acknowledges that the biblical story of the Exodus is not primarily about God's liberating people from slavery; but yet her community chose to read it that way nonetheless. Is this problematic? Is it laudable that Dickerson acknowledges how her community is handling the biblical text?
2. In addition to the commandments that Redding mentions, are there others of the Ten which Christians in your culture seem to break regularly?
3. Like the fifth commandment in a Confucian context, what other commandments might be difficult to follow in certain social and cultural settings? Are there any particular such ones in your context?
4. Was Egede's work benevolent and beneficial to the native Inuit? Or was it manipulating their language and culture in an attempt to control them?

CHAPTER 9

NUMBERS 22–24, 32, 36

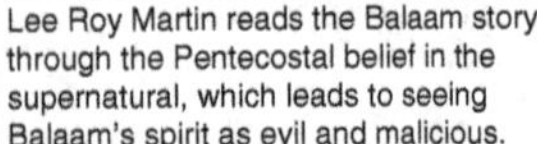
Lee Roy Martin reads the Balaam story through the Pentecostal belief in the supernatural, which leads to seeing Balaam's spirit as evil and malicious.

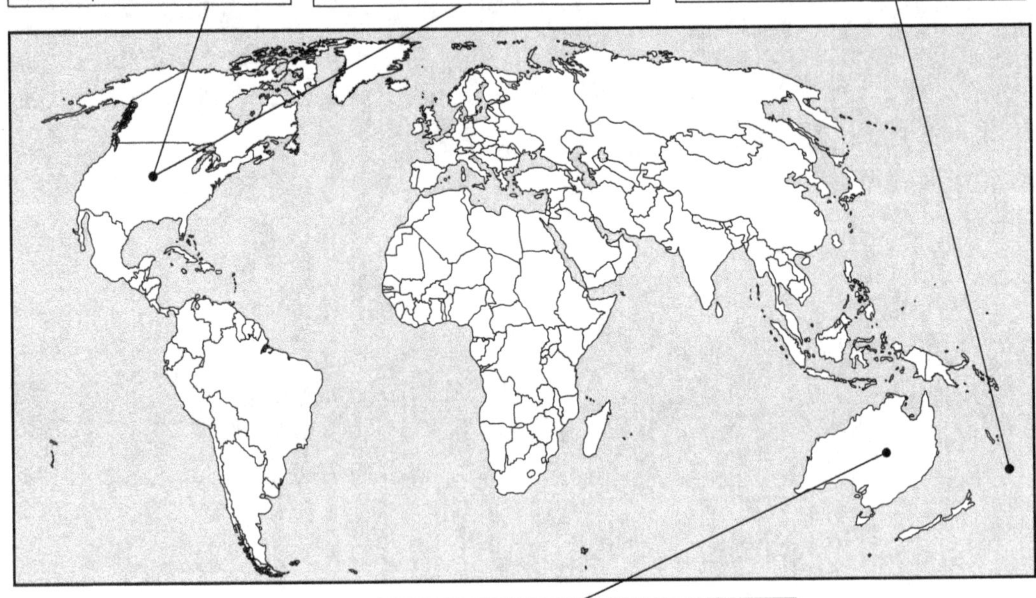
Tony Wing maintains that the Balaam narrative boils down to a simple story of doing what is right in the face of temptation, and God taking care of His people.
Jione Havea considers the story in Numbers 32 and the daughters of Zelophehad in Numbers 36 in the context of Western colonization of the islands of Oceania.
Roland Boer focuses on the way in which Numbers 22–24 justifies overrunning indigenous peoples, a situation akin to that of the native peoples of Australia.

READINGS

The Balaam Story through a Pentecostal Lens
Lee Roy Martin

The Balaam Narrative as a Story about Temptation and Protection
Tony Wing

Numbers 22–24 as a Justification for Overrunning Indigenous Peoples
Roland Boer

Numbers in the Context of Western Colonization of the Islands of Oceania
Jione Havea

The Balaam Story through a Pentecostal Lens

Lee Roy Martin (United States)

Enigmatic sorcerers... talking animals... otherworldly visitors... imminent battles... mysterious prophecies. No, this is not *The Lord of the Rings, The Chronicles of Narnia*, or *Harry Potter*. It is the biblical story of Balaam. We might wonder what significance this bizarre narrative offers to us who live in a technologically advanced world, where people are more concerned about Facebook hackers than malicious spells and incantations. A growing number of people, however, are showing a resurgence of interest in the supernatural world and spiritual realities. We are, in fact, faced with a multitude of spiritualities from which to choose. The belief in the supernatural is a vital component of my own Pentecostal faith, and accompanying that belief is the necessity for spiritual discernment. We are warned in the New Testament, "Do not believe every spirit, but test the spirits to see whether they are from God; for many false prophets have gone out into the world" (1 John 4:1).

Consequently, one of the many questions that emerges from a Pentecostal hearing of the Balaam story is not "Do spiritual forces exist?" but "Are all spiritual forces equally good, trustworthy, and benevolent?" The well-known sorcerer Balaam had been accustomed to engaging the spirit world by means of common ancient Near Eastern practices such as divination, reading omens, consulting ghosts, and necromancy (Num. 22:7; cf. Deuteronomy 18:10–12), but here he is confronted by a new spiritual force, one that he cannot manipulate, one that he cannot master. This new Spirit, the "spirit of God," comes upon him (24:1–2) and his "eyes are opened"; he "sees clearly"; he "sees a vision from the Almighty" (22:31; 24:3–4, 15–16). This Spirit demonstrates that Yahweh will not be resisted and his purposes will be fulfilled—purposes that include the blessing of God's people and their inheritance of the Promised Land.

It is repeated throughout the story that Balaam cannot curse Israel and that he can speak only the words that Yahweh gives him to speak (22:12, 13, 18, 20, 35, 38; 23:3, 8, 20, 26; 24:13). Still Balaam continues to assist Balak. Not once, but three times, Balak takes Balaam to a hilltop, offers sacrifices, and asks Balaam to pronounce a curse upon Israel. Each time Balaam can utter only blessings, and each subsequent oracle is more and more favorable to Israel, with the final oracle explicitly predicting Israel's defeat of Moab. Despite Yahweh's repeated insistence that Balak's plan will fail, Balaam continues to participate with Balak, in hope that Yahweh may change his mind and Balaam may receive his conjurer's reward.

We might wonder if Balaam's hopes are not grounded in a bit of truth. Has not Yahweh himself threatened to disown the Israelites (Exodus 32:10; Numbers 14:12), and has he not repeatedly stricken the Israelites with deadly plagues and other judgments (Exodus 32:35; Leviticus 10:2; Numbers 11:1, 33; 12:1–10; 16:31–35, 41–50; 21:6)? Thus, when Balak contacts Balaam and hires him to conjure a curse against Israel, we wonder if God might use Balaam as an instrument to destroy the remainder of the doomed Israelites. However, we learn that although God is prepared to punish his people, he will not allow Balaam to do his work for him. Therefore, God forces Balaam to proclaim blessings upon Israel, reaffirming God's ultimate purposes in bringing Israel into the land that had been promised to Abraham, Isaac, and Jacob. Israel had rebelled against God repeatedly, and they had suffered divine punishments, but Balaam affirms, "Yahweh their God is with them" (23:21). Yahweh is Israel's "king" (23:21), and he serves both as disciplinarian and as protector; therefore, Balaam admits that his sorcery is powerless against them (23:23). Yahweh will protect his people, a people that he has saved from slavery in Egypt (23:22; 24:8). Yahweh will fulfill his promise to bring Israel into the Promised Land (23:19). Therefore, within the narrative context of Israel's wilderness wanderings, the story of Balaam offers hope that God has not abandoned his people on account of their repeated episodes of unfaithfulness.

But if Yahweh never intended to allow the cursing of Israel, why did he choose to speak through Balaam at all? Why not simply put a stop to Balak's plan from the very beginning? And if Yahweh wanted to speak a word of blessing, why would he speak through a non-Israelite sorcerer? Perhaps the time had come in Israel's journey for a reminder of God's promises, and perhaps the word of blessing would have more impact if spoken from the "outside" rather than from the "inside."

Up to this point, the events in the story of the exodus and Israel's wilderness experience have been presented from Israel's perspective, with God, Israel, and Moses as the main characters. But here, the main characters are God, Balak, and Balaam—Moses is not mentioned at all, and Israel is not active in the story. The Balaam narrative, therefore, looks at Israel from the outside, at a distance. This perspective, called dramatic irony, is rare in the Old Testament. The oracles of Balaam are beautiful, powerful, and moving both in their content and in their unique origin. The same words spoken by Moses, Joshua, or Caleb would have been just as beautiful, but hearing the blessings from an enemy adds to their weight and significance.

Furthermore, the fact that Yahweh chooses to speak through Balaam demonstrates the way that God chooses to speak in the world. Yahweh is able to adapt to whatever situation may arise, and he is free to speak through unconventional means and through people that we would deem to be unqualified. Often in the Old Testament, God will choose a person to be his spokesperson. But here, Yahweh does not choose Balaam; rather Balak chooses Balaam to be his spokesperson, and Yahweh hijacks Balak's plan, choosing to speak through Balaam. This is neither the first nor the last instance of Yahweh's putting his Spirit upon a person whom he had not initially chosen. Earlier, Moses had chosen 70 elders, and Yahweh put his Spirit upon them and they prophesied (Num. 11). In a later example, the elders of Gilead chose Jephthah to be their leader, and Yahweh took advantage of the situation to put his Spirit upon Jephthah and empower him to deliver Israel. Here in Numbers, Yahweh does not initially choose Balaam as his spokesperson, but Yahweh adapts to the situation and orders the events to show that Balak is not in control.

Yahweh, however, does not choose to obliterate entirely Balaam's powers of volition. Yahweh is free to speak through recalcitrant Balaam, but Balaam retains some degree of freedom as well. He is free to continue in his selfish ways, seeking the "wages of wickedness," for which he is later condemned (2 Peter 2:15). Balaam's later actions in leading Israel into sin (Num. 25:1; 31:16) prove that, although he briefly abandoned divination and experienced the Spirit of God (24:1–2), he went back to his old familiar spirits, a choice which led to his demise (31:8). Balaam's spirit and the spirits of sorcery prove to be what the Bible calls "evil spirits," which are at odds with the Spirit of God and malevolent toward the people of God. The evil spirits of Balaam inspire him to deceive the Israelites, to behave immorally, and to resist the Spirit of God.

Lee Roy Martin (D.Th., University of South Africa) is Professor of Old Testament and Biblical Languages at Pentecostal Theological Seminary, Cleveland, Tennessee, United States.

The Balaam Narrative as a Story about Temptation and Protection

Tony Wing (United States)

College students in the United States find themselves in a very peculiar place. They are not children any longer, but they do not quite have the same responsibilities as adults. They have newfound freedom being away from home; they are forced to confront new situations. College is a time of transition for millions of students every year. Whenever there is transition, there is pressure. All students must deal with the pressure to abstain from doing evil.

"Evil" is a word that one only thinks about in connection with names like Hitler, but it can be much more subtle than that. Evil has to be faced from two fronts: from without and within. Evil is tenacious, and worst of all . . . it is desirable. It makes promises of wealth, love, peace of mind, power, or happiness. Even when one knows that what they are facing is not the right thing to do, it is nonetheless often tough to say no. While the evil a college student faces may not be in the same league as genocide and war crimes, fighting temptation has never changed.

While Numbers 22 stands out as having some odd similarities to Shrek (try not to think of the talking donkey as having Eddie Murphy's voice), it boils down to a simple story of God taking care of His people, and doing what is right in the face of temptation.

For Balaam, the evil offered came in the form of cursing the people of God. A rich, powerful ruler presented Balaam with the chance to make a name for himself and to set up a nice little nest egg to boot. Balaam prayed about the king's request and God told him to say no. It seems in the story that it was either an audible voice from God or a vision in a dream—either way a rather cut and dry response from Heaven—letting Balaam know that one doesn't curse God's people. Would one not guess as much? However, Balaam does not take the "no" at face value and continues asking God to be allowed to go.

For everyone else, knowing the difference between good and evil is not always as easy as it should have been for Balaam. Most people do not receive emails from God or late-night visions starring a host of angels to keep us on the straight and narrow. What they do have is a conscience and the rest of the Bible as a guidebook for righteous living. Yet, knowing the right thing to do is not always as simple as choosing to do it. Even if, like Balaam, one can say no to temptation the first time it rears its head, temptation usually will not stop at one attempt. Much like the princes of Moab and Midian, temptation keeps coming back with more attractive offers.

One may be thinking that their life is nothing like the story of Balaam though; but if one looks past the kings, talking animals, and promises of houses full of gold, then this story would align much more closely with anyone's life. Balaam was offered money in exchange for selling out the people of God, just as some might see dollar signs before their eyes if they cheat on their taxes or steal from the cash register at work. Balaam was asked to curse an entire people group, just as one might be tempted to curse (at) an ex-boyfriend or a particularly tough professor.

Obviously the stakes were much higher for Balaam, but the principles are the same. God was angered by Balaam's decision to question what God had told him. When God speaks to someone, they should not question it. No matter what is offered, be it fame, riches, honor, or love, it is wise to listen to the will of the Lord. There are always consequences if one decides to ignore what the Lord has asked of them. Luckily for Balaam, he had a friend who was there to help him in his time of need. Oddly enough, it was a donkey that could see angels and was given the gift of speech. For you, the voice that speaks sense in your time of trouble could be a friend, a parent, a pastor or priest, or even a stranger. God truly moves in mysterious ways, just as he did with Balaam's donkey.

How does this change the American college student though? If one is waiting on their pet dog to talk or a vision from heaven, then they have missed the point of the biblical story entirely. Read the rest of it in Numbers 23–24. The story takes another twist. Balaam finds himself with the king, looking out over the people of God. Face to face with the very person who has been tempting him, and without a place to run to, Balaam does the right thing. Instead of cursing Israel, he blesses them; and he does it four different times.

In Numbers 22, Balaam makes a number of mistakes; he falls in the face of adversity and temptation; but that did not mean he was without redemption. There is always a chance to do what is right in the end. Much of my ministry with college students is helping them realize precisely that point. No matter how big or small their mistakes may be, none of them represents the end of the world. Life goes on. God is forgiving. If students can learn how to face down temptation during the transition years of college, then maybe, just maybe, they will be better prepared to do so as they grow older.

Tony Wing (M.A., Christian Education) is Lay College Minister in Charlotte, North Carolina, United States.

Numbers 22–24 as a Justification for Overrunning Indigenous Peoples

Roland Boer (Australia)

The story of Balaam's talking ass in Numbers 22 has many possible angles, such as a reading that focuses on the animals: the ox licking up the grass (v. 4), the well-known talking ass (vv. 21–33), and the oxen and sheep sacrificed (v. 40). Most attention has concerned the talking ass and the angel. But I am interested in a different and even more complex problem, namely, the way the passage justifies overrunning indigenous peoples. In this case God condones the invasion, preventing Balaam from cursing the Israelites but ensuring that he blesses them. Balak and the Ammonites (along with some Midianites) are both justifiably terrified and yet thwarted in their efforts to prevent the invasion.

I read this passage from an equally complex situation in Australia, where all manner of justifications for overrunning the land of indigenous peoples have been and continue to be manufactured. Perhaps the most contentious term is *terra nullius*. Deriving from Roman law and meaning "land of no one," it designates a territory inhabited by people whose social or political organization is not recognized (i.e., they were regarded as far too "primitive" to have any society, let alone language). More technically, *terra nullius* designates land that has never been subject to the sovereignty of any state, or land over which any prior sovereign has expressly or implicitly relinquished sovereignty. *Terra nullius* means that any state can claim sovereignty merely by occupying the land. Outside Australia, the doctrine has been deployed variously in relation to Western Sahara, Greenland, New Zealand, and Canada, but the only location where it has been upheld is Antarctica, where *terra nullius* is vital for the Antarctic Treaty.

Terra nullius was deployed in Australia as a convenient fiction for colonization. Unable to understand the complexity and age of indigenous institutions and traditions, and unable to locate any leaders who might sign treaties, English colonizers simply did not make any treaties—unlike

North America, Africa, and New Zealand. Over the course of the 1800s, *terra nullius* became enshrined in law, gradually restricting Aboriginal rights: They could not sell, assign, or buy land, thereby ensuring that they could make no claim to possessing a land in which they had lived for over 40,000 years—the oldest continuous culture on earth.

However, in 1992, the doctrine was utterly overturned by the High Court in what is now known as the Mabo case. In response to a challenge brought by Eddie Mabo, David Passi, and James Rice, from the Meriam people of the Murray Islands in the Torres Straight, the High Court ruled that a concept of native title exists in common law; the source of native title is the traditional connection to or occupation of the land; that native title could be extinguished by the valid exercise of governmental powers provided a clear and plain intention to do so was manifest.

The story continues to gain in complexity, but what we find with the doctrine of *terra nullius* and the Mabo case is a complex effort to deny indigenous claims to a land, a denial which was then spectacularly overturned. In this light I read Numbers 22. Is the blessing-that-would-be-a-curse in Balaam's mouth also an effort at *terra nullius*, now of a theological variety? By blessing the Israelites (in Num. 23), does the text condone a story of invasion and occupation? Does God too become a player in this effort at theological *terra nullius* by—in the story—instructing Balaam not to do the bidding of Balak? Let us look at the story once again.

Immediately, the reader is struck by the fact that the story is told from the indigenous "point of view." The responses of the people of the land are mentioned, their fear and trepidation before the countless Israelites who have arrived to take their land. Are not stories of conquest usually told from the perspective of the victors, showing how cowardly, weak, sinful, and filthy the natives are (the last a drearily standard characterization of foreigners)? The initial impression is that this story does not do so, for here we have the perspective of Balak and the elders. Yet we should not read too quickly, for a basic question needs to be asked: Who writes for whom and why? Of course, we do not know the name of the author of this story, but it is clearly an Israelite story. If so, that means the perspective of the indigenous people is a constructed one, created to give a certain impression of those people. In other words, "point of view" is a technique of writing and not a reliable window into what people think or do.

It is a very clever narrative ploy, for we see through the eyes of the indigenous people, including Balaam. Yet the story attempts, precisely through that perspective, to make us sympathetic, not to those whose perspective we share, but to the Israelites, who are only ever the object of a distant gaze and of somewhat fearful rumor. In other words, the story wants us to feel that the invasion is perfectly justified and that the indigenous people are in some way not entitled to the land.

Noticeably, the story does not condemn the Moabites and Midianites for employing a diviner, Balaam. After all, God speaks intimately with Balaam. Instead, the story brings out all the big guns: God is on the side of the invaders; the prophet-cum-diviner is unable to curse them; even his donkey, oppressed and beaten as it is, can see the truth of the situation, even if the "seer" cannot.

For those of us accustomed to seeing God on the side of the good guys, we need to remind ourselves that in stories like this the representation of "God" is produced by the author(s). And this "God" ultimately reinforces the position of the author(s) and indeed editor(s)—especially when that position is presented through the point of view of the indigenous people. That is, not only do we have a theological *terra nullius* in this story but also a perspectival *terra nullius*, for their perspective on the whole story is colonized.

All the same, is there a "Mabo" moment in this story, a moment when the whole doctrine of *terra nullius* is overturned in all its many facets? I suggest that this moment appears from an unexpected quarter: What goes by the name of "Israel" is itself indigenous. What does this mean? The vast majority of biblical scholars agree that the evidence points overwhelmingly to the fact that Israel did not arrive as a foreign force, invading Palestine. Instead, Israel emerged from the people of Palestine, as did their religion, customs, and social and economic system. The implication is that the effort to discredit the indigenous people goes out the window, for those who try to do so are themselves from the same people. Either they discredit themselves along with everyone else or they recognize the legitimacy of those who are in the land.

Roland Boer is a cyclist, ship-voyager, and research professor at the University of Newcastle, Australia.

Numbers in the Context of Western Colonization of the Islands of Oceania

Jione Havea (Oceania)

Numbers 32 is cheeky, presenting the tribes of Gad and Reuben as if they are looking after their best interests, bordering on being ungrateful for and/or untrusting of God's promise. The wilderness journey was drawing to an end, and as Israel prepares to cross into Canaan, the Gadites and Reubenites requested that they possess the land on the east side of the Jordan (Transjordania), because it was just right for their livelihood. They asked to stay behind, and possess land outside of that which God had promised (32:1–5).

While their request is sensible, on account of their very great number of cattle, questions do arise. Did they expect the land God promised *not* to be good enough for them and/or broad enough for all of Israel? Were they scared of crossing their cattle for fear that some might drown in the Jordan? Did they not want to share their cattle with the other tribes of Israel? Were they scared and tightfisted?

Whatever the case may be, Israel as a whole does not seem to be satisfied with dispossessing the people of Canaan. They want also to dispossess the people on the other side of the Jordan. Indeed, Numbers 32 reads like the chronicle of the expansion of a predatory empire or the accounts of the outings of an insatiable chief, whose tentacles continuously reach out to grab and strangle. God's promise is not enough. Gilead will also be taken, sanctioned by an agreement between Moses, Joshua, and the heads of the Israelite tribes, with the Reubenites and Gadites (32:25–32). The land that God promised is not freely given. Unlike the time when Abram first arrived and seemed to move around unrestricted in the land, even though it was already occupied (see Genesis 12:4–9), this time Israel needs to fight for the land. And unlike the time when Jacob returned with his family and wealth to Canaan and was greeted by his brother Esau, this time it will not be easy for the Israelites to enter Canaan. This time they will take up arms for war, and all hands are required on deck. The Reubenites and Gadites are needed, suggesting that the resistance from the people of the land will be stronger. The war for the land will be fierce, and Israel will shed blood for the sake of God's promise. In this regard, the land is a bloody gift.

The Reubenites and Gadites complicated matters by requesting land that was not part of what God had promised, a promise that was already complicated because that land was the home of its first peoples. As if things were not complicated enough, Moses tightens the screw.

Whereas the Reubenites and Gadites were the primary claimants, Moses adds "the half-tribe of Manasseh son of Joseph" to the equation in 32:33–42. They too will have their inheritance in Transjordania. We are not told when and if they had asked for the same location, but the text is unwavering that Gilead was given to the Reubenites and Gadites (32:26) and then again to the half-tribe of Manasseh (32:39).

Many explanations are possible, but it is curious that the distribution of land was an ongoing struggle for this half-tribe of Manasseh. Numbers 32 sets up expectation for tensions between the two and the one-half tribes, but the text does not abide. Instead, it offers a romanticized view: "the two tribes and the half-tribe have taken their inheritance beyond the Jordan at Jericho eastward, *toward the sunrise*" (34:15, my italics).

The struggle of the half-tribe of Manasseh over inheritance was internal. Among the Manassites was Zelophehad, whose five daughters—Mahlah, Noah, Hoglah, Milcah, and Tirzah—brought a strong case before Moses, Eliezar, and the leaders because their father died without a son. They did not want his inheritance to be lost to someone else, which would mean that the name and memory of their father dies out with him. Their case led to a statute and ordinance in Israel the bottom line of which was that Israelite daughters can inherit land if they did not have brothers (27:1–11). Daughters would not inherit if there were sons, but these daughters made a significant difference in the customs of Israel.

In the end, however, the heads of the half-tribe protested and the daughters had to marry within their father's tribe (Num. 36). The book of Numbers closes with a counterclaim within the half-tribe of Manasseh, whom Moses pulled into the picture in Numbers 32 to inherit Gilead.

If I were to follow the plot of Numbers 32, I would wholeheartedly accept the reassigning of Gilead to the half-tribe of Manasseh, out of respect for the general flow of the book of Numbers, which closes by assuring that the half-tribe of Manasseh does not lose its inheritance. The forces seem to come together in order to establish the half-tribe in Gilead.

But since I opt to identify with Mahlah, Noah, Hoglah, Milcah, and Tirzah—the five daughters of Zelophehad—whose right to decide whom to marry was regulated because of a counterclaim by the elders of their tribe, I hesitate to endorse the right of the half-tribe of Manasseh over Gilead because that would mean dispossessing the Reubenites and Gadites. My hesitation is because I do not approve of disempowering women and men from deciding whom to marry, especially if the decision has to do with wealth and inheritance, and also because I do not approve of the dispossession of any people from their land. At this juncture, therefore, I lean in favor of the Reubenites and Gadites.

Because I am a native of Oceania, where small island nation-states are still under the shackles of Western empires—Tahiti and Kanak are colonies of France; Havai'i, Mariana, Guam, and one-half of Samoa are colonies of the United States of America—I refuse to accept any justification for the dispossession of the first peoples of both Canaan and Transjordania. Western empires bring their civilization, religions, values, and funding to help native people, and the result is the undermining, and in some cases the erasure, of indigenous wisdom, customs, and practices. Western presence has made natives live in their home islands as if they are foreigners. In this regard, Numbers 32 presents a haunting and seductive story. It is seductive because it can appease one into defending the Reubenites and Gadites against the claim of the half-tribe of Manasseh, and thus lose sight of the fact that they are dispossessors one and the same. And it is haunting because, as an account of dispossession, it pushes one to *be rooted* and at the same time, as in the reading offered herein, to resist when the text mimics one's roots. Israel was to Gilead as Western empires continue to be in Oceania.

In Numbers 32, the tribes of Gad and Reuben displace the first peoples in their preferred land and are displaced by one (half-tribe) of their own, inscribed and endorsed by Moses. This reading of Numbers 32 poses questions for readers, especially those who tune in to the power of stories and the maneuverings of biblical narratives: How may we read accounts of displacement and dispossession in contexts where displacement and dispossession (physically, economically, religiously, ideologically, theologically, internationally, and so on) continue and thrive? And how about when displacement and dispossession happen in the name of God, with the blessings and guidance of biblical, religious, or societal leaders? How might we learn to resist the colonial legacy, and the colonizing allure, of biblical texts?

Jione Havea is Senior Lecturer at United Theological College and School of Theology at Charles Sturt University, Parramatta, NSW, Australia.

QUESTIONS

1. Evaluate Martin's depiction of Balaam. If you were Balaam's attorney, how would you defend him in the face of Martin's reading?
2. What other "lessons" might one draw from this text? If you are a college student, do you find Wing's application of the story compelling?
3. Boer mentions, but does not explore, a reading that focuses on the animals. What insights would such a perspective offer?
4. Explain and evaluate the importance of the daughters of Zelophehad for Havea.

CHAPTER 10

DEUTERONOMY 6, 10, 16, 24

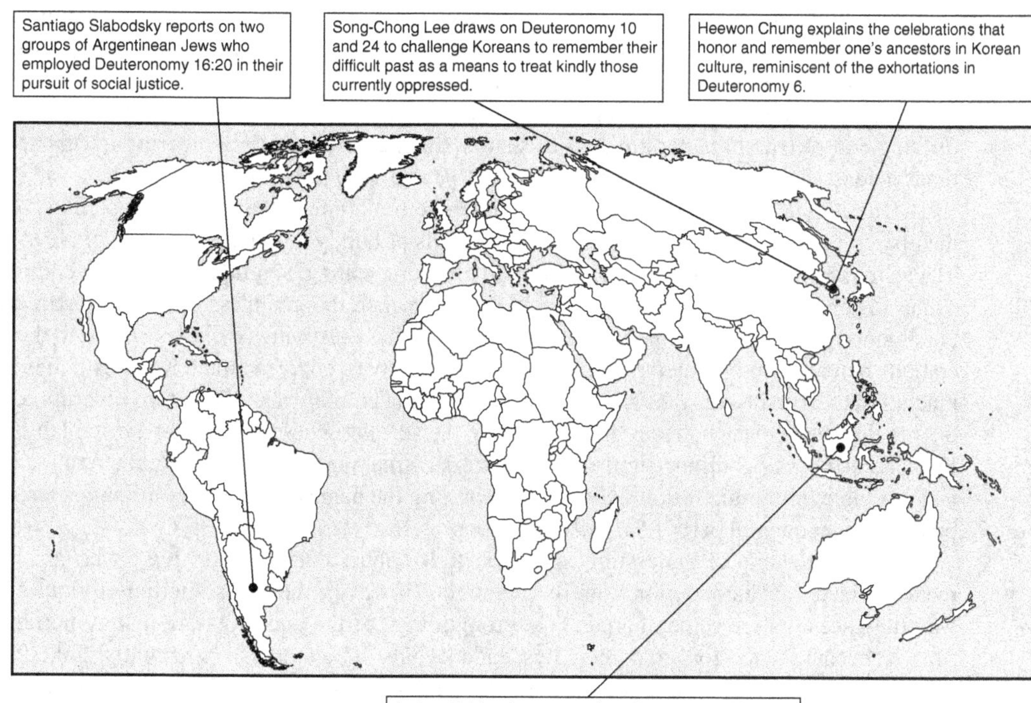
Santiago Slabodsky reports on two groups of Argentinean Jews who employed Deuteronomy 16:20 in their pursuit of social justice.
Song-Chong Lee draws on Deuteronomy 10 and 24 to challenge Koreans to remember their difficult past as a means to treat kindly those currently oppressed.
Heewon Chung explains the celebrations that honor and remember one's ancestors in Korean culture, reminiscent of the exhortations in Deuteronomy 6.
Andrea K. Iskandar suggests how Deuteronomy 10:17–19 can offer inspiration for Chinese Christians in Indonesia, who feel like aliens in their homeland.

READINGS

Korean Celebrations of Culture Compared to Exhortations in Deuteronomy

Heewon Chung (South Korea)

Throughout the world, various spiritual and religious traditions hold special celebrations to honor and to remember their ancestors and heritage. We see this in both Deuteronomy 6 and in certain aspects of Korean culture. The practice of remembering generations past has been a serious concern for many centuries in Korea. Living well for Koreans has to do not only with how they live but also with how they remember their ancestors. Koreans have traditionally believed that the ancestors are actively involved in the lives of people. In this perspective, in order for one to continue to live well, one has to respect his or her ancestors and to remember what they have done in their lifetime. What characterizes this special remembrance the most is offering *che-sa* (rite of veneration) to ancestors. Such ceremonial remembering occurs several times a year, such as *Chu-suk* (Thanksgiving Day) and *Sul-nal* (New Year's Day).

On *Sul-nal*, for example, sons and daughters return home to their surviving parents, revere their parents and the late ancestors, and hold festivals of family union in the season of New Year. The festivities involve family celebrations with drinking, eating, singing, and playing communal games. They give an opportunity for people to appreciate the goodness of life and help create bonds among all family members. An integral part of these festivities includes *che-sa* to the generations before them in remembering ancestors for another good year since Koreans believe that practicing this rite insures the family's prosperity in the coming year. Therefore, in gratitude for the life they have received from their ancestors, the surviving descendents set a ritual table with food and drink, pay obeisance to the late ancestors by making bows, and invite them to the ritual table. A table fellowship follows *che-sa*. Memorizing the names of ancestors through such ritual practices is an integral part of *Sul-nal* celebration.

During the rite of veneration and table fellowship, stories about those who are being memorialized are shared among family members. However, there is something unique in the way the ancestors are remembered. The wrongdoings of the ancestors are also remembered. This is because ancestors and their descendents are understood as spiritually linked: The misdeeds of ancestors are visited on their descendents, and conversely, action taken to help the ancestors will have a beneficial effect on their descendents. Therefore, descendents must eliminate their ancestors' impurities that they had done in their lifetime. Such purifying is achieved through granting unconditional forgiveness to the ancestors, which erases their misdeeds from the family's memory. Thus, the living begins a renewed relationship with those who have passed on.

This practice of remembering, however, demands some critique. From the perspective of the person wronged by the misdeeds, the family's demand for forgiveness may be experienced as revictimization without any due recourse for justice. At the same time, it could also be understood as another way of resolving conflicts, one way of putting an end to a distorted relationship and thereby liberating the victim/survivor from the power of the abuser.

Koreans are very conscious of making devoted efforts to eliminate their present misfortune by remembering the past misdeeds of ancestors. Knowing where one comes from and how one's heritage influences current events is a basic human need for survival in any culture. Regular remembering allows descendents to realize where they come from, how they shall live, and where they will go, and it solidifies family unity. Therefore, Korean families use the ancestor veneration rite on special days of the year as an occasion to teach the succeeding generations about the importance of remembering. This practice enables descendents to learn about ancestors whom they have not met in their lifetimes and to build relationships between generations. By so doing, ancestors and their deeds are not forgotten; they are remembered by the community of the living. It also allows descendents to deal with the reality of life and death on a regular basis, and it provides opportunities for them to continue to live in a right way. People become aware of their duty to behave properly and to avoid misdeeds and abominable actions which will adversely affect subsequent generations.

This Korean practice of remembering generations past has a number of implications for understanding Deuteronomy 6:10–25. In his sermon, Moses asks the people of Israel not to forget what Yahweh promised to the first three generations of patriarchs. He urges the people to remember Yahweh and the great ancestors who have laid the foundation for their lives. Moses reminds the people of Israel that they are connected to those who have come before them and that they will influence the lives of those who follow them. He then exhorts them to remember their ancestors' misdeeds during the time of wilderness wandering. In addition, he urges all the heads of Israelite families to teach their children to remember where they came from, so that they would know the great things Yahweh had done for his people. Moses concludes with the notion that the people of Israel can solidify their intergenerational ties and establish a right relationship with Yahweh by remembering the lives of ancestors and the promises given to them.

The practice of remembering helps us appreciate life that continues on through human connections over the generations. Deuteronomy 6 and *Sul-nal* remind us that it is so important to remember those that came before us, that we must take the time to reflect back with gratitude or sorrows on what our ancestors have done. More importantly, we must take the time to reflect with gratitude on God who made the way possible. Remembering the generations before us is a wonderful opportunity to turn grief into a positive expression of our gratitude to God, who laid the foundation for our lives. By remembering ancestors, one cannot help but worship God.

Heewon Chung is Lecturer of Old Testament at the College of Liberal Arts at Keimyung University, Daegu, South Korea.

Deuteronomy as Inspiration for Chinese Christians Living in Indonesia

Andrea K. Iskandar (Indonesia)

Chinese people in Indonesia are a minority ethnic, constituting approximately 3 percent of Indonesian people. Traditional Chinese belief is a blended faith, accommodating Buddhism, Confucianism, and Daoism. This faith is called *Sanjiao Heyi* (three teachings, harmonious as one) and is still held by many Chinese in Indonesia. However, there are also many Chinese in Indonesia who have converted to other religions, especially to Christianity. This happens mainly in economically more developed areas. This means that most Chinese in Indonesia are a minority both ethnically and religiously. Nonetheless, there is a widely held belief that the minority Chinese have control of 70 percent of Indonesian wealth. Despite the fact that there are many poor and homeless Chinese, it is often assumed that a Chinese person is likely to be a Christian and rich.

Now the majority of the Indonesian people are Moslems, and adult male Moslems (not women and children) attend weekly services on Friday at noon during an extended lunch time by walking from their work to mosques, which are available virtually everywhere. But Christians attend service on Sunday and they go to churches according to their own denominations, which may not be close to home. So, Christians—at least the affluent ones—drive their cars, which often creates traffic problems around uptown churches. But more than Sunday traffic jams, the general populace associates a Christian worship service with the giving of money as offering. This is not practiced by other state-sanctioned religions in Indonesia, so this gives the impression that in Christianity giving money to the church is a prominent way to show piety.

By contrast, Islam does not have offering as part of their weekly Friday service and mosques have no membership system as churches do. So when Moslems build mosques or need money for some major works, volunteers go to the streets with money containers to ask for people's charity. Of course, there are also Islamic institutions which employ more modern charity systems, such as using bank transfers and credit card payments, but still they would communicate their needs to the public and the public would respond by giving charity to these institutions, regardless of their institutional membership.

In fact, giving charity is a form of popular pietism in Indonesia. Giving money to beggars and street singers (who are easily found on overpasses, buses, and trains) is seen as a legitimate form of "social care" to the less fortunate; it is also understood as a way of giving offering to God. Many of these impoverished people are widows, invalids, and orphans living on the street without hope for education or a better future. Unfortunately, this kind of pietism is relatively unseen among Chinese Christian communities. Being more prudent with the disbursement of their money, Chinese Christians are likely to think, "They'd use the money for cigarettes anyway, so when we want to donate some money for a cause, we'd better do it through institutions which will provide, for example, scholarships." It is thus widely believed that "the rich Chinese Christian people" just don't care—they keep everything for themselves and when they do give, they give only to their own circles and causes, not to the people whom they actually meet.

Part of the problem is that the Chinese have been victimized for centuries by a series of policies imposed by Dutch colonial government and Indonesian "new order" government. This has led to serious ethnic violence, the last of which occurred in 1998 when many Chinese-owned properties were destroyed, and many Chinese men killed and women raped—an event still fresh in many people's minds. Indeed, Chinese communities were disenfranchised economically and forbidden to enter social, cultural, and political arenas. Although the condition has partially improved since the Refromasi of 1998, both the Chinese communities and those outside them continue to see the Chinese as "aliens who live among the native," despite the fact that the Chinese have been in Indonesia for many centuries prior to the segregation policies imposed upon them.

In this context, the idea presented in Deuteronomy 10:17–19—"God makes us aliens, lest we forget our calling"—offers inspiration for Chinese Christians in Indonesia today, who still feel that they are aliens in the land in which many of their families have lived for generations. This alienation has been deeply painful. However, God has blessed many people in this community so abundantly that they could be a blessing for others. They, indeed, can be a powerful tool of God's salvation, reaching out to people through big institutions and churches and, more importantly, through their personal encounters with people in need—orphans and widows and the invalids on streets, overpasses, buses, and trains. Then people outside the church will realize that the notions that "the rich Christians just care for themselves and not us" and "the church is only capable of taking care of her own" are just not true.

God, we might say, has made the Chinese Christian community aliens in our native land lest we forget who we are and where we're heading. Chinese Christians need to remember that the grand narrative of life is that we're all just pilgrims, aliens in foreign lands, heading toward our heavenly home. We can show the people around us that our God is a great God "who executes justice for the orphan and the widow, and shows love for the alien by giving food and clothing" (10:18).

Andrea K. Iskandar (M.Div., Cipanas Theological Seminary, Indonesia) is Chairman of the Board of Youth Ministry at Gereja Kristus Ketapang, Jakarta, Indonesia.

Deuteronomy as a Lesson on How to Treat the Oppressed

Song-Chong Lee (South Korea)

The book of Deuteronomy contains a profound message concerning outsiders, namely *strangers* and *sojourners*. Passages such as Deuteronomy 10:19 and 24:17–18 command the Jews to do justice to foreigners and the socially disadvantaged. Its implicit motivation, however, is more than the theme of social justice demanding equal and fair treatment or human rights. The life of strangers reminded the Jews of their suffering under the oppression of Pharaoh in Egypt and provided them with an existential reference point to convert and expand the orbit of their morality into the spiritual.

Prior to the conquest of the Promised Land (Canaan), foreigners were mainly the mixed multitude who had left Egypt with the Israelites; after their settlement in Canaan, they were the remnant of the conquered people. Moses commanded his people not to oppress and vex those strangers, and also to be proactive in protecting and helping them (24:19–22); indeed, the same civil and religious laws apply to everyone equally. The motivation and basis for such action was because the Israelites themselves were strangers in foreign lands. Even Abraham, Isaac, Jacob, and Lot were all aliens (Genesis 23, 26, 37). The Israelites were asked to refresh both their past memories and their spiritual identity and duty by looking at and caring for the life of the strangers.

The message and context of the Exodus was, and is, a very useful hermeneutical tool for the *minjung* theologians. The *minjung* theology was a Korean version of liberation theology in the 1970s and the 1980s; it made a tremendous contribution to helping the nation's democratization and protecting and improving the human rights of the people. The *minjung* theologians found the harsh reality of their oppressed people (*minjung*) and hope for their salvation in the story of the Israelite Exodus from Egypt. Korean people under a series of military regimes were identified with the Jews enslaved in Egypt and the strangers in the Jewish community. Although different in historical contexts, they were similar in that people's outcry was the primary source by which the *minjungeans* believed the saving work of God was initiated, revealed, and completed.

However, contemporary Korea seems to have already settled in her own Canaan. She has obtained democracy and achieved unprecedented economic success. The Korean churches have prospered more than ever. The majority of the Korean people in the twenty-first century would not identify themselves anymore with those oppressed in the 1980s. While Korean people are currently in the position of the liberated Jews, there is a newly emerging *minjung* with whom they can identify and from whom they can find a new spiritual and moral insight and injunction.

The new *minjung* in contemporary Korea are foreign workers and immigrants from developing countries and North Korean defectors. They are the sojourners who are in the most vulnerable position. Since the late 1990s, a great number of unskilled migrant workers and foreign brides have been brought in. As of October 2009, there were 680,000 registered foreign workers. The number of marriage immigrants reached 177,000 in 2010. Including undocumented workers, the total number of foreign residents has hit almost 2 percent of the entire population. The number of North Korean defectors is also increasing. Since the Korean War, about 6,000 North Koreans have defected to South Korea. Unfortunately, they are in the position of the Korean people of the 1980s. Like Korean *minjung*, they are the people who are suffering *han* (the feeling of unresolved bitterness). According to a recent Amnesty International report ("South Korea: Disposable Labour: Rights of Migrant Workers in South Korea," October 20, 2009.), foreign workers in South Korea experience abhorrent working conditions such as delayed payment of wages, violence by employers, and exploitation associated with immigration status. Female migrant workers are often subjected to "sexual harassment and violence at work." In one survey, 42 percent of a random sample of foreign workers said that they had been beaten on the job. Another survey shows that a large proportion of South Korean elementary school children do not want to make friends with kids from *Damunhwa Gajeong* (a multicultural family).

North Korean defectors, whose number has drastically increased since the 1990s, are also experiencing hardship in settling in South Korea because of pervasive stereotypes and discrimination. One survey shows that only about 2 percent of North Korean defectors' households in Seoul have one employed family member. The most common suffering that the new *minjung* is experiencing is reportedly discrimination. They are looked down upon in social value, marginalized in politics, and thought of as incapable of upward social mobility. Without a doubt, the traditional social value inordinately emphasizing ethnic and cultural homogeneity is one of the primary reasons.

Now, I would argue, is the time for Korean people to reflect upon who they are and what they went through in the 1970s and 1980s just as the Israelites did before their new era. Looking forward to their own Promised Land, Koreans have to refresh their memories. They must take good care of the strangers because they themselves were the *minjung*, who were politically oppressed and socially alienated. They must remember that we suffered in factories with inhumane working conditions and that we cried out in torture chambers of the KCIA (the Korean Central Intelligence Agency). They must break off their Confucian attachment to the value of *soonhyul* ("pure blood"), find a way to get along with people from different cultures, and care for them for a better society. For the Israelites, who were also obsessed with the value of homogeneity, Moses allowed the strangers to participate in sacrificial rituals, Sabbath, and even Passover, if circumcised. The fair treatment was important because it not only made his community strong and stable but it also was the primary character of God.

Although most Koreans have graduated from the class of *minjung* (the oppressed people), the category of the *minjung* itself has never disappeared. There are always around us strangers, sojourners, orphans, and widows who are not as capable of defending themselves. Foreign workers and brides from developing countries and North Korean defectors are the present self-image of the Korean past and a significant reference point from which we can continue to reflect on who we want to be. Strangers are not a burden but a self-portrait that makes us humble and continues to test and stretch further our spiritual and moral potential.

Song-Chong Lee is Assistant Professor of Religious Studies and Philosophy at University of Findlay, United States.

Deuteronomy as a Blueprint for Social Justice

Santiago Slabodsky (Argentina)

More than half a million Jews live in Latin America. They represent less than 5 percent of world Jewry. More than half of this population calls Argentina their home. Most Argentinean Jews immigrated to the region between the 1880s and 1940s. While the majority was escaping intense religious persecution in Christian Europe, a good number of Jews from the Muslim populated Middle East and North Africa joined them in looking for more open societies and new opportunities.

In Argentina, Jews encountered a predominantly Christian immigrant society. In more than 100 years after their arrival, Argentinean Jews were able to maintain their particularity while intensively collaborating with the construction of Argentina as a nation-state. This adaptation, however, encountered obstacles. Since the very beginning they faced discrimination. This discrimination was the result of a reproduction of European developments (that culminated in, for example, the Holocaust) and zealous nationalist schools of thought that attempted to construct a nation under the banner of religious uniformity (among them Catholic right-wing trends were predominant).

Among the Jewish groups confronting this discrimination, two of them are noteworthy. These movements, at different times, employed the Hebrew Bible in order to sustain their struggle. While there are a variety of passages in the Torah which call for justice (Exodus 23:1–9; Deuteronomy 10:17–19), in both cases Deuteronomy 16:20, "Just justice you shall pursue" was used to counter injustice toward the Jewish community and the Argentinean society at large. The first of these movements was the collective *Masorti* (my tradition), a group that fought against the genocide of a U.S.-endorsed military government between 1976 and 1983. The second was *Memoria Activa* (Collective Memory) that denounced the complicity of state powers for the collaboration and obstruction of investigations into an attack against the central Jewish institution in Argentina (AMIA) in 1994.

The first case was the collective *Masorti*. Between 1976 and 1983 a U.S.-backed military government took over power in Argentina. During this period there was a systematic plan to eradicate all opposition. At the end of this period, 30,000 young bodies and voices disappeared without leaving a trace. The *desaparecidos* (disappeared people) were kidnapped in the street or from their homes, schools, or places of employment, and, after being tortured for days, months, or years, were murdered. Most of their bodies have never been found. Of the total of disappeared people, 12 percent were Jews even though they represent less than 1 percent of the population. It is not a surprise that the perpetrators saw themselves as the fulfillers of both Catholic right-wing ideologies and local national-socialisms.

In those days a group of young, religious Jews, risking their own lives, reacted to the genocide. Under the banner of Deuteronomy 16:20, "Just Justice you shall pursue," they understood that they could not trust a corrupt and compromised judicial system to bring clarity concerning the disappearances. The movement started to join religious and secular resisters in underground organizations to confront the military dictatorship. The biblical call was a remembrance that only "just justice" could be contemplated, and to achieve it, sometimes, it was necessary to defy the unjust justice implemented by the status quo. The *Masorti* leader was American-born rabbi Marshall Meyer. He not only integrated the commission of notables who researched the genocide and incarcerated the perpetrators but also was honored by the democratic Argentinean government with the highest prize offered to a noncitizen, the "Order of General San Martin."

More than 10 years later, another group of Jews followed the example and took the same biblical verse as their banner. On July 18, 1994, the central community of Argentina (AMIA) was destroyed by a van-bomb attack, in which 86 were murdered, Jews and non-Jews, Argentineans and non-Argentineans alike. The institution, until then, was in charge of social welfare far beyond the Jewish community. While the Argentinean society was outraged and the government showed its solidarity with the victims, soon enough it was clear that the security forces and the government were implicated in the obstruction of justice. The official judicial channels, presumably independent, were politically compromised and a clear account of the events has not yet been achieved.

A group of activists, *Memoria Activa*, started to use the banner "Just justice you shall pursue" to confront the "unjust justice" they witnessed. This movement did not come about in a vacuum but retrieved the memory of the previous movement. In the 1970s several members of *Masorti* joined the mothers and grandmothers of the disappeared people in a weekly vigil, arguing for "just justice." For 10 years starting in 1994, the members of *Memoria Activa* gathered in a vigil the same day of the week at the same time of the attack to stand for justice. They did it in front of the palace of Justice and their closing prayer was Deuteronomy 16:20.

The cases of *Masorti* and *Memoria Activa* show the power of the Hebrew Bible to offer resources to people struggling to create a just society. Latin American Jews today still draw from the Hebrew Bible (as well as other sources of rabbinical literature) to engage in the struggle not only for the Jewish community but also for society at large.

Santiago Slabodsky is Assistant Professor in the program of Religion, Ethics, and Society at Claremont Lincoln University and in the School of Religion at Claremont Graduate University, United States.

QUESTIONS

1. What spiritual and religious traditions, if any, serve to honor ancestors and heritage in your community? How do they compare to those in Korean culture?
2. Read all of Deuteronomy 10 to see how verses 17–19, those cited by Iskandar, fit into the context. What observations do you make?
3. Analyze Lee's assertion that in Deuteronomy the fair treatment of non-Israelites was crucial because it not only strengthened the community, but it also was the primary character of God.
4. In your estimation, was the biblical text foundational in motivating the pursuit of justice or did the text serve only as a "resource" to support a desire for justice that was already present?

CHAPTER 11

JOSHUA 1–11

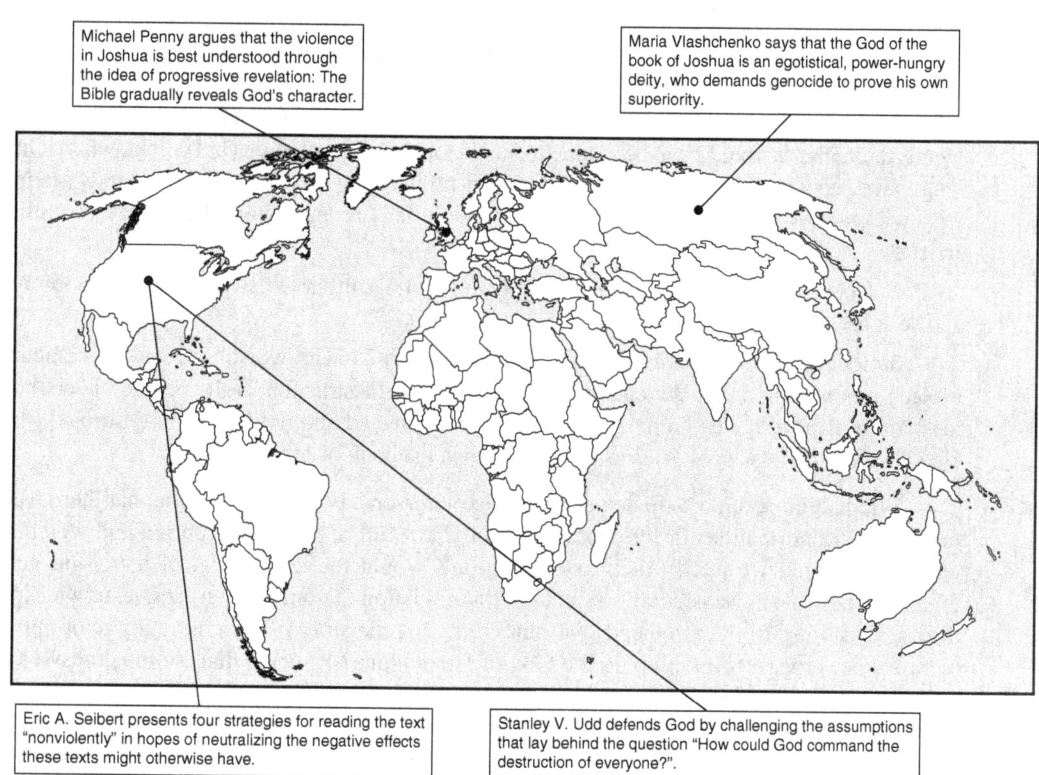

Michael Penny argues that the violence in Joshua is best understood through the idea of progressive revelation: The Bible gradually reveals God's character.
Maria Vlashchenko says that the God of the book of Joshua is an egotistical, power-hungry deity, who demands genocide to prove his own superiority.
Eric A. Seibert presents four strategies for reading the text "nonviolently" in hopes of neutralizing the negative effects these texts might otherwise have.
Stanley V. Udd defends God by challenging the assumptions that lay behind the question "How could God command the destruction of everyone?".

READINGS

Understanding Joshua through Progressive Revelation
Michael Penny

Four Strategies for Reading Joshua Nonviolently
Eric A. Seibert

A Defense of God
Stanley V. Udd

God as an Egotistical Deity
Maria Vlashchenko

Understanding Joshua through Progressive Revelation

Michael Penny (United Kingdom)

The book of Joshua is exciting reading and would make a spectacular big-screen, surround-sound movie, especially the destruction of Jericho with its collapsing walls. However, for many twenty-first-century Christians it presents a moral dilemma. Would God sanction the slaughter of so many people? Or did Joshua misunderstand? Should he have simply driven the people out of the land?

Here are some of the explanations people have put forward to justify Joshua's action.

1. There were actual giants in the land. When Moses sent spies, one of whom was Joshua, into the land of Canaan to see its agriculture and people, they returned and reported that Nephilim (giants) were in the land (Numbers 13:33). Depending on our understanding of Hebrew measurements, these giants would have been nine to ten feet tall, and excavations at Bashan, where Og was king, have supported this. There is also an earlier reference to Nephilim and there they are linked with wickedness, evil, and violence (Genesis 6). So it is probable that there were Nephilim in Jericho.

2. There was extreme sexual immorality in Jericho, similar to that in Sodom and Gomorrah, and so it had to be eradicated.

3. Jericho was not far from Ammon, the center of Molech worship. Some have suggested Molech was worshipped in Jericho as well, and hence its destruction. If the people of Jericho had repented of their religious failures, would God have relented and not had them destroyed (just as God does in other instances, such as the Ninevites in the book of Jonah)?

I find all three of these to be inadequate explanations. Even if we assume that there were in fact genetic abnormalities in Jericho, that the city was full of sexual corruption and worshipped other gods, could we justify their extermination? Would the destruction of abnormal genetic mutations be ethical? Was complete and utter annihilation the only way to eradicate widespread diseases resulting from extreme sexual immorality? Is the story of Jericho really about punishment for not properly worshipping the God of Israel alone? It seems that we must answer "no" to each of these questions.

There is a much better fourth option: progressive revelation. As we progress through the Bible, more is revealed about God and His character, and we see changes in what He requires from His people. The Law of Moses, given for the people of Israel in Exodus, was followed by them throughout the Old Testament, and into much of the New, but we read of the ordinances being abolished in Ephesians 2:14–16 and Colossians 2:14–17.

At one time it was right for a person to bring a lamb to be sacrificed when that person had sinned. However, when the Lamb of God who took away the sin of the world had come, died, and risen from the dead, such sacrifices were no longer part of God's will for His people. Likewise, in Joshua, we see the pronouncement to drive out the aliens from the land. However, grace and truth came through Jesus Christ (John 1:17). Few, in the Old Testament saw God "face to face," and the majority understood Him as "through a glass darkly." However, Christ is the incarnation of God—He is the express image of God (Hebrews 1:2) being the fullest revelation we have of God. As such we should pay far more attention to what He taught concerning the treatment of aliens and enemies.

He probably had in mind the occupying forces of Rome, the great national enemy of Israel, when He gave the command to "love your enemies, do good to those who hate you, bless [speak well of] those who curse you, pray for those who mistreat you" (Luke 6:27–28).

This was picked up and passed on by the Apostles: "If your enemy is hungry, feed him; if he is thirsty, give him something to drink" (Romans 12:20). However, Paul seems to have had *personal* enemies in mind, rather than *national* ones. If we are to treat our personal enemies in this way, should it affect the way we look upon our national ones? And how should the government of our country treat other nations which are poorer (economically) and weaker (militarily)?

Because Joshua's battles are in the Bible does not mean that it was God's intention that mankind should live in such a state throughout all ages. There is always the danger that we take certain episodes from the Bible and, instead of leaving them in their historical context, treat them as *truth for today*. In fact we should give greater weight to the later parts of God's revelation in the Bible than to the earlier ones. One final question remains: Did Joshua and the Israelites misunderstand God when they killed everyone in God's name? Or, did God in fact, at that particular historical moment, want Israel to slaughter their enemies, even if it is not what God wants His people to do today?

Michael Penny, originally from Wales, has pastored a church in Wisconsin for nine years and authored several major theological books; he edits Search *magazine for the Open Bible Trust in Great Britain (www.obt.org.uk).*

FOUR STRATEGIES FOR READING JOSHUA NONVIOLENTLY

Eric A. Seibert (United States)

The conquest of Canaan depicted in Joshua 6–11 is one of the most morally troubling passages in the entire Old Testament. The Israelites mercilessly massacre Canaanite men, women, and children, and they ostensibly do so in obedience to the will of God. Such indiscriminate killing not only raises serious ethical and moral questions but also casts a long shadow upon God's character. What kind of deity would issue such a morally reprehensible, genocidal decree? Of particular concern is the way this passage has been misused over the years by those wishing to acquire someone else's land. These individuals have co-opted this narrative to legitimate terrible acts of violence against indigenous people whose land they desire. The deceitful and murderous treatment of Native Americans by European settlers is but one of many examples of the way this story has been misappropriated and misapplied. Whenever sacred texts are used to encourage acts of violence, oppression, and killing, something has surely gone terribly wrong. So what can be done to avoid such destructive readings? How can the conquest narrative be read in ways that criticize rather than valorize the killing of "Canaanites," whoever they may be?

There are several strategies that can help us read this story *non*violently, in ways that do not legitimate future acts of violence. These reading strategies effectively neutralize the text's potentially lethal afterlife. One of the most rudimentary ways of reading this story nonviolently involves putting a human face on war. The battles described in the conquest narrative say very little about the human suffering that results from the experience of warfare. By and large, the participants remain nameless and faceless. The conquest narrative almost never reports the number of casualties, and very little attention is given to the actual battles themselves. For example, only two of the 27 verses devoted to the battle of Jericho actually describe the battle itself (6:20–21). Setting aside the question of whether this story actually happened for the moment, consider what is not included in these two verses. No mention is made of the raw terror the inhabitants of Jericho presumably felt the moment the walls came crashing down and the Israelites went charging in. Nor do these verses contain descriptions of pierced flesh, severed limbs, or decapitated heads. Also lacking are any tales of terrified toddlers clinging to parents or accounts of helpless babies being brutalized. But all these horrors—and many more—could be inferred from this brief battle report. Yet because these terrible deeds are never explicitly mentioned, many readers happily celebrate the Israelites' victory without ever contemplating the cruel realities of war.

Putting a human face on war means slowing down long enough to consider its devastating effects upon those who are directly—and indirectly—involved. It means recognizing that war does terrible things to individuals on both sides of the conflict; both victims *and* "victors" inevitably suffer harm. When the enormous human toll of warfare is taken into consideration, it is much more difficult to regard the violence of the conquest narrative as virtuous, much less exemplary.

A second strategy for reading this narrative nonviolently involves reading it from the perspective of the Canaanites. Most who read this story identify with the Israelites. But what happens when the story is read the other way around? What does the conquest narrative look like when read through the eyes of a Canaanite? From a Canaanite's point of view, Israel's behavior appears villainous rather than virtuous. From their perspective, the Israelites were hostile invaders intent on stealing their land. They were merciless aggressors determined to kill everyone in their path. Not even women or children were spared! Such behavior hardly seems praiseworthy. Reading this narrative with the victims rather than the victors causes us to see the story in a whole new light. We may find ourselves weeping with the Canaanites rather than celebrating with the Israelites. At the very least, reading the conquest narrative this way should keep us from simplistically appealing to such texts to justify acts of war and genocide in the world today.

A third strategy involves questioning the Old Testament's rationale for the conquest: (1) to punish Canaanite wickedness, and (2) to preserve Israel's religious purity and fidelity, since it is assumed that leaving Canaanites in the land would certainly cause Israel to go astray (see Deuteronomy 7:1–4; 9:4–5; 20:16–18). But are these compelling reasons for engaging in acts of genocide? Do they justify the slaughter of every Canaanite man, woman, and child? I think not. While the Canaanites may have been "wicked" in certain ways, it seems they were no more wicked than other people. Why would God punish Canaanite wickedness by ordering their annihilation while sparing other people who were at least as bad if not worse? Such a decree raises disturbing questions about divine justice.

The explanation that Canaanites needed to be killed in order to preserve Israel's religious purity is also quite problematic. It is hard to see how killing others can be spiritually beneficial. Moreover, while we might agree on the importance of protecting people from bad influences, we would not condone the actions of individuals who went around killing people because they thought their beliefs and practices might negatively influence others. Yet this is essentially how the Old Testament justifies Canaanite genocide. Killing Canaanites is justified as a means of preventing their religious beliefs and practices from negatively affecting Israel's. Such reasoning here, in which the ends supposedly justify the means, is morally bankrupt.

Ultimately, the Old Testament's rationale for Canaanite genocide is unsatisfying because it fails to address the most pressing and obvious problem, namely, the immorality of genocide itself. Genocide, an act which involves killing everyone—even the weakest, youngest, and most vulnerable—is never good, never moral, and never justifiable.

A final strategy for reading the conquest narrative nonviolently involves recognizing that its portrayal of God as warrior is a culturally conditioned construct, one that does not accurately reflect God's true character. In the ancient world, warfare was fraught with theological significance. Like others in antiquity, the Israelites believed that God commissioned wars and fought in them. They also shared the commonly held view that God was responsible for victory or defeat in battle. Given this context, it would seem that Israel's portrayal of God as a divine warrior says more about ancient Israel's worldview, and the cultural milieu out of which these texts arose, than it does about the true character of God. Thus, despite the way God is portrayed in the conquest narrative and related passages in Deuteronomy, there is no compelling reason to believe that God ever willed, commanded, or participated in acts of genocide.

The archaeological evidence also seems to support this conclusion. Many scholars do not believe the book of Joshua contains a reliable account of how the Israelites came into possession of the land of Canaan. This is due, in part, to evidence on the ground which suggests otherwise. Excavations at Jericho and Ai, for example, seem to indicate that these first two cities the Israelites reportedly conquered were actually uninhabited at the time. If that is the case, then it stands to reason that God did not hand over Jericho's "king and soldiers" (6:2) or Ai's king and people (8:1) as the text claims. Realizing that God never issued genocidal directives or willed the destruction of Canaanites significantly diminishes the conquest narrative's ability to do harm in the modern world.

By utilizing the reading strategies discussed here, it is possible to read the conquest narrative nonviolently. These same reading strategies can easily and profitably be applied to other problematic Old Testament texts as well. Reading nonviolently directly challenges the Old Testament's insistence that violence is sometimes necessary and that killing another person may constitute an act of obedience to God. Rather than appealing to such texts to justify acts of violence and war, ethically responsible readers will read them in ways that criticize and problematize the violence they contain, thereby neutralizing the negative effects these texts might otherwise have.

Eric A. Seibert is Associate Professor of Old Testament at Messiah College in Grantham, Pennsylvania, United States; he is the author of Disturbing Divine Behavior: Troubling Old Testament Images of God *and* The Violence of Scripture: Overcoming the Old Testament's Troubling Legacy *(from which this piece is adapted with special permission of Augsburg Fortress).*

A Defense of God

Stanley V. Udd (United States)

If God is purported to be good and loving, how can this be aligned with the clear commands in the Old Testament when God insisted on the slaughter of peoples including innocent children, as we see in the book of Joshua and elsewhere? There would seem to be an inconsistency here. How can a good and loving God command the destruction of infants and babies? This is understandably an oft-asked question by readers of the book of Joshua. But there are problems with the question itself, namely, there are a number of erroneous assumptions that lay behind the question.

First of all, the question assumes that the Canaanites are an innocent people and that God is simply pushing them out or killing them to make room for His people. You will recall that the ancestor of the Canaanites—Canaan—is cursed by Noah for the sexual sin that he perpetrated against his grandfather (Genesis 9:20–27). So the Canaanites are a cursed people. Their sin is an offence to God, but He is patient with them granting them time to repent. In the days of Abraham God indicates that the iniquity of the Amorites (Canaanites) is not yet complete (Genesis 15:16). So there was to be another four generations before God would bring judgment. I'm sure that God was waiting those many years hoping that some would repent of their wickedness (2 Peter 3:9). But eventually, God in His justice needed to remove these wicked people. Isn't it illustrative that at the destruction of the city of Jericho, God supernaturally destroyed the defenses to the city while at the same time preserved that portion of the city wall where the scarlet cord was hung from the window? God was simultaneously punishing the wicked and rescuing those who trusted in Him. He does not kill indiscriminately. Were not righteous Lot and two of his daughters rescued from the fiery destruction of the five cities of the plain? These people in Canaan were getting their just due—God was not killing for the thrill of the kill.

Second, the question assumes that the destruction of children condemns them to some dark destiny. The Bible, on the other hand, makes it very clear that with children there is a time before which the child knows enough to refuse the evil and choose the good (Isaiah 7:15 and 16). Children who die before they reach the age of accountability fall into the hands of a compassionate God (Jonah 4:10–11). To leave those children to grow up in such a wicked and vile setting would surely be less compassionate and virtually guarantee their condemnation. So, even the slaughter of innocent children is not the greatest possible evil. Did not Jesus say, "Let the little children come to me and do not hinder them, for to such belongs the kingdom of heaven" (Matthew 19:14)? Surely children who are truly innocent become inhabitants of heaven.

A third assumption is that the concept of "devoted to destruction" is simply the wonton murder of innocent people. The Hebrew word contains the idea that this action is a sacrifice to God—a symbolic act like a whole burnt offering. The Israelites were the weapon that God was using to appropriately discipline the Canaanites. Their death was the necessary atonement to cleanse the land for Israel. This act was a righteous act. Justice must be carried out. Indeed, Psalm 106:34–39 describes the consequences for Israel not carrying out fully God's command to destroy the Canaanites.

One final assumption is that God has no moral basis for making such bold commands. Such an assumption ignores the fact that all human beings owe their existence to God and God alone. "In Him we live and move and have our being" (Acts 17:28). He is their creator and as a result has a moral basis for expecting a certain level of morality. The Bible is very clear that no one is without excuse (Romans 1:19). On that basis alone God has the moral authority to judge people.

The righteousness of God is a verity. It is His most significant and most compelling attribute. It undergirds all that He does. It should not be questioned—even if we cannot adequately explain the ramifications or the logic of His actions. God is not capricious. He is not arbitrary. He is not cruel. But He is unquestionably just.

Stanley V. Udd (Th.D.) is retired Professor of Biblical Languages at Grace University, Omaha, Nebraska, United States.

God as an Egotistical Deity

Maria Vlashchenko (Russia)

I've seen various Study Bibles make comments such as, "Joshua's lessons are overwhelmingly positive ones," "Here the nation of Israel meets with unprecedented success," or "The book gives a fresh breeze of hope." But to me this is a terribly one-sided view of things. Certainly the stories told in Joshua 1–12 are about death and God's unfair treatment of the native inhabitants of Canaan. As someone outside the Jewish-Christian tradition, I do not identify with the conquering Israelites. The people of Israel, following God's direct command, storm through Canaan pillaging, raping, murdering, and burning the people and towns as they carry out a massive genocide. How can there be anything "positive" or "hopeful" about such brutal destruction? And make no mistake about it. This is genocide pure and simple. The Israelites deliberately and systematically wipe out the "the Canaanites, Hittites, Hivites, Perizzites, Girgashites, Amorites, and Jebusites" simply because they were not Israelites. These people represented different national or ethnic groups; they worshipped different Gods and had different religious rituals and practices. In the name of the Lord their God, the Israelites kill them all—men, women, and children. It reminds me of the quote in the short story "Seven Feet" by Christopher Fowler: "What's the point of organized religion if you can't exclude unbelievers?"

In the book of Joshua—indeed in the Old Testament as a whole—God is the God of the Israelites only. He is a nationalistic deity who fights against other peoples and other deities (cf. the story of the Exodus). He gives land, power, wealth, livestock, prosperity, and success to only one group of people. Those who are not Israelites are treated as not human. Thus they can be exterminated and their land taken by God's chosen people. While this is remarkable enough, what is even more amazing is that some religious people in the Jewish-Christian tradition defend God's genocidal action. How is this possible in the world in which we live? How is this possible when religious people claim that God is the God of everybody?

It is important to note that the native inhabitants of Canaan do not start the battles in the book of Joshua. All they wanted to do was to defend their land, their houses, their property, and their loved ones. The Israelites are the aggressors. They not only are the ones who violently possess land that is not theirs, but they also purposefully and willfully kill all the people. They do not try to negotiate with them or convert them. They just destroy them—all of them, people and animals alike, as if they were the same thing. God is very clear that the Israelites are not to leave alive anything that breathes (e.g., 11:14–15). Everything and everyone is to be "devoted to destruction for the Lord." How can this in any way be justified or defended? Think of all the blood, gore, and carnage. Think of all the infants slaughtered by the Israelites.

Positive lessons? Unprecedented success? Fresh breeze of hope? I don't think so.

It is also important to observe God's role in the story. Not only does he command the genocide, but he himself takes an active role in the military campaign. The text reports that God "hurled large hailstones down on them from the sky, and more of them died from the hailstones than were killed by the swords of Israelites" (10:11). God, then, is not only the motive behind the destruction of the Canaanites but also the principle and primary warrior for the Israelite cause. But even the Israelites themselves are in danger if they don't follow God's commands. When Achan took some goods which were meant to be sacrificed to God, he was given a death sentence. Not only was Achan to die, but his whole family and all his animals were stoned and burned to death as well (7:24–25). Once again, innocent people were terminated to satisfy God's wishes. If you are the Canaanites, you are in mortal danger of God's wrath. If you are the

Israelites, God might be on your side, but the moment you do not follow his exact commands, God will immediately turn on you and your whole nation. (This scenario reminds me of the book of Exodus, where God destroys the Egyptians in order to save the Israelites, and then a few chapters later is ready to destroy the Israelites for their idolatry, which only Moses' intervention prevents.)

In one sense, the book of Joshua, at least ostensibly, is about the fulfillment of the promise to Abraham: God gives the people of Israel the land on which Abraham's descendents will live. But in another very real sense it seems to be much more than that. The text itself says so. Speaking of Israel's enemies, we read: "For it was the Lord himself who hardened their hearts to wage war against Israel, so that he might destroy them totally, exterminating them without mercy" (11:20). In reality, then, the bloody stories in Joshua are not about God trying to complete a promise or about God trying to take care of and provide for his own people. No. God makes this crusade for himself to satisfy his ambitions, to prove that he is the only God, that his decisions cannot be questioned. He manipulates the hearts and minds of the Canaanites precisely so that he can exterminate them without any compassion. If God wanted to give the land to the Israelites, why not devise a more peaceful plan? Why not soften the hearts of the Canaanites so that no blood would be spilled? Instead, the book of Joshua presents us with an egotistical, power-hungry God, who demands genocide to prove his own superiority.

Maria Vlashchenko is from Khabarovsk, Russia; she attended the Academy of Economics and Law in Khabarovsk before moving to the United States to study.

QUESTIONS

1. What are the potential benefits and problems of using progressive revelation to account for the violence in the conquest narrative? What might Penny say to the idea that if revelation is progressive, then it must surely be continuing today?
2. In what sense is Seibert's reading "nonviolent"? What other terms might be used to describe his approach?
3. Are the biblical references Udd uses supportive of his interpretation? What other interpretations are possible for these passages?
4. Do you personally identify with the Israelites or the Canaanites? What people or groups might naturally identify with the Canaanites?

CHAPTER 12

1 SAMUEL 16–2 SAMUEL 21

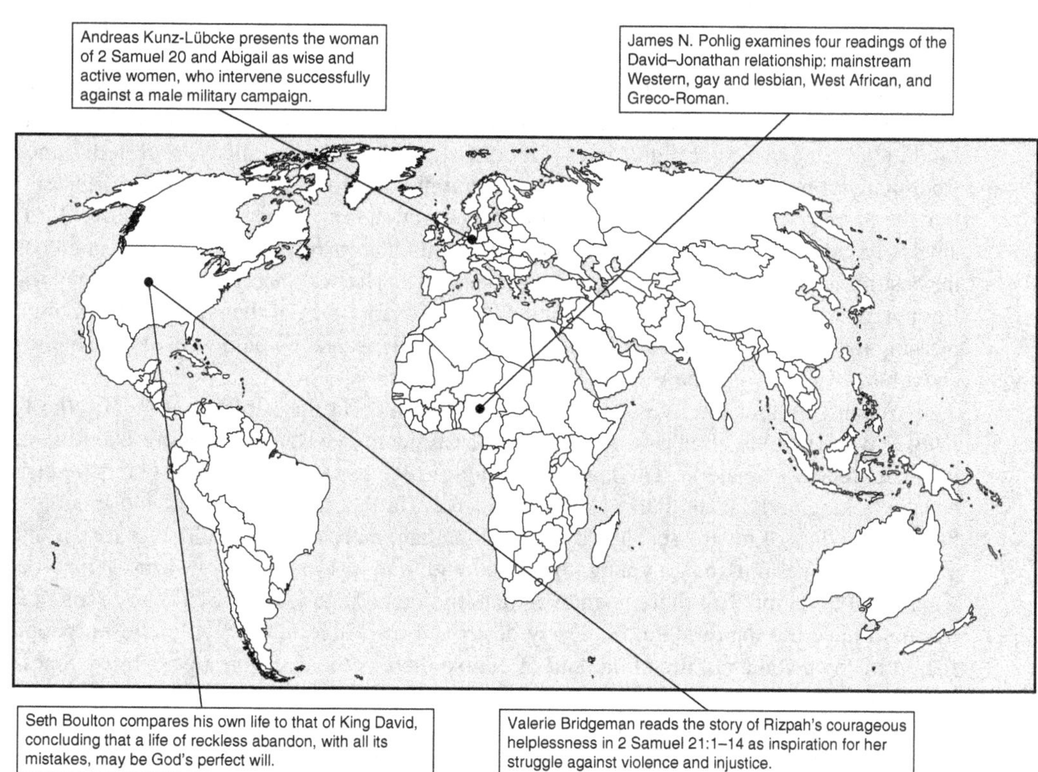
Andreas Kunz-Lübcke presents the woman of 2 Samuel 20 and Abigail as wise and active women, who intervene successfully against a male military campaign.
James N. Pohlig examines four readings of the David–Jonathan relationship: mainstream Western, gay and lesbian, West African, and Greco-Roman.
Seth Boulton compares his own life to that of King David, concluding that a life of reckless abandon, with all its mistakes, may be God's perfect will.
Valerie Bridgeman reads the story of Rizpah's courageous helplessness in 2 Samuel 21:1–14 as inspiration for her struggle against violence and injustice.

READINGS

The David Stories as Sanctioning a Life of Reckless Abandon
Seth Boulton

Four Interpretations of the David–Jonathan Relationship
James N. Pohlig

The Woman of 2 Samuel 20 and Abigail as Peacemakers
Andreas Kunz-Lübcke

The Inspiration of Rizpah's Courageous Helplessness
Valerie Bridgeman

The David Stories as Sanctioning a Life of Reckless Abandon

Seth Boulton (United States)

The truth of the matter is that even though my band never played a stadium tour or had our videos on MTV we were a huge commercial success. I lived the good life: I played the music I wanted to play every night; I had a band that consisted entirely of beautiful women who did whatever I told them to do; I partied when I wanted to party; I slept with the women that I wanted to sleep with; and when I felt like quitting, I just quit. Who wouldn't want to be that guy? I really, truly lived life with reckless abandon and if I had it to do over again, I would do it twice as hard and twice as fast.

Now I know that is not the testimony that most Christians are accustomed to hearing. I've tried and I just can't be sorry about any of it. My regrets are for the things I didn't do, things I didn't say, experiences I didn't have. Of course, this attitude has always met with opposition from many of my fellow believers, whose general philosophy is that the more you abstain from fun, the more godly you must be. I admit that moderation is an important part of life. But I have always found myself questioning whether these particular proverbial "fruits" that one bears are the best measure of one's commitment to God and the success of one's spiritual journey. In fact, I'm not even so sure that being a "Christian" is necessarily part of the equation for living a life pleasing to God. (One of my best friends is a lesbian atheist and I wouldn't change a single thing about her.) And I've got the Bible to "prove" it.

When I look at the lives of most of the great men in the Bible, specifically the life of King David, the man after God's own heart, I can identify. The life of King David is one of exquisite reckless abandon. The man sang songs, killed lions and bears and giants, led armies, became a king and danced half naked in the street (in that order), had lots and lots of wives, had lots and lots of mistresses, loved a man, Jonathan, more than he could ever love a woman, and, when he was old, took a young girl to bed with him just to keep him warm. Who wouldn't want to be that guy? But there is an even darker side to David: He sent a man to his death so he could have the man's wife, he nearly destroyed the kingdom of God's chosen people, he fought his own son and killed him, and of course there is the disturbing possibility that David raped a lot of women.

One could argue that it is recorded in Scripture that David repented for at least a few of these things. But when I look at the life of David, I don't see a man with regrets. If he truly regretted what he had done, he wouldn't have kept living the way he did right up to the end. Perhaps I am reading between the lines (but isn't that where the truth usually lies) or maybe I am focused too much on the big picture. Either way, on my reading, David did what he wanted and lived an amazing, beautiful life that really didn't necessitate an abnormal number of apologies. And if this is my example to follow, I think I've done pretty well and my Father in heaven is well pleased with me and is pleased that I have recognized the success in my accomplishments and all the other crazy things that I've done along the way and will do in the future. Indeed, I'm a lot like King David in all his imperfections. But I think we need to understand that most of what we call his imperfections was really just David living a successful life of struggle, love, frustration, ecstasy, and a vision for his own future.

Society may label our actions as acceptable or unacceptable, but the true measure of the man—whether he is hiding in a cave or sitting on a throne—is his own ability to take control of his life and live it the way he feels is right. I hope the reader doesn't construe as arrogant my comparison of myself to a great hero of the Bible. On the contrary I do not consider myself above any of the rules that govern us all. I am in fact humbled by the discovery that I bear some resemblance to the king. When the play *Death of a Salesman* was released, it was criticized by others for not being a true tragedy because its main character, Willie Lowman, was not royalty or of some aristocratic position (note his last name). If he was nothing more than a lowly salesman, how could his life have great tragedy? But, to my mind, because he was an American pursuing his dream he was in fact royalty. Any man in this country is the king of his castle and therefore has the potential for tragedy or great triumph. With this in mind, a comparison of every man and woman to King David is not only appropriate but needful in that we should understand our true potential for greatness and success. You are living the legend of you in all its archetypal grandeur. You are a great king and you may be criticized for decisions which go against the grain. But in the end, going against the grain with all of its mistakes and fumbles may be God's perfect will for all of us.

Seth Boulton was a successful full-time musician for many years; he is a born-again Christian who currently resides with his girlfriend and daughter in the United States.

Four Interpretations of the David–Jonathan Relationship

James N. Pohlig (West Africa)

Through the centuries, readers have been deeply touched by the account of David and Jonathan's friendship. It speaks of loyalty and intimacy of spirit, of Jonathan's heartbreak over his father Saul's treatment of David, and of David's heartbreak over Jonathan's tragic death in battle—themes that every age has found poignant.

However, cultures and subcultures interpret the nature of that friendship in different ways. Let us briefly look at four different interpretations, separated from each other by time and culture. First, mainstream Western culture has held up David and Jonathan as exemplars of same-gender faithfulness that has no sexual overtones. Second, the contemporary gay and lesbian movement tends to read the account as a not-so-veiled depiction of homoerotic love. Third, West Africans have their own view, which is superficially similar to the mainstream Western view but has a different cultural context. Finally, going back in time, we have a very good idea of how first-century A.D. Greco-Roman culture would have viewed that friendship.

Let us begin with mainstream Western culture. This view follows in the tradition of the ancient Greek myth of Damon and Pythias, in which each friend offers his life to the tyrant of Syracuse for the other. We take it that this model of friendship projects values that include the following: You hold each other's needs and well-being in higher priority than your own; you have similar likes and dislikes; you have similar outlooks on life; you enjoy each other's presence; you are happy to share one's own possessions with each other; and you find it safe and rewarding to share your deepest thoughts with each other. Such friendships often originate out of undergoing some extended experience or hardship together, such as schooling, military service, or common employment. In this model, David and Jonathan were strongly drawn to each other, but with no sexual overtones.

How their relative social statuses meshed is something of a riddle. David is presented as acutely aware before the king, Jonathan's father, of his humble background. If Jonathan bent over backward to befriend him, the reader is led to believe that Jonathan made nothing of it whatsoever. This point is important, because some current research on friendship emphasizes that social constraints tend to be as determinative of such relationships as personal proclivities. It is important to note that mainstream *American* culture, while affirming the nonsexual nature of this kind of friendship, at the same time does not accord it first place in the domain of the sharing of deepest thoughts and feelings. Americans assign this domain instead to marriage.

We turn now to the contemporary gay and lesbian movement, limiting our attention to the part of it that can be regarded as an outgrowth of contemporary Western culture. Perhaps the most notable early claim that David and Jonathan were homoerotic lovers came from Oscar Wilde at his trial in 1895 for sodomy, when he said in court: "The love that dare not speak its name in this century is such a great affection of an elder for a younger man as there was between David and Jonathan." Following today in Wilde's footsteps, it seems almost an article of faith among Scripture-oriented gays and lesbians to adduce in 1 and 2 Samuel indications that David and Jonathan were lovers. In this view, Jonathan concluded some kind of friendship pact with David because "Jonathan loved David as his own soul" (1 Sam. 18:3); in divesting himself of his robe and tunic in order to give them to David (1 Sam. 18:4), Jonathan is taken as offering sexual relations. David's piercing lament after his friend's death (2 Sam. 1:19–27) is often cited as well, especially verse 26: "I am distressed for you, my brother Jonathan; very pleasant have you been to me; your love to me was extraordinary, surpassing the love of women." This language is seen not only as intense but also as connoting sexual interest.

In West Africa, this friendship, however, would be instantly identified as that of two best friends. In Mbe of southeastern Nigeria, for example, the term *wuchi* is not simply "friend"; it specifically denotes the status of two men or two women who are bonded together for a long time, potentially all their lives. Developing a close affinity, each shares with the other deepest thoughts, fears, and desires to a degree that goes far, far beyond what is shared with a spouse. His wife is emphatically *not* a man's closest confidant; that role is taken by one's *wuchi*.

In the same vein, it is very common for West African cultures to completely prohibit public touching between any man and a woman, even if married. But it is very common for two men or two women to walk hand in hand. A Westerner, living in West Africa, must become accustomed to being led or accompanied by the hand of an acquaintance of the same gender. But this kind of physical touch expresses the male—or female—friendship that Africans would recognize in David and Jonathan. The statement, "Very pleasant have you been to me; your love to me was extraordinary, surpassing the love of women," would be seen as quite unremarkable among the Mbe people, for this would be expected of a man and his *wuchi*.

Finally, let us consider how the first-century A.D. Greco-Roman culture probably regarded the David and Jonathan account. Sexual activity in Greco-Roman culture did not essentially depend on personal relationships. It was instead an expression of social hierarchy. Men had relations with their wives, slaves, and prostitutes. Homosexual behavior was common, but it was never between male peers, but rather between men and boys. The Greek word *aretē*, although usually glossed as "virtue" or "excellence," was the essential characteristic of men and had an obligatory sexual component. A real man penetrated others, but was himself never penetrated. It was probably for this reason that male peers never had sexual relations; to do so would entail a loss of honor for one, if not for both. Since David and Jonathan appear to regard themselves as peers, Greco-Romans would probably not have considered them to be sexually involved. Furthermore, for Greco-Romans, homosexual relationships were, so far as we can tell, never considered much more than casual. Even man–boy relationships would have probably lasted only a few years. Long-term committed gay relationships were unknown. Thus, the biblical account suggesting a lengthy friendship between David and Jonathan would not have been considered sexual.

It is not known whether the Greco-Romans had any ritualistic oath or other device to establish a "covenant" of friendship such as Jonathan is depicted as setting up with David. But we do know that they had ideals of friendship, such as was expressed by the myth of Damon and Pythias. Besides this story, many relevant quotations have descended to us from the Greeks: "Be slow to fall into friendship; but when thou art in, continue firm and constant" (Socrates). "One loyal friend is worth ten thousand relatives" (Euripides). "What is a friend? A single soul in two bodies" (Aristotle). "Without friends no one would choose to live, though he had all other goods" (Aristotle). We therefore conclude that the Greco-Romans would have viewed David and Jonathan as an example of friendship worthy of that of Damon and Pythias.

We have considered four different cultural readings of David and Jonathan's friendship. Each one can be compelling to its respective cultural "insiders." The humanity that we share, however, with our transcultural "memory" of these two men makes us say to them, "Perhaps what you experienced was not exactly like what any of us today can experience, but we are sure that for you it was a powerful thing."

James N. Pohlig (D.Litt., Biblical Languages, University of Stellenbosch) has worked to analyze various West African languages, to bring literacy to them, to translate the Bible, and to author resources for Old Testament translators in general.

The Woman of 2 Samuel 20 and Abigail as Peacemakers

Andreas Kunz-Lübcke (Germany)

There are currently nine major conflicts taking place around the globe, each with more than 1,000 fatalities in the last year. Today, as I sat down to write this, the war in Libya broke out. In more than half of the conflicts (Afghanistan, Somalia, Iraq, Northwest Pakistan), military forces from Western democracies are or were involved. The reasons for the military engagement of the Western democracies differ and are sometime nebulous: The fight against terrorism, the overthrow of an illegitimate ruler, the establishment of democratic structures, the prevention of genocides, and others. All these conflicts have one thing in common: They are difficult to bring to an end. Here I propose that the narrators of two biblical stories in Samuel point to a successful strategy to end a conflict or to avoid it completely: send a diplomatic, peace-seeking woman into a group of violent men.

The story in 2 Samuel 20 is riveting. Under brutal general Joab, the siege becomes more heated. The ramp is headed up, the gigantic ram is assembled. Under the severe shocks of the siege-weapons a first outer wall begins to collapse. If the walls of the city are broken, every hope is lost. What will happen next is inevitable: torture and execution of leaders and defenders of the city and the deportation of the women and children. But wait. In the exact moment of the collapse of the first wall, a single woman appears on the top of a wall: "I am one of the peaceful and faithful in Israel, but you seek to destroy a city and mother in Israel! Why do you swallow the inheritance of YHWH?" (20:19). Only a few words are spoken—but they are effective words. The general stops the siege and explains the reason for his campaign. There is an insurgent behind the city walls: "Deliver this man and I will withdraw from the city!" (20:21). The wise woman negotiates "in her wisdom" with the people of the city. The insurgent is soon decapitated, his head flies over the city wall and the war is over.

2 Samuel 20 narrates an amazing story. During a siege of a city a wise woman appears on the wall and her argument is simple: Negotiations must be conducted *before* you are allowed to siege a city (cf. Deuteronomy 20: 10–12). But the woman on the wall, full of wisdom and politically eloquent, is not the only presentation of a woman within the story. After David hears of the revolt of Sheba, he takes his twenty "concubines" who were raped in public during the Absalom revolt, and detains them in a guarded house (20:3). Here they stay as "living widows." *And he never goes into them.* Twenty women enclosed by walls as living widows without the chance of motherhood on the one hand, and one woman on the wall of a besieged city (calling herself a city and mother in Israel) on the other. The story presents a very ambivalent picture of women's fate: to be a victim of male violence and power or to become a wise speaker and negotiator. To remain behind the walls of a prison-like house or to stand on the wall and rescue an entire city. The story contains extreme variations of women's fate.

The wise woman on top of the city wall who intervenes against an eruption of male-initiated violence is reminiscent of another wise woman—Abigail, who appears at the beginning of the David stories in 1 Samuel 25. David is full of wrath against Nabal, who refused to hand over a considerable quantity food. The reader is confused: Is David's demand against Nabal justified? Or does he act in a Mafia-like manner? The only thing that is clear is that he pursues a cruel strategy. "May God punish me, and even more if I let survive everybody who belongs to him *who pisses against the wall* until morning" (25: 22). These are not the words of a wise statesman; rather they are the words of a man who loses control over himself. Two men act like real men: The rich farmer refused to deliver a very small quantity of his yields. The other cannot accept the refusal. With the aid of 400 heavily armed men David leaves his camp. Four hundred armed men—the reader expects a great number of victims.

However, there is a countermovement in the story. Nabal, whose name means "fool," stands in stark contrast to Abigail, who is characterized as intelligent and attractive (25:3). When the wise beauty Abigail hears about the Fool's rejection of David's demand, she reacts instantly, approaching the disgruntled David with many gifts and a convincing theological argument: "Kill Nabal and his followers and become guilty before YHWH because you shed blood" (25:31). At her words, David relents. And what does the Lord think of Abigail and her actions? It's clear by his response: After 10 days he kills the paralyzed Nabal (25:38).

The scenario here is the same one as in 2 Samuel 20: An angry man with the aim to slaughter a great number of innocent people, a single male person who (innocent or not) is the reason for the assault, a wise woman who acts alone, the use of words to calm down the aggressive mind of the man, and the solution of the conflict by killing the single cause, thus preventing the death of many others.

These two biblical women can be contrasted to a woman in a similar situation in an Assyrian drawing of a siege on a hostile city. In this scene, there also appears a woman on the top of the wall of the besieged city. But here the woman is portrayed with a gesture of entreaty—she is a victim without hope of rescue—and the entire composition leaves no doubt that the city will soon be seized by the Assyrian troops. This highlights the uniqueness of the nameless wise woman in 2 Samuel 20 and of Abigail: They are wise and active women who interact successfully against a male war campaign.

This indeed is a hopeful end to a story of war: Lady Wisdom has beaten the General.

Andreas Kunz-Lübcke is Lecturer for Old Testament at the Missions Seminar in Hermannsburg and apl. Professor for Old Testament at the University of Leipzig, Germany.

The Inspiration of Rizpah's Courageous Helplessness

Valerie Bridgeman (United States)

Rizpah fascinates me. Her story in 2 Samuel 21:1–14 is horrific and inspiring at the same time. Rizpah's life was inextricably bound to David because he was a ruthless leader who "sanctified" his brutality by "seeking the face of the Lord." Rizpah was like many biblical women, a political pawn in a game of "who will be king."

I'm not sure when I first started reading and rereading this story. I just know at some point, it captivated me by its senselessness and by Rizpah's courageous helplessness. If I have to pick a time, I would say I started paying close attention to her crazy witness when my sons were teenagers in the 1990s. In Austin, Texas, where we lived at the time, gang activity had picked up and I was afraid of the streets' sway and the dangers of its allure to my middle-class sons. I was afraid of the OGs, the Original Gangstas, who were themselves kings of a certain sort. Because I was a community activist, I was keenly aware of the dangers. But like many mothers of those days, I felt helpless in the face of the pull of gangs and knew only that I would pray and stand vigilant.

Rizpah couldn't stop the violence against her sons and those of her sister-wife Merab, any more than those of us who were trying to battle gang life could stop the influence of gangsta life in our neighborhoods. Like King David, gang leaders wielded power that had impact on people caught in the crosshairs of their power grabs. Reading closely, it's easy to see that Rizpah and Merab were caught in the cross fire of David's power grab for Saul's kingdom. These seven sons were political collateral. And the pretext that their deaths were "revenge" for Saul's actions did not convince Rizpah, or me.

I like Rizpah's crazy stand for dignity for her dead sons, for her insistence that the public display of shame end. She reminds me of the worldwide movement, "Women in Black," the group that stands silently in cities throughout the world in protest against war and other forms of violence (http://www.womeninblack.org/en/vigil). Their witness, like Rizpah's, is both an acknowledgment that they have only the power of right in the face of violent regimes, militarism, and ongoing injustices. But Women in Black members believe they have the power of moral outrage and moral right on their side. Such stands are meant to shame the powers-that-be into doing right, while members also work for peace.

Another thing that strikes me about Rizpah's stance is that she looks crazy in this text. Really. She looks crazy, out on a rock protecting dead bodies from vultures by day and wild animals by night. And she does it for a long time. I often think, someone had to be with her, to relieve her while she slept. Someone *must* have stood with her, even if she started it on her own. Else, how did she survive? When did she sleep? How did she eat?

I am an African American woman who grew up in the 1960s in the United States, the height of the Civil Rights Movement. Many stories from that time feature a singular hero: Martin Luther King, Jr., speaking, Rosa Parks sitting on a bus, or Fannie Lou Hamer testifying before Congress. Though such individuals are lifted up in a singular way, the often-untold story is the cast of thousands of activists and supporters that made their action or voice possible.

Rizpah is one of those unsung heroes in the text, easily overlooked if one is reading only for David's sake. I don't want to be guilty of passing over her witness. Despite the text's insistence that the famine needed David to kill these threats to his throne, in the end we are told the famine didn't end until Rizpah's silent protest for dignity forced David to give the sons, Saul, and Jonathan proper burials.

All these years later, I continue to be intrigued by her.

Valerie Bridgeman is Associate Professor at Lancaster Theological Seminary, United States; she is an ordained preacher and published poet.

QUESTIONS

1. Evaluate Boulton's reading of the David stories. What do we learn about Boulton? About the biblical text? Do you identify with David in any way?
2. How do you understand the relationship between David and Jonathan? How, if at all, does Pohlig's discussion broaden your thinking?
3. What "successful strategy" might contemporary leaders learn from the women in Samuel about avoiding and ending war?
4. How do Bridgeman's life experiences inform her reading of Rizpah? Can you connect with Rizpah in any way in light of your experiences?

CHAPTER 13

ISAIAH 40–55

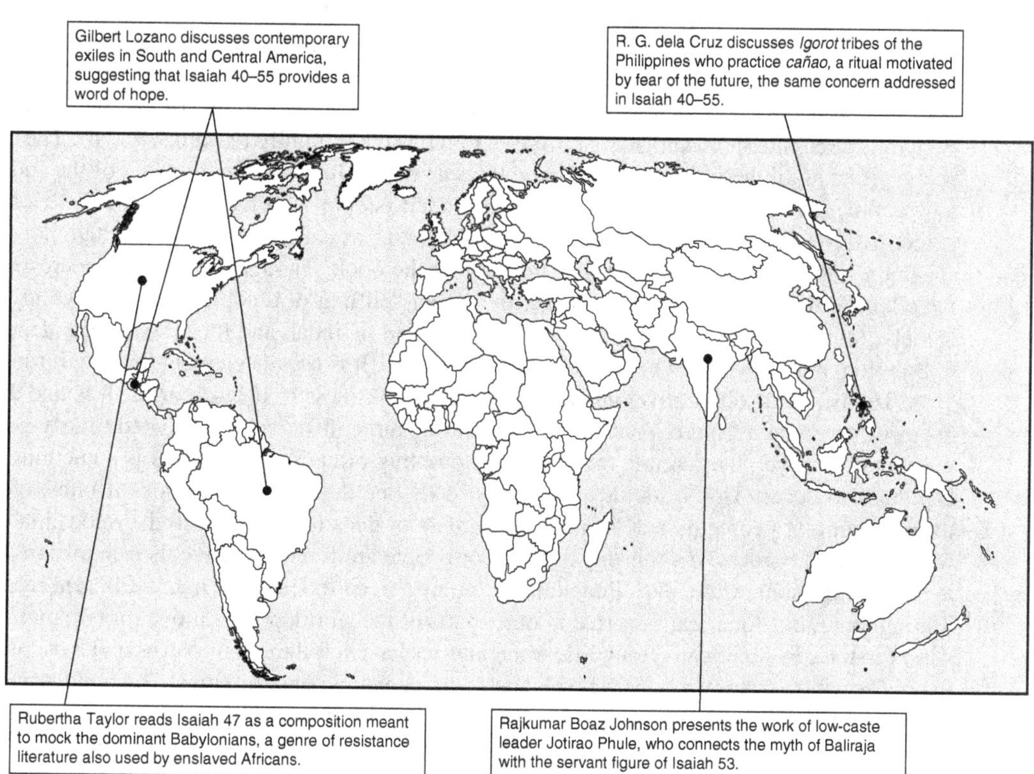

Gilbert Lozano discusses contemporary exiles in South and Central America, suggesting that Isaiah 40–55 provides a word of hope.
R. G. dela Cruz discusses *Igorot* tribes of the Philippines who practice *cañao,* a ritual motivated by fear of the future, the same concern addressed in Isaiah 40–55.
Rubertha Taylor reads Isaiah 47 as a composition meant to mock the dominant Babylonians, a genre of resistance literature also used by enslaved Africans.
Rajkumar Boaz Johnson presents the work of low-caste leader Jotirao Phule, who connects the myth of Baliraja with the servant figure of Isaiah 53.

READINGS

Words of Hope for Contemporary Exiles in South and Central America

Gilbert Lozano (Colombia)

In 586 B.C.E. the Babylonians captured Jerusalem, destroyed the Temple, and exiled many of the leaders. These events were a severe blow to the Judeans, for they marked the end of their nation. Three things resulted. First, the people's faith in their God YHWH was called into question. The Babylonian conquest meant that YHWH had been defeated by the more powerful Babylonian deities. Second, the destruction of the Jerusalem Temple meant that even if someone wanted to continue worshipping YHWH, the worshipper couldn't do that because the religious system and its structure had been dismantled. Third, the removal of the royal family to Babylon called into question God's promises to the Davidic family (2 Sam. 7:8–16). The composite effect of all these things endangered the survival of Judah as a nation and of the Judeans as a people. Isaiah 40–55 addresses a downtrodden people who had witnessed the violence committed by a powerful empire (43:1–2, 14, 17; 54:4), as can be seen from the "Do not fear" statements uttered more than 10 times throughout the book. Though we cannot underestimate the effect of those things on the Judeans, the actual splitting of a population into two groups, namely, those who were allowed to remain in the land of Judah and those who were deported to Babylon, must have been horrendous in its own way. It is on this element that I will focus.

Today people often travel hundreds of miles on business or pleasure trips. It is one thing, however, to go on a trip voluntarily. It is something quite different to be forced to leave one's homeland. And yet, the forcible removal and uprooting of entire populations is something that continues to occur. This leads us to ask, how does one define "exile"? Does it only refer to the relocation of people outside of national borders or does it also point to the relocation even within internal borders? To this day millions of people are forced to leave their homes in order to seek refuge somewhere else. People move or are forced to leave for many different reasons. Throughout Latin America, as is true in other parts of the world, people move for two main reasons. First, Latin Americans from different countries have left their hometowns and have moved internally within their own countries seeking better economic opportunities. The rapid urbanization of Latin American countries has been the result of this process. In this fashion, people from Brazil's northeast have left their impoverished states and moved to the megalopolises of São Paulo and Rio de Janeiro seeking to leave their poverty behind and to find a better life in the city. Many people have similarly left the countryside and relocated to the capital cities of La Paz, Quito, Lima, or Bogotá. Moreover, millions of people have left their homelands in order to seek a better future in other countries, especially the United States.

The second reason people have left their homes is to escape violence. Once again, there have been internal displacements of entire population groups. Due to civil strife within their countries, indigenous peoples have been forced to leave their ancestral homelands in several Central American countries, especially Guatemala and El Salvador. Then, there is the case of Colombia, which is going through one of the longer-lasting civil conflicts in the world. Since the 1960s, Marxist guerrillas have fought government forces for control of the land. In the late 1980s and early 1990s, the conflict was exacerbated by the creation of right-wing paramilitaries who fought the guerrillas. In the last decade other armed groups have been formed, leading to a veritable humanitarian crisis. These violent groups target mostly peasants (countryside inhabitants), but women (often the victims of sexual abuse), indigenous people, and Afro-Colombians are particularly vulnerable to exploitation as well. As a result, Colombia has the second-largest number of internally displaced people in the world. According to the UN Refugee Agency (UNHCR), there were close to 3.6 million people who were internally displaced in Colombia in 2010, and 115,000 refugees and asylum-seekers in neighboring countries—though it is likely that these figures are even higher. By any measure these are staggering numbers. But they are just that—numbers. They don't help us to see the unimaginable suffering of those who have been displaced, those who, like the Judeans, have been exiled from their homes.

In Colombia and elsewhere in South America, those struggles are the continuation of a long series of conflicts over resources and land that began with the arrival of the first Europeans on these shores. Control of natural resources and access to land continues to lead to the forcible removal of people everywhere on this continent. Oil companies seeking to dig often cause the migration of entire populations to new areas (e.g., Ecuador, Colombia). Even national governments set aside human rights or disregard popular sentiment in order to pursue grandiose development projects. For instance, the construction of the Belo Monte Dam in the state of Pará in central Brazil is causing the flooding of hundreds of square miles of ancestral indigenous lands. The people who have lived on those lands for thousands of years are being forced to leave in order to give way to a vision of development that has no regard for indigenous rights or international appeals.

What does Isaiah 40–55 have to say to those people? What connections can be made between that sixth-century book and the people today who are exiled both internally and externally? First, its message irradiates hope today, as it did in the past. To those experiencing exile, the book speaks of a God who sees their plight and encourages them (41:10, 13; 54:4). Second, the book announces judgment upon those who cause human suffering, whether individuals or empires (41:11–12; 47:1–15; 51:8–10). Lastly, throughout Isaiah 40–55 we find the witness, seen elsewhere in the Hebrew Bible, that YHWH sides with the defenseless (40:1–2; 41:17; 42:6–7; 43:1–4). This should inspire people of faith to work alongside God on behalf of suffering and displaced people. Indeed, although centuries separate us, Isaiah 40–55 continues to address important issues that we confront in our world and it continues to offer hope for the millions of exiles in South and Central America today.

Gilbert Lozano (Ph.D.) taught at Fidelis: the Mennonite School of Theology, Curitiba, Brazil, and is currently Associate Professor of Biblical Studies at Anderson University, United States.

Fear of the Future among *Igorot* Tribes of the Philippines

R. G. dela Cruz (Philippines)

Among the Filipinos living in the mountain ranges of the Cordilleras are the *Igorots*. In the Province of Benguet on the northern Luzon island, there are three prominent *Igorot* tribes: the *Kankana-ey*, the *Ibaloi*, and the *Kalanguya*. Although history remembers the *Igorots* as unconquered and uninfluenced by the Spanish colonization that brought Christianity to the Philippine Islands, many have since become Christians under the influence of American missionaries. I have been living in Baguio City since 1986, where I have developed good friendships and acquaintances with Benguet *Igorots*. Most of them are my fellow ministers of the Gospel and Christian believers.

The *Igorots* practice a ritual called *cañao*. It is a social/cultural and religious event. Although the Philippine Tourism Authority promotes *cañao* as a kind of grand cultural festival, emphasizing its sociological aspect, it is first and foremost a religious matter to common *Igorots*. Specifically, it is a ritual motivated by dread and fear of the future. The dance celebrations, the clanging sounds, and the eating festivities do not reflect the real purpose and the meaning for the person or family that sponsors the *cañao*. The *Kankana-eys*, the *Ibalois*, and the *Kalanguyas* in particular exercise their faith in the *cañao* ritual to stop a misfortune. If a person dreams about a tragedy, then a *cañao* must be done to abort the impending disaster. When a family experiences crisis and wants it to cease, a *cañao* is performed to solve the ongoing problem. These Benguet *Igorots* are willing to spend a huge amount of money and invite an elder priest shaman (*mambunong*) to lead the ritual. They will invite their family members, friends, and neighbors to join them. They butcher animals for meat to feed those who have come for the *cañao*, which makes it very expensive. It is a big community event. Even if the person or the family does not have the resources to hold a *cañao*, they will often borrow money to pay for the ritual because safety, peace, and harmony are dependent upon it.

Although many of the *Kankana-eys*, *Ibalois*, and *Kalanguyas* are Catholics or Protestants, they are still influenced by this fear of the future if *cañao* is not performed. It is indeed difficult to separate religion from culture. Many of them, however, find hope and comfort in certain passages from the Bible. One such text is Isaiah 41. Here the people of Israel are in exile—their nation has been destroyed. They have no king and no temple; the situation is bleak. They are in need of hope, of restoration; their fear of the future must be overcome. And this is precisely the word that the prophet gives. The declaration of God's oracle is plain: Those who trust in God have nothing to fear. When those who trust God are dismayed because of the enemy and forces of evil that are against them, God promises to strengthen and help them (41:10–11). God vows to eliminate their fear. The prophet proclaims that God is in control; there is no reason to live in dread. This message is deeply inspiring and encouraging for Christian *Igorots*. It encourages them, as it did ancient Israel, to be hopeful about the future; it gives them confidence that they will "thresh the mountains and crush them," that they will have the power to "make the hills like chaff," which the wind carries away (41:15–16)—and with it the crippling terror associated with *cañao*.

For many *Igorots* the question then becomes how should they approach *cañao*. Some argue that after becoming a Christian one should have nothing to do with *cañao* and other *Igorot* practices, like the rituals associated with the burial of the dead. They maintain that these are purely pagan practices which must be avoided. Many of the Protestant (Pentecostal, Baptist, Methodist, etc.) pastors and churches reason thus. On the other side, there are those (mostly Catholics and Anglicans-Episcopalians) who participate in the *cañao* because of its communal and social value. The former conservative group, for example, sees the use of gongs and the dances that are part of *cañao* as simple paganism that must be avoided. The gongs are meant to call the ancestral spirits and the dances to communicate with and appease the spirits of the dead, ideas which are contrary to the Christian faith, they would argue. On the other side, some Christian *Igorots* apply Christian content to the ritual forms. For them, the gongs and dances become a type of thanksgiving festival where the focus is now on God and his goodness.

Whether or not to continue practicing *cañao* is a hotly debated topic among *Igorot* Christians. But all can agree that passages such as Isaiah 41 offer a word of peace, hope, and security for those who are faithful.

R. G. dela Cruz is Lecturer at Asia Pacific Theological Seminary in Baguio City, Philippines; he is an ordained minister of the South Central Cordillera District Council of the Philippines General Council of the Assemblies of God.

Isaiah as Resistance Literature

Rubertha Taylor (United States)

Biblical scholars describe the literary structure of Isaiah 47 as a poetic composition of humiliation and mockery against the political structure of ancient Babylon. Various scholars classify some narratives and behaviors of enslaved Africans and their descendants under the same genre. In this project, I adopt James C. Scott's terminology to argue that Isaiah 47 and certain narratives and behaviors of captive Africans and their descendants classify as "weapons of the weak"—tools of resistance exercised behind a mask of public compliance. These parallel writings and behaviors deviate from a "norm" and provide subordinates a way to articulate a different reality. Isaiah 47 serves as an example that Israel, a subordinate nation, expressed themes that humiliated and dismissed Babylonian power.

Stories about my maternal second great-grandfather (a son of a slave woman and a white slave owner) and his descendants born into a segregated North America influence my interpretation of biblical exilic narratives. The information passed down to me from my grandparents and parents leads me to see memory, rituals, and the emergence of social leaders as tools of resistance—tools which are also present within the Israelites' exilic community. I believe this similarity demonstrates that North American captives and their descendants embodied biblical texts and that their experiences inform Isaiah 47.

Isaiah 40–55 is a compilation of thoughts that culminated into a unified, public poetic declaration of resistance against Babylon's dominancy. Isaiah 47 opens with a series of commands against the Babylonian empire. As a nation once entrusted with YHWH's people, the writer now refers to Babylon as a female disrobed of its glory with a dismal fate. At no place in Isaiah 47 is this nation given space to negotiate YHWH's vengeance. Moreover, the tone of this chapter deliberately taunts and indicts Babylon for its previous actions against Israel. Such a portrayal leads to the following question: What has led the author to make this bold declaration of Babylon's downfall?

To address this question through an African-American hermeneutic, I begin by recognizing false compliance and self-empowering messages as two covert forms of resistance operating in both social contexts. In regards to my African ancestors, public group resistance against African enslavement did not occur, for the most part anyway, after their initial arrival in North America. Those who survived the Middle Passage needed time to recover physically, emotionally, and psychologically from the horrific journey during which as many as half of the stolen Africans died. Apparently during this time of recovery, many of my ancestors began to make adjustments to living as captives in a strange new world; and yet, remembering their heritage as free people in Africa was paramount. This connection between memories and current thoughts created tension between forced compliance and an ability to think beyond physical and social restraints. As my ancestors came to know enslavement in North America, their memory produced states of mind that challenged their present social realities and made it difficult for them to perform work that misrepresented beliefs about themselves and their heritage. Consequently, covert forms of resistance began to develop and operate as means for survival.

Unlike the resistance of many Africans, public group resistance among Israelites occurred at the beginning of Babylon's invasion but faded away following the death of Gedaliah and other Judeans at Mizpah. A lack of information regarding exilic circumstances leaves many biblical scholars uncertain of social activities of the Israelites under Babylonian domination. What is certain is that many exilic passages encourage Israelites to remember their heritage as covenant people of YHWH. This indentured group considered itself servants of YHWH, not servants of the Babylonian empire. In so doing, the Israelites spoke with assurance of YHWH's redemptive powers as though there had been no hiatus in YHWH's presence or delivering acts.

The impact that memory has on autonomous forms of resistance includes individual and group ritualistic performances. To remember their heritage before living in captivity, my enslaved ancestors developed elaborate plans to practice African traditions and religious rituals in North America. They expressed themselves with music and, for those who were literate, creative writing. Their forms of expression also included images in art, stories about their homeland, and, in some cases, stories from the Bible. By combining African traditions with forms in the new world, my ancestors developed rituals that established self-identity, strengthened social bonds, and taught moral, social, and religious instructions. Still, for a number of them, this assimilation into a colonized North America did not result in absolute conformity. Instead, resistance in forms of conversations of empowerment, encouragement, contempt, and hope operated consistently beyond the purview of power holders.

Sermons, songs that promote divine deliverance, messages of contempt, and sorrow songs are all present in the exilic literature from the Hebrew Bible. A recognition of these forms is important for several reasons: First, it demonstrates that sermons encourage the Israelites to remember YHWH; second, it portrays songs of faith in YHWH as a redeemer even when YHWH is not actively involved; third, it refutes eternal slavery; and fourth, it shows that through lamentations the Israelites grieve as a collective nation. Given these four fundamental causes, the Israelite rituals serve to promote the importance of memory, faith, negation, and unity as tools for establishing modes of resistance. These tools of resistance encourage autonomous living identical to those of my African ancestors, namely self-identity, social bonding, and moral, social, and religious instructions. From this list, forms of religious instruction function as a primary cause for both groups' movement from covert to overt means of resistance.

Although my ancestors of African descent did not claim a covenant with a god as did the Israelites, religious instructions or beliefs were keys for developing an understanding of themselves in their new social context. For those captives who adopted Christianity as a major religion, some were influenced by biblical texts to lead insurrections such as the one led by Nat Turner in 1831. In a confession to his lawyer, Turner revealed that the Spirit of God told him to kill his enemies. His full confession, certain Negro spirituals, sermons, and writings all mirror Isaiah 47:3 and 6 in claiming that divine interruption into human affairs functions to initiate vengeance against social injustice and human exploitation. While this claim of divine interjection serves as a catalyst for social changes, it alone does not set in motion events necessary to transform a community; an emergence of social leader(s) and community participation are two other components.

A combination of God, social leaders, and community involvement merges religion with social issues, in which subordinate leaders emerge from the shadows of false compliance to announce God's intentions to change current social conditions and to organize people to carry out these transformations. Turner's announcement to four men of God's intention to reverse current social orders and his solicitation of them and others to carry out this divine mandate reflects Second Isaiah's announcement of a divine purpose for a new dispensation of peace and restoration to an exilic people and a call for the Israelites to declare collectively YHWH's intention to take vengeance against Babylon.

At a glance, the public declaration of Babylon's dismissal of power in Isaiah 47 appears abrupt. However, a close examination of this passage reveals YHWH's recognition of the Israelites' oppression and their faith in YHWH to deliver them. Their acknowledgment of and faith in YHWH suggests that the Israelites maintained forms of their preexilic relationship with YHWH throughout 70 years of exile.

As an African-American female biblical scholar, my reading of Isaiah 47 reveals that "weapons of the weak" such as memory, a practice of traditional rituals, and an emergence of social leaders can lead to open mockery against dominant forces. These bold proclamations clearly indicate that forms of resistance behind a mask of public compliance are *not weak*; rather, they provide subordinates a way to articulate a different normality that represents and supports beliefs about themselves and their heritage and shields them from an all-encompassing force of public humiliation and human exploitation.

Rubertha Taylor taught six years in the Bible Department at Lee University; she resides in Cleveland, Tennessee, United States.

The Myth of Baliraja Compared to the Servant Figure in Isaiah

Rajkumar Boaz Johnson (India)

Isaiah 53 is the grand finale of the so-called Servant Songs in the book of Isaiah. The unnamed servant is a royal figure, yet he is portrayed as disfigured (52:14), "despised and rejected" by humanity (53:3). The servant becomes the paradigm of the depths of sorrow, pain, and rejection. Nonetheless, the final song begins and ends in a note of hope: "See, my servant shall prosper; he shall be exalted and lifted up, and shall be very high" (52:13); and "Therefore I will allot him a portion with the great" (53:12).

Who is this "servant?" In Christianity, of course, it is Jesus. The New Testament quotes this text to describe the rejection and passion of Christ (John 12:38; Acts 8:26–35; Romans 10:16). In Jewish tradition, by contrast, "the servant" is generally understood to be the corporate people of Israel—that is, not an individual but the nation as a whole. In Western biblical interpretation, therefore, one is forced to choose between one of these two. Viewing Isaiah 53 and the Servant figure in the context of Eastern traditions, namely, in conjunction with the low-caste and outcaste people of India, offers us a different—perhaps even better—approach to the text.

More than 80 percent of the population of India comes from low caste (*shudra*), outcaste (*dalit* or *ati-shudra*), and the aborigine tribes (*adivasi*). Approximately 12–15 percent of the population consider themselves as high-caste Hindus: the priests (*Brahmin*), the royalty (*Kshatriya*), and the business castes (*Vyashiya*). These high-caste Hindus are said to be descendents of the Aryans or pure-blooded people who migrated to India from Central Asia. In high-caste Hindu texts, the low caste, outcaste, and aborigines are always described in very derogatory terms. For instance, *Manu Dharma Shastra VIII, 413–414* reads, "But the Shudra, whether bought or unbought, he may compel to do the work of a slave; for he was created by the self-existent (*svyanbhu*) to be the slave of the Brahmin." Based on texts like this, the low castes, outcastes, and aborigines of India have been treated very poorly and enslaved historically by the high castes.

In the history of India, there have arisen some low-caste saints who have revolted. Here I will focus on the writings of one such low-caste leader, Jotirao Phule (1827–1890), since he makes a poignant connection with the servant figure of Isaiah 53. Born a *shudra* in the Satara district of Maharashtra, Phule develops his theories on the emancipation of *shudras* and *ati-shudras* based on the stories narrated and songs sung among the low-caste people in Maharashtra. In an important book entitled *Gulamgiri* (Slavery), published in 1873, Phule sets out the task of demythologizing Hindu myths and reinstating the *shudra* narrative. That is, for Phule, Hindu myths are political and sociological tools used to denigrate and demonize the original inhabitants of India (the low castes, outcastes, and aborigine), and his objective is to counter those by elevating the stories of low-caste people.

One such story is the myth of Baliraja, which literally means the Sacrificial King. This mythological King Bali is also found in Hindu texts. However, in the Hindu texts he is described as an Asura (a Demon). One Hindu text, for example, reads as follows:

> In the beginning the demon Bali controlled the worlds. Then Vishnu became incarnate as a dwarf, and went where Bali was performing sacrifice. He became a Brahmin and asked Bali to give him the space that he could cover in three strides. Bali was pleased to do this, thinking that the dwarf was just a dwarf. But the dwarf stepped over the heaven, the sky, and the earth in three strides, stealing the property of the demon. He sent the demons and all their sons and grandsons to hell (Patala), and gave Indra kingship over all humanity. (Vayu Purana 2.36.74–86)

By contrast, according to the *shudra* myth of Baliraja, he is not an Asura (Demon). Rather he is the King of kings. Phule notes that in the *shudra* story, the Kingdom of Bali was global. "He was famous for his just wars... He was a champion of the downtrodden. He was a lover of music... He appointed an officer to dispense justice... We can see from this account that Bali's kingdom had spread far and wide" (*Gulamgiri*, 31). Bali presided over ritual sacrifices on the banks of rivers like Narmada—an act that commemorated the *shudra* idea of creation. The Aryan gods wanted to conquer Bali, so Vishnu took the form of a dwarf. He tricked Bali into giving him the amount of land, which he covered in three strides. With two strides he covered the heavens, the earth, and the netherworld. The third step was upon the head of Bali, who was killed and pushed into the netherworld (*patal*). The *shudra* story claims that Baliraja, the Sacrificial King, became the paradigm of sacrifice. However, he will come one day to establish his just kingdom, which the *shudras* and *ati-shudras* celebrate and anticipate with several festivals and rituals.

Although Phule never became a Christian, he was exposed to Christianity in a school established by Scottish Missionaries. He called Hindu myths "despicable lies," and considered himself and his followers to be Truthseekers. In his quest for truth, he discovered the connection between the suffering Messiah image in Isaiah 52–53, the suffering image of Christ in the New Testament, and the suffering Baliraja. This image of the "fallen king who will rise in the eschaton [end-times]," according to Phule, is the low-caste and outcaste image of the servant of Isaiah 53. The servant-king or *shudra*-king is killed by the high-caste invaders of India. Yet, one day he will arise to set up his kingdom—the Bali Raj. In low-caste thought, the suffering of the individual Baliraja is a paradigm for the corporate suffering of the low-caste people at the hands of the high-caste Hindus. Their rituals enable them to reenact the death of Baliraja. Yet, this Baliraja ritually arises once a year, to express their hope that Baliraja's kingdom will come one day.

In terms of the connection with Jesus, Phule writes, "Thus the prophecy of our venerable old ladies 'May Bali's kingdom come!' seems to have materialized when the Baliraja (Jesus Christ) was crucified by a few wicked desperadoes, and a great movement of liberation was set in motion" (*Gulamgiri*, 36). When Bali's kingdom comes, there will be complete salvation, and universal peace and justice for all. This is reminiscent of the hope which is expressed in the beginning and end of the final Servant Song in Isaiah 53 and of the hope which Christians find in the crucified Jesus. In short, the servant figure, according to Phule, is both the Christ of the Bible, and the suffering *shudras, ati-shudras,* and the aborigines.

Rajkumar Boaz Johnson was reared in one of the slums of Delhi, where he witnessed many of his young friends taken into slavery by high-caste Hindus; he is Professor of Biblical and Theological Studies at North Park University, United States.

QUESTIONS

1. How does the movement of people within or across the borders of your county compare to the movement of people discussed by Lozano?
2. What would you recommend to Christian *Igorots* debating whether or not to continue practicing *cañao*?
3. Comment on a number of specific verses in Isaiah 47 which illustrate Taylor's reading of the text.
4. Can the identity of the servant legitimately be all three: Christ, the corporate people of Israel, and the suffering *shudras, ati-shudras,* and the aborigines?

CHAPTER 14

EZEKIEL 1–24

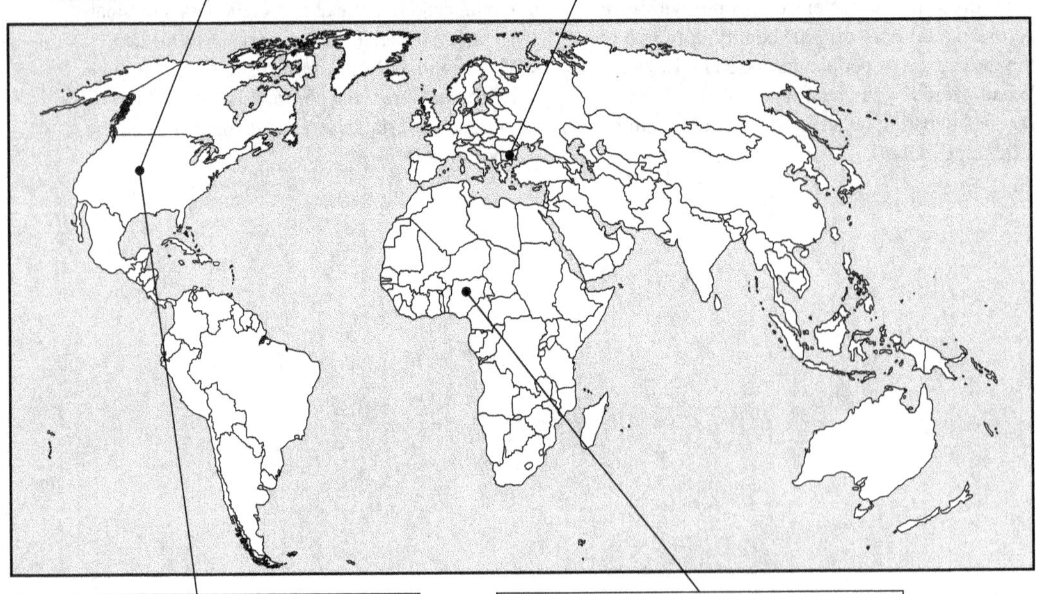
Aaron Koller studies God's mistreatment of female Jerusalem in Ezekiel 16 in light of literature on child sexual abuse.
Elizabeth A. Steger reads Ezekiel 16 in the context of her missionary work with orphans in Bulgaria, noting the hope and warning that the text offers the children.
John Fink compares Ezekiel's message to the doom and gloom of news networks, "talking heads," popular culture, and outspoken Christian activists.
James N. Pohlig explains the difference between shame cultures and guilt cultures, observing how Ezekiel 18 is a surprising move toward the latter.

READINGS

"Doom and Gloom" in Ezekiel and Today's News Networks
John Fink

God's Mistreatment of Female Jerusalem in Ezekiel 16
Aaron Koller

Ezekiel 16 as Hope and Warning for Orphans in Bulgaria
Elizabeth A. Steger

Ezekiel 18 in the Context of Shame Cultures and Guilt Cultures
James N. Pohlig

"Doom and Gloom" in Ezekiel and Today's News Networks

John Fink (United States)

At first glance, from a historical perspective, Ezekiel's place in history may seem very similar to our own. Finding himself in a time of conflict and upheaval, when the "status quo" had changed, Ezekiel identifies himself as an "exile" (1:1), claiming to see visions from God while amongst the insurgent forces of King Jehoiachin. The majority of his writings describe his encounter with "the glory of the Lord" (1:28) and how he was directed to serve as a prophet (a "watchman") of God's displeasure and harbinger of doom (2:3), with the caveat of "whether they listen or fail to listen—for they are a rebellious house—they will know that a prophet has been among them" (2:5). He describes the destruction of Jerusalem and the Temple as God's continued punishment of the Israelites (Ezek. 4–24), before closing with the prophesied restoration of a Jewish state and the construction of a new Temple (Ezek. 33–48).

We ourselves are surrounded by similar tidings of doom, gloom, and impending disaster, although we may not think of 24-hour cable news, "talking heads," popular culture, or outspoken Christian activists as modern-day Ezekiels. The news carries tales of horrors—past, current, and future—with self-proclaimed "watchmen" seeking to sculpt popular opinion as they feed on the fears and uncertainty of the times to gain viewership. Popular culture, such as the "History Channel," have embraced the so-called Mayan calendar "2012 Disaster" phenomenon, when the ancient long count calendar ends, marking the end of the current "age" and the transition to a new one. Fringe elements of Christianity, such as Westboro Baptist Church of Kansas, claim that the United States has angered God in various ways, including the legalization of abortion and same-sex marriage, going so far as to picket certain events with signs claiming that "God hates fags" and other divisive messages.

It is my belief that we find ourselves in a position much like Ezekiel. While our nation has not been crushed by outsiders and oppressed, with our citizens scattered to the winds, we do live in a time of warfare and strife, having deployed our military to engage enemies in other lands for nearly a decade now. Our economy is struggling, with millions of people having lost their jobs. Crime and other social hardships continue to run rampant. People in our time wax poetic for the past, remembering it much more fondly than the present, and hope for the future, sincerely wishing it to be better than today, while secretly dreading that it will only be worse. We are afraid, and because of that fear, we turn to whoever will provide reasons and answers for that fear.

Compare those thoughts to what the Israelites of Ezekiel's time must have felt, having been dominated by the Assyrians, the Egyptians, and the Babylonians, rebelling several times before finally being crushed by Nebuchadnezzar in 586 B.C., with both Jerusalem and the Temple being pillaged and burned and their people scattered into exile. They too were afraid of the present and future, either believing themselves unfortunate or having angered God and therefore suffering His punishment. Their present was unpleasant, their collective past, when they had a home and a cultural identity, was believed better, and the future was uncertain at best. They too were looking for answers and reasons for their punishment/misfortune wherever they could find them, whether those answers came from a rebellious leader who had grand hopes for the future or a priest who moved among them spreading the Word of God. Who amongst us, after all, enjoys being told we are or have done wrong?

Regardless of their message, we find ourselves surrounded by those who would be modern-day Ezekiels. The message of impending doom and destruction, either because we have displeased God or because of secular, scientific, or hypothetical reasons, are everywhere. Ezekiel's words could easily have been written today, and would quite possibly rocket to the top of various best-seller lists. This is not to say that I am declaring Ezekiel to be antiquity's equivalent of Glen Beck, Rush Limbaugh, Keith Olbermann, or Pat Robertson. I am merely attempting to draw a comparison between the tone of Ezekiel's writings and the messages and sources we are confronted with today. Perhaps some of these activists believe they are twenty-first-century "watchmen," reaching out with strident voices as they seek to make their understanding of God's Word understood, much as Ezekiel was charged. Perhaps they find us as equally stubborn and rebellious as God warned Ezekiel the Israelites would be (2:4). There is, on the surface, very little difference between a sign declaring "God hates fags" and Ezekiel declaring in the name of God that "he who eats at mountain shrines, defiles his neighbor's wife, oppresses the poor and needy, commits robbery, does not return what he took in pledge, looks at idols, does detestable things, and lends as usury and takes excessive interest" will not live (18:10–13).

John Fink has worked as a middle and high school band director, a special education teacher, and a police dispatcher.

God's Mistreatment of Female Jerusalem in Ezekiel 16

Aaron Koller (United States)

In Ezekiel 16 Jerusalem is personified as a girl: abandoned as a baby, saved by God as a foundling, and later taken by him in marriage. The bride takes her newfound possessions and newfound confidence and seeks many extramarital sexual partners, including the legendarily virile Egyptians and the Mesopotamians, but she is not yet satisfied. She is the antiprostitute, paying others for sex. Her husband undertakes to punish her, handing her over to her many lovers, who strip her naked, stone her, and cut her up with their swords.

Despite what some modern exegetes have written, it is clear that God does not care for the girl in even the most basic ways until she has reached sexual maturity. Rather than direct nurturance, he used some sort of magic formula to ensure Jerusalem's survival (16:6); he even left her unclothed and unwashed in the field. When God finally cleanses her (16:9), there are probably three bloods mingled: the hymeneal blood of her first sexual encounter, the menstrual blood showing her new maturity, and the birth blood in which she has been wallowing for more than a decade.

The deeply troubling images used in this chapter have provoked impassioned and thoughtful critiques by a generation of feminist scholars, and they have done well to identify the objectionable imagery used here. The failing of this scholarship is that it has not gone far enough in interrogating the text: It has often portrayed the offending imagery as a problem for *us* rather than for Ezekiel and his original audience, as if *they* would have seen nothing objectionable about humiliation and sexualization. The assumption, sometimes made explicit, has been that males will sympathize with the male in the story, and thus that the narrative spun by Ezekiel glorifies God's behavior and castigates everything done by female Jerusalem.

Two facts about myself prevent me from adopting this approach. First, I am male, but am repulsed by the behavior attributed to God in this chapter. Thus it seems to me that the sharp gender divide posited by some scholars, insisting that males and females will inevitably read the text differently, is an ironic misstep, which overessentializes the male–female dichotomy.

Second, as someone who grew up as a religious Jew, and who teaches Bible in a Jewish university, I am not prepared to accept the view that "we" ought to reject the text's portrayal of God, which was acceptable to "them." I instinctively feel myself to be part of the community addressed by the prophet. My "we" cannot insist on difference between "us" and the text's audience, because we *are* that audience. (I should add that I am a devout feminist, as well, but do not believe that to be relevant to the interpretation of this text, which is offensive to all humans.) One need not be part of the Jewish community to hold this view; some have argued that no listener would have sympathized with God as portrayed in this text. Indeed, the Talmudic Rabbis, who lived in a far more male-dominated society than ours, were apparently deeply troubled by this text: Some forbade its public reading in the synagogue (Bavli Megillah 25a–b). Most importantly, within the rhetoric of the text, the people of Jerusalem—the audience—is identified as the *female* Jerusalem, *against* the male God.

In certain contemporary societies this marriage would be considered statutory rape. Indeed, it would be child sexual abuse (CSA). The literature on CSA and its effects is huge. Many of the documented effects of CSA closely resemble the descriptions of Jerusalem in our text. One of the important points that emerges from this literature is that effects are not culturally specific. Psychologists have come up with a number of good hypotheses to explain this phenomenon, but the phenomenon itself is quite clear and has to do with psychological realities rather than cultural expectations. Even 2,500 years ago in Iraq, therefore, the same reality should have applied.

CSA is statistically associated with different types of risky sexual behavior, including multiple partners. In many cases, when CSA victims reach adulthood, their sense of betrayal resulting from the abuse may lead to a series of shallow, unfulfilling short-lasting sexual relationships, as part of a desperate search for a meaningful relationship. It must be emphasized: In our text, the girl had her first sentient encounter with another human being at around age 12, when an all-powerful male figure appeared, had sex with her, and entered into an eternal marital bond with her. Her later life was certainly unsatisfying, as she took all she had and gave it to potential lovers, enjoying the trysts but never feeling satisfied. Is this not clearly an example of a CSA victim in a desperate search for a redeeming relationship?

Ezekiel is psychologically perceptive, and depicts his characters with pathos and verisimilitude. Scholars have observed that later in the chapter, God is described as an abusive husband: He beats his wife because he suspects her of infidelity, and blames the abuse on the battered wife; he claims that these actions will bring his wife in line, and expresses satisfaction when she is cowed into submission. Jerusalem, in turn, is depicted as a battered woman, in a state of learned helplessness, hoping against hope that if she does not raise her husband's ire, he will not beat her again.

The question, then, must be this: Why would Ezekiel portray God in such an unflattering, even damning, light? It should be observed that Ezekiel is nothing if not consistent. In Ezekiel 23, he again describes Jerusalem's early life as one filled with uninvited sexual experiences. Referring to Jerusalem's childhood in Egypt, Ezekiel says, "there their breasts were squeezed, and there they pressed their virgin nipples" (23:3); that is, in their youth they were sexually abused, and the rest of the chapter essentially blames the victims. If Ezekiel's goal is to chastise Israel, why would he tell a story in which it is difficult not to pity her? If his goal is to explain God's actions, why would he tell a tale in which it is difficult to sympathize with God?

An answer must be sought in the literary-theological realm, since Ezekiel is fundamentally a book of literary theology. Perhaps Ezekiel chooses descriptions which undermine the character of God in order to make the point that the past does not matter in judging the present. That the present is independent of the past is, of course, a major theme of Ezekiel's theological platform (cf. Ezek. 14 and 18). Might it be that in his retellings of history, he specifically paints the origins of the relationship as one-sided and portrays God in a negative light, in order to avoid getting into an argument over whether in fact Israel owes God anything at all?

Hosea and Jeremiah claim that since God was beneficent to Israel, Israel's turn to others is betrayal. Ezekiel does not think that defining his generation's behavior as betrayal is dependent on what God has done for them. This leads Ezekiel to a radical conclusion: Jerusalem is bound by loyalty to God *even if God did nothing for them.* It may well be that God was not justified in initiating the bond; it may well be that Jerusalem's chafing at the bond is understandable and almost predictable. But a bond is a bond, and, Ezekiel says, there is no escape from it.

The suggestion is, then, that the use of the offensive images in Ezekiel is meant to force a theological reevaluation of claims Israel may make against God. Some of Ezekiel's contemporaries may have argued that God has lost their trust, since he is no longer acting toward them with love, beneficence, or kindness. By denying that God was ever good to Israel, Ezekiel undercuts any defense based on the claim that he has stopped.

Aaron Koller is Assistant Professor of Near Eastern and Jewish Studies at Yeshiva University, New York, United States.

Ezekiel 16 as Hope and Warning for Orphans in Bulgaria

Elizabeth A. Steger (Bulgaria)

As a nurse desiring to provide medical and spiritual care in Bulgaria, I have toured through a number of government-sponsored facilities for children of all ages. One houses beautiful infants that could easily be loved and cared for by any family, as well as babies with deformities that make them look more monster-like than childlike. These little ones live with conditions that could have been prevented or would never be left untreated in the United States.

Another is filled with children who are injured from hitting their heads against the wall, who cower in the corner, or who simply rock back and forth resisting touch. These same children sleep on vinyl flooring on their beds rather than a mattress covered with a sheet for the ease of the employees hired to provide care to the children. One orphanage is filled with happy toddlers who sing and play, seemingly unaware that there is any other type of life.

Then, there are the facilities that house older children, wild with energy, unsupervised, and craving attention. These older children are perfect targets for predators and perverts who lurk outside their doors. One of these cement homes shelters disabled young adults who would likely be unable to establish a life on their own because of their mental or physical challenges.

All of these children have something in common, the stigma of being outcasts. They are abused, abandoned, or unwanted. While some families cannot afford to provide for a child and consider it a kindness to relinquish their parental duties to the state, there are many terror-filled stories that seem to belong more in a horror movie than in the life of a child. One such story is that of two sisters I've developed a relationship with over the years. Both girls have mental impairments and were removed from an abusive household; one of them had been hit in the head with an axe by her mother.

Many of the boys in this same orphanage have begun cross-dressing and experimenting with homosexuality and many of the girls are overly sensual in their interactions with men, likely as a result of exposure to sexual abuse and the evil and darkness that surrounds them. They, too, are striving to fill a void.

Where can they find hope?

In Ezekiel 16, a story is told of a nation that was without the care and compassion of a loving parent. Israel had not always been solely Jewish, but God rescued her. He adopted her as His own. She would have perished without Him. He not only nurtured her as a child but, as she matured, he served as her Bridegroom and loved her fully and passionately. He clothed her in the finest garments and accessories as a queen.

God gave Israel every orphan's dream: love, acceptance, security, and provision as if they were royalty. He was worthy of complete trust and faith. After observing the plight of the orphans in Bulgaria, and the response that these children exhibit from the smallest gestures of kindness, I would anticipate that Israel would wholeheartedly follow God's instructions for her. I could imagine that much like Nadia, Vasilka, Tiho, and Greta freely express love, adoration, and affection in response to a piece of fruit, a soda, or a small gift, the Israelites would show an outpouring of heartfelt gratitude for the new life that God gave them. They were given a new identity that allowed them to leave a life filled with shame and isolation for a life full of promise.

However, Israel did not respond in this way to the Almighty. Instead, she rejected God and sought other lovers. Israel engaged in countless acts of idolatry and immorality without remembering her covenant with God. She rejected the One who had saved her from certain death. She took the gifts she was given and heartlessly offered them to another. Just as an undisciplined child becomes unruly and despised, Israel had turned into a self-centered, entitled, and depraved nation.

A response was needed. God allowed the Israelites to fall to neighboring countries and to experience the consequences of their sin. Suffering through the difficulties and challenges of living without the diplomatic immunity to which she had become accustomed got Israel's attention. Eventually, God did provide atonement for Israel's unfaithfulness and the covenant was restored, but Israel would endure shame for her actions and pain when she remembered the way she had so easily discarded her Redeemer.

God desires to adopt the discarded and rejected in society. This message is truly transformational and life changing to those who have lived in isolation and seclusion from the mainstream, with little to call their own. For them, a "forgotten" life is reality, but the opportunity to be adopted by God changes their identity completely. Like a newborn who is unaware of the dangers that await him as he is not cleansed and swaddled at birth, those orphans who do not know God are pursued by a compassionate Savior. God desires that none perish outside the atonement He offers.

The acceptance these children can find in a Savior who unconditionally loves them and communes with them is unlike any parental relationship they have ever had. Their past and present are encumbered by adults who, at best, are overwhelmed with hardships and impossibilities and, at worst, who exploit them. They are accustomed to having their dreams, desires, and individuality removed, rather than promoted. Few people offer them anything without expectations.

They see other children at school who go home to families who provide warm meals and hugs. In those families, if the children's hearts are broken, they have someone to reassure them that they will love again. If they are afraid at night, they have a bed they can jump into for security. If they are admitted to the hospital, there is a family member to stay with them. The orphans have none of this. Inclusion in the family of God may be the first time these "outcasts" have been included in anything of worth in their lives.

Understandably, the orphans may embrace the opportunity to become a child of God fairly readily. But once they have called upon God for salvation and rescue, it is tempting to quickly forget God, their first love. The worldly and base environment of the orphanage does not foster purity. The mentors in the Christian faith are few in this part of the world. If the converts fall away, Ezekiel 16 offers both warning and hope. God fully adopts a child, which includes discipline to align believers with Him. Consequences and shame result from rebellion and disobedience. However, God never forsakes His child.

The rejection God experienced in this passage and ultimately that Jesus faced on the cross was more pronounced than that of my friends in Bulgaria. He truly knows agony and feelings of abandonment. He has the remedy for ailments. He can heal hurts. He can bring peace beyond understanding, quell that nagging feeling of unworthiness to receive authentic love, which includes discipline.

While Ezekiel 16 offers answers and life for the orphan, the ability to enact principles of Christian living and instruction into the environment of the orphanage is challenging. It is difficult to overcome the many social concerns, language barriers, and personal demons that these children face. When a conversion to Christianity occurs, discipleship is extremely limited and may result in a faith that is easily set aside. My prayer for these lovely orphans is that they would be drawn to grace and that there would be a continual Christian influence available to foster an ever-deepening relationship with the One who calls them His children.

Elizabeth A. Steger (MSN, RN, NEA, FACHE) is Vice-President of Patient Care Services at Presbyterian Hospital in Charlotte, North Carolina, United States; she is involved in medical missions in Eastern Europe, especially with the orphanages of Bulgaria.

Ezekiel 18 in the Context of Shame Cultures and Guilt Cultures

James N. Pohlig (West Africa)

Should all members of a community suffer equally for their community's misdeeds? A "yes" answer is typical of so-called "shame cultures," but is not typical of "guilt cultures." These two terms, now standard concepts used in cultural analysis, were popularized in 1946 by American anthropologist Ruth Benedict in a very influential study of Japanese society.

Members of **shame cultures** evaluate themselves in terms of the good opinion and standing (i.e., honor) that they enjoy in the eyes of the community. For these individuals, "outward directed" personal honor, not an "inward directed" moral system, is the main motivator of personal behavior. One effect of this system is that one's misdeeds tend not to be considered to exist unless they come to the attention of other people. Moreover, because an individual's honor also partially depends on the good standing of the relevant collective unit—whether family, clan, tribe, and so forth—in the eyes of *other* collectives, the collective's honor must also be maintained at all costs.

Because the collective's good name reflects well on all its members, shame cultures find it far more important to maintain that good name than to punish the actual misdeeds of any one member. In the same vein, when the collective suffers loss of honor, this shame overrides any individual's possible innocence: All must suffer together. Either way, a shame culture individual evaluates himself in terms of how he is regarded by the collective.

The ancient Near Eastern cultures—including the Israelite culture—are regarded today as having been shame cultures. In shame culture thinking, YHWH's mass punishment of Israel would have been seen at the time as clearly justifiable. All society must openly suffer the loss of honor if it does wrong. Since YHWH's covenant community of Israel, as a whole, had embraced the worship of idols, YHWH turned against his own people in full view of all the surrounding nations and doomed them to disaster.

The open recognition on the other nations' part of the cause of Israel's shameful punishment is demonstrated many times in the Bible. For example, after Jerusalem falls for the last time in 586 B.C., the Babylonian commander himself tells the prophet Jeremiah, "The Lord your God decreed this disaster for this place...All this happened because you people sinned against the Lord and did not obey him" (Jeremiah 40:1–3). Again, "When her [Israel's] people fell into enemy hands, there was no one to help her. Her enemies looked at her and laughed at her destruction...All who honored her despise her...she herself groans and turns away" (Lamentations 1:7–8).

Having survived through the millennia in large numbers, shame cultures are today alive and well. Here are some incidents typical of shame cultures I witnessed in two different West African communities:

1. A local school's parents' association finds that its funds have been embezzled by the treasurer. In response, the association fires the treasurer...and then immediately reelects him to the same post! That is the end of the disciplinary action. In this way the group covers the fault of the individual—they certainly have no thought of legally charging him with a crime. To keep the treasurer as a member in good standing is seen as reflecting well on the association. The group's honor has a higher priority than the individual's guilt.
2. A young man among the Mbe people of southeastern Nigeria runs off with a girl from the same *ekuó* (family unit), an action that is prohibited by local custom, because a person cannot marry within the same *ekuó*. A village pastor goes to discuss the matter with him, and the two get into a fistfight. Afterwards, the young man goes to the police and swears out a warrant of assault and battery against the pastor. A policeman comes out to the village, arrests the pastor, and hauls him to headquarters. In response, the elders of the *ekuó* gather together and induce me to drive them in my vehicle into town. En route, we stop to buy a case of beer for the police station. In return for this mark of consideration, the sergeant releases the pastor. Moral of story: The appropriate social unit—in this case, the *ekuó* acting through its elders—covers the individual's offense. The collective's honor is maintained in the eyes of the other collectives.
3. Two teenage girls are caught shoplifting in the village market. I see them pass my house, stripped down to their underwear, and bedecked with palm fronds, being forcibly paraded through the village streets by a noisy crowd of jeering young people. Public humiliation—the loss of honor—is the punishment of choice in shame cultures.

While Ezekiel sits in Babylon, awaiting news of the expected final catastrophe for his beloved city of Jerusalem, the oracle that we call Ezekiel 18 comes to him like a conceptual lightning bolt:

> The word of the LORD came to me: "What do you people mean by quoting this proverb about the land of Israel: 'The fathers eat sour grapes, and the children's teeth are set on edge'? As surely as I live," declares the Sovereign LORD, "you will no longer quote this proverb in Israel. For every living soul belongs to me, the father as well as the son—both alike belong to me. The soul who sins is the one who will die."

The rest of Ezekiel 18 is a complex elaboration of this opening principle, which would eventually become a foundation stone of Western society and thought, that of the concept of personal responsibility, the bedrock of guilt cultures.

In contrast to shame cultures, we view **guilt cultures** as promoting the individual's interior knowledge of having done wrong, regardless of whether others know of it. If the misdeed happens to be made public, shame will indeed be experienced as an emotion—but the individual is motivated less by this exterior loss of honor than by the interior knowledge of having done wrong. The society usually insists that the individual must pay for his own misdeeds, regardless of how bad this may make the society look in the eyes of others. It is no accident, for example, that the U.S. Department of the Treasury maintains a Conscience Fund, which receives freewill donations from taxpayers whose consciences attack them for having defrauded the government. Their sole motivation is the knowledge that their internal moral code has been violated, and the pressure they receive from a guilty conscience.

In guilt cultures we find an emphasis on punishment and forgiveness as the remedy for one's misdeeds. It also becomes conceivable that a single individual could oppose the entire community on a moral question and actually be in the right. Moreover, Christianity's focus on the individual's stance toward God would be unthinkable without this foundation of personal responsibility.

Did Ezekiel 18 produce an immediate revolution in Jewish thinking? Not at all. In fact, Ezekiel 19 is a lament over the fall of Jerusalem, and Ezekiel 20 strongly emphasizes that their ancestors had been unfaithful to YHWH as well. The succeeding chapters are equally condemnatory.

But a seed was sown in Ezekiel 18, one day making it possible for Christ to preach the Sermon on the Mount and stress one's individual stance vis-à-vis God: "Blessed are the gentle... Blessed are those who show mercy... Blessed are those who are persecuted in the cause of right" (Matthew 5:5–10); "Be careful not to parade your religion before others... When you give to the poor, do not announce it with trumpets... When you pray, go into a room by yourself and shut the door" (Matthew 6:1–6).

On the other hand, the New Testament does indeed speak of Christians together as "the body of Christ" and "the new Israel." Just maybe the genius of Christianity is that it places a high value on both the individual and the collective.

James N. Pohlig (D.Litt., Biblical Languages, University of Stellenbosch) has worked to analyze various West African languages, to bring literacy to them, to translate the Bible, and to author resources for Old Testament translators in general.

QUESTIONS

1. In what ways does the comparison between Ezekiel and modern-day "watchmen" shed new light on the prophet's message? Does Fink's last sentence sum up the matter perfectly or does it go too far?
2. How might one further extend the insights that Koller makes as a result of reading through the lens of contemporary psychology? How would a victim of child sex abuse react to this text? Should such a person be discouraged from even reading it?
3. Assess Steger's comparison of orphans in Bulgaria to Israel in Ezekiel 16. Does it help "put a face" on Israel?
4. Is your own culture (and perhaps subculture) primarily a shame or guilt culture? How does this lens help you see your own culture differently?

CHAPTER 15

JONAH

Mariel Pons compares the challenges and contradictions of her city, Buenos Aires, to Jonah's life context and work.

Jonathan Seitz reads Jonah as a missionary, comparing the biblical prophet to the cross-cultural challenges he faces ministering and living in Taiwan.

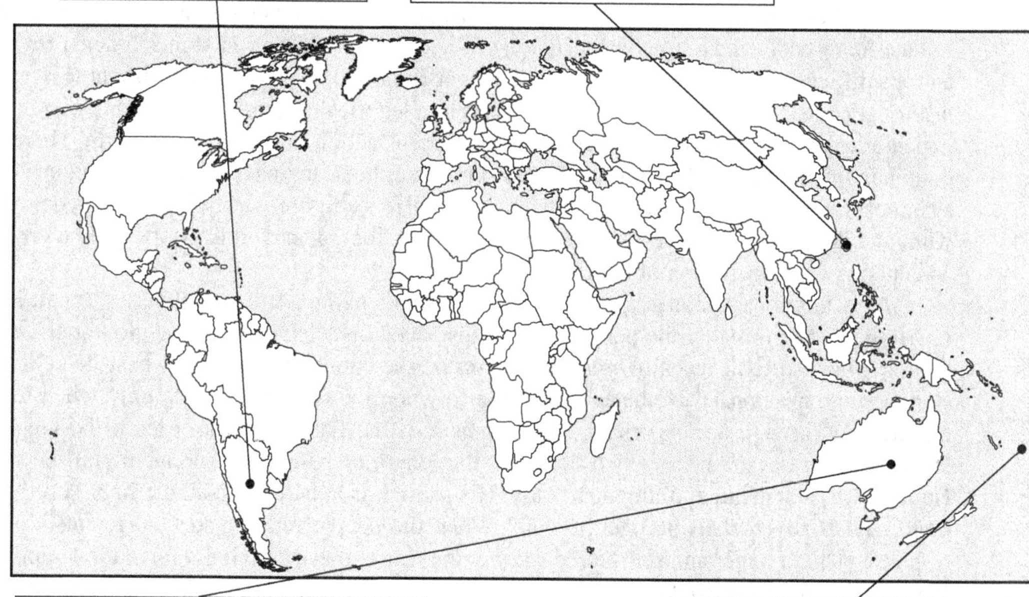

Jione Havea observes that the book of Jonah is full of surprises and reversals, the most notable of which is that Yhwh repents and decides to spare Nineveh.

Nāsili Vaka'uta, as an islander from Tonga, offers a reading of Jonah that is oriented toward the ocean *(moana)*, rather than away from it.

READINGS

Jonah as Missionary
Jonathan Seitz

A Tongan Island Reading of Jonah as Oriented toward the Ocean
Nāsili Vaka'uta

Jonah and the Challenges and Contradictions of Buenos Aires
Mariel Pons

Jonah as a Book of Surprises and Reversals
Jione Havea

Jonah as Missionary

Jonathan Seitz (Taiwan)

I did not expect to be "Jonah," but the name suits me. When I came to Taiwan to teach mission and religion, the president of my school gave me the Chinese name for Jonah. Where Jonathan abbreviates as "Jon" in English, it becomes "Jonah" in Taiwanese or Mandarin. Soon I took to joking that Jonah was the worst missionary in the Bible, but also the most successful, and I was not sure yet what type of Jonah I would be. However, as I have worn the name longer, I've come to see Jonah as an unflattering but often accurate portrait of mission and as a challenging foil for my work here. It has not been common to read Jonah as a missionary, but such a reading gives us new insights into Jonah the prophet and the challenges of mission today.

Theologians have almost always treated the story of Jonah allegorically, since it's so hard to take literally. We have to contort biology to keep Jonah stewing in stomach acids for days, and it's difficult to explain how such a vast conversion of Nineveh occurred without leaving any historical trace. Moreover, the story lends itself to allegorical interpretation, teeming with theological images of vengeance, disaster, repentance, resurrection, salvation, and rebirth. There's no dominant interpretation of Jonah, but he has sometimes been an image of the unrepentant Jew or a sign of warning and an example of what not to be. He's a figure starkly lacking in redemption, without a denouement that resolves the conflict, as in, for instance, Job. At the end he is sitting and cursing God's salvation of Nineveh.

As a missionary, Jonah's message is even more jarring. I like to think of Jonah as the archetype of bad mission, the patron saint of displaced preachers. He's not "missional," to use the new, faddish term recently created to describe the church's sending; at best he's "dismissional" or "remissional." He hates the people to whom he is sent. He goes only when forced, indeed only through the supernatural mechanism of the fish. He doesn't learn the language. He stays three days, during which he walks the length of Nineveh, denouncing all the while. He preaches judgment, and judgment only. His sermon is apparently a single line: "Forty days more, and Nineveh shall be overthrown!" When the people repent and God relents, Jonah's response is bitter anger and self-hatred for the role he has played in God's forced redemption of Nineveh. Jonah wishes that he had died instead of seeing his enemy saved. He reflects the worst tendencies of mission. The book of Jonah portrays the prophet-missionary as angry at God and Nineveh; he is moody and peevish and resentful of divine goodness given to others.

At the same time, Jonah shows God's great grace, which is also portrayed with comical hyperbole. Even animals are covered in sackcloth and every Ninevite turns to God. The God of the Israelites redeems their enemy, and God speaks clearly about God's love for all people: "And should I not be concerned about Nineveh, that great city, in which there are more than a hundred and twenty thousand persons who do not know their right hand from their left, and also many animals?" (4:11).

As a missionary, Jonah reflects a key duality: the recognition of human chauvinism and ethnic hatred and the affirmation of God's concern and grace. This duality is also reflected in our own cross-cultural work, where the missionary's primary task is to share God's grace, even though in daily life missionaries are inevitably stammering and confused. We are ordinary people who often take offense at the grace shown to others. In Taiwan, I'm keenly aware of the frailty of the missionary task, even as I admire its capacity to bridge cultures and provide new insights. Challenges are legion:

Incompetence A challenge of cross-cultural work is that we are constantly confronted with our difference. Language, custom, food, and celebration all change in a new context. Chinese is a famously difficult language for Westerners, with four tones and tens of thousands of characters. Taiwanese is in some ways even harder, with eight tones and many local oral traditions. Where the biblical Jonah shows no interest in the culture, language, or religion of daily life, most cross-cultural workers are deeply interested in these areas but limited by background and training.

Obsolescence I am a missionary serving at the Presbyterian seminary in Taipei. In the early twenty-first century, denominational mission has largely waned. The classical missionary apparatus has evaporated, and the few of us still related to the Presbyterian Church, the major Protestant church here, stay as guests. Where 2,000 Presbyterian missionaries served a generation ago, now there are 200 of us, mostly working in Presbyterian schools, churches, and hospitals. At my school, I am the youngest member of our faculty, and the least experienced. The church here does not *need* me.

Alienation I sometimes feel Jonah's sense of isolation and alienation, even though in truth we have a lot of support and many friends we can rely on here. One of the ironies of Christian expansion is that most Christians prefer to worship with those like themselves. Social scientists have noticed that while diversity may allow for pluralism and mutual respect, it often reinforces the sense of difference and may harden ethnic hatreds. Those living in multicultural contexts, ironically, are often more likely to distrust their neighbors. While we wish that living together automatically led to friendship, in reality it's never so simple.

Naivety and Disillusionment Mission faces many temptations. It is common to fetishize the place we live, to put a golden halo over it, but to largely ignore the differences. This may take the form of idealizing and simplifying local people, of becoming an uncritical advocate. The opposite side of such naivety is disillusionment or hatred. The honeymoon of early weeks of cross-cultural life may give way to an aggrieved or besieged mentality. Like Jonah, it's also possible to feel estranged and bitter. A not small number of missionaries leave after a short time, feeling defeated or abused, confounded by cultural difference. Many of us also aspire to "go native," to learn the language and culture and blend in. However, it's never that easy. Most of us struggle to become hybrid beings, ambivalent about our two cultures.

Jonah concludes with the prophet unconsoled. God, meanwhile, contrasts Jonah's anger with God's concern for humanity. God, seeing from all directions, replaces human anger with divine compassion. We find ourselves living and writing from one—or perhaps two or three—contexts that we know deeply, and yet most of the world remains off-limits to us. We may encounter this world superficially as consumers, readers, or travelers, but we rarely have a great depth of knowledge of any culture but our own. We may react with anger, as does Jonah, or sadness, fear, or even joy. Nonetheless, the book of Jonah concludes by reminding us that God's purview is greater than ours, and that while our human capacity often precludes forgiveness, much less compassion or love, God's grace extends even to the despised neighbor. For me, a wayward Jonah in a foreign land, the tale of the angry prophet, and a God who saves whole cities—even the animals—is good news.

Jonathan Seitz (Ph.D., Princeton Seminary) teaches at Taiwan Theological Seminary in Taipei as a Presbyterian Church (USA) mission coworker.

A Tongan Island Reading of Jonah as Oriented toward the Ocean

Nāsili Vaka'uta (Tonga)

Paddling across and around Jonah, I found myself caught up in two conflicting currents. One flows toward Nineveh, the other toward Tarshish. The "Nineveh orientation" calls for commitment and "obedience to the will of God, the same God who sent Jonah on his mission to Nineveh." This orientation resides in the claims of domination by one party and the need for submission by another. It involves imposition of one's interest and values upon others; it requires the suppression of other interests and values. It demands total "turning back" (conversion) from one's belief system and worldview. The current of the "Nineveh orientation" originates from either a divine command or action that directs toward an individual or a group. The "Tarshish orientation" stands in opposition to the "Nineveh orientation." It is one of resistance, confrontation, and departure. Its current originates from an attempt by an individual or a group to resist and depart from a dominant force, be it human or divine. Both currents, however, are oriented toward dry lands.

As an islander from Tonga, I am not interested in such orientations, because I am from a region (Oceania) that has more ocean space than land space. We perceive and value the ocean (the *moana*) differently from its portrayal in Jonah 1 and a large part of the Hebrew Bible. The *moana* in Jonah 1 is constructed as a destructive force, an instrument of God's wrath. It respects no one. It is there at the service of Yhwh, even if it means compromising the lives of innocent people (e.g., sailors), who do not deserve to suffer. The trouble at sea in Jonah 1 happens for one reason: to drive Jonah toward dry land, Nineveh. For that reason, I would like to offer an alternative reading; one that is oriented toward the *moana*, rather than away from it. I will attempt herein to give Jonah 1 a *moana* reading.

This *moana* reading is based on the following island insights. First, the *moana* (ocean), the huge watery space we call Oceania, is a shared home for islanders. It is a home that none of us owned; we all belong to it. Second, the *moana* largely defines our identity. Besides referring to ourselves as islanders, we are also proud to call ourselves at times "peoples of/from the ocean" (Tongan, *matu'a mei tahi*). Third, the *moana* is a source of food; it is our "oceanic garden." Fourth, the *moana* links islands together. It is not a boundary that divides, but one that connects islands and islanders. Fifth, the *moana* is an accommodating space, a place of difference. Oceania is home to different island cultures, yet they share a common watery heritage. Sixth, the *moana* is vast and deep. The vastness of the *moana* counters the continental (or land-based) view of islands as small, peripheral, and insignificant. The *moana*, the home to our islands, is immeasurable. The depth of the *moana* resists the common misunderstanding that anything is fathomable. One's view is *ipso facto* defined by one's limitations. To claim otherwise is an illusion.

This *moana* reading of Jonah 1 begins by acknowledging its limitations. First, the focus is strictly on the ocean space (the sea) as presented in the story, and all the events that happened therein. Second, I enter the story through that watery space; the space Jonah chose as his escape route away from Yhwh; the space Yhwh used to exhibit his might; the space where Jonah encounters the "people of the sea," the sailors. It is in that space that I sneak into the story, to listen to the conversations and to witness the unfolding of events. Third, I read as an Oceanic islander, but I do not speak for all Oceanians. As the *moana* is a space of difference, so is *moana* reading. It is always plural, multidimensional, and diverse. My reading is but one amongst many, and I can only read Jonah 1 through the limits of my eye/I as a Tongan.

What new insights, if any, can this *moana* reading bring out of Jonah 1? First, the ocean offers a different space of encounter. Boarding the Tarshish-destined ship, Jonah has the company of people who were different from him in terms of faith, and perhaps culture. The sea serves as a multireligious (and multicultural) space. Whereas in-land Yhwh demands conformity and conversion, everyone at sea worships his own god. The well-being of the whole group comes before promoting one's value and belief. In the midst of crisis, each person works for the common good. Second, we know very little about the identity of those at sea except that they are referred to as captain and sailors; they are "peoples of the ocean." Like islanders, the ocean is part of their lives. The ocean defines who they are.

Third, the ocean links and connects. Whereas in the story the ocean is seen as an instrument of Yhwh's wrath, a *moana* reading focuses on the connections and links that the ocean allows. Geographically, the ocean connects different places such as Israel and Tarshish (despite the obscurity of its location). Socially, it connects people together such as it does to those on the ship. Religiously, it brings different faiths together; even the sailors respect Jonah's deity. The ocean, despite the trouble Yhwh caused, accommodates the difference amongst the sailors themselves, and between them and Jonah. On dry land, however, that sense of belonging and accommodation is blurred by a demand to repent.

Fourth, the ocean serves as a space of freedom. If freedom means having the opportunity to make decisions for oneself, the ocean offers Jonah that opportunity. Instead of praying for help, he opts to sleep. Why would one ask for help from a deity who comes after him with terrifying force and aggression? Jonah's decision brings out two different perceptions of the divine. To the captain and sailors of the ship, the divine is a source of help, whereas in Jonah's case the divine is controlling, demanding, and requires conformity and unreserved respect for his sovereignty.

Fifth, and finally, the ocean, the *moana*, the watery space, offers Jonah a home away from dry land. When the crew suspected Jonah to be responsible for the situation at sea, they did not force him out of the ship. Nor did Jonah ask that he be saved. Instead, he made an odd request: "cast me into the sea." Two points are worth noting: (i) At sea, Jonah puts the well-being of others before his own, and (ii) like an islander, he prefers to make the ocean, the *moana*, his home, rather than going with the flow of the current toward Nineveh.

The story continues with the narrator's attempt to take Jonah on to dry land, out of the *moana*, toward Nineveh. However, as an islander, I would rather remain in the ocean—the place where difference is accommodated, and freedom is not compromised.

Nāsili Vaka'uta, a Tongan, is Lecturer in Biblical Studies and Oceanic Hermeneutics in the School of Theology at University of Auckland and Trinity Methodist Theological College, Auckland, New Zealand.

Jonah and the Challenges and Contradictions of Buenos Aires

Mariel Pons (Argentina)

Buenos Aires, La Boca, southern quarter in the great city, suburbs, harbor, sailors, immigrants, poverty, exclusion…church. We can apply this description to many of the cities in the world. Although the book of Jonah does not specifically describe the wickedness of the city of Nineveh, perhaps it was much like my city, Buenos Aires. We suffer from a large gap between the rich and the poor, which is especially difficult on the many poor children; increasing individualism without any authentic social relationships; abuse of the environment—both water and land; increased violence, especially against women; and a failure to love each other and God.

These contexts, like Jonah's, have their own contradictions. In light of these challenging circumstances, many times we choose the comfortable belly of the great fish. We hide in those safe places where we are surrounded by like-minded people. We think that we bring light to these dark spaces with our thoughts and our many words, all the while praying and recognizing and claiming a merciful, kind God—just like Jonah. But, like Jonah, we find it difficult to get out of our comfort zones, difficult to see the world in new and unexpected ways, difficult to truly share the love and mercy of God when it appears in surprising places and unanticipated ways. How many times do we fight the temptation of thinking that nothing can change; and then if something does change, we get annoyed, as if some great injustice has occurred? How many times without moving from our own quarter, our own world, are we in fact escaping to Tarshish?

One aspect in Jonah's story that draws our attention is the literal and metaphorical use of the number "three." Focusing on that number helps us to rethink our faith and the way to share it, but mainly the way to live it.

Jonah's actions occur in three scenarios: The first one is in the ship in his attempt to flee. Here, despite his resistance to heed the Lord's call, we see that Jonah is courageous enough to tell the truth when confronted by the sailors. He knows that he is the cause of the storm (1:9–10) and he knows what must be done in order for the storm to cease (1:12). He then finds himself inside the great fish for three days, where he recognizes the loving care of God. Jonah, it seems, has a conversion experience, as he now goes to Nineveh.

Second, Jonah arrives in Nineveh—a large city that takes three days to walk across. Interestingly, the text reports that Jonah went only one day's walk into the city before stating, rather tersely, that Nineveh will be destroyed. Surprisingly, the people of the great city, from king to animal, repent of their evil ways. In response, God too changes his thinking and decides not to destroy the city (3:10). So far, everyone has changed their thinking: Jonah, the Ninevites, and God.

But the third scenario provides yet another change. Under the pumpkin plant or *ricino*—a plant in which each leaf has three seeds—Jonah is unable to accept the fact that God has chosen to save Nineveh. He cannot deal with God's change of mind and the love and compassion that God shows to all of his creation—even the enemies of Israel. Jonah had proclaimed God's mercy in his prayer in the belly of the fish. But now he is not able to live what he had proclaimed. Instead, he is upset with God for showing love and mercy on the people of Nineveh; he even claims that he knew that God would save the city, which is why he fled in the first place (4:2). Jonah is so distraught that he wants to die (4:3); but he apparently still holds out "hope" that God will destroy Nineveh, as he sits down on a hill outside the city to see what will happen. He then becomes even more despondent when the plant that was shading him withers and dies. And he defends his right to be upset about the plant. In response, God asks Jonah a question, comparing Jonah's concern for the plant with God's concern of Nineveh. The book ends here. We do not know Jonah's answer. Does Jonah turn to the God who is able to be moved by his creatures or does he continue to be annoyed because he gives Nineveh the possibility of a new existence?

By ending in this fashion, the book of Jonah calls each of us to answer that question for ourselves and our communities of faith. Like Jonah, my context in Buenos Aires is complex and fraught with contradictions and challenges. As we wrestle with the ambiguities of life, we must actively listen to God's word and, at the same time, truly see the world around us and be moved by it.

The name Jonah means "dove." This recalls the dove that Noah sent out from the ark, a dove which announced a new earth, a fresh, clean start. It also anticipates the dove that descended on Jesus at his baptism, signaling that God was about to do something new in the world, that God's kingdom was breaking in on the messiness of life. The book of Jonah, concluding as it does with a question, calls us to given an answer. Will we live out the love of God in our own contexts of contradiction—even if that love does not always seem fair? In each of our realities we are asked for an answer. The decision is open.

Mariel Pons (B.S., Theological Studies) is a Pastor in the Evangelical Methodist Church, Argentina.

Jonah as a Book of Surprises and Reversals

Jione Havea (Australia)

Before Jonah arrives at Nineveh, the narrator expects readers to trust the judgment of Yhwh and so to believe that the Ninevites were a bad people who deserved to be crushed (1:1). Any half-decent reader, Jewish or otherwise, who is aware of the doings of the ancient Assyrian empire, whose capital was Nineveh, would concur. No one in her or his right mind dare speak up on behalf of Nineveh—just as today no one dare defend Nazi Germany. The bad guys, the enemies, deserve to be destroyed. But the book of Jonah is full of surprises and reversals.

The story indeed contains several incredible turns: a prophet does not follow orders, a sea rises and calms abruptly, a big fish swallows a man whole, a man survives in the belly of the fish for three days and three nights, a crew of believing sailors, and swiftly repentant city folks. Oh, so incredible! If those are incredible, difficult to accept as true, why should one accept Yhwh's perception of Nineveh? Why should one accept the narrator's portrayal of non-Hebrew sailors and Ninevites as if they were unthinking seaweed who drift to wherever the waves take them? If (literary) context matters, the incredible turns of events in the story problematize the very mission of Yhwh. In other words, Yhwh's perception of Nineveh is just as "too good to be true" as the story of Jonah is.

Surely, Yhwh can't be wrong! The story of Jonah has duped many readers on this very issue. Readers' allegiance to Yhwh, carried by thick theological clouds, veils their eyes from the one critical characterization of Yhwh in the story: Yhwh repents (Jon. 3:10). Divine repentance is not an unusual characterization of Yhwh in the Hebrew Bible. Before the great flood, Yhwh repents of having created humanity (Genesis 6:5–8) and the upshot was destruction. Later on in the wilderness, to the contrary, Yhwh repents of wanting to destroy the chosen people, deciding to spare them instead (Exodus 32:11–14). This time, Yhwh spares the Israelites. Similarly, but benefitting a different group of people, Yhwh repents and decides to spare Nineveh in the story of Jonah. If repentance is acknowledgment that one has made a mistake, in action and/or in perception, the same is true of Yhwh also. Indeed, Yhwh can be wrong!

Remarkably, Jonah claims that he knew from the outset that Yhwh was "ready to relent from punishing" (4:2). Thus, to follow Yhwh's command and go to Nineveh was an utter waste of his time, so Jonah set off for Tarshish instead. I consequently sympathize with Jonah because Yhwh permits the survival of the Assyrian empire—the wicked oppressors.

The story ends with Yhwh asking a question that could also be understood as a declaration: "And should I not be concerned about Nineveh, that great city, in which there are more than a hundred and twenty thousand persons who do not know their right hand from their left, and also many animals?" The final scene, then, is of an inconsolable and discomforted or, more appropriately, un-comfort-able Jonah. And rightly so, for Yhwh's repentance spares the capital of one of the empires that oppressed Jonah's people. Yhwh's compassion for Nineveh is good for Nineveh but problematic for Jonah and the Israelites. Readers are thus torn between looking out for the interests of Nineveh and identifying with the cause of Israel. The story of Jonah is fascinating in this regard, for readers are discomforted no matter with whom in the story they identify.

Jione Havea is Senior Lecturer at United Theological College and School of Theology at Charles Sturt University, Parramatta, NSW, Australia.

QUESTIONS

1. Seitz sees Jonah as a bad missionary. How could one rehabilitate Jonah's image?
2. What is the most compelling insight of Vaka'uta's *moana* reading? On what point(s) might it be challenged?
3. Evaluate Pons's connection between the wickedness of Nineveh and Buenos Aires.
4. Based on your particular social, cultural, and religious location, who are some of the people or groups for whom no one "in her or his right mind dare speak up"?

CHAPTER 16

MICAH 3, 6

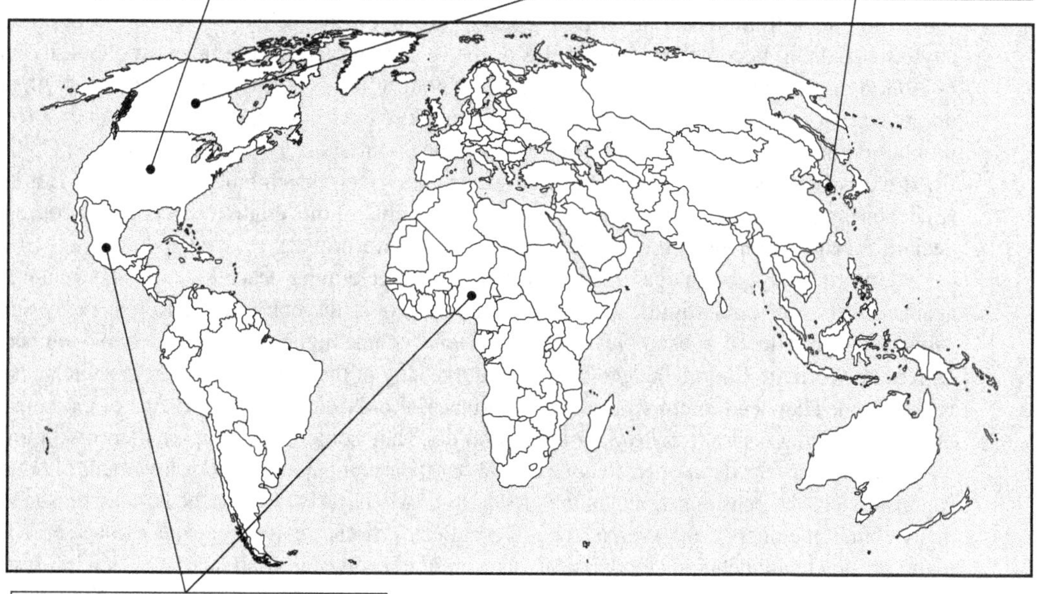
Rebecca T. Alpert inverts the order of Micah 6:8's three commands in light of her identity as a Jewish lesbian: love God/yourself, love others, seek justice.
Shannon E. Baines details the plight of the poor living in downtown Toronto and presents Micah 6 as a text of hope for them.
Hyung Won Lee reads God's accusation and punishment against the leaders of Israel in Micah 3:5–12 as a word of warning to greedy preachers in Korea.
James N. Pohlig explains the values and views of "The Image of Limited Good" societies and offers an interpretation of Micah 6 through that lens.

READINGS

MICAH 3 AS A WARNING TO GREEDY PREACHERS IN KOREA

Hyung Won Lee (South Korea)

Micah 3:5–12 is a part of God's accusation and punishment against the leaders of Israel and Judah in the eighth century B.C. It shows that the religious leaders, that is, the prophets and the priests, were just as responsible as the political and social leaders in keeping their countries just and holy. Their false leadership and sins result in the total devastation of the country and the agony of the people (3:12). Verses 5–6 describe the false prophets' twisted motives of greed or economic expediency. In order to achieve personal gain and materialistic abundance, their sole theme in preaching became that of peace "when there was no peace" (Jeremiah 6:14). The images of proclaiming "peace" to the congregation who give them delicious and nutritious foods "to bite with their teeth," while preparing to wage war against the ones who do not give anything to them, become vivid examples of the twisted motive of the false prophets. In verses 6–7, God announces harsh punishment against them: total darkness, no vision, no divination, no answer from God, and total shame and disgrace. Micah's own "vision statement" for his prophetic ministry in verse 8 indicates some of the essentials of being a true prophet: (1) being filled with divine power, justice, and might which are given through the Spirit of the Lord, and (2) declaring transgression and sin to the people. "Might" in this context refers to the courage to declare transgression and sin of the people without compromise.

Unfortunately, the image of the false prophets' proclaiming peace to some and waging war against others transcends time and space. In the context of the churches in Korea, many similar cases can be introduced as examples: Some ministers become highly sensitive every November and December when the Church budget (including the raising of the minister's salary) for the next year is discussed. They tend to emphasize the importance of providing for the servants of God, and the blessings which are sure to follow for those who do. They sometimes compare their own ministry with that of their friends in order to complain about their comparatively poor treatment in housing, car, insurance, and pensions. Some of the greedy ministers eagerly wait for the holiday season when many church members bring presents or gift certificates. Some revivalists expect to be served in a luxurious hotel with delicious foods as well as with brand new shirts and pants—which has become a custom. Reservation at a golf course during or after the revival makes them happy. Some of them are boastful of the expensive gifts they receive from the revival meetings at which they preached.

If they are treated well, they proclaim peace and divine blessings to the congregation. On the contrary, if their expectation is not met, they express their dissatisfaction in their sermons by proclaiming the themes of divine judgment and curse. In order to gain more offerings, the emphasis of the sermon is put on the materialistic blessings given to the one who offers to God wholeheartedly. In addition, some false preachers prophesy during the revival meeting that the Lord designated some rich elders or deacons to give a certain amount of money (usually a large sum) to the church or even a brand new car for the pastor. While this is not true of every minister, of course, it is a problem nonetheless.

The negative impact of greedy false preachers is enormous. Their preaching as well as greedy lifestyle becomes a bad witness of the true stewardship of Korean Christians in general. Church members have to bear severe financial burdens in order to satisfy the crooked desires of their leaders. In addition, the misuse of offerings results in the reduction of funds available to help the needy, evangelize nonbelievers, and perform overseas mission work.

Churches in Korea have been growing rapidly over the last 125 years since missionaries from the United States started churches, hospitals, and schools here. Currently, over 10 million people, one-fourth of the entire Korean population, are protestant Christians. There are around 50,000 protestant churches in Korea. Over 20,000 missionaries are sent out to other countries around the world. There are presumably many theological, sociological, and ecumenical reasons behind this rapid and steady growth. But one thing is for sure: The growth is the result of the faithfulness of Christian ministers who have served the people of Korea with a sincere motive like one the prophet Micah expressed: "I am filled with power, with the spirit of the Lord, and with justice and might, to declare to Jacob his transgression, to Israel his sin." While preparing and leading early-morning prayer meetings throughout the year, Christian ministers in Korea ask for the fullness of the Holy Spirit every day and its accompanying gifts of power, justice, and might. They also remind themselves of the "vision statement" as Micah expressed in 3:8.

There is a saying among Christian ministers in Korea handed down from their ministerial predecessors: "Be prepared to be hungry; be prepared to be moved to another church; be prepared to be martyred." This saying helps them to be alert when greed darkens their spiritual insight and personal gain interferes with their motives for ministry. It helps them to treat their congregation with justice and equality and to be cautious of the prejudices which hinder their just and righteous service to the people. It also helps them to be the contemporary "true" prophets of God not only by declaring transgressions and sins of the congregation but also by providing true repentance for them.

Micah 3:5–8 is a crucial passage for contemporary ministers around the world. It teaches Christian leaders what to avoid (greed), what to expect when they become false preachers (total spiritual darkness, no vision, no divination, no answer from God, and full of shame and disgrace), and what to remember in their daily ministries (the necessity of the fullness of the Lord and its gifts and the solemn calling of preaching the Word of God without compromise).

Hyung Won Lee is Professor of Old Testament at Korea Baptist Theological University/Seminary, Dae Jeon, Korea.

A Jewish Lesbian Interpretation of Micah 6:8

Rebecca T. Alpert (United States)

Micah 6:8 offers an ideal framework for examining Jewish lesbian concerns. Here the prophet summarizes his understanding of "what is good" as follows: "Do justice, love well, and walk modestly with God." Micah's threefold precept suggests three areas of particular concern: how to live with and present oneself in the world (how to walk modestly with God), how to establish social relationships (how to love well), and how to make the world a better place (how to do justice). My interpretation inverts the order of Micah's precept. Micah culminates with the individual's relationship with God in keeping with his theocentric (God-centered) worldview. From my human-centered perspective, I begin with the individual's relationship with God, expressed through her relationship with herself. It is this relationship that enables her to love others, and then to translate that love into acts of justice for all humanity, which is for me the ultimate goal.

The process begins where Micah ends, with the enigmatic phrase, "walk humbly with God." I interpret this statement to be about the way an individual understands her own place in the world. I assume that the way in which a person approaches her own life will determine her ability to behave ethically toward others. A central Jewish precept demands that we love our neighbors as ourselves. Commentators have understood this to mean that we can only learn to love our neighbors if we learn to love ourselves.

Walking with God is a metaphor for the way each person approaches her own life. It is a way to conceptualize one's innermost feelings and thoughts. It is not necessary to hold a traditional concept of God, or to imagine God in human form, to appreciate this metaphor. To see oneself walking with God requires a vision of God as the most important value in life, which is with us always and everywhere. God may be in the image of a human being, but God could also be a power, force, feeling, idea, or anything that helps one perceive holiness in the world.

As Jewish lesbians, we begin with the assumption that we can only walk with God if we know and accept ourselves for who we are. Walking with God requires self-knowledge. Those who walk with God know their way and consciously claim a path in the world. They are guided by the understanding that all human beings are holy, having been created in God's image. They respect the mysterious process, whether it derives from nature or society that makes them women who are erotically attracted to other women and who prefer to build their lives with each other. This is not an easy task to accomplish. I share my own coming out story as an example.

I grew up knowing that I was strongly attracted to members of my own sex. But everything I saw in society—movies, popular songs, my parents' relationship, Bible stories—pointed to heterosexuality as the norm. I often had crushes on girls and women teachers and had sexual relationships with girlfriends in high school. Yet as an adolescent I would never have called myself a lesbian; I assumed I was going through a stage. When I was growing up, lesbians were found in bars, underground magazines, and pulp novels. They were assumed to be poorly adjusted women who wanted to be men, not courageous women who dared to be different. I did not want to be one of them.

For me, focusing on my Jewish identity provided a perfect alternative to exploring my sexual identity. I married, became a rabbi, and had two children. Despite my wishes to the contrary, the strong erotic attraction I felt toward women never left me. At some point it became clear to me that I needed to make a choice. It was then that I left my marriage and developed a primary relationship with a woman.

Coming out to myself, calling myself a lesbian, was not an easy thing to do. I had achieved status and visibility in the Jewish world as a rabbi, and I was afraid that if I came out I would be forced to give that up. I was concerned that people I had worked with would be uncomfortable around me or that they would no longer respect my ideas and judgments.

But at a certain point I developed a strong conviction that it would be better if people knew, and that I couldn't worry if they did or not. I came out because I got tired of hiding and lying; it had a corrosive effect on my soul. In coming out I experienced a sense of pride in being a lesbian. I gained peace of mind and a sense of freedom unattainable in the closet.

The second part of Micah's precept is about loving well. Loving is the connection we make to others, whether in intimate or social relationships. Loving well in social relationships means respect for the other person; loving those with whom we are intimate involves passionate feelings and intense closeness in addition to respect. Loving well forms the link between individual self-acceptance (walking modestly with God) and universal justice. We cannot love others unless we accept ourselves. And we cannot bring justice to a world where people do not know how to treat others with whom they are in relationships.

While loving well is applicable to heterosexuals and lesbians alike, the concept raises issues that are particular to lesbian lives. There are differences in the ways that lesbians create loving networks with people around us. Lesbians also have a different perspective on coupled relationships and on the bearing and raising of children. Looking at the subject of loving through a lesbian lens contributes a new perspective to the ongoing Jewish conversation about human relationships.

Typically, Jewish families are created through biological ties, institutionally sanctioned marriage, adoption, and conversion. Jews inherit or claim a place in the Jewish community. We may choose to belong to a different religious or secular community from our family of origin, but for most of us, our primary connections to Judaism are set in our early lives.

Lesbian connections are not based on biological ties. Like converts to Judaism, most lesbians are not raised by parents who share our orientation. Unlike converts, the children we raise are mostly not like us either. Our lesbian family is a loosely defined network that incorporates our parents, children, and other family members who are willing to support us along with friends, former lovers, and members of their families.

It is imperative that the Jewish community comprehend and support the new concept of family that is derived from the context of Jewish lesbian existence. Changing the concept of family also demonstrates the need for new forms and rituals to celebrate our lives.

I now end where Micah began, with "doing justice." The commitment to do justice requires us to go beyond our own lives and to look at larger issues in the world around us. In the conception of Micah's precept that I describe here, these efforts are intrinsically interconnected. We cannot make a choice between accepting ourselves, caring for our circle of loved ones, and doing justice in the world. These efforts must be woven into one framework.

What, then, is the justice that we seek? Our goal is to live in a world where every person has what it takes to satisfy basic human needs: food, clothing, and shelter. Where every person has the opportunity for health care, safety, education, and work. Where all people have the opportunity to participate in decisions that affect their lives. Where nations do not make war against one another. And where the planet itself, and all that lives on it, is treated with dignity and respect. These are the goals of a just society.

When we work for justice, we do it as Jewish lesbians. It is important that we maintain our cultural heritage and identity, and bring the wisdom that this heritage provides into our work in the world. Guided by Micah's precept we have a set of goals to work toward: Begin with self-acceptance, continue with love within our close communities, and reach beyond ourselves to demand and create a world within which there is justice for everyone. These goals are not for lesbian Jews only. This is a model for the transformation of Judaism from a lesbian perspective that derives from our interpretation of the biblical text.

Rebecca T. Alpert (Rabbi) is Associate Professor of Religion at Temple University, Philadelphia, Pennsylvania, United States.

MICAH AND HOPE FOR TORONTO'S POOR

Shannon E. Baines (Canada)

I will provide a reading of Micah 6 from the perspective of the poor living in a densely populated neighborhood in downtown Toronto where alcoholism, drugs, prostitution, violence, and poverty are visible to the naked eye. This will be based on my firsthand experience as a frontline resource worker at an inner-city Christian mission which helps people to participate more fully in society.

The poor come in many shapes, colors, and sizes in this tightly knit community. Whether children in households have one parent/guardian or both parents present, these families work hard to try to make ends meet. Many people, including senior citizens and those with physical and mental disabilities, depend on government assistance for survival. While people who are fortunate enough to attain subsidized housing tend to reside there over the long term, others wait patiently for affordable housing units to become available. In the meantime, they live with friends or family, in rooming houses, or small, cramped apartments, sometimes in substandard conditions. As an alternative, there are a few homeless shelters in the area, which are usually quite full on any given night.

The area has a high population of immigrants who have come to Canada seeking a better future for their families, only to find themselves working long hours in jobs that do not necessarily utilize skills acquired in their home countries. For those immigrant families that are fortunate enough to establish themselves financially, they leave this area and move to safer neighborhoods in the city or even further out into the suburbs. One can hardly blame parents for wanting a better standard of living and a better environment to raise their children. The lure of drugs, gangs, prostitution, criminal activity, and violence looms in the streets, alleyways, schoolyards, parks, and lobbies of apartment buildings day and night.

Some officials impose suffering on the poor living in this inner-city neighborhood. It could be the social assistance worker who treats the single mother poorly, without dignity and respect, and either fails to inform her of the full range of benefits that she and her child are entitled to under the government program or delays receipt of these benefits. Some employers discriminate against people living in the neighborhood by passing over their employment applications. Police enforcement in the area is rather severe and unfair especially in dealing with the youth. Municipal authorities and developers are working to improve the inner-city neighborhood through regentrification, but their plans displace some of the poor either temporarily or permanently to other parts of the city where services are more limited.

The poor not only experience suffering by institutions and authorities but also by members of their own community. Whether it is the local crack-addicted prostitute who is trapped by her addiction and the controlling, violent pimp who won't let her go free or the senior citizen who is rightly afraid to venture out after dark for fear of being attacked. Landlords provide a slow or nonexistent response to urgent repair requests for basic water and heat. Tenants who cannot afford to move into better accommodations are forced to live in these circumstances.

The poor have suffered much more than has been briefly mentioned here. But today they have entered into a local courthouse to hear a case that is of utmost importance to their lives. Ironically, they are not there in support of a friend or family member, as is often the case, but have come to witness an almost inexplicable historical event. The small courtroom where this case is being held is packed beyond capacity.

What is so special about this particular case that has attracted so much attention in this community? People who have treated the poor unfairly in any way are on trial and are being called to give an account of their actions before the almighty God. Apparently, these defendants should have known to seek justice, enact mercy, and walk humbly with God (Mic. 6:8), but they did nothing that was required of them. Witnesses have been called to provide testimony to the injustices that they have inflicted on the poor. These are no ordinary witnesses. They are absolutely impeccable in their credibility and have been in existence for a long time, watching and listening to every word and deed of these defendants. Countless stories of abuse, oppression, and injustice of every kind imaginable are being vividly retold. The evidence is overwhelming. God cannot and will not let any of these perpetrators go unpunished, for they have been judged guilty in all respects. Though the exact nature of the sentence has yet to be determined, the reaction of the poor as they witness the trial is overwhelming: joy, exuberance, and shouts of celebration pour out into the hallways of the courthouse. The windows and doors cannot contain their excitement.

Finally, after many years of either silent suffering or voiced frustration, justice has prevailed. This is real justice stemming from God which convicts the perpetrators and puts an end to the suffering of the poor. There is renewed hope of real restoration in the lives of thousands of poor people in this community. The native Canadian or the disabled person on social assistance will now soon be diagnosed and treated adequately with the utmost dignity and respect. The single father working multiple jobs to make ends meet will soon be able to spend time with his children instead of leaving them alone, susceptible to the lure of gangs. Many young people who have been stereotyped by authority figures will soon be treated fairly with all false accusations being dropped. Whether it is the fear and shame of being teased and bullied or other forms of violence, locals will soon be able to go about living their lives in a safe environment. The prostitute who has been struggling for years to break away from her pimp is finally free to seek a better quality of life. The countless families who have struggled to attain adequate work and pay will be able to provide for themselves and even help their neighbors. The coveted subsidized daycare spaces which have been so limited for poor-income families will become abundantly available, thus freeing up time for parents to attain meaningful employment or pursue educational dreams during the day.

In sum, Micah 6 can provide hope for the poor who experience injustice, suffering, and oppression—hope that one day their situation will improve. In the midst of daily suffering, the poor who have committed their lives to God know that God is close at hand, hears their prayers, and will give them strength and courage to persevere. At the same time, Micah 6 can inspire us not only to act justly towards the poor but also to become an advocate on their behalf. We are called to intervene and help the poor because they often do not have the knowledge, resources, power, influence, or voice to defend themselves. A reading from this perspective sensitizes us to the reality of suffering and God's justice, and provides a glimpse into how peoples' lives and communities may be restored.

Shannon E. Baines is a Ph.D. candidate at McMaster Divinity College, Hamilton, Ontario, Canada.

"The Image of Limited Good" in Relation to Micah

James N. Pohlig (Nigeria, Mexico)

Micah 6 is part of a metaphorical legal charge that YHWH brings upon Israel, his covenant community. He had brought the nation up from Egypt, releasing them from slavery. He had given them leaders to explain his pact with the new nation: that he would be their God and that they would worship and follow him. One part of the agreement with the nation was that Israel would act as a just society by following YHWH's covenantal laws.

What is the American notion of justice? Surely there is a heavy individualistic bias to our version of justice. It is for this reason that, when Micah 6:8–15 calls for justice among God's covenant people, we see this call as an emphasis on the individual's rights vis-à-vis the rest of society, especially the organized, influential, and powerful parts of society. Democracy, after all, seems to depend on the sincere belief of the vast majority in society that everyone has the same rights before the law as the next person. On the economic level, Americans are not willing to see fellow citizens starve or suffer unnecessarily in other ways. But we still do not tend to condemn vast differences in personal wealth. Bill Gates is admired, not generally condemned.

However, American anthropologist George M. Foster presented in 1965 a theory that he named "The Image of Limited Good" (ILG), which he applied to so-called "peasant societies"—societies that are for the most part closed to economic growth from outside themselves. Foster and others had observed that in various regions of the world, many such societies seemed to view things of value—and not only material goods!—as existing in limited quantities, and never enough to satisfy everyone's wants, at least for very long. This proposed cultural view is seen as producing significant effects, as shown in the following examples.

In southeastern Nigeria in the 1950s, an American church established a seminary at which eventually a local Nigerian became the first national professor. Because of his salary, he became the first in his village to have electric lights at home and to own an automobile. But one day he was put on trial as a witch by his village. Fortunately, he survived the experience; not all accused witches do. Moral: A sudden increase in wealth is often viewed with suspicion in ILG societies, on the assumption that the culprit has acquired more than his fair share of goods. If one's economic position significantly improves because of employment or relationships *outside* the community, this event tends to be regarded in a better light; it is evident, after all, that the villager has not taken more than his share of *local* wealth. In this situation with the professor, however, such was not the case.

In Huautla, in southwestern Mexico, Mazatec women are (or should be) known for the exquisite embroidery on their clothes. When American linguist Eunice Pike asked one of the women, "Who taught you how to do this?" the answer came back, "I just know how." Again, when she asked a village baker how he had learned to bake bread, she was told, "I just know." Pike could find no Mazatec who would acknowledge to have learned anything from another villager. Moreover, Pike once taught a Mazatec woman to read her newly written down language. At the woman's request, Pike then taught her eldest daughter. When she desired to teach the next daughter as well, Pike suggested that the mother teach her, but she shied away from doing so. Several children learned to read from Pike, but they themselves steadfastly refused to teach others. Pike eventually deduced that within ILG societies, one cannot appropriate another's know-how without being considered as stealing it (from Eunice V. Pike, 2008, "The Concept of Limited Good and the Spread of the Gospel." Forum of Bible Agencies International. Available online).

In addition, Foster ("Peasant Society and the Image of Limited Good," in *American Anthropologist*, 1965 [67:2]: 293–315) offers the following examples.

1. In Tzintzuntzan, Michoacán, Mexico, land is increasingly limited because of population growth. No villager has enough land to become wealthy by farming, only enough to hopefully eat throughout the year. Even the best of human interrelationships—friendship, affection, and love—seem to be jealously guarded. On one occasion, Foster brought a villager to his own home in California. Near the end of his stay, his guest told him that his brother was working nearby, but that he did not want to give him any of his own joy in being in Foster's home.

2. Among the Buganda, the largest ethnic group in Uganda, a woman does not want to become pregnant if she has not yet weaned her previous child. There is a risk of the unborn baby being jealous of its elder sibling and poisoning the mother's milk in revenge.
3. In rural Mexico, it seems common for men to feel their masculine nature to be threatened if their wives want a share of their authority at home. Every wife should be beaten once in a while, to reinforce the point that the male is in charge.

Peasant societies said to possess the ILG tend to have coping mechanisms in common. For example, an unexpected financial windfall is liable to be spent in throwing a huge feast for the village. In the ILG view, this villager is preempting accusations of undue greed by "giving" the money back to the community. Again, leadership roles tend not to be willingly accepted, because one's increase in prominence might have an unsettling effect on local harmony: After all, there is only so much prestige to go around.

What would a reasonable ILG interpretation, therefore, of our Micah 6 passage look like?

- "To act justly" (6:8): Justice amounts to not wanting more than your fair share of what is good, whether it is tangible or not. Humbleness is simply knowing your proper place and sticking to it.
- "your ill-gotten treasures" (6:10): How is gain dishonest? When it is made at the expense of the others in the community, leading to a breakdown in community harmony.
- "dishonest scales [and] a bag of false weights" (6:11): Dishonest scales and weights are bad, not primarily because they violate the truth, but because they enable unequal accumulation of wealth at others' expense, thereby endangering community peace.
- "her rich men are violent" (6:12): The rich men are violent because ILG assumes that *it is through violence that they became rich*. Westerners would likely regard this "violence," as do some commentators, to be a disregard for the law, which may show up as the seizure of another person's property, as giving false witness in court, or as bribing judges, other civic leaders, or priests. But ILG communities will regard violence here as first and foremost the undue appropriation of more than one's equitable share of a good.
- "Therefore, I have begun to destroy you, to ruin you because of your sins" (6:13–15): God's judgment will fall on a society like this in the most characteristic form imaginable—there will be even a greater shortage of the limited good than ever.

James N. Pohlig (D.Litt., Biblical Languages, University of Stellenbosch) has worked to analyze various West African languages, to bring literacy to them, to translate the Bible, and to author resources for Old Testament translators in general.

QUESTIONS

1. How does Lee determine true from false prophets/pastors? How might his criteria be assessed?
2. Explain why Alpert inverts the order of Micah 6:8. Which one is "better"—Alpert's version or the biblical version?
3. If you were in charge of improving the conditions described by Baines in Toronto, how would you go about it? Would religion or religious ideas factor into your equation?
4. How does the notion of an ILG society help to analyze the dynamics of your own culture? Are there instances in your context where people think and act as if goods and resources are unlimited?

CHAPTER 17

PSALM 22, 23, 42, 148

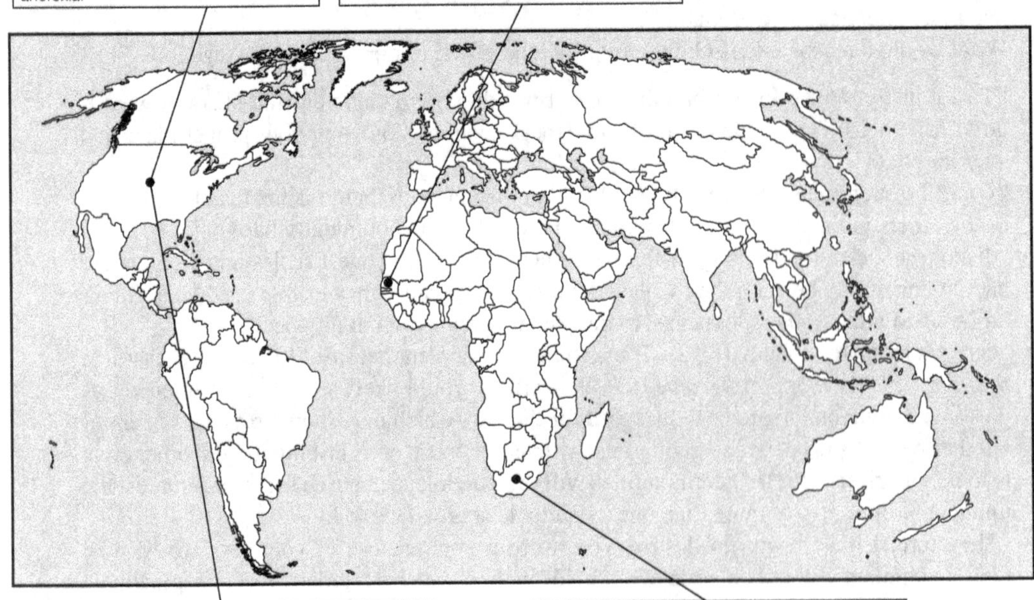
Amy Lambert comments on the opening verses of Psalm 42 from the perspective of those who struggle with the eating disorder anorexia.
Danielle Smith reads the shepherd metaphor of Psalm 23 in light of her knowledge of West African shepherds and through a Christian lens.
David Aftandilian reads Psalm 148 in light of the Native American idea of other animals as people like us, capable of sensing and relating to the divine.
Zacharias Kotzé shows how Psalm 22 is naturally understood in Africa as a spell against the attacks of a witch who is responsible for physical illness.

READINGS

Psalm 22 as an African Spell
Zacharias Kotzé

A Christian Reading of Psalm 23 and West African Shepherds
Danielle Smith

Psalm 42 and Anorexia
Amy Lambert

Psalm 148 and the Native American View of Animals
David Aftandilian

Psalm 22 as an African Spell

Zacharias Kotzé (South Africa)

Psalm 22 is one of many prayers of lament in the book of Psalms. It became famous in the Christian tradition because Jesus quotes its opening lines on the cross: "My God, my God, why have you forsaken me?" Much of its content constitutes complaints against an obscure enemy, and is therefore also called an enemy psalm. Interestingly, the enemy is described by means of animal imagery in verses 13–17, which has intrigued European and Western scholars. Although I am of European descent, I would like to attempt an interpretation of the enemy in Psalm 22 from a traditional African perspective.

Although many Africans have become Westernized, the majority still make use of traditional methods in dealing with illness, misfortune, and death. Like the peoples of the ancient Near East, Africans traditionally ascribe hardship and trouble to evil forces. More specifically, it is believed that certain people have the ability to cause harm through the practice of witchcraft. As a result, most Africans have a perceived enemy who is held responsible for all evil that befalls them. Even feared illnesses, such as HIV/AIDS, are commonly ascribed to powerful witches. In order to protect themselves against magical attacks, Africans go to a traditional healer who furnishes them with spells and herbal remedies for their protection. In addition to traditional African spells, some Africans also use the Psalms as incantations in an attempt to secure health, wealth, and good fortune. Viewed from an African perspective, Psalm 22 may be interpreted as a spell against the witch who is held responsible for a severe physical illness in the supplicant, particularly one that involves loss of bodily fluid.

Viewed from a European perspective, the psalmist's description of his infirmities is obscure: "I am poured out like water, and all my bones are out of joint; my heart is like wax; it is melted within me. My strength is dried up like a potsherd, and my tongue cleaves to my jaws; and you lay me in the dust of death" (vv. 14–15). In verse 17 the supplicant further says that one can count all his bones. No doctor would be able to make a diagnosis from the above description of suffering, but it is clear that the psalmist emphasizes the motif of dryness. This is evident from the images of water pouring out, the melting of the heart and intestines, and the dryness of a potsherd and dust. In the ancient Israelite worldview, dryness is associated with weakness. Similarly, the Sothos living on the hot, arid plateau of the South African Highveld, for example, would use images of dryness to describe discomfort. In short, dry is bad.

Interestingly, the psalmist seems to ascribe his illness/discomfort to the attack of his enemies. The above description is enclosed by references to animals attacking the supplicant in verses 12–13, and then again in verse 16: "Many bulls have surrounded me; strong bulls of Bashan have encircled me. They gaped open wide their mouths, as a ravening and roaring lion...For dogs have surrounded me; a band of evildoers has encompassed me; they pierced my hands and my feet." In their interpretation of these verses, some scholars have pointed to the numerous depictions of dangerous deities and demons as animals in the iconography of the ancient Near East. On a cylinder seal from Uruk in ancient Mesopotamia, for example, the "bulls of the pit" are depicted with the bodies of bulls, snake-like necks, and the gaping mouths of ravenous lions, much like the description of the "bulls of Bashan" in verse 13. Incidentally, "Bashan" is sometimes used as a synonym for "Yam," or "Rahab"—the ophidian sea-monster as Yahweh's enemy—in the Psalms. However, in view of the fact that the enemy is described in both human and animal terms, the majority of interpreters view the references to animals as metaphors for the strength and ferocity of the psalmist's human enemies.

From an African perspective, however, the mixture of animal and human elements is commonly associated with the witch. For example, in South Africa, it is believed that the Pedi night-witches transform into animals at night and go around scavenging. In the South African Lowveld, witches are thought to have the ability to combine elements of various animals, as well as humans, to take on the form of monsters with superhuman strength. Witches are suspected of meeting up with other witches at night, not only to go around stealing but also to cause illness by feeding on humans. It may be significant that the Zulus call HIV/AIDS *isidliso*, a word that is derived from the Zulu word for "to eat." In Nigeria, too, witches claim that they drink human blood day and night. From a traditional African perspective, therefore, the enemy in Psalm 22 may be viewed as a monster-like witch familiar in spiritual form who eats away on the flesh of the supplicant.

Some scholars have suggested that the Psalms contain magical formulas that were used as protection in ancient Israel. In this view, the psalms originally constituted incantations against demonic forces and witchcraft before they were reinterpreted by later editors who tried to rid them of their superstitious nature and dress them in a Yahwistic cloak. Still, traces of magical formulas can be detected. Psalm 22 is addressed to the "hind of the dawn" (v. 1). The Hebrew word for "hind" also refers to an ancient Canaanite moon-goddess type who was commonly invoked in spells. Also, the word for "dawn" is the Hebrew equivalent of the Ugaritic name of a well-known protector god associated with the dawn in the Ugaritic texts of Ras-Shamra. Not surprisingly, the word is associated with protective magic in the Old Testament. Similar to the peoples of the ancient Near East, Africans believe in the power of words and names. Many of their spells include various names of deities that are to be repeated several times. From an African perspective, the prayer in verses 19–20 may be regarded as an invocation to the deity who is called "my Strength."

Psalm 22 constitutes a remarkable text with a long history of development and interpretation. The words that Jesus quoted from the cross and the motif of enemies dividing the psalmist's clothes have captured the attention of Christians from a Western background. For those Africans who seek in the Psalms magical elements for everyday use, however, the psalm is most naturally used as a spell against the attacks of the witch who is believed to be responsible for some physical illness involving dehydration.

Zacharias Kotzé (Ph.D.), an Afrikaans-speaking South African, is a postdoctoral research fellow in Old Testament and Ancient Near Eastern Studies at the University of Northwest, South Africa.

A Christian Reading of Psalm 23 and West African Shepherds

Danielle Smith (Senegal)

My first memories as a child are of my life in West Africa. Although I was born in the United States, at 10 months of age my family moved to Sierra-Leone as missionaries. In 1997 we moved to Senegal and I spent the majority of my formative years in the northern part of that country where nomadic lifestyles were the norm. This setting has deeply impacted how I now view the Bible.

A theme of shepherding is woven throughout the Psalms, including the well-known Psalm 23, in which David compares God, the shepherd-king, to an earthly shepherd watching over his flock. In Western Africa there is a nomadic people called the Peul, who are known for their Bedouin lifestyle as keepers of cattle, sheep, and goats. Their livestock is the measure of wealth and social status. For them, shepherding is more than work or tradition; it is a way of life that offers meaning and purpose. Shepherding consumes them to the point that, when grass becomes sparse, they move their entire clan and all their belongings to the next location in hopes of better fields. In comparing God to a shepherd, we recognize that God is with His people and that He is always looking out for them, even when such care creates an inconvenience for God Himself. To be a shepherd is a sacrifice, a sacrifice not only of time and effort but of safety.

A well-known African proverb says, "That which does not kill a shepherd never kills the whole herd." The caretaker is the first line of defense and he is trained to let absolutely nothing get past him. As long as he is alive, he will fight the predator in order to save his sheep. To me, this shows that in the same way, God does not give up on His children; He fights for them and even gave His own son's life to save them. A shepherd would never knowingly or intentionally lead his flocks into danger (v. 3). Like the Peul, God plans everything around His flock; He leads His sheep down the safest paths to protect them from eternal death and suffering.

In sub-Saharan Africa, water and greenery tend to be sparse and sand is found in an overabundance. To remain healthy, shepherds have to find food and water for their livestock even during the dry seasons when rivers and lakes dry up. To not be in want (v. 1) does not imply comfort, but necessity; we are not promised the best or easiest life, but rather to be provided for if we follow our Shepherd. As sheep we are vulnerable, weak, and do not know how to take care of ourselves. Sheep blindly follow their shepherd and they obey all his commands without questions or hesitation. Occasionally, while driving in the rural areas of West Africa, you may find flocks of sheep unattended, roaming around. They know their way home, but during the day they may wander about wherever they please. Because of this, many sheep are killed by oncoming traffic while crossing the road. This is a picture of the sheep that have walked astray, who know where they should be but, without their shepherd's guidance, fall into traps. How often in the Old Testament is Israel presented as electing to follow false shepherds instead of Yahweh? Their lives, like those of the wandering sheep in Africa, become casualties of injustice, violence, and depravation and they represent the stark consequences of living outside the care of the Good Shepherd.

There is hope for us, however, when we walk through these difficult and dark times because God is still with those who follow Him. In verse 4 we read, "Even though I walk through the valley of the shadow of death, I will fear no evil, for You are with me." A shepherd is with his sheep not in a theoretical way, but in a tangible, real way and there is no greater proof of this real love than the coming of Jesus into this world. He was dedicated to his cause—suffered rejection, ridicule, and mocking from humans, yet still risked his life to save us. He was the Good Shepherd (John 10:11) who, unlike the hirelings, laid down His life in the face of danger. Shepherds cannot be cowards, running at the first sign of distress. They must be brave and, above all, ready, vigilant at all times to defend their sheep; they must be willing to suffer pain in order to save just one little lamb. In the final verse of this Psalm, David reveals the overarching theme of the chapter about the need for us as God's sheep to wholeheartedly follow the true Shepherd in trusting obedience. Unlike those exposed to danger by blindly wandering through life, David reminds us that the life of the faithful will be marked by goodness and love.

If we trust, He will guide. He will not abandon us in the face of death because His paths are safe. He will not deliver us to our enemies; rather He will anoint our heads with oil. He comforts and guides. He provides and it overflows. Most of all, He welcomes us one day to live forever in the Great Shepherd's house.

Danielle Smith spent her early life in Senegal and is currently studying cultural anthropology in the United States.

PSALM 42 AND ANOREXIA

Amy Lambert (United States)

In recent American culture, there is a perpetual focus upon food: the good and bad foods, the diet plans around food, how to prepare food, how to eat this food versus that food, and how to eat the foods you want and still lose weight. And the list continues on. In the midst of this societal craving, a group of people stay hidden behind this socially acceptable mask: those who struggle with an eating disorder called anorexia. It is through this lens that I wish to comment on Psalm 42.

Anorexia nervosa is an eating disorder in which an individual becomes obsessed with her weight and the intake and output of food. A person who struggles can be severely underweight and still restrict her nutritional intake in order to lose more weight. As the disease progresses, the mind is literally consumed with thoughts on food. However, the current environment of diet mentality in America creates a space for such individuals to hide within plain sight.

Throughout the starvation process, an anorexic learns ways to dim the body's hunger cues. Though an anorexic may feel hungry, over time, those cues are dulled and the ability to recognize hunger and the body's needs are also undone. As the stomach shrinks and the body's processes slow down, an anorexic can honestly say, "I am not hungry" despite the fact that she may not have eaten for days. A young anorexic woman once wrote in her journal to God:

> To eat again, after fasting for days and weeks leaves me feeling nauseous and sick. It is so disgusting that food is put in front of me and I recoil. The mere whiff of food turns my stomach. It seems at this point that starving would be easier than the painful reintroduction of food. I even spat out my communion wafer last week because it caused me to gag to have a foreign object in my mouth. People keep asking in complete shock—aren't I hungry? It takes everything not to laugh at their foolish ignorance.

Whereas hunger can dim over a time of starvation, thirst only becomes more intense as the body has no water. It is medically known that a body can go weeks without food, but fatal dehydration can occur in three days if the body has no water. An anorexic is well aware of her thirst, and she also knows that with enough liquid, she can temporarily drown her hunger and maintain her life. It is here that liquids become lifesaving. For an anorexic, because there is such a lack in proper amount of nutrition, the body becomes dehydrated more quickly than under normal circumstances. The young woman again pens to God:

> My body…my weakened heart and kidneys…my bones…my mind…my very soul thirsts though. My thirst is never satisfied. It is barely quenched these days. The less I eat and the longer I drink diet sodas in order to create a deceitful semblance of energy—the stronger the intensity becomes. Even when I drink water incessantly, it vanishes instantly as though I have not even put the glass to my lips. I wish this pain would go away—the way my emotions are numbed because of no food. And yet…it persists.

She is writing about a desperate thirst caused from dehydration intensified by starvation. As time wears on, thirst moves from a nagging feeling to an intense burn. From the intense burn and desire, thirst becomes a raging need that causes the mind to hallucinate and the skin to dry and crack. Extreme thirst moves into severe pain that a simple glass of water is unable to tame.

It is here that the opening verses of Psalm 42 ring out with new meaning. When the soul thirsts for God, the "living God," the suffering or recovered anorexic becomes vividly aware of the extremity of such words. How much does the soul ache and groan when its very life source is pushed away? The human soul (brought to life by the very "breath" of God as explained in Genesis) yearns, desires, and needs the living God in order to be quenched. A few months later, this same young woman once again writes to God:

> I saw a deer today lapping up water from a stream. Psalm 42 came rushing back to me—so suddenly I stopped what I was doing to reread the passage. My own body will always be in need of water. Just as that deer innately knows that it must have water to function and exist—my body will always need water and my soul will always need you. Those days, months and years that I fed and watered my being with my eating disorder withered my soul. How amazing it is to know that my soul will never be fully quenched. God, just as a deer escapes a dangerous situation and like the psalmist who experienced exile, may I always remember that in the good and the bad times, I am always in need of you, the Living God.

Amy Lambert (M.Div., Duke Divinity) is currently working as an Intern Pastor for ordination in the Universal Fellowship of Metropolitan Community Churches.

Psalm 148 and the Native American View of Animals

David Aftandilian (United States)

In Psalm 148, we find all of creation united in praise of God. Not just people but also the sun, moon, and stars, the depths of the ocean, fire, frost, and wind. Among this vast chorus of voices raised in grateful worship of thc Creator are those of animals from all the cosmological realms: sea monsters, wild animals, cattle, creeping things, flying birds, and humans.

Although differences between the animals are noted in this passage, especially in terms of what part of creation they inhabit, we do not see a hierarchy among them. This contrasts with other biblical texts, such as Genesis 1:26, which have been interpreted to mean God has subjugated other animals to humans. Instead, Psalm 148 directs our attention to the commonalities we share with other animals, rather than our differences from them. Specifically, all animals, including humans, are described as having the capability to recognize the divine and to honor God through worship.

Many stories of animals and saints in the Catholic tradition also describe animals as capable of recognizing the divine, praising God, even asking for and receiving the sacraments. Nor are Judaism and Christianity the only world religions to see animals in this way; similar visions exist within Buddhism, Hinduism, Islam, and, most prominently, indigenous spiritual traditions, including those of Native North Americans.

Among the Muscogee Creek and Cherokee, for example, animals are viewed as very much like people (both of these native nations used to make their homes in the Southeast, and today live both there and in Oklahoma). The animals can talk, think, create social and political organizations, pray and perform ceremonies, and have souls. For example, Creeks describe the other animals as meeting in council to decide whether and how to create the lands on the flooded earth (Frank Speck, "The Creek Indians of Taskigi Town," *American Anthropological Society Memoirs* 2(2):1907, 145–146), and the Cherokee speak of bears doing dances of thanksgiving and panthers performing the Green Corn ceremony, one of the most important annual ceremonies known to the Southeastern tribes. The Cherokee even say that certain animals, such as bears and rattlesnakes, were once humans; therefore, the Cherokee feel they have a direct kinship relationship to the other animals (James Mooney, *Myths of the Cherokee* [New York: Dover Publications, 1900], 324, 327–329).

The animals are also seen as different from humans in Native American conceptions. But unlike some Judeo-Christian interpretations of Genesis 1:26, which ascribe superiority to humans because we are the only beings created in God's image, Native American sacred stories of creation often refer to humans as having been created last and *least.* For example, in Creek, Cherokee, and other native creation stories, birds and water animals existed in the world before humans were created; this means that these other animals have more practical and spiritual knowledge than we do. They are therefore referred to as our elder brothers and sisters, worthy of respect because of their seniority. Furthermore, other animals also have greater spiritual power than we do, which they can choose to use to help or harm us. Owls, for instance, can share their power to see beyond this world with Creek medicine people, helping them with divination (John R. Swanton, *Creek Religion and Medicine* [Lincoln and London: University of Nebraska Press, 2000], 621). But when humans started killing too many animals, both Creek and Cherokee traditions say the animals retaliated by creating diseases that could cripple or even kill disrespectful hunters (Mooney, 250–252; Speck, 148–149).

Among the Creek and Cherokee, these ideas of other animals as people, like us, but also peoples with greater practical knowledge and spiritual power, have inspired a series of natural laws or ethical norms that regulate human relations with other animals. First, humans should treat other animals with the respect that is due to elder relatives. Ways to demonstrate this respect include thanking hunted animals for the gift of their lives, only hunting as many animals as we need to survive, and not wasting any of their bodies. Contemporary Cherokee storyteller Edna Chekelelee, for example, explains that when you hunt a deer, you should only kill one, and you should not waste any of the meat (Barbara Duncan, *Living Stories of the Cherokee* [Chapel Hill and London: University of North Carolina Press, 1998], 129–130).

Second, humans should give something back in return for what the animals give to us; this principle is known as *reciprocity,* and it is one of the most important ethical norms among Native Americans. Respect and thanks are two things we can give back to animals. But perhaps more importantly, we also have a responsibility to care for the other animals in at least two senses—to protect their habitats and numbers, and to perform stories, dances, and ceremonies of world renewal on their behalf. In Native American traditions, every being has its proper role to play in the world; that of humanity is primarily to perform these world renewal ceremonies which involve our sacrifice for the good of all creation. We might compare this concept to contemporary reinterpretations of Genesis 1:26 by religious environmentalists, who read this passage as speaking of our stewardship responsibility to take care of all creation—"to till and tend" the Garden we know as Earth (Genesis 2:15).

How, then, might we read Psalm 148 in the light of Native American conceptions of other animals as people like us, capable of sensing and relating to the divine, and worthy of our respect and care? If animals are capable of worshipping God, as Psalm 148 clearly says they are, this shows that Judeo-Christian traditions, too, often describe the other animals as similar to us. Just as the gift of animals' lives to hunters necessitates a reciprocal relationship between animals and humans among Native American peoples, so too does the shared ability of other animals and humans to praise God suggest that Jews and Christians also ought to recognize a reciprocal relationship between themselves and animals. Furthermore, the similarity between animals and humans in Psalm 148 might also lead us to rethink our theologies of animals, to shift them from focusing on what makes humans different to what makes us similar to other animals.

David Aftandilian is Assistant Professor of Anthropology at Texas Christian University; he is the editor of What Are the Animals to Us? Approaches from Science, Religion, Folklore, Literature and Art.

QUESTIONS

1. Reread all of Psalm 22 carefully, assuming that it is a "spell against the attacks of the witch." What new questions and insights emerge?
2. Does one need Smith's knowledge of shepherds in Africa to fully understand the meaning of Psalm 23?
3. Read carefully the rest of Psalm 42 through the eyes of someone who has suffered from anorexia. What insights can be gleaned? What questions arise?
4. What significance might one draw from the fact that in Psalm 148 not only animals but also "sun, moon, and stars, the depths of the ocean, fire, frost, and wind" praise God?

CHAPTER 18

PSALM 137

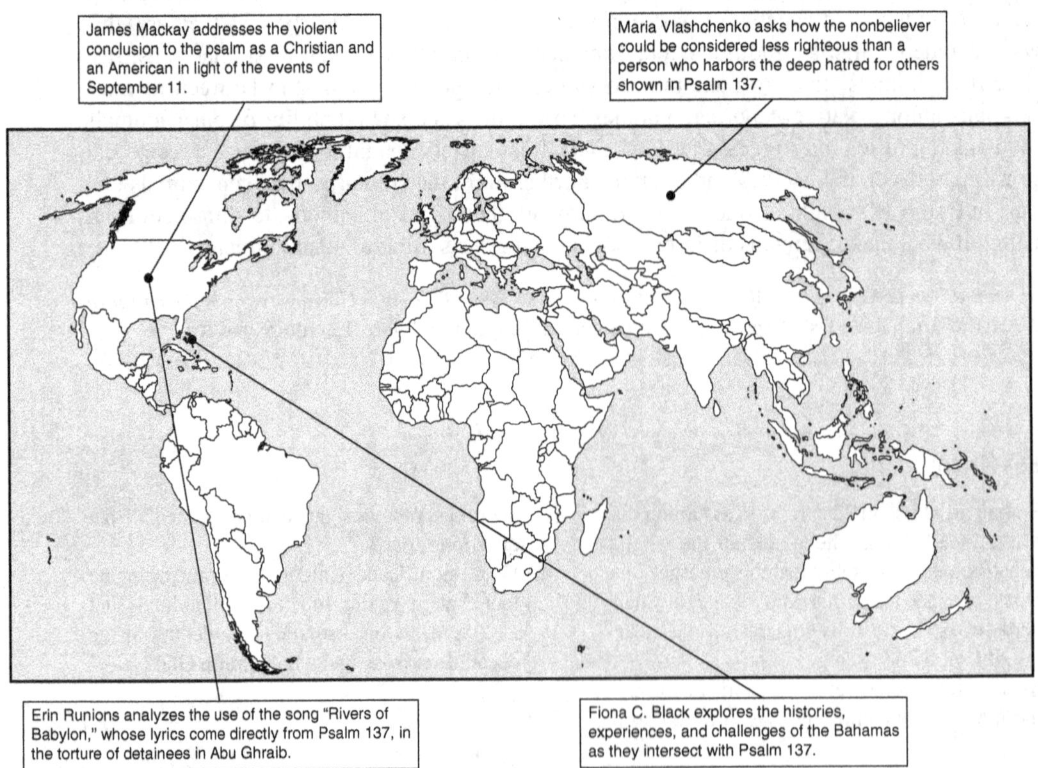
James Mackay addresses the violent conclusion to the psalm as a Christian and an American in light of the events of September 11.
Maria Vlashchenko asks how the nonbeliever could be considered less righteous than a person who harbors the deep hatred for others shown in Psalm 137.
Erin Runions analyzes the use of the song "Rivers of Babylon," whose lyrics come directly from Psalm 137, in the torture of detainees in Abu Ghraib.
Fiona C. Black explores the histories, experiences, and challenges of the Bahamas as they intersect with Psalm 137.

READINGS

Psalm 137 and the Histories, Experiences, and Challenges of the Bahamas
Fiona C. Black

"Rivers of Babylon" and the Torture of Detainees in Abu Ghraib
Erin Runions

The Violent Conclusion of Psalm 137 in Relation to 9/11
James Mackay

Righteousness and Hatred in Psalm 137
Maria Vlashchenko

Psalm 137 and the Histories, Experiences, and Challenges of the Bahamas

Fiona C. Black (Bahamas)

Christopher Columbus came to the Caribbean, observes Samuel Murrell, with a sword in one hand and a Bible in the other. Subsequently, the Bible was used there to form and dominate colonized peoples. Over the last few centuries, however, through Christianization, the Bible has become central and highly valued in the spiritual lives of many Caribbean peoples. Here I will consider the applicability of Psalm 137 to the Caribbean context. This is a significant text, since it voices the pain of exile; provocatively considers migration, loss, and belonging; and has interpretive/cultural connections to African diasporas. Herein, I explore some of the histories, experiences, and challenges of one Caribbean context (the Bahamas), along with the issues of migration, diaspora, and memory. These come into sharp focus in the Psalm, which offers a complicated message to ancient and modern audiences alike.

I operate out of a specific interpretive environment, which I bring to my reading of the biblical text. I write as a Caribbean (Bahamian) immigrant to a multicultural country, Canada. I read as one who is thinking about the Bible in connection with a web of colonial relationships, past and present, and to a host of traumatic, migratory, historical events. I also consider these matters in connection with poetics, since I am convinced that texts such as Psalm 137 are able to focus matters concerning identity and subjectivity in ways that are distinct from narrative texts.

Geographic, linguistic and historico-cultural variety abounds in the Caribbean. Aboriginal peoples first occupied the Caribbean; once largely exterminated, these were followed by a rapid influx of millions of diverse African peoples. Moreover, Dutch, Spanish, French, British, and South Asian colonial roots are all present here, which include the diversity one would expect from disparate African and European religions and cultures. Added to these historical resonances are the dynamics of contemporary immigration to the region.

In the Bahamas specifically, the picture is just as varied: The current population includes descendants of slaves or transplanted slaves, of loyalists expelled from America, of British colonialists, and so on, as well as a large, changing population through the influx of Haitian migrant workers and illegals, tourists and off-shore buyers. Like many other Caribbean nations, the Bahamas' socioeconomic and cultural situation is complex, suffering from extremes of wealth and poverty, with attendant problems around social issues, health care, education, and housing. The country also appears to be consolidating its energies into tourism and development, arguably beneficial for the economy but troubling for nationals, since it causes displacement and limitation of industry. Proudly independent since 1973, the predominantly Christian Bahamas finds itself between two colonial powers: a historical but still influential British past, and an economically and culturally impactful American present. Consideration of the Bible's problematic past and its potential to heal is both beneficial and necessary. To the Bahamian context, therefore, which is growing, changing, increasingly disconnected from its cultural roots, and troubled in many ways, it is plausible that the Bible has something to contribute in a positive way.

Highly applicable for the Caribbean context in general, Psalm 137 laments the calamity of exile and the desolation of displacement and lost generations; it also emboldens the desire for retribution. In this way, as a type of memorialization of the Middle Passage—the forced migration of Africans across the Atlantic—the psalm addresses the historical memory of Bahamian and other Caribbean peoples. Indeed, the psalm profoundly articulates loss of all causes—the loss of land, the desire to remember what is gone, the recognition that return is not possible. For the present day, this text might also address the failure of Bahamians to hold on to the land that is now theirs, to work it, to live off it, to own it, since they are being edged out by ongoing development and off-shore ownership. As they negotiate their past and their present, the psalm speaks to the myriad cultural and spiritual concessions that must be made. Thus, for the collective history or memory of Caribbean peoples, the psalm "fits" in many ways. And yet, it is not just the subject matter of the psalm that makes it work for the Bahamian context; it is also its mechanisms of memory and affect. Like other laments, the psalm carries the concept of memory in its interpretive cache—it works as a vocabulary for grief and loss, because it has worked this way originally, and for others over time throughout its interpretive life (e.g., in the Rastafari community through music). Memory, therefore, is both linked to specific events and transcends them. The psalm also, however, problematizes memory. It is there, at the speaker's insistence (indeed, he stakes his health on it); he also, however, struggles to let go, to end what ails him. Do not forget, but do forget, he seems to be saying. This multifaceted aspect of memory constitutes the very essence of the speaker: It defines his experience, but equally seems essential to allow him to have a voice, to continue his life.

To explain this another way, we might say that the lamenting language of Psalm 137 (and others) is affective—that which, though specific and descriptive, can also modulate its speakers. In other words, it helps actually to constitute the subject in lament, since people are formed by their experiences and by the descriptive language they use. Thus, lamenting language has longevity and variability. Since it is able to shift in these ways, describing past and present events, and in essence describing subjects in a state of loss (which one could argue all Caribbean peoples are—though we need to be cautious of creating a nostalgia for an imagined past), it is an excellent model for describing the subject "on the move," or in a state of flux.

This seems an apt way of understanding Bahamian life and culture—as in a state of flux. That model takes into account the Bahamas' historical past, its current disjuncture from the land, and the perceived loss of culture and society through cultural and geographical proximity to America, tourism, disenfranchisement of its peoples, and social problems, such as rape, incest, legalized homophobia, immigration, economic enslavement, and so on. This idea of shifting or fluctuating subjectivity—which is mirrored by repetitions and inversions in the language of the psalm itself—reflects the hybrid identities of Caribbean peoples, in all the ways they are constituted. It pushes them not to identify wholly with land lost *or* new, but to negotiate their existence somewhere in between.

One aspect of the psalm remains for comment: the troubling, violent ending. Violence forms the immediate memory of the speaker, but it also speaks to his past (colonial power) and future (revenge to be exacted). So visible is it, in fact, that the speaker makes it excessive: It is inflicted upon children; it is aimed at destroying generation; it is the vile taste in the mouth that comes after grief. Here, the contours of the psalm engage the contemporary Caribbean listener to think hard about violence, both as it operates excessively in our midst and as it frames the experience of the displaced. In the psalm, violence indicates that the rivers of Babylon are in places turgid and muddied, offering no clear reasons for, or solutions to, displacement. Through remembrance, community and resettlement appear possible in the psalm, but anger and violence are never far behind. The psalm, in other words, crosses from here to there, from lament to violence, from desolation to contempt, in ways that ought to leave us uneasy.

Perhaps the violence here suggests that Bahamians look more closely at the neocolonization at work in their midst. They might look to the violence of their own peoples by government or by society, where these turn a blind eye to failures of education and protection of the weak, and to the cultural losses of stories and traditions. At the same time, Bahamians might also look at the ways that the practices and structures of violence are reinscribed, as, for instance, through the quasi-enslavement and displacement of Haitians, who are brought in (or whose illegal entry is allowed) to service the tourist industry, but who are denied citizenship and other benefits of society.

Perhaps, though, it is possible to learn from contradictory texts and the painful realities of migration that might be represented there. Psalm 137 signals that "to belong" means we must not attempt to fix identity and claim those factors that come with it (voice, power, privilege), but be comfortable in their failure to contain us. In other words, contradictory texts and migrations teach us how better to understand ourselves, and potentially to create diasporas and communities that embrace migration and change in better ways. It might be that such work is what is needed for the Bahamas as it looks to its past and attempts to articulate its present.

Fiona C. Black is Associate Professor and Head of the Department of Religious Studies at Mount Allison University, Sackville, NB, Canada.

"Rivers of Babylon" and the Torture of Detainees in Abu Ghraib

Erin Runions (United States)

Psalm 137 is a powerful and disturbing text. Equally powerful and disturbing is the fact that it was used in the attempt to break detainees in Abu Ghraib, the U.S.-operated prison in Iraq, where Iraqi prisoners were subjected to physical, psychological, and sexual abuse and torture. Boney M's song, "Rivers of Babylon," whose lyrics come directly from Psalm 137, was one of the songs played at ear-splitting volumes to wear down the prisoners. Haj Ali Shalal—the man whose experiences match the now-iconic photo of the hooded man on a box—reported being subjected to high-volume repetitions of the song. The inclusion of "Rivers of Babylon" in the "torture playlist" at Abu Ghraib reveals much about the belief system that enabled other atrocities.

Chosen no doubt for its reference to captivity in Babylon, and perhaps also for its quickly maddening disco beat and repetitive tune, we might wonder to what degree Shalal's interrogators thought through the song's cultural, mythical, and allegorical reverberations. The song repeats and slightly modifies the first four verses of Psalm 137, a text that expresses agony over the Babylonian exile of the Judean elite in 597 and 586 B.C.E. A refrain is included from Psalm 19, asking that the song be acceptable to God.

Did U.S. soldiers think through the implications of playing this particular incarnation of this biblical text as a form of psychological stress? In what theological world might they have thought their actions acceptable in God's sight? Even if the most minimal planning was operative, the thick strata of irony and ambiguity surrounding this musical selection beg for exploration.

At the very least, the decision to play "Rivers of Babylon" at Abu Ghraib indicates that an allegorical-mythical figure of Babylon was grafted onto Iraq in some way. Aided by a long apocalyptic interpretive tradition, the story of Babylon conquering ancient Israel (Judah), destroying the temple, and exiling God's people is read as one moment within an ancient mythical and spiritual struggle that continues into the present. In the apocalyptic tradition, Babylon becomes a transhistorical symbol of tyranny, evil, and godlessness, most clearly embodied by the figure of the Whore of Babylon in Revelation 17. Such evil must be fought, by any means necessary, or so the logic goes. In this case, Babylon seems to stand in for Iraq, since Iraq is where ancient Babylon was actually located, while ancient Israel becomes the United States.

Yet the allegory is somewhat ambiguous. For instance, to whom do the song's captives refer—weeping by the rivers of Babylon and refusing to sing in a foreign land? U.S. servicemen in Iraq? The detained Iraqis? In neither instance does an allegory to the situation in Iraq work as expected. The first possibility would suggest that U.S. forces occupying Iraq were somehow captive, which they were not. The second interpretation would somehow put U.S. soldiers in the position of the ancient Babylonian captors, which, given the usual associations with Babylon, they might reject. Moreover, what does it mean when a country like the United States, which likes to think of itself as beyond slavery and other civil rights injustices, plays a song about freedom to people they are torturing? An ambivalence about Babylon emerges. The use of the song at Abu Ghraib perhaps suggests that the United States is more like Babylon than it would like to think. The ambiguity of the allegory shows how the United States can think of itself as victimized (weeping by the rivers of Babylon), and at the same time, be oppressors (emulating Babylon).

Though the song quotes only the first few verses of Psalm 137, we must also consider the troubling final lines of the psalm: "O Daughter of Babylon, doomed to destruction, happy is he who repays you for what you have done to us—he who seizes your infants and dashes them against the rocks." The psalmist dreams of a violent role reversal, in a way that might telegraph a repeating pattern of cross-identification through the ages, so that U.S. soldiers can feel like captives and captors at the same time (Israel *and* Babylon). Did this biblical text in any way, even unconsciously, justify the heinous, often sexualized, abuse of men, women, and teenagers at Abu Ghraib? Revenge has the unfortunate trait of making seem righteous what would otherwise be considered woefully wrong.

A number of biblical scholars have tried to understand the violent ending of Psalm 137 as an understandable response to acute oppression, often citing the Holocaust as a scenario through which one could possibly understand the psalmist's rage. These biblical scholars are acting in the best of faith, honestly trying to make sense of a difficult passage. But the problem is that when Babylon (and subsequently Iraq) is identified with Nazi Germany, the ancient empire is further mythologized as somehow spiritually associated with one of the terrible evils of the modern era. Once put into uncritical hands, these associations and connotations justify military strategies that would not otherwise be permitted. Imitation of the ending of Psalm 137 becomes thinkable.

These, indeed, are the dangerous pitfalls of biblical interpretation. It is easy for contradictory truths to materialize when ancient texts are used to represent cosmic truths of good and evil, which are then applied to shifting contemporary geopolitical ambitions. Even if the soldiers were not biblically literate or thinking through all the implications of their choice of songs, these verses are part of the fabric that has formed a cultural attitude toward Babylon, which, as their particular musical choice of interrogation technique shows, has been vaguely particularized to Iraq, the U.S. occupation, and the war on terror.

But why make so much of this one incident now, so many years after Abu Ghraib has closed? Because torture is still under discussion, and the way we think about the Bible can influence national consciousness and attitudes toward what happens in war. We should reflect carefully on how the Bible comes to be used as torture, and what responsibility we have in that scenario. We might worry about the way we allegorize good and evil, the portability of allegories, the harm they do when literalized, and the way that they can subtly reflect actual power relations.

Erin Runions is Associate Professor of Religious Studies at Pomona College, United States.

The Violent Conclusion of Psalm 137 in Relation to 9/11

James Mackay (United States)

The book of Psalms is filled with songs of praise to God, expression of hope, trust, and confidence that God will be with us. Psalm 137, however, is different. The writer of this text is being held captive by his enemy—he is a modern-day prisoner of war (POW). He has been forced from his homeland into slavery in another land. He and his people have gone from having freedom and liberty to facing exile and possible death. They find themselves in Babylon, which is modern-day Iraq, having given up on all motivation and praise (v. 2). Their Babylonian captors torment them by mockingly demanding a song about their now-destroyed homeland, Zion (v. 3). The writer asks rhetorically how he could possibly sing such a song in light of his awful circumstances. Indeed, the first four verses are sad and depressing. The writer is exhausted.

But he is also resilient—and angry. In verses 5–6 he vows to keep the songs of Zion in his heart. He refuses to forget his home, his country, his family, and his life. He not only takes joy in thoughts of Jerusalem, but also, in verses 7–9, he takes delight in imaging the destruction of the enemy. He calls for revenge on the Babylonians and their children, not just as enemies of Israel but as enemies of God. And he does not hold back his venom, expressing the desire to see the heads of the Babylonian children dashed against the rocks.

This can be a very confusing text for Christians today. Aren't we supposed to love our enemies as Jesus commanded in the Gospels? Shouldn't we pray for those who persecute us? So what do we do with the rage expressed here in Psalm 137 (and a few other places in the Psalms)?

Sometimes we face great obstacles and life-changing moments. For most Americans our country changed on September 11, 2001, when Muslim extremists attacked our way of life and killed thousands of innocent people simply because we are different from them. Now we find our nation's military spread across the globe fighting and deterring terrorists like this. Stateside citizens have lost some of their freedoms as they are subject to more scrutiny at public events, embarrassing pat downs at airports, and other intrusions into our daily life that did not exist prior to 9/11. In essence, then, the scenario is this: We have an enemy that has killed our people with no cause, has enslaved us to a life of heightened and invasive security concerns, and has made us live with the constant fear of another attack upon our people.

So do we simply forgive the terrorists and forget everything that they did? Absolutely not. To do so would be irresponsible and not biblical, as we learn from Psalm 137. This is an enemy that is clearly against human rights and has declared war upon the United States, the rest of the world, and God. We must respond; we must retaliate in order to defend ourselves, our nation, and our way of life. This is precisely the sentiment that is voiced by the writer of Psalm 137. This is not to say that we should kill or smash terrorist babies' heads against the rocks, but we should rise against our enemy and destroy them. There is a big difference between an adversary that is out to rob you of your coat and one that is out to do nothing short of kill you and your loved ones. As is evidenced by 9/11, we are dealing with the latter. As the writer of this psalm recognizes, the only way to protect your family against such foes is to do your best to remember your nation, your people, and your heritage, and to trust God through the pain, suffering, and loss of the life that we once knew. With God's help we can overcome the enemy.

James Mackay served nine years in the army and is currently a Sergeant in the Indiana National Guard.

Righteousness and Hatred in Psalm 137

Maria Vlashchenko (Russia)

For religious people, the book of Psalms contains songs, poems, and hymns that proclaim the glory of God and his power. The psalms show not only the Lord's supremacy over people, nations, and indeed the entire world but also his love toward humanity. But for a nonreligious reader, such as myself, the book of Psalms represents something else. Namely, the book is filled with psalms of hate and loathing toward those who do not believe in God. Nonbelievers are associated with all forms of wickedness and evil. All kinds of aspersions are cast at them. But why?

The book of Psalms divides people into two groups—righteous and wicked—from the very beginning: "Blessed is the man who does not walk in the counsel of the wicked or stand in the way of sinners or sit in the seat of mocker" (Ps. 1). This black-and-white way of viewing the world continues through the remaining psalms. There is no gray. There is no third option. One is either faithful and righteous and on God's side or a nonbeliever and wicked and opposed to God. But what about the person who simply chooses by his or her own will to have beliefs about God which are not in line with the Judeo-Christian tradition. What if one is a member of another religious tradition? What if one simply believes in a "higher power" without believing in the existence of the God of the book of Psalms? Or what if one believes in no God at all? Does that automatically make them wicked and evil?

The book of Psalms pulls no punches. It represents "wicked" people as "sinners," "mockers," who have a "heart filled with destruction," have a "deceitful tongue," are "bloodthirsty," and "love delusions and seek false gods" (Pss. 1:1; 4:2; 5:6, 9, 10). And that is just to name a few aspersions in the first couple of chapters. But is that right? Making a choice to believe or not to believe doesn't make one person good and right and another evil and wrong. Not every person who does not believe in God is evil, bloodthirsty, and full of lies. Yes, there are undoubtedly some people who do fit this description. But certainly a belief in the Judeo-Christian God is not the primary determining factor between who is righteous and who is wicked.

Moreover there is a real and remarkable paradox here. When we read through the psalms we find plenty of places where the psalmist, the righteous believer in God, is the one who is "bloodthirsty" and has "a heart full of destruction." The writer calls on God to destroy his enemies—using graphic and offensive language to do so. To take just a few examples, Psalm 58 says concerning the wicked, "Break the teeth in their mouths, O Lord...Let them vanish like water that flows away...like a stillborn child, may they not see the sun." Then "the righteous will be glad when they are avenged, when they bathe their feet in the blood of the wicked." This is disturbing rhetoric and language. How can a "righteous" person ask a supposedly "holy" God to kill their enemy so that it dies like an aborted fetus? Is this a religious tradition that a nonbeliever should be drawn toward? Surely this blurs the simple black-and-white world that the book of Psalms envisions?

While many other Psalms could be quoted, I will mention only one more. In Psalm 137, the writer again uses explicit imagery to express loathing and hate toward the enemy, in this case the Babylonians who have defeated Israel. Here the "righteous" psalmist proclaims, "Happy is he who repays you for what you have done to us—happy is he who seizes your infants and dashes their heads against the rock" (v. 9). While we can perhaps sympathize with the psalmist's suffering, still, how can these be the words of a good, religious person? How can any decent human being take joy in seeing an infant smashed to death? Belief in God—any God—does not give one license to say such things. How can the nonbeliever feel that they are less righteous than a person who harbors such deep hatred for others? Who, really, is the wicked person here?

Blaming "the wicked" for all one's misfortunes and calling on God to utterly destroy them is not only offensive to us nonbelievers, but it is also an example of religious hypocrisy. How can someone ask God to "Banish [the wicked] for their many sins, for they have rebelled against you," while also pleading with God to "Remember not the sins of my youth and my rebellious ways" (Pss. 5:10; 25:7). If the psalmists recognize that they themselves have been sinful and rebellious, it seems deeply misguided for them to call down curses on the wicked. Don't they see themselves under such curses? Don't they see the irony in all this?

Maria Vlashchenko is from Khabarovsk, Russia; she attended the Academy of Economics and Law in Khabarovsk before moving to the United States to study.

QUESTIONS

1. Explain and evaluate how Black connects Psalm 137 to life in the Bahamas. In her view, how can Psalm 137 "contribute in a positive way" to the Bahamian context?
2. Find a version of Boney M's song "Rivers of Babylon" on the Internet and reflect on its use in torture tactics. Try to imagine it played at high volumes as Runions mentions.
3. How do Mackay's experiences as a soldier shape his interpretation? How does Mackay's belief in God play into his thinking?
4. Evaluate Vlashchenko's critique of Psalm 137 and other biblical texts. How would a believer in the Judeo-Christian God respond? Could a believer "side" with Vlashchenko?

CHAPTER 19

PROVERBS 31

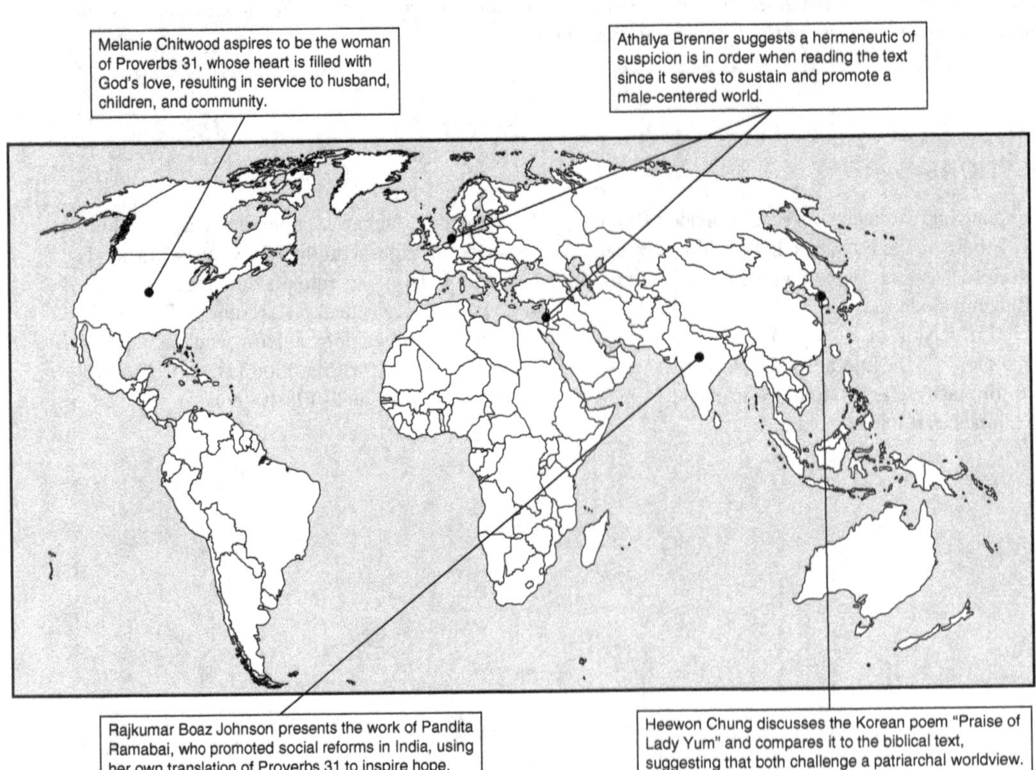
Melanie Chitwood aspires to be the woman of Proverbs 31, whose heart is filled with God's love, resulting in service to husband, children, and community.
Athalya Brenner suggests a hermeneutic of suspicion is in order when reading the text since it serves to sustain and promote a male-centered world.
Rajkumar Boaz Johnson presents the work of Pandita Ramabai, who promoted social reforms in India, using her own translation of Proverbs 31 to inspire hope.
Heewon Chung discusses the Korean poem "Praise of Lady Yum" and compares it to the biblical text, suggesting that both challenge a patriarchal worldview.

READINGS

Aspiring to Be the Woman of Proverbs 31

Melanie Chitwood (United States)

When I first read the description of the woman found in Proverbs 31:10–31, I thought, "She's not just an excellent wife, as described in verse 10. She's Superwoman and Betty Crocker combined, and I am quite sure I cannot be her." Knowing, however, God had a reason for including in Scripture the example of this godly woman, I decided to dig deeper.

Scholars tell us this passage describing the qualities of a godly wife was birthed from a mother's lessons to her son, a young prince. Since her son would one day be king, this wise mother knew how important his future wife would be. With the 22 letters of the Hebrew alphabet in sequential order as her guide, the mother creates an acrostic poem, with each verse describing an essential trait of an excellent wife. This poem would have been repeated often in the home, even memorized so it would be buried in the prince's heart and mind.

Although retold by the male writer of this passage, I appreciate how this description of a godly woman stems from the life of a woman who has "been there—done that." As a wife and mother herself, she is still doing that, turning her heart to God and seeking to obey Him in all she does. This real-life advice from another woman encourages me, helping me to believe that being like the Proverbs 31 woman is not an unattainable ideal but a worthy goal.

Along with providing a profile of a desirable wife, this poem also provides us with an example of the kind of godly woman, single or married, God wants us to be. We see the woman described in the New Living Translation as "virtuous and capable." Other versions of Scripture use the word "noble" (NIV) or "excellent" (NAS). For each, the Hebrew root word *hayil* can be translated as strength, capability, or valor. So the question beginning this passage could be worded as, *Who can find a strong woman? Or who can find a capable woman?*

No doubt about it, the Proverbs 31 woman "is energetic and strong, a hard worker" (v. 17). She works diligently around her home, serving her children and husband, and reaching out to the community. She plans and prepares meals, attends to clothing needs, and invests in business ventures to profit her household, to name a few of her many tasks. And all without the modern conveniences of a dishwasher or washing machine!

She's a woman not only with physical strength but also with strength of character. She is trustworthy and her husband is assured that she will "greatly enrich his life" (v. 11). She's generous to those in her community. She's at peace, "without fear of the future" (v. 25). She is wise and kind.

Because Proverbs 31 describes so many of the woman's strengths, it's easy to be intimidated by her and mistakenly to think I couldn't possibly be like her. Surely she must be gifted with superpowers or have an unusual bent toward homemaking. However, to truly understand this woman and to see her as the real woman she is, we need to take a look at what's behind her "to do" list.

Tucked in a verse at the end of the passage is the key to explain the source of this exemplary woman's strength: "Charm is deceptive, and beauty does not last; but a woman who fears the Lord will be greatly praised" (v. 30). Her excellence overflows from a heart which respects, trusts, and obeys God. One commentator sums her up perfectly: "Her heart is full of another world, even when her hands are most busy about this world."

She's not a picture of what a woman can do or become overnight. Rather she's a portrait of a woman who has spent a lifetime choosing moment by moment, day by day to be the woman God wants her to be. As I make daily choices to seek God, I find that just like the Proverbs 31 woman, I too will be a woman whose heart spills over with God's love, resulting in love and service to my husband, children, and community. I will be a rare and beautiful treasure, a woman whose heart and life belong to God.

Melanie Chitwood serves with Proverbs 31 Ministries (proverbs31.org), a Christian organization for women; she is the author of What a Husband Needs from His Wife *and* What a Wife Needs from Her Husband.

READING PROVERBS 31 SUSPICIOUSLY

Athalya Brenner (The Netherlands, Israel)

Proverbs is considered a "wisdom" book, a teaching for life, but I wonder whether this collection, including the poem in Proverbs 31, indeed contains "wisdom" that is universally applicable and useful for past as well as contemporary readers.

I am a woman scholar, Jewish, a native Hebrew speaker, a first-generation Israeli born to immigrant Ostjuden parents, a-religious, a mother to a son, divorced, living in Amsterdam and Haifa, teaching Bible and Jewish studies in Amsterdam and Israel, of working-class origins, a feminist with left-oriented political opinions. The world in which I live and with which I identify myself cannot be defined, simply and straightforwardly, as "Western." Rather, I see myself as both Orientalized and Westernized. And, importantly, I belong to a secular world, even though my business is to study and teach texts that are, by Western and non-Western cultural consent, religious texts. Thus, my attention to matters of faith lags far behind my interests in literary structure, forms, and content; issues of gender and class; epistemological questions; and the biblical text's influence on early twenty-first-century life, mine and that of others. It is no hardship or sorrow for me to concede that, in Proverbs, "religion" functions as a general background for sustaining societal stability and the politico-economic status quo. The advice dispensed in Proverbs is largely conventional and conformist—it promotes continuation rather than change. Obedience and authority are valued above independence and original thought. Agism (in the sense of age superiority) is the order of the day. In short, the status quo that Proverbs wants to promote and sustain is one which privileges elite-class, urban, educated males. Thus, I have many good reasons for not accepting Proverbs' counsel as universally applicable. A hermeneutic of suspicion when reading Proverbs 31 is indeed in order.

To appreciate the dynamics of Proverbs 31, we must begin in Proverbs 1–9. Here advice is dispensed from a parent to a "son," or from an "elder" or "elders" who are "wise," while the target audience is imaged implicitly or explicitly as male, young, "foolish," "ignorant," "insensitive," and in need of instruction and teaching. Whether this implies an actual family teaching praxis or rather a teaching situation at schools where elder persons prepared younger males for the privileged life of public office, scribal activity, or economic viability remains uncertain. What can be deduced, though, is the class situation in which such counsel could be formulated and transmitted: urban elite class males that had the leisure, money, and inclination to invest in the continuance of their ways through the training of whoever needed prompting in the right direction. That the producers as well as the consumers of this training were males seems to be borne out by the texts themselves, as well as by the preoccupation with female figures, personifications, and metaphors.

Throughout Proverbs 1–9 there is an interchange of father/mother's "instructions" to presumably a young son(s). It is filled with propaganda for the attractions of a feminized and eroticized Wisdom figure, and descriptions of a fatal Other woman (Loose or Strange Woman), whose assessment is obviously negative. The parents try to persuade the son—and ignorant male customers/readers in general—to follow Woman Wisdom with promises of health, wealth, and the good life, rather than sex. Her direct opposite, Woman Folly, also goes out into the street to attract customers but, as the Other woman, her attempts to promote hidden pleasures are inexplicably deadly, although her powers of persuasion are considerable.

The last section of Proverbs, once again, displays a deep concern with women and femaleness/femininity. Proverbs 31:10–31 is an acrostic poem that draws a portrait of a virtuous wife who works round the clock, keeps her family, and is commercially active, in addition to doing all traditional female crafts and tasks. She carries out economic transactions and is Yhwh-fearing, charitable, wise, and a source of praise and comfort for her sons and husband.

Proverbs' opening and closing units, then, foreground some points that are endemic to the collection as a whole and meaningful for understanding it. To start with, these units serve as the book's frame and its framework: All the other units are enveloped by or embedded in the frame. The frame contains much discourse that is concerned with femaleness and femininity—more specifically, it elaborates the roles of a legitimate wife/lover and mother over against illicit sexual ties of a man with Other women. This is in keeping with Proverbs' general interest in safeguarding the family as an ongoing, [re]productive social institution. This impulse makes sense for social continuation and self-perpetuation. At the same time, it betrays a male anxiety about the social project it promotes.

The curious persona or metaphor of woman as Wisdom, an erotically portrayed wife/lover and female teacher of commonsense, is deeply meaningful for identifying the underlying wishes and anxieties about the promoted social order of Proverbs. It would make no sense to advance and sustain a female Wisdom figure at the beginning of the book (Proverbs 1–9) and to attribute a teaching function to the virtuous wife at the book's ending (v. 26), if such a function was unimaginable for regular wives and mothers. The prominence of Woman Wisdom suggests an appreciation of womanhood—more specifically endogamous wifehood and motherhood—that is overtly absent from the androcentric (male-centered) world order advocated. Thus, a mixed and at least dual-layered message to and about women is implicit in the book of Proverbs.

The virtuous wife who closes Proverbs is a paragon of virtue: no wonder that Jewish husbands still recite the poem to their wives today, either at their wedding or on Shabbat eve. Incidentally, as I have learned recently, in some Orthodox Jewish communities the poem is recited also at the graveside during a deceased woman's funeral service (in Haifa); I have no idea whether an unmarried woman receives the same ritual treatment. At any rate, during her lifetime, such a wife is convenient to have, since she has everything, apart from beauty (v. 30). Like Wisdom, she is "far more precious than rubies" (v. 10). In fact, she is the personification of the metaphorical/metaphorized or personified Woman Wisdom of Proverbs 1–9. The essence of feminine/female achievement is a woman who has totally adapted to her required role. This is the ultimate male victory: a useful woman, the complete antithesis to the woman Other. Presumably, the final goal was for this exaggerated blueprint for wifely behavior to be taught by mother to daughter—after all, the virtuous woman does have the capacity to instruct wisely!

Athalya Brenner is Professor of Bible at the University of Amsterdam, The Netherlands; and Tel Aviv University, Israel.

Pandita Ramabai's Translation and Use of Proverbs 31

Rajkumar Boaz Johnson (India)

English translations of the Bible usually describe the woman of Proverbs 31:10–31 as a "capable wife" or "wife of noble character" or as a "virtuous wife." But these translations miss the main meaning of the Hebrew words *eshet chayil*: strong woman. By contrast, Pandita Ramabai translated it correctly and lived it.

Pandita Ramabai was a woman from India who intensely grappled with the question of the place and meaning of womanhood in late nineteenth-century and early twentieth-century India. She was also the first woman to have translated the whole Bible into a low-caste Indian language, Marathi. Indeed, she was the first woman to have translated the whole Bible into another language anywhere in the world. Research in the thought and writings of Ramabai make it clear that two things were paramount in her mind: injustices in India against women and injustices against low-caste/outcaste people. Ramabai's impact on India was so great that in 1989, a hundred years after the founding of Ramabai Mukti Mission (the House of Salvation), the government of India acknowledged her legacy with a commemorative stamp. The official brochure with the stamp reads as follows:

> Pandita Ramabai (1858–1920): Pandita Ramabai was a social reformer, a champion for the emancipation of women, and a pioneer in education. Left totally alone by the time she was 23, Ramabai acquired a great reputation as a Sanskrit scholar. Deeply impressed by her prowess, the Sanskrit scholars of Calcutta University conferred on her the titles of "Saraswati" and "Pandita." She rebelled against the caste system and married a shudra advocate, but was widowed at 23, having a baby girl. In 1882, she established the Arya Mahila Samaj for the cause of women's education in Pune and different parts of Western India. This led to the formation of the Sharda Sadan in 1889, a school which blossomed into an umbrella organization called Pandita Ramabai Mukti Mission, 40 miles outside Pune. In 1896, during a severe famine Ramabai visited villages of Maharashtra with a caravan of bullock carts and rescued thousands of outcaste children, child widows, orphans and other destitute women and brought them to the shelter of Mukti and Sharada Sadan. A learned woman knowing seven languages, she translated the Bible into her mother tongue—Marathi—from the original Hebrew and Greek. Her work continues today, a memorial to her life and path.

Ramabai wrote quite widely describing the state of the Indian woman. She wrote in her work *A Testimony of our Inexhaustible Treasure*:

> There were two things on which all those books, the Dharma Shastras, the sacred epics, the Puranas... were agreed: women of high and low caste, as a class, were bad, very bad, worse than demons, and that they could not get Moksha (salvation) as men. The only hope of their getting this much-desired liberation from Karma and its results, that is, countless millions of births and deaths and untold suffering, was the worship of their husbands. The husband is said to be the woman's god; there is no other god for her.

In the same token, commenting on injustices against low-caste and outcaste people in society, she wrote (*A Testimony*, 7):

> The same rules are applicable to the Shudras, the untouchables. The Shudras must not study the Veda and must not perform the same religious acts which a Brahman has a right to perform. The Shudra who hears the Veda repeated must be punished by having his ears filled with liquefied lead. . . . His only hope of getting liberation is in serving the three high castes as their lifelong slave.

Ramabai's life's work was dedicated to setting right these two injustices. She spent the last 18 years of her life translating the whole Bible into Marathi, the local language of Maharashtra, a state in India. Her translation makes it clear that the issue of injustice was topmost on her mind. For instance, she did not use the word *Parameshvar* for "God," as do other vernacular translations. *Parameshvar* is the God who introduced and propagates injustices against low-caste/outcaste people and women in Hindu mythology. Instead, Ramabai used the word *Deva*, which is the term used by low-caste/outcaste people to refer to God. This God frees the downtrodden masses and women from the oppression of high-caste people and gods. Further, Ramabai taught the languages of the Bible to the low-caste girls she rescued from prostitution, child widowhood, and poverty. In a sad—but perhaps fitting—note, the Bible Society of India, which was dominated by high-caste men, did not accept her Bible translation.

Ramabai describes the woman of Proverbs 31 as a Saduni Bai, that is, "mentally, emotionally, physically, and spiritually strong woman." This is distinct from other Marathi and Hindi translations, which describe this woman as a Bhali Patni, that is, an "innocent, dutiful, devoted wife." In Indian culture, this is obviously the model of a woman, even in today's society. The English translations we mentioned above (virtuous, capable, noble) are not as misguided as the Indian vernacular translations, but they nonetheless are inferior renderings. Indeed, Ramabai's translation is closer to the meaning of the Hebrew words, *eshet chayil*, the strong woman. The choice of these words makes it clear that Ramabai was very keen on setting right the place and meaning of womanhood in Indian society.

We further note that Proverbs 31 concludes with the words, "Many women have done excellently, but you surpass them all." The Hindi and the Marathi renders the word "women" as *stree*. In Hindu mythology *stree* are women who serve high-caste men, and in the Hindu concept of heaven, they serve men there as well. Ramabai avoids the word *stree* and renders instead, "Many daughters have done mentally, emotionally, physically and spiritually strong deeds." Without a doubt, Ramabai's translation sought to give the women of India, and especially the girls she rescued from terrible conditions, an emancipatory model of womanhood.

In sum, the "strong woman" of Proverbs 31 becomes the model for Ramabai and all the young women who found their home at Ramabai Mukti Mission, women who endured injustice in the Indian context of that time, as so many do even today.

Rajkumar Boaz Johnson was reared in one of the slums of Delhi, where he witnessed many of his young friends taken into slavery by high-caste Hindus; he is Professor of Biblical and Theological Studies at North Park University, United States.

"Praise of Lady Yum," Proverbs 31, and a Challenge to Patriarchy

Heewon Chung (South Korea)

Ancient Korea was a patriarchal society, in which women were regarded and depicted as unskilled, dependent, and unwise in many aspects. Yet, a few songs and stories in honor of the "wise woman" were recorded in certain genres of literature in ancient Korea. One such example is a poem entitled "Praise of Lady Yum," which describes the virtuous deeds of a wife. Its author is Nubaek Choi (?–1205), a high-ranking official of the *Korye* dynasty. After the death of his wife, Kyognae Yum (1100–1146), he composed the poem to commemorate her virtue, and later inscribed it on a massive monument as a tribute to her and to instruct his descendents. The following is the abbreviated translation of the poem:

> As a person, my wife was pure and modest. She was very literate and well understood moral obligations. In speech, appearance, skill, and conduct, she was superior to others. Before marriage she ably served her parents; after marriage she was extremely diligent in wifely ways. She was the first to perceive and carry out the wishes of the elders, and with filial piety she nourished my now deceased mother. In good and bad fortune, in congratulations and condolences, she could share the feelings of immediate family members, in-laws, and neighbors. There was no one who did not praise her.
>
> When I was involved in military matters, she endured hardship in our poor home and often made and sent military uniforms. And when I was a palace attendant, she used every means possible to supply delicacies to present to the king. How she followed me through all of these difficulties for twenty-three years I cannot entirely record.
>
> One day she said to me, "You are a man of letters. Mundane matters should not be important to you. I consider providing clothes and food for the family to be my task." When I was promoted to a drafter of royal edicts and proclamations, my wife, showing her happiness in her face, said, "It seems we have almost seen the end of our poverty." I responded to her, "Being a policy critic is not a position to earn a rich stipend." My wife said, "If suddenly one day you are standing in the palace court with the king arguing over an issue, even if I am forced to wear a thorny wooden barrette and poor cotton skirts and carry heavy burdens in making our life, I will accept willingly." These were not the words of an ordinary woman.
>
> I continued to be promoted many times and successively received higher stipends. In looking at my family's present situation, however, it is not as good as in the days when my wife struggled to make ends meet. How could anyone say my wife did not have wisdom? When my wife was about to die, in leaving her last instructions to me and our children, all her words were wise and worth listening to.
>
> When she died, her age was forty-seven. Her epitaph reads: "I, your husband, pledge not to forget you. That I am not yet buried together with you gives me great pain. Because of you, the children will live in harmony and expect to be prosperous forever."

This poem praises a woman who followed the four basic obligations of the traditional Confucian teaching for women: moral conduct, proper speech, proper appearance, and womanly tasks. She was filial to parents-in-law, harmonious with neighbors, and obedient to husband.

Notably, however, the wife is acclaimed as a wise woman for her individuality: She was literate, intelligent, and wise enough to instruct her husband although women in the period were excluded from formal education. In fact, the male-oriented society of ancient Korea believed that women should not be educated because they might discharge the duties appropriate to their role. Given this ethos, she went beyond cultural and societal views of stereotypical gender roles; she elevated herself to becoming an integral member of a multigenerational family unit and a paragon of virtue for the public. Lady Yum, therefore, significantly changed the status and image of wife from that of submissive spouse and caregiver to that of an advisor and helpmate.

As one can easily notice, "Praise of Lady Yum" demonstrates a number of striking lexical parallels and thematic correspondences with Proverbs 31:10–31. The biblical poem also praises the active good works of a woman in the ordinary affairs of family and society. She is depicted as having wisdom, diligence, modesty, compassion to the poor, administrative skill, liberality to neighbors, prudent speech, and judicious instruction. For these reasons, she was praised by her husband, children, and neighbors. Overall, the wise woman in Proverbs 31 represents more than simply a model for performing everyday tasks of marital life—she is more than simply a woman whom the young males dream of. Her astonishing capacities and wisdom overturns an ancient sociocultural ethos that a woman's role was to bear children and equip them for survival in a male chauvinist society.

In this framework, "Praise of Lady Yum" and Proverbs 31 offer a moment for reflection on the matters of gender role and gender equality in our society. Particularly, it is critical for Korean immigrant communities and other contemporary immigrant groups in the United States, mostly from non-European, Third World countries. For example, while only a small proportion of married women participate in the labor force in South Korea, the vast majority of Korean immigrant wives work outside the home. Their increased economic role and the persistence of their husbands' traditional patriarchal attitude and ideology cause marital conflicts and tensions in many immigrant families. Indeed, most Korean husbands have not modified their rigid form of patriarchal ideology brought from Korea because they are socially segregated from mainstream U.S. society. Furthermore, men's role as provider and their social status have significantly weakened with immigration.

What do Proverbs 31 and "Praise of Lady Yum" say to those who cherish a patriarchal ideology or a male chauvinism? As indicated above, the poems picture the wise wives as indispensable helpmates and advisers, and as the foundation for the peace and stability of the family. They also depict the female as a person-in-community and indicate the capabilities of women in cultivating and maintaining a web of social relations. Even though the poems still retain some aspects of reality for women in patriarchal society as "the way it is," the wives represented in the biblical poem and "Praise of Lady Yum" set themselves as examples in male-oriented societies to show that women can take active and authoritative roles in communities. Therefore, these two poems provide worthy interpretive and cultural rationales to dismiss a male-dominated mind-set and a patriarchal worldview.

Heewon Chung is Lecturer of Old Testament at the College of Liberal Arts, Keimyung University, Daegu, South Korea.

QUESTIONS

1. Assess Chitwood's reading of the biblical text. Is it accurate to describe the woman of Proverbs 31 as Superwoman and Betty Crocker combined?
2. Why is Woman Wisdom an important part of Brenner's reading? Explain what Brenner means when she says that a "mixed and at least dual-layered message to and about women is implicit in the book of Proverbs."
3. Compare and contrast the social and cultural context of Ramabai and the writers of Proverbs 31.
4. Imagine a conversation between Lady Yum and the woman of the biblical poem. How might they sympathize with and critique each other?

CHAPTER 20

JOB

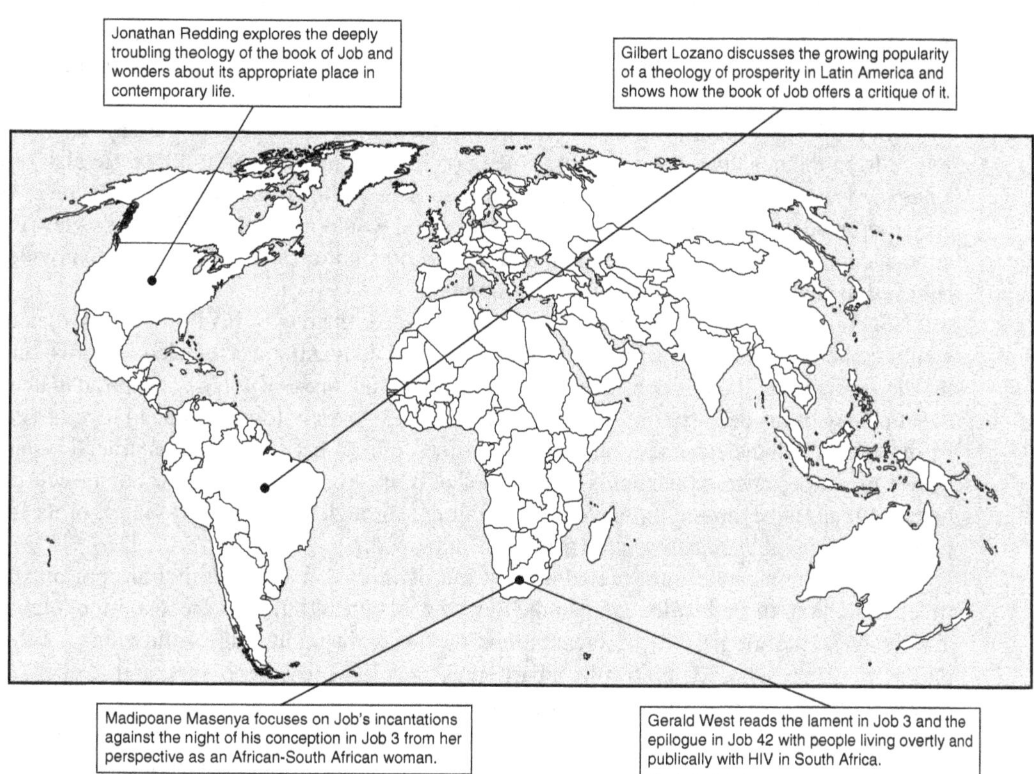

Jonathan Redding explores the deeply troubling theology of the book of Job and wonders about its appropriate place in contemporary life.
Gilbert Lozano discusses the growing popularity of a theology of prosperity in Latin America and shows how the book of Job offers a critique of it.
Madipoane Masenya focuses on Job's incantations against the night of his conception in Job 3 from her perspective as an African-South African woman.
Gerald West reads the lament in Job 3 and the epilogue in Job 42 with people living overtly and publically with HIV in South Africa.

READINGS

An African-South African Woman's Perspective on Job 3
Madipoane Masenya

Job 3 and 42 and Their Relation to People Living with HIV in South Africa
Gerald West

Job's Critique of a Theology of Prosperity in Latin America
Gilbert Lozano

The Troubling Theology of Job and Its Place in Contemporary Life
Jonathan Redding

An African-South African Woman's Perspective on Job 3

Madipoane Masenya (South Africa)

An African Proverb says, *bošego ga bo rone nta.* When translated it means: A night cannot remove lice from the seams of clothes. Its underlying tenor is that it is difficult to work efficiently in the night because dangerous experiences are usually linked with the night. The night thus cannot be safe; it cannot be trusted. Perhaps it is no wonder that acts of witchcraft in African cultures were and are still basically linked with the night. In Job 3, Job is not only scared of the night but also of the night's darkness and all the images which were conjured by the ancients when they thought about the night. He has a great distaste for the night, believing that nothing good could come from the night, that *bošego ga bo rone nta.*

Several observations are in order. First, in the incantations against the day he was born, Job calls on the negative, the night, to come upon his day and mess it up (3:4). He also reflects a narrow view of God and even a distaste for God. It is assumed that as the day becomes darkened, deprived of light and thus blackened, Job's God would not seek it! Has Job's view of creation suddenly changed? Was the night and its darkness not created by the same God who was believed to have been responsible for all of creation?

Second, as for the night of his conception, just like the day of his birth, Job wishes that it would come into oblivion (3:3). Even though Job 3 is conventionally labeled as Job's curse of the day of his birth, there is considerably more focus on the night of Job's conception than on the eventual day of his delivery on Mother earth. That the two are intricately bound together cannot be disputed. Nonetheless, the foregrounding of the night of his conception is crucial because it shows the importance of women's bodies, not only in providing a suitable home/security for human life at its beginning but also in nurturing life through the very early stages of its formation, influencing it even before its arrival on Mother earth.

Third, the incantations leveled against the night of Job's conception are not only three times more than those leveled against the day of Job's birth, but they are also more elaborate. The images emerging from the incantations on the night include the following: (1) intense darkness, (2) sadness, (3) no fertility/ barrenness, (4) light-less/dark stars, and (5) permanent darkness. In Job's view, that night must not only be darkened, but it should never have been fertile! The night's provision of suitable space for the fruitful sexual relationship between Job's parents is viewed with distaste by their offspring. Job particularly shuns the fact that his mother's womb became fertile ground for the beginning of his existence. For Job, the night cannot and should not be trusted, *bošego ga bo rone nta!*

Contrary to Job, from my perspective as an African-South African woman, the night does in fact have the capacity to remove lice from the seams of clothes, *bošego bo rona nta*! Why? First, it is on that night that a woman played a critical role in the process of cocreation. Second, had it not been for that night, where would Bible readers have gotten the story of a devout man whose relationship to God could apparently not be tampered with by what he perceived to be God's unjust dealings with him? Third, Job's character affords readers with a rare model of a male human being who faces the pain caused by grief with both frankness and humanness. Fourth, through Job's lament, the reader is also provided with a positive view of death and the place of the dead. A Bible reader coming from the Two-Thirds World is naturally empowered by Job's observation that in and through death, the ground is level: both the great and the small, royalty and those with no royal blood, the rich and the poor, those designated wicked and those designated righteous. All these will be and are united in death. Yes, that night which gave birth to the beginning of Job's life *e rona nta*! It can remove lice from the seams of clothes. It can thus be trusted.

An important issue here is Job's attack on his mother's reproductive organs. He curses the cervix of his mother's womb (3:7–10) and attacks his mother's thighs and breasts (3:12). Job's attack on his mother's body and reproductive organs does not resonate with the sociocultural reality of an African woman in South Africa. In African cultures, one who wants his or her rival to feel the real pinch will swear at them by swearing at their mother's private parts. Job's misogyny is revealed not only in his distaste for women (women's anatomy) but also in his lack of respect for women as human beings in their own right. Job does not have any appreciation for the importance of the human womb—a symbol of life for all human beings, irrespective of their gender and age. Life was precarious in Job's day, given the risks entailed in pregnancy and the birthing processes, especially without modern medicine. How could Job trivialize such crucial processes?

Job, who probably played a lesser or no role in communal mothering and never tasted what it means to carry a human being in the womb, has the luxury to speak about the female body as he so deemed fit. In his anger, he can simply say, "Why did I not die at birth, come forth from the womb and expire?" (3:11). It is indeed disturbing to note Job's lack of sympathy for someone (and their anatomy) who had treasured a human being and nurtured life in her womb for nine months. Only outsiders to female anatomy can in their moments of distress wish that their mothers' wombs were their tombs!

What about the life of a woman in such circumstances? Distressed men, such as Job whose misery has also inspired him to long for the tomb, apparently do not want to die alone. No! Their mothers, these women who should have possessed failed wombs, were then expected to serve as their son's graves. In essence, these mothers have a responsibility to accompany their sons to their own tombs!

In this vein, one wonders whether Job's assault on female anatomy is an indication of the control which men as property-owners (then and today) had/have on the bodies of those who are powerless. One thinks of powerless women today whose bodies are controlled by men: sex slaves, prostitutes, and girls and women from the Two-Thirds World who are used for sex trafficking by the rich—not to mention the many married women, widows, and daughters who fall into the same category. Job's assault of female anatomy follows the same line of thinking: Men control the bodies of women.

Job's lament reveals his problematic view of reproductive female anatomy, which is not helpful for (African) women, especially those who must struggle with the loss of a child. Such women are likely to be more pained after reading Job 3 than they were before they began. Another African proverb states thus: *Tswala ga e gane ka teng fela, le ka gare e a gana,* which is translated as: Birth (it) does not only fail inwardly, even on the outside it does fail. This proverb is usually cited by parents who had raised deviant children, children who dared to swear at their mothers. If Job had an African mother, not only would she have cited the preceding proverb, Job's African mother would have out of frustration leveled the following incantation at him for all that he said against female anatomy: *bakgekolo nke ba go dule godimo!* This means "Would that the old midwives would have sat on you immediately after your delivery onto Mother earth!"

Madipoane Masenya (ngwan'a Mphahlele) (Ph.D.) teaches in the Department of Old Testament and Ancient Near Eastern Studies at the University of South Africa.

Job 3 and 42 and Their Relation to People Living with HIV in South Africa

Gerald West (South Africa)

Since the 1950s the haunting sounds of the following lament have been heard in South Africa, at funerals, mostly, but also in political marches and in church. "*Senzeni na?* What have we done?/ *Sono sethu, ubumyama?* Our sin is that we are black?/ *Sono sethu yinyaniso?* Our sin is the truth?/ *Sibulawayo!* They are killing us!/ *Mayibuye iAfrica!* Let Africa return!" In the 1980s this song could be heard almost daily, and definitely on Saturdays, when the communities gathered to bury those murdered by the apartheid regime.

Unfortunately, a decade and a half after liberation we still sing this song. The terrain of struggle has shifted from political liberation to economic liberation, and the related struggle for deliverance from HIV and AIDS. Funerals are still the primary social location of this song. "*Senzeni na?* What have we done?"

In our work with people living overtly and publically with HIV, the Ujamaa Centre for Community Development and Research has turned to the book of Job. With the poet Mzwakhe Mbuli we have wondered, "Why are there so many more funerals than weddings?/ Do you [God] know that our graves are overcrowded?" Trusting in the solidarity of God, we have had the courage to ask hard questions. Experiencing in our bodies the life-giving effects of antiretroviral treatment, we have had the luxury of time to lament. Like Job we have turned to interrogate God.

Here at the Ujamaa Centre we have undertaken Contextual Bible Study, where we read parts of the Bible with a group of people living overtly and publically with HIV. As we explored Job 3 together with this group, a young man, one of the few men at that time to participate, voiced his despair, declaring that he knew exactly how Job felt, fantasizing about his death. Trembling with emotion, he told us how he had had to fight the desire to take his own life after he was diagnosed as HIV-positive. He had managed, he continued, to live "positively," drawing deeply on the support of the group. But, he declared, turning directly to me as one of the facilitators, our reading of Job 3 had reignited the smoldering desire for death. Why should he not, he asked me, take his own life?

It was a moment of utter terror for me. I realized I had made a terrible mistake in offering this text to the group. In that moment of complete panic I looked to my cofacilitator and colleague, Bongi Zengele, hoping desperately that her wisdom would offer a word of guidance and hope. Instead, she embraced and calmed me with her wonderful smile, silently encouraging me to trust the Contextual Bible Study process. So, doing what facilitators do, I turned to the group and asked them if they had anything to offer our brother. But he interrupted this attempt to draw on the resources of the group, stood and pointed at me, and said, "No, why do *you* say I should not leave this place and take my life?" He was insistent that I respond. Again, I looked in alarm at Bongi, and again she smiled. So I turned to the text, saying that though Job, like him, had fantasized about his own death, using an array of images, he had not contemplated taking his own life. He had directed, instead, his desire for death toward God, imagining the many ways in which God might have brought about his death at birth (3:3–19) or before he had experienced his current troubles (3:20–26). Though Job continued to lament his life, I said, he seemed to accept that his life was in God's hands.

Remarkably, my turn to the logic and flow of the text seemed to satisfy him, and he nodded and sat amongst us again. But I now felt the need to respond to his outburst, fearing that he might feel he had done "the wrong thing" by so openly lamenting his life. So I carried on, following the poetic narrative through to the end, summarizing briefly how Job refused to restrain his lament in the face of his friends' arguments, how Job even refused to retract his lament when finally he came face-to-face with God (38–42:6), and how in the prose epilogue God commended Job for "having spoken of/to God what is right" (42:7). It seemed to me, I concluded, that both what and how Job had spoken to/of God was appropriate, given Job's reality.

Others now rejoined the discussion, sharing their own doubt, fear, and despair. After nearly three hours together, Bongi brought our time together to a conclusion, inviting us to breathe deeply in unison and to pray for one another. We were exhausted but strangely at peace. It was then that we were asked whether we would be willing to do this same study of Job with their families.

Returning the notion of lament to the lives of those whose churches insist on the retributive theological trajectory of Job's friends (that all suffering is deserved) was clearly a liberating experience for the group members. But what was it that they wanted their families to know? Was it that lament was a "biblical" and therefore legitimate aspect of their (and the Christian) faith? Was it that Job refused to accept the dominant theological tradition of his (and our) time? Was it that Job persisted in his integrity (2:9) before his friends and even God? Was it that God affirmed Job's mode of engaging with God?

Each aspect of the poetic Job may have resonated with the group's members. But I suspect that it is probably the last mentioned element that resonated most clearly: By drawing their attention to how God responds in 42:7, I was offering them a potential line of connection with a God who takes a clear stand with the stigmatized Job over against Job's friends.

Job 42:7 seems to be pivotal point for those who are HIV-positive. The shift from verse 6 to 7 is massive, for we now leave the "private" domain of a dialogue between Job and God and enter the public domain. First, God, in front of Job's friends, takes sides with Job. Second, God then involves the whole community, by calling upon the friends to perform a public ritual, for which they are required to obtain resources—cattle, sheep, fire, knives—from Job's local community. Having in this manner drawn Job's community into the discourse, God then has Job praying, publically, for his friends, who in their folly have not, God repeats, spoken of/to God what is right (42:8). We are to imagine, I suggest, an audience of those who have stigmatized and withdrawn from Job listening and watching as God takes sides with Job. They then become participants, contributing to and so becoming implicated in the ritual that redeems the friends and reintegrates Job into his community. This, I think, is why the Bible study group wanted us to do the same study with their families.

And what might be the result of such a public affirmation? The answer can be found in 42:11, where the restoration of Job is not magical, but involves the acceptance and support of the whole community: All his brothers and sisters and those who had known him before came and consoled him and comforted him and ate with him.

The fundamental restoration is the restoration of a stigmatized Job to his community. "A person is a person because of other people" is the core value of African society, and yet the stigma associated with HIV has eaten away at us, devouring our communities. But if God is for us, who can be against us? If it is clear to the families of those who are HIV-positive that God stands with the infected, how can the family cast them out?

Gerald West teaches at the Ujamaa Centre in the School of Religion and Theology at University of KwaZulu-Natal, South Africa.

JOB'S CRITIQUE OF A THEOLOGY OF PROSPERITY IN LATIN AMERICA

Gilbert Lozano (Brazil)

The so-called theology of prosperity, or Prosperity Gospel, is spreading like wildfire throughout Latin America. Preachers from several theological strands have realized that this is a good marketing tool and that the masses are attracted to a message that speaks of earthly rewards instead of heavenly ones, and the gifts that God can bestow on the faithful. One watches with amazement as the masses are led to believe that the central message of the Bible is their own prosperity and enrichment.

A few years ago this message was restricted to Pentecostal churches, and then it was picked up by the neo-Pentecostal movement, a loose conglomerate of churches that attracts large crowds due to their emphasis on miracles and on the belief that the individual is the proper locus for God's actions in the world. In other words, the concerns of individuals have taken center stage. Religious services have little teaching, and biblical readings are selected mostly from those parts of the Bible that talk about blessings and promises. The neo-Pentecostal movement revolves around charismatic leaders who guide their flocks with hardheaded tactics. Religion has entered the realm of entrepreneurship. The leaders and their followers stand in a symbiosis in which the leader is able to lead because of his (for it's mostly, if not exclusively, a male-directed movement) capacity to innovate in religious matters. Likewise, the followers' entrepreneurship is tested in their ability to respond positively to the message by way of acting out the promises, for example, by starting new businesses and by making increased financial contributions to the churches. Entrepreneurship is also seen in the innovative theological concepts and practices that are being developed. In this sense, every church meeting is supposed to need a new practice, a new anointment, new ecstasies—for instance, blessings in which the believer is endowed with the strength of animals, and so forth.

It can be argued that a self-serving attitude motivates many who attend those services. It's a reciprocal *quid pro quo*, an exchange of commercial proportions whereby the believer gives something to God expecting to receive something in return. This new brand of faith is eminently a pragmatic one—people do such and such because it works and it is the best course of action for success.

The messengers of prosperity promise their audiences rich rewards based on texts largely taken from what scholars call the wisdom tradition. They use an assortment of proof texts without any other connection if not the common assurance of blessings. Texts such as Proverbs 12:2, "The good obtain favor from the LORD," and Proverbs 22:4, "The reward for humility and fear of the LORD is riches and honor and life" are commonly recited as proof texts of what awaits the faithful who follow these churches' doctrinal line and who contribute generously. I have heard this text from Deuteronomy used in those churches: "The Lord will make you the head, and not the tail; you shall be only at the top, and not at the bottom—if you obey the commandments of the Lord your God, which I am commanding you today, by diligently observing them" (28:13). Unfortunately, these messages lack ethical appeal, or an other-oriented ethical direction. The only ethical option or line pursued at those services is that of adhering strictly to the church's rules and giving tithes and other financial contributions. The prevailing ethics seems to be one of self-interest that puts individuals and their happiness in the center stage with promises of long life (Proverbs 3:1–2; 9:11), safety (Proverbs 12:21), and above all, wealth and prosperity (Proverbs 8:18–21; 22:4; Psalm 1:3).

This theology of prosperity has enormous appeal. However, it only takes a little empirical evidence to know that life is just not always easy or rosy colored. In fact, life for most people around the world is hard. Countless millions still suffer from the lack of the most basic of things, such as food and sanitation. In Latin America many people go to bed at night without having had a single decent meal during the day. Poverty in this continent is endemic, and this is true from the countryside to the great urban areas. Moreover, religiosity doesn't seem to help. Latin Americans are amongst the most religious and fervent of people on the planet, and yet their misery continues at alarming rates. In fact, the neo-Pentecostal message of earthly rewards is just a variation of the Catholic teaching that the impoverished people of these lands would be rewarded by God in heaven. The neo-Pentecostals have simply anticipated the time of the rewards, bringing them to this life. It's questionable, however, what world-changing orientation this message may cause among followers.

The message of God-given prosperity was questioned already in antiquity. The book of Job contains a sophisticated rebuttal to it. The book consists of three rounds of speeches between Job's friends—initially Eliphaz, Bildad, and Zophar, and lastly Elihu, who are defenders of the traditional classical wisdom. The theory behind the wisdom theology is simple. It proposes that if a person behaves a certain way, then she will receive rewards. Conversely, bad things (curses) will derive from not following the teachings of the sages. It's all very mechanical because the world is supposed to function almost like a machine.

The book of Job opens with a wager between Yahweh and Satan whereby Job is a mere pawn in a cosmic plot. Job begins by lamenting his birth and wishes to have been stillborn (3:1–16). Job's friend Eliphaz responds that righteous people don't suffer and that it's good to be punished by God. Today we would say that he defends the view that suffering holds lessons for people. Job, however, insists on his innocence (6:25–26), and refuses to accept his suffering (7:11). Bildad, the second friend, points out that God makes no mistakes (8:3)—Job's suffering must be justified. Job again points out that his trial is unfair since nobody can win a case against God. Job wishes for a fair trial based on justice. At this point the third friend, Zophar, emerges. He appeals to the mystery of God. Job accepts that, but he retorts that his friends have defended God, assuming Job's culpability. Elihu, the last friend to appear, argues that God does not pervert justice (34:12).

Job's friends accuse Job of obstinacy for his reluctance to confess the sins that undoubtedly were the cause of his misfortunes. The "friends" defended that system of rewards for good behavior and curses for wrongdoing. Moreover, their intent was to persuade Job to recognize the folly of his ways and to confess his sins. Job, however, defended his innocence and argued vigorously for his right to speak even before God. Furthermore, he pointed out that the wisdom system doesn't really work: There are evil people who enjoy long and prosperous lives and pious or just people who have died prematurely. Job complains bitterly against God in 10:1–22. He asks to be left alone. In fact, he accuses God of scheming to destroy him (21:27), while the wicked seem to do quite well (21:7–16).

God finally shows up in Job 38–41. God's speech stresses his power and knowledge, which contrast with humanity's insignificance (38:4–39:30). Job apparently admits that because he interrupts his defense (40:3–5). At the end, ironically God sides with Job, and not with those who had defended God. The book of Job, in short, gives a severe blow to a simplistic understanding of wisdom in a mechanistic fashion. Life is more complicated than that.

The book of Job corrects many of the distortions seen today in Latin America in the preaching of a theology of prosperity. This magnificent book stands as a witness that it's just not possible to manipulate the divine—that is, to reduce faith simply to a transaction that guarantees prosperity and happiness, and where the believers can expect to have it all here on earth.

Gilbert Lozano (Ph.D.) taught at Fidelis: the Mennonite School of Theology, Curitiba, Brazil and is currently Associate Professor of Biblical Studies at Anderson University, United States.

The Troubling Theology of Job and Its Place in Contemporary Life

Jonathan Redding (United States)

The perplexing and discomforting God in the book of Job makes few pastors and ministers enjoy preaching and teaching the text. A quick reading of the first two chapters may make the reader believe that God turns a blind eye as "the Accuser" ("Satan") orchestrates a plan that destroys Job's livestock, kills his sons and daughters, and covers Job's body in sores. Closer reading only worsens the portrayal of God's character because the text explicitly states that pious Job suffers as the result of a capricious wager between God and the Accuser. God's eventual reappearance and the content of God's response to Job (in Job 38–42) further denigrates the deity and troubles the reader. Job's heavenly bully seems fallacious compared to modern liberal religious idealisms, and my attempts to interpret this God from my progressive Christian perspective only obfuscates my understanding of God's actions.

My life has been easy and simple; I have never gone to war, nor have I ever experienced great physical anguish or trauma. America has no mass genocide or violent totalitarian leader in its brief history. Thus, I speak of suffering as I see and experience it occurring around the world. Unimaginable evil happens daily and Job's presentation of God makes this evil even more irreconcilable and horrifying. Nothing within the book provides idyllic resolutions.

Many children's sermons and countless childhood Vacation Bible School themes have a common message: God is loving and would never willingly harm anyone; therefore, being afraid of God is unfounded and misguided. Job's God shatters these youthful romanticized notions and makes one rethink the supposed benevolence of God. If Job's presentation of God is true, then God is responsible for the world's suffering and God is culpable for horrific events like the Holocaust or the genocides in Rwanda. Banal phrases such as "it is all part of God's plan" arise in the aftermath of catastrophic tragedies, and though the words are trite and arguably inappropriate, they do hold out hope that everything, even disasters, has a purpose. But the problem is that what befalls Job because of God's actions is trivial and purposeless, as God admits in 2:3. It was a perverted, pointless bet. There is no divine plan.

Job laments his life and mourns inconsolably. He cries to God seeking answers and God remains silent for over 30 chapters. When God does ultimately respond, the Accuser is gone and God alone speaks with Job. God's retort is just as appalling as the initial bet because God reminds Job of his lowly humanity and states that God is the one who created and upholds the universe. In summary, God asks Job, "What place do you or any human have in questioning me?" All humans, even the virtuous like Job, are to remain subservient as God's subjects. God is unapologetic and never shows remorse or regret; God essentially reprimands for Job questioning God's judgment. God's speech is akin to a schoolyard bully spitting and rubbing dirt on the child he or she has just beaten. Job's apparent acceptance (42:6) of his place as a mere pawn within God's cosmos is disheartening because God makes Job's life dispensable, which in turn questions the value of human existence. In the end, God restores and doubles what Job had previously, which Job enjoys with reverence and humility until his natural death.

To speak frankly, God is unjust in Job. The deity authorizes the Accuser to make sport of torturing and killing innocent people. God remains silent as Job mourns his unjustified circumstances. God's response is pompous, arrogant, and downright frightening. God's restoration of Job's belongings and family is belittling because God seems to believe that replacing what Job lost atones for God's behavior. Ask a mother and father who lost a son to a drunken-driving accident or a widower who lost a young wife to cancer: Would a new son or spouse compensate for the initial loss? Surely the answer would be a resounding "no." God's act of replacing dead children—ten of them no less!—severely diminishes the importance of human life: God seems to equate life with something that could be acquired from the local department store.

My reflections on God's character in the book of Job settles on a simple question: What place does the book have in contemporary life? Should people console mourning loved ones and friends by reading Job? Or should the entire book be in an editor's trash can? Job raises more questions than it answers, which may be intentional. Perhaps the author compiled this story as a personal therapeutic act as he or she attempted to reconcile recent catastrophes. Maybe the writer wanted to challenge traditional notions of divine omniscience and justice by writing something so outlandish that readers had no choice but to reconsider their assumptions and conclusions regarding God, suffering, and evil. It is also conceivable that the author genuinely felt this was how the world worked and composed this narrative as a reminder of humanity's insignificant place within creation. The text leaves the reader seeking answers.

What we can assert, however, is that the book's presentation of God contributes to the Bible's theological cacophony. The Bible's disharmony is an intrinsic and inflexible product of human effort, which gives readers the right to question, dispute, speculate, and deny its claims. The book of Job shows one individual's (or individuals') view of God and the world. Thus, the book must be placed within a broader understanding of scripture that encompasses humanity's limited understanding of the past and its idealized perception of the present. Making Job's theology doctrinal—elevating it to the status of truth—degrades the value of lived experience and discredits the simple hope that inspires humanity into daily living. If we take nothing else away from the book, we can find solidarity with long deceased humans as they struggle and live amidst chaotic evil.

Jonathan Redding is a student at Wake Forest School of Divinity and a parttime Minister with Youth and Families at Peace Haven Baptist Church in Winston-Salem, North Carolina, United States.

QUESTIONS

1. Assess Masenya's suggestion that Job's words are an indication of a social context in which women's bodies are seen as the property of men. Imagine how Job might respond to Masenya on this point.
2. Evaluate West's response to the young man contemplating suicide. Does West accurately interpret the text of Job 3? Does it matter?
3. How might a Prosperity Gospel preacher respond to Lozano?
4. Evaluate Redding's notion that God and Satan make a "wager" in Job 1 and 2 and his argument that God's speech in Job 38–41 is arrogant and frightening. How might one compose a counter-reading on these two points?

CHAPTER 21

SONG OF SONGS

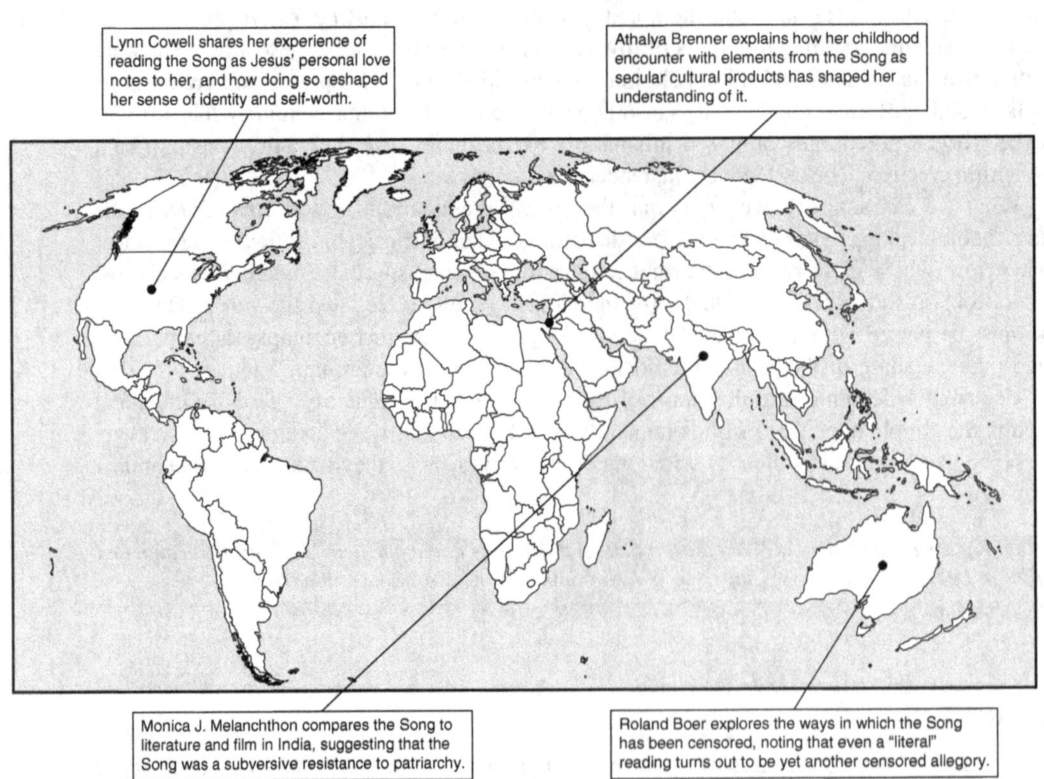

Lynn Cowell shares her experience of reading the Song as Jesus' personal love notes to her, and how doing so reshaped her sense of identity and self-worth.
Athalya Brenner explains how her childhood encounter with elements from the Song as secular cultural products has shaped her understanding of it.
Monica J. Melanchthon compares the Song to literature and film in India, suggesting that the Song was a subversive resistance to patriarchy.
Roland Boer explores the ways in which the Song has been censored, noting that even a "literal" reading turns out to be yet another censored allegory.

READINGS

A Comparison of the Song to Literature and Film in India
Monica J. Melanchthon

Hearing the Song as a Secular Cultural Product
Athalya Brenner

The Song as Jesus' Personal Love Notes
Lynn Cowell

The Song as a Censored Allegory
Roland Boer

A Comparison of the Song to Literature and Film in India

Monica J. Melanchthon (India)

Discussions of sexuality in India invariably begin with attention to a time in India's "ancient" past when public expressions of sexuality were not considered taboo. The extant Kama Sutra and the narrative surrounding it perhaps contributed to this impression, a product of colonial history, nationalist aspirations, and European theorizing that sought to present a free and sexually liberal Orient (East) that was in variance with a prudish and repressed Occident (West). But any discussions of Indian sexuality need to go beyond the Kama Sutra since that text restricts our understanding of modern manifestations of sexuality in India. India is diverse and so also its sexual cultures. Today, one sees small-town magazines and women's magazines which are part of a semi-illicit circuit of debate and discussion on sexuality, drawing participants that are not part of official or dominant discourses on sexuality and sex-education. These magazines have created a forum for nonmoralizing discussions on desires, fantasies, anxieties, and intimacies. These in my estimation are peripheral and marginal discussions on and constructions of sexuality. They are perhaps radical and liberating but considered perverse and not welcomed; they are policed by the State and the dominant culture that seeks to protect India from bad influences.

I see the Song of Songs as a similar text that perhaps arose as a peripheral and marginal text in the contesting and disorienting context of postexilic Israel. It was a time when, in the interests of the community and its identity, restrictions and proscriptions were inscribed on the bodies of women, considered to be the conduits of tradition and culture, objects of regulation and control. It is within such a context that the Song explores the subject of love and sexuality with a sense of candor and freedom of expression. At times, love is all passion, blazing and fierce. At times it is all compassion, gentle and reserved. The theme of love seems to act as a prism resolving a variety of attitudes toward women and the subject of desire. The Song can best be described as a reaction to the male essentialist description of feminine character, the female body, and female sexuality, longing, and desire. It resists patriarchy and articulates an unapologetic subjective female worldview on these issues in a traditionally restrictive patriarchal culture, and presents a female sexual self that will not be silenced or belittled by the normative injustices of the status quo. The author presses for the worth of a woman's being as body, affirms it as a form of feminine empowerment, and celebrates it, and the varied dimensions of her being as woman positioned in a patriarchal frame of reference.

The Song is part of our scriptural tradition. Could the Song have been included in the canon in an effort to integrate sexuality and spirituality? Was sexuality regarded as an integral part of life, a gift to be honored and enjoyed? Is this why this Song of Love was made part of the canon? The history of interpretation of the Song does not seem to point to this possibility. The subversive nature of the book and its potential to disturb a male-dictated society has been to a large extent domesticated and suppressed by rendering the Song as an allegory for the yearning of the devotee for God. Seen in this way, the inclusion of the Song was a way of co-opting it to diminish its revolutionary potential, its social and political dimensions, and to undermine its constructions of sexuality, particularly that of women.

In the Indian context, it is this allegorized reading that is emphasized. When one is led to see it primarily as a metaphor for love between the divine and the human being, one misses the subversive and the resistant nature of the Song. Read from the perspective of the Indian woman who, by and large, lives a life of unwilling compromises within given/imposed circumstances, the Song is preeminently a protest against the male control of the female body and the silence into which it has been coerced. The author mines the boarded up space that is the woman's body, loosens the fetters that have bound and shrunk the woman's body, and offers them to the world. As a means of protesting the silence into which it has been coerced, the female body keeps imprinting on itself all the seasonal changes as being wrought continuously by nature. A discerning reader and an engaged interpreter in tune with women's experience of subjugation and discrimination, of violation and pain would be able to recognize the Song's capability of engendering subjective epiphanies, of perhaps producing inner tremors resulting in the inner renewal and transformation of the woman in relation to her body, her relationship to her lover, and her perception of the self.

The fact that the book is presented as a song is of exceptional significance for the Indian reader, for there is a strong Indian tradition of narrating mythology, history, tales, and the like through song and dance, but particularly expressions of love. The form comes from Indian theater. Songs are considered a natural mode of articulation, to express emotions, advance the narrative, provide catharses, and entertain. Anyone who is familiar with Indian films would recognize that a majority of the songs are about love and sung by people in love. The backdrop for these love songs in Indian cinema is often the outdoors, in beautiful natural surroundings, lush green meadows, snowy mountain tops, flower-filled gardens, or architecturally grand settings in India, but more often in foreign locales. The viewer is transported to a different world. Devised as visual pageants, these songs are often contrived as "dream sequences," permitting change of costume and location, thus, expressing the inexpressible, and inviting the viewers to indulge in the pleasure of looking, while actors display their physical beauty and exhibit themselves as pure objects of desire to be visually feasted upon by their fans. If the camera makes strategic moves offscreen to shots of birds and trees, this is quite enough to suggest activities that the censors might not approve of. Filmmakers go through great lengths to showcase emotions through rain, and wind, from delicate sensuality to aggressive. Indian filmmakers make no attempt to conceal the fact that what is shown on the screen is a creation, an illusion, a fiction heightening the fantasy. Anything can happen that would not normally happen in the real world. For the majority poor in India, the film and the song provide temporary escape from daily troubles.

I cannot help but question if the Song of Songs is part of a dream. Was a woman in a traditional Israelite society able to exercise such sexual liberty in real life? What might the repercussions be? Even more noteworthy are the Song's appreciation of the verdure and variegation of nature and its description of the settings/locales of the meeting of the two lovers, its metaphors drawn from nature, to showcase their love, desire, and sexuality. For example, in Song of Songs 2, the woman can hear the leaping and the bounding of her lover across the mountains and hills, even from afar. The natural setting helps enhance the beauty of love. It stresses the notion that love cannot be confined to time and place. It helps the couple see beyond their mundane environments and their immediate problems. It transfigures the most ordinary of circumstances and transforms their immediate surrounding into a place of beauty and wonder. This interweaving of metaphors drawn from nature with the human experience of love and desire is significant and appealing, and strengthens the solacing camaraderie between nature and the human being. The Song seems to be saying that love and desire are natural, innate, and cannot be legislated, curtailed, or controlled.

The Song of Songs is first and foremost the cry of the female body in its essential yearning for love and the delight that can be found when in union with the body of a lover. The Song therefore may be part of a dream, a fanciful depiction, or even reality. Either way, it is purposeful and provides opportunity for academic and textual activism for the sake of the woman. To a liberated reader, the Song connotes the joy of freedom. To a reader still suffering from oppression and fear, the Song may be perceived as a fantasy, a dream, an escape into a space that she yearns for—something to hope for, to look forward to, to fight for. In either case, the Song has the potential to enter the beings of women; it provides women the opportunity to shake its quiescent images into wakefulness for the purposes of emancipation.

Monica J. Melanchthon is a Professor in the Department of Old Testament Studies at Gurukul Lutheran Theological College, Chennai, India.

Hearing the Song as a Secular Cultural Product

Athalya Brenner (Israel)

Imagine living with the Song of Songs (henceforth, SoS) in Hebrew, as a secular cultural product, without and before knowing it's a biblical text. "I am dark and/but comely." That is not SoS 1:6 but a popular song on the radio, in Radio Times Israel of pretelevision days (i.e., pre 1967). It is sung by a well-known female singer of Yemenite descent. Her Hebrew diction is Sephardi (Oriental), perhaps exaggerated. The tune is certainly Oriental.

"My beloved is mine and I am his" (2:16; 6:3) is another song, once again performed by a female voice. It is also a formula uttered by many brides under the *chuppah* (bridal canopy), a modern addition to the male-biased orthodox ceremony that is the law of the land for Jewish marriages.

"Many waters cannot quench love" (8:7). A piece of folk wisdom, isn't it? "I went down to the nut orchard . . ." is a song and a folk dance. "Folk" in both cases since most people who quote the former and dance the latter don't know or remember who was the inventing source or the choreographer; both are quoted, sung, or danced by many. The dance is easy to learn and danced by couples, normally heterosexual.

There are more lines to be cited. Kisses sweeter than wine. I am the lily of Sharon. My beloved is . . . All seem to be public property, known by all, sung by all, danced by many, part of the cultural milieu, and needing no explanation, or an inquiry into their origin.

And then, one day, I think I was in my mid-teens, it was Pesach (Passover), and we were all tired after reading part of the *Haggadah* and doing the *Seder* (the Pesach family ritual, according to its text) and eating the traditional Ashkenazi heavy meal, when my father—who managed the proceedings, as befits a paterfamilias-for-a-day—started intoning some text; and from within my state of being depleted with good but too plentiful food, I started hearing, not songs set to music, but a recitation of lines I knew full well outside this annual occasion. The lines quoted above. And looking at the *Haggadah* text, and the explanations thereof, I made a discovery: Those songs, sayings, dances I grew up on, practiced in earlier then teenage life, were part of a biblical book—the SoS. For, in Jewish tradition, the SoS is read on Passover: in some communities, such as my source community, on the *Seder* night and at home; in others, at the synagogue, on Passover weekend. It is one of the Five Scrolls (together with Ruth, Lamentations, Qoheleth, and Esther) that are ritually recited, annually, in Jewish Holy days.

The fact that I had met and practiced—so to speak—the SoS before I knew it was "biblical" undoubtedly shaped my understanding of this biblical text; or, at the very least, this is how I see it in hindsight. Also, the way I met those texts has been influential, consciously or otherwise, in my scholarly but far from "objective" interpretation: It takes but little self-awareness to realize this. And, I believe, this has also given me an edge for understanding the "original" settings, or a little of them—and by so writing, I don't wish to sound superior or arrogant. This is what may happen when the cart precedes the horses. So here is how I view the SoS.

- The SoS is just that: songs. Not poems or lyrics to be read, recited, but texts performed to music. That the music is lost to us is a great pity; but that the Hebrew words, *shir ha-shirim*, mean "song of songs" and not "recitation of lyrics" is made abundantly clear by my cultural experiences.
- Most of the SoS songs, as set to music, that I heard in my life prior to discovering that they were biblical, were performed by female singers. Hence, it is natural for me to acknowledge not just an equal, but in fact a superior, presence of females in the SoS. Women in these poems seek their lovers actively, more so than their male lovers seek them. Women's voices comprise more than 60 percent of SoS lyrics, once we count the lines of lover women as well as the "Daughters of Jerusalem" chorus lines. Women lovers move more, act more, say more, are more articulate, and are more prominent. When we watch a play, a TV program, don't we assume that the actor who has the most lines, who performs the most actions, and who is seen the most is the chief actor? There you go then. Moreover, a female voice starts the proceedings (1:2–4) as well as ends them (most of SoS 8 to its very end). The love credo, the definition of love as strong as death or stronger than death, is uttered in a female voice (8:6–7).
- There is no "Father's House" in the SoS, just a "Mother's House" and brothers who seem ineffective as guardians of female sexual modesty (1:6; 8:8–10). Again, no problem. With so many female voices trilling, female power—even within the "Mother's House" and not outside it, where the City Guards may restore patriarchal order (3:3; 5:7)—is obvious. In love, if not necessarily in the world.
- In my childhood and youth I heard many singers, more females than males, singing SoS lines, at times as they appear in the Bible, at times fragmented or joined. These were not always the same singers, not even when the same lyrics were used. It is therefore no hardship for me to view the SoS as a *collection* of love lyrics. I don't need to speculate about a plot, or other unifying elements, or one single heterosexual couple, or a single romantic triangle (Solomon–shepherd–damsel). For me the variety of singing voices represents a variety in the SoS itself. This variety is eventually harnessed by editorial skill into a structure that climaxes in the middle of the book (4:8–5:1), then unfolds similarly in a chiastic manner on both sides of the climax.
- Is the SoS a wedding collection? Some scholars, from Origen on, would have it so. My early experiences of it undoubtedly make it easier to understand that, although a wedding for King Solomon is mentioned in SoS 3, the book is not a wedding collection; it doesn't celebrate an official union, and it certainly doesn't celebrate the otherwise foremost reason for marriage in the Bible—giving birth to offspring.
- The life contexts in which I first "met" SoS texts—secular, nonallegorical, young, completely unattached to matrimonial or theological situations—make it easier for me to view this biblical book as a collection of love songs, nothing more or less, so popular that its existence could not be suppressed; a solution would and did entail allegorical interpretations, but this is a different story altogether.

In sum, I grew up as a native Israeli, Hebrew speaker, daughter of immigrants from Eastern Europe. Most of the SoS for me was music, dance, geography, romance, life, before it became a biblical text. It took decades before I understood how my life context influenced my scholarly, definitely feminist reading.

Athalya Brenner is Professor of Bible at the University of Amsterdam, The Netherlands; and Tel Aviv University, Israel.

The Song as Jesus' Personal Love Notes

Lynn Cowell (United States)

Are you like me? Do you tend to gravitate toward certain books of the Bible, while avoiding other parts of God's Word? This is exactly what I did until I discovered something. I was missing out. I was missing some of the best parts about knowing God, because sometimes His love notes to us are hidden.

Unsure about its content, the Song of Solomon was one of the books I avoided. I knew that to some it is a picture of the passionate love that occurs between a groom and his bride, and to others a poetic metaphor of the love of Christ for his bride, the church. But what really was in the book?

A friend encouraged me to delve right in. She helped me realize I could personalize it to find hidden love notes from God. I began to look at the Song of Solomon from a different perspective; rather than see it as a book about God and all those "other people," I began to put myself into the verses. I was amazed at what I saw.

When I put my name into a passage in Song of Solomon 6, it felt like God was whispering directly to me: "I think you are so beautiful, Lynn... Let me start at your feet and go all the way to your head. Your toes are so pretty... they each should have a ring on them and then be slipped into soft and lovely slippers fit for a princess. Your hands are so soft, with fingers that are slender and feminine... a diamond placed on each one. Your arms are strong and defined, but perfect for a lady... they each deserve silk gloves to your delicate elbows. Your cheeks are smooth and rosy, surrounding a smile that is captivating. Just looking at your hair makes me want to run my fingers through it and never stop!"

Read that passage again. Listen to the powerful words. They are very emotional! I was shocked when I found words like these in the Bible. I had never known that God could have these feelings—that Jesus could feel *this* way about me. I had grown up following Him, knowing Him as my shepherd, savior, and friend, but I had never seen this side of Him before!

As we read Song of Solomon, it can bring perspective to our lives. This book can help us see another side of our multifaceted God. Genesis 1 tells us that we are made in His image; part of that image is an emotional being. While our walk with Him should not be based on emotions, emotions are a part of it. Love is a huge part of it. He doesn't just want to be the God that I serve; He wants to be the God I love. This book lends itself to helping us love our God.

I started reading His "love notes" over and over and over again. Exploring these treasure-filled verses changed me. I began to understand God felt a strong love for me. I also began to change. As I filled my mind and heart with these words of love from Jesus, loneliness, low self-esteem, and fear left me—there was no room for them! I began to see myself differently. The desperate need to be perfect inside and out began to fade.

Listen to *these* powerful words: "All beautiful you are, my darling; there is no flaw in you" (4:7). The word "flaw" in Hebrew means defect, blemish, shame, or defilement. I began to see that when He looks at me, He is not disappointed in me. He doesn't see the things I see. He sees what He created and He says that it is good. He sees the one He came to die to forgive: His own.

God says it again in 5:2, "Open for me, my sister, my love, my dove, my perfect one." Sounds strange? How can He say, "my perfect one"? He calls you perfect because when He sees you, when you have accepted Jesus as your Savior, He doesn't see your sin—He sees His forgiveness. He's cleansed us; that's what He sees. His word reassures us that we belong; we are loved. "My lover is mine and I am his . . ." (2:16) settles feelings of rejection and loneliness. This is what we were created for: to love and to be loved.

Lynn Cowell (www.LynnCowell.com) is author of His Revolutionary Love: Jesus' Radical Pursuit of You.

The Song as a Censored Allegory

Roland Boer (Australia)

Censorship is the context in which I wish to read the Song of Songs, since the Song has always had to deal with censorship of some form or another. Censorship seems undesirable when someone else is doing it to you, but necessary when you are imposing it on someone else. In theory, most of us would prefer to see no censorship at all (in the name of freedom of expression); in practice, we will come down in favor of some form of censorship: denial of the Holocaust in World War II, inciting hate crimes against people due to their gender, religion, or ethnic identity—these acts and others are forbidden in many countries. Undesirable but unavoidable—that sums up the dilemma of censorship.

As I write, in Australia the furor over censorship hinges on the Internet. It may be easy to rant and rave about censorship in China or to decry the closing down of the Internet during the 2011 revolutions in Egypt, Tunisia, or Libya, but when it comes closer to home, the question becomes touchier. The Australian government is in the process of imposing a series of Internet filters in order to block "undesirable" content. Much of that filtering applies to extreme political views, especially to what now goes under the name of "terrorism," but mostly it applies to graphic sexual material (violence, animals, and so on). And that is where this legislation has a direct bearing on my reading of the Song of Songs.

The Song with its acknowledged sensual and sexual tone has always attracted the censor's black tape. To begin with, it was one of the last texts to be included in the canon of the Hebrew Bible. Why? As a collection of poems that is all about the fecundity of nature, and the blend of human lust and love, it does not mention God at all, let alone offer any religious teaching. With its references to breasts, night sprinkles, hands in "latches" or on "bolts" (4:5; 5:2, 4, 5; 7:3), so much so that one can almost hear the slapping, squelching, and groaning of sex, more than one question was raised about the Song's status as authoritative and canonical, especially in the first and second century C.E.

So that the Song might become acceptable, three factors played a role. The claim of Solomonic authorship was one (it is, on this level, a product of his virile and lusty youth), and the use of the Song in rituals, especially the Day of Atonement, was another. These two are already subtle acts of censorship and theological appropriation. But the third factor is the most interesting of all—interpretation itself. The Song was read allegorically; that is, it really speaks about Israel's relationship with God, or later for Christians about the Church's and God's love for one another. So we find Rabbi Aqiba's famous and oft-quoted statement, at least as it appears in the Mishnah:

> Heaven forbid! – No Israelite man ever disputed concerning Song of Songs that it imparts uncleanness to hands. For the entire age is not so worthy as the day on which the Song of Songs was given to Israel. For all the scriptures are holy, but the Song of Songs is holiest of all.

You really are one of us, Aqiba is saying, but you just didn't know it. This is not merely a classic case of subtle interpretive censorship, shifting the troubled status of the Song and making it central, but it actually protests too much, going overboard to make the Song fit in: Not just holy, not a latecomer to the party who stands alone at the edges, the Song is in fact the "holiest of all." So much so that, as far as Aqiba is concerned, there was no dispute over the Song—but only if the Song is read allegorically.

This issue came back to haunt interpretation of the Song when this allegorical reading was discarded and a more "literal" sense gained ground. Tied in very closely with the Renaissance and Reformation, and appearing at about the same time as pornography was invented in the early sixteenth-century, the Song now becomes a collection of poems about human lust and love. Yet even here censorship is crucial: It must, it was argued, be lust between a heterosexual couple, preferably "betrothed" to one another. It cannot be a homosexual couple, for instance, or the expression of lust between multiple partners (such readings are perfectly possible with the Song and do no violence to the text). Once again, the Song has had to deal with the heavy hand of the biblical interpreter's censorship.

Yet all of this has a final and unexpected twist: Any reader of the Song finds precious little explicit and graphic sex described or celebrated. Instead, the Song is full of animals cavorting, of plants budding, flowers popping, of pollens and smells in the air. Indeed, a close reading reveals a text full of fluids, liquids, juices, running over and around the lines of the text. If it is about sex, then it is sex well beyond human engagement, for the sex we find in the Song is of a much wider realm that includes endless flora and fauna.

What are the implications for the so-called "literal" interpretation in which the Song is about human lust? That reading turns out to be yet another allegory, for the "literal," sexual meaning must be read at another level from the text itself. In that respect, interpreting the text as an expression of heterosexual lust is not different, at a formal level, from seeing it as an expression of God's love for Israel and/or the Church. It is hardly "literal" at all. The implication is clear: Both interpretations are forms of theological and scholarly censorship. So what would an entirely uncensored reading look like? Is it possible?

Roland Boer is a cyclist, ship-voyager, and research professor at the University of Newcastle, Australia.

QUESTIONS

1. Explain and evaluate Melanchthon's claim that the Song is subversive. What parts of the Song might counter this claim—that is, what part(s) might not "resist patriarchy"?
2. How does its place within Scripture influence one's interpretation of the Song? If it were not part of a religious text, how would the Song be read differently?
3. Assess Cowell's approach—identifying its potential problems and benefits. Does she appear to perceive a sexual element to the Song?
4. If Boer is right that both literal and allegorical readings are forms of censorship, then indeed what would an uncensored reading look like?

CHAPTER 22

RUTH

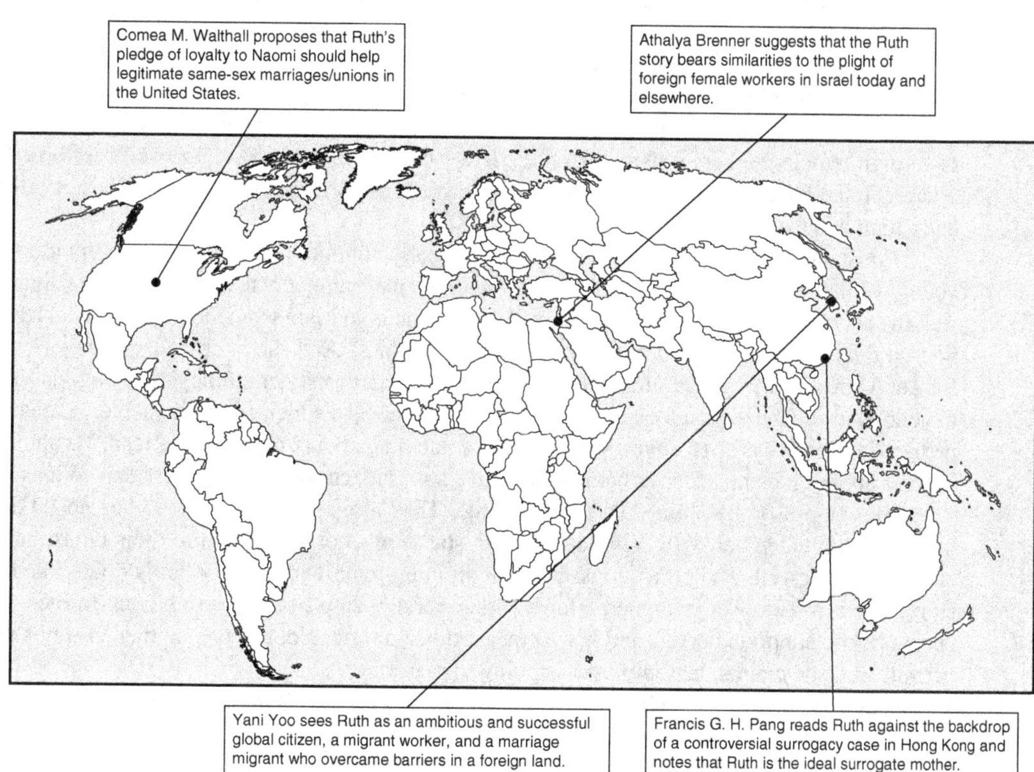
Comea M. Walthall proposes that Ruth's pledge of loyalty to Naomi should help legitimate same-sex marriages/unions in the United States.
Athalya Brenner suggests that the Ruth story bears similarities to the plight of foreign female workers in Israel today and elsewhere.
Yani Yoo sees Ruth as an ambitious and successful global citizen, a migrant worker, and a marriage migrant who overcame barriers in a foreign land.
Francis G. H. Pang reads Ruth against the backdrop of a controversial surrogacy case in Hong Kong and notes that Ruth is the ideal surrogate mother.

READINGS

Ruth and the Plight of Foreign Female Workers in Modern-Day Israel
Athalya Brenner

Ruth as a Successful Global Citizen, Migrant Worker, and Marriage Migrant
Yani Yoo

Ruth's Relevance to the Same-Sex Marriage Debate
Comea M. Walthall

Ruth as the Ideal Surrogate Mother?
Francis G. H. Pang

Ruth and the Plight of Foreign Female Workers in Modern-Day Israel

Athalya Brenner (Israel)

Why did Ruth accompany Naomi to Bethlehem (Ruth 1)? Commentators attribute Ruth's decision to accompany her mother-in-law to her love for Naomi, or to her commitment, or other ideals. But I have read it differently for some time. A nonidealizing possibility is that for Ruth, a widow, going to a foreign country with her former mother-in-law is preferable to staying behind in her country of origin. This is as good a reason for her becoming a temporary, that is, a migrant worker—in the fields, for food for her and for her mother-in-law, a reason not stated in the biblical text but supported by her situation as narrated.

This reading, and my publications on it, was reinforced by what I knew of the situation of foreign female workers in Israel from the late 1980s. In turn, the reading itself reinforced my interest in the legal and social situation of those workers. So let me imagine Ruth's story differently than it is usually done.

Early one morning, you come back from an early summer party, you chance upon a fairly young woman wandering. She's on her own, wearing an evening gown. She seems to be aimlessly walking about. While she is definitely dressed up, her hands and skin seem those of a manual laborer. So you think to yourself, "Not a prostitute, but who knows? And she is obviously foreign"; since she can't speak the language properly, you can hardly understand her although her lingo is similar to your own somehow. You look more closely and she seems disoriented and unstable. Is she drunk perhaps? Or on drugs? Moreover, she mumbles something about "the man, the man." Is she hurt? No, she doesn't look molested or harmed. You're a good citizen so you have a problem. What to do?

So you notify the police. The police come. They arrest the woman, who has no ID documents, and threaten her with deportation. Still, she seems not to respond to their interrogations and threats too well. The police must bring in an interpreter, and this is what is done. She has a story: She is a widow, a foreigner, a farmworker nearby, employed by a rich local farmer. With her work she supports herself and her former mother-in-law. No, she has neither visa nor work permit. But, she claims, her employer is going to marry her.

The cops laugh: Such Cinderella stories don't happen so often in our insular society. Rich local farmers don't marry their foreign female workers so easily. But since the woman has made a claim that might affect her personal status and the case, they have to call in a lawyer. The woman may be eventually deported, but no deportation is possible without a court order, even when the facts seem clear. And anyway the woman has a right to public legal defense.

The lawyer calls the rich farmer named as employer and future husband, and the alleged mother-in-law. He finds out the woman has told the truth. She is indeed a migrant worker. The farmer has promised to marry her and intends to keep his promise. Alas, nevertheless, she remains an illegal alien, thus a candidate for speedy deportation.

The matter is brought before the judges. The farmer is passionate in his plea for the woman and their relationship, while the woman and her former mother-in-law remain silent. In order to help solve the legal problem, the woman hastily converts to Judaism. She and the local rich farmer marry on the spot. Eventually, as decorum dictates, the woman has a son by the rich farmer. The son seems to belong to the former mother-in-law, somehow.

Now, obviously, this is the story of Ruth, grandmother to King David, foremother of Jesus (Matthew 1). A skit similar to this appeared several years ago in *Ha'aretz* ("The Land"), an Israeli newspaper, just before *Shavu'ot* (Pentecost), when the biblical Scroll (Ruth) is traditionally read in the synagogue. It is worth noting that *Ha'aretz* is a left-of-center and totally "secular" newspaper. Its general editorial policy is to promote Israeli/Jewish culture, even help to shape it, but Bible study is not privileged. The fact that such a skit/article was published witnesses not only the Israeli public's fondness for biblical stories, especially those that belong to the recurrent annual liturgy, but also that the Ruth story can be read as bearing similarities to the plight of foreign female workers in the Israel of today.

Ruth is usually romanticized. She is read as the righteous, never self-serving widow. The motives attributed to her are of love and loyalty, not only to Naomi but also to the god of Israel, and to Boaz. Readers are happy to point out that, although a Moabite, she is integrated into Judahite society and royal gynealogy, a counterexample to the foreign wives driven out of the community in Ezra's times, perhaps a counterstory to that same driving-out story. Although the matter of levirate marriage is far from clear in the Scroll (for instance by comparison to the law in Deuteronomy 25:5–10), commentators prefer to gloss over the difficulty and also project later Judaism's view of Ruth as an enthusiastic proselyte.

But the truth is that Ruth follows Naomi, and her god (1:16–17), dramatically but without stating her reasons. Does she love Boaz, does Boaz love her? Is there lovemaking on the threshing floor? Who knows? There are no references in the biblical text in this regard. Is Ruth selfless? Not necessarily. She looks after Naomi and she loves her according to the woman neighbors (4:15), but she certainly looks after her own interests as well. She is married; she has a son. However, lo and behold, once Ruth gives birth, she disappears from the scene. She doesn't even have the privilege of holding her son, or naming him; she recedes, is swallowed by the local culture. And she remains The Moabite, always, forever, without fail.

Foreign workers, in Israel, and elsewhere, migrate looking for employment. They do so mostly because what awaits them in their source community is worse than the indifference that might await them in their target community. In that sense, they don't really have a choice. They work hard for their employers, and their hard work is sometimes recognized. They may migrate elsewhere, and they may manage to "catch" a husband and stay. But, in most cases, they will remain foreign. Assimilated, if you wish, but not integrated into the target community. Perhaps you've met such women in your neighborhood, looking after elderly people, or children, or performing menial tasks, at the bottom of society and the social ladder, originally perhaps from Mexico, or Latin America, or the Philippines, or Eastern Europe? If you consider the similarities between such migrant workers and the Moabite Ruth, perhaps you'll read her story differently. Perhaps you'll ponder the fact that she is not even allowed to hold her own babies in her lap: This falls to the lot of Naomi, former mother-in-law but a local dame.

Athalya Brenner is Professor of Bible at the University of Amsterdam, The Netherlands; and Tel Aviv University, Israel.

Ruth as a Successful Global Citizen, Migrant Worker, and Marriage Migrant

Yani Yoo (South Korea)

This essay sees Ruth the Moabite as an ambitious and successful global citizen, a migrant worker, and a marriage migrant who overcame human and customary barriers in a foreign land, Israel. The background of this reading is the recent global phenomenon of migration. With globalization, more people are becoming migrant workers, including women from the so-called developing countries who marry men in the so-called developed countries. They are called marriage migrants. Some countries receive migrants and others send them.

My country, Korea, is one of the receiving countries. Although in general Koreans have good intentions toward migrants and there are many nongovernmental organizations (NGOs) working for them, it is correct to say that the Korean government does not treat migrants fairly; severe forms of sexual, cultural, racial, economic, and other discriminations are committed against migrants. Koreans have lived as a monoethnic group for hundreds of years and have only recently begun to learn to live with people from other ethnic backgrounds. From this backdrop I read the story of Ruth both from the perspective of a citizen of a receiving country and from my own experience of having had been a temporary illegal alien while studying in a Western country.

I call Ruth a global citizen because of her crossing national borders, being a migrant worker in a foreign country, and being a marriage migrant because of her marriage to a national of the receiving country based on an economic reason. Although Ruth is a foreigner, a widow living with her mother-in-law, young, and poor, she is determined not to just survive, but to succeed in a new land. She has two major hurdles to overcome to fulfill her goal: local people and customs.

Ruth faces the cold responses of people. To begin with, her mother-in-law Naomi is an immediate stumbling block for her to build a new life. Naomi knows many locals but would not connect Ruth to them. This unwilling ally seems to be depressed, unable, and unkind. Naomi tries to expel her daughters-in-law out of her life. While Orpah says goodbye, Ruth stubbornly remains. In Bethlehem, Naomi does not look for ways to make a living although she had patrimony to claim and knew what to do about it. She knows of dangers in the field which may befall a foreign young woman but does not give Ruth any advice about it when the latter leaves for gleaning for the first time. It is only after Ruth's gleaning and her mention of the field owner Boaz that Naomi offers information about him as their possible supporter (2:20) and comes up with a honey trap using Ruth as the bait (3:3–4). We doubt that the honey trap is Naomi's only option. It is at the expense of not just Boaz's honor, but also Ruth's.

If Naomi is not so considerate of Ruth, the Bethlehemite women are even more so. At the beginning and end of the story, they converse with Naomi but never with Ruth. There is no report that Ruth was welcomed by women in the field, whereas there is an exchange of greetings between Boaz and his workers (2:4). Being a woman does not guarantee solidarity among women.

Men in the field can be sexually or otherwise violent to women as they may "meet" (2:9) and "touch" (2:22) the latter. No male relative steps out to offer any long-term social security to Ruth and Naomi. The *goel,* the nearest male relative who has the right to redeem Naomi's land, denies the right (4:6, 8). The male elders are portrayed as those who mix up practices of two customs of the levirate (taking off the shoes; cf. Deuteronomy 25:5–10) and the *goel* (Leviticus 25:24ff.). Although Boaz said and did nice things to Ruth in the field, he has not offered any fundamental solution to Ruth and Naomi. He seems reluctant to follow the progress of events after spending a night with Ruth at the threshing floor. Women chose and entrapped him. No wonder that there is no further interaction described between the couple other than the typical patriarchal report, "Boaz took Ruth and she became his wife. And he went to her and the Lord gave her pregnancy" (4:13).

Ruth as a foreigner takes advantage of not knowing the local laws and customs or she pretends not to know them. First, Ruth challenges the regulation of gleaning in the empty field. For her, it only makes the poor continue to remain poor. So she boldly asks to glean among the sheaves, demanding more than the custom in quality and quantity. Boaz concedes, saying to his workers, "You must also pull out some handfuls for her from the bundles and leave them for her to glean" (2:16). Ruth finds in this nice owner of the land a good target for her new future.

In her report to Naomi after the night at the threshing floor, Ruth twists Boaz's words about barley. He gave her the barley, simply saying, "Bring the cloak and hold it out" (3:15). But Ruth lies to Naomi by reporting that he said, "Do not go back to your mother-in-law empty-handed" (3:17) and thus nudges her mother-in-law in the ribs so that she can plan for the young woman's future.

Second, Ruth demands Boaz to carry out the levirate and the *goel* duties although he is not the immediate male to have the right to do it. It is understandable that she as a foreigner mixes up the two customs, but Boaz and the men in town mimic her in combining the two. Perhaps the text is mocking Boaz and the elders, pointing out that they cannot handle their own customs correctly, let alone use them to control a foreigner: Institutions and cultures born long ago do not work even for locals, not to mention for newcomers.

The genealogy at the end sums up Ruth's final victory. Only three generations after this first migrant worker, a king is born to her family. When viewed from the perspective of the locals, this is a radical proclamation. This bold genealogy can be read as a challenge to any people who deny the rights of migrants. Here we remember that the book of Ruth is the only book in the Bible which is named after a foreigner.

In sum, originally Naomi and her family had migrated to Moab to avoid famine. We do not know whether the Moabites were nice to them. Now a Moabite migrated to Bethlehem and the natives must decide whether or not they will be good to the foreigner. But regardless of their actions, the new migrant finds ways to survive and thrive. In our globalized world, people with new faces in foreign lands can read Ruth as a global citizen's success story, even if it is bittersweet. Although Ruth initially faces a number of barriers, she eventually becomes the great grandmother of Israel's greatest king. The book of Ruth points us to a place that does not have classes among people, where migrant workers are not paid much less than the locals. Our reading of Ruth can empower global citizens and nomads who must start new lives in new lands. It can also challenge the locals who think they lose opportunities because of migrant workers. Indeed, Ruth destroys national borders and demands that we have broader worldviews.

Yani Yoo is Lecturer in Old Testament at Methodist Theological University, Seoul, South Korea.

RUTH'S RELEVANCE TO THE SAME-SEX MARRIAGE DEBATE

Comea M. Walthall (United States)

Ruth 1:16–17 is a powerful testament of undying affection between two people: "Entreat me not to leave thee, or to return from following after thee; for whither thou goest, I will go, and where thou lodgest, I will lodge. Thy people shall be my people, and thy God my God. Where thou diest will I die, and there will I be buried; the LORD do so to me, and more also, if aught but death part thee and me." These words are often read at wedding ceremonies and used in sermons to illustrate the ideal love and passion that spouses should have for one another. What is most interesting about the verses, however, is that they are not words spoken between a man and a woman, but they are the words of a woman, Ruth, spoken to the mother of her deceased husband, Naomi, who is also a widow; both women are without sons.

To understand the full impact of Ruth's decision to "cleave" to Naomi, we need to put ourselves in the mind-set of the time. When Ruth was written, women had only two acceptable places in society: They could be a daughter in their father's household or a wife in their husband's household. A woman without a man had no social standing. There are several stories in the Old Testament about widows who almost starved to death because they had no man to take care of them. The context makes Ruth's decision to stay with Naomi almost unbelievable in light of the social vulnerability of a widow, let alone, two widows together.

The book of Ruth may be a brief four chapters, but for a woman, it is very powerful. Out of 66 books in the Bible, Ruth is one of only two books named for a woman (the other is Esther; also Judith and Susanna if including apocryphal texts). Ruth is also the only book in the Bible dedicated to the history of a woman. For a queer woman, understanding the context of Ruth and Naomi's precarious social position and Ruth's decision to stay makes the relationship between the two women even more powerful.

I had heard Ruth 1:16–18 twice, as part of wedding ceremonies, without knowing the context, but still appreciating the significance and power of such words between two people pledging to be together until death do them part. It was not until 1994, when I saw the film *Fried Green Tomatoes* that I decided to *really* read the book of Ruth for myself and to try to understand the context of those words. In the film, the characters Idgie and (appropriately) Ruth display subtle undertones of a lesbian relationship. For a budding lesbian on the cusp of understanding her own sexuality, reveling in the subtle relationship of the film's characters and the biblical reference (used in the film to convey a message from Ruth to Idgie) left me curious.

Ruth, indeed, was an epic discovery for me, when in 1994 I was unsure and somewhat at odds with what to believe about my feelings and my religion (especially in conjunction with one another). The book of Ruth has been a study for me throughout my life. In college I used it as a reference for papers in both women's studies and religious studies. Further inquiry led me to discover the connection between Genesis 2:24, "Therefore shall a man leave his father and his mother, and shall cleave unto his wife; and they shall be one flesh," and Ruth 1:14, "And they lifted up their voice and wept again; and Orpah kissed her mother-in-law, but Ruth cleaved unto her." The Hebrew word "cleave" that is used in Genesis 2:24 to describe how Adam felt about Eve (and how spouses are supposed to feel toward each other) is the exact same word that is used in Ruth 1:14 to describe how Ruth felt about Naomi.

Ruth's vow to Naomi has been used to illustrate the nature of the marriage covenant. The irony lies in the fact that across the United States, thousands of years after the story of Ruth and Naomi was scribed, it remains illegal for same-sex couples to make the same covenant. Often opponents of same-sex marriage or unions reference the Bible to support claims that two people in love can only get married if they are of opposite sex. It is interesting that those opponents seem to skip over Ruth 1:16–18. These words were originally spoken by one woman to another, their tale important enough to survive years and a multitude of biblical edits. The power of Ruth's vow to Naomi has played a significant role in the covenant for many new husbands to their wives. One day, Ruth's vow will (legally) bind me to my "wife" of almost nine years, defeating the scorn of those who skipped the Bible's eighth book.

Comea M. Walthall has Bachelor's degrees in Psychology, Biology, Religious Studies, and Sociology; she is currently working in retail sales and is a GLBTQ Youth Outreach Advocate.

Ruth as the Ideal Surrogate Mother?

Francis G. H. Pang (Hong Kong)

In late 2010, the eldest son of a Hong Kong (HK) real estate tycoon announced that he became a new father of triplets. Since he did not disclose any information about the identity of the mother of these babies, rumor has it that he hired a surrogate mother in the United States to give birth to his three sons. Since having male offspring is a big concern for the traditional Chinese and his father was very vocal in expressing his desire for a grandson to carry the family name, the public had little problem accepting the rumor. When his younger brother's wife failed to produce sons, it was not very difficult for the public to connect the dots and see the attempt of the elder son to father sons as a competition among the two of brothers to gain favor in the eyes of their old father. Unfortunately, this has come at a time when popular sentiment toward the rich is vastly negative due primarily to the alarming level of income disparity in HK. Therefore, when the picture of the proud grandfather holding his three newborn "grandsons" hit the newswire, it sparked a heated discussion regarding the morality of such an endeavor.

Although surrogacy is nothing new in the West, it has always been a rare and controversial matter in HK because of religious beliefs and traditional Chinese morals. After the story of the triplets came to light, the press criticized the family for disrespecting human dignity and ignoring the children's rights. The church in HK also sternly condemned the family, contending that getting male offspring for self-interest through surrogacy is immoral and ignores the children's right of growing up in a healthy family. Furthermore, there is also a legal issue here. A decade ago the government of HK passed a bill on the use of human reproductive technology, restricting it to a strictly noncommercial basis and only under special circumstances (e.g., a legally married but infertile couple). Technically, a surrogate license will only be issued to someone who is willing to bear a child for a family without any monetary arrangement and who will subsequently give up the custody right of the newborn baby in order for the donor to adopt the child. Under such stringent rules, there has not been a single successful application for surrogacy since this legislation, presumably because it requires a high degree of sacrifice on the part of the surrogate. Since pregnancy involves considerable amount of mental stress and physical risk, it is rather difficult, if not impossible, to measure the value of such endeavor in monetary terms. The subtle yet inevitable conflict of interest between the donor (biological parents) and the surrogate mother in a commercial surrogacy arrangement is inevitable. Thus, in essence, the aim of this law in HK is to discourage any commercial surrogacy arrangement to safeguard children's rights and avoid endless courtroom drama on custodianship.

Reading the book of Ruth under this cultural context and particularly using this incident as a backdrop, several things stand out to the reader regarding the role of Ruth. First, throughout the narrative Ruth has been referred to as a Moabite (2:2, 6, 10, 21; 4:5, 10). This seemingly unnecessary title helps the reader to connect this story of the origin of the Moabites (Genesis 19:30–38). The episode of Lot and his daughters is in fact a story that involves metaphorical surrogacy. These two stories share some similar plot elements. Both narratives involve an old man sleeping with a young girl(s). Although it is not stated explicitly in Ruth, the reader can easily infer from conversations that Boaz is an old man (3:10). In both stories the male protagonist becomes intoxicated and unable to recognize the woman lying/sleeping with him. These features in Ruth allude to the Lot narratives to remind the reader of the Moabite origin of Ruth, the descendent of a gestational surrogacy.

Second, the fact that the child Ruth gives birth to is called Naomi's son (4:17) and is nursed by her also resembles the circumstance of the present-day surrogacy arrangement. The threefold blessing of Boaz by the legal assembly (4:11–12) supports this reading. Three names (Rachel, Leah, and Tamar) that were mentioned in the blessing link the story of Ruth and Naomi to two narratives in Genesis. Both narratives involve a woman bearing a child for another woman/family. It is also stressed in these narratives that the status of a woman in ancient times is anchored in childbearing, thus when a woman cannot bear a child for her husband, it sets a perfect stage for surrogacy arrangement. For example, in the Jacob narrative both Rachel and Leah ask their handmaid to sleep with Jacob (Genesis 30).

As noted by scholars, the similarities between the Tamar narrative (Genesis 38:1–30) and the story of Ruth are overwhelming. The narrative explicitly compares Tamar to Ruth by the statements of the elders (4:11–12). Both stories involve a family moving to foreign soil, mixed-marriage with a Gentile woman, and the deaths of a spouse and two sons. In both stories, the reader witnesses the female protagonist removing her widow's garments, which changes her social status and breaks the social and physical boundaries, to try to obtain a child for the levirate rights owed to her deceased husband. Finally, both narratives contain an element of surprise. Judah (the donor) does not know Tamar's (the surrogate mother) intention and her identity when he sleeps with her. Similarly, when Ruth follows Naomi's plan and uncovers Boaz's feet (lower body), he does not know Ruth was lying with him until the middle of the night (3:7–8).

The story of Ruth and Naomi can be viewed as the biblical surrogacy arrangement *par excellence*. Neither the donor nor the surrogate mother uses the child to gain an upper hand in the family (contra Rachel and Leah). Ruth as the surrogate mother also demonstrates excellent moral character (contra Tamar)—she does not fight for her own interest but rather considers the interest of her donors (Naomi and to a lesser extent, Boaz). The donors also demonstrated genuine concern for the surrogate. In fact, if we plot the story in modern-day HK, Ruth might even pass the stringent requirement by the government of HK and be granted a surrogate license. The narrative clearly demonstrates that the custody right ended up belonging to Naomi. Ruth does not use the baby to gain any benefit from the donor's family, neither financially nor in terms of social status. Although one can argue that she finally finds a patron for herself, Ruth is definitely as good a metaphorical surrogate mother as one can find in the Old Testament.

Francis G. H. Pang, originally from Hong Kong, is a Ph.D. candidate at McMaster Divinity College, Canada.

QUESTIONS

1. Construct a vignette, as Brenner does, from your culture that compares to the story of Ruth.
2. How does the experience of migrants and/or marriage migrants in your culture compare to Korea as described by Yoo?
3. Assess Walthall's reading of Ruth. Is she justified in using Ruth 1:16–17 as support for gay marriage?
4. Evaluate Pang's intertextual approach (drawing on other biblical stories). What particular insights does it bring to a reading of Ruth? Are there other biblical or nonbiblical texts to which Ruth could be linked?

CHAPTER 23

LAMENTATIONS

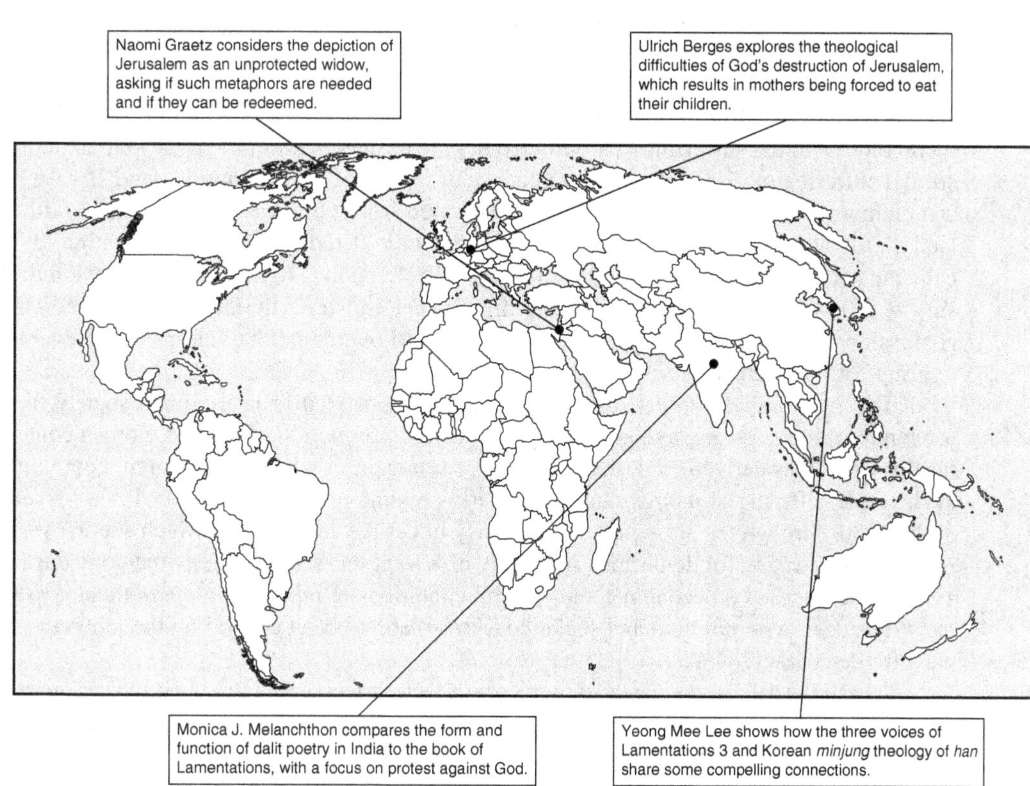
Naomi Graetz considers the depiction of Jerusalem as an unprotected widow, asking if such metaphors are needed and if they can be redeemed.
Ulrich Berges explores the theological difficulties of God's destruction of Jerusalem, which results in mothers being forced to eat their children.
Monica J. Melanchthon compares the form and function of dalit poetry in India to the book of Lamentations, with a focus on protest against God.
Yeong Mee Lee shows how the three voices of Lamentations 3 and Korean *minjung* theology of *han* share some compelling connections.

READINGS

THE THREE VOICES OF LAMENTATIONS AND KOREAN *MINJUNG* THEOLOGY OF *HAN*

Yeong Mee Lee (South Korea)

Life is full of joys and sorrows. The book of Lamentations deals with the agony experienced during a time of extreme suffering. It was a time when a mother was forced to eat the flesh of her own child. Nothing captures the degree of the suffering more vividly than this graphic image. In facing such extreme suffering, the human reaction can be quite diverse. The biblical reaction to the suffering found in Lamentations 3 provides a good analogy to Korean *minjung* theology of *han.*

Lamentation 3 introduces three voices of "I," "He," and "We," each of which show their reaction to the suffering. "I" reminded people of the disaster (vv. 1–24) and explains the special suffering of "He" who suffers because of the sin of the community (vv. 25–39). "He" is a member of the community. But He is separated from others as the one who is faithful to God and is waiting for salvation. He bears the agony of the community upon him. "I" then calls the people to return to God immediately. "We" responds to him with confession of their sin (vv. 40–47). The responses of these three bodies illustrate the importance of communal confession of sin and the collective responsibility to overcome the suffering and eventually to bring forth salvation.

The term *minjung* refers to those who are marginalized from the main society through economic, cultural, social, and gender discrimination. *Minjung* theology is a Korean contextual theology that was derived from the communal confession of sin and the church's commitment to share the suffering of *minjung* under the Park's regime in the 1960–1970s. It was developed in the 1980s through the struggle for democracy under the Jeon regime which suppressed *minjung*'s demonstration for democracy in the city of Kwang Ju. While *minjung* theology during the 1960–1970s focused on economic and cultural conditions of *minjung*, *minjung* theology during the 1980s dealt with political and social concerns that had been evoked by the *minjung* movement for democracy.

During the 1970s, the death of two Korean factory workers highlighted the seriousness of the suffering of *minjung*. Mr. Jeon Taeil, a worker in a textile trade company, struggled for the basic legal rights of labor and burned himself as a sacrificial action for the request of legal compensation. He asked for keeping the labor standard of working eight hours a day. Ms. Kyeong Sook Kim, a worker and the leader of the union of a wig trade company, was killed during a forced dispersal of the workers by a large and strong police force. Several theologians and ministers who worked in the Protestant Urban Industrial Mission had joined them in their struggle. They also called upon society and the religious community to participate in communal confession and advocacy for change.

Minjung theologians further developed the collective experience of suffering through the concept of *han*. *Han* is a Korean term for an underlying feeling of the oppressed people. It is an accumulation of suppressed and condensed experiences of oppression. Many Korean folk songs express *minjung*'s *han*. *Han* is very deeply rooted in Korean history and culture. The country's entire way of life has been profoundly shaped by it. It is a culturally complex entity. Koreans have suffered numerous invasions by powerful surrounding nations to the point that the very existence of the Korean nation has come to be understood as *han*. Also, under Confucianism's strict imposition of laws and customs discriminating against women, the existence of women was *han* itself.

Han is moral evil originating and promulgated by imperialistic, feudalistic, and ideological power, in addition to gender discrimination.

Lamentations 3 and Korean *minjung* theology of *han* share some compelling connections. First, *minjung* theologians represent the "I" of the biblical text. The "I" explores the situation of the suffering and the agony of "He," namely, people like Jeon Taeil and Kyeong Sook Kim. The "I" plays a role in bringing the community's attention to the suffering and helps them to realize its social dimension; eventually it evokes the participation of the community into the struggle for resolving the agony.

Second, just as the biblical text explains "S/He" bears the sufferings because of the sin of the community, so too *minjung* theology perceives that the suffering of *minjung* is not an individual matter but is the reality of oppressive and miserable social existence. The lament of "S/He" and the *han* of *minjung* is not just the sound of weeping, but is also a prophetic voice that motivates the action of the community.

Third, as "We" confessed their responsibility for the suffering of "He" in Lamentations 3, so too Korean churches shared the responsibility of *minjung*'s suffering. In the stage of *han*, of hopelessness and despair, the Christian faith community must not be silent but share the suffering of *minjung* and be "a priest of *han*." The community participates in the process of comforting and healing of *minjung's han* and breaking the vicious circle of violence. With the evoking voice of "I" and solidarity of "We," the *han* of *minjung* (S/He) will transform into a prophetic voice for change.

Yeong Mee Lee (Ph.D.) is Associate Professor of Old Testament Studies at Hanshin University, Seoul, South Korea.

Lamentations and the Form and Function of Dalit Poetry

Monica J. Melanchthon (India)

One of the more significant, concrete, and palpable achievements of the dalit struggle and movement in India is dalit literature. Dalits were traditionally denied any access to learning and all fields of intellectual activity were barred. Their cultural and creative activity was either denied or considered debased and vulgar. The situation today is almost totally changed, as even mainstream critics recognize dalit literature as a valid, robust, and progressive genre. It has challenged assumptions of prevalent theories of literary critics and aesthetics. It exposes the atrocities of higher societies with burning anger and hatred and calls for ruthless vengeance against the society and people who have created inequality—indeed, it is rejection of the all-embracing conventional Hindu world vision. The literature aims at total revolution and uplift of the entire lower classes. It has become propagandist and collective, rather than individualistic in nature; it express the aspirations and frustrations, convictions and courage of the community.

Dalit poetry to some extent bears many parallels to the Hebraic tradition of lament, both individual and communal, through which are expressed alienation, suffering, grief, anger, and the questioning of God. Dalit poetry's ultimately positive purpose of life affirmation, emotional release, remembering, and communal healing allow this form of poetic metalanguage to resonate with the lament traditions of the Hebrew Bible, for it has become a literature of extreme situations, a literature of survival.

The occasion for the poems in the book of Lamentations was the watershed event of 587 B.C.E.—the destruction of Jerusalem which greatly influenced developments in Israel's religious thought and practice. The five poems, authored perhaps by different poets during or soon after this event, give us a glimpse of the horror and grief of the survivors and their expression of primal outrage through the medium of language. As survival literature, Lamentations stresses the need for survivors of any calamity or oppression to give verbal or written expression to the experience of pain. The poems are a deliberate opportunity to give vent to the full horror, distress, and agony that has been experienced, providing an invaluable vehicle to remember and recount the diverse aspects of the assault. By giving expression, the community is enabled to face the calamity and to come to terms with the many dimensions of the suffering inflicted on the community.

Furthermore, a major theme is protest, but more specifically it is a protest against God who inflicts pain and suffering and sanctions destruction of God's own people (1:1–10; 2:1–10; 4:11–16). While there is an acknowledgment of sin on the part of the people, God is also placed alongside the "enemy" as being responsible for the acute suffering. God as betrayer is perhaps one of the most disturbing features of the book, as the deity is approached with anger and reproach (2:20).

Unlike the Hebrew laments, many dalit poems do not mention the divine, perhaps because of the atheist/Buddhist leanings of the poets. Neither is their cry addressed to a deity nor is the deity blamed. There is hard questioning of the caste system and its proponents. Hence, the resolution of crises, the annihilation of caste, and the attaining of freedom are only possible by means of resistance and revolt against the oppressor and the unjust social system. Hope is articulated in secular terms. Where the divine is mentioned, as in the Hebrew laments, there is no fear of offending God, nor are there any religious qualms from being acrimonious with God.

In another stream of dalit poetry, God is not seen as the source of suffering, but as a cosufferer. Dalit gods are spirits of ancestors and deified heroes and leaders. These gods are also stigmatized and discriminated and hence suffer along with the community. The divine is therefore constructed from the perspective of dalit limitations rather than from the vantage point of the "power" of the dominant-caste groups. The shrines, temples, and abodes of dalit gods are polluted places and their Gods, muted and disfigured, are as helpless as the people. Such conceptions of dalit gods therefore seem to aid in the process of catharsis and coping with the crisis.

Inherent in such dalit poems and the Hebrew laments is a rejection of religious optimism that shies away from examining suffering in its multiple dimensions or an optimism that sanitizes God by removing God from the ugliness of suffering and pain. This is made possible by the fact that the Hebrew conception of God as the one who identifies with the poor and suffering, the one who suffers "along with," is rooted and derived from the experience of the oppressed and marginalized. If God is responsible and has to be blamed, so are the people.

I would like to believe that embedded within the accusation against God, in the anger, the questioning, and the reproach against God in Lamentations is also a poetic critique of the Israelite community for its silence in the face of oppression, its passivity, its complicity. If it is a reminder to God that the human situation is not as it should be, it is also a reminder to the community that all is not as it should be. God and the community as covenanted partners are called to act and must act. The cause of the Lamenter is God's cause and vice versa. They raise their voice in pain, do not flinch from naming the sorrow of the circumstances, and insist that they be transformed. By articulating such pain, by naming their own volition in the suffering and calling on God to act, the book of Lamentations rouses the community into action. Through description of the situation, the grief and the sorrow, and the questioning of it, the community, and perhaps God as well, finds the answers and the directions for a better future.

Monica J. Melanchthon is a Professor in the Department of Old Testament Studies at Gurukul Lutheran Theological College, Chennai, India.

The Theological Difficulties of God's Destruction of Jerusalem

Ulrich Berges (Germany)

There is no doubt that YHWH, the God of Israel has an impressive record of violent depictions in the Hebrew Bible. There are more than 600 entries in the OT where nations, kings, or individuals are depicted acting violently against each other. But nearly 1,000 times it is affirmed that YHWH smashes, destroys, and kills peoples, nations, or individuals. Approximately 100 times it is stated that the God of Israel ordered the death of persons. What are we to say and think about passages in which even innocent children are the object of God's wrath and anger? Can we still consider God's actions against children as part of his legitimate rule and dominion? Are they simply paying the price for the sins of their fathers and mothers (cf. Exodus 34:7; Numbers 14:18)? Are there theological reasonings to justify that kind of violence against children—or ought we to call it what it really is: pure violence!

There is no other book in the Hebrew Bible in which the wrath and violence of YHWH are depicted in such gloomy colors as in the book of Lamentations. In 1:12–16 he behaves like a terrible enemy against Jerusalem and Zion. The personified city as mother of her inhabitants plays here (as elsewhere in Ancient Near East) the role of the female goddess who speaks and acts on behalf of the victims of divine wrath and anger. God's fierce anger went as fire into her bones, he spread a net for her feet, turned her back like a hunted animal. He bound her transgressions into a yoke and handed her over to those she could not withstand. These images depict the destruction of Jerusalem by the hands of the Babylonians. The cruel fate of the population is highlighted in 2:11–13 when the poet looses control of his emotions when seeing children dying in the arms of their mothers: "My eyes are spent with weeping; my stomach churns; my bile is poured out on the ground because of the destruction of my people, because infants and babes faint in the streets of the city" (v. 11). That's not enough: Like a news-reporter on the battlefield he directs his camera and microphone on the fainting and starving children. Thus he witnesses their last words: "They cry to their mothers, 'Where is bread and wine?' as they faint like the wounded in the streets of the city, as their life is poured out on their mothers' bosom" (v. 12). This is a very touching scene: Not often does the Old Testament show the last moments in the life of the victims of violence and war. Here it does: The bosoms of the mothers become the graves of their children!

These are very dangerous pictures and politicians in our days try to be sure that such scenes are not shown in the news on TV. The so-called *imbedded reporters* in modern wars are not allowed to report scenes like these! Where does that reluctance come from? Why censor the *real reality* of war? Because the images of dying children tell the real truth—not the truth of the powerful, but of the innocent victims!

At those places where rational justifications become insufficient to explain God's wrath and violence, critical voices are heard. The culpability of Jerusalem and her prophets is strongly affirmed (2:14, 17) and there can be no doubt about the right of YHWH to punish the evil city and her leading class, but the violence he employed or did allow to be employed against her was totally out of proportion. Even in his anger, YHWH is bound to his own standard of justice and ethical behavior. In very dramatic words, mother Zion holds YHWH himself responsible for all her grief (2:20–22). She addresses him as the real cause of her suffering and that of her children: "Look, YHWH, and consider! To whom have you done this? Should women eat their offspring, the children they have borne? Should priest and prophet be killed in the sanctuary of the Lord?" (v. 20). The situation is very much that of a female victim confronting her male aggressor who should acknowledge the enormous pain he caused. God himself should see and consider *to whom* he did all this, namely, to her beloved children (2:19–20; cf. 2:11).

In contrast to YHWH who apparently lost control of his passion in his fierce anger, mother Zion does not loose her composure, because there is no hair tearing, skin gouging, or loud hysterics, which are the normal elements in Ancient Near Eastern depictions of mourning women and goddesses. Zion's lament is voiced in critical terms against the one who slaughtered infants in the streets and priests and prophets in the sanctuary (2:20). At first glance, the death of the temple officials seems to be an anticlimax but the parallelism with the dying children has to be taken seriously. Like mothers who lost their children, YHWH looses his religious personnel. The perversion of mothers eating their children stands parallel to God not preventing his priests and prophets from being killed in the sanctuary. As the motherly bosom symbolizes warmth and nutrition, the sanctuary stands for prosperity and life. Thus the center of life has become a deadly trap.

In 2:21 Zion underlines three times YHWH's violence: "*you* have killed...*you* have slaughtered...*you* didn't pity." Interesting enough, no objects are named, but it is absolutely clear that Zion's children are meant. That YHWH acts *without showing mercy* is never stated in the Psalms or in other prayers in the Hebrew Bible, but it is well known from the prophets, especially from Ezekiel.

Can one imagine something of more cruelty? YHWH killed and slaughtered without pity those children mother Zion had given birth to and had raised up. Thus God is no less cannibalistic than the mothers eating their own children (cf. 4:10). In none of the Assyrian texts are mothers the ones who eat their children: Thus the poets of the book of Lamentations intensified the borrowed language from the Ancient Near Eastern environment.

The perversion of the mother–child relation is stressed by the characterization of the mothers as "compassionate" using the Hebrew word which relates to the "motherly womb." Like the mothers in Zion boil their offspring, YHWH consumes the foundations of his beloved city. But there is a fundamental difference between the mothers in Zion and YHWH: The former were forced to do what they did because the latter did not restrain his wrath. Should YHWH not have been obliged to restrain his anger in the face of dying children and the forced cannibalism of their mothers? Why didn't he act according to what he himself had urged from the aggressors of Israel (cf. Jeremiah 25:8–14)? Do ethical standards apply to every one else but not to YHWH? The voice of mother Zion is the voice of all the innocent victims: There is no human reality so dark that it can't be brought before YHWH.

There is no philosophical solution to the question of God's justice (theodicy) but only the practical solution of keeping the hope alive. Zion doesn't get an answer from God, as her children didn't get an answer to their plea for bread and wine (2:12)! The answer is given in the middle of the third poem (3:31–33). There the suffering person who experienced God as "antishepherd" who afflicted him with the rod of his wrath, driving him into darkness without light, comes to the conclusion: "The Lord will not reject forever. Although he causes grief, he will have compassion according to the abundance of his steadfast love; for he does not afflict out of his heart." This practical solution of steadfast hope does not stand as the great finale at the end of the book of Lamentations but rather in its very center surrounded by lament and protest. Therefore, hopeful faith in YHWH and fierce protest against him are not antagonistic attitudes but "brothers in arms."

Ulrich Berges is Professor of Old Testament Exegesis at the Catholic-Theological Faculty at the University of Bonn, Germany.

The Depiction of Jerusalem as an Unprotected Widow

Naomi Graetz (Israel)

On the ninth day of the month of Av, the Jewish people commemorate the destruction of the first temple by the Babylonians (586 B.C.E.) and the destruction of the second temple by the Romans (70 C.E.) by fasting, reading the book of Lamentations, and special prayers of lament. In commemorating these destructions, some of us also remember the Holocaust and other tragedies that have befallen the Jewish people. Some observant Jews remember this date, and the three weeks preceding it, by abstaining from eating meat, not listening to music, and by not participating in any joyous event.

In Lamentations 1:1–2 Jerusalem is described as a widow after the destruction of the Temple. The theological intent of Lamentations 1 is to justify God's destruction of the Temple in Jerusalem as punishment for sin. The disaster that befell the community is because of the sin and infidelity of the people, not God's failure. The widow accepts the blame and says, "The Lord is in the right, for I rebelled against His word" (1:18). Indeed, Jewish theology tends to be self-blaming for what has happened: "On account of our sins, we have been exiled from our land [Israel]" goes the refrain in prayers Jews recite on certain Sabbaths. But is a "widow" guilty of sin? Should we be blaming ourselves for being the subject of God's aggression? Our modern sensibility suggests that perhaps we should be blaming the Angry God who has caused the destruction. For a believing Jew, this is not a blasphemous stance, for in our tradition there is a heritage of doubt and protest.

The depiction of Jerusalem as an unprotected widow (usually lumped together with the stranger and the orphan), abandoned by her husband/God, destroyed by her supposed protector can be seen as a metaphorical justification of abuse of women by men. Israel is not only abandoned by God, but she is also considered responsible for her own downfall—and therefore deserving of punishment. However, widowhood could be constructed positively; it could mean freedom from an abusive marriage. Today more women are single by choice and widowhood has become a normative, not a deviant, status. Yet there are many who still think they (or others) are missing something when they are not married. Widowhood, therefore, is naturally constructed as loss (of more than just the husband) and not gain.

The rabbis sense that it is unjust to blame the widow as a sinner, so they say she is not a real widow. She is in the situation of a woman whose husband has gone off for a while—leaving her as a "grass widow." It could not be that Jerusalem, or the people of Israel, can be likened to a real widow. Were that to be the case it would imply that God is dead! She is not a real widow, just like one whose father or husband has gone abroad and who intends to return to her, for it is said that Israel and Judah are not widowed from their God (Jeremiah 51:5).

The use of negative feminine metaphors to depict God's relationship with Jerusalem is both dangerous and powerful. There is a midrash in which God is likened to a heroic figure with great strength. He hits another man and the man immediately dies from the blow. This hero then goes into his house and hits his wife and she withstands the blow. Her neighbors say to her, "All the great athletes have been killed from one of the hero's blows—but you are able to survive more than one blow." She answers them that "he hits *them* with all his might, out of anger, but to *me*, he gives what I am able to take" (presumably out of love). In a continuation of this same midrash, the rabbis ask, why it is that the people of Israel can stand up to God's anger? The answer is this: It is because God hits us and then returns immediately and re-creates us. This is the comfort that Israel can take in their unique relationship to God.

But why do the prophets and rabbis need such myths and metaphors to depict their relationships with God? What, if any, are the redeeming possibilities of studying such texts? Here I will mention three other suggestions, before referring to my own.

David Blumenthal suggests a theology of protest in response to the possibility that abusiveness is an attribute of God. He writes that the definition of abuse is when the punishment is out of proportion to the sin. In his mind, God is sometimes abusive, and in wrestling with this truth, one must acknowledge and react to it. Blumenthal raises the question of how God does *teshuva* (repentance). The acknowledgment of abuse by the abuser is not enough. There must be a commitment never to abuse again. Obviously the abused person has to accept the commitment and accept reconciliation; but even with it, it is difficult to maintain a relationship of mutual trust with the abusing God. This is part of a theology of protest and sustained suspicions which are a proper response to God's abuse. The book of Lamentations is clearly understood as a possible response and reaction to God's specific abuse of the Jewish people.

Walter Brueggemann perceives lament as a "genuine covenant interaction" between us and God. He points out that when lament is absent, a cover-up and a practice of denial and pretense characterizes our relationship with God. When lament is allowed we can criticize God for not functioning properly. Lament happens when God's dysfunction reaches an unacceptable level, when the injustice is intolerable and change is needed. In lamenting, we are recognizing the abusiveness of God, and we are also rejecting that aspect of Him or Her.

J. Cheryl Exum proposes a three-fold way of dealing with gender-biased prophetic rhetoric. One strategy is to pay attention to the differing claims these texts make on their male and female readers. The second is to recognize the violent representations of God's sexual abuse of a nation personified as a woman and to expose this "prophetic pornography" for what it is. Finally, she suggests looking for competing discourse to uncover evidence of the woman's suppressed point of view in biblical texts.

Picking up on Exum's final point, I try to re-create a world in which women had a place. I find this a legitimate and necessary enterprise. It is a way of contributing new insights and/or perspectives to our Bible. Modern feminist midrash attempts to redress the misogynist tendencies of traditional mainstream midrash. The consequences of a patriarchal worldview for us are clear. Conventional attitudes toward women are still being transmitted to us as part of our heritage and too often we respond unquestioningly to these views as if they were absolute truths. Women should not have to identify against ourselves. On the one hand, we must seek out old texts where women appear and bring them to the surface; on the other hand, as part of our theology of protest against previous and present abuse, we must be revisers and revisionists. With new vision we bring new perspectives to the old text, and in doing so, we contribute to the ongoing work of revelation.

Naomi Graetz taught English for 35 years at Ben Gurion University of the Negev, Israel; she is the author of a number of books on women in the Bible and Midrash.

QUESTIONS

1. Lee focuses on Korean *minjung* theology of *han* as it connects to Lamentations 3. How might it connect to other elements of the book? In what ways might it not fit particularly well?
2. In addition to the one mentioned by Melanchthon, what other differences exist between dalit poetry and the book of Lamentations?
3. Reflect on your experiences of news reports of wars. Analyze Berges' claim that the reality of war is censored to promote the agenda of the powerful. Is the book of Lamentations also somewhat censored in this regard?
4. Elaborate on the "dangerous and powerful" nature of "negative feminine metaphors" in Lamentations. In this vein, explain what Graetz means when she writes, "Women should not have to identify against ourselves."

CHAPTER 24

EZRA AND NEHEMIAH

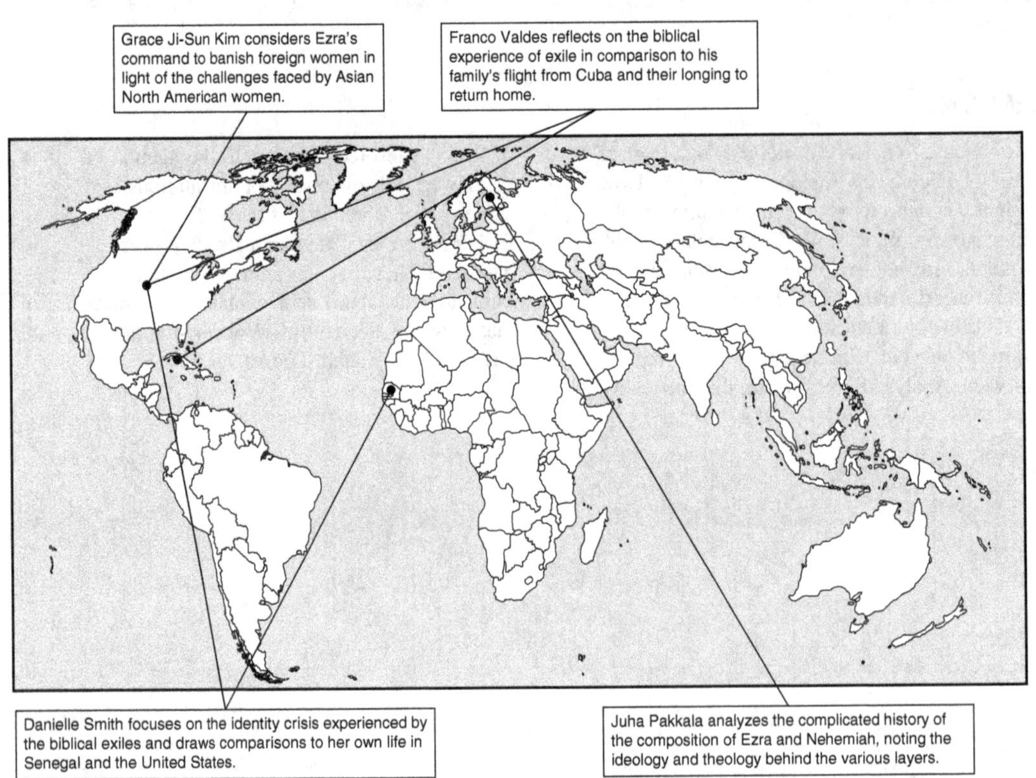
Grace Ji-Sun Kim considers Ezra's command to banish foreign women in light of the challenges faced by Asian North American women.
Franco Valdes reflects on the biblical experience of exile in comparison to his family's flight from Cuba and their longing to return home.
Danielle Smith focuses on the identity crisis experienced by the biblical exiles and draws comparisons to her own life in Senegal and the United States.
Juha Pakkala analyzes the complicated history of the composition of Ezra and Nehemiah, noting the ideology and theology behind the various layers.

READINGS

Asian North American Women and Ezra's Banishment of Foreign Wives
Grace Ji-Sun Kim

A Cuban Reflection on the Biblical Experience of Exile
Franco Valdes

A Few Personal Thoughts on the Identity Crisis of Biblical Exiles
Danielle Smith

The Complicated History of the Composition of Ezra and Nehemiah
Juha Pakkala

Asian North American Women and Ezra's Banishment of Foreign Wives

Grace Ji-Sun Kim (United States)

When Nehemiah chastises the Jews who had married foreign women, he reminds them that Solomon's foreign wives turned his heart away from the Lord and caused him to sin despite the great favor he received from God (1 Kings 11). In Ezra 9, Shecaniah suggests they make a covenant with God and send the foreign women away. Ezra makes the elders of Israel swear to do as they had said originally, and he sends messengers to inform all the returnees that they must appear in Jerusalem within three days or face confiscation of all property and excommunication from the congregation. Three days later, the whole congregation arrives and sits trembling in the rain waiting for Ezra to address them. Rebuking them for their unfaithfulness, he commands them to separate from "the peoples of the land and from the foreign women." When the meeting concludes they establish a commission, and three months later 113 men send away their wives.

In the Bible, foreign women and wives become pawns to be negotiated or dismissed by various peoples—men, religious leaders, even other women. Perhaps the story of Abraham sending away Hagar and her son can be viewed as a justification to dismiss the foreign wives and their children. Foreign women in the biblical narratives were often discriminated against both racially and religiously. They were identified as pagan, non-Jewish women whose idolatrous practices would draw the returnees back into the very sin that had precipitated the Exile. Thus, the foreign women became the scapegoats. Rather than the failings of the political leadership, the foreign women were blamed for Jahweh's anger. Ezra 9 exposes some of the horror of the casting away of foreign women, which had great consequences for the family, community, and the nation. These women had little control over their circumstances and often found themselves as expendable commodities.

This image of casting away "undesirable" women has perpetuated the continuous domination and scapegoating of women. They are viewed as inferior and simply as "the Other," which has allowed terrible acts of violence, dominance, sexual objectification, and slavery. Scapegoating was literally a tradition in Jewish culture—a goat would take on the sins of the people on the Day of Atonement and be cast away. The goat is an innocent creature blamed and punished for the sins, and often distracts attention from the real causes to problems. Likewise, the foreign women in Ezra are seen as creatures to take on the sins of the people, one of which is the issue of purity. The female body represents the abject (hopeless, miserable) which must be expelled, and everything maternal and female are represented as unclean. In many ways, knowingly or not, this is still occurring in our context today.

The history of Asian North American immigration involves more than 100 years in North America and much of this was plagued with hardship, turmoil, difficulties, and perseverance. Coming to North America is a difficult transition for many immigrants who face the challenge of living with a new culture, language, and religion. From the beginning of immigration, Asian North American women have been viewed as the foreign wives of Ezra's assessment, polluting the pure strain and angering God.

As immigrants came into the United States, the white Europeans were treated differently from Asians or people of color. Europeans entered the United States through Ellis Island in New York, which was essentially a processing center. Immigrants simply had their identification checked by officials and then they were registered to enter America. Asians, on the other hand, came through Angel Island in San Francisco Bay, which was essentially a prison. While European immigrants at Ellis Island waited a couple of hours or overnight before they were allowed to enter the land of milk and honey, Asian immigrants at Angel Island had to wait weeks, months, or even years. Whereas 2 percent of Europeans who applied for entry were sent back, Asians were sent back at more than 10 times that rate. The difference in treatment toward these two groups of people was race. It was not that European immigrants were any healthier or smarter than Asian immigrants; it was rather a difference of color. The Japanese government actually did their best to send only the smartest, most educated, and healthiest to America. However, this did not matter in the eyes of white immigration officials who already had negative views of Asians.

While white European immigrant women are able to quickly assimilate into the dominant Western culture, Asian immigrant women are obviously foreign. It does not matter how many generations they live in North America, their "yellow" skin will continue to mark them as a "foreigner." The portrayal of Asian North American women as the perpetual foreigner leads to racism, subordination, objectification, and discrimination. Since they experience a double discrimination as "foreign" and "women," they are easily cast away as unimportant members of society. Their experiences of racism and sexism often go unnoticed and therefore ignored by others.

Discrimination still continues in interracial marriages. During and after the Korean War, there were many American GIs who married Korean women. This interracial marriage was viewed negatively by the Korean society as impure, thus violating the pure Korean society. To add to this problem, when the American GIs returned to the United States, these wives were often ostracized and isolated from the rest of the American community. There was a sense of disdain by both the American society and the Korean immigrant community. Thus these wives became triply despised by three different social groups. To make things worse, some of these Korean women were abandoned by their GI husbands as the men eventually found Caucasian American women to remarry back in the United States. Many still used the purity code to justify this discrimination.

It is necessary to move beyond the way Ezra 9 dealt with these very pertinent issues. The question of foreign women and intermarriage is essentially about hybridity and purity. It is crucial to recognize that everyone is a hybrid and to rejoice in the differences. Hybridity brings together and fuses while at the same time maintaining separation: If one is a North American Korean woman, she is both North American and Korean, and therefore different—in a positive way—from North American women. Hybridity brings insight into analyzing the notion of the foreign women in Ezra 9. The foreign women of Ezra's day, just like Asian North American immigrant women, were living lives of hybridity as they were bordering on different religions, cultures, and heritages. Rather than banishing these women as the scapegoats of our issues, we need to embrace, welcome, and celebrate diversity, and find a richer way of being together in community.

Grace Ji-Sun Kim (Ph.D.) is Associate Professor of Doctrinal Theology at Moravian Theological Seminary, Bethlehem, Pennsylvania, United States.

A Cuban Reflection on the Biblical Experience of Exile

Franco Valdes (Cuba, United States)

The Cuban American people mostly reside in South Florida, the place I call Home. Even now, that I live elsewhere, South Florida remains my "Home," the place I was born and raised. This thought is one that is embedded in Cuban Americans today, even more so in Cubans who have immigrated to the United States in the last 30 years and are now even American citizens. This feeling of Home is a very strong sentiment to Cubans; their small Cuban neighborhood, their friends, and their families all play part to this significant attachment.

Before we continue, it is important to have an abridged history lesson of both the political revolution in Cuba and the biblical one in Jerusalem. Cuba, backed by the United States, was under control of a communist government ruled by Fulgencio Batista. Attacks against Batista started in 1953 on Moncada Barracks in Santiago and ended in 1959 when Batista finally fled the country. During these six years of war people began to understand the inevitable future of the country. Many of them fled Cuba and came to the United States before it was too late. Today, the doors remain closed, and the thousands of now South Floridians have no choice but to accept their new residence, away from their real Home.

At the end of the year 2012, Cuba will have served over 53 years under Fidel Castro and his administration and many more under a communist government, including Batista's reign. That is over five decades of poverty, hunger, suffering, and hardship that the Cuban people have had to cope with. Still, the Cuban people residing in South Florida do not call the United States their Home. My father, who came to the United States in 1984, is now an American citizen and even receives help from the U.S. government; in conversation he will still attest to Cuba being his real home and only residing here temporarily: "I live here and I have family here, but this is not my country." That view will never change.

Traveling back in history many centuries we come to read about the Assyrian empire, ruling the Middle East from 900 B.C.E. to 607 B.C.E. The Kingdom of Judah was client to this vast territory. After a few years of war, the Babylonians overthrew the Assyrian Empire in 599 B.C.E. and two years later, the city of Judah fell as well and was destroyed by the Babylonian ruler Nebuchadnezzar. Nebuchadnezzar appointed Zedekiah to be king of the territory not knowing that he would revolt against him in the future. Zedekiah entered into an alliance with the Egyptian Pharaoh Hophra and attempted to take back Judah. Nebuchadnezzar once again succeeded and in 587 B.C.E. destroyed the city walls, Temple, and the houses of the most important citizens. During this time many people fled to avoid the destruction, seeking refuge in neighboring cities such as Moab, Ammon, and Edom.

The thought of leaving behind everything you have ever known is a very difficult decision. Leaving your family, your home, your job, your security, your values, and anything else you own is a decision that every person in exile has made. Each situation may be different but the feeling is always the same. It is tough to know the specific conditions in which people left Judah, but as a Cuban American, I know the conditions in which people have left Cuba. My father, mother, uncles, and aunts have all shared with me their stories of escape. Speaking to my mother about this brings her to tears; she misses Home deeply and painfully. She left everything to come to the United States and avoid the cruel world inside Cuba. Although she does not regret her decision, she feels as though she has lost her identity and has completely disconnected herself from her past, her memories, and her family who still remain in Cuba.

In theory both moments in history, Israelite and Cuban, have many similarities. Both, for example, coincide with a lack of democracy and a lack of freedom. There is a crucial difference, however. Nehemiah 1 and 2 feature a theme that not a single Cuban American can relate to: returning Home, rebuilding, and rejoicing. This part of the story has not yet been written for Cuba and the Cuban American people. This longing for Home in the Cuban American people's hearts is persistent. We hope that one day—before our time on this earth is done—that part of the story will take place. This hope is what keeps so many of them so close. South Florida is not only a safe haven for these people, but it is also a very close geographical location to their Home. One day they hope to be able to go Home and experience the joy of the returning Israelites: the end of hardship and the establishing of a new country, the regaining of their identity and rejoining a community that they were forced to leave years ago, the rejoicing in and reconstructing of their past and their memories. This possibility, tragically, remains far away for Cuban Americans. Times only get tougher in Cuba, making a place so beautiful and so close feel yet so distant and destroyed.

Franco Valdes (B.A., Latin American History, University of Virginia) is a first-generation Cuban American from Miami.

A Few Personal Thoughts on the Identity Crisis of Biblical Exiles

Danielle Smith (Senegal, United States)

The books of Ezra and Nehemiah are essentially a story about an identity crisis, one in which the Israelites struggle to define who they are as a people. Are they defined by their past as the nation of Israel? Are they defined by their present as a part of the Persian Empire? Or is it a common faith that binds them, regardless of their political and national status and geographic location? Having grown up in a missionary family and lived in various African cultures, I can relate to this struggle. There is a constant battle between the American roots of my family and birthplace, and my African heritage, as I had spent the majority of my childhood in Africa. While residing in America I was in the racial and religious majority and yet I thought in ways that were culturally different; whereas, in Africa, I was distinctly in a racial and religious minority but found I was more culturally attune to the African way of living. Each location required a thoughtful reflection on who I was. When seen through these cultural dynamics, Ezra's actions are those of a servant of God who is attempting to unite the Israelites through the rebuilding of their Temple—a Temple that served as a symbol of their faith and the very heart of what brought them together as a nation in the first place. In the final analysis he is seeking to bring an identity to a dispossessed people whom God was returning to the Promise Land and the faith of their fathers.

King Cyrus allowed the Israelites to return to Jerusalem in order to rebuild the temple which had been destroyed previously by King Nebuchadnezzar. Therefore, the heads of the Israelite families prepared their things and moved to Jerusalem and the surrounding towns in hopes of renewing their covenant with God as they attempted to reestablish the destroyed temple. As the "newcomers" struggled with moving and starting such a great task, however, they met opposition from hostile people around them.

To me this recalls my first year in an African school. As the only white person in the entire school and not knowing any French at all, I was definitely a misfit in their eyes, as well as in my own. They did not understand me or why I was so different and they could not relate to me or my ways. Consequently, I remember the seemingly endless days of students pulling at my hair because it was long, blonde, and so different from their own, or kids always begging for money with the assumption that every white person was wealthy. It wasn't until many months later that the kids began to warm up to the idea of having a foreigner amongst them. Much like the era of Ezra, in African societies, racial identity often assumes religious affiliation. For example, the Wolof of Senegal will assume that any fellow Wolof is a Muslim and therefore anyone seeking to integrate into their community will come under intense pressure to espouse Islam. Similarly with the Jews, surrounding areas did not welcome them as they brought their own traditions and history with them. They sought to rebuild something unique to their own culture amongst the people of an entirely different one. What is important to remember is that the resistance they met was created by their attempt to be faithful to God; we, too, can expect similar hostility until God gives us a clear direction on how to engage with those around us.

As time went on and the Israelites became more accustomed to their surroundings, they started assimilating with the people around them. They began intermarrying and following the foreign customs of their neighbors. Just before my freshman year of high school, my family left Senegal indefinitely and moved back to America. I was faced with a new home, a new school, and a culture with which I was not very familiar. My first reaction was to push away from conforming to the cookie-cutter American image because of my loyalty to my African roots. However, being different can be exhausting, especially as a young teenager, and I soon found that I just wanted to be "normal." I began dressing, talking, and acting like what I thought was the typical American. It was not simply an outward appearance with which I was struggling, but an inner perception.

Throughout the book of Ezra, we see a fundamental struggle of identity amongst the Israelites who were tired of being oppressed and whose tendency was, just like me, to blend in with the society surrounding them. All who have ever experienced the process of cultural adaptation understand the challenges of integrating into a new environment without assimilating. Integration means to become a participant in the new society but assimilation occurs when one surrenders their very identity in the pursuit of being accepted by their new neighbors. At the core of this decision is the question of personal beliefs, personal faith. How far will one go just to fit in?

Unlike Nehemiah, who focused on political restoration, the heart of Ezra's message was the spiritual restoration of the people of God. Ezra sought to bring the Israelites' focus back to their faith and God thus making it the essence of their identity. There were practical consequences concerning intermarriage and enculturation with the surrounding nations. It is a stark reminder that faith does impact daily life. While the New Testament does not espouse a racial bloodline from Abraham, the Good News does declare that the bloodline of Jesus will cause separation from the world when it seeks to alter our identity in Christ.

When God is at the center of our worldview it affects our practical decisions. Like the Israelites, who we marry and what we build (the Temple) are expressions of our faith. Every generation has to make the critical choice of conforming to the world around them or being transformed by the truth of God's Word. Whether in Africa or in America, the day-to-day decisions I make are part of the worldview that God is instilling in me. In Ezra's time, God was seeking a people no longer held in captivity by alien beliefs or influences; rather their identity was to be in the God of Abraham, Isaac, and Jacob. The same can be said today: God is still seeking a people who live according to their identity in Christ and not that of the culture around them. It is the most practical form of the concept called holiness.

Danielle Smith spent her early life in Senegal and is currently studying cultural anthropology in the United States.

The Complicated History of the Composition of Ezra and Nehemiah

Juha Pakkala (Finland)

The story of Ezra in Ezra 7–10 and Nehemiah 8 describes the coming of Ezra from Babylon. The story has a very complicated history. It is the product of successive editors and authors who made several substantial additions and other modifications to the text before it became too holy and canonical to be changed any further—that is, the version we now have in the Bible. For a better understanding of the text's various contexts of writing, it is necessary to distinguish between the main editorial stages. The final text does not do justice to the various contexts where the text was produced. By peeling back the layers in the text, we can observe the development of Jewish identity in the Persian Empire.

It should first be stressed that the story in Ezra 7–10 and Nehemiah 8 was originally an independent story and not intended to be read with Ezra 1–6, the story of the building of the temple, or with the Nehemiah memoir in Nehemiah 1:1–7:4. Dealing with different aspects of the restoration of Judah and the Jewish community (Temple, Law, and City), these originally independent stories were later combined to form a single composition. In order to tie the Nehemiah memoir with the Ezra story, Nehemiah 8 was relocated from its original position between Ezra 8 and Ezra 9.

In the oldest part of the story Ezra is portrayed as a scribe who was skilled in the Law of Moses (Ezra 7:6). He returned to Jerusalem to discover that the people who had remained in the land had lived without the Law and, against the Law, taken foreign wives. Consequently, Ezra was commissioned to annul the mixed marriages and expel the foreign wives as well as their offspring from the Jewish community. The story ends with a reintroduction and reading of the Law. The main message of this story is that the Law of Moses has been reinstated in Judah after the Exile and that the Jewish community now must live according to it. This story was written in a strongly Law-oriented Jewish community, which apparently paid little attention to the Temple and its practices. In fact, the Temple is not even mentioned in the oldest Ezra story. It is also significant that the Law is introduced from Babylon. Although one has to be critical of the historical value of the events that are described in the story, the idea that the Law derives from the Babylonian Jewish community may have a historical kernel.

Ezra's prayer in Ezra 9 is a later addition. The main intention of the prayer was to reflect the mixed marriage crisis with Israel's history and with the Torah's commandments, some of which are quoted. The prayer portrays the Jews as recurrent sinners who have violated Yahweh's commandments in the past and have done so again by taking foreign wives.

The next main editorial phase emphasized the community of those who returned from the Exile. This so-called Gola-community was assumed to form the backbone of the Jews, and corresponding changes were made to the text. Whereas the older text is based on the existence of a community of Jews who had remained in the land, the focus of attention is now the returnees. The Gola-community was assumed to have sacrificed alone (Ezra 8:35); they alone were summoned to Jerusalem to resolve the mixed marriages (Ezra 9:7) and only they take part in the celebration of the feast of booths (Neh. 8:17). Even the mixed marriage crisis is assumed to have been caused by the returning exiles (Ezra 9:4), although it contradicts the whole idea of the original story, which implies that those who had remained in the land had been living without the Law. The Gola-additions are found throughout the book of Ezra, which implies that Ezra 1–6 had now been combined with the Ezra story.

Artaxerxes' edict in Ezra 7:12–26 was added after the model of other similar documents of the Persian authorities found in Ezra 1–6 (e.g., Cyrus' edict in Ezra 6:3–5). Although these documents are unlikely to be authentic, their addition implies that the authors perceived the Persian authorities in a positive light and that an imperial authorization for the reestablishment of the Jewish community was considered important. In comparison, many biblical authors relate negatively to the Babylonian and especially Assyrian empires. However, it is probable that the Persian documents were written only after the destruction of the Persian Empire.

The final editorial stages primarily deal with the Temple and priestly issues. Ezra's mission was gradually made more priestly, so that he became a carrier of the temple vessels and the leader of returning priests (Ezra 8). In this process Ezra, originally only a scribe, was made a priest because a nonpriest could not have led such a priestly mission. Ezra was also given a priestly genealogy deriving from Aaron (Ezra 7:1–5). The development of the text reflects the increasing importance of the priests in the community where the Ezra story was transmitted. The older text did not fit well the conceptions of these final priestly editors. They assumed that the priests should have a more important role in the society and thus the text was changed accordingly. For example, in the older text, Ezra reads the Law to the people (Neh. 8:3), but a later priestly editor added that Levitical priests were needed to explain it to them (Neh. 8:7–8).

The Ezra story shows how important the Law had become for the preservation of the Jewish identity after the destruction of the Temple in 587 B.C.E. It implies a full reorientation from a temple-focused religion of the monarchical times to a religion centered on the Law of Moses. The oldest Ezra story is based on theological conceptions that do not necessitate the existence of the temple. It was created in a social and ideological setting that had to cope with a templeless time. The Law of Moses in effect replaced the Temple as the way to serve God. Temple-centered conceptions reemerged after the rebuilding of the Temple, and this change in the ideological setting is also reflected in the Ezra story. Successive redactions gradually added the involvement of priests and Temple-related issues throughout the story.

Because of the editorial changes, there is a certain tension between the Temple and the Law in the story, but this is a reflection of the tensions in the Jewish communities of the Second Temple period. The different Jewish parties were, in part, created out of the bipolar background of Judaism. It is evident that the various solutions to the relationship between the Law and the Temple created tensions between the religious parties. On the other hand, because it contained both the temple and the law aspect, the Ezra story could be used as a source of inspiration for the Temple circles and the Law-oriented circles. The amalgamation of the Temple and Law in the Ezra story guaranteed its success and acceptance in the Hebrew canon.

The Ezra story is a prime example of a biblical text going through substantial revisions. Instead of seeing these textual changes as distorting history, they provide substantial evidence about the social, religious, and ideological changes taking place in the context where the text was transmitted. In fact, the events that the story describes may not be the most important history that the text bears witness to. The textual changes and the historical changes they imply may be more important than what the text tells us about the events in the fifth century B.C.E.

It should also be added that these changes kept the story relevant for the developing Jewish community. Without the changes, the text might have become irrelevant because it would not have addressed issues of the new circumstances. The destruction of the Second Temple in 70 C.E. meant that the basis for the Temple-oriented texts suffered considerably. With its Law-based aspect, the Ezra story was well suited for the new situation. The Ezra story became a central text in Judaism after 70 C.E., and with it Ezra as the advocate of the Law became one of the most important Jewish heroes.

Juha Pakkala teaches in the Department of Biblical Studies at University of Helsinki, Finland.

QUESTIONS

1. Explain and evaluate Kim's point that "everyone is a hybrid" and that one should "rejoice in the differences."
2. In addition to the ones mentioned by Valdes, what are some other similarities and differences between the Cuban and Israelite contexts?
3. How does your cultural context compare to that of Smith and Ezra–Nehemiah in terms of associating racial identity with religious affiliation?
4. How does Pakkala's analysis shed light on Ezra–Nehemiah? What assumptions and problems might be identified with his approach?

CHAPTER 25

BIRTH OF JESUS

Matthew 1–2; Luke 1–2

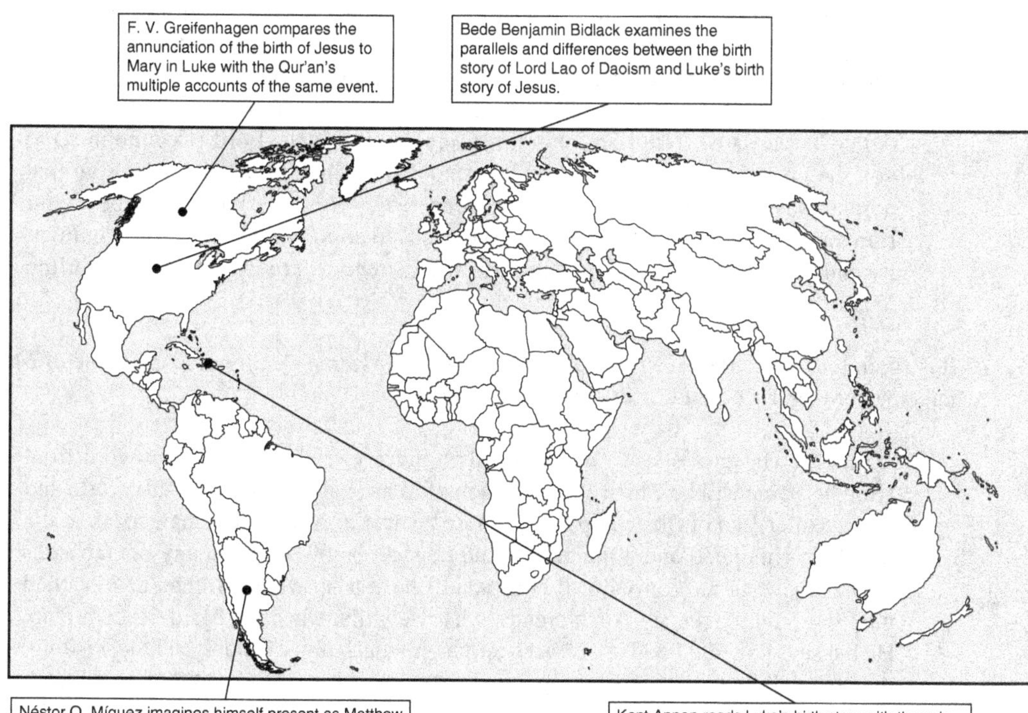
F. V. Greifenhagen compares the annunciation of the birth of Jesus to Mary in Luke with the Qur'an's multiple accounts of the same event.
Bede Benjamin Bidlack examines the parallels and differences between the birth story of Lord Lao of Daoism and Luke's birth story of Jesus.
Néstor O. Míguez imagines himself present as Matthew writes of Herod's slaughter of the children, drawing parallels with other atrocities of history.
Kent Annan reads Luke's birth story with those in Haiti, focusing on their understanding of the phrase "no room at the inn" for Mary and Joseph.

READINGS

The Annunciation to Mary in the Qur'an

F. V. Greifenhagen (Canada)

The annunciation by a divinely sent messenger to Mary of the birth of a special son is narrated not only in Luke's gospel (1:26–38) but also in the Muslim scripture, the Qur'an, originating with the prophet Muhammad in the seventh century C.E. in Arabia. There the story is told not just once, but twice. In Surah 19 *Maryam* ("Mary") 16–21 we read thus:

> 16 Relate in the book (the story of) Mary, when she withdrew from her family to a place in the East. 17 She placed a screen (to screen herself) from them; then We sent to her our angel, and he appeared to her as a man in all respects. 18 She said, "I seek refuge from you to (Allah) most gracious; (come not near) if you fear Allah." 19 He said, "No, I am only a messenger from your Lord (to announce) to you the gift of a righteous son." 20 She said, "How shall I have a son, seeing that no man has touched me and I am not unchaste?" 21 He said, "So (it will be); your Lord says, 'That is easy for me, and (We wish) to appoint him as a sign to humanity and a mercy from Us'; it is a matter (so) decreed." (Translation by 'Abdullah Yusuf 'Ali, 2001)

It is again found in Surah 3 *Ali 'Imran* ("The Family of 'Imran"—'Imran is the name of Mary's father according to Qur'an 66:12 and 3:35) 45–49:

> 45 Behold! The angels said, "O Mary! Allah gives you glad tidings of a word from Him; his name will be Christ Jesus, the son of Mary, held in honour in this world and the hereafter, and of (the company of) those nearest to Allah. 46 He shall speak to the people in childhood and in maturity. And he shall be of (the company of) the righteous." 47 She said, "O my Lord! How shall I have a son when no man has touched me?" He said, "Even so: Allah creates what He wills; when He has decreed a plan, He but says to it 'Be,' and it is! 48 And Allah will teach him the book and the wisdom, the law and the gospel. 49 And (appoint him) a messenger to the children of Israel, (with this message): 'I have come to you with a sign from your Lord, in that I make for you out of clay, as it were, the figure of a bird, and breath into it, and it becomes a bird by Allah's leave. And I heal those born blind, and the lepers, and I quicken the dead, by Allah's leave. And I declare to you what you eat, and what you store in your houses. Surely therein is a sign for you if you did believe.' " (Translation by 'Abdullah Yusuf 'Ali, 2001)

Furthermore, the Qur'an alludes to the annunciation in two other verses. Surah 21 *al-Anbiya* ("The Prophets") 91: "And (remember) her who guarded her chastity: We breathed in to her of Our Spirit, and We made her and her son a Sign for all peoples." And Surah 66 *al-Tahrim* ("Prohibition") 12: "And Mary, the daughter of 'Imran, who guarded her chastity; and We breathed into (her body) of Our Spirit; and she testified to the truth of the words of her Lord and of his Revelations, and was one of the devout (servants)." (Translation by 'Abdullah Yusuf 'Ali, 2001.)

The qur'anic versions of the annunciation to Mary accord with Luke's story in many respects. An angel announces that she will bear a son, to which she responds with bewilderment since she is a virgin. Her virginity, however, is no obstacle, for God is able to create a child within her without a human father. The Qur'an unpacks the angel's more terse assertion in Luke's gospel that "nothing will be impossible with God" (1:37) by having the messenger explain that when God decides anything, God merely needs to say "Be!" and it is—it is thus easy for God to do what is impossible for mortals. God's Spirit is involved in the miraculous conception in both the biblical and qur'anic accounts, and in both versions the child will be named Jesus. Mary devoutly accepts the message in both Luke and the Qur'an, although her assent in the Qur'an is not explicitly verbalized as it is in Luke. Finally, like the account in Luke, both of the fuller qur'anic accounts of the annunciation are preceded by the story of the annunciation to Zechariah, who, as in the biblical version, distrusts the announcement and is struck mute.

There are also differences. The Qur'an is not interested in details such as the town where Mary lives, and it omits entirely the sign of Elizabeth's pregnancy and any mention of Joseph. The qur'anic versions especially highlight the chastity of Mary by depicting her as withdrawing alone from her family and screening herself from them (19:16–17), a motif that leads to a heightened sense of Mary's alarm when she is approached in her seclusion by the messenger, whom the Qur'an describes as appearing like a human man in all respects. Mary, fearing molestation, needs to warn him off by seeking refuge with God. In an atmosphere charged with sexual danger, more explicit than the confusion or perplexity she experiences in the Lukan account, Mary displays proper propriety. Finally, one of the titles to be given to her son in the Qur'an is "son of Mary," a name that stands out as unusual in a patriarchal context in which descent was reckoned from one's father, and thus it serves to emphasize even further Mary's virginal status. (The title "Jesus son of Mary" appears in Mark 6:3, but seems there to be used as a slur against him.)

But the biggest differences lie in the description of the son that will be born to Mary. In the qur'anic accounts, he is not named "son of God"; nor is his career portrayed as that of a king, although he is called Christ or Messiah. Rather, the Qur'an emphasizes his qualities of righteousness and honor, and describes his career in terms of learning the holy scriptures and being sent as messenger to the children of Israel with miraculous powers of healing, animation of dead matter, and foreknowledge. This depiction accords with the prophetic paradigm applied by the Qur'an to all those that it names prophets; namely, that they are righteous folk who function primarily to bring a message from God to a specific people, encapsulated in a book, and confirmed by miracles.

Interestingly, some Muslim commentators have discussed whether Mary herself functions as a prophet in that she receives a "word" from God (3:45). While this "word" is usually glossed as a mere reference to God's command "Be!" by which Jesus is miraculously conceived, it bears an uncanny resemblance to the divine *logos* or word which is used of Jesus in the Gospel of John (1:1–18). Rather than some willful misunderstanding, the Qur'an has here redirected emphasis on Jesus as God's word, and on his miraculous conception, away from indications or proofs of his divine status to demonstrations of the divine creative power of God. Even Jesus' miracles, the Qur'an insists, are performed by God's permission (3:49).

In shifting the focus in this manner, the Qur'an gets behind the postbiblical Christian doctrinal ideology of Christ's status as God. Luke, for instance, depicts Jesus mainly as subordinate to God (see especially the early Christian preaching described in Acts, such as 2:22–24; 3:13, 17–26; 4:27–28), joined to God by the Spirit but not identical with God. Overall, the Qur'an attempts to steer a middle course between what it sees as the excessive claims made about Jesus by Christians, on the one hand, and the rejection of Jesus and his significance by Jews, on the other. The Qur'an rejects the interpretation, found in Jewish literature, of the story of Jesus' birth from a virgin as a cover-up of fornication but it does not go as far as Christians in deifying

Jesus even though Jesus clearly has a preeminent status among the prophets in the Qur'an. The Qur'an's versions of the annunciation to Mary, with their insistence on her chastity and virginity equally and her submission to God's will, as also her son's submission, can trigger a reading of Luke's account of the annunciation uncoupled from later theological overlays.

F. V. Greifenhagen is Associate Professor of Religious Studies at Luther College, University of Regina, Canada.

THE PARALLELS AND DIFFERENCES BETWEEN THE BIRTH STORY OF LORD LAO AND JESUS

Bede Benjamin Bidlack (United States)

Laozi was a philosopher of ancient China and is traditionally considered the author of *Daode jing* and the founder of Daoism (Taoism). Over time he became revered as a deity; indeed by the second century A.D. he was worshipped as Lord Lao. In Daoist beliefs, Lord Lao comes down when the ways of humankind fall into grave error, wander from the Dao—the Ultimate Reality in the Daoist worldview—and need instruction on how to get back into harmony with the Dao. He appears to the ruler or to a person who later becomes a religious leader as a result of the encounter.

In sixth-century China, Daoists and Buddhists were competing for royal favor and met in a series of court debates. The question concerned who was prior: Laozi or Buddha. The tradition with the older religious founder was considered the superior religion. To prove the superiority of Daoism over Buddhism, Daoists looked to the *Scripture of the Conversion of the Barbarians* (*Huahu Jing*). The *Scripture* was written from a tradition of transformations of Lord Lao when he descended into the world on a regular basis to provide guidance to rulers and to reveal sacred scriptures.

The central story of the *Scripture* tells of how Lord Lao traveled West, transmitted the *Daode jing*, then continued to convert the Indians to Buddhism, which Daoists understood as a diluted form of Daoism. A later version of the story escalated the polemical character of the text: Laozi and his companion Yin Xi journeyed to the West; there was an exchange of banquets with the barbarian kings; Laozi and Yin Xi underwent ordeals; after emerging from the ordeals, they punished the barbarians for their unbelief; they tried to civilize the barbarians with Buddhist precepts; Laozi left to convert other lands, while Yin Xi remained and was known as the Buddha. In these narratives, Lord Lao was the creator of the universe, a supporter of rulers, the source of scriptures, and the personification of the Dao. The *Scripture* describes the arrival of Lord Lao this way:

> In those days, in the reign of Tanjia of Yin with the year star in *gengshen*...the Highest Venerable Lord came down from the eternal realm of the Dao. He harnessed a cloud of three energies and strode on the essence of the sun. Following the rays of the nine luminaries, he entered into the mouth of the Jade Maiden of Mystery and Wonder. Taking refuge in her womb, he became a man.
>
> In the year *gengshen*, on the fifteenth day of the second month, he was born in Bo. Nine dragons sprinkled water over him to rinse and wash his body then they transformed into nine springs.

> At that time, the Venerable Lord had white hair. He was able to walk upon birth. A lotus flower sprouted under each step he took. After nine steps, he pointed to heaven with his left hand, to the earth with his right hand and announced to the people… "I shall reveal the highest law of the Dao. I shall save all things moving and growing, the entire host of living beings."

While the birthing of Lord Lao contains many parallels with that of Jesus, four differences are apparent at the outset. First, Dao is not equivalent to God, as it is impersonal and not above the universe, but it *is* the universe. This is a monistic worldview. Therefore, Lord Lao, the embodiment of the Dao, is the universe as well. Second, Lord Lao is not the son of the Dao, as Jesus is the Son of the Father. Lord Lao is a particular divine person who is accessible to the world. Third, this is one of many of Lord Lao's appearances, but Jesus comes only once. Fourth, Laozi's body itself is different from any person's body, although it is very real and of flesh and bone. His body is the representation of the Dao accompanied by mythical markings—such as white hair at birth or bone protrusions on the forehead —that are rich symbols and points of meditation. The marks are similar to those attributed to the body of the Buddha in Mahayana Buddhism.

The interaction with Buddhism in the court debates and elsewhere resulted in a free exchange between Buddhism and Daoism. The birth narrative shows close links to the stories of Buddha's birth. By adopting the birth story and other elements of Buddhism, Daoism claims itself as a universal religion and Lord Lao as the seat of all creation and the source of all teachings, particularly of Buddhism. But what about the similarities with Jesus?

The birth of Laozi is situated in history, even to the date and location, as is Jesus' birth in Luke. In contrast to Jesus' annunciation, Lord Lao's conception is told with a spectacle of light and energies, but he ends up, like Jesus, in the womb of a woman of cosmic importance (Luke 1:26–27), where he became man. His birth is accompanied by dragons, which not only serve to represent nature—as do the presumed animals in Jesus' stable (2:7)—but also angels, insofar as they are beings that travel between heaven and earth (2:9, 13). Immediately at birth, Lord Lao is able to walk and talk—an image analogous to Jesus' advanced wisdom at a young age (2:46–47). Finally, he is identified as the savior of the world (2:11).

Authors of both Luke and the *Scripture* tell of events and characteristics of the descended deity to express that the child will be different from ordinary people and will do something great. The experience of the divine coming into our world is too fantastic for common words. The event is beyond our normal experience, so special words or literary devices are necessary to tell it. The images draw attention to the special identity of these people. Noticeably, both are identified as saviors. But what does it mean for Lord Lao to be a savior and is that the same role that Jesus has?

Salvation as the end of earthly struggles was such a radical departure from Chinese thought that an outside influence cannot be ruled out. Up until that time, dynasties were empowered by a Heavenly Mandate that bestowed on the sovereign, and therefore the entire kingdom, the power to provide prosperity, security, and integrity. A dynasty rose by receiving *de,* "virtue" or "power," from Heaven. Upon wandering from the Dao, the Heavenly Mandate and its *de* would be rescinded by Heaven, causing the downfall of the kingdom. It would be given to the next dynasty, which would follow the next predictable fate of rise and fall.

In texts like the *Scripture*, Lord Lao brings salvation to the kingdom, which was the cosmos to the ancient peoples of China. "Salvation" does not mean redemption from sin, but harmonization with Dao. Lord Lao harmonizes by making several appearances to rulers at times when they have wandered from the Dao. Upon following his divine teachings, the kingdom regains harmony with the Dao and is on the right track for reaching the final age, the Age of Great Peace. In this way, Lord Lao saves little by little until the Age of Great Peace blooms and a perfect harmony with the Dao endures on earth forever.

The *Scripture's* focus is not on the final age, but on the claim of the conversion of the barbarians, as its title states, thereby establishing Daoism as the superior religion over Buddhism. In the court debates, Lord Lao's dramatic birth, acceptance of disciples, and movement to the West were primarily for the purpose of converting those beyond China's borders.

Bede Benjamin Bidlack is Assistant Professor in the Department of Theology at St. Anselm College, United States.

Herod's Slaughter of Children and Other Atrocities throughout Time

Néstor O. Míguez (Argentina)

The Feast of the Holy Innocents was established in the Christian calendar in memory of the slaughter of the children of Bethlehem, which was ordered by Herod upon hearing of the birth of the one who would be Messiah, as we read in Matthew 2. In the story, Joseph receives a warning in a dream and flees with Jesus and Mary, but the remaining children in the village are murdered.

Matthew did not allow the memory of the homicidal Herod to be erased. Herod repaired the temple but destroyed the people. He obtained the throne, backed by the (Roman) Empire, and ends up killing the children of his own people to avoid losing his own unjust power. Soldiers against children, weapons against weeping: terror as the king's method. He who fears losing his throne cannot help but see threats at every turn. But what of the mothers of the innocent who refuse to be comforted.

From my Argentina, I stand alongside Matthew as he writes his gospel. I sit at his worktable and say to him: "For centuries, the commentators will debate if your account is historical dear Matthew, if it squares with the facts, or how theologically to justify the death of the innocent to save the life of the savior. Go ahead and include these details, brother. History will prove them true. I can tell you, from my sad experience that the facts align with your account. Time and again the unjust allies of the Empire—the powers that be—perpetuate their power by killing the innocent. They call it 'preemptive war' or 'collateral damage.' Sad copies of Herod."

I go on, "What is more, Matthew, I know those mothers who refuse to be comforted. They have names: Azucena Villaflor, Adela Antokoletz, Nora Cortinas, Hebe de Bonafini, Estela Carlotto. Some have suffered the same fate as their children; some have died. Others live on, refusing to be consoled, refusing to lower their hands—ceaselessly marching in circles in front of Herod's home, in the town square of uprisings and deaths, the square of the people and of treasons, demanding on behalf of their children. Their white headscarves are an emblem of pain turned to struggle—those mothers who refuse to be comforted because their pain is a part of their struggle. They are the untiring grandmothers who trace the footprints of horror because they know that there they may find, hidden away, the heirs of their dreams."

I carry myself away with my own words, forgetting Matthew and going on: I see those beloved faces—some known, some unknown—equally lovable in their expression of terror. I, like Matthew as he writes, am a witness of the facts even as I speak. "Cry out, mothers of pain and of hope. Do not cease to cry out throughout the centuries, you mothers of Rama and Bethlehem. Alongside the mothers of Iraq and Gaza, and again of Bethlehem. With the mothers of Auschwitz or of Armenia, and the mothers of all the genocides of humanity's senseless history. Weep and cry with the mothers of all our indigenous peoples of America, decimated in their own lands by the homicidal zeal of the conquistador in search of gold and power. Cry with the mothers of Soweto, of Hiroshima, with the millions of mothers of the holocausts of the innocent that pride, ambition, and prejudice sow in our history. With the mothers of Biafra and Haiti, seeing their children die from imposed hunger, from calculated misery. Join your worn voices with the mothers of children born with deformities due to senseless pollution of lands and waters, or in the hells let loose by the napalm of Vietnam. Join together with millions upon millions of those voices that have witnessed the crushing of the heads of children by the homicidal hordes that the empires and their allies, stocked with arms and money, have unleashed time and again on defenseless peoples. May your cries of terror resound forever, without ceding to the offers of comfort from those who purchase consciences. Do not listen to the sweet words with which those preachers of undignified reconciliation wish to soften you. May you never cease in your determined lament, that unceremonious demand for life, the endless marches around the town squares; may the demand for justice that rises from the bottom of the centuries and remains to this day never be silenced, so that the Empire may never sleep without feeling, even if it covers its ears, that its massacres have not been forgotten."

Matthew looks at me, astonished. The names are strange, the situations familiar. "Write, dear Matthew, brother. Write. Your words call out to thousands throughout time. History will sadly corroborate your story, your gospel encouragingly faithful. Keep writing this mirror of the human soul, keep going and don't stop until the necessary resurrection," I say to him, as if the Spirit had not already told him.

Néstor O. Míguez is Professor of New Testament Studies at ISEDET, Buenos Aires, Argentina.

Reading Luke's Christmas Story with Those in Haiti

Kent Annan (Haiti)

It was Christmas Eve in Haiti seven years ago. My wife, Shelly, and I were living there and had gathered on our porch under the palm trees and starry sky with a dozen friends and neighbors. We'd shared a meal of rice and beans and all the fixings. The plates had been cleared away.

Dusk settled, conversation continued, and someone suggested reading the Christmas story. We got our Creole Bible, lit a kerosene lamp, and one of our neighbors, a young man with a strong clear voice, read aloud the narrative of Jesus' birth from the gospel of Luke. The story was read a couple of times and then Shelly or I (can't remember who) asked what stood out to people.

We were informally using *lectio divina*, an ancient approach to reflecting on Scripture that we had adapted and were using as part of a Christian education program with churches and schools in Haiti.

After hearing the story a couple of times, everyone was invited to share their thoughts on what they heard. And everyone did, from young (seven years old) to not-so-young (a couple in their late sixties) to in between.

There were comments about Christ entering the world as a child, comments about Joseph and Mary's faithfulness, and then the discussion began to focus on the phrase: "There was no room for Mary at the inn." Except in the Creole version this read, "There was no *place* for Mary at the inn," a slight variation that seems inconsequential.

At least it did to me. When I heard the verse read that night I understood, as I always had, that literally the inn had no rooms left—a full house, a first-century version of a flickering neon "No Vacancy" sign.

But our friends on the porch understood it a little differently. To them, "No *place* for her in the inn" didn't so much mean that there wasn't a vacancy, but that there was no place for someone *like* Mary in the inn. There was no place for someone who had just ridden in on a donkey. There was no place for someone dressed in peasant clothes. No place for someone who came from the nowheresville of Nazareth. No place when you don't have money, because, let's be honest, if you have enough money you can always find a place.

One neighbor who is a farmer said, "If Mary and Joseph would have been wearing nice clothes and had lots of money, there would have been a place for them. They would never have made her give birth with the animals."

"Yes," someone else said, "they would have treated them differently if they had money."

"And that is just how it is for us too," said the farmer, speaking again. "If we tried to go to one of the good hospitals in Port-au-Prince, there would be no place for us. If we tried to go to one of the hotels in the city, they would see our clothes and shoes, and they would know we're peasants. There wouldn't be a place for us either."

The conversation paused, a silence acknowledging the truth of his words.

"But isn't it amazing," spoke up another friend, "that our Lord chose to come to this earth through a woman who had no place, who was given no place. And even more amazing, God came to earth with good news to tell us: *that we do have a place*! He came to tell us, 'You have a place here as a child of God. And you have a place after this. In fact, right now my Father is preparing another place for you too.' "

There was another pause, but this time it was a silence of peace and of hope.

It was a holy moment I'll remember for the rest of my Christmases. It permanently changed how I hear that phrase in Jesus' birth story. So what happened?

We listened with people who were, in many ways, different from us. Our economic, racial, educational, national, and cultural backgrounds are very different from the friends we were sitting with. Some of these neighbors had no formal education and lived close to the edge of survival. Something happens—or at least can happen—when we listen together. The hermeneutic imagination expands. I then hear not only as myself, but also have a chance to hear through the ears/experience of the person sitting next to me. This can happen in another country or in a small group in your neighborhood. For example, I hear with increased intensity and specificity if listening to a Psalm of lament while sitting next to a woman whose husband just died. If we also listen to each other's reflections on the Bible, this possibility opens up even more.

We listened in another language. Our experience reflected what Frederick Buechner wrote in *Wishful Thinking*, "If you have even as much as a nodding acquaintance with a foreign language, try reading the Bible in that. Then you stand a chance of hearing what the Bible is actually saying instead of what you assume it must be saying because it is the Bible."

We listened to Scripture. There are so many differences, but we were brought together by a common story: the story of Jesus. That's the reason we were gathered on that eve. That's what led us to open a book that everyone, despite our differences, holds dear.

We listened in a way that ensured everyone present could participate. Some literate and some not. I don't think anyone there had finished high school, and at least a few were illiterate and probably had never spent a day in school. But we didn't think about education levels when it was happening. We had been (and continue to be) carefully developing how to approach Christian education in a country where about 50 percent of people are illiterate, so there is pedagogical strategy behind using *lectio divina*, which can be done by listening even if you can't read. But as it happened, we were just there with friends, thinking about Jesus' birth, and finding a way to share a meaningful moment together.

We listened to each other. Really listened.

We listened for God. This feels like an outrageous move of faith sometimes, but also the reason to go to the Bible. Since my faith wavers at times, I'm glad we can listen for God together, lean on each other. Maybe I'll hear something of God, but if not, maybe someone else will hear a whisper and let the rest of us know.

It's not that you couldn't get this insight sitting in your church or reading alone at home. But that didn't happen for me. It happened with these friends on that porch in Haiti.

The night was meaningful, hopeful, and peaceful, but the undercurrents of what is radical and gritty about faith were also right there in the midst of the story and the interpretation. In the shared reading. In the shared lives. In the work for justice that was—and is—ahead.

Kent Annan (M.Div., Princeton Theological Seminary) is author of After Shock *and* Following Jesus through the Eye of the Needle*; he is codirector of Haiti Partners.*

QUESTIONS

1. How do the biblical details, in contrast to the sparse nature of the Qur'an, influence one's reading experience?
2. Bidlack states that one of the purposes of the *Scripture* was to convert those outside China's borders. What was Matthew's and Luke's purpose in composing their birth narrative (they may be different)?
3. Imagine Matthew's response to Míguez. What is your response to Míguez's imagined conversation?
4. What other elements in Luke's story—besides Mary and Joseph having "no place"—might resonate with Annan's group?

CHAPTER 26

SERMON ON THE MOUNT

Matthew 5–7

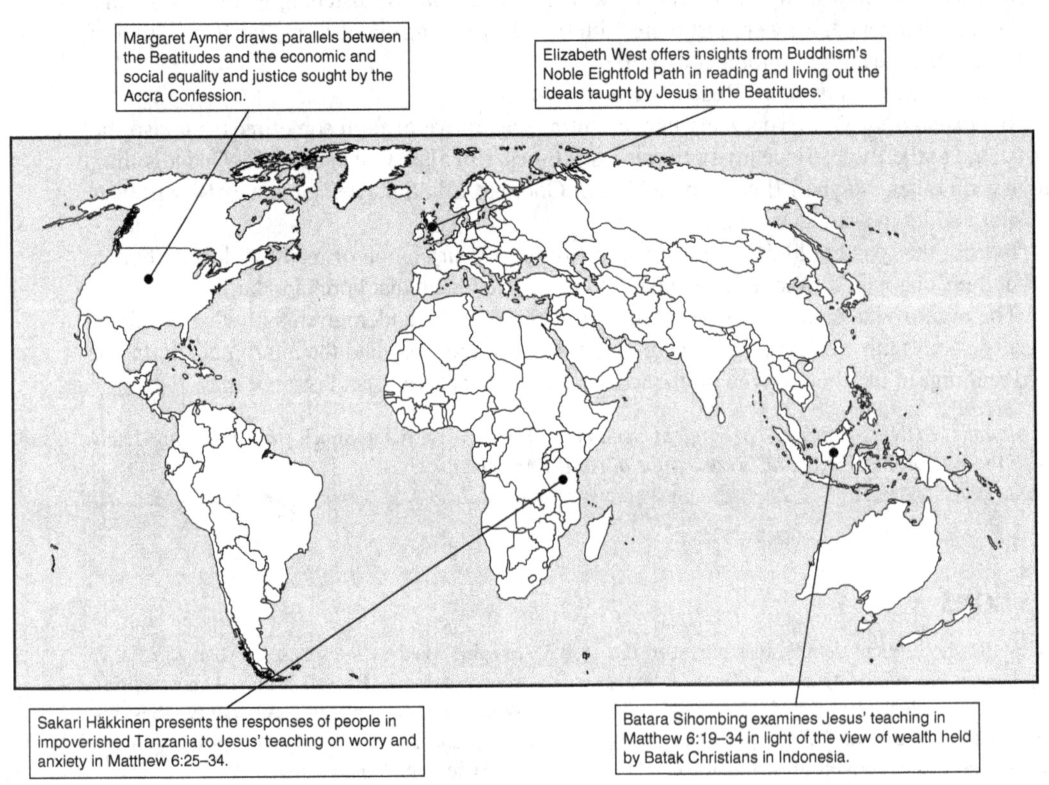
Margaret Aymer draws parallels between the Beatitudes and the economic and social equality and justice sought by the Accra Confession.
Elizabeth West offers insights from Buddhism's Noble Eightfold Path in reading and living out the ideals taught by Jesus in the Beatitudes.
Sakari Häkkinen presents the responses of people in impoverished Tanzania to Jesus' teaching on worry and anxiety in Matthew 6:25–34.
Batara Sihombing examines Jesus' teaching in Matthew 6:19–34 in light of the view of wealth held by Batak Christians in Indonesia.

READINGS

Comparing Buddhism's Noble Eightfold Path and Jesus' Beatitudes
Elizabeth West

The Beatitudes and the Accra Confession
Margaret Aymer

The Sermon on the Mount in Light of Wealthy Batak Christians in Indonesia
Batara Sihombing

Reading Matthew 6 with Those in Impoverished Tanzania
Sakari Häkkinen

Comparing Buddhism's Noble Eightfold Path and Jesus' Beatitudes

Elizabeth West (United Kingdom)

The Beatitudes can be usefully revisited with Buddhist insights. The eight simple statements of Jesus known as the Beatitudes contain the very essence of his teaching. Most Christians think they know them well. However, their richness can be lost because our minds are loaded with conditioned beliefs and perceptions. We may have been taught to understand them in a particular way that prevents us from seeing them in other, perhaps deeper, ways.

The transformative power of the Beatitudes lies in the fact that they are written in the present tense and imply realization here and now. They are not promises for the future or for the afterlife! They are states of being that as Christians we are meant to enter into here and now. The Beatitudes are a course in how to be "blessed." More than simply being happy, "blessed" suggests a profound sense of unshakable well-being that comes from the transformed self and not the acquisition of wealth or power.

In 1994 I was privileged to be present at the John Main Seminar in London. His Holiness the Dalai Lama, who had agreed to comment on passages from the Christian Gospels from a Buddhist perspective, led the seminar. The moment when he read the Beatitudes was one that those present will never forget. The power of that moment lay in the fact that he so embodied what he was reading. There was a sense of having *met* Christ. That a member of another religion could be such an icon of Christ was a profound lesson. Here we saw one who truly lives the way Jesus lived. He who embodies Christ's teaching and values becomes truly as Christ, whether they are members of the institutional religion set up in his name or not. It was clear to all that His Holiness lives in this state of unshakable well-being to which the Beatitudes call us. His joy radiates to all around him in spite of all he suffers from the situation of Tibet and his people. Here is a living example that happiness here and now is a very real possibility.

The Noble Eightfold Path of the Buddha consists of the following:

Balanced view (or Right seeing or Right view);

Right intention;

Right speech (or Positive speech);

Right action (or Wholesome action);

Right livelihood (or Harmless livelihood);

Right effort;

Right mindfulness (or Awareness);

Right samadhi *(a difficult word to translate—possibly meditation/contemplation)*

The Eightfold Path of Buddhism is also a list of means to happiness. In fact it is the expansion of the Four Noble Truths, which is the truth that tells us how to end suffering. "Suffering" is not a very accurate translation of the Sanskrit word *dukkha*; a closer translation would be unsatisfactoriness. *Dukkha* is a state of dissatisfaction which our minds create around the situations of our lives. This then is the Buddha's list for achieving the cessation of suffering which is the opposite of happiness. The list clearly shows that my suffering is self-created and that my happiness and that of others are inseparable. What I do to be happy must also make others happy or at least not increase their suffering. We cannot be happy at the expense of others. This is a mistake people often make.

The term *right* in the Noble Eightfold Path implies an approach that will lead to freedom. It means to be true, on course, being in such a way that will enable us to be happy. One meaning of the Greek word for sin is "to miss the mark." Such an interpretation enables us to see sin as something that destroys happiness, both for ourselves and others.

The Buddha also stressed that we cause our own suffering and that nothing outside ourselves can make us suffer. Sin brings its own consequences rather than it being the punishment of God. This is something we Christians need to ponder deeply to free ourselves from the fear that the old teaching on sin tended to engender. The fear of hell enhances the fear of death, and fear is the greatest block of all to living in the fullness of life that Jesus came to bring us. This fullness of life is enshrined in the teaching of the Beatitudes. All the Buddha's teaching is focused on the attainment of those mental states that eliminate suffering for ourselves and the ways in which we cause suffering to others.

His Holiness the Dalai Lama points out repeatedly that the one thing all human beings have in common is the desire to be happy and to avoid suffering. Whether a religious person, a businessperson, a politician, or a criminal, each still has the desire for happiness as a basic motivation; the difference lies in the way one expects to find that happiness.

Some people do not think they deserve to be happy and it is reflected in a number of ways. Some feel that they are too unworthy and sinful for happiness, that they should be punished and suffer instead. The sad thing is that this can be a deeply held yet unconscious view that prevents happiness from being present. Others feel that it is wrong to be happy when there is so much suffering in the world. Yet if one is not happy it only adds to the suffering in the world! If we are unhappy how can we help and heal others? Thus it is very important to seek to heal any sense we may have that we do not deserve to be happy.

"Blessed are the poor in spirit for theirs is the kingdom of heaven." This short sentence sums up one of the truths that is at the very heart of the Buddha's teaching. He pointed out that one of the main reasons we suffer is because we fight life, clinging to what we want and pushing away what we do not like. If we can free ourselves from craving after "worldly things," this is the first key to true happiness. It is not about whether or not we have them, it is about our attitude toward them.

"Blessed are the pure in heart; they shall see God." Purity of heart follows from poverty of Spirit. Perhaps this is the Beatitude we as Christians are inclined to take least seriously. Yet the Buddha taught that it is possible, if very difficult, to eliminate suffering in this life and live in harmony with all that is. Enlightenment can be seen as being full of the light of the Divine Presence—that ultimate mystery which cannot be grasped in words, but which is the birthright of every human being. The Buddha refused to speak about "God" because words can never contain that mystery; he chose rather to give people the means by which to attain that state in which they would no longer need words.

Blessed are the gentle (meek), merciful, and the peacemakers. From the Buddha's teaching, it is clear that we cannot truly be any of these things until we have at least a small measure of poverty of spirit and purity of heart. The Buddha spoke of Four Immeasurable Qualities or Divine Abidings: Loving-Kindness, Compassion, Empathetic Joy, and Equanimity. These qualities grow out of letting go of ourselves and turning toward the Truth, the Divine. We cannot love and care for others until we glimpse who we truly are.

How do we do this? How do we reach purity of heart? The answer is contained in the Buddha's teaching on Meditation and Wisdom, which helps us to control our minds so that we can become aware of the true nature of reality. Teachings on Contemplation have largely been pushed aside and forgotten in Christianity, but today there is a hunger in the world as never before to discover who we really are and to find true happiness. The Eight Beatitudes sum up this path. The Buddha's teaching and the meditations he taught can help us do just that, whatever our spiritual background may be. The Buddha and most of his followers today are not interested in converting people to their "religion," but rather in offering all the ways they can to help humankind grow in happiness and well-being and so bring about in the world those qualities Jesus laid out in the Beatitudes.

Elizabeth West (M.A., World Religions) was a Catholic nun for 30 years, teaching in the United Kingdom and Africa; she founded the Buddhist Christian Vedanta Network for those who find themselves practicing the teachings of more than one faith.

The Beatitudes and the Accra Confession

Margaret Aymer (United States)

In 2004, the World Alliance of Reformed Churches, a global organization of Protestant churches, convened in Accra, Ghana. From that meeting came a confession called "Covenanting for Justice in the Economy and the Earth," known today simply as the Accra Confession. In the Accra Confession, the churches said, in part (Accra 19):

> We reject the current world economic order imposed by global neoliberal capitalism and any other economic system, including absolute planned economies, which defy God's covenant by excluding the poor, the vulnerable, and the whole of creation from the fullness of life. We reject any claim of economic, political, and military empire which subverts God's sovereignty over life and acts contrary to God's just rule.

This and other portions of the confession were considered scandalous by rich Christians in Europe and the United States of America. However, the confession was not saying anything that Jesus had not already said in the Beatitudes millennia ago.

The Beatitudes occur in Matthew and Luke and, although different, are complementary. Jesus' first four beatitudes in Matthew hold up as honorable the "poor in spirit," the "mourners," the "meek," and those who "hunger and thirst for righteousness" or justice (5:3–6). These four groups of people are really one group, the group that the Accra Confession calls "the poor, the vulnerable and the whole of creation." In Jesus' day, poverty and poverty of spirit were not considered inevitable. It was caused by persons who had taken too much of the limited goods of society for themselves, leaving others poor. This is why Zacchaeus is hated (Luke 19); he has grown rich on the backs of his fellow citizens. It is also the reason why the rich man, who could not see poor Lazarus at his front door, is condemned (Luke 16).

What Jesus only implies in Matthew, he states outright in Luke. Not only are those who are "poor," "mourners," "hungry," and "persecuted" honorable, but those who are "rich," "laughing," "stuffed," and "well-spoken of" are shameful (6:24–26). Jesus does not sidestep the issue. He points squarely at those who have profited on the backs of the poor and says, "Shame on you."

The Beatitudes reveal that the Accra Confession is not saying something new, but something very old: that the concern of heaven is with those who are powerless on earth, and that it is the business for people of faith to be thus concerned also. It goes further, however, to charge that those who would have the concern of heaven today are those facing the underside of neoliberal economic globalization.

The Accra Confession is not only a condemnation of the policies that cause poverty and want, however. It is also a pledge as people of faith to stand with those who have been harmed. It reads (Accra 26):

> We believe that God calls us to stand with those who are victims of injustice. We know what the Lord requires of us: to do justice, love kindness, and walk in God's way (Micah 6:8). We are called to stand against any form of injustice in the economy and the destruction of the environment, "so that justice may roll down like waters, and righteousness like an ever-flowing stream."

This too is an echo of the Beatitudes. For, if the first verse of Jesus' Beatitudes in Matthew excoriates those under an unjust economic system, the second verse honors those who work for justice. Jesus upholds "the merciful," "those with integrity," "the peacemakers," and "those who are persecuted for the sake of righteousness" and justice as being equally the concern of heaven. The call to the disciples is to stand with "those who are victims of injustice" as people of mercy, integrity, and peace.

However such a stand does not come without a cost. As the Accra Confession affirms, "We believe in obedience to Jesus Christ, that the church is called to confess, witness, and act, even though the authorities and human law might forbid them, and punishment and suffering be the consequence (Acts 4:18ff). Jesus is Lord."

And, once more an echo is heard from the mountain on which Jesus preaches the Beatitudes in Matthew. "Blessed are you when people revile you and persecute you, and say all manner of evil against you falsely for my sake" (5:11). There are, both in contemporary and ancient times, consequences to standing with those who suffer and against those who profit. The consequences may be financial, social, or, in the case of Jesus himself, mortal danger. Nevertheless, there are consequences.

Despite the parallels between the Beatitudes and the Accra Confession, the Beatitudes are rarely seen as a radical text; and they are certainly not the source of condemnation that the Accra Confession has been. Perhaps what makes some people uncomfortable with the Accra is that it dares to ask this question: Who are the blessed poor today?

Note: In 2010, the World Alliance for Reformed Churches joined with other global Protestant bodies to become the World Communion of Reformed Churches (WCRC). The WCRC has also adopted the Accra Confession.

Margaret Aymer is Associate Professor of New Testament at the Interdenominational Theological Center in Atlanta, Georgia, United States.

The Sermon on the Mount in Light of Wealthy Batak Christians in Indonesia

Batara Sihombing (Indonesia)

Corruption is a well-known phenomenon in Indonesia. Indonesia is declared by the international economic institutions as one of the most corrupt countries in the world and the champion of corruption in Asia. It has faced economic crisis since 1998 when Suharto was forced to step down. Many factories have closed, the price of goods has risen steadily, and the rate of crime is high. It is publicly acknowledged that the well-known *KKN—Korupsi, Kolusi, Nepotisme* (Corruption, Collusion, Nepotism)—is the reason behind the crisis. Greed seems to have played an important role in making Indonesia morally and economically bankrupt.

In fighting this corruption the Indonesian government has established a *Komisi Pemberantasan Korupsi* (Corruption Eradication Commission). As a result, during the present time, we often hear that many high-ranking government officials—ministers, generals, governors, mayors, legislators, diplomats, and so on—have been imprisoned due to their corruption. But there is no easy way to eradicate greediness for wealth. People tend to have the bad eyes ("greedy") instead of good eyes ("generous") in dealing with money (Matt. 6:22–23). They are not aware that the eye of a greedy person is never satisfied with his or her share. The lover of money will never be satisfied with money. People store up treasures on earth instead of in heaven (6:19–20). So, it is understandable that their hearts focus on earthly materials (6:21).

When we look at the position of Indonesian Christians, particularly the Batak Christians (6 million) to which I belong, we find that they too have contributed to Indonesia's moral bankruptcy. The Batak place much importance on wealth. Their three highest values are *hamoraon* ("riches"), *hagabeon* ("fecundity"), and *hasangapon* ("honor"). Every adult Batak knows these ideals.

The traditional Batak orients their life to these three objectives with a high competitive element. The reason for such orientation is that the Batak people entered modern Indonesia only at the beginning of the last century. Thus, their values originate from their old religion. These ideals bring about covetousness toward all sorts of positions that can give prestige and toward material possessions. Many Bataks abandon their villages in the Batakland and move to new places in order to attain riches, honor, and fecundity.

Further, the Batak desire for wealth can be seen from their *umpasa*, that is, the proverbial prayers to God, the giver of wealth. The use of *umpasa* is very popular among the Batak especially in cultural functions. There are more than 47 *umpasa* which express a strong wish to be wealthy. Although several Batak proverbial requests also point out that wealth should be obtained in appropriate ways, their main goal is to be wealthy no matter what it takes and to attain the praises and admiration of family and friends. For example, every Christmas and New Year many Batak families return to their villages or their parents' home. In this homecoming visit, many of them come with new cars and bring many kinds of presents for their families who are delighted to receive such gifts and to admire their success. Conversely, those who are less (or even not at all) successful are looked down upon by villagers. This is the major reason why many unsuccessful persons, especially the young people, do not return even though they have not seen their parents for years. Being unsuccessful and poor is shameful.

However, people hardly question the means of obtaining these riches. Many are young professionals, government officials, or businessmen. Their salary alone would not enable them to enjoy such wealth. So, where do they get their riches? The answer is, most likely, by corruption. It is not difficult to imagine that in a community which highly values the rich, people will employ whatever means necessary to accrue wealth. But, as Jesus reminds us, one who has an evil eye or greedy eye will become evil (6:22–23). Besides, love of money will bring about evil things in life (6:24). Jesus encourages people to have wealth in an honest and just way, "to strive first for the kingdom of God and his righteousness, and all these things will be given to you as well" (6:34).

It is clear that the Batak face the danger of mammon, the idolatry of materialism. Satan has used mammon as a means of challenging God's plan for the Batak people. In this case, unchecked greed has brought about the bankruptcy of the Indonesian economy, a high rate of unemployment and poor people, and increased crime. Jesus says, "You cannot serve God and mammon" (6:24).

Batak and Indonesian Christians should faithfully serve God. They should store up treasures in heaven by sharing what they have with those who are in need (6:19–21), and they should avoid taking the treasures that do not belong to them. They should be generous givers because God is also generous to them (6:22–23). In so doing, they walk in the way of righteousness (6:33–34), and do not need to be anxious (6:25, 31, 34) because God will provide for their needs (6:32–33).

Batara Sihombing is a Pastor of Huria Kristen Indonesia *(HKI) Church; he also teaches Biblical Studies at the Divinity School of Silliman University, Dumaguete, Philippines.*

Reading Matthew 6 with Those in Impoverished Tanzania

Sakari Häkkinen (Tanzania)

The village of Kinywang'anga is one of the poorest in the Iringa district in the middle of Tanzania. It consists of approximately 1,000 inhabitants who all make a living from their own little farms ranging from one to ten acres in size. Almost all of them would be considered peasant farmers. There is one primary school with five teachers. Even though the teachers receive government pay, each also has a small farm with some cattle. In addition, there are two religious leaders in the village, one a Lutheran evangelist and the other an Anglican priest. They also have farms. There are no other professions among the inhabitants of the village and no one goes to work outside of the village.

People from three different tribes—the Hehe, Bena, and Kinga—live in Kinywang'anga. These tribal names are also the names of the languages spoken in the village. There are no cars. There's only one tractor and a few bicycles. Despite the lack of transportation, people make weekly visits to neighboring villages to meet with relatives and friends and sometimes to try to find medical treatment, though health care is a constant challenge. Also, in recent times HIV and AIDS have struck the village more heavily than most parts of the world, making nearly one in every four adults HIV-positive.

People in Kinywang'anga are totally dependent on the products of the earth. If there is no rain, there is no crop and they are in danger of starvation. The last time this happened was in 2000. Other catastrophes might destroy the crop as well. There are no barns or other storehouses in the village which enable them to keep surpluses to use during hard times or to sell as a way of providing additional income. However, the village grows sunflowers, which are pressed for their oil and sometimes sold to people travelling the main road, which is two miles outside the village. In 2008 a water pipe system was built for them, so now they have a place from which to fetch water. There is no electricity in the village.

The villagers live in traditional African clay houses with grass roofs. They are very poorly dressed; many people have no shoes. Approximately 50 percent of the population is comprised of children. According to international standards, the people in Kinywang'anga live in absolute poverty—that is, under $1.25 a day.

I discussed Matthew 6:25–34 with the villagers. The text was not read from a book with leather covers, but rather performed in narrative style. In Tanzania the oral culture and narrative tradition is still alive and well. By telling the stories from memory I tended to get their first reactions, which may have been different had I simply read to them from the Bible. Some of the villagers were non-Christians, so they were not too closely acquainted with the text beforehand. Even the Christians heard the narrative differently compared to the way they had heard it in local church. I had hoped to have a lively discussion of the poverty stories in the Gospels, and I most certainly did. Often the religious authorities (a pastor, an evangelist, or some other religious leader) were present, but I politely asked them not to take part in the discussions since they are professionals and I wanted to hear the voices of ordinary people. They agreed to my request, but I usually visited their home afterwards so that they did not feel left out. I also asked the people gathered at the meeting place to set aside their understanding of the story if they had already heard it and to listen as if they were hearing it for the first time in their lives. At the meeting there were some 20 people present, from both genders and all ages, and approximately 10 of them took part in the discussion.

In Kinywang'anga people sometimes have no food at all, clothing is meager and they have enjoyed the "pure" water from the pipes for only a couple of years now. In normal years they have enough food, but it is quite simple and not very nutritious. In Kinywang'anga the context for this gospel passage is totally different from that of my own country of Finland as well as most Western countries; instead it is quite close to the conditions of first-century Galilean villages, the original context of Jesus' teaching. It is important to note, however, that the religious and cultural context of the people in Kinywang'anga is not identical with that of the first audience. Key terms in the passage such as "heavenly Father," "Solomon in all his splendor," "Gentiles," "strive first for his kingdom and his righteousness" would have resonated with first-century Jewish listeners differently from the Tanzanian poor, who would be without an important context for understanding the passage.

The meeting took place in an outside area in the shade. During the time of year that we met, the "flowers of the field" were very beautiful and everything was green; the "birds of the air" flew over us and sang (6:26, 28). A lively discussion followed the performance of the text. The discussion was opened by an elderly man who said, "Maybe Jesus spoke these words because he found that the people had very little faith. He wanted to teach them about faith." I suppose that what the man meant by "faith," was *trust in God's care*, but I am not sure. Another man said, "Jesus found people so keen on material things that they forgot the spiritual things and God. They were concerned about food, clothes, and other things, but not God." A woman said that if someone came to say such words to her, she would think that this person is not good. "It would be better if somebody would tell me a better way how I could manage my life in order to get things and not to say 'Do not worry.' " Another said that a person who said such things would be considered "mentally disabled" by the villagers. The Lutheran evangelist interjected, "Some worry is understandable, because we need many things, but one should not worry about things that are beyond one's ability to influence or control, for example, weather. It is, however, good to plan your future." When I asked if they knew anyone who did not worry about tomorrow, they strongly denied knowing such a person. The same elderly man who started the discussion, said, "Jesus knew the people and their problems and needs, so he wanted to give them a change, a new perspective, a new way of thinking." I asked, what would happen if they stopped worrying about daily food and drink and clothing and just trusted in God? Someone said that then life would be very bad. Another said that it is a matter of faith. If the people believed what Jesus said and stopped working they would have thought everything comes automatically, without human involvement, if they just believed. A young woman with a baby said, "The speech of Jesus must have divided the people in two groups: some had faith and thought that 'this is true, why worry,' while the others thought 'this is not possible.' Faith is the main topic of Jesus' speech." One man said that if you trust God, you will have everything you need.

In further discussion over sodas we found a tentative solution for this problematic text. If someone is worried, he or she soon becomes depressed and is not a joy to his or her friends and relatives. So it is better not to worry too much about worldly things that you cannot do anything about, but instead to rejoice with family and friends for all the good we have.

It became clear to me that the *Do Not Worry* passage is difficult to comprehend in a village where people are living in ongoing poverty. The villagers tried to find a spiritual message in the saying, maybe because they found it unreasonable to live a careless life, as Jesus seemed to be advising. They interpreted the saying in the light of the kingdom of God (6:33), which they seemed to have understood as spiritual.

Sakari Häkkinen is the dean of the Lutheran diocese of Kuopio, Finland.

QUESTIONS

1. What practical and philosophical differences, if any, are there between the Beatitudes and the Noble Eightfold Path? Is the idea that "nothing outside ourselves can make us suffer" consistent with the biblical text?
2. Aymer treats the Beatitudes in Matthew and Luke 6 as complementary. What differences might be noted between the two versions, and which one, overall, is more in line with the Accra Confession?
3. How might Batak Christians respond to Sihombing's criticisms? How might they argue that the Beatitudes support their actions and desires?
4. Assess Häkkinen's interview techniques and questions. How would you have approached the opportunity to discuss the Sermon on the Mount with people in Tanzania?

CHAPTER 27

PARABLES OF JESUS (PART I)

Luke 10:25–37; Matthew 13:24–30; Matthew 25:1–13

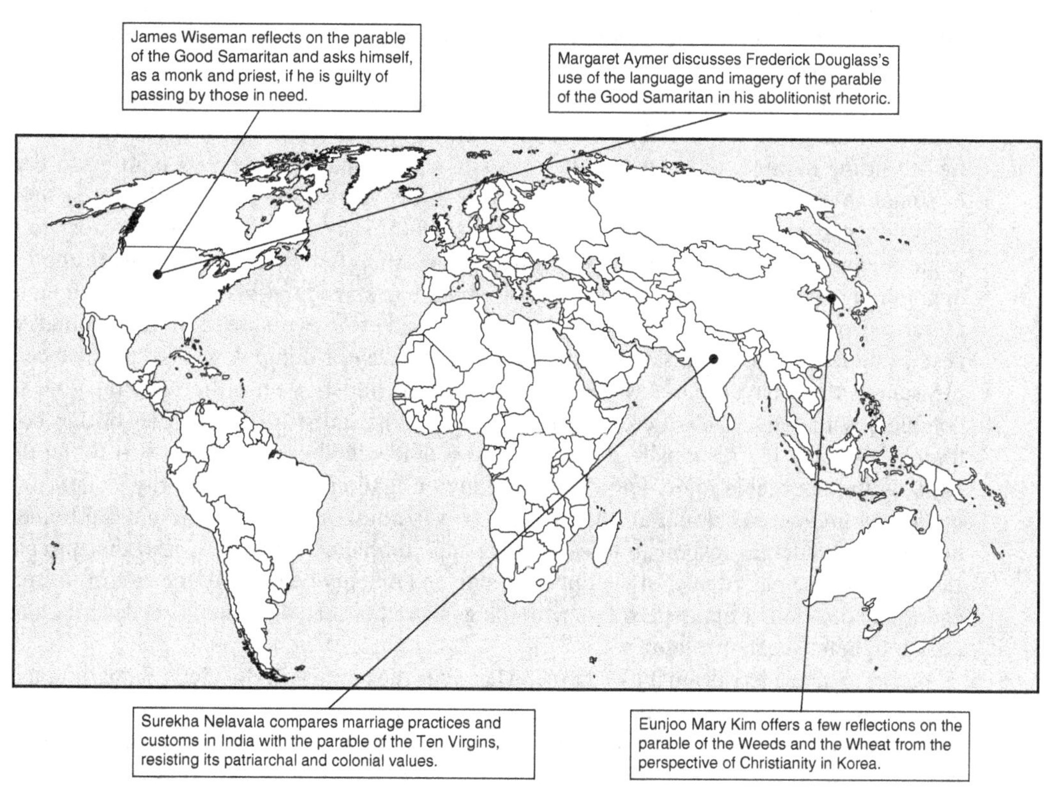

James Wiseman reflects on the parable of the Good Samaritan and asks himself, as a monk and priest, if he is guilty of passing by those in need.
Margaret Aymer discusses Frederick Douglass's use of the language and imagery of the parable of the Good Samaritan in his abolitionist rhetoric.
Surekha Nelavala compares marriage practices and customs in India with the parable of the Ten Virgins, resisting its patriarchal and colonial values.
Eunjoo Mary Kim offers a few reflections on the parable of the Weeds and the Wheat from the perspective of Christianity in Korea.

READINGS

The Parable of the Good Samaritan and Those in Need

James Wiseman (United States)

As a monk, I have taken a vow of poverty. Although in the technical sense that vow means that I own no possessions, the fact that my monastic community provides everything I really need for my work (including the assurance of three meals a day and a room that is well heated in winter and air-conditioned in summer) means that I am in fact a member of the white middle class in what is generally considered the most powerful country in the world. It is within this context that I reflect daily on passages from the Bible, including some that are definitely challenging and even discomforting.

Being an ordained priest as well as a monk, I am particularly challenged by Jesus' parable of the Good Samaritan, for I have to ask myself to what extent I, like the priest and Levite in the parable, pass by "on the opposite side" instead of actively coming to the aid of someone in need. I will never forget the day a few years ago when a religious sister who had dedicated her life to helping the homeless took me and a few other ministers to visit a site under one of the freeway bridges here in Washington. What we saw were the living quarters of about 20 homeless men, each of whom had staked out his own spot with an array of cardboard boxes. Each man's bed was just a blanket or two spread on the ground, or at best a dilapidated mattress salvaged from some alleyway or dump. Our visit took place on a pleasant summer day, but as I write this, we are in the midst of a headline-making cold spell, complete with snow and a fierce northwest wind. What must life under that bridge be like tonight? What is my responsibility toward the people who are presumably still living there? I can, with impeccable logic, tell myself that my obligations toward all of my students at the university prevent my doing all that that sister was doing to befriend and aid the homeless, but do my academic responsibilities absolve me completely? Might I, like that priest and Levite, really be passing by on the opposite side and thereby be running the risk of ultimately ending up on another opposite side—with the goats rather than the sheep—as described in the Last Judgment scene in Matthew 25?

Or, to take a less dramatic example, what does the parable of the Good Samaritan tell me about how to treat the many people begging for money on the downtown streets of my city, their numbers larger than ever in this time of widespread unemployment? True, I cannot give generously to everyone who asks (and actually have very little pocket money myself), but I will always remember something that another religious sister once wrote—that the worst pain experienced by any beggar is to be totally ignored, to have passersby avert their eyes so as not even to see him or her, to reduce the beggar to the status of a nonentity, a nobody. Is not the parable warning me to avoid walking literally "on the opposite side" of the sidewalk, calling me instead to look the beggar in the face and give, if not a monetary donation, then at least a pleasant word? Here, too, all sorts of "logical escapes" are possible, such as the sensible reminder not to encourage the panhandling that in many areas is illegal anyway, but I dare not forget that Jesus was not particularly interested in enforcing man-made laws when other higher values were at stake.

Jesus was also insistent that his followers avoid too many words, whether when praying or on other occasions, and that they turn instead to doing what is required of them in particular circumstances. In this parable, it is important to notice that Jesus doesn't directly answer the lawyer's question about a certain fact ("Who *is* my neighbor?") but talks about *behavior*, about how to *act* toward people whom we are inclined to avoid. In asking his questions about what is required to inherit eternal life, the lawyer was interested in boundaries, ones defined perhaps by "being in the Abrahamic covenant" or "being recognized by the religious elite as righteous." What he got instead was a story that brought home the effacing of any and all boundaries for love and compassion. Jesus was saying that none of his followers dare circumscribe their concern by placing anyone outside the scope of their concern, regardless of the other's religion, race, or nationality. Note that in the parable there isn't even mention of the nationality of the man who had fallen in with robbers. We might well assume he was a Jew, but for the Good Samaritan race didn't matter. He simply came to the aid of a person in need, no questions asked.

As often in the Gospel accounts of Jesus' interaction with others, he concludes with a question of his own: "Which of these three, in your opinion, was neighbor to the victim of the robbers?" Receiving the only possible reply—that it was the one who treated him with mercy—Jesus concludes with the words, "Go and do likewise." What does this mean for me? Or for you?

James Wiseman is a Benedictine monk at St. Anselm's Abbey in Washington, D.C., and a professor of theology and religious studies at Catholic University of America, United States.

FREDERICK DOUGLASS'S USE OF THE GOOD SAMARITAN IN ABOLITIONIST RHETORIC

Margaret Aymer (United States)

It was 1846 in Paisley, Scotland. Before a gathered audience stood African American abolitionist Frederick Douglass, condemning the Free Church of Scotland for its decision to accept financial assistance from southern U.S. slaveholders.

> Every imaginable excuse for slaveholding was brought forward by these men eminent for their learning—men who claim to be the heaven-appointed instruments for the removal of all sin. I heard these men, standing up there, appealing to the sympathies of those who heard them to remember the slaveholder, and not one rose who spoke of remembering "those in bonds as bound with them." They were called on to look on the difficulties in which the slaveholder was placed. Their manacled bondmen were not thought of for a single moment, but, like the Levite of old, they "passed by on the other side."
>
> (Douglass, "The General Assembly of the Free Church" in *The Frederick Douglass Papers: 1841–46* ed. J. W. Blassingame, vol. 1 of *The Frederick Douglass Papers*; Series 1: Speeches, Debates and Interviews; [New Haven and London: Yale University Press, 1979], 427; quotation marks added to offset biblical quotes, Hebrews 13:3 and Luke 10:32 respectively)

No audience member, raised as they were with the King James Version of the Bible, could have missed Douglass's allusion to the Good Samaritan. The Levite who "passed by on the other side" was too familiar a story. What they might not have seen coming, though, was how Douglass identified the body lying on the side of the Jericho road.

Jesus, of course, does not identify the body. That's not the point of his story to the lawyer in Luke 10:25–37. Instead, Jesus identifies the sworn enemy of the people of Judea, a Samaritan, as the only one of the three who understood what it meant to be neighbor. The scandal of Jesus' story is his command to the lawyer to "go and do likewise," that is to go and be at least as good as a Samaritan.

Douglass, by contrast, is directly interested in identifying the body on the side of the road. For, until his audiences could see the body, they would not be able to distinguish the Samaritan from the much more well-respected holy persons that might pass by. So, like a forensic pathologist, Douglass metaphorically stoops down to examine that unidentified body. Then, standing, he pronounces it to be the slaves of the antebellum South in the United States of America. He makes this pronouncement not as a white abolitionist but as one of those very slaves, a run-a-gate slave using his voice on behalf of the bodies he sees in sharp focus.

Once Douglass identifies the body, he is able to extend the Samaritan metaphor in his series of passionate speeches against U.S. chattel slavery. He draws, for example, a sharp distinction between the religion practiced in the Free Church of Scotland that was accepting money from slaveholders and what he calls "true religion." True religion "sends its votaries to bind up the wounds of those who have fallen among the thieves," as the Samaritan did, while the religion of the Free Church and of all allies of slaveholders "leaves the bruised and the wounded to die" (*The Frederick Douglass Papers* [series 1: Speeches, Debates and Interviews, vol. 2: 1847–54, ed. J. W. Blassingame, New Haven and London: Yale University Press, 1982], 99–100).

Similarly, when his friend and ally, William Lloyd Garrison was being excoriated as an enemy of the United States for his abolitionist stance, Douglass was able to argue that Garrison, unlike the slaveholders, had put his body, voice, even life on the line on behalf of the body on the side of the road—the 3 million enslaved women, children, and men of the deep South. Garrison, thus, was not the enemy but the Samaritan, an example to be followed.

Perhaps most scandalously to those in the United States is that Douglass's identification of the body forces the churches of the antebellum South into the uncomfortable position of being the bandits who created the body on the side of the road in the first place. He is fairly explicit in this charge, arguing at one point that "slavery with gags and bonds lived and had its being under the American church—and . . . the church . . . served to weave its fetters and bind the chains by quotations from scripture" (*The Frederick Douglass Papers,* vol. 1, 369).

In so doing, Douglass goes beyond taking Jesus literally to taking him seriously. But he takes him seriously, not as a lawyer with privilege who has the authority to determine what it is and is not legal to do on behalf of one's neighbor. Instead he takes him seriously as one who sees the implications of Jesus' words not only for the lawyer but for him and the millions like him who find themselves lying on the side of the road.

Margaret Aymer is Associate Professor of New Testament at the Interdenominational Theological Center in Atlanta, Georgia, United States.

The Parable of the Weeds and Wheat from the Perspective of Korean Christianity

Eunjoo Mary Kim (Korea)

Here I offer a few reflections on the parable of the "Weeds and the Wheat" found in Matthew 13:24–30 from the perspective of Christianity in Korea. Christianity was introduced to Korea in two different historical epochs. The first time was during the high peak of the Yi dynasty in the eighteenth century. Some government officials and liberal Confucian scholars who visited China as delegates or envoys of the dynasty met Roman Catholic missionaries and obtained Christian literature written in Chinese. They were fascinated by its new teaching about God, humanity, and the way of life, and wanted to spread the good news of Christianity to their families, villagers, and the larger community. However, it was not good news to the authorities of the dynasty, governed by Neo-Confucian principles and systems based on the hierarchical order of classism and sexism and the polytheistic religious practices and cultural tradition. For them, Christian believers who followed the religious and moral teaching of Christianity that emphasized monotheism and egalitarian love were "weeds," dangerous and harmful to their grain field. In order to protect the "wheat" growing in their traditional cultural and religious soil, they hastily made every effort to pull the weeds out of the field before they quickly spread all over their grain field. As a result, Christianity was banned in Korea, and tens of thousands of early Christians in Korea were persecuted and martyred.

The second tide of Christianity in Korea was led by Protestant Christians during the late nineteenth century. Since the 1870s, the Yi dynasty had been on a downward path and Korean society was in chaos politically, socially, economically, and religiously. Neo-Confucianism, which had provided the moral and religious foundation for the society, was no longer the stronghold of the people's morality and the social system and order. The corruption of the government and religious leaders; the military threats of Japan, China, Russia, and other foreign countries; and severe drought, plagues, and dire poverty had caused local and national revolts. The suffering masses felt discontent and despair with the existing social order and the conventional cultural and religious teaching. They yearned for a new religious and moral guidance that was able to restore their social stability and personal and communal well-being.

The government's persecution of Catholicism continued until the early 1870s. In the following decade, however, the government officially opened a door to Christianity and welcomed Christian missionaries by making a Treaty of Amity with the United States in 1882 and with other Western countries shortly thereafter. Immediately, Protestant Christian missionaries from the United States and other Western countries entered Korea, and many Koreans and their political leaders welcomed it as a new leading spirit, alternative to the traditional Confucian and Buddhist formalities and the rigid literati mentality.

Indeed, Christianity has contributed to transforming the Korean soil. The "good seed" grew and multiplied its fruits in the Korean soil, overcoming turbulent hardships in particular seasons with the Koreans: During the period of the Japanese annexation of Korea (1910–1945), many Christian believers fought against Japanese imperialism and militarism. They were involved in the independence movement, even at the cost of their lives, and their churches played a major role in providing the oppressed colonized people with a spiritual home, in spite of horrible persecution executed by the Japanese authority. During and after the Korean War (1950–1953), churches in South Korea made unparalleled relief efforts and encouraged the people with a hopeful message for their future. During the 1960s and the 1970s, when rapid social changes, spurred by the processes of industrialization, modernization, and urbanization, generated culture shock and feelings of anxiety and displacement among the people, the Christian church embraced those weary people. Moreover, Korean theologians and ministers who were influenced by Korean liberation theology (*Minjung* Theology) actively participated in both the labor movement and the democratic movement and struggled with and for the oppressed against military dictatorship during the 1980s.

The public's favorable view of Christianity based on its positive social and political impacts and the zeal of Christian leaders for evangelism have contributed to a conspicuous increase in the membership of the church. Today, about one-third of South Korea's 45 million people identify themselves as Christian. They dominate Korean ethos and culture as the majority group in the multireligious and pluralistic Korean society.

Obviously, the Korean field is full of Christians. But, it is questionable whether it is a field of wheat or of weeds. It must not be overlooked that many Christians and their churches are consciously or unconsciously creating and exacerbating numerous complex problems and issues within and beyond the church, such as denominationalism, sexism, consumerism, and Christian triumphalism. In many cases, for example, the message that is proclaimed behind the pulpit is no longer the gospel of Jesus Christ, who suffered and died on the cross, but the gospel of prosperity and positive thinking, co-opted by popular human wishes and worldly desires. Many Korean missionaries dispatched to Asia, Africa, South America, and other continents are agents of Christian triumphalism who think their mission is to conquer the world with their denominational doctrines and dogmas, which is *the* gospel for them. The more critically we reflect on contemporary churches in Korea through the biblical lens, the more we find in them characteristics of weeds that are unfruitful rather than those of wheat that bear grain.

In the parable in Matthew 13:24–30, the servants urgently report to the householder about weeds growing in his field and request of him permission to get rid of the weeds. However, the householder does not permit his servants to pull out the weeds from the wheat immediately, for he is worried that his servants might uproot wheat plants along with the weeds by mistake in this early season. Instead, he orders them to allow both the weeds and the wheat to grow together in his grain field until harvest time. When the time comes, everything will be clear by its fruit: Without grains, it is obviously a weed that must be thrown to be burned, and with ripened grains, it is obviously wheat that must be stored in the householder's barn.

Ironically, Matthew describes this mixed, ambiguous field of the householder as the kingdom of heaven here and now, in which God is present and rules with patience and compassion. In this kingdom, it is uncertain who is to be burned and who is to be stored in the barn, for God's measuring stick in the harvest time will be different from ours (cf. Isaiah 55:8–9). As H. Richard Niebuhr has suggested, the self we loved might not be the self God loves, the neighbors we did not prize might be God's treasures, the truth we ignored might be the truth God maintains, the justice which we sought because it was our own might not be the justice that God's love desires, and the righteousness God demands and gives might not be our righteousness but be greater and different.

What, then, if non-Christians, whom Christians believe to be weeds unless they are converted to Christianity, turn out to be wheat in God's coming reign? What if heretics and minority Christian groups, whom mainstream Christians label as weeds, turn out to be wheat in God's sight? Or, what if those who confidently believe that they are good Christians turn out to be weeds without fruit in the harvest time?

It is grace that the kingdom of heaven is different from our kingdom on earth, in which we hastily sort out the bad from the good and throw them to be burned. It is gracious that God does not weed us now but patiently waits until we bear the good fruit of the Spirit—love, joy, peace, patience, kindness, generosity, faithfulness, gentleness, and self-control (Galatians 5:22–23)—a hundredfold, 60, or 30 times.

Eunjoo Mary Kim is Associate Professor of Homiletics at the Iliff School of Theology, Denver, Colorado, United States.

A Comparison of Marriage Practices in India with the Parable of the Ten Virgins

Surekha Nelavala (India)

Jesus explains his teachings using parables, which is an effective communication method that uses known subjects in order to introduce new or unknown concepts. For instance, to explain the nature of the kingdom of God, an unknown concept, Jesus uses many parables with which the people can easily associate and resonate. Therefore, the parables rely on the day-to-day life of his social context in order to make the unknown contexts far more comprehensible. Therefore, on the one hand, Jesus' parables help to simplify the complex subjects of his teachings, and on the other hand, they are the resources for understanding the social context of the ancient Palestinian society, its values, culture, and norms.

The parable of the bridegroom and the ten virgins in Matthew 25:1–13 is one such parable used to explain the nature of the kingdom of God, while also revealing social customs and norms. In this parable, Jesus uses a wedding setting as a metaphor, in which the roles of the bridegroom and the virgins, along with their privileges and stereotypes, bear many similarities to the wedding and marriage context of India. Thus my questions and interpretation of the text come mainly from my own social location and a perspective informed by Indian culture, values, challenges, and observations. My interpretive approach to the parable is from an Indian feminist perspective. First, as an Indian contextual reader, I try to emphasize the social context presented in the parable, while comparing and contrasting it with the specific Indian context. Second, as a feminist reader, I use the feminist lens to understand and interpret the parable while being mindful of the significant impact that the text has on the common people.

In my encounter with the text, this parable leaves me uncomfortable regarding the way in which it could read in an Indian context where the bridegroom, or potential bridegroom, is always in demand, and assumes a higher status. It also makes me uneasy because of the dichotomization of the ten virgins, some as wise and some as foolish, judging by whether or not they found favor with the bridegroom. This parable demonstrates the patriarchal nature of the context that it is portraying. The parable characterizes one bridegroom against the ten virgins, although most scholars conveniently interpret them as bridesmaids instead of potential brides. In the parable there are 10 women fighting for one man, and whoever is able to find favor with the bridegroom will, in fact, make it to heaven.

A similar story plays out in many ways in the lives of Indian women. As an Indian woman, when I read this text, I am deeply affected by the fact that male privilege and female discrimination are widely prevalent as accepted norms in current Indian society. In the arranged marriages, which are predominant in Indian society, the men are always in demand, and the women are regarded as fortunate if they are somehow favored by men for marriage. As the wise virgins in the parable are equipped with extra oil, the wise virgins of India and their families must be equipped with dowry and wedding-related expenses. These kinds of stereotypes are not unique to the marriage setting in patriarchal cultures but rather apply to almost all spheres of life. For instance, a woman is considered a good cook only if she can satisfy her husband's taste, which is not necessarily a reflection of her culinary skills, although it is considered a vital qualification for a wife. Similarly, a virgin is considered worthwhile only when she is liked by the groom's family and the groom. In an arranged marriage system, the potential bridegroom and his family visit the bride's family to assess and judge the bride's beauty and familial qualifications, such as her cooking, cleaning, and working skills. A young girl is presented to the potential groom's family at her best, sometimes with added exaggeration. In addition, the real wisdom and preparedness of the virgin is tested by discussing the dowry with her parents. Whoever can afford the anticipated dowry is highly regarded as the wise family of virgins, and others are often criticized as foolish if they cannot marry off their daughters when qualified grooms approach them.

In the parable, the description of the wise virgins is that they are the flawless ones, the ideal virgins who are always eager, ready, and at the service of the man. In this parable, the virgins wait so long that they eventually fall asleep. The wise virgins are extra careful and equipped enough to meet the bridegroom at his arrival, but the foolish virgins do not have what they need. The wise virgins do not take any chances when it is a matter of impressing their potential bridegroom, whereas the foolish virgins take it easy. This parable reinforces the status quo of male privilege and female discrimination. The delay of the bridegroom communicates his privilege while the virgins eagerly wait for him. The same privilege is not a possibility for the virgins. The five virgins who do not meet the bridegroom at his arrival are forever denied their opportunity to be potential brides to the qualified groom.

What made the so-called foolish virgins unprepared and unequipped? Do they not understand that they do not share the same privilege of delayed arrival as the bridegroom? However, after the bridegroom arrives, he does not wait for the other five virgins who went out to fetch some more oil. The man of the parable enjoys his full privileges to take his time and delay his arrival, while the women wait for him at the expense of their sleep and lamp oil. Once he is ready, he responds harshly when the five virgins return, saying that he does not know them. The bridegroom metes out the severe punishment of abandonment for the late women, and he provides no explanation for his delay. This parable offers a clear example of male privilege and female marginalization.

Jesus' words offer no challenge to the status quo, but rather use it as an example to explain the kingdom of God. As an Indian reader, for whom this parable is not just a metaphor but a real experience, my interpretive stance is not only to learn about and understand the kingdom of God but also to feel genuine fear about the status of males and females in the kingdom of God. If God perpetuates equality, justice, and liberation, how should this parable be interpreted as it simply reinforces male privilege? As an Indian feminist reader, I challenge both the metaphor and also the concept of the kingdom of God that contains patriarchal and colonial values of power and privilege rather than justice and liberation that are the true values of God's household.

Surekha Nelavala is a Mission Developer at Global Peace Lutheran Church in Frederick, Maryland, United States.

QUESTIONS

1. How does Wiseman's context, which he explains in the first paragraph, shape his reading of the biblical text? How do you think he himself would ultimately answer his final question? How would you answer it?
2. What particular insights does Douglass's handling of the biblical text offer? Should Jesus have focused more on the identity and body of the victim?
3. What would Kim say about the status—wheat or weeds—of "liberal Confucian scholars" or those who banned Christianity in Korea? Is there any basis for exclusion or condemnation of any group or individual?
4. How does Indian society, as described by Nelavala, compare to your particular cultural context in terms of gender discrimination in marriage practices. How could your context be brought to bear on the parable?

CHAPTER 28

PARABLES OF JESUS (PART II)

Matthew 20:1–16; Matthew 25:14–30; Matthew 13:33
and Luke 13:20–21; Matthew 13:1–23

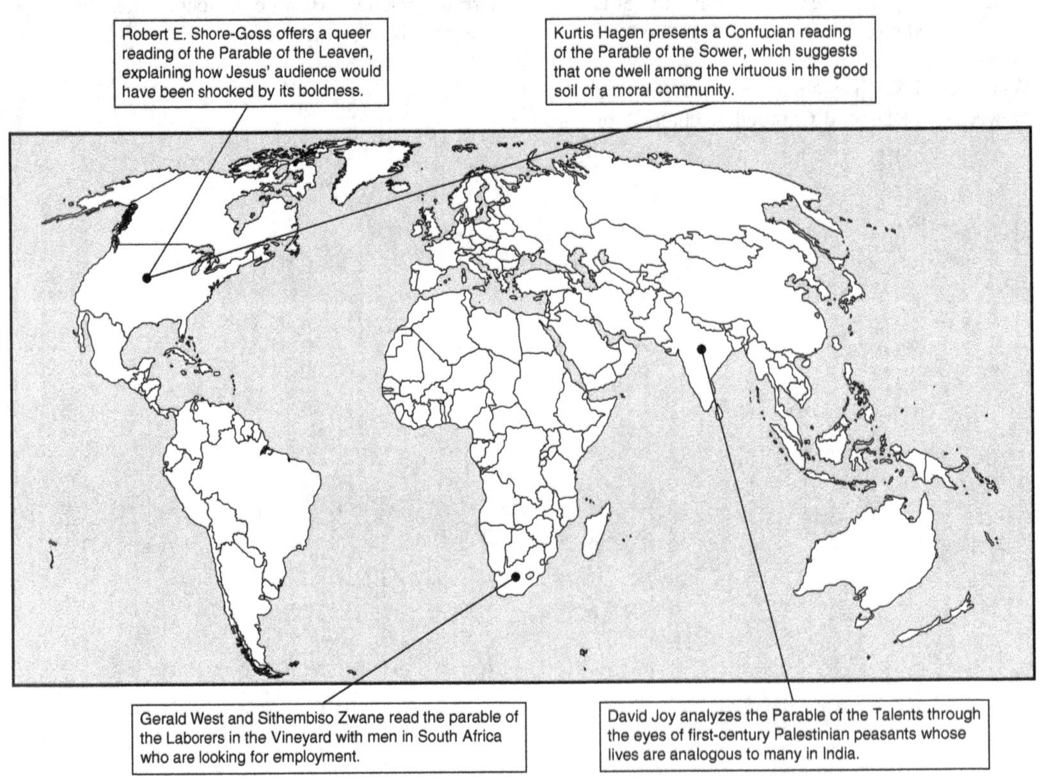

Robert E. Shore-Goss offers a queer reading of the Parable of the Leaven, explaining how Jesus' audience would have been shocked by its boldness.
Kurtis Hagen presents a Confucian reading of the Parable of the Sower, which suggests that one dwell among the virtuous in the good soil of a moral community.
Gerald West and Sithembiso Zwane read the parable of the Laborers in the Vineyard with men in South Africa who are looking for employment.
David Joy analyzes the Parable of the Talents through the eyes of first-century Palestinian peasants whose lives are analogous to many in India.

READINGS

THE PARABLE OF THE LABORERS IN THE VINEYARD AND THE UNEMPLOYED IN SOUTH AFRICA

Gerald West and Sithembiso Zwane (South Africa)

Every day groups of men, some South Africans and others from the southern African region, sit on the side of the street in downtown Pietermaritzburg, South Africa, waiting for work—a scene repeated in nearly every city in our country. Some have the tools of their trade with them, such as shovels and trowels, while others hold only their meager lunch in their hands. They are our day-laborers. Most of them have some trade or work experience, but others have few formal skills, offering nothing more than their willingness to work. All of them are the flotsam of capitalism's relentless pursuit of profit, whether in the guise of the racial capitalism of apartheid or the more recent globalized form of neoliberal capitalism. They are among the products of systemic forms of economic exploitation going back more than three centuries.

The Theology and Economic Justice Programme of the Ujamaa Centre for Community Development and Research, in the School of Religion and Theology at the University of KwaZulu-Natal, has noticed these men and has begun to work with them. On a regular basis we have "hired" them for the day to spend time with us reflecting on the role that biblical and theological resources play in their lives. To demonstrate our commitment to socioeconomic justice, we compensate them for a full day's work and we also use our networks among a range of faith-based and nongovernmental organizations to assist these men in finding more permanent employment. At first apprehensive about the ideo-theological "work" we offer them, the men now eagerly embrace this opportunity to "do theology." They are contributing to a project called Contextual Bible Study, in which the resources of socially engaged biblical scholars and these casual workers are shared in order to construct a worker's theology. Among the texts we have read together is Matthew 20:1–16. We have approached this parable in a number of different ways, offering both "capitalist" and "socialist" readings of the text.

Initially this text was used to explore a socialist vision of society. In this collaborative reading, we would focus on the recognition the parable gives to the reality of day-laborers and the equitable payment to each according to their need. However, our longing for such a socialist vision was not enough to silence the features of the biblical text that stood over against such a reading. For while we overtly take up the Bible as a resource for economic survival, liberation, and life, and while we discern a prophetic socioeconomic trajectory weaving its way through the literary and sociohistorical contexts of the Bible, we are committed to respect the detail of particular biblical texts, recognizing that just as socioeconomic contestation is central to our own South African context it is also central to the sociohistorical sites of production of biblical texts.

In this case we were regularly troubled in our readings by the class identity of the "landowner," and his autocratic manner in hiring, paying, and dealing with the complaints of the day-laborers. We were also worried about his payment of the minimum wage and his delegation of the task of payment to "his manager." Most of all we were disturbed by the landowner's capitalist sounding rhetorical question, "Am I not allowed to do what I choose with what belongs to me?" The detail of this text aroused our hermeneutic of suspicion, and we wondered if this parable *should* be read in a liberative manner. Clearly it *could* be read as supporting aspects of socialism, but only if we ignored some of its detail. Was there a way, responsible to the detail of the text, to read this text within our socialist ideo-theological orientation?

Our determination to read this text economically was frustrated by the refusal of much of biblical scholarship to even engage with this dimension of the text. We were drawn therefore to William Herzog's reading of this parable, identifying with his notion of Jesus as "pedagogue of the oppressed," and his location of this parable within the realities of the conflictual interface between "agrarian societies and traditional aristocratic empires" (*Parables as Subversive Speech: Jesus as Pedagogue of the Oppressed* [Louisville: Westminster/John Knox, 1994], 85). Read from such a perspective the contours of the parable are clearer. The owner of the vineyard is likely an absentee landowner, a member of the economic urban elite, employing a manager to handle the daily affairs of the vineyard, and engaged in a form of agriculture that produced a crop that can be converted into a luxury item (wine), monetized, and exported. Unable to calculate how many laborers he will need, such is the extent of his landholdings, the owner must make a number of trips to the agora to hire workers. Regular assessment of the number of workers he needs also enables the landowner to keep his workers to the minimum necessary to harvest the crop within the designated time period. Furthermore, by hiring small numbers of laborers during the day the landowner exercises his unilateral power, negotiating only with those hired at the beginning of the day for the minimum daily wage, but leaving the wage for those hired later in the day indeterminate (vv. 4, 7). For in a context of chronic systemic unemployment and underemployment, the day-laborer is in no position to insist on a just wage. Far from being generous, then, the householder is taking advantage of an unemployed workforce to meet his harvesting needs by offering them work without a wage agreement. By telling a story in which the landowner is actively involved in the economic process, Jesus foregrounds the socioeconomic contestation of his time, making the usually invisible absentee landlord visible and so setting up a direct encounter between the elites and the expendables.

The arbitrary power of the landowner is evident in the payment process. His power is signaled in the delegation of his manager to make the payments, but is fully manifest in his deliberate flaunting of protocol by refusing to pay the first-hired laborers first; by making the first-hired wait until last he flaunts his power and shames them. The dignity of those who have worked all day demands a response, and so they risk a protest (vv. 11–12), speaking back to power, invoking the principle of equal pay for equal work. Singling out their spokesperson (v. 13), the landowner condescendingly reminds the resisting workers of their contractual agreement, knowing full well that the day-laborers were never in a position to negotiate anything other than the minimum wage, and then goes on to dismiss their complaints, reiterating his right to do what he pleases with his power (v. 14), and concluding by blasphemously asserting that the land which has systemically been coerced from the very peasant farmers who are now day-laborers belongs to him (v. 15). At this point the systemic violence beneath this text becomes palpable.

The Contextual Bible Study we have constructed to explore both the "socialist" and "capitalist" interpretive possibilities of this text generates considerable excitement and discussion. Most participants are unfamiliar with multiple ways of reading the same text, and most are unfamiliar with an overtly socioeconomic reading of the Bible. The discussions within each group are usually animated and intense, for we as participants have much at stake in our reading, particularly those who yearn for decent work but whom our economic system consumes as casual workers.

Gerald West and Sithembiso Zwane are coordinators at the Ujamaa Centre in the School of Religion and Theology at University of KwaZulu-Natal, Pietermaritzburg, South Africa.

Reading the Parable of the Talents with Palestinian Peasants and Those in India

David Joy (India)

The parable of the Talents in Matthew 25:14–30 has spawned volumes of interpretations from various viewpoints. Unfortunately, the parable has been misused to subjugate the weak, the vulnerable, the less privileged, and the voiceless. For example, in India migrants and the lower caste are inevitably branded as people with less talent and worth; and the parable has been interpreted as support for their continued oppression. Likewise, the parable has been used to promote capitalism which typically leads to the suffering of those who cannot produce capital, "for whoever does not have, even what he has will be taken from him" (25:29). Thus, there is a significant need to launch a fresh reading. This article is an attempt to read the parable through the eyes of the peasants of first-century Palestine, whose lives in many ways are analogous to a large portion of the population of India. I believe that such a reading will bring out the liberative meaning of the parable and the Gospel truth which it contains.

Many parables of Jesus reflect the fact that Palestine was occupied by Roman forces during that time. Thus, the sayings, parables, and miracles of Jesus need to be studied against the context of Roman colonialism. Such an approach is particularly relevant in today's world where millions of people become migrants and homeless due to liberal economic (capitalist) policies. Our so-called subaltern-cultural reading is concerned with the location, condition, and mind-set of the ordinary people in Jesus' audience and their everyday world. In this particular parable, it pays special attention to the third servant. Why is he afraid of the master? Why is he treated so harshly? What reaction is the audience supposed to have to the servant and the master?

To answer these questions we must pay attention to the social, cultural, and economic context of first-century Palestine, as a number of modern commentators have done quite well. This parable, for instance, assumes a context in which a household had compliant slaves who would make every effort to benefit materially and socially their master in order to exemplify faithful discipleship (i.e., the first two servants). The text offers no critique of this socioeconomic structure or of the particular activities of the obedient slaves, which may very well involve accumulating wealth at the expense of others (v. 24). The audience, then, is supposed to supply the critique. Namely, they are to recognize that the "specific socioeconomic commitment of the master and the activities of the first two slaves are not to be imitated" (Warren Carter, *Matthew and the Margins: A Sociopolitical Religious Reading*, [Bangalore: TPI, 2007], 488).

This reading is supported by several factors in the text. First, the third servant claims that the master has acquired his wealth through dishonest means ("harvesting where you did not sow and gathering where you did not plant," v. 24). Remarkably, the master himself affirms the truth of this (v. 26). Surely, the audience is not meant to approve of this unethical behavior. Second, the master's response to the servant seems obviously cruel and unfair, not to mention exaggerated and absurd. The "worthless" servant has his one talent confiscated and given to the servant with 10 before being expelled from the house—which again is hardly a response to be admired. In sum, though this parable might smack of capitalism, it is more clearly a critique of it, which Jesus presumes the audience will actively supply.

The parable, then, is one which presents the vulnerability of the oppressed class in Palestine. More specifically, it calls attention to the world of retainers—people who are part of the system of social dependency for survival—in the household of a powerful elite. The audience's sympathy for the wounded psyche of the fearful and helpless servant can translate into a motivation to work on behalf of the homeless, migrants, and all dispossessed people in India, or any other economic context which exploits a segment of the population. Perhaps it can also inspire the disenfranchised to stand up and demand dignity. In the name of social and political power too many people have been denied the basic necessities of life for too long. In this parable, Jesus challenges such political and economic systems by affirming that everyone ought to have a rightful place in God's just world.

David Joy is a Presbyter of the Church of South India, South Kerala Diocese, and a Professor of New Testament at the United Theological College, Bangalore, India; he has authored a number of books.

A Queer Reading of the Parable of the Leaven

Robert E. Shore-Goss (United States)

Jesus' parable of the leaven appears in Matthew 13:33 and Luke 13:20–21. The text stresses the action of the woman who has concealed the leaven in three measures of flour until the flour is entirely leavened. Typically, clergy and churches have understood the point of the parable as proclaiming that a small amount of leaven will pervade a large amount of flour, nearly 50 pounds. It is interpreted in the same ecclesial interpretation of the parable of the mustard seed: Small beginnings of God's reign will produce large consequences. The action of the woman hiding the leaven in the dough is preached as a positive action.

Generally, queer Christians do not read the scripture from the lens of heterosexuality. We read the scriptures as gay, lesbian, bisexual, transgendered, or intersexual folks with our own life contexts and our own particular histories within a given community. Queering the text is a reading strategy of the queer community to read and appropriate the texts for themselves. In other words, it is a reading strategy that disrupts the traditional heterosexist interpretations of the scripture. We read the scriptures as outsiders of many churches, for we have been marginalized by many Christians because of our sexual-orientation differences and gender variances. Our reading of this parable of the leaven is comprehended from the social context of queer folks as outsiders. We understand ourselves as leaven within many Christian churches.

As outsiders, we recognize the subordinate status of the woman who conceals the leaven in the dough. Jesus understands that women will have a role in the implementation of the reign of God. First, that is problematic for many first-century C.E. Jewish holiness groups who find women more susceptible to pollution and impurity than men. Women in the Jewish tradition of the day, as in other Mediterranean cultures, were associated with the unclean, the religiously impure, through her monthly menstrual cycle. Men were more structurally aligned with religious purity and holiness. Could the kingdom come about or result through women and other devalued peoples who are marginal, often unseen, and expendable?

Second, the word "hidden" is perhaps better rendered "concealed" and has a negative sense in the metaphorical language of the parable. The obvious question that many clergy fail to ask about this parable is this: What if the woman was caught for concealing the leaven in the huge amount of dough? Would she be punished for her subversive action? Why is the fact that she stealthily placed the leaven in the dough stressed in the parable? The baker will be surprised to see the dough rise. Was this bread of leaven used for the Passover feast?

Many closeted LGBT Christians have acted stealthily, concealing their true lives from family, friends, church, and society. I concealed my life as a gay Jesuit priest for several years. The Catholic hierarchy labeled homosexuals as "intrinsically evil, objectively disordered." Homosexuals were impure and polluted in their erotic desires and lives, just as women were in first-century Judaism.

While closeted, I was able to subvert institutional pastoral practice and to release gay and lesbian Catholics burdened from guilt in their struggles to be good Catholic Christians and to be themselves. For example, I remember a lesbian Catholic who lived with a female lover for over 20 years being denied absolution in confession unless she left her lover—all this as she was undergoing surgery with a great deal of risk. I was able to do even more as an out gay priest after I was released from the Jesuits because I was gay and in love. There are many stories of LGBT folks who hid the leaven in different churches and social organizations to make them more humane and compassionate to the lives of queer folks.

Another significant metaphor is the leaven. Leaven in the ancient Mediterranean world was understood as "unclean, impure, or corrupt." In Hebrew Scriptures, there is an identification of leavened bread with the ordinary days of the year, and unleavened bread with the high holy days. Leaven becomes a metaphor for corruption, the impure, and the ordinary. One creates leaven by taking a piece of bread and storing it in a damp, dark place until mold forms as the bread rots and decays. Thus, leaven became a natural symbol for putrefaction, impurity, decay, and corruption, and by extension, leaven became associated with moral impurity and corruptions (Hosea 7:4). Likewise, in the New Testament leaven is equated with corrupt teaching (Mark 8:15) or associated with sexual immorality (1 Corinthians 5:8).

So the three elements "woman," "conceals," and "leaven" form a trinity of paradoxical images in the parable of the leaven that few religious figures would employ to speak about the reign of God. God's reign, Jesus affirms, is like moral corruption. But it is contextually different from the leaven or teachings of the Pharisees and Herod. The three images denote an agency that expands and transforms the three measure of dough into leavened bread. Jesus' audience would have been shocked or silenced by the boldness of the parable. Jesus in his teachings on compassion and his table fellowship with suspect or stigmatized men and women transgressed Jewish holiness/purity codes. In fact, the assembly, who delivers Jesus before Pilate, levels the following charge: "We found this man perverting the nation..." (Luke 23:2). This sums up Jesus' ministry of God's reign that perverted various notions of purity and pollution.

The language of purity/pollution has been reinscribed today in the strong moral rhetoric of contemporary religious conservatives and fundamentalists. Same-sex sexuality is characterized as disgusting, an abomination, sinful, perverted, intrinsically evil, and a threat to family and Western society. Employing rhetorical purity strategies of saving and protecting our children from homosexual marriage, they depict same-sex marriage as a contagion eroding "American traditional family values." Indeed, "queer" and "leaven" are functionally synonymous in many contemporary Christian purity maps. Queer folks blur the boundaries of contemporary Christian maps of sexual purity with the infusion of arguments for same-sex marriage or marriage equality, the creation of LGBT families of choice, and the right to gender transition. Like the woman in Jesus' parable, queer Christians insert their leaven of marriage equality and the right to family into the dough of Christian churches.

Imagine when the baker mixes up the 50 pounds of dough with the leaven mold and the dough rises. His reaction might well be similar to the Christian right's reaction upon discovering the spread of marriage rights of same-sex couples in several U.S. states and among several Christian denominations.

Queer readers would describe this insertion of leaven into the three measure of dough a "que-eruption" of heterosexist thought. For Jesus says the leaven—those queer folks and all morally throwaway people—will be instrumental to bring in the reign of God. There will be a shock how the three measures of dough will surprisingly arise, and it is already too late, for God's reign will already be expanded through queer leaven. A queer reading of Jesus' parable of the leaven recaptures its original shock value and brings new leaven into contemporary Christian purity codes.

Robert E. Shore-Goss (Ph.D., Comparative Religion and Theology, Harvard University) is the gay Pastor of the MCC Church in the Valley; he is author of Jesus ACTED UP: A Gay and Lesbian Manifesto *and* Queering Christ: Beyond Jesus ACTED UP.

A Confucian Reading of the Parable of the Sower

Kurtis Hagen (United States)

Here I will offer a Confucian interpretation of the parable of the Sower found in Matthew 13:1–23. Let me begin by discussing Mencius, the second great Confucian thinker of China's classical period, who told a parable reminiscent of the one in Matthew 13. According to Mencius' parable, barley seeds grow similarly when they are sown during the same season, in similar conditions, and are similarly cultivated. However, he points out, "There will be differences, due to differences in the quality of the soil and the distribution of rainfall, as well as in human efforts" (*Mencius* 6A7). That is, the seeds are basically similar, but outcomes may still vary if the conditions vary. We should also consider the compatible metaphor for which Mencius is most famous: People are born with "sprouts" of benevolence, appropriateness, ritual propriety, and wisdom (*Mencius* 2A6, 6A6). So, to "bear fruit," from this perspective, would involve fully developing these "spouts," and ultimately contributing to the increased harmony of the world: "If one were able to fully develop them, that would suffice to nurture and protect all within the four seas" (*Mencius* 2A6). On the other hand, if someone does not become virtuous and caring, it is not because he or she was a "bad seed," Mencius suggests, but because the development of his or her sprouts was thwarted by environmental conditions (*Mencius* 6A8).

In the parable of the Sower, placement is critical: where each seed falls determines its outcome. And yet, could *we* each be somehow responsible for whether or not we are "sown on good soil" and "bear fruit"? From a Confucian perspective, at least, our placement is neither merely a matter of chance nor of predetermined fate. For our "fate," as it is understood in Confucianism, is influenced by our own choices. As Mencius put it, "A person who understands 'fate' (*ming*) does not stand beneath a wall that is about to collapse" (*Mencius* 7A2). Indeed, our responsibility for our own placement is a theme repeatedly emphasized in the Confucian tradition. Confucius, for example, said, "It is the presence of benevolence (*ren*) that make a neighborhood admirable. If one chooses not to dwell among benevolent people, whereby can one achieve wisdom?" (*Analects* 4.1) Similarly, Xunzi, the third great Confucian thinker of the classical period, writes thus:

> If one finds good friends to associate with, then one can witness faithful service, living up to one's words, respect, and deference being put into practice. In their moral character they will make daily progress with respect to benevolence and appropriateness,

> without even realizing it, for it is proximity that makes it so. On the other hand, if they dwell with the morally inept, then they will hear of deceit, slander, cheating, and fakery, and will witness debasement, wonton depravity, and corruption in action. Without even noticing, they will be doing terrible violence to their moral character, for it is proximity that makes it so. (*Xunzi*, Book 23, "Innate Dispositions are Detestable")

From the Confucian perspective, then, the parable of the Sower evokes the value of having morally cultivated associates. It is a lesson about carefully choosing one's neighbors, friends, and general social environment. Associating with the virtuous will be fruitful. It will help one develop into a virtuous person oneself—a model of exemplary conduct. One will then be a good neighbor and friend of others, and thus not only bear fruit oneself, but many times over, as Jesus' words "some a hundredfold, some sixty, some thirty" seem to likewise suggest. Similarly, Mencius remarks, "Some are exceeded others by twice, five-fold, or even countless times, because they are unable to make the most of their potential" (*Mencius* 6A6). This multiplying effect is possible because, as Confucius says, "The moral power of the exemplary person is the wind; that of the petty person is the grass. When the wind blows over the grass, it will surely bend" (*Analects* 12.19). The message a Confucian draws from the parable of the Sower, then, is practical and sensible: Hearing of the proper path, but not understanding it, one will fail to fulfill one's potential to grow fully as a person, and to contribute to others. Hearing of the proper path, rejoicing in it, but not dwelling among the virtuous, one will ultimately fail as well. But if one hears of it, and commits to it, in the good soil of a moral community, one will both fulfill oneself, and have a significant transformative influence on others. So, choose your neighbors and associates wisely.

Kurtis Hagen is Assistant Professor in the Department of Philosophy at State University of New York, Plattsburgh, New York, United States.

QUESTIONS

1. Based on your own careful assessment of the biblical text, which is the better reading of the parable—the socialist or capitalist one? How do you suspect that your own economic context and views influence your response?
2. Assess Joy's interpretation of the parable of the Talents. How does it compare to your own reading?
3. How do the citations of other biblical texts help to support Goss's argument?
4. Based on Hagen's Confucian interpretation, how might one revise or improve Jesus' parable?

CHAPTER 29

TEACHINGS OF JESUS (PART I)

Luke 4:18–19; Matthew 15:4–9; Mark 12:38–44; Mark 7:24–30 and Matthew 15:21–28

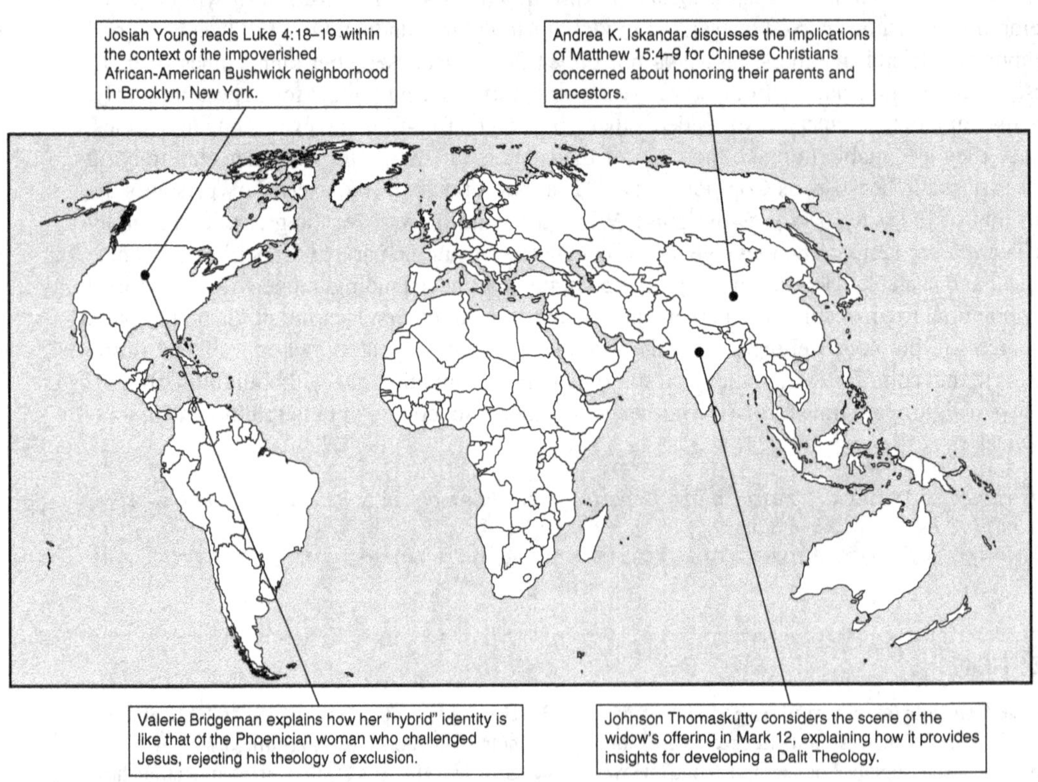

Josiah Young reads Luke 4:18–19 within the context of the impoverished African-American Bushwick neighborhood in Brooklyn, New York.
Andrea K. Iskandar discusses the implications of Matthew 15:4–9 for Chinese Christians concerned about honoring their parents and ancestors.
Valerie Bridgeman explains how her "hybrid" identity is like that of the Phoenician woman who challenged Jesus, rejecting his theology of exclusion.
Johnson Thomaskutty considers the scene of the widow's offering in Mark 12, explaining how it provides insights for developing a Dalit Theology.

READINGS

Luke 4 and the African-American Bushwick Neighborhood in New York
Josiah Young

Honoring Your Parents and Ancestors
Andrea K. Iskandar

The Widow's Offering and Dalit Theology
Johnson Thomaskutty

Personal Reflections on the "Hybrid" Identity of the Phoenician Woman
Valerie Bridgeman

LUKE 4 AND THE AFRICAN-AMERICAN BUSHWICK NEIGHBORHOOD IN NEW YORK

Josiah Young (United States)

I grew up in Bushwick, a neighborhood in Brooklyn, New York. Life there in the 1960s was fatal for many African-Americans, especially underclass males. They died young from substance abuse and homicide. The hostility of the public school system and the aggression of law enforcement agencies toward them did not help. Neither did their dysfunctional households. The escalation of crime coincident with the hard drugs that flooded the "community" seemed to suck them in like a black hole. Unfortunately, places like Bushwick continue to exist today. Black males are among the most uneducated and unemployed caste in America. The black residents of Bushwick and other ghettos still suffer from crime, segregation, poor schools, and early death. Regentrification policies add to their misery by displacing them, forcing them to move to other depressed areas or rendering them homeless.

Perhaps Luke 4:18–19 is pertinent to these sad circumstances, for it depicts Jesus of Nazareth as bringing "good news to the poor." By the time one reads Luke 4, one knows Jesus is the Christ, the "Son of the Most High," from the time his mother conceived him by the Holy Spirit's power. He has triumphed over the "devil" in the aftermath of his baptism and anointing with the Spirit of God. So none is surprised when the Christ, reading from Isaiah in Luke 4:18–19, says "the Spirit of the Lord is upon" him and has anointed him to make the blind see and set the oppressed free. He proclaims "the year of the Lord's favor," which alludes to the Jubilee year, in which the Hebrew elite were to release their Hebrews slaves. None is surprised that he fulfills the prophecy as he heals and feeds the poor. And after the Romans put him to death, the Christ rises bodily from the dead. He is exactly who he said he was—God's anointed.

Many Bushwick folk brave the dangerous streets on Sunday morning just to hear the powerful words of the Gospel; for the words do provide hope for the oppressed. They long for "the year of the Lord's favor" and trust that it is coming, for Christ's sake. Their hope motivates them to challenge their adversity and work for the betterment of humankind. But the Jubilee was the year the Hebrews set their Hebrew slaves free and kept their *non*-Hebrew slaves ("the aliens") "as a possession" for their children (Leviticus 25:44–46). No Jubilee for them. Luke's parables that feature master–slave relationships make me wonder whether he had the Hebrew or the "alien" slaves in mind (cf. 12:41–48). Is there good news for Bushwick's African-Americans, of whom Luke never heard? Are they like the "aliens" without Jubilee rights?

I think that the Gospel of Jesus Christ is broader in scope than the Jubilee that is only for some. It must be broader than that if it is to be taken seriously. Otherwise, the Gospel would lose much of its power to instill hope in the oppressed and in anyone else who hopes that the Kingdom of God is for all creation. I, then, cannot confine the Gospel to slave codes far more ancient than Luke's gospel. The narratives of the risen Christ break through such antiquated practices precisely because they promise that a new creation is coming and has already come in the glorified Christ. May it come for the rest of us soon (and very soon).

Josiah Young is Professor of Systematic Theology at Wesley Theological Seminary, Washington, D.C., United States.

Honoring Your Parents and Ancestors

Andrea K. Iskandar (China)

"I have 2 siblings. Both of them are now Christians and I'm the only one left. If I convert to Christianity as well, who will take care of our parents and ancestors? Who will take care of their altar and keep on praying for them? Please don't ask me to dishonor my parents and ancestors." Such an empathic statement is not uncommon among Chinese people when they're challenged to accept Jesus as their savior. In this context, Matthew 15:4–9 is an important and encouraging passage to consider.

Chinese people are known for the high respect they give to their parents and ancestors. Upon a person's death, an expensive festival is due. The deceased's children and relatives will prepare a set of "living provision" to ensure the deceased's well-being in the afterworld. Depending on the family's wealth, the provision may include a large mansion, a villa and its furniture, fancy cars, a couple of maids and servants—all of which are beautifully made of colorful and expensive papers—as well as a large amount of afterlife bills. These are all meant to sustain (or even increase!) the deceased's lifestyle and well-being in the afterlife compared to the one he or she had while alive. At the end of the burial or cremation ceremony, the deceased's children and relatives will burn all of them as a way of sending these provisions to the afterlife. It is believed these crafts made of fancy papers will be transferred into real stuff in the afterlife, so a burnt Jaguar paper craft would turn to an actual Jaguar as a means of transportation in the next world. The process of respecting the deceased doesn't end there. After the body is buried or cremated, an altar will be kept in the family's houses for generations with the deceased's photograph hung above it so his or her descendants will continue praying and burning some afterlife bills that function much like monthly stipends for the deceased to sustain his or her lifestyle and well-being in the afterlife until reincarnation.

Apart from the expensive paper accessories to be burned, a number of food offerings are also involved. From the mourning days prior to the burial or cremation ceremony, and continuing for many years afterwards, there are highly exquisite and expensive foods involved in the offering. All these actions constitute "honoring the parents and ancestors." Furthermore, this culture knows no such thing as "empty nesters." Grown-up adults in most cases still live with their parents until they get married, and as both parents and children grow old, parents will live near to or in the same house with their children. Grandparents are highly involved in rearing their grandchildren and married children are responsible for taking care of their aged parents. Although retirement houses are available, letting one's parents stay in a retirement facility may be deemed as a sign of disrespect and neglect, a gesture of unwillingness to hold responsibility toward parents.

It thus becomes a serious barrier for many people of Chinese descent to convert to Christianity, fearing that no one else will take care of their parents' and ancestors' well-being in the afterworld. Converting to Christianity is understood as neglecting the care of one's parents and breaking away from one's family. Christian converts are often labeled by their parents as disrespectful children who are not concerned about their parents and ancestors—indeed, this is a very serious accusation which would be akin to having your parents spit on your face for abandoning them and dishonoring the family's name.

Then the following questions arise: "Can I follow Jesus and yet still honor my parents and ancestors? But then again, how can I honor my parents and ancestors while I neglect my service to their altar? Which one should come first: God or my parents? Can I make peace between the first and fifth commandments—how do I worship God alone and still adhere to ancestral traditions?"

A part of the issue that is rarely mentioned, however, is that this respect to parents and ancestors has often been overvalued at the expense of the actual respect shown to parents while they are still alive. It's not strange to find children who devotedly prepare the food offering on the parents' altar, but during their parents' life they would often be involved in arguments and fights, not to mention never taking their parents to a restaurant to enjoy the kind of fancy food now offered to their parents' soul in the afterworld. As for the parents, when they accuse their children of disrespectful behavior, they are often worried more about their children's devotion to them after their death (for it involves their well-being in the afterworld) and less about these children's actual devotion to them in the current life.

Matthew 15:4–9 helps to clarify the stand of the Church in face of such accusation that "you cannot convert to Christianity without being disrespectful to your parents and ancestors." It helps the Chinese families and parents realize that the Bible actually puts a high emphasis on respecting parents. Believers are not expected to give to God at the expense of taking care of their parents. Instead, provision for parents' well-being is to be put ahead of offerings given to God. One cannot honor God without honoring parents.

Jesus speaks in terms of tangible (financial) gifts to parents while they are still alive. Applying Jesus' teaching in today's context, we might conclude that if one has enough money to treat one's parents to a fancy meal, then one ought to do that instead of offering them exquisite food after their death.

Of course, it is evident in this passage that Jesus expects his followers to be respectful of parents not just in terms of material provision but also in terms of relationships. He expects people to have a right heart, a proper attitude (vv. 8–9). Children should not quarrel or speak disrespectful words to their parents. Such honor and respect, we might say, surpasses the demands of the Chinese cultural tradition. In sum, Matthew 15:4–9 provides a comforting and corrective passage to people of Chinese descent who worry about the well-being of their parents as a result of their conversion to Christianity.

Andrea K. Iskandar (M.Div., Cipanas Theological Seminary, Indonesia) is Chairman of the Board of Youth Ministry at Gereja Kristus Ketapang, Jakarta, Indonesia.

The Widow's Offering and Dalit Theology

Johnson Thomaskutty (India)

The Dalits, the majority community of India, are politically powerless, socially untouchable, economically poor, and religiously voiceless. Even today casteism is practiced in several parts of the country, by which the interests of the elite are protected. Dalit women of India are victims of patriarchal and androcentric customs as well as natural and accidental catastrophes. They are still victims of a cruel and oppressive socioreligious order. The customs of the society traumatized the feelings of women, especially Dalit women, in the past and even now it hurts their identity. Many of them are homeless, jobless, starving, sick, oppressed, exploited, persecuted, robbed, raped, hungry, and dying.

Today, the Dalits are eagerly waiting for a paradigm message of transformation and equality to overcome the dehumanizing structures. Mark 12:38–44 is just such a text which provides powerful insights for developing a Dalit Theology. In this passage Jesus targets his criticism primarily toward the scribes due to their neglect and exploitation of the widows, the helpless people. In the story, Jesus is seated upon a bench watching the people bringing their contributions to the Temple treasury. Jesus' position beside the Temple allows him to observe a succession of rich contributors who come and deposit their coins. Many of those donating large sums were wealthy landowners who lived in or near Jerusalem; others were Jewish businessmen and merchants who had journeyed to Jerusalem for the Passover holiday. In contrast to the rich who contributed large sums, the woman tossed in two tiny coins. The coin referred to here (lepton/mite) was the smallest in circulation in Palestine. The widow's two coins were all that she had—it was the sum total of her possessions, which constituted a day's wage, a puny amount.

Jesus was in sharp conflict with the Judaism of his time and the crucifixion was the end result. The theme of Mark's Gospel—the Son of Man came not to be served, but to serve and give his life as a ransom for many—connects well with the story of the needy-poor-widow-woman. Jesus raises the status of the woman before the rich; that is the climax of this rhetorical irony. In Mark's Gospel, one of the primary teachings of Jesus is about discipleship: the one who "acts," rather than the one who speaks. In 8:34 Jesus says, "whoever desires to come after me let that one deny self, and take up his/her own cross, and follow me." Here, it is obvious that discipleship requires complete denial, that is, total surrender to Jesus Christ. The widow in 12:41–44 represents and reaffirms such a model of discipleship, as she rendered her whole livelihood.

The story of the poor widow was told not merely for preaching purpose, but to turn the human acumen toward the moral and spiritual responsibility for a transformed life. Jesus' people-oriented approach for transformation provides us a frame for molding a theology of liberation and emancipation here and now. The first and the foremost task in our mission for and of Dalits is to give them hope that they are "new people" and no more "no people." That is what we comprehend from the story of the needy-poor-widow-woman. In India, poverty is not simply an economic problem. This problem is produced and perpetuated by a system of exploitative structures which makes the rich richer and the poor poorer. It is similar to the scribal-and-widow woman tension within the Markan story.

The widow in Mark 12 is a victim of an imbalanced society in which she was oppressed as poor, subjugated as a woman, and dehumanized as a widow; she was indeed suffering from triple-oppression. A Dalit Christian woman is a woman, a Dalit, and a Christian. There is in India a tradition defining what each of these identities involve which is so strong that a Dalit Christian woman can be described as thrice handicapped or thrice alienated on the basis of her gender, her caste, and her membership in a minority religious community (i.e., Christianity in India). The Women's Movement in India has emphasized that Dalit women are the dust of dust in Indian society—the thrice oppressed, brutalized, and abused not only by the upper castes/classes but by Dalit men too.

While the rabbis walked around in long robes, the widows ended up with tiny coins; while the rabbis were greeted with respect, the widows were considered a public disgrace; while one people group was comfortable with their best seats, the other was without a place to lay their heads; and while one constructed their own splendorous mansions including the Temple, the other had their houses devoured. These caricatures go well with the context of lower caste–higher caste or poor–elite disparity in the Indian scenario. The presentation of the Markan widow over against the giant men can be taken as a symbolic expression of a social reality. The life-situation of the widow in the narratives of Mark provides paradigmatic rhetoric for us to apply to the life-situation of India.

Dalit women who are victims of patriarchal constraints within the Dalit-fold itself are emerging as a volatile force to challenge the status quo. They are the targets of sexual abuse by upper castes in a context of caste/class clashes, of state-sponsored violence in various forms, and of domestic violence in the hands of their own men. The widow of Mark 12 is a living testimony for all the widows, oppressed women, and all the Dalit people in India and elsewhere around the globe. She must not be looked at merely as a historical monument; instead we must place her into the real-life situation of all the oppressed and exploited classes as a directive force for transforming the dehumanizing structures that are prevalent in the contemporary global scenario.

Not only in this story but throughout all the Gospels, Jesus stood firm for the causes of the marginalized and identified completely with them. Just as Jesus sided with the vulnerable as a prophet of social transformation, so too in the present-day situation the church should raise its prophetic voice on behalf of the Dalits, especially the Dalit women of India.

Johnson Thomaskutty is Assistant Professor of New Testament and Greek Language at Union Biblical Seminary, Pune, Maharashtra, India.

Personal Reflections on the "Hybrid" Identity of the Phoenician Woman

Valerie Bridgeman (United States)

I am a hybrid woman, born in the rural countryside of the Deep South of the United States, but with a city sensibility. I love the cacophonic sounds of many languages clashing in the air—sounds I've only heard in a big city. I love foods and music from a variety of cultures perhaps because I am the embodiment of a clash of cultures—England slave-owning great-great-great grandfather, Cherokee great-great grandmother, the Africans somewhere in my ancestry. Thus I am mixed, perhaps like the Phoenician woman from Syria (Mark 7:24–30 and Matthew 15:21–28).

I grew up on my maternal parents' farm. My mother's mother, Callie, was part Cherokee and African, a "root worker" who somehow kept us well with the potions and teas she concocted. Healing was her profession. She knew the gift of the land. Perhaps like Jesus. And she always fascinated me. Callie was a woman of few words, but she had sharp eyes and missed very little. She could tell when someone was sick or emotionally distraught. She was fierce. I admired, loved, and feared her at the same time. I remember her performing the esoteric act of "talking fire" out of our bodies should we get burned. And it worked. Healing is a part of my Native American/African heritage.

I also am an African American mother of sons. My daughters are my goddaughters and my granddaughter. Like most mothers, I worry about my children, especially when they are in any kind of distress—physically, economically, spiritually, or socially. My children learned this phrase when they were growing up: "My mama is like a she-bear with her cubs." I inherited my fierce protectiveness of my children from the maternal lineage from which I derive. I have learned that not every mother feels this fiercely, but I do. I always did. And I was never good at hearing "no" when it came to my children. Once, when my son got into a conflict at school, the principal insisted that he would have to be expelled, even though it was not his fault. There was a "no tolerance" policy that was unbendable, he said. That principal told me I had no choice besides the one he offered. I rejoined, "I always have choices, even if it means worrying you until I get what I want." And I did win that battle of wills. I fought for my son despite what seemed insurmountable "rules." That is the spirit of the Syrophoenician woman who approached Jesus. And the spirit of my mother and grandmother, and I imagine, their mothers before them.

And I am a biblical scholar, a preacher, and an artist. All these contexts are really one context. I am an African American mother-scholar-preacher-artist who engages texts with an eye toward liberation and healing. I always want to know how a text may help us live fully and freely in light of God's love for all humanity. For me, the salvation that Christians speak of is not salvation without the ability to live an abundant life.

Jesus' encounter with this woman strikes me for several reasons. The first issue is that he is in her country. He is the foreigner, not her. He goes away, on "vacation," to get away from his daily work of teaching, healing, leading. He is, it seems, a welcomed and honored guest among people who do not share his heritage or his religious history. They accept him. And they want to hear from him. Difference is a gift, another one of my truly held beliefs. And she, this Syrophoenician woman, is "at home" in her land. She approaches Jesus with deference and respect. If one were not paying close attention, Jesus' answer might make you think she is the one out of place, the foreigner. If one only had his reply, one would believe that she was out of order. But she approaches him like many before her.

She is fierce, and will not be put off by Jesus' seeming disinterest in her plight. She will not be insulted. She will not be demeaned. She has a sick child and will suffer whatever indignities she must for her child's survival. As an African American woman, the ability to allow insults to bypass you in order to get justice is a necessary trait. And make no mistake; the encounter is in fact very insulting. There is no way to soften the derogatory sound of "dog" rolling off even Jesus' tongue. The statement simply is pejorative. But she refuses to be deterred. It is her tenacity that is compelling in the text. It is her insistence that her daughter—and by default, all the Phoenician daughters and sons from Syria—deserve the same care and healing as the "house of Israel." She becomes the testimony that the ministry of Jesus is not limited to "his kind."

As an African American woman who remembers the harsh realities of segregation, I know the insult of feeling "less than" because of someone else's presumed superiority and priority. My mother, Bernice, was a proud woman who taught us that we were just as good as anyone else in the world. She taught us that we deserved to be treated with dignity and respect. And while she taught her children that, the world did not always oblige us her lessons. Sometimes, we suffered indignities and disrespect because we were African American. Sometimes, white people seemed to question whether we should even breathe the same air as they did. So this text is a confrontation of cultures, of prejudices, xenophobia, and of expectations. It prods me every time I read it or preach from it. These cultures are not in isolation. How could they be, if Jesus could walk easily into a "foreign" territory? There wasn't that much physical distance. And, it wasn't as if Jesus didn't know what it was to be an outsider, since he would have known that Joseph fled to Egypt when he was born in order to protect him—a stranger in a strange land. Despite the presumed differences, it seems Jesus and this woman were more alike than they were different.

I have preached about the need for health care for all from this text; I've preached that in a culture wealthy with bread, no one should have to settle with crumbs from a full table. I've preached a mother's love can be fierce and that she rejected Jesus' theology of exclusion. She challenged him. That seems daunting in a Christianity that has been taught not to question anything, certainly not Jesus! She is the heroine in this story; she exemplifies God's grace to all humanity and she demands it from the savior of the world. In this story, healing from demonic oppression is just the final moment of redemption. Redemption begins when she challenges Jesus to be the savior of the whole world, and offer the feast of God to more than just his kind. That is good news.

Valerie Bridgeman is Associate Professor at Lancaster Theological Seminary, United States; she is an ordained preacher and published poet.

QUESTIONS

1. How are the residents of Bushwick like and unlike the "aliens" for whom there is no Jubilee?
2. How would Matthew 15:4–9 be appropriated in your cultural context in comparison to Iskandar's interpretation of it?
3. According to Thomaskutty, in what sense is the widow to be emulated? And in what sense is Jesus to be emulated?
4. How does Bridgeman's personal background and identity shape her reading of the biblical text? What elements of your background and identity might yield interesting insights on the story of the Syrophoenician woman?

CHAPTER 30

TEACHINGS OF JESUS (PART II)

Luke 20:20–26, Matthew 22:15–22, and Mark 12:13–17; Matthew 3:10; Matthew 7:16–20; Matthew 12:33; Luke 13:6–9; Luke 18:18–30

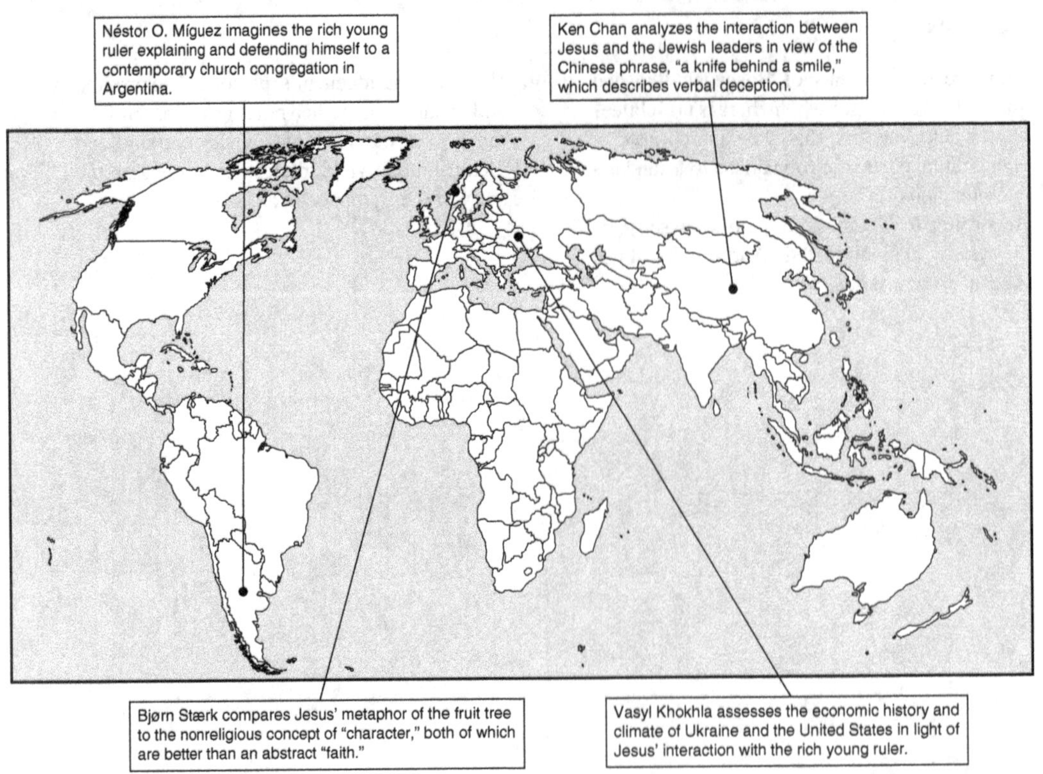
Néstor O. Míguez imagines the rich young ruler explaining and defending himself to a contemporary church congregation in Argentina.
Ken Chan analyzes the interaction between Jesus and the Jewish leaders in view of the Chinese phrase, "a knife behind a smile," which describes verbal deception.
Bjørn Stærk compares Jesus' metaphor of the fruit tree to the nonreligious concept of "character," both of which are better than an abstract "faith."
Vasyl Khokhla assesses the economic history and climate of Ukraine and the United States in light of Jesus' interaction with the rich young ruler.

READINGS

"A Knife Behind a Smile" and the Interaction between Jesus and Jewish Leaders

Ken Chan (China)

The religious leaders did not like Jesus. They felt threatened by him because he was gaining a popular following for his reputation as a miracle worker. Jesus also interpreted scripture (the Old Testament) differently from them. This was uncomforting. They could lose their power over the Jews. They might be out of a job soon.

Their response was to get rid of Jesus, and they needed an excuse. So, in Luke 20:20–26 (as well as in Matt. 22:15–22 and Mark 12:13–17) we read that they watched Jesus carefully, and then they sent out spies to catch Jesus in his words. The spies pretended to be "righteous" people (20:20), and they started off by flattering him: "Teacher, we know that you speak and teach rightly" (20:21). This was a lie. They came to Jesus precisely because they did not believe he "teaches rightly." They hoped to catch Jesus off guard by tricking him with the question: "Is it proper for us to give tax to Caesar, or is it not?" (20:22). The text is ringing with alarm bells, telling the reader that here is a trap.

The Chinese have a phrase to describe this type of verbal deception. We call it "a knife behind a smile." Cantonese (a dialect of Chinese spoken in the southern part of China, including Hong Kong) calls it "a deadly snake behind a smile." For example, it may appear strange that a Chinese who meets you for the first time would treat you like you were the king—strange, until you later find out that the information that was gathered about you had been used to your disadvantage. This is the reason that many Chinese guard information about themselves tightly. When they are asked a question about themselves, they often try to divert the topic of conversation, or fall silent, or ask you a question instead, so as to avoid having to answer the question you had first asked them.

Jesus responded to this trap graciously. He knew what they were up to (20:23), but he did not get angry or yell back. Like a classical Chinese gentleman, he dealt with the problem while remaining calm. The first thing he did was to ask for a denarius coin (20:24). He turned this situation into an object lesson: He taught the crowd how to resolve the apparent conflict between loyalty to the State and to God. Like a good Rabbi, he began by asking a question: "Of whose image and inscription does it have?" For him, paying tax to the Roman government does not equate with denying the authority of God. Jesus was loyal to the absolute claim of God, and yet he recognized the temporal authority of the State in matters such as taxation. Jesus put each thing in its place when he said, "Give the things of Caesar to Caesar, and the things of God to God" (20:25). His statement sounds great to a Chinese because it fits the Rule of the Median as taught by Confucius. The best way forward should address all concerns.

While the religious leaders spent considerable time plotting against Jesus, Jesus was able to respond immediately. This shows that Jesus knew what he believed in. The urgency of the situation revealed the core of himself—a man who knew the will of God and how to apply it in daily life. Jesus gave a good answer. He also acted within his culture by responding indirectly. He busted the fallacious premise that was hidden in the question. But his aim was not to defend himself and save his skin; rather, his desire was to teach the truth on this occasion.

The spies were dumbfounded, since "they were not strong enough to seize upon his words before the people" (20:26). They even had a tinge of admiration at his superb answer. At the end, all they could do was to be silent. This was an unexpected reversal of events. Jesus was supposed to lose face and credibility before the people, but the spies ended up in those shoes. Their silence was their way of minimizing their embarrassment when they had failed to trap Jesus. The irony through it all is that Jesus was not even concerned about whether he would lose face. Jesus knew he was in good standing with God, and he had nothing to be afraid of.

The nonliteral use of words, questions, and facial expressions in the Chinese culture is not always meant for ill, but miscommunication frequently occurs because of it. Often, a Chinese person will come up to you and apologize about something for no apparent reason. It is because that person was reading your facial expression and thought that you were displeased about something. For that person, making a preemptive apology is the best way to clarify any possible misunderstanding before it blows out of proportion and destroys the relationship.

This, in turn, makes it hard to ask a real question. Since a question is often used as (and interpreted as) a verbal criticism, many Chinese simply do not ask questions in public even if they have a burning question. For fear of being misinterpreted, they will (a) leave the question dangling, (b) get the information from a third party, or (c) deduce the answer based on what they already know.

Another cultural norm that blocks communication is that Chinese are expected to agree with one another no matter what. Conformity to the norm is also strongly encouraged in a typical Chinese Christian church. The desire for uniformity makes problem-solving difficult when divergent opinions genuinely exist within the church. It is a generally accepted principle that conflicts can only be resolved by analyzing the alternative positions and rationally weighing their pros and cons. Yet, it is hard to have a real discussion in a Chinese church, since harmony is emphasized. A so-called discussion is often only a beautiful veneer on the outside of a stew of garbled emotions. Such communities would even deny that there is a problem, until the pent-up feelings erupt, and the community splits.

This passage helps me, as a Chinese, to reexamine the distance between my words and feelings, what I actually think and what I say. And when someone with malicious intent comes my way, my job is to (a) see through the trap, (b) be calm, (c) examine my conscience, (d) get rid of the fear of man, (e) speak and teach God's truth in a culturally acceptable way, and (f) apply the Rule of the Median.

Ken Chan (Ph.D., Biblical Studies) is a linguist translator with SIL International serving in East Asia.

The Metaphor of the Fruit Tree and the Concept of Character

Bjørn Stærk (Norway)

In the Christian faith that I grew up in, it is your faith that saves you, not good deeds; but your actions are a reflection of your faith, a demonstration of the role Jesus has in your life. The idea is that only God can see what is in your heart, and in the end that's all that really matters, but everything you do in your daily life, all your actions and choices and habits, reflect what is in your heart. Your actions are not only a demonstration of your relationship with Jesus but a demonstration to nonbelievers of the power and goodness of your religion.

This is a powerful idea. A less religious word for a similar concept is "character." Your actions reflect what's inside of you, your essence as a person. It is your character that makes you good or bad, but your actions display that good or bad character to the world.

Nonbelievers often overemphasize the role of good deeds in Christianity. There's a reason for this. Good deeds are something we can understand and respect, unlike faith, a concept even Christians can find difficult to comprehend. You can only fully understand faith by having it, but anyone can understand good deeds. Anyone can look at what you do and say, "Yes, this is a person who does good things. There must be something good on the inside that causes this."

All of this can be summed up in that perfect metaphor of the tree interwoven throughout Jesus' teaching (e.g., Matt. 3:10; 7:16–20; 12:33; Luke 13:6–9). Just as good trees produce good fruit and bad trees bad fruit, so it is with people. This is an idea that is relevant far beyond Christianity itself.

As an atheist, I am not very interested in faith. I think faith is a morally questionable ideal. But I like the metaphor of the fruit tree, the idea that your actions can be used to judge your character, and I think it shows us a way for different worldviews to coexist without compromising their integrity.

Think about how people with different interests and abilities find a way to get along in daily life. We're rarely fortunate enough to be able to spend our time with people who are exactly like ourselves. We have to deal with people we like but who aren't perfect, people we don't have much in common with, and some people who are just awful. We do this with the help of social lubricants.

One of these is politeness, maintaining a friendly, somewhat ritualized facade, while hiding your innermost thoughts from strangers. Another is keeping your distance, not forcing yourself into other people's lives. You don't have to like the local shopkeepers, just find ways to deal with them without getting into a fight. So you smile, because it's polite, and you don't tell them about your personal life, because they don't want to know. To get along with other people, we restrict ourselves, but we get something valuable in return, so we accept it.

Now think of groups of people, groups with different worldviews. Some of them are religious worldviews; others could be philosophical or political. In the past, everyone who lived near you thought like you, but today we're surrounded by people of different cultures, different faiths, and different ideologies. Again we need a lubricant, some way to make it easier to deal with groups with alien ideals.

Just as the instinct of individuals, beneath all the layers of social indoctrination, is to demand that everyone should think and behave just like ourselves, so it is with groups and their worldviews. All faiths and ideologies would prefer if the whole world could be organized according to their ideals. It would feel so good. And many worldviews go through phases where they try to do just that; they try to impose their views by force.

Eventually they learn better. Just as a person who tells everyone they meet exactly what they think is wrong about them won't make many friends, a worldview that imposes itself through force will be feared, hated, and resented. It may succeed at forcing itself on people, but at a high cost. Modern Christians still live in the shadow of their authoritarian ancestors. In my own country, Norway, anyone who professes a strong personal faith in God risks being associated with authoritarian Puritanism. People will look at you as if you may at any moment rise up and shout, "That looks fun. Let's MAKE IT ILLEGAL!" It's a prejudice, but the prejudice was caused by earlier generations of Christians who wanted to regulate society according to their ideals and force everyone to live by their standards.

So the dilemma of the believer today is this: You have what you believe is a good faith, a true faith, and you want other people to see that, and adopt it themselves. But they don't always want to listen to you. They laugh at you. They live by what you consider to be deeply immoral ideals. And even if you find a political majority for your views, using power to impose your views will not make anyone adopt your faith; it will just make them bitter.

So you remember the metaphor of the fruit tree, and you say to yourself, "I will act out the ideals I believe in. I will live my life as a testimony to my faith. And I will do this together with my family, and my friends, and my congregation. In this evil world, full of hate and despair and sorrow, our community will be an island of good, of hope. People will look at us and wonder what it is that makes us so content. We're only human, but we are humans who strive toward a wonderful ideal, with the aid of Heaven. Sometimes we will do things that are wrong, and people will notice that. But we will regret our mistakes, and try to make up for them, and we hope people will see that too. And they will at worst respect us, and at best become curious about what it is that we have that makes all this possible."

And that is the tree that bears good fruits, or, more accurately, the tree that is so confident that it is willing, even eager, to be judged by its fruits. Imagine a world where all faiths and all philosophies and ideologies think like this. A world where we promote unpopular ideals by living them in practice, and setting a good example. All of us. As individuals, or as groups.

Not everyone can live out all their ideals, but everyone can do it to some extent. Everyone can think of themselves as ambassadors from a better world. We can see other worldviews not as enemies to fight, but competitors to outshine. This doesn't mean that we necessarily see our actions as the core of our ideals, but that we see actions as our chief way of interacting with those who follow other ideals.

And perhaps we will produce good fruits, and be judged by them. Or perhaps we are wrong and produce rotten fruits, but at least we did our best to make the world a better place, without forcing ourselves on anyone. That's something I think most of us can appreciate, no matter what we believe in.

Bjørn Stærk is a software developer from Norway; he is an atheist and former Christian, and writes a blog at http://max256.bearstrong.net.

Ukraine, the United States, and Jesus' Interaction with the Rich Young Ruler

Vasyl Khokhla (Ukraine)

After the collapse of the Soviet Union in the early1990s, Ukraine became an independent nation. Although Ukraine was officially proclaimed a democracy in 1991, numerous traces of the Soviet past still remain. A swift shift to democracy and capitalism, or "shock therapy" as some economists term it, drove many people to extreme poverty. The gap between the rich and the poor widened. Life in much of Ukraine remains bleak today. Having grown up in Kalush, Western Ukraine, I have witnessed this firsthand. Now that I am studying at a University in the United States, this is the question I ask myself: Why aren't democracy and capitalism working in Ukraine while they are bulwarks of prosperity and development in the United States?

To my mind, the religious, specifically Christian, heritage of the United States has made a big difference. The teachings of Jesus have had a significant impact. In Jesus' encounter with the wealthy young ruler in Luke 18, we see one of many places where Jesus promotes the distribution of wealth, without rejecting the initial accumulation of it. It is to be noted that Jesus instructs the man to "sell all that he owns and give the money to the poor." The man must essentially sell his business, perhaps much like merger and acquisitions that take place today which often drive the economy. The rich man is to share the proceeds of his successful and sound business with the less fortunate in his community. He is to be socially responsible.

The United States, unlike Ukraine, was founded on Christian values in which the ethics of sharing as advocated by Jesus had an important place. This generated a strong trust among people, which, in turn, facilitated business transactions. Trust became the social capital that laid a foundation for a free and ethical enterprise. While the main aim of capitalism is to generate profit, if Americans were setting up business with the sole goal of becoming rich, I doubt they would thrive. If they were simply pursuing their own gain and not worrying about the needs of others, they would not get very far. However, Americans are known as the most giving nation in the world. This is, I believe, due in part to people taking seriously Jesus' words to share with the poor. American business people usually remember their duty to help the community. Indeed, as Max Weber's classic work, *The Protestant Ethic and the Spirit of Capitalism*, explains, Christian values have influenced the success of capitalism.

Ukraine, on the other hand, is a former Soviet Union country where practices of religion were suppressed. Lenin, one of the founding Soviet leaders, felt that Karl Marx was right when he said, "Religion is the opium for the people." Although some people in communist Ukraine worshipped God despite severe persecution, the attitudes of atheism prevailed. With the collapse of the USSR, people received freedom of religion, which led to the emergence of a myriad of religious organizations, including Protestant ones (the predominant religion in Ukraine is the Orthodox Church). Yet, many people are still nonreligious, a direct result of the atheism that was prevalent among Communists, the major political party in the Soviet Union.

Although Democracy brought hundreds of new political parties to Ukraine, the problem is that the politicians in these new parties of the "democratic era" consist of so-called "repainted" Communists. The very same Communists in the Soviet Union assumed a role of democratically elected representatives in the independent Ukraine. Independent Ukraine has thus experienced much corruption and embezzlement, severely hindering economic growth. Instead of showing concern for the well-being of the people, such politicians stuff their own pockets. They indeed represent the antithesis of the ethics of sharing taught by Jesus in Luke 18. As atheists, they have no fear of God, no religious principles to guide them, and as a result they exploit and manipulate the economic system to their own advantage. This has caused the moral erosion of the nation. People distrust such politicians. The majority of the citizenry feel hopeless. Alcoholism is very prevalent.

In my view, then, what Ukraine needs is for people and politicians to live out the Christian ethic of sharing. In order to share, one must first acquire and accumulate, which the young ruler in Luke 18 had done, without any condemnation from Jesus. As the young man discovered, sharing can be difficult, unnatural even. But it is what Jesus calls people to do—and it is what people in the United States in fact do. In my perspective, the success and efficiency of the American capitalistic system is a result of America's religious heritage and tradition, specifically their willingness to follow Jesus' sharing praxis outlined in Luke 18.

Vasyl Khokhla was born in Kalush in Western Ukraine; he is currently working on a law degree in Ukraine and a finance degree in the United States.

The Rich Young Ruler's Imagined Self-Defense to a Contemporary Church in Argentina

Néstor O. Míguez (Argentina)

Buenos Aires City, Sunday morning. The regular worship of a middle-class Presbyterian Church, with a gentle charismatic influence. The service was moving along as usual. The songs and prayers came and went without incident. The time came for the reading of the Scriptures. A sister read the passage indicated by the pastor, Luke 18:18–30. The congregation listened to the reading with unction, rising to its feet. A prayer was offered, asking for inspiration for the message. The pastor begins to step up to the pulpit when, suddenly, out of nowhere, a strange figure occupies the pulpit—a man richly dressed, but in a style fitting with the first century. We do not recognize the language, but we suddenly begin to understand. He breaks into speech:

> Ah, it is so easy for you! Once again you will preach about me, and I will be mistreated—I know already. I am the bad guy, the one who rejected salvation. For centuries I will be labeled as the one who could not say "Yes," the one who rejected Christ. This isn't fair. I was seeking eternal life and now as it turns out, I have eternal shame.
>
> But I want you to hear the other side of the story. As you know, I am a ranking official in my nation and I want to act justly and do right. The majority of my friends and other government and temple officials mistrusted Jesus. He is a rabble-rouser, they said, he mingles with the wrong crowd, and he has connections to the rebel. A lawyer, an expert in the Law, told me that he had interviewed Jesus personally. He told me how it had happened: He had gone to where Jesus was staying, and the people were asking him all kinds of questions. My friend intended to test Jesus on this topic: "What can I do to inherit eternal life?" he asked. Jesus questioned him on the Law—him of all people, an expert in the Law. My friend answered, "Love the Lord your God...," but knowing something about how Jesus thinks, he added, "Love your neighbor...." Jesus told him that if he kept these commandments, he would live. And because the lawyer insisted, Jesus told him a parable about a Samaritan who had helped someone who had fallen into the hands of bandits. And he exhorted him to go and do likewise. It was an intelligent answer. The lawyer was left perplexed. That story had many elements, but Jesus demonstrated the wisdom of the teachers. I was interested in hearing a bit more.
>
> I wanted to meet Jesus for myself. So when I knew Jesus was nearby, I headed out in his direction. I wanted to have good relations with him, and at the same time, the question of eternal life had been an unsettling one for me. I needed to know more. So I went to him and asked him the same question the lawyer had. I was eager to elaborate on that exchange; I had already prepared a few more questions in case I received the same response.
>
> But his initial response surprised me. I called him "good teacher." I was polite, much more so than is expected of a prince when speaking with a village carpenter—his notoriety as a wise man notwithstanding. I expected a response that was equally polite. "Why do you call me good?" he asked, in front of the crowd. I was disconcerted. "God alone is good," he added. Was there a reproach hidden in those words? Was he indirectly denouncing those in my position, saying that nobody is good—as elevated in status as he may be? My mood became uncertain. His follow-up questions reassured me. They had to do with the commandments that relate to one's neighbor. I

could see that his response was heading down the same path as the one he had given the lawyer. I replied that yes, I knew the commandments and had endeavored to keep them since I was a boy.

And it was true. I know we government officials have a bad reputation, but as I told you, I try to be honest in my work. I truly do want to obtain eternal life. I was formed in the faith of my elders and I do not want to lose that heritage. I know of the righteousness that comes by the Law of Moses and I try to live according to it. Jesus' initial response lifted my spirits.

But that sense of reassurance wouldn't last long. "One thing you lack," he told me. What could be lacking? Could there be anything more to being righteous than remaining faithful to God, keeping his Law? As a Pharisee, we keep not only the written law but all of the precepts. We undoubtedly seek that everyone might know the Law and keep it. "One thing you lack." I opened my ears.

And then the phrase that has been my nightmare for centuries was pronounced: "Sell all that you have and give it to the poor, and then come follow me." I didn't know how exactly to respond. You here at this meeting, along with many others, are followers of Jesus, so I ask you: Has he asked you the same thing? How many here have sold everything they have to follow Jesus? Did he not ask everything of you as well? Not something, *everything*. Did he ask everything of you, as he did of me? Did you give it to him? Have you given it to the poor? I don't see many heads nodding. I see that many have golden rings. I saw many cars at the door. I also saw many poor people in the streets, and I know that this enormous city is surrounded by shanty towns where children die in hunger. Have you shared your goods with them? And if so, why is there still so much poverty, and you are at ease in this Church?

If you are Jesus' followers, and still hold your goods, then you have been treated more kindly than I have. Is that fair? Jesus didn't simply ask for something, a part, whatever it may be; he asked for everything. Of course I left very sorrowful, I tell you, very sorrowful, a sorrow that lasts even to this day. You think I don't feel that burden. I have lost eternal life, and it is only by some unexpected miracle that I stand before you today.

As if that were not enough, as I left, I heard Jesus himself saying that it is very hard for a rich man to enter the kingdom of heaven. Ah, but for God nothing is impossible, Jesus says to you, and you are at ease. Well it doesn't put me at ease—he gave me no answer that would be of aid to me.

I arrived at home and told my wife: You can't imagine how she reacted! She was extremely upset. She reacted like anyone else in her situation might: "Who does he think he is? You have responsibilities: You have to look presentable for the temple functions, to receive Roman ambassadors, and I can't accompany you without a decent bracelet or an elegant necklace. You can't get rid of everything. So much depends on you and you have to have what's necessary to fulfill your obligations. You are not to blame for your large inheritance. Of course, a poor carpenter knows nothing of these things... Giving everything to the poor... What do we live on from then on? You sell, you give up everything, and in 15 days neither we nor they have anything. I know you're a conscientious person, that you're concerned, but that doesn't work. There must be another way to be generous. All this has done is embitter you. In any case, why did you go to ask a simple carpenter who knows nothing of government responsibilities?"

Look, the other day I received a man named Zebedee, an older man who had come to ask for my help because his sons had gone after Jesus and had left him alone. The man is a fisherman, and now has to take care of the entire family because his sons listened to Jesus and left with him. Who will watch over Zebedee and his family now? No, nothing is as simple as it seems. Zebedee's wife lost her mind and trails after Jesus, asking him to reserve a special spot for her sons, one to the left, the other at the right hand, when he comes in his Kingdom. So they weren't that generous or disinterested either, leaving everything just to receive more. If we politicians do that, along come our critics and call it cronyism, clientelism; but when Jesus does it they call it grace.

You might say I'm resentful, bitter, that I see everything in a negative light. It's just that I've heard too many dreamers who think that this complicated world can be fixed with a little good will and generosity. You have to understand what it is to be in a place of authority, to understand the tensions one suffers. And Jesus, instead of helping me, made it more difficult.

Others—nearly all others—have decided to follow Jesus, and keep their things as if he never said these words. I stayed on the outside, because, honestly, I can't do what he asked me. But I'm still looking for an answer. Help me find it.

Néstor O. Míguez is Professor of New Testament Studies at ISEDET, Buenos Aires, Argentina.

QUESTIONS

1. How does Chinese culture as described by Chan encourage individuals to act in ways that resemble both Jesus and the "spies"? Why does Chan take his "lesson" from Jesus rather than from the "spies"?
2. Compare and contrast Jesus' metaphor of the fruit tree (note the larger context of the biblical passages) with Stærk's explanation of "character."
3. Assess Khokhla's reading of the biblical text. Was Jesus asking the rich young ruler to be "socially responsible"? Did Jesus accept his accumulation of wealth?
4. What is your response to Míguez's imagined "rich young ruler"? What is Míguez trying to do: inspire you to sell all that you have? Cause you to side with the ruler? Or something else?

CHAPTER 31

MIRACLES OF JESUS

Matthew 9:27–30; Mark 4:35–5:1; Matthew 8:5–13

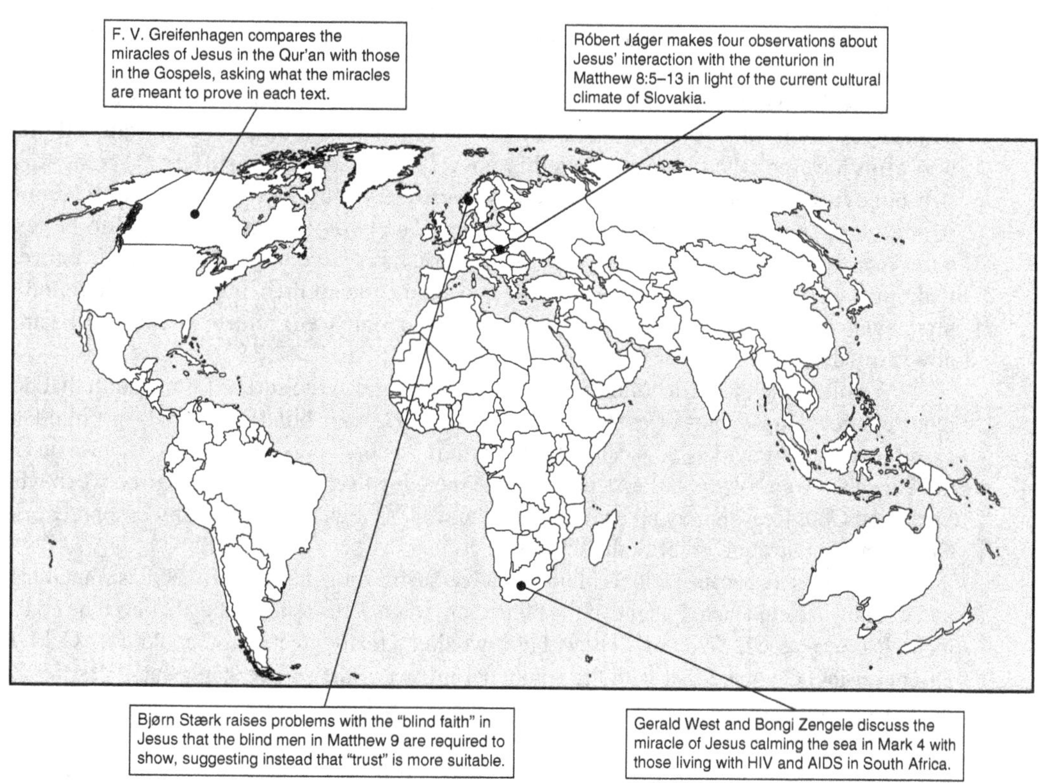

F. V. Greifenhagen compares the miracles of Jesus in the Qur'an with those in the Gospels, asking what the miracles are meant to prove in each text.
Róbert Jáger makes four observations about Jesus' interaction with the centurion in Matthew 8:5–13 in light of the current cultural climate of Slovakia.
Bjørn Stærk raises problems with the "blind faith" in Jesus that the blind men in Matthew 9 are required to show, suggesting instead that "trust" is more suitable.
Gerald West and Bongi Zengele discuss the miracle of Jesus calming the sea in Mark 4 with those living with HIV and AIDS in South Africa.

READINGS

The Trouble with "Blind Faith"
Bjørn Stærk

Reading the "Calming of the Sea" with Those Living with HIV and AIDS in South Africa
Gerald West and Bongi Zengele

A Comparison of Jesus' Miracles in the Qur'an and the Gospels
F. V. Greifenhagen

Four Observations about Jesus' Interaction with the Centurion
Róbert Jáger

The Trouble with "Blind Faith"

Bjørn Stærk (Norway)

In the story in Matthew 9:27–30, Jesus heals two blind men. It is their faith that heals them. Jesus tells them so. He asks them to believe, and says he will heal them according to the strength of their belief. There are many similar stories in the Bible. God does not like to be tested. He does not perform miracles on demand. Faith comes first, genuine faith, and then miracles may—or may not—come later. You don't approach Jesus as some service provider, with a remedy that may or may not work. He sees your heart, so in your heart there must be faith.

Most Christians who have heard these stories throughout the centuries have found themselves living in times of few miracles. The blind remain blind, the mortally ill die. The best of us have perished in wars, slaved in poverty, starved, and/or suffered. Seeing this, and still believing in a good God who watches over everything and wishes us well, requires a strong faith, stronger than the faith in this story. The two blind men only had to believe for a few seconds before they were healed. Most Christians have to go through their entire lives without a sign like that, and they are still expected to keep their faith. Faith that God has a plan, even when bad things happen. Faith that Jesus really will return, and it may be any day now. Any day.

We often use the term "blind faith" to describe an extreme sort of faith, a faith that doesn't require rational arguments or evidence. But, really, all faith is blind. Faith that isn't blind, that is based on reason or evidence, is called trust. Faith is when you do not have proof, but you choose to believe anyway. We talk of a "leap of faith," meaning that faith is the bridge between what we know and God. Reason may take you part of the way, as it has done for many rationally oriented Christians, but at some point faith takes over.

It is precisely because faith is blind that it has such a romantic appeal. There is something cold about asking for evidence. Imagine if the blind men, when Jesus asked if they believed he could heal them, had responded, "We don't know, but it would be really great if you could try." Cold. Rude. Disconcerting. Compare that with the emotional impact of the simple statement, "Yes, I believe," uttered so often in the Bible, in prayers, and in our stories. Faith is romantic. Faith is beautiful. Faith is inspiring.

But the faith that brings victims of disease to Jesus in the Bible is the same faith that brings people today to faith healers, psychics, homeopaths, and other providers of questionable remedies. It is faith that, for some, creates the bridge from sanity to insanity, peace to violence, pragmaticism to fanaticism. The direction of the leap is different, but the essence of faith is the leap itself.

Faith that isn't blind is called trust. Do an experiment: Take the role faith plays in Christianity, and replace it with trust. In this version of the story, Jesus asks the blind men, "Do you trust that I'm able to heal you?" They say, "Not quite, but some people say you can, and you seem like you mean well, so we're willing to try." He heals them, and asks, "Now do you trust me?" They say, "Yes, now we do." A relationship has been built. It has a concrete basis, and can be built upon further.

Now think of someone who does not live in the age of legends and miracles, perhaps someone who lives today. We can have faith in God, that's easy, but can we "trust" that God oversees the world, and has a plan for everyone and everything? On what basis? The miracles today are few and far between and always tainted with the suspicion of fraud or delusion.

Faith comes beforehand, and is indefinite, absolute. To demand faith is an aggressive, dominant act. Trust comes afterwards, and is built, gradually, over time. Faith is binary, either there or not. Trust has many levels. Trust is not cold and cynical. It is the essence of friendship and love. But it requires some evidence, some reciprocal signals of ability and good intent. We trust our friends because of what we have been through together, and what it has revealed about their character. We do not approach strangers, as Jesus often did, and say, "Become my friend. Trust that I mean you well." "Why should I?" will be their answer.

And that should also have been the answer of the blind men in Matthew 9. It was wrong of Jesus to demand faith from them, and all the other people who approached him for healing, beforehand. It was wrong of him to be angry with people who asked him for proof (e.g., Matthew 16:4; Mark 8:12). It was wrong to build Christianity on faith, when it should have been built on trust.

Humans are both rational and social beings. Faith demands that we restrict our rational abilities, abilities that are part of who we are. Trust allows us to use both our rational and social abilities to their fullest. Faith is a temptation we should learn to avoid. Our ideal, instead, should be trust.

Bjørn Stærk is a software developer from Norway; he's an atheist and former Christian, and writes a blog at http://max256.bearstrong.net.

Reading the "Calming of the Sea" with Those Living with HIV and AIDS in South Africa

Gerald West and Bongi Zengele (South Africa)

The Ujamaa Centre, a community development and research organization, reads the Bible among communities of the poor, marginalized, and working class, with the explicit purpose of participating in God's emancipatory project by working toward social and personal transformation. As part of these Contextual Bible Studies, we have developed a study of Mark 4:35–5:1 with those who are living with HIV and AIDS. Compelling conversations have emerged.

We asked participants the following questions:

Question 1: Retell the story in your own words in "buzz groups" of two. What is the text about?

Question 2: Who is sailing the boat? What is Jesus doing in the boat?

Question 3: When and why do the disciples wake Jesus?

Question 4: What are they afraid of?

Question 5: What are we who are living with HIV and AIDS afraid of?

Question 6: Is Jesus in "the boat" with those living with HIV and AIDS? If he is, is he asleep or awake?

Question 7: If Jesus is still asleep, how do we wake him up?

Question 8: If he is awake or if he were to waken, what would we want him to do?

Question 9: What does this story challenge us to do?

Question 1 opens up space for the group members to share whatever their impressions of this text might be. It is an important question because it establishes that anyone in the group may participate and that any response is acceptable. This question makes it evident, even to new members, that the facilitator is just that, a facilitator and not the "expert" voice.

Questions 2, 3, and 4 return the participants to the biblical text. In this case there is no in-depth probing of the literary features of the text or of the world behind the text. Here the readers simply return to read the text again, giving the text its own voice, and affirming that the text does indeed have a voice. Questions 5, 6, 7, and 8 then shift back again to the readers' reality, in an overtly contextual reading, ending the process with an action plan.

Question 1 generates a host of responses, ranging from answers like faith, fear, anxiety, the power of God, a miracle, to Jesus teaching his disciples. Question 2 often elicits some surprise, as participants notice that it is the disciples who are in control of the boat, not Jesus. They are the ones with expertise in sailing, not Jesus. This detail becomes significant later when they respond to Questions 6, 7, and 8, all of which emphasize the agency of the Bible study participants (all of whom are HIV-positive). Some participants notice that Jesus is asleep "on the cushion," and wonder why Mark has given us this particular detail. Perhaps, some suggest, this is to reassure us that Jesus is only unaware of the danger facing the disciples because he is so comfortable. Jesus is not uncaring. He is exhausted by his teaching and so has fallen asleep, but without the pillow he would probably have woken by himself as the boat became more and more violently shaken by the wind and the waves. Others venture that Jesus is being uncaring, making himself comfortable while the disciples struggle with the task of sailing the boat in increasingly difficult conditions.

Question 3, with its dual focus, reflects on how the disciples only wake Jesus when the situation is no longer in their control, when "the boat was already being swamped" (v. 37), in the expectation that he might or will be able to help them. Jesus is significant, and at times just his presence is enough, without his active involvement; but at other times he is expected or required to act in a form of participation that exceeds presence.

Question 4 already begins to shift the readers, in most cases, to their own realities, for there is not much in the text to interrogate with regard to this question. Obviously the disciples were afraid of dying (v. 38), but perhaps their fear was heightened by the very presence of Jesus with them. Perhaps they felt some responsibility for him, for he was not, after all, a fisherman, and so would not be familiar with this kind of situation. But more importantly, he was their leader, and so there was the weight of responsibility to protect him. Furthermore, Jesus had given their lives new meaning and so to die now, with him, was a situation worthy of dread. These reflections, however, are intimately linked to the fears of the group's members, who fear not only for their own lives but also for the lives of those for whom they are responsible, particularly their children. They too have discovered a new sense of "life" (*ukuphila*) since their diagnosis as HIV-positive, especially since they joined the group.

The shift to the readers' realities is decisive in Question 5, moving directly from text to participants' contexts. Those living with HIV and AIDS have much to fear. Our government is only gradually rolling out antiretroviral (ARV) treatment, so not everyone who needs ARVs is able to obtain them at the appropriate time. Even when we are able to access ARVs, the stigma associated with taking the medication is as severe as the stigma associated with being HIV-positive. Added to this is the fear of not having sufficient nutritious food to allow the body to cope with the toxic ARV drugs. Then there is the fear that one's body will develop resistance to the particular cocktails available in our country, where we do not yet have second-or third-generation drugs (as Western countries do). But the deepest fear is not living long enough to see one's children go to school or to be reconciled and accepted by one's family.

Question 6 is the question around which the whole Bible study is based. It is derived from the discussions of this text before the Contextual Bible Study itself was developed. In informal reflections around this text Bongi Zengele heard one of the discussants declare, "It is time for Jesus to wake up!" Probing, she discovered that this is what some of them felt when they read this text, though they were not sure they should feel or say such things about Jesus. And so the seed of "an-other" theology was sown! Question 6 opens up formal space, within the safe sacred site of a Bible study, to delve more deeply into this embodied cry: "It is time for Jesus to wake up!"

Question 7 continues to encourage the participants to do theology, invoking our own participation in God's work. Questions 8 and 9 move the study to its conclusion, inviting participants to envisage and plan for transformation. We usually ask participants to work toward concrete "action plans," beginning with an immediate action that can be taken, then planning an action that requires some additional time and resources but which is nevertheless feasible within their context, and finally to imagine a plan of action that might be possible if there were appropriate resources.

What emerges in Contextual Bible Studies such as this, if the group is a sacred and safe space, is that the embodied theologies of the participants find forms of articulation. Such emergent articulations are what South African theologian James Cochrane calls "incipient theology" (*Circles of Dignity: Community Wisdom and Theological Reflection* [Minneapolis: Fortress, 1999]). Incipient theology is a product of the corporate embodied experience of the group, who draw both on the resources of their own bodies and the biblical text to bring to articulation what is inchoate. So in this case, though this same group of people have affirmed in other Contextual Bible Studies that Jesus stands with them over against stigmatizing society, they are also able to bring to words another part of their lived reality, namely a Jesus who is in some sense asleep. And, as they said, "It is time for Jesus to wake up!" Here is the beginning of a profound theology of both God's presence and absence in the context of HIV and AIDS.

Gerald West and Bongi Zengele are coordinators at the Ujamaa Centre in the School of Religion and Theology at University of KwaZulu-Natal, Pietermaritzburg, South Africa.

A Comparison of Jesus' Miracles in the Qur'an and the Gospels

F. V. Greifenhagen (Canada)

Miracles are extraordinary events seen as resisting normal human explanation and therefore attributed to divine intervention. The Gospels are replete with accounts of the extraordinary deeds or miracles of Jesus, involving either the healing of humans—by cures, exorcisms, or resuscitations from the dead—or the demonstrating of power over the natural world, such as turning water into wine, calming storms, and miraculously feeding many people.

The Muslim scripture, the Qur'an, originating with the prophet Muhammad in the seventh century C.E. in Arabia, also attributes miracles to Jesus: In Surah 2 *al-Baqarah* ("The Heifer") 87, the Qur'an quotes God as saying, "We gave Jesus, the son of Mary, clear (signs) and strengthened him with the Holy Spirit" (Translation by 'Abdullah Yusuf 'Ali, 2001). In two other passages, the Qur'an more specifically describes various miracles of Jesus.

Surah 3 *al-'Imran* ("The Family of 'Imran") 46, 48-49:

> [46]He shall speak to the people in childhood and in maturity. And he shall be (of the company) of the righteous... [48]And Allah will teach him the Book and Wisdom, the Law and the Gospel, [49]And (appoint him) a messenger to the Children of Israel, (with this message): "I have come to you, with a Sign from your Lord, in that I make for you out of clay, as it were, the figure of a bird, and breathe into it, and it becomes a bird by Allah's leave: And I heal those born blind, and the lepers, and I quicken the dead, by Allah's leave; and I declare to you what ye eat, and what ye store in your houses. Surely therein is a Sign for you if ye did believe." (Translation by 'Abdullah Yusuf 'Ali, 2001)

Surah 5 *al-Ma'idah* ("The Repast") 110, 112–115:

> [110]Then will Allah say: "O Jesus the son of Mary! Recount My favour to thee and to thy mother. Behold! I strengthened thee with the Holy Spirit, so that thou didst speak to the people in childhood and in maturity. Behold! I taught thee the Book and Wisdom, the Law and the Gospel and behold! thou makest out of clay, as it were, the figure of a bird, by My leave, and thou breathest into it and it becometh a bird by My leave, and thou healest those born blind, and the lepers, by My leave. And behold! thou bringest forth the dead by My leave. And behold! I did restrain the Children of Israel from (violence to) thee when thou didst show them the clear Signs, and the unbelievers among them said: 'This is nothing but evident magic.' "... [112]Behold! the disciples, said: "O Jesus the son of Mary! can thy Lord send down to us a table set (with viands) from heaven?" Said Jesus: "Fear Allah, if ye have faith." [113]They said: "We only wish to eat thereof and satisfy our hearts, and to know that thou hast indeed told us the truth; and that we ourselves may be witnesses to the miracle." [114]Said Jesus the son of Mary: "O Allah our Lord! Send us from heaven a table set (with viands), that there may be for us—for the first and the last of us—a solemn festival and a sign from thee; and provide for our sustenance, for thou art the best Sustainer (of our needs)." [115]Allah said: "I will send it down unto you: But if any of you after that resisteth faith, I will punish him with a penalty such as I have not inflicted on any one among all the peoples." (Translation by 'Abdullah Yusuf 'Ali, 2001)

In these two passages, the Qur'an attributes the following seven miracles to Jesus:

1. **Speaking to the people in childhood and maturity (3:46, 5:110).** The Arabic phrase is understood as meaning "from the cradle as at a mature age," indicating that Jesus miraculously spoke as an infant. The Qur'an elsewhere tells the story of how, when Mary returns to her family with the infant Jesus, they suspect her of unchaste behavior, and Jesus speaks up in her defense (19:27–33). The Qur'an here echoes the Christian Arabic Infancy Gospel, one of the New Testament apocryphal writings, which also depicts Jesus as speaking as an infant from the cradle. Among the biblical Gospels, only Luke narrates the somewhat analogous story of a precocious 12-year-old Jesus astounding the teachers in the Temple with his questions and responses (Luke 2:41–52).

2. **Breathing life into a bird made from clay (3:49, 5:110).** This miracle, while missing from the canonical Gospels, is narrated in the second- or third-century C.E. Infancy Gospel of Thomas as one of the miracles Jesus performed as a child—there he fashions twelve sparrows from mud, claps his hands, and they fly off. The qur'anic version is distinct in that Jesus' action evokes the Qur'an's description of God "creating" Adam out of "clay" and then "breathing" life into him (38:71–72).
3. **Healing those born blind (3:49, 5:110).** The Arabic word used here specifically refers to those who have been blind from birth, which intensifies the miraculous nature of these healings. While the Gospels narrate several accounts of Jesus healing various blind persons, only the story in the Gospel of John (9:1–12) specifies that the blind man has been blind from birth.
4. **Healing the lepers (3:49, 5:110).** The Gospels of Matthew, Mark, and Luke describe Jesus as healing lepers.
5. **Resuscitating the dead (3:49, 5:110).** In the Gospels, three specific stories of Jesus raising the dead are found: a widow's son, the daughter of Jairus, and Lazarus.
6. **Declaring what people eat and what they store in their houses (3:49).** These words can be understood as indicating that Jesus had miraculous foreknowledge of what people were eating and storing in their houses. However, it is also possible to interpret these words as portraying rather Jesus' authority to legislate what people can eat and store in their houses, just as Jesus in the Gospels claims the authority to interpret and modify the laws of the Mosaic Torah, and the traditions that have developed around it.
7. **Providing a meal from heaven (5:112–115).** Here the Qur'an describes Jesus' disciples requesting a table set with food from heaven; Jesus subsequently prays for God to provide this miracle. This qur'anic story indirectly echoes the feeding miracles of Jesus in the Gospels; that the table comes from heaven and signifies a "solemn festival" also echoes Jesus' discourse about the bread from heaven in John 6, and the Gospel accounts of the Last Supper and the institution of the Christian Eucharist.

The Qur'an's list of Jesus' miracles includes both healing and nature miracles, overlapping with those found in Christian sources, both canonical and apocryphal. By including miracles from the latter, the Qur'an rehabilitates early Christian traditions that were marginalized because they did not become part of the surviving official Christian biblical canon.

The Qur'an, as usual when it narrates material also found in the Bible, does not provide many details. It neither narrates specific miracle stories of Jesus nor gives the particulars of the persons affected or their circumstances. At the most, the Qur'an tells us that the miracles of Jesus were directed to the "Children of Israel" as "Signs" (3:49–50, 5:110), that the Holy Spirit was involved (5:110), and that disbelievers dismissed these miracles as nothing but magic (5:110). Similarly, "signs" are the favored designation for miracles in John's Gospel (e.g., 2:11, 57), Luke's Gospel especially emphasizes the power of the Spirit behind Jesus' deeds (4:1, 18, etc.), and the early Christians had to defend themselves against the accusation that the miracles of Jesus were mere magic.

What are the miracles of Jesus meant to communicate or prove? This concern, instead of narrative details, seems to be the Qur'an's intent. Miracles play a part in the stories of most of the biblical or Arab prophets mentioned in the Qur'an; they function as one of the "signs" of God meant to convince, or at least refute, disbelievers who reject the message of a prophet. The miracles of Jesus thus function in like fashion to those of previous prophets such Abraham and Moses.

Traditionally Christians, however, have argued that Jesus' miracles are proof of his divinity, as Jesus in John's Gospel seems to suggest: "Even if you don't believe me, believe the miracles. Then you will know and understand that the Father is in me and I am in the Father" (10:38). Yet miracles are not unique to Jesus; they are part of the career of prophets in the Hebrew Bible, and the practice of miracles is continued by the Christians after the death and resurrection of Jesus.

In fact, the portrayal of Jesus in Luke's Gospel and Acts seems to accord more with aspects of the qur'anic depiction of Jesus than with the postbiblical Christian doctrinal ideology of Christ's divinity. Luke presents the miracles of Jesus as proof that God is working through Jesus, not of Jesus' own divine power, as evident especially in the early Christian preaching described in Acts, where, for instance, Peter notes "how God anointed Jesus of Nazareth with the Holy Spirit and with power; how he went about doing good and healing all that were oppressed by the devil, for God was with him" (Acts 10:38). The Qur'an, in its description of Jesus' miracles, likewise repeatedly emphasizes that these extraordinary actions are done "by God's leave." Miracles from this perspective are signs of divine activity, not of divinization.

F. V. Greifenhagen is Associate Professor of Religious Studies at Luther College, University of Regina, Canada.

Four Observations about Jesus' Interaction with the Centurion

Róbert Jáger (Slovakia)

The healing of the centurion's servant in Matthew 8:5–13 is an important and compelling story. A key aspect of this scene is the presence of the centurion—a stranger, an outsider whose faith Jesus admires and underlines as one of the most important attitudes required for the full realization of the eternal destiny of humans (dining with the patriarchs in the Kingdom, v. 11). Jesus was a Jew; the centurion was a Roman. Jesus followed the religious laws; the centurion did not and would have been seen by Jews as a theologically "worthless" person. The centurion is thus both ethnically and religiously an outsider.

The overall interpretation and the focus on certain aspects of a biblical passage are dictated by the individual context of any interpreter, and the case is no different with me. I grew up in a small village in Eastern Slovakia on the border with the Soviet Union in the context of arrogant communist oppression, where human individuals were of no worth. It was a mixed community—Slovaks, Hungarians, Gypsies, and Ruthenians—with a healthy sense of mutuality and Christian solidarity. On the other hand, in school we were forced to accept the official and only legitimate atheist worldview: the leading role of the Communist party, the nation as the owner of all goods, and the total mental obedience to this worldview. Anyone who dared to express something else or publicly practiced his or her faith was exposed to mockery, not to mention political persecution. What was of ultimate importance was the Communist party and its "glorious future," which never came. Thanks to God. Nevertheless, now after 20 years of freedom, a new division is felt in Slovakia: the "orthodox" versus "outsiders." This is true in any aspect of social life—politics, culture, education, and geographical and ethnic relations—in our very tiny country.

When the former Czechoslovakia was split into the Czech Republic and Slovakia in 1993, Slovakia suffered from a tragic lack of constructive efforts for national and economic growth. As a result, there was a pathological search for enemies responsible for all negative elements in the life of the country, which the political elite used (and sometimes still use) to cover up unprecedented thievery of national and financial resources. The new enemy became the Hungarian minority living in Slovakia (about half a million people). The Slovak–Hungarian political tensions within the country and on the international level are well known in Europe. Moreover, today migrants from the East—especially from Russia, Ukraine, Romania, China, Vietnam, and Southeast Asia—are another emerging source of social and political tensions. It is in this context of "orthodox insiders" and "foreign outsiders" that I make the following four observations about the story of Jesus' interaction with the centurion.

First, the centurion's attitude is the example of faith to be followed. He asks for healing not for himself or his family, but rather for a person of lower rank. The centurion must also humble himself by coming to an itinerant Jewish preacher. His faith is attitude in action, demonstrating a strong social and human empathy. Reading through the eyes of my sociocultural context, the strangers coming from the East coincide with the centurion. These migrants take care of each other. They have good, close relationships and a newcomer is never left out. Their mutual support is incomparable with the growing selfish relations of the individuals of my society. For example, the increasing number of older persons left alone in various institutions is alarming. There is no one to take care of them; people are not taking care of their parents and grandparents. The strangers (the migrants from Russia, Belarussia, Ukraine, and so forth) are the ones who help them. Whose faith is better? Those who go regularly to church but forget parents in hospices or those who are close to each other and more significantly take care of the parents and grandparents of strangers? The stranger is pictured as a challenge to Christians of all times.

Second, being Christian and hating any nation or nationality is an absurd contradiction. There are two basic political streams. The nationally (Slovakian) oriented Christians who openly despise those who are not ours (Hungarians, migrants). On the other side, there are the silent Christians who are not standing up fully for the truth and rights of others. In my reading, Jesus' judgment on the sons of the Kingdom in verse 12 points to the false self-esteem of the righteous and orthodox: they have no compassion for the aliens, which will cause them to be cast out. Moreover, such attitude lowers the cultural and moral profile of the nation as such. So besides their eternal fate (thrown into outer darkness), it brings about political and cultural condemnation here and now.

Third, Jesus' immediate positive answer to the centurion's request challenges our attitudes toward aliens. To ignore a stranger on any level of life equals ignoring Jesus himself, who did not despise or disregard strangers and outcasts. Jesus broke the cultural and social boundaries. So should Christians in Slovakia (and elsewhere).

Finally, Jesus' attitude absolutely challenges a kind of "traditional" understanding of faith, that is, ritualism. Unfortunately, the quality of Christian faith is still measured by church attendance, while the social, political, and cultural impacts of faith are seen as something accidental. The opposite ought to be case. This is the first instance where Matthew uses the term "faith." It is significant since the unfolding of the concept of discipleship and faith starts here. To be Jesus' true disciple requires having both the stranger's attitude and Jesus' openness to the stranger.

Róbert Jáger is lecturer and researcher in New Testament Studies in the Faculty of Theology Aloisinianum, University of Trnava; and priest of the Greek Catholic diocese of Kosice, Slovakia.

QUESTIONS

1. Critique Stærk's discussion of the difference between "faith" and "trust." How would you discuss faith and trust in terms of your own life?
2. In addition to the benefits that West and Zengele mention, what are some potential challenges and difficulties, indeed risks, of conducting Contextual Bible Studies?
3. What are some reasons one might give for favoring the biblical version of the miracle narratives over the qur'anic version? And vice versa?
4. How might one challenge Jáger's reading of the biblical text? For instance, is the centurion acting selflessly and humbly?

CHAPTER 32

JOHN 1–10, 16

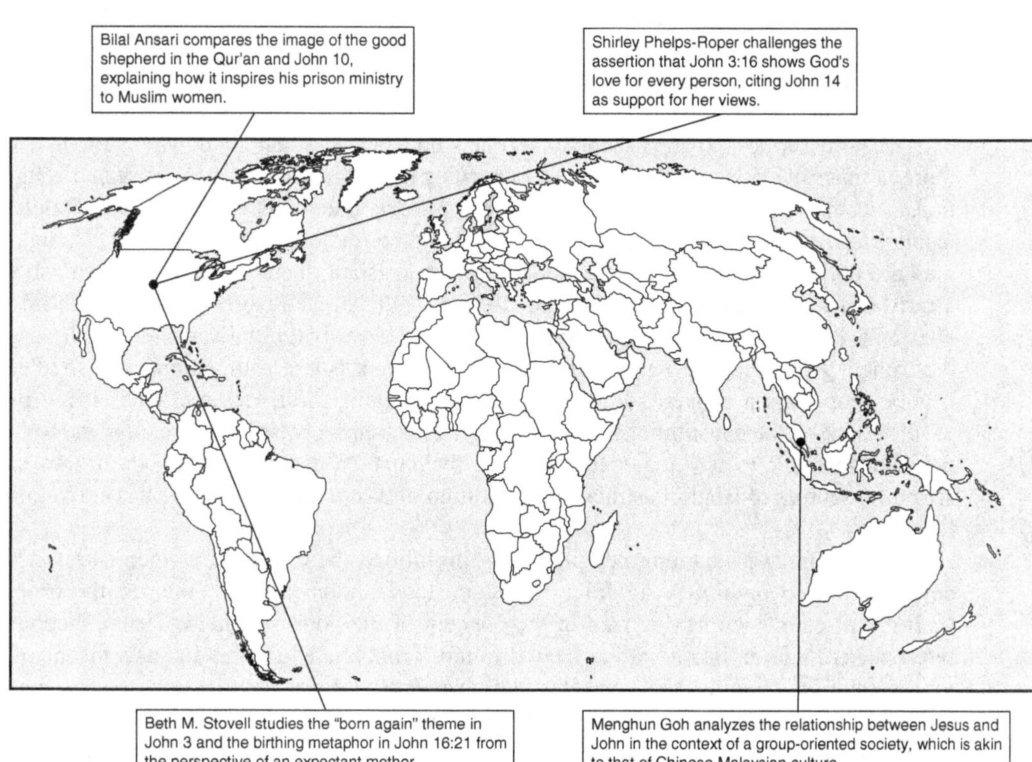

Bilal Ansari compares the image of the good shepherd in the Qur'an and John 10, explaining how it inspires his prison ministry to Muslim women.
Shirley Phelps-Roper challenges the assertion that John 3:16 shows God's love for every person, citing John 14 as support for her views.
Beth M. Stovell studies the "born again" theme in John 3 and the birthing metaphor in John 16:21 from the perspective of an expectant mother.
Menghun Goh analyzes the relationship between Jesus and John in the context of a group-oriented society, which is akin to that of Chinese Malaysian culture.

READINGS

The Image of the Good Shepherd as Inspiration for a Prison Minister
Bilal Ansari

Jesus and John the Baptist in the Context of a Group-Oriented Society
Menghun Goh

A Mother's Perspective on the "Born Again" Theme and the Birthing Metaphor
Beth M. Stovell

Does God Really Love Everyone?
Shirley Phelps-Roper

THE IMAGE OF THE GOOD SHEPHERD AS INSPIRATION FOR A PRISON MINISTER

Bilal Ansari (United States)

Shepherding is the sacred, theoretical, and practical metaphor used to explain the ministry of pastoral care in both Hebrew and Christian scriptures. In the Gospel of John, Jesus identifies with the concept of the good shepherd, reminding his audience of the prophetic call and covenant of care, "I am the Good Shepherd; and I know and recognize My own, and My own know and recognize Me" (10:14). The teachings of Islam also employ the good shepherd metaphor, which for me is a call lived out through American prison ministry, specifically pastoral care for Muslim women behind bars.

Jesus describes the good shepherd as one who would risk and lay down his life to care for those in times of crisis and need (10:11). Observing the lack of religious ministry and congregational worship for Muslim women in American prisons, one might conclude that Islam has no parallel for Jesus' concept of the good shepherd and no tradition of pastoral care. Though only men are obligated to attend congregational prayer in Islam, there are religious texts showing clearly that women are not to be prevented from congregational worship. Yet, prison ministry is extended only to Muslim men in American prisons. So why do I uncharacteristically care for the "other" gender behind bars when there is no apparent Islamic obligation to do so? Perhaps it is because I am a convert and my Christian upbringing influences me. Or is it my pledge of allegiance to the constitutional "free exercise of religion clause" that compels me to be the only Muslim male to accept a contract to care for female Muslim inmates? No. In fact, sacred scriptural sources of Islam illustrate a rich tradition of pastoral care which is my motivation and inspiration.

The prophet Muhammad emphatically prohibited the denial of women's free right to congregational worship. As in John 10, Islam does wholeheartedly embrace the prophetic tradition of care as contextualized in the concept of the good shepherd. Jesus' shepherding reference is found in Islam both as a condition of prophetic education and as a means of pastoral formation. Imam Bukhari narrates in his *Sahih of al Bukhari* collection two relevant narratives: one that places the profession of shepherding as a prerequisite of all prophets and the other that illustrates its essential elements. In one narration in volume 7, a person addresses the prophet Muhammad saying, "(O Messenger of God!) Have you ever shepherded sheep?" He said, "There has been no prophet but has shepherded them" (Book 65, Hadith #364). John 10:2 analogously explains this, "He who enters by the door is the shepherd of the sheep." In Islam the doorway is understood as inner piety and outer conformity to the teachings of the Qur'an and Sunna of the prophet Muhammad. The second narrative in volume 1 clearly explains that the entrance door of the good shepherd is spiritual care of the heart: "I heard the Messenger of God as having said this: He who guards against doubtful things keeps his religion and honour blameless, and he who indulges in doubtful things indulges in fact in unlawful things, just as a shepherd who pastures his animals round a preserve will soon pasture them in it" (Book 2, Hadith #49).

It is evident that Jesus' references to the good shepherd in John 10:11 and 14 are echoes of earlier scripture from Prophet David in Psalms 23 and 28:8. Jesus described the courageous ability to care for others in a crisis as a quality of good shepherding and the lack of that care in the shepherd as other than true pastoral care (John 10:12). And comparing how the Hebrew scriptures present the prophet Moses with the qur'anic presentation, we find that the story of

Moses in the Qur'an is told more often than any other prophetic narrative, marking the importance of Moses to Islamic thought and practice. The prophet Muhammad—before congregational worship was made law for anyone—was given the Islamic scriptural references of the good shepherd in the story of Moses. In the Qur'an, a chapter called The Narratives (28:22–28) describes at length Moses' crisis, qualities of care, and his formation as a good shepherd just before his prophetic calling. In the Hebrew Bible a comparative description of this narrative is given in Exodus 2:15–21. Both of these narratives relate to John 10:16 in that Moses proactively seeks to care for the women shepherds and their flock, until God made their flock his flock by employing him as shepherd, and this led to Moses hearing God's voice and heeding His call. Islamic scripture showed the way of pastoral care in Islam is through the door of proactively caring for the well-being of women. This is supported and emphasized in qur'anic exegesis as the model of how to become a good shepherd and emphasizes that Moses' pastoral formation and care lasted 10 years before his call from God.

Furthermore, the strong support for women's congregational worship is found in a *sahih* (reliable) hadith. This hadith refers to the very earliest Muslim community after the passing of the prophet Muhammad. It helped preserve women's free exercise of congregational worship when early Islamic law became established. 'Umar Ibn al Khattab, one of the early companions of the prophet Muhammad, became the second caliph of Islam (the second successor to Muhammad) and he essentially functioned as the supreme justice of the Muslim polity. 'Umar's son narrates an example from 'Umar's wife as an empowering example of women's right to congregational worship (and a prime element of the pastoral voice) in Islam. In *The Sahih of Imam Bukhari* (volume 2, book 13, number 23), 'Ibn (son of) 'Umar narrates:

> One of the wives of 'Umar ('Ibn Al-Khattab) used to offer the early dawn and the late evening prayer in congregation in the mosque (at a time when it was completely dark and quite dangerous on the streets). She was asked why she had come out for the prayer as she knew that her husband 'Umar disliked it, and he has great (self-respecting jealousy). She replied, "What prevents him (my husband and supreme justice of Islam) from stopping me from this act?" The other replied, "The statement of the Messenger of God: 'Do not stop God's women from going to God's Mosques' prevents him."

To my mind, in this narrative the prophet Muhammad succinctly conveyed the compassionate pastoral care tradition of the good shepherd to those who followed him just as Moses, David, and Jesus had before him. Muslim women behind bars should be allowed congregational worship and pastoral care. We know good shepherding in Islam and claim it as our own, a continuity that exists in Islamic scripture with the earlier Hebrew Bible and the Gospel of John. The strong pastoral voice in Islam can be witnessed in the foundational texts of Islam itself, but it is only heard by hearts who perceive that voice as the *central* voice and who preserve the good shepherd metaphor as a *normative* model for the spiritual guidance of Muslims, both male and female.

Bilal Ansari is the son of a Christian minister and Muslim imam; he currently serves as an Islamic Faith Leader for the U.S. Department of Justice, Bureau of Prisons, at the Federal Correction Institution in Danbury, Connecticut, a female prison.

Jesus and John the Baptist in the Context of a Group-Oriented Society

Menghun Goh (Malaysia)

The world of the Gospel of John—indeed the biblical world in general—was a group-oriented society in which acquiring honor and being shamed affected one's social identity and status in the community. To a large extent, a person's worth and credibility were often tied to her or his group membership. If the group, especially the leader(s), had a good reputation, its group members would also have similar honor. The identity of the group and its members were closely intertwined. As such, the notions of honor and shame, whether acquired or inherited, permeate such spheres as economics, culture, sexuality, politics, ethics, and religion. Living in such a world, one would want to accrue, or at least maintain, honor and avoid words and deeds that can bring shame to one's group. One's actions affect not only one's own person but also the public reputation of her or his friends and family for generations. For instance, in John, the Jews insistently claim that they are from the lines of Abraham (8:31–41) and Moses (9:28–29)—this bolsters their honor and credibility. Likewise, Nathanael's reply "can anything good come out of Nazareth" illustrates the concept of group shame (1:46).

This type of group-oriented way of thinking also informs the worldview of many Chinese Malaysians. A Chinese (Confucian) sociocultural value highly regards the teacher figure. A Chinese proverb says, "Even if the person teaches me just one day he will be my father-like figure for life." Thus, when someone shows disrespect toward her or his teacher, it not only shames the person but also her or his family and close associates. The idea is that if the family has taught the person well, she or he will not disregard the teacher. Furthermore, those who remain in close contact with such a person (can only) suggest that they too think and behave similarly; otherwise they would not be associated. It is through this group-oriented lens that I offer a few comments on the relationship between Jesus and John the Baptist as it is presented in the Gospel of John. Indeed, in light of my background and context, it is only natural (and valuable) for me to focus on the identities of Jesus and John as they are linked to their groups via honor and shame.

The first thing that strikes us about the Jesus–John dynamic is that John is continuing to baptize (3:22–4:3), even after John has explained that his understanding of water baptism is to manifest Jesus to Israel (1:31). This is odd. Upon the revelation of Jesus, one might expect John to stop baptizing and work with the Jesus movement. It is therefore ironic that even though John continued to baptize, this Gospel, unlike the Synoptics, does not attribute to him "the Baptist" title. After all, did 1:6–8 not say that God sent John to witness so that he might testify for Jesus and so that all might believe *through* him? This "through" shows the importance of John as a medium or witness for *all* to believe in Jesus.

The significance of "testifying" in the Gospel of John is noteworthy when we find that almost half of the occurrences of witnessing in the New Testament appear in this book (33 of 76 times). Likewise, the content of witnessing occurs 14 times, out of 37 times in the New Testament. If witnessing in the Gospel, which requires firsthand knowledge, is related not only to testifying to facts but also to confessing and proclaiming the truth, then it is puzzling that—although two of John's disciples followed Jesus upon hearing John's witness (1:35–42)—John's other disciples felt envy when they saw "all" people going to Jesus (3:26). In fact, not only does the Gospel say that the disciples confirm John's witness for Jesus in their complaint (3:26), it also has John forcefully say to them that "you yourselves testify for me that I said *I am not* the Christ" (3:28)! Jesus' retort to those who wanted to rejoice in John's light despite John's witness for Jesus is also puzzling (5:33–36; cf. 2:24–25). It appears that even though John's witness about Jesus is true (10:41–42), the Gospel portrays Jesus as not trusting human witness.

Several comments are in order. First, the Gospel reduces John's baptism to witnessing (contra the Synoptics). Such reduction heightens the significance of baptism; without it Jesus would not be revealed to Israel (1:31–34). John 4:1–3 further links baptism with discipleship. Second, if witnessing requires firsthand experience, then how could John witness effectively if he and his movement remained separated from the Jesus movement?

Third, in a collective honor-and-shame society, it is unlikely for one to be honored while the other in the same or related group shamed. For the Gospel, John must be a very honorable figure (cf. 1:19–28; 5:33–35); otherwise it would not have him witness for Jesus. Yet, the Jesus and John movements do not seem to work together. Besides the public tensions in 3:22–26, the attempts to "subordinate" John (1:6–9; 5:33–40; 10:40–42), and the mention of John's disciples following Jesus while John and many other disciples did not (1:39ff) show conflicts between the groups. In a "limited good" worldview, moreover, John's saying in 3:30 that Jesus must increase and he must decrease could give bad press for the Jesus movement. Who would want someone testifying for him to become less while he himself becomes greater? In a group-oriented society, it is more likely that the related individuals and groups either increase together or decrease together. Further, if the Pharisees revered John, it is puzzling that they would criticize and even plot against Jesus to whom John bore witness. Lastly, the conversation in 3:26–28 seems like a double-edged sword that highlights not only the misunderstanding and unwillingness of John's disciples to receive his witness concerning Jesus but also John's competence and authority as a revered *rabbi*.

Given this ambivalent portrayal of John and his disciples from the perspective of *collective* honor-and-shame sociocultural values, the tension between the Jesus and John movements thus also suggests the conflict between Jesus and John. As we cannot easily separate the individual identity from her or his associated groups, our interpretation cannot simply focus on individual figures without considering their social positions in the groups with which they are associated. Now if the text does (re)present the tension between Jesus and John, we cannot help but ask about the role and function of John in the Gospel, especially when John is the figure whom Jesus refers to the most in the four Gospels. This question is noteworthy because if John's witness can bolster the credibility of the Jesus movement, the ambiguity and ambivalence in his words and deeds can also engender unease and suspicion toward the movement. It is therefore not too surprising that the Gospel tells us that while Jesus acknowledges John's witness, he is also troubled by it (5:33ff). In the end, the Gospel tells us that the ultimate witness, and hence honor, comes from God, who honors those who honor God, despite the fact that such honoring may dishonor the social norms and bring shame to oneself (5:36–44). This conception of honor and shame that is not bound by social conventions reminds Chinese Malaysians not to absolutize our framework of honor-and-shame values, especially when it can become hierarchical, and thus, discriminating and stifling to the betterment and transformation of life.

Menghun Goh is writing his dissertation in the Department of New Testament & Early Christianity at Vanderbilt University, United States; he lived in Kuala Lumpur (Malaysia) for 18 years.

A Mother's Perspective on the "Born Again" Theme and the Birthing Metaphor

Beth M. Stovell (United States)

In Nicodemus' encounter with Jesus in John 3, being "born again" or "born from above" by the Spirit is the central theme. While many have discussed the idea of "spiritual rebirth," this passage has not been read in light of the actual experience of childbirth. Here I will offer a reading of John 3 through the eyes of expectant mothers and mothers who have recently given birth, and compare this passage on birth in the Spirit to other passages in the Old and New Testament that discuss birth.

As any mother knows, birthing can be a terrifying and dangerous experience; it brings a woman near to death for the sake of creating a new life. This experience of crisis in birth was even more terrifying in the ancient context, where women frequently died during childbirth, and, even more frequently, babies died in the process. Expectant mothers often felt greater anxiety as the birth approached, not knowing exactly when the birth would take place or whether they or their child would survive. When an expectant mother or a mother who had recently given birth approaches the biblical text, such experiences could not help but come to the forefront of her mind.

Throughout the Bible, God is depicted with maternal and birthing metaphors. In the Old Testament, God's descriptions as mother or as one giving birth are often juxtaposed with traditionally male metaphors such as God as Divine Warrior, God as Father, God as Artisan, and God as Husband. For example, in Isaiah 42 Yahweh is described like a birthing mother calling out and like a warrior yelling a battle cry. The authors of the New Testament also use the metaphors of childbearing and mothering in various ways, including: describing the birthing role of the Spirit (John 3:3–8), of Jesus Christ (1 Peter 1:3, 23; 1 John 2:29; James 1:18), and of God in spiritual transformation (1 John 3:9; 4:7; 5:4; 5:18); predicting the effect of Jesus' death and resurrection on the disciples (Matthew 24:8; Mark 13:8; John 16:21); describing the relationship between the disciples and the Church (1 Thessalonians 2:7); and discussing birth by the flesh versus birth by the Spirit (Galatians 4:29; John 3:6).

These other uses of birthing metaphors provide insight into the use of the birthing metaphors in John 3. Here the Spirit is the giver of a second birth that leads to seeing and entering the kingdom of God. This birth is contrasted with physical birth in two ways: first, through Nicodemus' somewhat humorous question regarding returning to one's mother's womb as an old person, and second, through the differentiation Jesus provides between birth of the Spirit and birth of the flesh. As is typical of John's theology, this differentiation is more than simply a differentiation between spiritual and physical birth. It is describing the believer's need to be born anew through cleansing.

Yet, should this new birth given by the Spirit be understood as purely "spiritual" and in no way connected to physical childbirth? What is included in this second birth? Reading this passage in light of the experience of childbirth provides a way of considering this passage anew. In the Old Testament, the metaphor of childbirth is associated with universal and personal crisis and includes the possibility of pain and death. When dealing with John 3, this element of the metaphor is often overlooked; yet elsewhere in John's Gospel the same understanding of childbirth as a metaphor for crisis is present. For example, in John 16:21, Jesus describes the experience of his death and resurrection as being like a woman who when she is giving birth has pain because "her hour has come" (which echoes "his hour had come" in reference to Jesus' death), but when her child is born, she does not continue to recall her pain (even if she remembers it), because now she has the joy of the newborn child.

The language used in John 16:21 mirrors the language used in Isaiah 42:14 by the use of the same verb "to give birth." In the same way that Yahweh is pictured like "one giving birth" in Isaiah 42:14, the experience of Jesus' death will be for the disciples like a woman who "gives birth." John 16:21 also uses language that echoes John 3's discussion of "birth from the Spirit" with its use of the verb "born." The ability to enter the kingdom in John 3 through the "birth" of Spirit is also similar to John 16 which compares the experience of the joy following the resurrection to the joy of when a child is "born."

Reading with an awareness of the echoes between John 3 and John 16 helps correct the general conception of the birth metaphor in John 3. Many commentaries speak of the "birth" in John 3 as simple and painless because it is spiritual rather than physical, as though a spiritual stork dropped the child off in a nice neat package. Yet it is unlikely an ancient reader would have read the birth metaphor apart from its original implications of crisis, particularly if the reader were a mother or mother-to-be. Even Nicodemus' response suggests that ancient readers would think of physical childbirth when they read John 3. Jesus' clarification that this birth is spiritual and not physical does not necessarily remove the implications of possible pain and/or crisis. Metaphors often move from an original physical referent (like physical birth) to something more abstract (like spiritual birth), and to understand the metaphor, one must understand the physical referent first.

In fact, two other indicators in the passage suggest that pain and crisis may be a part of the metaphorical entailments of being "born again" of the Spirit. First, Jesus' description of the movement of the Holy Spirit as unexpected in terms of its comings and goings may reflect the unexpectedness of the birth process. There is a sense of expectancy in labor and a constant sense of unknowing. In ancient times, one did not know specifically when labor would occur. The same is true for mothers today. The baby comes when it wants and with it comes the pain of childbirth, but also (as Jesus points out in John 16:15) the expectation of great joy to follow.

Another indicator of the pain and crisis involved is how the metaphor of birth is joined to the metaphor of the Son of Man being "lifted up" for the purpose of "eternal life." Repeatedly in John, this concept of the Son of Man being lifted up refers to the hour of Jesus' death, that is, his "lifting up" upon the cross by crucifixion. The reader is told that this is the means by which "everyone who believes will have eternal life in him." Not surprisingly, birth and life are interweaving metaphors, but this second birth and this eternal life must be precipitated by Jesus' death and suffering on the cross. Similar to John 16, this picture of death and resurrection, suffering and exaltation of the Son of Man should be understood as part of the underlying imagery of the second birth pictured in John 3.

This has particular impact as one continues reading John 3 and sees the description of the Father giving his Son in John 3:16. When one thinks in terms of the potential loss of life inherent in childbirth and then combines this with the notion of inheritance, the idea of God the Great King giving his one and only Son highlights the dashed hopes that families felt frequently with the death of a newborn son. Such a hope was writ large in the situation of ruling families. For the Father to give up his only Son could potentially mean the loss of every hope, yet the second-half of John 3:16 immediately turns this possible loss into absolute hope. Because this Father has given *his only Son*, all other fathers and mothers have the hope of *their children* never perishing.

Beth M. Stovell is Assistant Professor in Biblical Studies in the School of Theology and Ministry at St. Thomas University, Miami Gardens, Florida, United States.

DOES GOD REALLY LOVE EVERYONE?

Shirley Phelps-Roper (United States)

God loves everyone is *the* single greatest lie that man or Satan has ever told and John 3:16 is always cited as support for it. It is the central theology of all phony Christians worldwide. Have you questioned how many times the actual words "God loves everyone" appear in the Bible? Or who said these words? Or how many times Jesus said, "God loves everyone"? As a matter of uncontroverted fact, the phrase "God loves everyone" never appears in the Bible. Period. In other words, the most famous Christian notion of God of our time—repeated without measure or limit in this sinful and adulterous generation—NEVER APPEARS IN THE BIBLE!

What about John 3:16? Does it say anything remotely close to "God loves everyone"? Of course it does not! It says, "For God so loved the world that he gave his only begotten Son..." The word translated "world" is the Greek word *kosmos*. It does not refer specifically to humans, certainly not to all humans, and certainly not you individually. In my experience most of the faux-Christians who cite John 3:16 stop halfway through the verse. This is where they would like the verse to stop. Here is the part they leave out: "*that whosoever* believeth in him should not perish, but have everlasting life."

It is clear, then, that if you do not believe, you do not obtain everlasting life and in fact Christ says just two verses later that you are "condemned already" (3:18). That's right; many of this world are walking dead men, condemned to eternal damnation and in the fullness of time will land in hell as condemned men! What does Christ say about the condemnation of man as John 3 continues? He states "that men love darkness rather than light because their deeds were evil," and "*everyone that* doeth evil hateth the light, neither cometh to the light, lest his deeds should be reproved" (vv. 19–20). The Holy Spirit closes John 3 in a dramatic and unambiguous fashion that blows straight to hell the notion that God loves everyone: "He that believeth on the Son hath everlasting life: *and he that believeth not the Son shall not see life; but the wrath of God abideth on him.*" God's hatred is his perfect determination to send the unrepentant to hell for eternity.

Satan concocted "God loves everyone" to ensnare the ungodly and the children of disobedience to believe there is no accountability in this life or the life to come for their filthy sins. The Prince of the Power put it in the hands of sinful men so they could multiply their stupid words to obfuscate the Consuming Fire's great Day of Judgment. But Satan, the great deceiver, says there is no wrath coming! This generation thinks the mere assertion of "God loves everyone" will wash away their adultery, fornication, sodomy, idol worship, abortion, murder, thefts, and drunken reveling. Here is what the servants of God say with all their hearts: "RUN! THIS DOOMED AMERICAN THEATER IS ON FIRE! RUN! FLEE THE WRATH TO COME!"

"God loves everyone," really? Here is how it all turns out according to Revelation 21:8: "But the fearful (cowardly Christians), and unbelieving (Jews, Muslims, Hindus, etc.), and the abominable (Sodomites), and murders (abortionists, the military, and criminals), and whoremongers (fornicators, adulterers, Sodomites), and sorcerers (drug addicts, alcoholics, witches), and idolaters (those that make and worship graven images and bow down to Santa Clause and the like), and all liars shall have their part in the lake which burns with fire and brimstone: which is the second death." God obviously does not love these people whom he daily torments in the fiery lake of hell.

So who is to blame for this bogus reading of John 3:16 and the proliferation of the "God loves everyone" lie? The pastors of this generation are to blame! They are paid fat salaries and fat pensions to lie and to gloss over the sins of fornication, homosexuality, remarriage after divorce, killing on the battlefield, and paying homage to all forms of godless consumerism. God condemns the preachers that scatter his flock, just as he condemned the false prophets in Old Testament times (e.g., Jeremiah 5 and 23).

It was not always so.

The famous American Puritan and Congregationalist pastor Jonathan Edwards (1703–1758) wrote about God's wrath as God's dominant characteristic in his sermon "Sinners in the Hands of an Angry God":

> The God that holds you over the pit of hell, much as one holds a spider, or some loathsome insect over the fire, abhors you, and is dreadfully provoked: his wrath towards you burns like fire... You are ten thousand times more abominable in his eyes, than the most hateful venomous serpent is in ours. O sinner! Consider the fearful danger you are in: it is a great furnace of wrath, a wide and bottomless pit, full of the fire of wrath, that you are held over in the hand of that God.

Edwards as representative for his generation took the Bible seriously and concluded that God hates people. You may have heard it said that "God hates sin, but loves the sinner." The Bible never says that anywhere. That is yet another lie propagated by wicked Christian leaders. Not only is God's hate of sinners implied in his wrath toward them, but God explicitly states that he hates workers of iniquity in texts such as Psalm 5:5. Furthermore, God simply appoints some humans for his hatred, having done neither good nor evil, before they were born, in order to fulfill God's purpose. God, for instance, declares his hatred for Esau in both Malachi 1 and Romans 9. The Bible not only does not say that "God loves everyone," but it includes assertions to the contrary: God hates some people (some before they were even born).

So, who does God love? From one end of the Bible to the other, including in the Gospel of John, we find one repeated answer: Those who obey God. Among the many passages we could cite are John 14:21, "He that hath my commandments, and keepeth them, he it is that loveth me" and 14:23, "If a man love me, he will keep my words: and my Father will love him."

God loves only those who believe in Him and obey His commandments. The rest will burn in eternal torment. Therefore, run from the "God loves everyone" farce, as your soul depends upon it!

Shirley Phelps-Roper is an attorney and servant of the God of all creation in the last minutes of the last days.

QUESTIONS

1. In light of Ansari's observations concerning Islamic texts and traditions, speculate as to why there is "a lack of religious ministry" for Muslim women in prison.
2. How does a group-oriented, honor–shame culture compare to your cultural context?
3. Reread the story of Nicodemus in light of Stovell's observations. What "spiritual pain" might be involved in being "born again"?
4. Assess Phelps-Roper's reading of the biblical text. How would the "wicked preachers" of this generation respond to her?

CHAPTER 33

GOSPEL OF JOHN

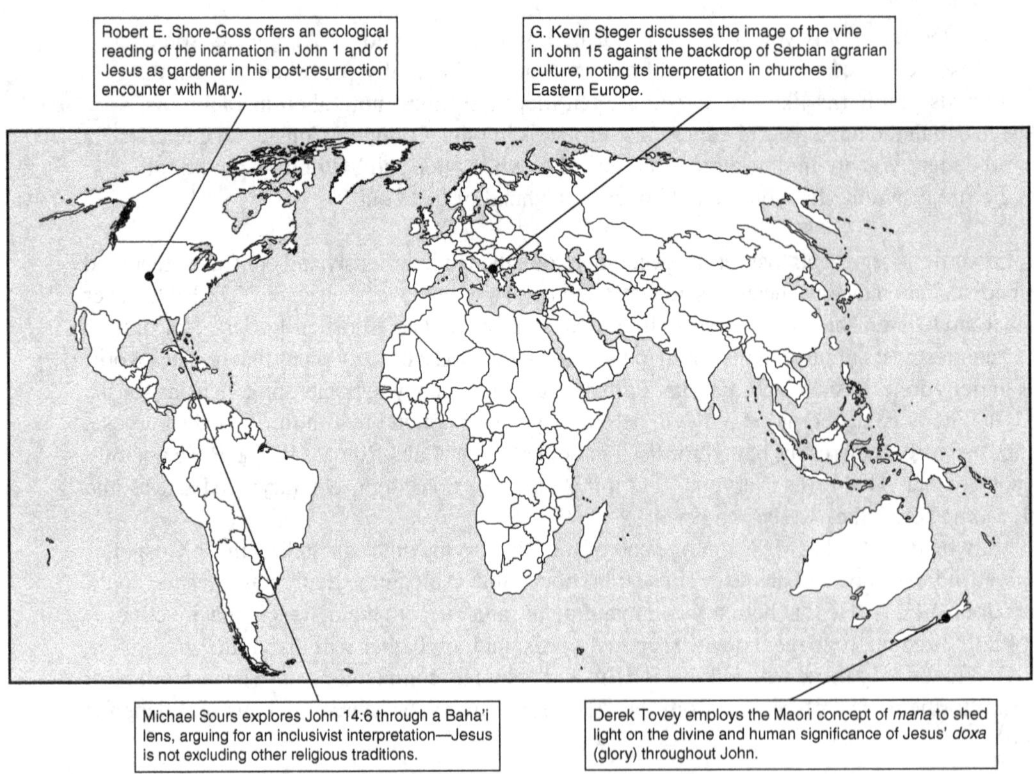

Robert E. Shore-Goss offers an ecological reading of the incarnation in John 1 and of Jesus as gardener in his post-resurrection encounter with Mary.
G. Kevin Steger discusses the image of the vine in John 15 against the backdrop of Serbian agrarian culture, noting its interpretation in churches in Eastern Europe.
Michael Sours explores John 14:6 through a Baha'i lens, arguing for an inclusivist interpretation—Jesus is not excluding other religious traditions.
Derek Tovey employs the Maori concept of *mana* to shed light on the divine and human significance of Jesus' *doxa* (glory) throughout John.

READINGS

An Ecological Reading of John 1 and Jesus as Gardener in His Encounter with Mary
Robert E. Shore-Goss

The Image of the Vine against the Backdrop of Serbian Agrarian Culture
G. Kevin Steger

An Inclusivist Interpretation of John 14:6 through a Baha'i Lens
Michael Sours

The Maori Concept of *Mana* as a Vehicle for Understanding *Doxa* in John
Derek Tovey

An Ecological Reading of John 1 and Jesus as Gardener in His Encounter with Mary

Robert E. Shore-Goss (United States)

The Green Christ of Breton Cavalry painted by French artist Paul Gauguin in 1889 depicts the women at the cross taking down the body of Jesus. The painting is embedded in the wild Breton landscape of France where Christ's body is green, prophetically signifying that his death was green—bringing life to the interconnected network of life. I have found this painting profoundly symbolic with a human Christ within a "this-worldly" landscape and incarnationally embedded in the ecological network of life. *The Green Christ* is interwoven with the Breton landscape, and his green coloring signifies growth and life for all. Women and the Earth herself accept the crucified and ravaged body of Christ. For me, Gauguin's Green Christ prompts me to read anew John's Gospel from an environmentally green context.

A number of environmental Christian theologians read the incarnation in John's Gospel (1:14) from an ecological context. It has produced ecologically sensitive readings of the scriptures. For example, New Zealand theologian Neil Darragh (*At Home in the Earth* [Auckland: Ascent Publications, 2000], 124) comments on consequences of "the Word becoming flesh" to the biosphere, the web of interrelated ecological relationships that make up the Earth: "To say that God became flesh is not only to say that God became human but to say also that God became an Earth creature, that God became a sentient being, that God became a living being, that God became a complex Earth unit of minerals and fluids, that God became an item in the carbon and nitrogen cycles."

The incarnated Christ became a part of the Earth's ecosystem. God's incarnation became a deep incarnation into the fleshy biological life of the Earth, to include human bodies and all the bodies of other creatures and plants themselves, and is now evolving creation in a radically new way. God becomes incarnated from microscopic level to the macro-biosphere of the Earth. God communicates God's divine life to all flesh. This conforms to the theology of Ireneaus that "God became human so humanity can become divine." God's incarnation finds its dramatic apex in the death and resurrection of Jesus, specifically in the story of Mary Magdalene at the garden tomb (20:10–18).

On the first day of the week, Mary Magdalene discovers the stone of the tomb of Jesus rolled away. Mary looks into the tomb to see two angels in white, one sitting at the head of Jesus and the other at the feet. They ask her, "Woman, why are you weeping?" Magdalene responds, "They have taken away my Lord, and I do not know where they have laid him." Mary's epiphany vision deepens with her longing. The narrative possibly alludes to Song of Songs 3:1–4, where a dark-skin woman searches for her male lover, asking the city guards if they have seen her lover. Earlier allusion to the Song of Songs is found with the spices of "myrrh and aloe" used to anoint the dead body of Jesus. The same combination of the spices is found in the description of the dark-skin woman in Song of Songs 4:14. Magdalene's longing to find the human body of her Lord within a garden furthers my ecological reading of the narrative. Magdalene's yearning for her Lord is shared by green Christians who identify the body of Christ with the Earth.

The polyvalent symbolism of the garden tomb is reminiscent of Jesus' parable "unless a grain of wheat falls into the earth, it just remains a single grain; but if dies, it bears much fruit" (12:24). The garden tomb is a liminal space that reenacts the parable—where death and life are symbolically mingled, bearing the fruit of eternal life.

In one of the beautiful scenes of mistaken identity, Mary supposes that the risen Jesus is the gardener. She pleads, "Sir if you have carried him away, tell me where you have laid him, and I will take him away." What if in her misperception of the risen Christ, Mary spoke prophetically that the risen Jesus is indeed the gardener. Eco-theologian Edward Echlin writes, "Mary's initially mistaking Jesus for the gardener is profound irony with many connotations. Jesus in fact is the Gardener, the New Adam, as the open side on the cross intimates, Master of the garden earth, the One in whom, with whom and under whom all human gardeners garden" (*The Cosmic Circle: Jesus and Ecology* [Dublin: Columba Press, 2004], 125–126).

Jesus appears to her in the garden, symbolic of Eden restored to a new fullness and the cosmos coming to life fully within God. She recognizes the gardener as her Teacher only when he calls her by name. She is the disciple that Jesus predicts in John 16:20 who will "weep and mourn" and have pain turned into joy. Her inclination is to touch or to cling on to Christ. She holds on to Jesus but Jesus tells her that she cannot continue to hold this way as his resurrection transformation is not completed until his body becomes transformed from one plane of existence into the entire ecosystem. The resurrection of Jesus is not only the radical transformation of the crucified Christ but the "green" transformation of all things in God. All things become interconnected through the risen Christ as he is the vine connected to the branches and God is the vinegrower (John 15). This strengthens the irony of the mistaken identity of Jesus as the gardener. The risen Christ now assumes the divine position of vinegrower or gardener.

Resurrection is the final green event, a transfiguration of all things—an incarnational ripening and greening of human life and the cosmos. For John's community, there was no doubt that what God was doing for the whole cosmos and humanity had been done to Jesus in the dark hours before Easter dawn. In other words, gardening is a resurrection activity of God's Spirit, for what God did to Jesus, God has been doing from the beginning—saving and bringing life from death. God calls Jesus back into God's life to green the world.

Magdalene and the other disciples were called to follow in the steps of the gardening Christ. They were invited to participate in the important job of cocreating, coparticipating, and coliving with the Spirit in giving life to the garden and bringing that garden to the fullness God intends.

But our garden, the Earth, is dying, and human beings are responsible for killing the garden. All resources are required to heal, nurture, cultivate, and restore health to God's garden. In their drive for overconsumption and reckless disregard for long-term consequences of carbon emissions to the atmosphere, humanity has impacted our fragile ecosystems with global warming. There are fore-signs with shifting weather patterns, oceans warming and coral reefs dying, intense storms and floods, and rapid melting of the polar ice cap. In watching the ABC graphic novel *2100*, my congregation was horrified by the possibilities of billions of climate refugees with oceans rising meters above current sea levels if we do not change our overconsumption of fossil fuels, develop alternative green technologies for power, and modify our lifestyles. As a result our church became one of the totally green churches in Los Angeles.

We are called to be healers of the wounds of the Earth—making amends for our sins of consumptive greed and heads in the sands. It starts with a personal conversion that began on Easter Sunday when Christ appeared to Magdalene in the garden and invited us to participate in the mission of caring for the Earth. Resurrection is about gardening the Earth and nurturing life on the Earth for God.

Robert E. Shore-Goss (Ph.D., Comparative Religion and Theology, Harvard University) is the gay Pastor of the MCC Church in the Valley; he is author of Jesus ACTED UP: A Gay and Lesbian Manifesto *and Queering Christ: Beyond Jesus ACTED UP.*

The Image of the Vine against the Backdrop of Serbian Agrarian Culture

G. Kevin Steger (Serbia)

My mother was raised on a farm in Northeast Texas. She had regular chores to do including stereotypical things like milking the cow and weeding the garden. She grew up with an understanding of the relationship man had with the land. My wife's parents were also raised on farms in East Bell County in central Texas. They grew up feeding the chickens and planting seeds in that seemingly miraculous black dirt that would grow anything. They developed calluses on their hands pruning cotton plants and picking that white gold, so they also understood the necessary connection man has with the land. Different from so many of my parents' generation, I grew up in town. I attended school, church, and cub scouts, all within a few blocks of our home in a nice neighborhood in the good part of town. The only connection I had to the land was that it tethered me to a lawnmower every Saturday whether I liked it or not. I remember asking my Sunday school teacher why Jesus taught so often with agricultural themes. The kind old Mr. Alex explained, "Well, it's because that's what the people knew." He continued, "Everyone in Jesus' day was dependent upon the produce of the land, so in one form or another, they were all connected to it."

I understood about as much as a 10-year-old could, but it would be many years later, as a young man stepping foot in Eastern Europe that I really began to understand the significance of passages like John 15:1–8. After visiting Serbia for the first time, I understood the significance of the image of the vine. The subsistence culture of so many in Serbia is directly tied to the land and its stewardship. Consequently, there is a deeper understanding of things like pruning and harvesting. On my way to Serbia, I passed through beautiful river valleys in Central Europe covered in vineyards that were initially planted by the Romans 2,000 years ago. Across Europe, wine and spirits are important parts of their culture, mainly because they are products of their ancient land. Each region has their own varietals of which they are very proud, having an understanding of the hard work involved in their production as well as the emotional investment in creating something uniquely their own. In Serbia, grapes are used certainly to make wine, but perhaps more importantly they are also used to make *Rakia*. *Rakia* is to the Serbian people what Vodka is to the Russians. Every family makes their own version and serves it in shots before every meal, including breakfast. They believe it promotes healthy digestion. The connection they feel to the fruit of the vine is an integral part of their identity as Serbs.

In John 15:1, Jesus explains to the disciples, after they have just shared the Last Supper, that He is the vine and His father is the gardener. He used this metaphor because the vineyard, the grapes, and the wines of the local area were an important part of the community's identity just like for the Serbs. They understood the sanctity of the growing process; therefore, Jesus chose the metaphor of the vineyard.

Jesus spent an incredible amount of time in his days on earth challenging the hypocrisy of the Pharisees. He was especially concerned that the Pharisees seemed more concerned about appearances than actual spirituality. Jesus' vine metaphor includes a sharp statement against hypocrisy stating that the gardener "cuts off any branch in me that does not bear fruit." According to Jesus, those who look as though they belong in the family of faith, those who seem to be attached to Him, if they bear no fruit, are cut off from the vine. Perhaps they were never actually part of the vine in the first place.

Eastern Europe's evangelical population is small. They are small because they must compete with the state-supported Orthodox Churches. Any religious group that does not fall into the very strict government definition of acceptable religious organizations is considered a cult. So, most of the evangelical groups in countries like Serbia and Bulgaria are considered a cult. They have no official classification or acceptance from the government.

Because the evangelical churches in Eastern Europe are often persecuted, their leadership places a high value on church identity. If a member of the church is bearing no fruit, they are confronted by the church leadership and encouraged to participate in the life of the church or be cut off. Church discipline is certainly encouraged in John 15, but few churches today genuinely practice it, except for these churches in Eastern Europe. While teaching a course at the Novi Sad Theological College in Novi Sad, Serbia, I became aware of a rather high-profile church disciplinary action in the area: One of the leaders in a prominent evangelical church was a wealthy businessman. In their annual review of contributions, the Board of Elders discovered that this man did not tithe. The elders confronted him and gave him an opportunity for repentance, which he disregarded. After some time passed, they made a further decision to excommunicate him. Across the larger evangelical community in the region there was general agreement that the action taken by the elders was not only appropriate but also necessary. Every member of the church—as a "branch" on the vine—has an important role to play, and if they are not participating, then they must not be a genuine Christ follower and are cast out from the fellowship. Those that remain "in the vine" are expected to bear fruit.

G. Kevin Steger (D.Ed.Min.) is the CEO/Founder of Light over Europe Ministries, Inc., an organization dedicated to the advancement of the Gospel of Jesus Christ all over the European Continent.

An Inclusivist Interpretation of John 14:6 through a Baha'i Lens

Michael Sours (United States)

I was baptized in the Church of England and spent my formative years growing up in the American "Bible Belt." In this Christian-dominated culture the Gospel was readily available and was ever present in daily conversations. However, by the time I was a teenager I began to learn about other faith communities, in particular Hinduism, Buddhism, and Islam. I became fascinated with Buddhist and Islamic art. I was impressed by the teachings of the Buddha and the anticlerical poetry of Muslim mystics like Hafez. But early in this journey of discovery, I learned that many of my Christian family and friends viewed my interests in other faiths as troubling. I was soon schooled in a conservative form of Christian exclusivism. Stated concisely, Jesus claimed that He was the only way to God, the only truth, the only life. Verses like John 14:6 were interpreted to mean that the followers of other faiths were lost, doomed to perish in Hell or in a lake of fire in the final days. Some of my Christian friends even believed this gruesome fate awaited other Christian denominations, such as Catholics and Mormons.

If it were possible to look beyond the confines of Christianity and find only God-haters perpetrating cruelty and injustice, reading John 14:6 in such an exclusive way might be easier. But this is not reality. There are people in other faraway places who are just as devoted to God, just as charitable and caring as Christians in Texas. In many parts of the world, deeply religious people pass their lives without ever hearing the message of the Gospel. In fact, this has been true for most of human history. Can it be that God is so uncharitable and His grace so limited that He cares so little for the souls He created? And would God judge harshly even those who have encountered Christianity and rejected it when it came to them alongside the barrel of a gun or with foreign diseases that decimated their populations and destroyed all that was dear to them? Why do some people get to learn about Christianity in the most favorable circumstances while others only encountered it in ways that would convey the opposite of Jesus' own example? I could not imagine that God would be less compassionate, less fair, and less understanding than mere human beings.

At an early age, the problem of religious pluralism became one of the central questions of my personal religious life. It was Bahá'u'lláh's answers to this problem that attracted me to the Baha'i Faith. At the core of Bahá'u'lláh's teachings is the belief in the oneness of religion. Bahá'u'lláh taught that all the religions have "proceeded from one Source, and are rays of one Light." But if they are one, why are they so different? He explained that each successive revelation unfolds in accordance with "the varying requirements of the ages in which they were promulgated." In effect, there is only one religion and Bahá'u'lláh's followers, the Bahá'ís—like Jews, Christians, Buddhists, Hindus, Zoroastrians, and Muslims—all belong to this same true religious heritage.

Buddha, Moses, Jesus, Muhammad, Bahá'u'lláh, and others were like the sun, shining light on all peoples each new day. We can give the sun a different name each day, but no matter how many days the sun sets and rises again, it is always the same sun. It is the same light that gives life wherever it shines. This more loving view of God explains both why religion is so universal and why some differences exist between them. And with these teachings in mind, I could understand why every Faith proclaimed itself as the "only way."

Many Christian friends were unsatisfied by such general explanations. They wanted me to reconcile my acceptance of other religions with the particular claims of Jesus Christ found in the Bible. Because Bahá'u'lláh presents a forceful defense of the Gospel in His writings, a Baha'i cannot brush aside Jesus' claim as unreliable. Bahá'u'lláh stresses that God's redemptive testimony is available to everyone. He ardently defends the Gospel against its critics who claim that the true record of Christ's teachings has been lost or corrupted. God protects and renews His redemptive message. It is a theological principle that can be applied to the scriptures of any Faith. And its truth is demonstrated in the spiritual efficacy of the message that still survives in the different holy books. All Faith communities have pious believers, remarkable leaders, inspired mystics, saints, and martyrs. And those personal transformations were inspired and informed by Scripture regarded as sacred and authoritative. If we argue that one community possesses the genuine Word of God and others do not, then where is the superiority of that sacred book over other books that have shown the same transformative powers?

Bahá'u'lláh provides the principles for reconciling the age-old claims that have divided the followers of other Faiths. And, for His followers, it becomes an act of faith to read the Scripture—all world Scriptures—through a lens that is free from cultural prejudices. Just as Christians have reconciled seemingly conflicting verses between different books because they regard them as holy and authoritative, a Baha'i can read the Scriptures of many faiths as the one Word of God. He writes, "Purge thy sight… from all earthly limitations, that thou mayest behold them all as the bearers of one Name, the exponents of one Cause, the manifestations of one Self, and the revealers of one Truth." If we can see past the outward names and cultural differences, we can come to know the Buddha in Christ and Christ in the Buddha. We can hear the same way, truth, and life—the same one voice of God speaking through them all.

When I read the Gospel of John, the book Christians cite most often to convey an exclusivist message, what stands out most is the Gospel's prologue that describes the Messiah, the "Christ," as a preexistent reality and light of the world. Jesus is both the historical Messiah, and also much more—the one divine Reality that transcends place and time. In His example, as recorded in the Gospel of John, Jesus lives a life of devotion to God, compassion, and self-sacrifice. He rejects materialism and violence, and urges social justice and virtuous living. In John's description of Jesus' significance and in the particulars of His teachings and example, Jesus provides a theological and ethical way for understanding His words, "I am the way, and the truth, and the life; no one comes to the Father but through Me." In context, Jesus is not making a distinction between Christianity and Judaism, or Christianity and Buddhism, or Christianity and any other religion, but a distinction between the Light he represents and the darkness of materialism, the ethical and virtuous way that leads to God and the ways that do not. It is a distinction between morality and immorality, between truth and falsehood, between love and hatred. It is about "the Way," "the Truth," "the Life," not about the different names used by Jews, Christians, Buddhists, or Muslims to designate the same reality. The context isn't other religions. Rather than rejecting Judaism, Jesus affirmed it. When he criticizes, it is the conduct of followers, not the Faith itself.

Understanding John 14:6 in this way liberates us from a view that inevitably reduces God to an image of our own prejudices. And, instead of feeling like the members of an exclusive and superior club, this interpretation calls us to live fuller and more meaningful lives as believers, whatever religious tradition we follow. Rather than a mere matter of ideological correctness or believing in a particular theology of Jesus or belonging to the right group with the right name, this interpretation means that the way of salvation requires that we follow Jesus' example. It is an interpretive approach that can be applied to similar "exclusivist" verses in the Scriptures of other Faith communities.

The oneness of God and the oneness of religions are central Baha'i teachings, and the promotion of fellowship between faith communities is important to the Baha'i mission of promoting world peace. This makes understanding these types of verses and being able to explain them important to Baha'is.

Michael Sours is a Baha'i and an award-winning author of a number of books on the relationship between Christianity and the Bahá'í Faith; he has been involved in many interfaith activities.

The Maori Concept of *Mana* as a Vehicle for Understanding *Doxa* in John

Derek Tovey (New Zealand)

Among the strategies and the rhetorical devices that the author of John uses to present his understanding of Jesus is his use of the concept and language of "glory" (*doxa*). This concept provides a way of establishing the status and honor of Jesus, both as a character in the story and as portrayed in the dynamics of the narrative, so that readers, by understanding Jesus' honor and status as both ascribed and achieved, may accept the Gospel's claim for Jesus as the Christ and as God's Son (20:30–31).

Here I examine the concept of *doxa* (glory) by drawing analogically upon the Maori concept of *mana*. Not only does this help to illuminate the Gospel's use of *doxa*, but it also provides a way of mediating the dichotomy between a "theological" understanding of Jesus' glory which emphasizes his divine status over against a "view from below," which sees that *doxa*, or "glory," as manifest in and through a human character. I must state at the outset that I write as a Pakeha (European) New Zealander, and I am very dependent upon secondary literature, by both Maori and non-Maori scholars, for my understanding of *mana*.

The noun, *doxa*, is used 18 times in John's Gospel (and the verbal form appears in a variety of cases and tenses 22 times). In ancient secular Greek, it had two basic meanings. One was "opinion" in the sense of the perspective or thoughts on a matter that one held and was prepared to defend. The other sense of *doxa* referred objectively to one's standing or repute in the eyes of others. This sense most likely contributed to its choice by the translators of the Greek Septuagint (LXX) to translate the Hebrew word *kabod*. This could refer to a person's status, importance, worth, dignity, rank, and position of power: It conveyed the sense of a person's *gravitas*, a person's inherent authority and prestige. In the Septuagint, *doxa* was also used of God's glory, and so represented God's radiance, and divine mode of being.

Mana, like *doxa*, is a big concept. It has a wide range of meanings that cannot quite be captured in English. To have *mana* is to be a person who has prestige, status, charisma, dignity, and influence. To have *mana* is to have authority and power of control (sovereignty) over people or something (like land), or to have authority and control in certain contexts. Furthermore, as a concept *mana* is closely associated with *tapu*, which itself has a range of meanings. It can refer to the fact that a person or thing is placed under a religious or spiritual restriction, so that the person or thing that is *tapu* is "holy," or even "consecrated" and "set apart," or that the person or thing is off-limits as "polluting," or "unclean," even "dangerous," depending on the context. The fundamental feature of *mana* is that it is ultimately something that is received from God (or "the gods" in ancient Maori understanding); the power from which *mana* is derived is spiritual and supernatural in nature.

It is important to understand that, though everyone is born with *mana* inherited from one's parents and inherent in being human, the degree of *mana* inherited depends upon one's parents' rank and social status. While individuals of high rank in ancient Maori society inherited an initial store of *mana* by birth, they could increase or decrease their *mana* by their own actions. Moreover, *mana* was also "given" to an individual by the community: It derived from the recognition and respect given to an individual by others. Hence, *mana* as a social value was both *ascribed* (by one's birth or primogeniture and by the recognition of others) and *achieved* by one's own actions and abilities.

The pertinence for our reading of John's Gospel in drawing an analogy between *mana* and the concept and language of *doxa* lies precisely in the way in which the concept of *mana* sees a link, or continuum, between the human and divine. In John, the *doxa*, or *mana*, of Jesus is seen "from below" through his works or "signs," for instance, as much as it is portrayed "from above" through the claims made by the narrator, or by Jesus himself. The narrative portrays honor as both ascribed to Jesus and as achieved by Jesus. As characters are challenged by Jesus to accept his status, or *mana*, as demonstrated by his works, so the reader is to understand and recognize Jesus' *mana* on the basis of the narrative.

The prologue in John 1:1–18 is, *par excellence*, an example of how the narrator outlines Jesus' ascribed honor, that is, his status as "the Word" who is the same as God, and who is, in fact, God's only begotten Son. Is it too much to say that this is the narrator's way of establishing Jesus' "primogeniture"? I would argue that the author of the Gospel begins precisely in this way in order to establish that Jesus' status as God's Son is ascribed. When the narrator says that the Word has "lived among us" and that "we have seen his glory, glory as of a father's only son" (1:14), he does not just mean that we have seen in him the divine splendor of God shining forth, but rather we have seen and come to understand his true status, we have recognized his *mana* as One who is one with the Father. This "oneness" with the Father is something that Jesus asserts again and again in the Gospel, in different ways and contexts. In John 17:5 we have an instance where Jesus directly claims this honor: "So now, Father, honor me in your own presence with that status/honor/*mana* that I had in your presence before the world existed."

It is the achieved, or acquired, status or honor of Jesus that the author is particularly concerned to convey to the reader. The signs, those miraculous deeds that Jesus does, are intended to make clear to all who have eyes to see (e.g., 10:31–39) what Jesus' status really is: the true *mana* that he has. This, I suggest, is made explicit in the very first sign Jesus performs (2:1–11). At the conclusion of this event, when Jesus has turned the water into wine, the narrator comments that in this first sign Jesus revealed his "glory" (his honor/status/*mana*) and his disciples believed in him. In 11:4, at the outset of what may be taken as the last miraculous sign, Jesus says that the raising of Lazarus will function to bring "glory"/honor both to God and "the Son of God" who will be "glorified"/honored through it. In this way the author has the "glory" (*mana*) of Jesus revealed in his actions as a human being: "Flesh" and "glory" combine, just as the two words appear "side-by-side," as it were, in 1:14.

The Gospel also shows Jesus engaging in verbal defense of his *mana* through challenge and riposte, claiming that those who are truly alive to the import of his actions would recognize the "honor" that he is due, and the honor that he shares with God (e.g., 5:39–47; 10:31–39; 14:11).

It is important to note that the rhetoric about Jesus' honor particularly coheres around his "hour," a theme that is developed in such a way in the narrative leading up to Jesus' crucifixion that the reader is led to see that Jesus achieves honor through the dishonor of what is done to him in his "hour of suffering" (cf. 12:20–28, esp. vv. 23, 28; 19:1–3, 5, 16–25). The author of John presents the human character Jesus who attains honor by his actions. But these actions bespeak a *mana* that is more than merely human: This true, divine status of Jesus is reinforced by the narrator, who refers to Jesus' ascribed honor in the Prologue, and by the discourse of Jesus in which Jesus also makes claims for this divine status, and challenges his interlocutors to accept this on the evidence of his works. But, above all, this is a *mana*, and a style of seeking honor, that subverts human conceptions of honor.

Derek Tovey is Lecturer in New Testament at the College of St. John the Evangelist, and the School of Theology at University of Auckland, New Zealand.

QUESTIONS

1. Find *The Green Christ of Breton Cavalry* on the Internet and place your interpretation of it in dialogue with the comments by Goss.
2. How would religious groups in your culture react to the excommunication of the wealthy businessman? What is your response?
3. How might an exclusivist reading of John 14:6 attempt to refute Sours's interpretation?
4. Is there a concept analogous to *doxa* or *mana* in your cultural context that might be brought to bear on a reading of Jesus in John?

CHAPTER 34

CRUCIFIXION AND RESURRECTION OF JESUS

Matthew 28, Mark 16, Luke 24, John 19–20

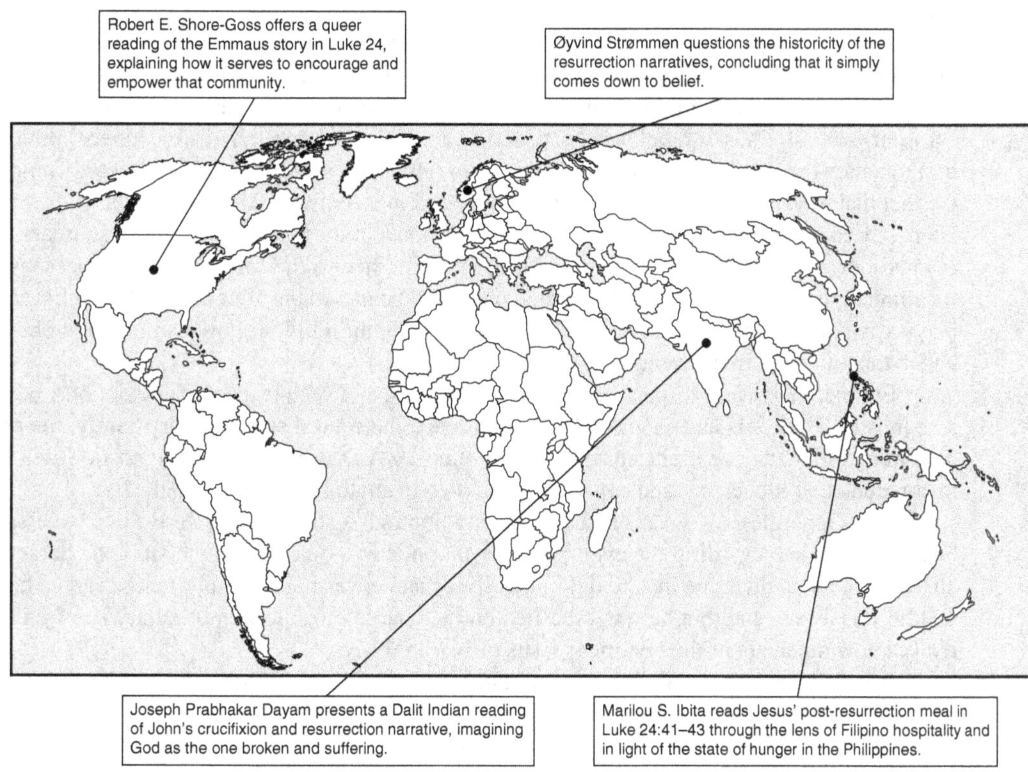

Robert E. Shore-Goss offers a queer reading of the Emmaus story in Luke 24, explaining how it serves to encourage and empower that community.
Øyvind Strømmen questions the historicity of the resurrection narratives, concluding that it simply comes down to belief.
Joseph Prabhakar Dayam presents a Dalit Indian reading of John's crucifixion and resurrection narrative, imagining God as the one broken and suffering.
Marilou S. Ibita reads Jesus' post-resurrection meal in Luke 24:41–43 through the lens of Filipino hospitality and in light of the state of hunger in the Philippines.

READINGS

Questioning the Historicity of the Resurrection Narratives
Øyvind Strømmen

Jesus' Post-resurrection Meal through the Lens of Filipino Hospitality
Marilou S. Ibita

A Dalit Indian Reading of John's Crucifixion and Resurrection Narrative
Joseph Prabhakar Dayam

A Queer Reading of the Emmaus Story in Luke 24
Robert E. Shore-Goss

Questioning the Historicity of the Resurrection Narratives

Øyvind Strømmen (Norway)

Norway is often seen as a bastion of secularism, and even of atheism. And it is true; to most Norwegians religion plays a very limited role in daily life. Only about 3 percent are regular churchgoers. In one poll, 44 percent said they believe in God, 29 percent said they are in doubt, and 27 percent said that they do not believe in God at all. The Norwegian Humanist Association is one of the largest such associations in the world, and it is by far the largest such association per capita.

And yet, this is only half the story. Eighty-five percent of Norwegians remain members of the Lutheran State Church. And what about myself? I did not grow up in a Christian family, but I did grow up in a community with many conservative Christians and Christianity was omnipresent in my school. Thus, a rebel was born, and as a youngster I was a hard-line atheist, doing my best to annoy the theologist we had as a teacher in religion in secondary school, secretly enjoying the fact that it was a subject I'd soon be able to avoid in its entirety. How naïve? Just a few years later, I became gradually more interested in religious studies. Why? As many scholars have pointed out, some of them with quite a bit of embarrassment, the secularization process which for some time was seen as inevitable turned out not to be inevitable after all. In 2013 religion still plays a major political and societal role. Without studying religion, how can one even hope to understand many current events?

For me, increasing respect came with my studies; and with respect, came doubt. I became an agnostic. Thus, it is as an agnostic that I approach the central story of Christianity, the resurrection narrative, an event placed sometime around 30 A.D. And it is as an agnostic I will have to conclude that it does not and *can* not come down to anything other than belief.

First, regardless of what certain Christian apologists may claim, we do not have strong historical sources regarding the event, or—for that matter—on Jesus as a historical character at all. Most of us might agree that he did in fact live, that he was regarded as a teacher and a healer, that he was a Jew, and that he was crucified on the charge of sedition; but otherwise, we do not really know much about the historical Jesus of Nazareth.

According to traditional Christian understanding, the Gospels of John and Matthew were written by eyewitnesses. Modern research, however, has shown that there are good reasons to doubt this claim. In any case, it does not seem likely that any of the Gospels were written before 70 A.D., 40 years after the reported events. There might have been earlier writings, such as the hypothetical Q source seemingly used by both Matthew and Luke, but if there were, they have been lost. This of course raises an interesting question: Would you today believe a story about a man rising from the dead in the 1970s, a story not written by an eyewitness, a story published 40 years later and peddled to you by a rather small—yet increasingly successful—new religious movement? Or would you consider it, perhaps, as a fanciful fable?

If you are a Christian, and this *does* provoke you (it should not, really), you might want to consider a very real parallel, namely the question of the historicity of the prophet Muhammad. Once again, we have few sources except distinctly Islamic ones, most of which are of a later date. There is a Greek anti-Jewish text called *Doctrina Iacobi* from around 640 A.D., which mentions "a false prophet amongst the Sarasenes." There is a Jewish apocalyptic text from the late eighth-century mentioning a prophet of the Ismaelites. And there is a mention of Muhammad by the Armenian bishop Sebeos, recorded around 660 A.D. While this certainly gives us reason to consider Muhammad as a real historical person rather than as an imagined hero, it does not tell us much about the historical Muhammad, and I have met quite a few Christians who regard his prophethood as nothing more than a fanciful fable.

As with Muhammad and the Muslims, it is possible to find some non-Christian sources mentioning or, at least, referring to Jesus or the Christians. The Jewish historian Flavius Josephus mentions him twice in his *Antiquities of the Jews* from 93 A.D. The Babylonian Talmud mentions "Yeshu" a few times. Pliny the Younger advises on how to deal with Christus-worshippers in a letter to Emperor Trajan from around 112 A.D. None of these sources mention the resurrection, though. The first non-Christian to even touch upon that topic was Lucian of Samotasa, a Greek satirist—think of him as a Jon Stewart of his age—writing in the second century. He ridiculed the Christians, portraying them as gullible fools. Then came Celsus, who wrote the first known comprehensive attack on Christianity—a work called *The True Word*—sometime around 170–180 A.D. The work itself has been lost, but fragments are known—thanks to a reply written by Origen, a later Christian scholar. Celsus disregards the resurrection as a story from "a half-frantic woman, as you state, and some other one, perhaps, of those who were engaged in the same system of delusion."

Of course, none of this disproves the resurrection narrative. It does show, however, that there is no such thing as historical *evidence* for the story, regardless of what the Gospels say, and regardless of numerous daring claims made by Christian apologists. It shows that the story itself was so fantastic, that it was met with disbelief even in a time when *magic* was considered as a very real phenomenon and where *Gods* were seen as active participants in the world of men.

It is worth noting that there are many early Christian texts which do not share the focus on resurrection. The Gospel of Mark, for example, by scholarly consensus originally ended at 16:8 (all the earliest manuscripts end there). Verses 9–20 appear to have been added later in an attempt to bring it in line with the other three Gospels. It is indeed striking that the earliest written biblical gospel does not (at least originally) contain a story of Jesus' resurrection. The aforementioned hypothetical Q source used by Matthew and Luke focuses almost exclusively on the teachings of Jesus and does not include a resurrection story. The noncanonical Gospel of Thomas—which has been dated as early as 60 A.D.—merely contains a number of sayings by Jesus, and mentions neither miracles nor the resurrection. Likewise, the Gospel of Mary seems to present Jesus' teachings as a way to inner spiritual knowledge and it rejects the idea that Jesus' suffering and death provided a path to eternal life. Indeed, one could argue that if it were not for Paul's focus on the significance of the death and resurrection of Jesus that those beliefs would not have become central to the faith. Even Paul's own understanding of the resurrection is not entirely clear. Some have reasoned that he believed only in a spiritual—not bodily, physical—resurrection based on passages such as Acts 9 and 1 Corinthians 15.

None of this tells us much more about the historical Jesus or about the historicity of the resurrection narrative, of course. It does, however, reveal that the story of early Christianity is a story of heterodoxy, rather than of orthodoxy, of conflicting ideas rather than of a shared faith, which leads to a final point: Even the four Gospels do not agree on what happened that first Easter morning. Four conflicting accounts do not make for good historical evidence. But one can still believe.

Øyvind Strømmen is a journalist and writer; he has studied religious history, and is currently particularly interested in the impact of religion on dietary habits.

JESUS' POST-RESURRECTION MEAL THROUGH THE LENS OF FILIPINO HOSPITALITY

Marilou S. Ibita (Philippines)

The post-resurrection meal in Jerusalem (Luke 24:41–43), often eclipsed by the meal at Emmaus (vv. 13–32), contains a very significant detail as the *last* of the 10 meal scenes of Jesus in Luke's Gospel. It affirms and sets the evangelist's seal to the theme of table-fellowship that evokes a specific picture of Jesus, sheds light on an aspect of his proclamation of the Kingdom of God, and presents a challenge to discipleship. Hence, reading the Lukan meal scenes, especially Luke 24:41–43, as a Filipina Christian with our meal-oriented culture vis-à-vis the problem of hunger in the Philippines is a challenging task.

One of the most important expressions of Filipino hospitality is table-fellowship with friends and family, expected and unexpected visitors, and even with strangers. *Kain tayo!* (Let's eat), *Salo tayo!* (Let us partake [of food and drink]) are variations of an invitation to table-fellowship. It could be an elaborate or everyday meal, a simple snack or a sharing of whatever meager food one has. The list of venues is endless: one's own home, a food chain outlet, a park, a beach, a bus, or a place under a mango/coconut tree. Differences in economic and social backgrounds influence the quantity and quality of what is offered. However, the driving force behind it remains the same: to share food and drink with others because one is a *kapwa* (the other is a person like one's self).

The level of *pakikipagkapwa* is detectable in Filipino table-fellowship through the kind of food and drink served, the type of tableware, and the way guests and hosts relate to one another. *Pakikipagkapwa* is humanness at its highest level where the *kapwa* (other) is *sarili na rin* (oneself). *Pakikipagkapwa* is rooted in the concept of shared inner self and recognition of shared identity, not just smooth interpersonal relationships. *Kapwa* embraces both the categories of *ibang tao* (outsiders) and *hindi ibang tao* (insiders). In table-fellowship, one can detect the level of relationship between partakers. The *ibang tao* (outsider) category moves from *pakikitungo* (level of amenities) to *pakikibagay* (level of conforming) and *pakikisama* (level of adjusting). The *hindi ibang tao* (insider) category consists of two levels: *pakikipagpalagayang-loob* (level of mutual trust) and *pakikiisa* (level of fusion, oneness and full of trust). The progression of relationships from being an outsider to an insider is evident in the quality of relationships expressed in the meals, with *pakikitungo* as the shallowest and *pakikiisa* as the deepest. The food and drink served varies from elaborate and expensive ones in the *ibang tao* (outsider) category when the parties involved try to gain each other's confidence to that of being able to serve daily fare in the *hindi ibang tao* (insiders) category. The tableware changes from those infrequently used to those that are utilized daily as partakers become more at home with each other. What I want to highlight here is how the visitor grows from being a guest toward becoming a cohost with the host and a coservant at table when the deepest level of relationship has been achieved, enabling the former guest to be one with the host and help serve the new guests.

Yet the richness of the meal-sharing culture questions and challenges the state of hunger in the Philippines. We have enough food but not everyone has the power to buy food. The November 2010 survey indicates that there are about 3.4 million Filipino families who suffer from hunger. This report shows that we lag behind the UN Millennium Development Goal (MDG) No. 1 of eradicating extreme poverty and hunger by halving the proportion of those who suffer hunger between 1990 and 2015. Our own context, nevertheless, is but a small reflection of the shocking news in 2009: mid-way through the UN MDG drive that began in 2002, we have reached the 1 billion mark of people suffering chronic hunger worldwide.

How does this contrasting background influence my reading of Luke's meal scenes? First, I want to focus on Jesus at table with different kinds of people and explore Luke's characterization of Jesus, of God's kingdom, and of discipleship in these texts, particularly in 24:41–43.

In dialoguing between the meal scenes where Jesus is the protagonist and my own context, I notice that the Lukan Jesus' role at table keeps on changing. In Galilee, Jesus is first the guest of Levi, a despised tax collector (5:29). Then he is a guest of Simon, a law-abiding Pharisee (7:37). Does Luke imply that just as Jesus can be the guest of these seemingly extreme examples, he can be a guest of those who fall in between? Nevertheless, at the close of his Galilean ministry, the Lukan Jesus changes his role to that of host and feeds a hungry multitude (9:15). In this part of the journey, Jesus is not confronted directly by those against his kind of table-fellowship.

In Jesus' ministry on the journey to Jerusalem, he is pictured as the guest of many people: of women (10:38–42), of another Pharisee (11:37–54), of a ruler who belonged to the Pharisees (14:1–24), and of a chief tax collector, Zacchaeus (19:1–10). It is notable that just before entering Jerusalem, the last two hosts of Jesus remind us of the first two hosts that he had. However, there is an intensification of the characters with whom Jesus shares table-fellowship since one is a *ruler* who belonged to the Pharisees and the other a *chief* tax collector. At this juncture and in contrast with his Galilean experience, Jesus addresses direct antagonism from people he dines with (11:53–54; 14:1) and from all others who disapprove of his brand of meal-sharing (15:2; 19:7).

Despite the disapproval of many, Jesus continues his inclusive table-fellowship. In Jerusalem, there is only one meal scene but it epitomizes an inclusive table-fellowship: his farewell meal or the Last Supper (22:14–38). Here Jesus is the host who gives himself to his disciples, even if one will betray him and another will disown him (vv. 14–23, 31–34) and the rest will abandon him. With his disciples' misunderstanding of roles at table, Jesus affirms that he is among them as one who serves (v. 27). In Luke, Jesus' table-fellowship contributes to his crucifixion.

Luke, however, continues to emphasize table-fellowship in the post-resurrection accounts showing that Jesus and his brand of table-fellowship overcome death. The disciples recognized the Risen Jesus at table as a guest who is also a host (24:13–35, especially 29–31). Then in the next scene in 24:41–43 Jesus is back to his initial role as a guest, indicating an invitation to follow him in the cyclical roles at table.

From the foregoing, I glean that the Lukan Jesus can be characterized as cyclically changing his roles at table. It reminds me of the changing roles at table in Filipino table-fellowship. Jesus as a guest shows that we are guests, recipients of God's providence just as Filipinos strive to serve the best for their guests. Yet, Jesus changing roles suggests that we cannot be guests forever. We are called to be hosts, too, like Jesus at the end of his Galilean ministry and at the Last Supper. Lest one become conceited for providing food and drink, Jesus shows that being a host is coupled with being a servant. Hence, Luke portrays his post-resurrection appearances by underscoring table-fellowship in Emmaus and ending with the one in Jerusalem. Jesus' cyclically changing role as guest–host–servant at table consequently challenges his disciples to follow what I call Jesus' meal-ministry that proclaims a facet of God's kingdom as a banquet for all.

How do these insights relate to hunger? They ask Christians to be cognizant of their own table-fellowship and the changing roles of Jesus at table. The dialogue creatively challenges them to embody his example in the different contexts in which they find themselves whether as a guest or a host or servant at table. To do so, Christians and Christian communities need to be informed and active participants in the demanding, complex issue of hunger by contributing in ways that uphold economic, political, and sociocultural rights that affect the food security, food self-sufficiency, and food sovereignty of peoples. In this way, everyone, not just a few, can have enough nutritious food at table every day. The UN MDG goal of reducing the number of hungry people in the world and eventually eradicating hunger can be achieved. This would indeed be an expression of God's dream of a banquet for all.

Marilou S. Ibita is a Filipina, Roman Catholic Christian, and a doctoral researcher at the Katholieke Universiteit Leuven, Belgium; she has served at the Institute of Formation and Religious Studies at Maryhill School of Theology and St. Vincent School of Theology, Quezon City, Philippines.

A Dalit Indian Reading of John's Crucifixion and Resurrection Narrative

Joseph Prabhakar Dayam (India)

On the Christmas Eve of 2007 Dalit Christians in Khandamal in Orissa, India, were brutally attacked. While they were preparing to gather around the manger to celebrate life found in the baby Jesus, they were paraded to the outskirts of their vicinities. The persecution that began on that Christmas day continued and found greater expression in the year that followed. At least 50 people were brutally killed and several thousands displaced. It was told by the victims that some were butchered and at least one was buried alive. A nun was raped and several were forced to renounce their faith. Churches were set on fire and priests were beaten. Their houses were looted and fields were burnt. The symbol that strikingly conveys their context is the gruesome cross with the grotesque body of Christ on it. One may write off this incident as an isolated one. Mass murders like that in Khandamal may not occur every day. However, Dalit (those who were considered as untouchables and polluted in the caste structure that determines the identity and social location of an individual and communities) life in India is marked by suffering.

In a context of such despair and death, where do we, as Dalit Christians, locate hope? John 19:38–42 echoes the faith of the Church about Christ. Both the Apostle's creed and the Nicene Creed profess that Christ, the God incarnate, had suffered, died, was buried, and was raised to life. Such is the faith of the Dalit Christians as well.

In this text the writer brings together three Christian symbols which were central to the faith of the Church. He was crucified, buried, and raised to life again: Golgotha, grave, and the garden. These were the occasions for the Son's glorification.

It is intriguing that even though Christ as God incarnate is the central theme of John's Gospel, he does not mention any of the birth or the infancy narratives. Rather, his passion narrative is quite lengthy. He describes the way in which the powers of the day collided and unjustly put Jesus to death. He makes the slyness of the scribes, prejudice of the priests, and the cowardice and the cunningness of Pilate responsible for the death of Jesus. The place where he was crucified was a public place where everyone could see what would happen to a blasphemer and one who engages in treason. Sure it was a political murder of someone who was presented as a breaker of the law, as a rebel, a subversive usurper, and pretender. John painstakingly narrates the gruesomeness and paints the picture of the grotesque body hanging on the cross. The way of the cross in this Gospel is an excruciating journey. It was a painful political path for Jesus. For his disciples who left everything and followed this man, it was a betrayal of their hopes. The one whom they believed would institute God's reign is hanging there, being mocked, pleading for a drink, and finally giving up his spirit. The one in whom they supposedly experienced the presence of God hangs on the cross naked and God-forsaken.

While the cross of Christ depicts the grotesqueness of his death, the grave declares the irrevocability of it. It appears to be the end of any hope for the community of Jesus. It looks as though his movement was a failure, the hopes that he evoked were fake. He is like any other messianic pretender. The one who is supposedly the Word of God which creates all that is and on which all reality constantly depends has fallen silent. It is the absolute abandonment of God experienced by the One who claimed to be present with the Father in eternity.

Incongruously, it is in these sites of God's absence that the Gospel writer locates God's presence. It is through these shameful and ridiculous symbols that John unfurls the wisdom of God: a scandal to the worldly wise and the power of God to the one who is being saved. For the Gospel writer, Jesus unveiled God by living among humans, proclaiming and practicing the good news of God's presence among us, walking the way of the cross, and finally by being interred. He was God crucified and God buried.

The Gospel of John alone mentions that there was a garden in the place where Jesus was crucified. Accordingly, the place where Jesus was crucified was also the site of his resurrection. It is likely that by placing the grave in the garden the Gospel writer has his eye on the resurrection morning. While Golgotha and the grave obscure any view of the horizon of hope, the garden where the grave becomes empty opens up a new horizon of hope. By raising Jesus from the dead, God declares him to be the Son who was with him from eternity. By the raising of the Son from the dead, by turning the grave—the location of death, into a location of life, God gives meaning to the cross and the grave.

By placing Golgotha, the grave, and the garden together, the Gospel writer suggests that these three sites are revelatory symbols. If Christ is the God incarnate, he is God crucified, God interred, and God raised to life. It is in and through these sites that God manifested God's perfections.

How do they relate to the context of the Dalits?

1. It opens up a possibility to imagine God as the Dalit. In the event of the Father experiencing the death of the Son and the Son experiencing the abandonment by the Father, the human experience of pain, suffering, and death are taken into the very life of God (Jürgen Moltmann). God who is manifested in the incarnation of the Son is the God crucified and God interred: the one who is pierced, broken, torn asunder, killed, and buried. God is the broken one who took upon Godself the Dalitness (the word "Dalit" literally means, the broken, crushed, and torn asunder which is used by the "untouchables" in naming themselves). If in the cross of Christ God has identified and expressed God's solidarity with the extremities of human predicament and pain, I suppose it is theologically legitimate to engage in such imagination. In the incarnation of God in Christ, not only did God come to us, but humanity also is taken into the life of God. In this passage of human into the life of God, God takes into Godself the human brokenness, pain, and pathos. Therefore one could imagine God as the Dalit.

Both for a Jew and a Greek, and for an Indian alike, the grave is a polluting site. For a Jew, since contact with anything dead is a "polluting" act, the holy one of Israel could never enter into such a site. For the Greek, since the spirit is eternal and matter is evil, an interred God is unthinkable. Christian faith in the one who is crucified, buried, and raised brings pollution into the language of the perfections of God. If incarnation is a necessity in the life of God for God's self disclosure, then I suppose pollution is a necessity in the life of God. In the death, burial, and resurrection of Christ, God manifests Godself as the Pained and the Polluted One, the Dalit. Perhaps, one could imagine pathos and pollution as the divine perfections.

2. Dalit lives are characterized by pain and death. These are the lives, symbolically speaking, nailed to the cross and interred. Their lives seem to be Godforsaken and God seems to be an abandoning God. How do Golgotha, grave, and the garden speak to us in such a context? Could we suggest that in Dalit persecution Christ is persecuted, in their cry for liberation Christ is shouting aloud: "Why God, Why God, Why have you forsaken us?" In this cry, God experiences the death of God's children and turns their graves into a garden. Surely God would raise them to life. It is precisely in these grave-like situations God acts, bringing life to the dry bones, turning the grave into a garden. This habitat of the Dalits is the location of Christ's resisting and God's life-renewing activity.

Joseph Prabhakar Dayam, a theologian and an ordained minister of the Andhra Evangelical Lutheran Church, is an Associate Professor in Christian Theology at the United Theological College, Bangalore, India.

A Queer Reading of the Emmaus Story in Luke 24

Robert E. Shore-Goss (United States)

Concerning the Emmaus story in Luke 24:13–35, John Dominic Crossan writes, "Emmaus never happened, Emmaus always happens." (*Jesus: A Revolutionary Biography* [Harper: San Francisco, 1994], 197). Crossan considers the Lukan narrative unit a metaphoric condensation of early followers of Jesus who continued to experience his resurrection appearances over a period of time and associated his presence with his actions of interpreting the scriptures and the continued practice of commensality.

The story of Cleopas and the unnamed disciple walking toward Emmaus has long been recognized in queer faith communities. For queer Christians, the two disciples are separated from the main body of Jesus' male disciples, huddled in Jerusalem. They are physically outside the inner circle, and they may have left in sadness and disgust over the failure of the body of disciples to be present to Jesus at his crucifixion. The death of Jesus has become a crisis, generating emotions of fear and anxiety mixed with feelings of loss and grief. Clearly, the text is a story of grief over the loss and death of Jesus.

The two disciples are grieving at the loss of Jesus, but they are joined by a stranger who walks with them, and the disciples speak to the stranger about their hopes, dreams, betrayals, and deadly loss. They express to him how they have given their hearts to Jesus, his message and practices, and how they had hoped that Jesus would set them free. The two are astounded by the reports of the women who went to the tomb. They are separate from the mainstream male leadership in Jerusalem; they are queer outsiders, perhaps even two lovers. They raise the women's story with the stranger because they are processing the death of Jesus with the proclamation of the empty tomb. They tell their story to the stranger on the road. It takes a stranger to hear the story of two outsiders.

The stranger explains from the scriptures how Jesus had been charged with perverting the nation and queered all religious expectations and that through his ministry, suffering, and death, the Christ entered into glory. God has not disappointed them, for God raised the queer Christ. The stranger speaks to their estrangement and alienation, but they are also emotionally open to speak about the pain of their lives. Many translesbigay folks feel out of place within many churches since those churches have taken Jesus away from them with their exclusionary practices. Churches have absented Jesus from their lives by directly excluding them from community or making it impossible to love and remain within the community.

Stopping at Emmaus, the two queer disciples invite the stranger to stay with them for the night and share a meal with them (queer folks love meals as a time to deepen their communal bonds of friendship). They extend the stranger hospitality at their table. Their hearts yearned for Jesus' presence, and as outsiders they intuitively recognized and felt an embodied connection to their own experience. They included him in their meal with openness and a warm welcome—remembering that open table hospitality was a significant feature of Jesus' ministry. Jesus practiced an egalitarian commensality, an inclusive lived practice of the parable of the Great Supper (Luke 14:15–24). During the meal, he "takes, blesses, breaks, and gives" them the bread. These gestures are mimetic rituals that Jesus set up during his ministry of open commensality and during his last meal. Jesus took and blessed, but they clearly recognize him in the distinctive last gestures—breaking and giving. These were the functions of women and slaves. The risen Jesus takes the role of a woman or slave in breaking and distributing the bread. The eyes of the disciples are opened, and they recognize Jesus in the transgression of social roles.

Their eyes were opened with the mimetic rituals. They function as a memorial linking object that evokes a memory of Jesus that actualizes a sense of presence. Their lives changed, for they complete the ritual of the bread, recognizing Jesus in the midst and in their own life experiences. The disciples recognize their lives in the bread. Jesus takes bread; blesses their experiences of brokenness, pain, exile, and alienation; and transforms the bread of their lives into himself. The breaking of the bread creates hope, actualizes the presence of the risen Christ, and forms them into church. The risen Jesus is not the possession of the community back in Jerusalem alone but also abides in the word of scripture, in the bread broken, and queer embodied lives in community. Though physically absent, Jesus is present through scripture, the breaking of the bread, and the community fostered by a memorial practice linked to Jesus' original practice of open commensality. The moral of the narrative is "Do not neglect to show hospitality to the stranger, for the stranger can be the risen Christ." It is also a warrant that exclusion is not a practice of open commensality.

Their queer experience finds hope in God's vindication of Jesus' queer ministry and death, for Jesus was charged by the high priests with "perverting the nation" (Luke 23:2). Their hearts were once again set on fire as they once heard Jesus' proclamation of the good news in his ministry. The despondent community of the male apostles did not enkindle the fire of hope but the simple repetition of the hospitality and kindness reconnected them to God and the risen Christ. The story of Emmaus highlights that the risen Christ walks with us in our human pain, grief, and confusion.

The story of Jesus is not finished as the opening quote from John Dominic Crossan: "Emmaus always happens." Crossan's insight is correct that the followers of Jesus then and even now encounter the risen Christ in the ways Luke describes. The narrative is repeated in queer Christian lives. One such story is that of the founder of MCC (Metropolitan Community Church), the Rev. Troy Perry.

Perry took an ad out in a gay Los Angeles magazine, *The Advocate*, announcing a worship service for gays and lesbians. At that first service on October 6, 1968, 12 people responded to the ad and came to the service. Toward the end of the worship, Perry offered a prayer over the bread and grape juice and invited those who had been excluded to come and receive communion. He dramatically and spiritually ritualized the inclusion of those queers excluded from their churches' politics of the table. They had been denied access to the ritual Christian meal because of their sexual orientation. Rev. Perry opened a sacramental gateway for not only gays and lesbians but also for bisexuals, transgendered folks, and alienated heterosexuals.

This ritual is now repeated in all MCC Sunday worships at the end of the communion table prayer with the invitation: "You neither need to be a member of MCC, nor any church nor even be a Christian. All are welcome to God's table." In that simple ritual proclamation, there is embodied a mimetic invitation of open inclusion and egalitarian commensality—that the unconditional grace of God is available to all people and equally available to them. God surrounds all human beings from birth to death with unconditional love and compassionate care. This gift of love is nothing other than God's self-communication of divine love and forgiveness. There are three notions embodied in MCC's ritual to the open commensality. First, God's grace is radically inclusive and without conditions. Second, no one is turned away. Finally, every person is loved equally by God. This ritual invitation has become the core mission of MCC: radical inclusive love.

Queer folks look for the risen Christ outside many denominational Christian churches. They have discovered the absence of the risen Christ in the lack of welcome and hospitality in hostile and exclusive churches. As they discover Christ outside the traditional faith communities in open commensality, they realize their responsibility to journey back to the community. Their healing, openness, and reflection lead them to follow the trajectory of Cleopas and the unknown disciple. With courage and renewed lives, they leave their exile to tell the story how Jesus was found in their queer lives and stories and how the breaking of the bread made them into a community, empowered by the risen Christ. The risen Christ's breaking of the bread transforms the two queer disciples into church. Each time queer followers gather together in faith and remember the meal that Jesus celebrated, they create a queer Church.

Just as Cleopas and the unknown disciple, the queer church travels back to the mainstream churches, bringing the message of the power of Christ's resurrection discovered in their embodied, erotic experiences. They embody the risen Christ in radical inclusive churches, and the recognition of their embodiment of the queer Christ motivates them to return to the larger community to bear witness to the queer Christ in their own lives and inclusive practices of table hospitality and love. They now have the power to transform the despondent and disembodied community, to change the hearts of its members so that they can recognize the presence of the risen Christ embodied in queer disciples. It is only their embodied return that prepares the community to welcome and hear the risen and embodied Christ in their midst.

Robert E. Shore-Goss (Ph.D., Comparative Religion and Theology, Harvard University) is the gay Pastor of the MCC Church in the Valley; he is author of Jesus ACTED UP: A Gay and Lesbian Manifesto *and Queering Christ: Beyond Jesus ACTED UP.*

QUESTIONS

1. What might constitute evidence for the historicity of Jesus and the resurrection? Why does Strømmen say that his observations should not provoke Christians?
2. Examine carefully each of the biblical texts discussed by Ibita and assign each character or group to one of the categories from Filipino table-fellowship.
3. What texts from John does Dayam have in mind when he says, "John painstakingly narrates the gruesomeness of the cross and paints the picture of the grotesque body hanging on the cross"?
4. Assess carefully Goss's handling of the biblical text, not his ideological orientation.

CHAPTER 35

ACTS 2

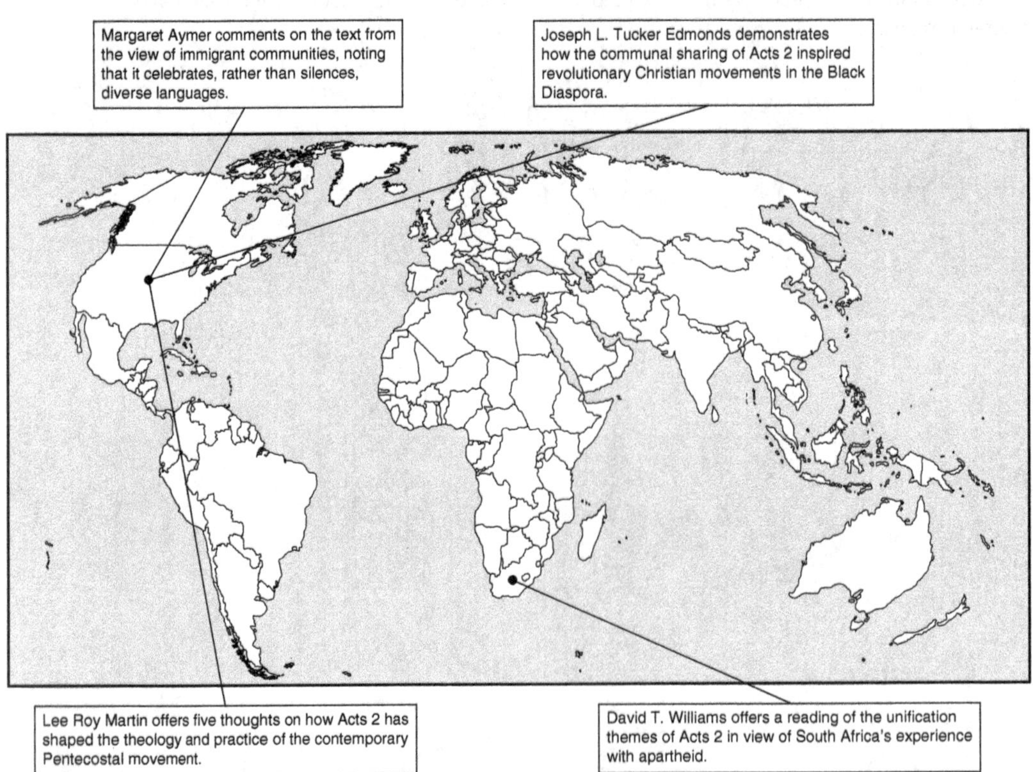
Margaret Aymer comments on the text from the view of immigrant communities, noting that it celebrates, rather than silences, diverse languages.
Joseph L. Tucker Edmonds demonstrates how the communal sharing of Acts 2 inspired revolutionary Christian movements in the Black Diaspora.
Lee Roy Martin offers five thoughts on how Acts 2 has shaped the theology and practice of the contemporary Pentecostal movement.
David T. Williams offers a reading of the unification themes of Acts 2 in view of South Africa's experience with apartheid.

READINGS

Pentecost's Diverse Languages from the View of Immigrant Communities
Margaret Aymer

The Influence of Acts 2 on Revolutionary Christian Movements in the Black Diaspora
Joseph L. Tucker Edmonds

The Unification Themes of Acts 2 in View of South Africa's Experience with Apartheid
David T. Williams

Five Thoughts on Acts 2 Relating to Theology and Practice in the Pentecostal Movement
Lee Roy Martin

Pentecost's Diverse Languages from the View of Immigrant Communities

Margaret Aymer (United States)

When one is an immigrant, voluntarily or involuntarily, any trace of home can draw your attention, distracting you from whatever it was you were doing. This is particularly true for the sounds of home, words of a language or a dialect you may have not heard used publicly for many years. We immigrants are used to exchanging our languages for that of our host country, either learning an entirely new grammar or having our dialects "corrected" to match the dialect of the majority culture. All nations do this in one way or another. It is a way of gaining control over "the other" and maintaining a sense of national unity over against the "Babel" that threatens to split apart any nation.

And so, in our daily lives, we speak and act as though we are part of the dominant culture. However, when we immigrants come together, when we drop the need to translate ourselves into someone else's culture and their accents and music, food and rhythms of home emerge, and we find ourselves suddenly emancipated. We find freedom in being able to affirm all of ourselves, instead of hiding parts of who we are for the sake of the uncomfortable majority. It is no wonder that those who fear the encroachment of us foreigners blanch at the sight of our flags flying at our festivals or cringe when we sing "their" national songs in our languages and rhythms. They sense the palpable freedom in the air that comes from being whole.

In many ways, Roman-dominated Jerusalem would have been no different. Those who walked its streets would have spoken either Aramaic, the language of the land, or Greek, the language of commerce and of the Roman military. Immigrants to the city, like immigrants today, would have found themselves exchanging their languages for those spoken by the majority of residents, for only in this way could one survive. Most of them would probably have spoken Greek. Greek was, in many ways, the language of domination. It was the way in which Rome gained control over all of disparate groups under its rule, over the "Babel" that always threatened to split apart the empire.

Against this context, the Pentecost narrative stands in stark relief, like the bursting of a Mediterranean-wide "ethnic festival" on an otherwise ordinary day. As Luke narrates the story, after the Spirit descends on the Galileans, themselves set apart from Judeans by their accents (Luke 22:59), they begin to speak in other, or as we might say today "foreign," languages. The languages are quite distinct and represent a roll call of the nations from around the Mediterranean basin (Acts 2: 9–11).

The sound of languages other than Aramaic or Greek would have been a curious enough sign of something different and potentially holy afoot. But a more poignant moment happens when the languages are heard. For, at the sound of their languages being spoken, immigrants to Jerusalem do what immigrants always do when they hear the sounds of home. They turn toward the languages to hear more. The coming of the languages is not simply a sign of the power of God. It is, as many immigrants can attest, a signifier that this "new thing" is a place of emancipation, of self-expression, of home.

To be sure, these are immigrants (2:5), and not pilgrims in town for the Pentecost feast, as is often proclaimed. It is these immigrants, outsiders and foreigners with "strange" maternal languages and flags and accents, that make up the congregation for Peter's famed sermon and that constitute the first members of the early church in Acts 2. They come together not because they feel the need to translate themselves in order to survive, but rather because the Spirit of God has chosen to translate the good news and the church to them, to signify that the sounds of the church are sounds of home.

Of course, the gathering drew mockers. Gatherings of "others" always do. The charge of drunkenness, of being somehow less than upstanding aimed both at the Galileans and tangentially at the accents and languages so strange to majority ears, is a polemic intended to reset the dominant order. Not unlike the unkind mocking of accents that so many of us know, the charge is that something in these different sounds and words is not quite right.

In response to this charge that somehow the sounds of difference are harmfully transgressive, Peter declares, in the words of the prophet Joel, the kinship of all of the languages present: the majority and minority ones, the silenced and the spoken. For, in Peter's proclamation that God will pour out God's Spirit on all flesh, sons and daughters, old and young, Peter is also declaring that all present, yes even the immigrants, are witnesses to that greatness in their maternal tongues and dialects, accents, and rhythms.

In Acts, the promise for salvation changes the rules about immigrants; for Acts does not require of us self-translation and it does not need, as empires do, to silence Babel for the sake of control. Indeed, Acts celebrates Babel in all of our rich linguistic diversity. And into the polyphony, God translates God's own self through the Spirit for the sake of the people. And all over Jerusalem, heads turn and people gather. For they hear the sounds of home.

Margaret Aymer is Associate Professor of New Testament at the Interdenominational Theological Center, Atlanta, Georgia, United States.

The Influence of Acts 2 on Revolutionary Christian Movements in the Black Diaspora

Joseph L. Tucker Edmonds (United States)

While capitalism is dominant in the contemporary global village and is often conflated with freedom in its Western formulation, capitalism is not without its detractors and critics. For a number of groups the narrative of capitalism has not only included the trade of goods and items that enrich their lives, but for many in our global neighborhood, capitalism has been rooted in the trade of certain people and insensitivity to the needs of many. Capitalism for certain communities has been a narrative of horror, disenfranchisement, and violence. As a result, many of these communities have looked to the Bible for resources to challenge and reshape capitalism. The book of Acts, and especially the second chapter of Acts, continues the countercultural narrative of the gospel that challenges the exclusivist (especially among religious elite), imperial, and masculinist biases of the first century and beyond. Acts pushes the boundaries of the biblical narrative (especially the Gospels) where the individualized acts of the miracle-working Messiah and his small group of disciples is extended from the inner circle to a larger group of men and women who are charged to speak prophetically and transform creatively the very contours of local and global communities. It is in the Acts narrative that power and control are effectively loosed and shared. Moreover, the loosing of the tongues (glossolalia) on the Day of Pentecost functions as a metaphor for the decentralization of power and the locus of control from the elite to the entire community. It is a radical re-visioning of autocratic and dictatorial forms of control, and it signals a shift to democratic and power-sharing modalities. Here I will address the ways in which democratic participation and communal modes of power and profit sharing in the first-century community were as countercultural then as they are now. I will also suggest that the *post-glossolalia* moment led to a reorganizing of the early church community and provided compelling options for revolutionary Christian movements in the Black Diaspora in the twentieth century.

The "glossolalia event" or the speaking in tongues moment (Acts 2:4) is critical in the biblical narrative, for it represents an important shift in who has access to divine revelation and what happens when divine revelation rests in the hand of the many rather than the few. This moment reflects a radical reordering as it not only signals a critique of the elite-dominated Jewish community but is also an expansion and fulfillment of the biblical and gospel narrative. The quoting of Joel 2:29 by the leader of the nascent Christian community highlights the unique and auspicious nature of this moment. God is pouring out God's self not only on the elite or well connected but also on the Galileans who could be understood as the weak, marginalized, and oft-forgotten group of Israel. More importantly, in this moment not only is it poured out on the weak and marginalized men, but also this revelation from God is given to both male and female Galileans in the presence of those who might otherwise degrade or ignore them. The revelation that is given to the "servant" or the weak in Acts 2 is one that is not only heard by the elite and the Jewish community that is meeting in Jerusalem for a high holiday, but also it is understood by them and signals a shift in their orientation. Moreover, the shifted orientation of the early Jewish/Christian community from elite-led and indifferent to suffering to communally focused has relevance for Black Christian movements and their quest for freedom in the modern era.

The particular shift that is highlighted in this passage is a reconception of power and participation that challenges the foundations of what would in the first century be understood as imperial or elite rule and in the modern era is conceived as the foundation of capitalism. While we tend to focus on the glossolalia event, the important part of the Acts narrative for many Christian movements in the twentieth century is the reshaping of their freedom projects in light of the voices (the Galileans, the servants, the women) that are now audible in the postglossolalia moment. Black freedom as described by Christian or Christian-derived projects like Rastafarianism and the Nation of Islam in the beginning of the twentieth centuries, Martin Luther King and the civil rights movement in the middle of the twentieth century, and the anti-apartheid Christian movements in South Africa in the latter half of the century was a critique of elite-dominated, profit-oriented structures and practices. Freedom was not a continuation of the modern project and the way that it had previously unfolded, as that project was one that denied and degraded Black and Africana subjects and was predicated upon individual ownership and profit maximization at all costs. The postglossolalia moment in the Africa Diaspora re-visions the very parameters of freedom and participation by listening to those people that had either been commodified, destroyed, or ignored by the elite or those committed to profit maximization. The communal ethos of Rastafarianism and their commitment to local and communal self-sufficiency, the mass boycotts during the Civil Rights and apartheid eras, and even the emergence of small tight-knit communities based on shared economic empowerment like the Nation of Islam and the early Black Pentecostal communities argued for a rejection of profit and self-interest in favor of holding many things in "common" and working together to "give to anyone in need" (Acts 2:45). The Acts narrative in these communities became a space for disenfranchised and often disempowered people to lay claim to God's voice and to use it radically to resist the forms of modernity and capitalism that desired to destroy them and people like them. In this regard, the Acts narrative or Pentecost is not simply about the spiritual act of speaking in tongues, but it is the ways in which God's revelation to God's people can be connected to acts of liberation and freedom for everyone, even, or especially, the weak and disenfranchised among us.

Joseph L. Tucker Edmonds is Assistant Professor of Africana Studies and Religious Studies at Indiana University-Purdue University, Indianapolis, United States.

The Unification Themes of Acts 2 in View of South Africa's Experience with Apartheid

David T. Williams (South Africa)

The essence of the political problem is how to get people who are different in so many ways to live together. How can they be persuaded to treat each other in a humane way without injustice and oppression?

The last half of the twentieth century witnessed a solution to the problem in South Africa that was to become notorious, and to add a word to the global vocabulary, "apartheid." It was the expression of a belief that peaceful coexistence was not really possible, so the best solution was to keep peoples apart. Although obviously inspired by political and social ideology, the sadness was that attempts were made to justify it biblically. At the same time, although it could have been established in justice, it was not, and the blatant inequality and oppression outraged many in South Africa and the world.

The experiment ended, after a long struggle, with elections in 1994, and the emergence of what Nelson Mandela and Desmond Tutu envisioned as a "rainbow nation" with the welding of disparate elements into one nation. Will the South African attempt succeed when so many other nations have continued to experience tremendous internal friction, and when the splitting of countries has been a not infrequent event? Welding different groups together is by no means a simple endeavor.

The second chapter of the book of Acts starts with the recognition of the existence of several distinct groups, which had come to Jerusalem with one purpose, but which were decidedly different. Yet by the end of the chapter there had been the emergence of a group which was characterized not by the word "separation," but by its opposite, "together" (2:44, 46).

In itself what was recorded in Acts 2 was dramatic enough, but the rest of the book relates something even more striking, for the world of the day witnessed the practice of an apartheid beside which the South African version fades into insignificance. Jews maintained a rigid separation from Gentiles, especially from their neighbors in Samaria. Perhaps there was a similarity of cause in that the Jews saw their distinctiveness in a belief that God had chosen them (Deuteronomy 7:7). Likewise, even if it may be argued that the British must be reckoned culpable in their attitudes to the nonwhite population of South Africa, the belief of the Afrikaners that they were the chosen people of God reinforced and motivated an ethos of separation.

What emerged from the events recorded in Acts 2 was not a dull uniformity. The early Church was not a manifestation of communism. Even if there was an amazing practice of sharing, it was not equality, but an expression of love, the fruit of the Spirit, so that nobody was any longer in need. It was not very long before the original enthusiasm of sharing came under pressure in the story of Ananias and Sapphira (Acts 5), but the very existence of the story witnesses to the continued existence of private property. The story highlights that at the same time there was an openness, both in the sense of willingness to share material possessions, but also of not hiding personal secrets from each other. What had been produced was called *koinōnia*, active sharing (2:42), through which differences between people were not just removed, but that the needs of all would be met. Paul would later describe the interaction of people in the Church in terms of the members of one body (1 Corinthians 12:4f), where each is distinct, but where there is a process of mutual interaction and support.

This vision prefigures the dream that Nelson Mandela and Desmond Tutu have of a South Africa renewed after the horror of apartheid. The picture that is often used is of a rainbow nation, where color is obviously prominent in a way in which it was not in the early Church, but where the key idea is of diversity in unity.

But there may be an unfolding tragedy in South Africa. The dramatic events of Acts 2 can only be explained by the coming of the Holy Spirit. He has been described as *vinculum amoris*, "bond of love," where his action in the world is an expression of his role in relating the Persons of the Trinity. Later theology spoke of *perichōresis*, the interpenetration of the Persons so that they are absolutely equal while preserving distinction. It is this that he produced in the early Church.

Churches were very active in the transition from apartheid. The process of struggle was undergirded by an enormous amount of prayer both within and outside South Africa. The transition was held up as morally correct and in accordance with biblical norms. Then after the transfer to democracy, there was a process of "Truth and Reconciliation," inspired and chaired by Desmond Tutu, again an acknowledgment of God's hand in the whole process. This was only to be expected in a country where the majority of the country claimed to be Christian.

But South Africa has declared itself a secular state, and the accepted policy is pluralistic, no doubt acknowledging the existence of significant minorities from other faiths. The modern ideal of tolerance is upheld, and there is no longer a belief in the correctness of Christianity; it is one belief among others, as is common in the Western world. A not insignificant factor is the belief that Christianity was used to justify apartheid. Religious education is no longer a school subject; theology in universities is diminishing and under pressure. The contrast with the attitudes of the apostles is striking.

The society that is emerging is one of disparity. Far from the sharing of the early Church, South Africa is one of the most unequal societies in the modern world, with all the associated danger of unrest and conflict. The divisions are no longer rigidly along racial lines, although race is far from insignificant, but the economic divide is just as painful, even if it is seen not in skin color but in expensive clothes and cars.

While Peter, in his initial sermons, could trumpet the resurrection of Christ as evidence for the reality of the gospel, and while the "resurrection" of South Africa can likewise be seen as evidence for the reality of the action of God in the world, the appeal that Peter made to accept and to change, to "save yourselves from this crooked generation" (2:40), is increasingly falling on deaf ears.

Nonetheless, the miracle of Acts 2, and the subsequent miracle of 1994, provides hope, even confidence, that God would act again. While praying for, and expecting this, as they were at the start of Acts 2, Christians should emulate the disciples, who, although they could not really anticipate the coming events, were nevertheless acting in a way consistent with them, anticipating them as they were "together in one place" (2:1).

David T. Williams, originally from the United Kingdom, has served as a missionary in Southern Africa since 1971; he is currently professor of systematic theology at the University of Fort Hare, South Africa.

Five Thoughts on Acts 2 Relating to Theology and Practice in the Pentecostal Movement

Lee Roy Martin (United States)

"PENTECOST HAS COME TO LOS ANGELES" was the front-page headline for the inaugural issue of *The Apostolic Faith*, the newspaper published at the Azusa Street Mission by African American pastor William J. Seymour. The Azusa Street revival included extraordinary expressions of worship and witness, such as glossolalia, miracles, dreams, visions, healings, and prophecies. Many people questioned the validity of these experiences—opponents labeled the revival as fanatical at best and demonic at worst. Sympathizers were curious, but they were also puzzled about the meaning and significance of the manifestations. Seymour's paper was an attempt to defend the revival against its critics, to encourage the faithful, and to articulate for the inquisitive the meaning of the miraculous events. Seymour concluded on the basis of Acts 2 that Los Angeles was experiencing a last days' outpouring of the Holy Spirit that was meant to restore Apostolic Christianity to the world.

Seymour and other Pentecostals observed in Acts 2 a parallel to their own experience. The disciples of Jesus were filled with the Holy Spirit and began to speak in all kinds of tongues. The Jewish pilgrims who were in Jerusalem for the annual feast of Pentecost were astonished at this unexpected behavior. It was not a part of the usual Pentecost ritual; rather, it was something new and different. Many in the crowd, made uncomfortable by the disciples' vigorous praise of God, scoffed at them and accused them of debauchery. They said condemningly, "These people are drunk." Others were curious and asked, "What does this mean?" Peter stood forth and offered an answer to the question. Citing the prophet Joel, he declared that the unusual events signaled God's intent to pour out his Spirit upon all people. Furthermore, this Holy Spirit was flowing from Jesus Christ, whose crucifixion and resurrection ushered in the day of salvation.

Following the lead of Peter and of early Pentecostals, I would offer at least five answers to the question, "What does this mean?" First, the events of Pentecost mean that God is faithfully fulfilling his promises. Through Prophet Joel, God had promised that in the last days he would pour out his Spirit "upon all people" bringing charismatic gifts and activities such as prophecy, dreams, and visions to "sons and daughters," to young and old, and even to the poor and marginalized. The promises of Joel are echoed by John the Baptist who, in reference to Jesus, declares, "He shall baptize you with the Holy Spirit" (Matthew 3:11). Jesus himself assures his disciples saying, "I will pray to the Father, and he shall send you" the Holy Spirit (John 14:15). Then, just before his ascension into heaven, Jesus instructed them, "wait in the city of Jerusalem until you are clothed with power from heaven" (Luke 24:49). Therefore, in answer to the question, "What does this mean?" Peter responds, "This is that which Joel predicted and which Jesus promised." Peter insists further, "This promise is for all of you, for your children, and even to everyone who is far away" (Acts 2:39). Consequently, Pentecostals understand that we are living in the last days, that God is now faithfully fulfilling his purposes, and that Jesus Christ continues to pour out his Spirit upon believers everywhere.

Second, the events of Pentecost signify that Jesus Christ is alive, that he is active in the world, and that he has been exalted as Lord over all. Everyone in Jerusalem knew that Jesus had been crucified and buried, but only a few had knowledge of the resurrection. On the basis of the Spirit's outpouring, Peter argues that Jesus is alive (2:32–33). According to Peter, the Holy Spirit has come on behalf of the Lord Jesus to empower and guide the Church's witness to the world.

The ministry of Jesus and the Kingdom of God would not cease, but it would continue through the Spirit-empowered ministry of the Church.

Third, God's outpouring of his Spirit means that he is offering his love and grace to the entire world. Another section of Joel's prophecy that Peter cited promises, "And it shall come to pass that whosoever shall call upon the name of the Lord shall be saved" (2:21). Peter extended the offer of salvation to his listeners saying, "Repent and be baptized… and you shall receive the gift of the Holy Spirit" (2:38). This Pentecostal version of salvation declares that God's power is available and sufficient to deliver from any power that binds or oppresses. In most cases, salvation is a spiritual work, and those who repent will be delivered from the power and corruption of sin. Salvation can also mean deliverance from the power of drugs, alcohol, and other life-controlling substances and addictions. In still other contexts salvation might mean liberation from political and social oppression.

Fourth, the events of Pentecost mean that God continues to work in new, exciting, and surprising ways. The Church can at times appear to be fossilized, predictable, and powerless. In such times we may attempt to produce vitality and spectacle through our own ingenuity and creativity, but in Acts 2, the spectacle was of divine origin—"there came a noise from heaven like a rushing mighty wind" and "there appeared tongues like fire." These heavenly signs were demonstrations of God's visitation with inbreaking, transforming power. On the Day of Pentecost the onlookers were "amazed and perplexed" (2:12). Like those spectators, we do not enjoy uncertainty and ambiguity. It seems that the Church has now excluded any manifestations of God's presence that might result in amazement and perplexity. We are unsure how we should evaluate and respond to the signs that accompany God's visitation. God, however, desires to visit us in surprising ways; we must not attempt to confine him in our theological box. Only when we entertain him in new ways will we be able to recognize his contemporary presence and relevance. We must overcome any overreliance upon the familiar, the traditional, the certain, the ritualistic, and the predictable. We must invite and welcome divine interventions, prophecies, healings, miracles, and other manifestations of God's presence. For Pentecostals, this means that we should expect to be filled with the Holy Spirit just as the apostles were filled on the Day of Pentecost, and we should expect the same kinds of miraculous manifestations that occurred in the book of Acts. We pray for the sick with the expectation that God will heal them. We anticipate that our worship services will include utterances of tongues and prophecies from clergy and laity alike. We assume that, at any time, God may speak directly to us through a dream or a vision. As God pours out his Spirit, he continues to show himself to be the God of the present.

Fifth and finally, the outpouring of the Holy Spirit transforms Jesus' followers into a community of prophets that bears witness to the gospel. On the Day of Pentecost, the Spirit-filled believers "spoke in other tongues" (2:4) and proclaimed "the wonderful works of God" (2:11). The prophetic gift is not confined to select individuals; it is for "all people." It is not limited to certain categories of leaders or to particular classes of people. Joel foresaw the day when men and women of all ages and all social groups would prophesy (2:17–18). It is Jesus' own prophetic ministry of "miracles, wonders, and signs" (2:22) that serves as the paradigm for his Spirit-filled Church.

In sum, when Joel speaks of new voices and new visions, he anticipates neither the perpetual rote repetition of the old voices nor the nostalgic recitation of old visions; instead, he announces the eruption of new voices and new visions—sons and daughters will prophesy; new dreams and visions will break the old wineskins; and those on the margins will find themselves at the center of God's exploits, as he again brings salvation. The new voices and new visions seek to refresh and reshape the ancient theologies and usher them into new contexts.

The universal and indispensible Pentecostal testimony is that God never ceases to be intensely active; that is, he continues to speak and work through and among his people for the sake of his Kingdom in the world. From Azusa Street until now, Pentecostals everywhere have insisted upon the present reality of God's presence to save, sanctify, fill with the Holy Spirit, heal, and reign as coming king.

Lee Roy Martin (D.Th., University of South Africa) is Professor of Old Testament and Biblical Languages at Pentecostal Theological Seminary, Cleveland, Tennessee, United States.

QUESTIONS

1. Is there an imposed dominant language in your cultural context? How might Aymer's comments on language be brought to bear on the place in which you live?
2. Explain what Edmonds means by the "post-glossolalia moment." How does his reading integrate both a political-economic and spiritual dimension?
3. What parts of Acts 2 support Williams's statement that the Christian community was not "a manifestation of communism"?
4. Evaluate Martin's application of Acts 2 to spiritual and religious life today. What insights does such a connection bring? Are there possible problems in making such a link?

CHAPTER 36

ROMANS

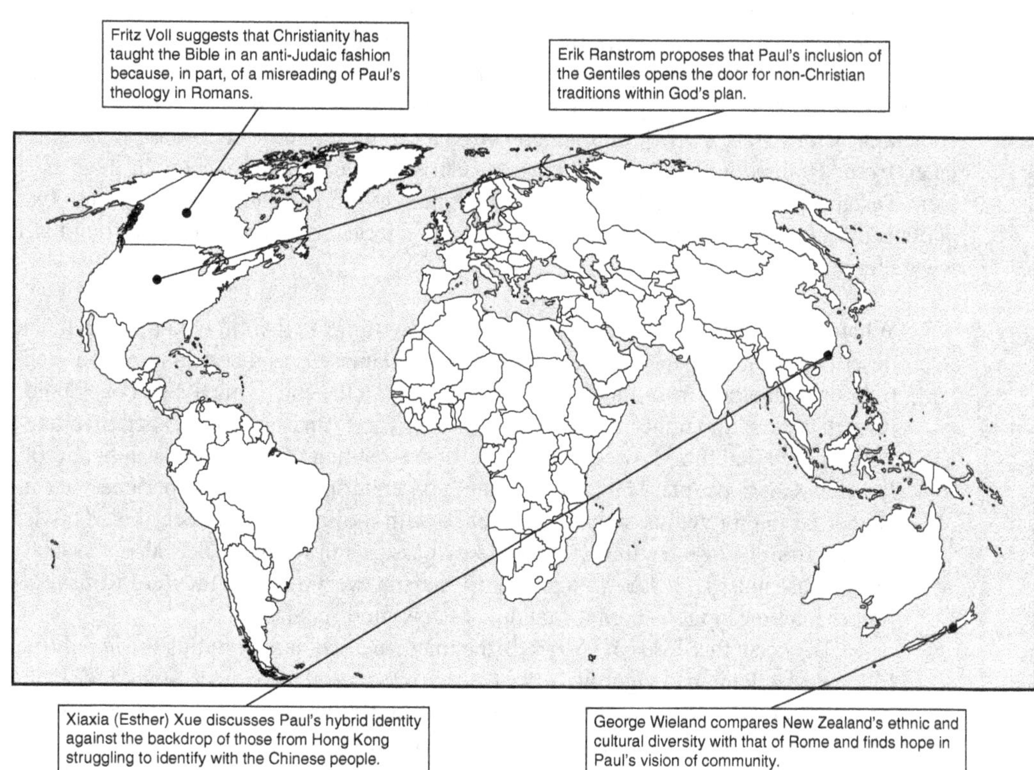

Fritz Voll suggests that Christianity has taught the Bible in an anti-Judaic fashion because, in part, of a misreading of Paul's theology in Romans.
Erik Ranstrom proposes that Paul's inclusion of the Gentiles opens the door for non-Christian traditions within God's plan.
Xiaxia (Esther) Xue discusses Paul's hybrid identity against the backdrop of those from Hong Kong struggling to identify with the Chinese people.
George Wieland compares New Zealand's ethnic and cultural diversity with that of Rome and finds hope in Paul's vision of community.

READINGS

Anti-Judaism as a Result of Misreading Paul's Theology in Romans
Fritz Voll

Paul's Inclusion of the Gentiles as an Opening for non-Christian Traditions
Erik Ranstrom

Paul's Identity against the Backdrop of the People of Hong Kong
Xiaxia (Esther) Xue

New Zealand's Ethnic and Cultural Diversity and Paul's Vision of Community
George Wieland

Anti-Judaism as a Result of Misreading Paul's Theology in Romans

Fritz Voll (Canada)

On the whole, Christianity has taught the Bible in an anti-Judaic fashion for 2,000 years, and it is still going on as if neither the Holocaust nor the foundation of the state of Israel ever happened. There is hardly a book on Christian biblical theology written before the 1950s and 1960s that is not anti-Jewish. When I discovered this in my own theological library, I had to throw out all books printed before this time. The New Testament cannot stand on its own; it is based on Judaism, its history, that is, on the Jewish Bible, the Church's "Old Testament." However, instead of admitting this freely, Christianity did its best to develop a "theology of contempt" (Jules Isaac) which dominated Christian thinking until the 1960s. What follows is taken from "Re-reading Paul—Guidelines for Christian clergy and teachers in their use of the New Testament with reference to the New Testament's presentation of Jews and Judaism" published by the Council of Christians and Jews, Victoria, Australia. It can be found at http://www.jcrelations.net.

> What is clear from a careful reading of Paul's writings is that he would never have described what happened to him on the road to Damascus as a conversion from one religion to another, from Judaism to Christianity. To the end of his life he considered himself a Jew, a member of the People Israel. The Damascus road experience and what ensued, led him, however, to a new understanding of himself as a Jew and of Israel as God's people. It was a profound and enduring religious experience but it cannot be interpreted as signaling a breach with the faith of his ancestors. This is evident from a close reading of several key passages in Romans. It is also a crucial insight that must be acknowledged by Christians everywhere if they are to have a proper relationship to and understanding of Jews and Judaism.
>
> To accept that Jesus of Nazareth, the man crucified under Pontius Pilate, whose followers he, Paul, had vigorously persecuted, was indeed alive, necessitated for Paul a profound reassessment of the nation to which he belonged. Just as, in the context of God's grace, it led to discovery in his own life of a hitherto unsuspected subtle sinfulness and resistance to God, it led also to a similar judgment on the nation as a whole, one that collapsed the vision of a holy nation separate from the surrounding nations of the world.
>
> Let us be quite clear: This pessimistic view of Israel in moral terms was a judgment made by a Jew within Israel. It was a judgment made in earlier times by many of the prophets of Israel. It was one being made in Paul's time by other Jews who shared his apocalyptic worldview, such as the members of the community who wrote the Dead Sea Scrolls, the author of the Fourth Book of Ezra, and evidently by John the Baptist. It was a prophetic view that in no sense implied a rejection of the Jewish nation but rather a summons to conversion in view of the coming judgment of God.
>
> Central to his personal experience of call was the conviction on Paul's part that it was his distinctive God-given task to summon the nations of the world to share in this movement of repentance centered upon but not confined to Jews. Israel had always acknowledged righteous Gentiles and, at the time of Paul, many people from

the nations were attracted to the monotheism and ethical uprightness of Judaism. Paul, however, fought for and served a more radical vision, one that by no means all his fellow members in the messianic Jesus movement shared. In Paul's view, the nations of the world would come to the God of Israel, not as converts to Judaism but precisely as Gentiles. They were not to take on circumcision and the ritual obligations of the Torah. Nor, through a rigorous imposition of the purity laws, were they to be made to feel second-class citizens when the community gathered to celebrate, worship and eat (Galatians 2:10–21).

Paul found scriptural validation in his reading of God's dealings with Abraham. Jewish writers before Paul had pictured Abraham as the first proselyte. Paul took this notion much farther. In Abraham's simple faith in God's promise that he would have a son and heir contrary to all the evidence, a faith that put him right with God ("justified" him), Paul saw prefigured a pattern whereby the nations of the world could find acceptance and salvation. In God's promise to Abraham that all peoples would be blessed in his descendents (Genesis 22:18; 26:4) he found scripture's indication that the final people of God would be made up of Israel and a vast constituency of believers from all the nations. Paul's view of salvation history gives priority to the covenant God made with Abraham over that made with Israel at Mt Sinai through Moses. After all, Abraham was justified before, not after, he was circumcised—thus circumcision was not a requirement for justification (Rom. 4:9–11).

This new understanding did not diminish for Paul his self-understanding as a Jew; nor did it depreciate the role of the Jewish people. Rather, it emphasized the place of each in the conversion of the nations to faith in the God of Israel.

Paul rejects the imposition of Torah upon Gentiles for two basic reasons. In the first place, as already mentioned, that imposition destroyed Gentile identity in a way contrary to God's will as explained to Abraham. Secondly, and this is a more contentious point, he believed that as an instrument of moral regulation it could not stand up to the ingrained power of sin in human beings. Paul's analysis in Romans 5–7 (5:20; 6:14–15; 7:5, 7–25; also 3:20; 4:15) of the nexus between law and sin is where he gives greatest offense, seemingly intolerable offense, to Jews and Judaism. What he is trying to do, however, is to dissuade Gentile converts from looking to Torah as a sure means of restraining the impulses and temptations to return to their old pagan pattern of life. Against this, Paul believed that the law would for them be useless, indeed, counterproductive. It would actually provoke rebellion and make matters worse (Rom. 7:5, 7–13, 14–25).

Paul makes it abundantly clear that the problem lay not in the law itself, which he insists remains "holy and righteous and good" (Rom. 7:12), but in the indwelling power of sinfulness in unredeemed human nature. So, for instance, when Paul speaks in Rom 8:2 of "the law of sin and death'' from which "the law of the Spirit of life has set me free," he is in no way identifying the Law of Moses with sin and death. The "law" of sin and death is the regime of sin in human life, which the Torah, in his view, is powerless to remedy. That judgment about the Law's impotence is made, as noted already, primarily with Gentiles in view.

When Christians read Paul's remarks about the Law (Torah) as God's general abrogation of the Law and apply these remarks to Jews and insist that Jews have to become Christians, they in fact deny God's covenantal faithfulness to the Jewish people (Rom. 11:29). For almost 2,000 years, since its separation from Judaism and beginning with the Church Fathers, Christianity has taught an anti-Judaism that contributed to anti-Semitism and the Holocaust.

Deeply shocked by the murder of 6 million Jews perpetrated by mostly baptized German Protestants and Catholics, the Catholic Church and most mainline Protestant churches the world over have since the late 1960s repented and reconsidered their theology of Judaism, among them Anglicans/ Episcopalians, Lutherans, and Reformed churches. They now recognize the lasting validity of God's covenant with God's people Israel and have begun to reread the New Testament in light of this recognition. Some evangelical churches, however, continue their anti-Judaic teaching and try to convert Jews to Christianity.

It takes time for the countless official statements of the churches to filter down to people in the pews. Many people baptized and confirmed as Christians will continue to know the Bible only in an anti-Jewish interpretation, as they were taught as children in Sunday schools and confirmation classes, especially if they don't continue to attend church services any longer.

Fritz Voll established the website Jewish–Christian Relations (www.jcrelations.net), to which he contributes as translator.

Paul's Inclusion of the Gentiles as an Opening for non-Christian Traditions

Erik Ranstrom (United States)

It is certainly worthwhile, even necessary, to consider whether the Bible itself has a global perspective. In our own time, the rise in popularity and increased legitimacy given to interreligious dialogue is pressuring Christians to relax and even eliminate claims of revealed truth. After all, as some have argued, hasn't the "pretension to be a 'chosen people, a royal priesthood, a people set apart' led to exclusivism, chauvinism, and expansionism"? The moral force of the question sometimes results in evacuating the meaning of the Bible altogether in favor of a shapeless, formless, least common denominator universal "religion" of morality and spirituality. Christians, however, should not renounce their faith or their belief in the truth of the biblical tradition in light of this challenge. The New Testament is not alien to such questions. The New Testament was written in pressure situations where "insider" and "outsider" debates generated interethnic and intrareligious conflict and debate. Much of this was caused by the New Testament God who worked in surprising and often unpredictable ways among those who were not thought to have anything to do with God (Gentiles). I believe that Paul's letter to the Romans has something to say to this contemporary, global sensitivity.

Unlike other correspondences that he had with churches throughout Asia Minor and Greece, Paul had never been to Rome and had no relationship with the Roman Christians. Paul was reaching out to them primarily because he needed to rally support for his missionary expedition to Spain. Establishing relations with the Roman Christians was going to be complex for Paul since it was his writings that in part had led to inflammatory relations between Gentile Christians and Jewish Christians there. The Gentile Christian community was most likely disparaging the venerable Jewish tradition, perhaps following an interpretation of Paul's legitimation of the Gentile mission and Gentile Christian identity in Galatians. The Jewish Christian community, indignant at being dishonored by the traditionally dishonorable Gentiles, responded with condescension by relying on stereotypes of the "nations" and their immorality. We can imagine Paul's situation very much like our own, interrelated, interreligious world, where our words and actions are never allowed the "privacy" of their limited audiences but get caught up in different, more strained contexts. Paul is very much like the "crisis" interreligious theologian today, having to do theology and address issues in a setting where much is at stake.

Paul begins Romans with a "plight" narrative in 1:18–32 that describes the Gentiles and their situation before God. God's grace and truth was indeed given to the Gentiles but was rejected. The Gentiles relied on their "lower nature" rather than on God's truth, and Paul introduces a laundry list of vices that ensued: wickedness, envy, evil, greed, malice, disorder. Now a first-century Jewish-Christian audience reading this opening to Romans would have nodded their heads in approval. What Paul narrates in 1:18–32 would have been a very familiar Jewish invective against the Gentiles and would have been viewed as an unequivocal victory for their claims to superiority. Finally, Paul had taken their side, and the Gentile Christians are put in their place. Yet, this is where Paul surprises them, for in the very next chapter, Paul accuses the Jews of failing to uphold the Law and deluding themselves that they would "escape God's judgment" (2:3). As Paul says, "For there is no distinction; all have sinned and are deprived of the glory of God" (3:23).

We can learn from this too, for often Christians compare religious traditions unfavorably; the Sermon on the Mount is compared to violence in other religious traditions, the "preferential option for the poor" is compared with the historical abuses of the caste system. When we maintain such lopsided comparisons and contrasts, we are making the same error as the Roman Jewish Christians, and need Paul to remind us of our sin, of our own lack of righteousness.

It is crucial to note that Paul in Romans doesn't stop with a universal condemnation. Condemnation in Romans serves only to undercut claims of superiority that were causing conflict and division within the community. It also sets the stage for the insight in the very next line (3:24) that Jewish and Gentile Christians both "are justified freely by his grace through the redemption in Christ Jesus." Just as Gentile Christians and Jewish Christians are impartially judged, they are also impartially redeemed in Christ. There are no exceptions in either judgment or salvation; all have fallen, all have been redeemed, and all are assured of divine forgiveness and divine presence. Now some will be quick to counter that this impartial redemption for Paul applies only to Christians, those who have through baptism entered into this universal community of salvation won by Christ. It can be argued by these well-intentioned contemporaries that in the ancient, Jewish-Christian world Gentiles may have been representative of inclusion, but more is required today.

But, I would argue, there needs to be a place for members of non-Christian religious traditions within God's plan. Anything less is too parochial. Now, Paul didn't have this question in mind in the first century, but today, we can bring the revelatory text of Romans into conversation with contemporary questions. To address this concern, let us discuss Paul's treatment of Abraham in Romans 4 and its contemporary, global, interreligious implications.

Paul had to answer the question, who is in the community of salvation? Only the Jewish Christians? Only the Gentile Christians? Paul mediates this conflict by hearkening back to the prototypical figure of Abraham. Abraham is the ancestor of God's community of salvation; everyone in this community is somehow related to Abraham. What aspect of Abraham's existence was deemed by God to be constitutive of the community of salvation? Is it available to all, or only to some? Paul maintained that what made Abraham righteous in the sight of God was Abraham's faith, so that whoever has faith shares in that same righteousness, now consummated in Christ. Paul's theology here was liberating for the Christian community at Rome because faith is not something exclusively tied into a particular ethnic identity; rather it is a human invariant. Therefore, Jew and Gentile are both kin in this community of faith.

Abraham is often referred to today as the "father" of Jews, Christians, and Muslims; this is in many ways quintessentially Pauline: Through Abraham all three of these faith traditions are united. But this can be extended beyond even the three "Abrahamic faiths" into other faith traditions and people of goodwill, keeping in mind the twentieth-century Catholic Christian German theologian Karl Rahner who spoke of the presence of the theological virtue of faith among non-Christian religious traditions and all people of goodwill. This faith is a mysterious reality, perhaps known fully only to God alone, but like Paul, Christians place their trust in the impartiality of God's favor and salvation, and bring healing and communion to a world torn by interreligious indifference, suspicion, and hostility.

Erik Ranstrom is a Teaching Fellow in the Department of Theology at Boston College, United States.

Paul's Identity against the Backdrop of the People of Hong Kong

Xiaxia (Esther) Xue (Hong Kong)

Some postcolonial scholars argue that an identity is not grounded in geography (where you are from), but rather in the retelling of the past. Hong Kong was under British (colonial) power for a century and a half before it was returned to Mainland China in 1997. For those of us from Hong Kong, it is difficult to identify with those Chinese people who haven't been under the British power because we have been highly influenced and even transformed by the British culture. One example is that we do not know how to speak the official Chinese language (Mandarin). For most of us, it is much easier to speak English than Mandarin. We somehow are stuck in between two cultural identities. On the one hand, we desire to be identified with our traditional Chinese cultural heritage, so we begin to learn Mandarin and build up relationships with people in Mainland China. On the other hand, Hong Kong culture has been Westernized. Thus, in some sense, we struggle between two cultural systems. Gradually we have come to realize our new hybrid identity by integrating our colonized cultural system into our current Chinese context.

It is in this context that I read the oft-discussed passage in Romans 7:14–25 where Paul, I propose, is also struggling with reconciling various religious and cultural identities. The members of the church in Rome to which Paul was writing contained both Jews and Gentiles who believed in Jesus as the Christ. Like those of us in Hong Kong, the Jewish people were subjected to foreign forces for centuries prior to Jesus. They experienced the various dominations of Assyrian, Babylonian, Persian, and Roman empires. During those periods, the Jewish people and their culture were transformed. One of the most notable influences is that the Seleucid king Antiochus IV (175–64 B.C.) attempted to abolish the sacral constitution of Jerusalem and Judaea and tried to assimilate his Jewish subjects culturally and religiously to the Hellenistic way of life. In 6 A.D. Judaea was made a Roman province, and it was given two-tier administration (an appointed Roman provincial governor and a Jewish high priest). Some of the provinces of the

Roman Empire assimilated Roman civilization so that their inhabitants came to think of themselves as Romans. By some estimates, there were between 40,000 and 60,000 Jews in Rome by the beginning of the first century A.D., as many as in Jerusalem itself.

In the book of Romans, Paul, as a representative Jew who was torn between two cultures, is speaking to other Jews describing his struggle with his past cultural identity. As a Hebrew born of Hebrews, he was a zealot, a persecutor of the church (Philippians 3:5–6). Ruled by a pagan polytheistic Roman Empire, Paul's concern for the national and religious life of the Jewish people impelled him to seek the independence of the nation and the restoration of the glory of the temple by the Messiah. Paul was driven to purify the nation by totally observing the law and persecuting people who spoke against the law (Stephen). Also, it was important for an honorable Jew to maintain inherited status in the "limited-good" culture of the first century. So, Paul's insistence on adherence to the laws of his tradition shows his desire to seek his identity in the historical past.

However, Paul's encounter on the way to Damascus had a series of transforming consequences, namely the realization that his zeal for the traditional Jewish culture and law had been misguided. Thus, when Paul talks about "wishing to do good, but doing evil instead," he does not mean that he does not have the ability to perform good. What he is referring to is that he sought to follow the will of God by persecuting Christians and confirming his identity in the root of the Jewish tradition, but what he had done in reality was to oppose the true Messiah by persecuting the Church. Similarly, when in Romans 7:17–18, 20 Paul reiterates "sin dwells within me" and "nothing good dwells within me," he is not referring to his inner evil self, or the evil impulse inside human beings. Rather, according to Romans 1, the sin of human beings is the ignorance of God, and seeking one's identity within themselves. Thus, "they became futile in their thinking" (1:20). Paul's zealous behavior demonstrates his seeking to establish his own righteousness in the Jewish laws. This demonstrates the power of sin "dwelling within me," which can refer to a certain force driving from a culturally twisted social system to push people to achieve certain religious or political goals. This zeal for their original identity led Jewish people into conflict with the very God they wanted to serve.

In 7:14–25, then, Paul is retelling his past story from his Christian perspective. It is a description of the struggle for a new self-understanding and way of being peculiar to the Jewish believer in Jesus. It is crucial to note that Paul does not simply reject the system of his Jewish tradition (e.g., the law) when he retold his story. He admits the good of the law (7:12). Moreover, the law is spiritual (v. 14), and could do many things for those who embrace it. Paul delights in his innermost with the law of God (v. 22). Now, however, Paul has arrived at a new stage of his understanding of the law, namely that faith in Christ establishes the law. Therefore, the new identity that Paul wishes his Jewish people to understand is a hybrid identity. Paul challenges his hearers in the Roman church to define their past in light of the new story of being in Jesus Christ.

In sum, Paul and the first Jewish followers of Jesus experienced a crisis of their cultural identity reminiscent of that experienced by those in postcolonial Hong Kong. In Romans 7:14–25 Paul looks back on his preconversion identity as a zealot for the Torah. He explains how the very heart of his religious devotion led him away from the will of God. Paul's new identity in Jesus Christ made him realize that this conflict lies not only within Paul himself but also among his pious Jewish people. Akin to our postcolonial cultural identity, Paul views his new hybrid identity as not totally ruptured with his past, but rather continuous with it. Paul, after all, does not become a Gentile after his conversion.

Xiaxia (Esther) Xue was born in FuJian, China, and studied in Hong Kong for many years; she is now a New Testament Ph.D. student at McMaster Divinity College, Canada.

New Zealand's Ethnic and Cultural Diversity and Paul's Vision of Community

George Wieland (New Zealand)

Auckland is New Zealand's largest city, with a population of 1.3 million. With almost 40 percent of its population comprising people born outside New Zealand it is increasingly diverse. Currently around 11 percent of the city's population is of Maori descent (indigenous people of New Zealand), 56 percent is European (descendants of nineteenth-century settlers or more recent arrivals), 15 percent have Pacific Island heritage, and the most dramatic increase over the last two decades has been in Auckland's Asian population (from Taiwan, Hong Kong, South Korea, India, the People's Republic of China, etc.), which now stands at around 19 percent of the total.

Many of those who have migrated to New Zealand have brought with them strong traditions of Christian faith, and others have found faith here. Pacific Island churches are prominent in some parts of Auckland and more than a hundred Chinese and a similar number of Korean congregations meet, some in their own church buildings but most in local schools or in premises belonging to other churches. To those may be added Russian, Iranian, Vietnamese, Ethiopian, Brazilian, Japanese, Afrikaans, and many other groups. As in many cities around the world, however, immigration and increasing evidence of diversity has been challenging for some who regard themselves as "traditional New Zealanders" and fear a dilution of what they regard as their cultural identity. Such responses are also found in many churches, even toward immigrants who share their Christian faith.

Reading Romans in this context (I myself moved to Auckland from Scotland 11 years ago) has thrown into sharp relief aspects of Paul's message in this letter that I had paid little attention to before. Rome, like contemporary Auckland, was a large multicultural city. It was ethnically and culturally diverse, with the addition of multiple gradations of social status, political influence, and wealth. Christian faith had first been brought to Rome by Diaspora Jews, residents of Rome's large Jewish quarter who had made the journey to Jerusalem for the festivals and had experienced the astonishing events of Pentecost and the subsequent proclamation of Messiah Jesus. By the time Paul wrote his letter, the church had evidently spread beyond the Jewish community and there were several groups of believers meeting in various homes, probably ranging from crowded tenements to the villas of the better-off. It's quite probable that these home-based groups would have comprised clusters of similar people, with particular attitudes and ways of behaving, and that there might have been some reluctance to have much to do with other groups who were different.

That wasn't good enough for Paul! He pleads with them, "Welcome one another, therefore, just as Christ has welcomed you, for the glory of God" (15:7). The "one another" who come into view in Romans 14–15 are believers who have different opinions and practices concerning food and drink and the observance or otherwise of particular days. Reading in ethnically diverse Auckland, these sound very much like cultural distinctives, and specifically the different norms that would have shaped the attitudes and behavior of people brought up in various Jewish and Gentile environments in the Roman world.

Rather than being an argument purely about ethical choices among Christians who varied principally in their stages of spiritual maturity, the issue that Paul was addressing seems to have had a lot to do with the challenge of cultivating authentic community across barriers of social, ethnic, and cultural difference.

But why does this matter? If churches are growing, worshiping, and witnessing within their own ethnic groups, is intercultural fellowship really a gospel priority? Rereading the familiar text of Romans with such questions in mind brings to the fore a dimension of the gospel that a more individualistic focus obscures, namely, that in it God brings together into one people those who had been ethnically and culturally separate. The gospel is the startling message that through God's Son, the Davidic Messiah, the Gentiles—the *ethnē*, the nations of the world—are called to belong to the one people of God, receiving together the gift of salvation (1:1–6). Paul is not ashamed to take this gospel to the heart of the empire, the multicultural city of Rome, because it is the power of God for salvation to everyone who has faith, to the Jew first and also to the Greek (1:16).

This theme runs through the letter's magnificent sustained exposition of the gospel. Romans 1–3 argue that all, of whatever ethnic identity, are under the power of sin, and that God deals with all on the same basis, that of faith in Jesus Christ. Romans 4 demonstrates that Abraham is the ancestor not only of those who could claim biological descent from him but of all who share his faith in a God who gives life to the dead. Romans 5 traces the problem of sin back beyond the Law that was given through Moses to the first human ancestor, Adam, and declares that God's gracious answer to that problem in Jesus Christ meets the need not only of Moses' disciples but of Adam's whole family. Romans 6–8 expound the new identity and the new life of those who become children of God through union with Christ rather than through any particular ethnic affiliation. Romans 9–11 wrestle with what this new vision of a family of God means for the more exclusive understanding of Israel as God's family, and offers the illustration of Israel as the olive tree that God had planted and cultivated, from which unfruitful branches had been pruned, but into which wild, uncultivated branches from among the nations were now being grafted.

When Paul turns in Romans 12–15 to spell out what all this means for the Christian community in multicultural Rome, his appeal has to be heard as not directed primarily to individual believers and their ethical choices, nor even to house churches regarding their internal relationships, but to the whole diverse people of God in Christ in that city. They are to be a family living for the glory of God as they break free from the ungodly assumptions, attitudes, and ambitions prevalent in their environment and radically reshape their thinking according to what God intends for his world (12:1–2). So in place of pride and competitiveness there is humility and mutuality; in place of indifference or a desire to retaliate there is love and generosity; in place of self-protective withdrawal from wider society there is respectful participation and love in action (Romans 12–13).

This includes how the believers are to relate to one another. Romans 14–15 turn out to be not an afterthought, but a major goal to which the argument of the letter has been leading! If the gospel really is the power of salvation for all, then that astonishing scope has to be seen and experienced in the community of those who are being saved. This, says Paul, is how God is glorified: "May the God of steadfastness and encouragement grant you to live in harmony with one another, in accordance with Christ Jesus, so that you may together with one voice glorify the God and Father of our Lord Jesus Christ. Welcome one another, therefore, just as Christ has welcomed you, for the glory of God" (15:5–7).

A string of Old Testament quotations (15:9–12) reinforces Paul's point that it is God's intention to gather the nations together with Israel to receive his mercy, to praise him joyfully, to live as one people under the rule of his Messiah.

Looking across my city, I hear in Romans 14–15 a series of rebukes to the kind of attitudes that obstruct relating in Christ across barriers of difference. There are the judgmental attitudes toward Christians whose practices and opinions are different from mine (14:1–13), the woefully inadequate vision of the kingdom of God that focuses on those differences rather than what really matters (14:17), the failure to look for and do what builds up the community and particular people within it (14:19; 15:2). I glimpse in these chapters the exhilarating prospect of people of all cultures and languages praising God joyfully as one (14:11; 15:5–12). I recognize more fully than before that this diverse but united worshiping and mutually accepting community is what God intends and is the goal for which Christ gave himself (15:8–9). It is what Paul longed to see, and it must also be what I hope for and strive toward among the still too fragmented Christian community in Auckland.

George Wieland is Lecturer in New Testament and Director of Mission Research and Training at Carey Baptist College, Auckland, New Zealand.

QUESTIONS

1. Read carefully the relevant passages from Romans and assess Voll's argument concerning Paul and the Law. What, if any, counterpoints could be made?
2. In what ways are the writings/views of both Paul and Ranstrom a reflection of their particular historical and cultural location?
3. What are the strengths and weaknesses of Xue's reading of Romans 7:17–18, 20?
4. What are some of the specific challenges of "cultivating authentic community"? How and why might those in Rome and Auckland resist Paul's and Wieland's call for a "united worshiping and mutually accepting community"?

CHAPTER 37

EPHESIANS

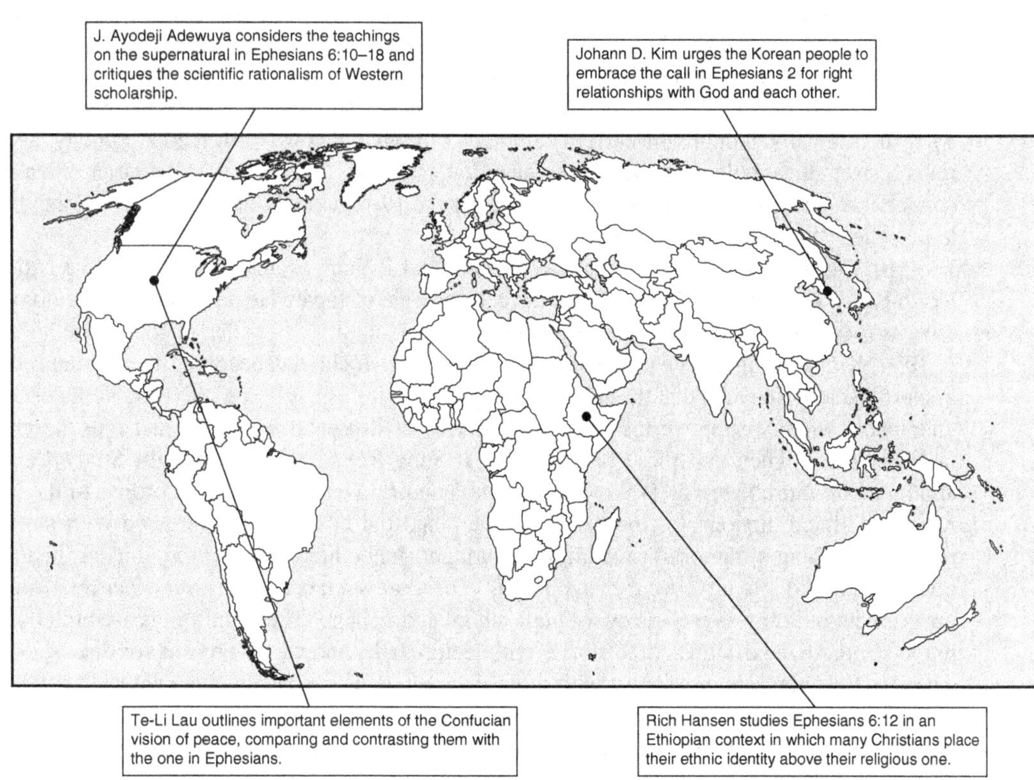

J. Ayodeji Adewuya considers the teachings on the supernatural in Ephesians 6:10–18 and critiques the scientific rationalism of Western scholarship.
Johann D. Kim urges the Korean people to embrace the call in Ephesians 2 for right relationships with God and each other.
Te-Li Lau outlines important elements of the Confucian vision of peace, comparing and contrasting them with the one in Ephesians.
Rich Hansen studies Ephesians 6:12 in an Ethiopian context in which many Christians place their ethnic identity above their religious one.

READINGS

A Call for Koreans to Practice Right Relationships with God and Each Other
Johann D. Kim

Ephesians 6:12 in an Ethiopian Context
Rich Hansen

The Supernatural in Ephesians and a Critique of Scientific Rationalism
J. Ayodeji Adewuya

Comparing Ephesians and the Confucian Vision of Peace
Te-Li Lau

A Call for Koreans to Practice Right Relationships with God and Each Other

Johann D. Kim (Korea)

Since 1945, the tiny nation of Korea has been divided into two nations because of ideological differences. South Korea is a capitalist nation, while the North is communist. There are also major religious differences. North Korea follows the path of Juche (translated "self-reliance"), while the South has become increasingly Christianized. Into this context of division, strife, and tension between North and South Korea, we can turn to Paul's call in Ephesians 2 for unity in Christ as a source of hope for the future of Korea.

The first major Christian revival in Korea occurred with the arrival of missionaries in 1907 in, ironically enough, the current capital city of what is now North Korea, Pyongyang. The revival swept the whole country, with some reports showing that more than a quarter of a million conversions occurred within a year. Indeed, after the 1907 revival, the city of Pyongyang began to be called "Jerusalem of the East."

In 1945 things changed dramatically when Kim Il-Sung established the separate nation of North Korea when it was liberated from the colonial rule of Japan. He developed an ideology that took its root in Marx-Leninism but soon became a personality cult called Juche. Since his death in 1994, Kim Il-Sung has been worshiped as a god and Juche has become the national religion in North Korea. The idea that the Juche ideology functions as a religion in North Korea becomes undeniable when we realize that they have places of liturgical functions just like the church in Christianity. They call these places "Kim Il-Sung Revolutionary Thought Study Centers" and there are more than 450,000 of them in the country. Here is where, according to the North Korean political dictionary, "the party members and the laborers are equipped with the comrade Kim Il-Sung's immortal revolutionary thought, Juche ideology and the glorious history of revolution in order to advance the revolution." There are such centers at every factory, office, or government building as well as every high school and college. These buildings are built according to standardized designs: three stories with lecture halls and various rooms for discussion and study. In the cities, any work unit with more than 100 workers has its own center. In rural parts of the country, at least every other village has a center. These centers are maintained with utmost care in order to keep them spotlessly clean. Inside the center, the portraits of Kim Il-Sung and Kim Jong Il (his son and successor) are prominently displayed. People are expected to enter the centers without wearing coats and shoes.

In stark contrast, in South Korea Christianity has grown to be one of the largest religions in the nation (Buddhism being the other major one), with close to 10 million followers, nearly 30 percent of the population. However, the numerical growth of Christianity in Korea does not tell the whole story. Numerous reports of corruptions and scandals in the Korean churches have seriously undermined its credibility among the public, where the church ranks dead last in trustworthiness in opinions polls. The essential problem is Mammonism: money, greed, and power. Indeed, the rapid economic growth in the last quarter-century swallowed the gospel of Jesus and spit out a new type of religion mixed with the powerful and sweet gospel of prosperity, which has, unfortunately, mesmerized many. The church is in crisis. If in the north, Juche replaced Christianity, then in the south, Mammonism has replaced it.

In Ephesians, Paul argues that it is God who unifies the universe under the lordship of Jesus Christ, his Son. Paul declares that "you were dead through the trespasses and sins" (2:1). But Jesus defeated "the ruler of the power of the air" on the cross and we were made alive together with Him in resurrection because of God's abundant mercy and love toward us. Paul argues that we have been saved by the grace of God so that no one can boast—it is the gift of God (2:8–9). Not only did God save us by His grace, but also He prepared beforehand "good works" for us to carry on with our lives. In 2:11–22, Paul delineates the nature of the good work that God prepared for us: It is none other than to work to be "one new humanity" (2:15) in Christ who broke down the dividing wall of the hostility and became our peace (2:14). Paul uses Temple imagery to explain this process: "In him the whole structure is joined together and grows into a holy temple in the Lord; in whom you also are built together spiritually into a dwelling place for God" (2:21–22). The vertical restoration of humanity's relationship with God results in the horizontal restoration of relationship between people.

This is the message that the Korean people must embrace. This is the good news of God that is being spoken to them. Both in North and South Korea, people are still following their passions of the flesh, its desires and senses (2:3). It appears that very few Christians have survived the long period of persecution in the North. Likewise, it seems that very few faithful and renewed Christians have survived in the tainted churches in the South. However, if we know the power of God who raised Jesus from the dead, we also believe that it is possible for us to see another revival in Korea, not just in the South, but also in the North, and the Korean people will become one again in the Lord. With Paul, we confess, "there is one body and one Spirit, just as you were called to the one hope of your calling, one Lord, one faith, one baptism, one God and Father of all, who is above all and through all and in all" (4:4–6). Amen.

Johann D. Kim is Associate Professor of New Testament at Colorado Christian University, United States.

Ephesians 6:12 in an Ethiopian Context

Rich Hansen (Ethiopia)

Human life flows through various "structures of existence" that give coherence to our lives—government, family, religion, social expectations and traditions, and so forth. One's clan, tribe, or ethnic group is a prime example of these structures that bring order and cohesion to life for many of the world's people. In Ephesians 6:12, Paul warns that these structures of existence can be invaded by and even taken over by evil powers. When he speaks of the "principalities and powers," he is referring to the fact that good structures God created for the benefit of the world (Colossians 1:16) have been warped from their good purpose and now stand in opposition to God and Christ (Colossians 2:8).

Human government is a perfect example. Paul speaks of the positive role of the "governing authority" as God's servant in Romans 13; yet in the book of Revelation we see this same Roman government vilified as the "beast"—the instrument Satan uses to bring horrible persecution to the early Christians. An even better example is the Old Testament law, which the Bible repeatedly tells us was God's gift to his people. Yet Paul is just as clear in Galatians that this law has mutated into an enslaving legalistic power, keeping people from Christ. Theologian Stanley Grenz offers this helpful summary:

> Despite God's good intention for the structures, however, they can be manipulated for evil purposes. In this manner, what God intends as a means to promoting community can actually weaken it. Rather than aiding people in building community, the powers enslave them. Structures become a channel for evil, whenever they are pressed into the service of evil ends (Theology for the Community of God [Grand Rapids: Eerdmans, 1994], 233).

So the structures God intends for good, to bring meaning and stability to human life, can (and often *do*) become warped and evil.

Here in Ethiopia, as in much of the global south, ethnic identity is *the* primary structure that not only tells people "who they are" but makes life both meaningful and livable day-to-day. Ethnic diversity—Ethiopia has more than 80 distinct people groups—enriches the society in the same way biological diversity enriches our natural world. But exactly because ethnic identity is such a primal structure of existence, it is always susceptible to be co-opted by the "principalities and powers" to spawn great evil. The Hutu versus Tutsi ethnic cleansing in Rwanda in which more than 800,000 died was a dramatic demonstration of what continues to happen under the radar of worldwide attention. About two years ago, deadly conflict erupted between two tribal groups in western Ethiopia, tragically including Christians taking up arms to fight one another, sometimes even members of the *same congregation*. Ethnic identity trumped Christian identity.

However, when Christians consider their ethnic identity, we encounter a paradox. Unlike Islam, which forces Muslims worldwide to worship in the Arabic language, Christianity promotes exactly the opposite—planting faith and worship as deeply as possible in every indigenous language and culture. In Ethiopia, vast resources are being expended translating the Bible into many tribal languages because we Christians believe so strongly (especially after the mistakes of the nineteenth-century mission colonialism) that every human being has the right to grow as a disciple of Jesus Christ without having to reject his or her own ethnic/cultural identity.

But *tribalism*—giving ultimate loyalty to one's own ethnic group—is idolatry. Tribalism is always lurking around churches here, ready to snatch what God intends for good and turn it toward evil. Particular tribal groups, who jealously guard the leadership positions for their own tribe and are unwilling to share power with those from other tribes, dominate most Protestant denominations in Ethiopia. Minorities are made to feel "second class" by those in the majority. Churches split and withdraw from one another over which language to use in worship.

Ethiopian Christian leaders struggle mightily against ethnic identity being co-opted by the "principalities and powers" and turned into the false god of tribalism. However, they are not alone. The Apostle Paul engaged in the same struggle throughout his ministry. Listen to his own confession in Philippians 3:4–7: "If anyone else thinks he has reasons to put confidence in the flesh, I have more: circumcised on the eighth day, of the people of Israel, of the tribe of Benjamin, a Hebrew of Hebrews; in regard to the law, a Pharisee; as for zeal, persecuting the church; as for legalistic righteousness, faultless. But whatever was to my profit I now consider loss for the sake of Christ." Eugene Peterson in his modern English paraphrase, *The Message Bible*, translates the last verse with extra punch: "Compared to the high privilege of knowing Christ Jesus as my Master, firsthand, everything I once thought I had going for me is insignificant—dog dung."

In his words we can recognize Paul's subtle pride in his own ethnic heritage. Paul is *not* saying everything about being a Jew is "dog dung." He is not criticizing his Jewishness in and of itself anymore than in other places he criticizes the Old Testament law in and of itself. No, it is *to what purpose* that ethnic identity (or the law) is used. Whenever Paul's ethnic heritage gets in the way of following Christ... whenever people assume they are part of "God's people" simply because they are Jewish, or Amhara, or Oromo... whenever, in short, ethnicity is overrun and bent toward evil by the principalities and powers... *then* Paul will set aside his heritage and be sure everyone in his church knows it. In relative terms, his new identity in Christ is far *more* important to him than his ethnic identity.

Paul's radical Magna Charta of human identity is this: "There is neither Jew nor Greek, slave or free, male or female, for you are all one in Christ Jesus" (Galatians 3:28). This is the challenge for church leaders here in Ethiopia—where ethnic identity is still "everything people have going for them" to get ahead, to belong, to survive. Church leaders here are challenged to walk in the Apostle Paul's sandals, let his mind-set shape their own personal agenda, and then declare that Christian identity always trumps ethnic identity as passionately and as courageously as Paul does. Will outsiders look at the church and see the same ethnic rivalry, nepotism, and even violence they are accustomed to seeing between tribal groups in every other sector of society? Or will they look at the church and see Christians not denigrating their ethnic heritage but setting it aside whenever necessary in favor of their far greater identity as "*one in Christ Jesus*"?

Rich Hansen is Professor of Systematic Theology at Ethiopian Graduate School of Theology, Addis Ababa, Ethiopia.

The Supernatural in Ephesians and a Critique of Scientific Rationalism

J. Ayodeji Adewuya (United States)

Ephesians 6:10–18 is perhaps one of the clearest descriptions in the New Testament of the nature of the spiritual warfare that believers face. Yet its interpretation is less than clear due to cultural influences. Paul does not call the believer to enter into spiritual warfare. He simply announces it as a fact. The fact that our real battle is not against flesh and blood is lost on many Christians, who put all their efforts in that direction. This passage informs us of the nature of our divine weapons, which imply the nature of the struggle that we are in.

Proper preparations are the key to executing a successful war. One aspect of preparation is to know the enemy's capabilities and limitations. C. S. Lewis makes the perceptive observation: "There are two equal and opposite errors into which our race can fall about the devils. One is to disbelieve in their existence. The other is to believe, and to feel an excessive and unhealthy interest in them. They themselves are equally pleased by both errors, and hail a materialist and a magician with the same delight" (*The Screwtape Letters* [New York: Macmillan, 1961], ix). Perhaps at no other time is C. S. Lewis' observation more important than in the twenty-first century. Western scholarship is dominated by antisupernaturalistic rationalism in which the mention of evil powers in the New Testament is as a myth that needs to be removed in order to make the message suited to a postmodern scientific age. Such understanding not only refuses to share the first-century Mediterranean worldview concerning the spirit world but also argues that supernatural powers are incapable of interfering with, or interrupting, the natural realms of cause and effect. Other scholars, although recognizing and accepting the presence and reality of the supernatural forces as described by Paul, nonetheless diminish their primary malevolent influence. As such, the powers are considered to refer to good angelic powers rather than to hostile demonic forces. These interpreters also suggest that the powers refer to social, economic, and political structures that affect people's everyday lives. Thus, these powers constitute "a collective symbolization of evil" and the "collective weight of human existence." These interpretations are different from Africa, where there is a deeply rooted belief in a mystical power or force in the universe. As such, there is no difficulty in accepting the existence and reality of the influence of evil spirits. Without doubt, the African and the first-century Mediterranean share similar beliefs about the spirit world. Thus, the African understanding of Ephesians 6:10–18 is closer to Paul's than that which prevails in the Western hemisphere.

Paul describes the enemy in rather vivid terms. It is completely irrelevant if the particular opponent we face is a "principality," a "power," or a "ruler of the darkness of this age." Collectively, they are all members of spiritual hosts of wickedness in the heavenly places. They are all part of a spiritual army that is organized and established into ranks and under the headship of Satan, the devil, who comes against us with his wiles. These are not just "the world of axioms and principles of politics and religion, of economics and society, of morals and biology, of history and culture." Such a view is reflective of people in the Western hemisphere who downplay the existence of real evil forces that wreak havoc in the world. Paul believed in the personal character of the powers of evil in the universe.

Paul lists several items of the believer's armor in the order in which they would be put on. Together they comprise the *panoplia* worn before taking the field. First is the belt of truth to deflect the lies and tricks of the devil. The "breastplate of righteousness" stands for uprightness and integrity of character. But this moral rectitude and reputation for fair dealing results directly from the appropriation of Christ's righteousness. Christians are not to seek their protection in any works of their own but only in what Christ has done for them and in them.

Once the breastplate has been fitted into position, the soldier puts on his strong army boots. The Christian soldier must have the protection and mobility that come with one's feet "shod with the preparation of the gospel of peace." The Christian soldier is then to "take up the shield of faith." For the Christian this protective shield is faith, both in action and in its objective content. With such a shield, the believer can extinguish all the incendiary devices flung by the devil (v. 11). The Christian's shield effectively counteracts the danger of such diabolical missiles not merely by arresting or deflecting them, but by actually quenching the flames to prevent them from spreading.

The Christian's only weapon of offence is "the sword of the Spirit." "The word of God" is the divine utterance or speech, the powerful spoken word. Finally, Christians are to "pray in the Spirit on all occasions." By doing so, they can stand firm and true, successfully resisting all enemies and spiritual foes only as they remain in the spirit of prayer, ready always to cry unto the Lord and lay all their needs before him.

In brief, in Ephesians 6:10–18, Paul not only assures us that there is a spiritual war but also warns us that apart from utilizing the weapons which God has provided for us, we are hopelessly underpowered. If we plan to win the battle, we must rely on provisions and resources beyond human capabilities.

J. Ayodeji Adewuya is Professor of New Testament at Pentecostal Theological Seminary, Cleveland, Tennessee, United States, and a Fellow at Manchester Wesley Research Centre, Didsbury, Manchester, United Kingdom.

Comparing Ephesians and the Confucian Vision of Peace

Te-Li Lau (United States)

Ephesians and the Confucian *Four Books* (a collection of four key Confucian texts) both share a grand vision of peace. The Ephesian vision of peace encompasses the household, the local church, the heavenly church, and the cosmos; the Confucian vision of peace likewise encompasses the household, the state, the empire, the world, and the cosmos. Moreover, both demonstrate a complex relationship between ethics, politics, and metaphysics. Putting both texts in conversation may therefore provide insights for a fresh perspective of Ephesians. Here I will briefly outline important elements of the Confucian vision of peace, compare and contrast them with Ephesians, and conclude with some implications for reading Ephesians.

The Confucian *Four Books* is traditionally ascribed to Confucius and his school. Confucius lived during the Eastern Zhou period (770–256 B.C.E.), a time of great political upheaval that saw the dissolution of old feudal structures. Framed within the chaos and anarchy of this period, Confucius and his disciples created a vision of peace that attempted to recapture the stability of the glorious past as witnessed in the Western Zhou Dynasty (1100?–771 B.C.E.). This vision encompasses several elements:

1. The Confucian vision of peace is dominated by the concept of harmony. Harmony is not static uniformity; it is the dynamic unity and tensive balance that forms when one pole constantly adapts to the push and pull of other poles. Such a harmony or perfect balance is brought about by proper practice of the rites that reflect the underlying pattern or principle of all things in the universe. Although originally developed within a religious context, the concept of rites gradually expanded into a complex system whose scope includes norms of acceptable behavior in all aspects of human life: from liturgies in various ceremonies, such as weddings and sacrifices, to norms regulating social conventions, such as receiving a guest, and to rules of conduct in the minute details of life, such as sweeping the floor.
2. Confucianism envisions peace in multiple concentric circles of focus: individual, household, kingdom, and the cosmos. At the individual level, peace is the full realization of one's innate good moral nature, the maintenance of perfect balance in all aspects of life, and the uniting of one's feelings, thought, will, and action. At the household and the kingdom level, peace results from the acceptance of one's preordained social station in life and the fulfillment of one's moral and social obligations within the social and political hierarchy. At the cosmic level, peace ensues when all beings realize their innate principle, proceeding according to their nature and the Way of Heaven.
3. The means of attaining peace within the multiple concentric circles of focus starts with the moral cultivation of the individual. Only individuals who have fully realized their nature and become a sage are able to develop the nature of others through a ripple-like effect, thus bringing harmony first to their immediate household, then their kingdom, and then the entire world. The moral influence of the sage does not, however, stop at the human social world; it also encompasses the cosmic and natural order. Sages who manifest absolute integrity form a trinity with Heaven and Earth, participating in their transformative and generative processes which ultimately bring balance and peace to the cosmos. The sequence for implementing the vision of peace is thus laid out as follows: Individual → Household → Kingdom → World → Cosmos.

4. Given the political context in which Confucius lived, the primary frame of reference for his vision of peace is the state, and the intended audience includes the intellectual elite, political advisers, and rulers. If the Confucian vision of peace begins with the moral cultivation of the individual, then the primary individual in focus is undoubtedly the king. When the king acts virtuously, he will effect the ethical transformation and renewal of the people as they imitate his example.

We turn now to a comparison with the Ephesian vision of peace. Ephesians was written to various Christian communities in Asia Minor who were familiar with the Jewish Scriptures, not least of which is the creation account in Genesis (Eph. 3:9). The Ephesian vision of peace is therefore located within a context of initial cosmic order followed by a rupture and chaos that necessitates a reconciliation and uniting of all things under Christ. This larger context differs from Confucian thought as it does not seek to recover the past but to forge a new cosmic order, a new creation (2:10, 15; 3:9; 4:24). Further comparison with the Confucian vision of peace can be laid out as follows:

1. While Confucianism is dominated by the concept of harmony and balance, the Ephesian vision of peace is communicated by a cluster of terms including "peace" (2:14, 15, 17; 4:3; 6:15), "reconciliation" (2:16), "unity" (4:3), "submission" (1:22; 5:21, 24), and "oneness" (4:4–6). Moreover, while Confucian harmony is brought about by meticulously following the prescribed rites at every social level, the Ephesian vision of peace is brought about by means of Christ's death on the cross. Christ plays such a vital role in the Ephesian vision of peace that not only is he the *basis* for peace, he is also the *locus* (1:10; 2:13; 3:6) and the *personification* (2:14) of peace.
2. As in Confucian thought, Ephesian peace operates at multiple levels. In the human sphere, peace is the elimination of ethnic enmity between Jews and Gentiles, the use of individual gifts for building up the ecclesial body, and the maintenance of household codes within a framework that presents God in Christ as the true *pater familias*. In the spiritual sphere, peace is the reconciliation of believers to God and their incorporation into the body of Christ. In the cosmic sphere, peace is the summing up and uniting of all things under the headship of Christ (1:10).
3. In contrast to Confucian thought, Ephesians considers the basis for attaining peace not to rest on human effort but on the prior work of Christ. Due to Christ's sacrificial death, believers are reconciled to God and consequently to one another; due to Christ's subjugation of the cosmic powers, cosmic peace is inevitable. Ephesians nevertheless stands in the tension of the "already" and "not yet." The Ephesian vision of peace has been decisively inaugurated, but its full realization will only occur in the coming age (1:21; 2:7). Standing in this tension, the church must embrace the unity brought about by the Spirit (4:3) so that it can function as the proleptic symbol of the future perfect unity under Christ. The existence of a united church then proclaims to the evil spiritual powers that their authority has been broken and that their demise is certain.
4. The primary frame of reference for the Ephesian vision of peace is the church, and the intended audience is not the leaders of the church but its members. As an intentional community or voluntary organization, the church seeks to transform members with different worldviews and backgrounds into a unified body politic. Central to this goal is the formation of a common pool of values (4:4–6); a common communal history that recalls their election before the foundation of the world (1:4) and their formation through the death of Christ (2:16); and a common understanding that they are no longer strangers and aliens, but fellow citizens and familial members within God's household (2:19).

Finally, we can consider some of the implications for reading Ephesians. The ability to compare meaningfully Ephesians with the overtly political Confucian texts confirms the presence of political elements in Ephesians. Nevertheless, one must not ignore its theological character. It is therefore best to understand Ephesians as a politico-religious letter on peace that lays the framework for constructing a new communal identity within the reality of Christ's supreme rule. Ephesians lays out the foundational narrative of the community, explaining that believers were predestined before the foundation of the world. It also guides the church to embrace the certain hope of a fully restored cosmos in the coming age (1:10, 21; 2:7). Ephesians, however, does not only present past and future aspects of the ecclesial community in relationship to God's decisive act in Christ; it also stresses the present mission of the church. By setting ethical standards for the community and presenting their present life as a conflict with malevolent spiritual forces that threaten ecclesial unity, Ephesians urges the church toward peace so that she can function as a testimony to the power of God's plan of reconciliation in Christ. In a time where the church is still divided by cultural, ethnic, geographical, and socioeconomic factors, the message of Ephesians is still powerfully relevant today.

Te-Li Lau, originally from Singapore, is Assistant Professor of New Testament at Trinity Evangelical Divinity School, Deerfield, Illinois, United States; he is the author of The Politics of Peace: Ephesians, Dio Chrysostom, and the Confucian Four Books, *from which this essay is taken.*

QUESTIONS

1. How are Juche and "Mammonism" alike? How are they different?
2. How, if at all, is Paul's "ethnic heritage" different from the context in Ethiopia?
3. How do your own views about the existence of evil spirits compare to Adewuya's? What arguments would you make in support of your position?
4. Which vision of peace do you find more appealing, the Confucian or Ephesian one?

CHAPTER 38

PHILIPPIANS 2

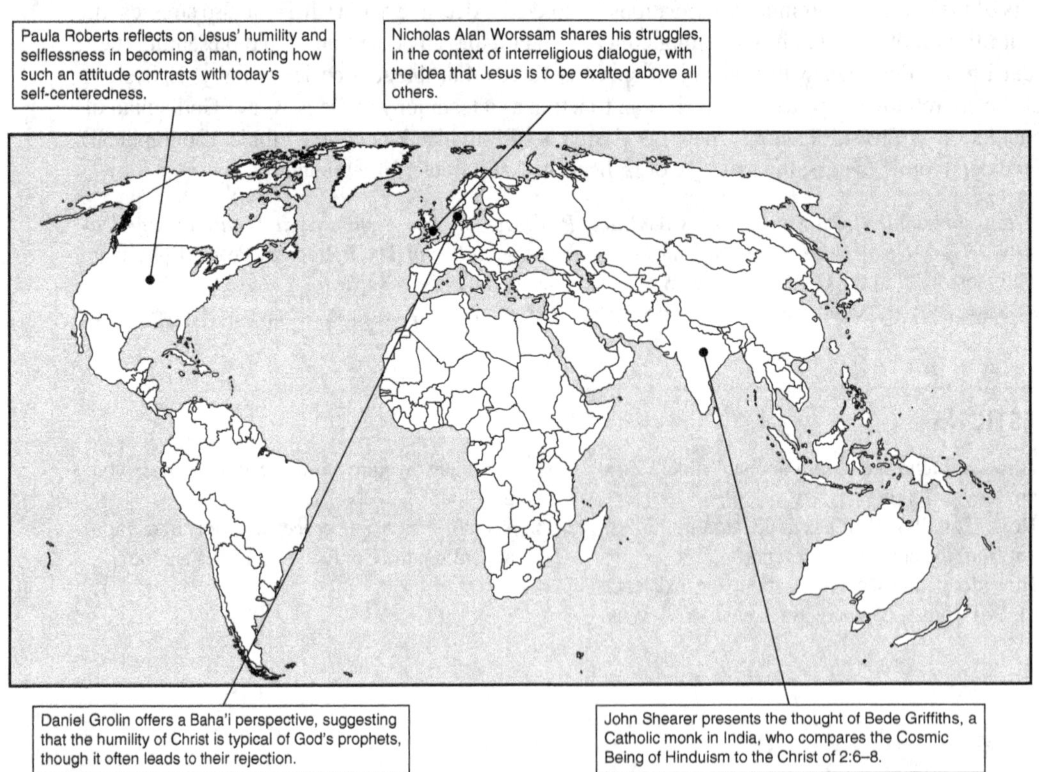

Paula Roberts reflects on Jesus' humility and selflessness in becoming a man, noting how such an attitude contrasts with today's self-centeredness.
Nicholas Alan Worssam shares his struggles, in the context of interreligious dialogue, with the idea that Jesus is to be exalted above all others.
Daniel Grolin offers a Baha'i perspective, suggesting that the humility of Christ is typical of God's prophets, though it often leads to their rejection.
John Shearer presents the thought of Bede Griffiths, a Catholic monk in India, who compares the Cosmic Being of Hinduism to the Christ of 2:6–8.

READINGS

How to Read "Jesus Exalted above All Others" in the Context of Interreligious Dialogue

Nicholas Alan Worssam (United Kingdom)

One passage that I have inhabited for many years comes from Philippians 2:5–11. It is a beautiful passage, probably in its original form a hymn that Paul has adapted for his letter, filling out the earlier statements with explanatory phrases. As such it is one of the earliest statements of Christian belief, one of the hymns to Christ that the first Christians sang in the catacombs or in their own homes in the gray light of their early morning meetings. It is a hymn that glorifies Jesus for his role in the salvation of humankind, showing his descent from heaven as Son of God, his saving death and resurrection, and exaltation in glory. It is a kind of creed, a forerunner of the more formal and fully developed Christian doctrinal statements (e.g., Nicea).

But it is also a problematic passage, particularly for those of us who have been involved in interfaith dialogue or who have drawn deeply from the wells of wisdom in other religious traditions, such as Buddhism. Is it true that Jesus is exalted above all others, and that every knee will bend at the name of Jesus, submitting to him as Master and Lord? To the ears of a Buddhist, this passage can sound triumphalistic and overbearing. As such, it requires careful examination if it is to be understood in a way that makes sense of our contemporary experience of the encounters of different faiths.

In fact, however, there are many ways of understanding this passage from Philippians, rooted in the text itself, yet open to a wider embrace of other religious traditions. First, Paul exhorts his readers to have "the mind of Christ," which is in itself a bridge to the Buddhist emphasis on the mind as the focus of the spiritual path. It is a mind of love, compassion, sympathy, and joy (three of the Buddha's "Divine Abidings"). For Paul, as for the Buddha, it is a mind that moves radically beyond self.

Second, this passage is not necessarily about a divine redeemer descending from above. There are many New Testament scholars who see this rather as a meditation on the role of Adam, and of Christ as the new archetypal "everyman." Philippians 2:6 speaks of Christ as being "in the form of God," but this is an echo of Genesis 1:27, where it says that "God created humankind in his image." Likewise, in Colossians 1:15 Paul says that Christ is "the image of the invisible God." Christ, then, is to be understood as the new Adam.

Paul then goes on to say that Christ "did not regard equality with God as something to be exploited" (or grasped). As with the Buddha, it is attachment, particularly to self, that is the root cause of suffering. A truer response is that of self-emptying (*kenosis*), though a Buddhist would nuance this by encouraging the realization that there is in fact no self to grasp. For the Christian, this grasping of equality with God is the sin of Adam, which Christ rectifies by his relinquishment of all grasping at self. Adam and Eve literally grasp the fruit of disobedience, thinking to gain the knowledge of good and evil, and so fall into the primordial dualism of self and other, gain and loss, life and now-inescapable death. Christ, however, humbles himself, accepting death, not holding on to one side of the life–death continuum. His divinity is expressed by his letting go of divinity—his life lived by nonattachment to life or death.

Just as the Buddha teaches that the path to enlightenment is open to all, so the new Adam, Christ, shows us the way to a new humanity, revealing a death to self in which we are all encouraged to share (Phil. 3:10). The death of Christ is an inclusive event, in which everyone who dies to themselves and lives by the power of the Spirit of God may participate. Christ's death is ours, just as we share in the power of his resurrection. All are linked to the Adam recapitulated in Christ: "For as in Adam all die, so in Christ will all be made alive" (1 Corinthians 15:22).

But then we get to the tricky part of Philippians 2: "Therefore God also highly exalted him and gave him the name that is above every name, so that at the name of Jesus every knee should bend." Does this mean that the particular name "Jesus" is above every name, and that at the name "Jesus" every knee shall bow? That is the traditional understanding and what I had always, despite my interfaith embarrassment, felt to be the unavoidable interpretation. But to really understand this passage I think we need to ask again: What is the name that is given to Jesus? I suggest that it is the unspeakable name YHWH, first revealed to Moses at the burning bush (Exodus 3:14). YHWH means something like, "I am who I am" or simply "I AM." With added vowels for pronunciation, "Yahweh" is really a breath, a sound of sheer silence.

When this concept is translated into Greek, we get further clues to this divine name carried by Jesus. YHWH in the Greek becomes ό ών, pronounced *Ho Ōn*, and translated The One Who Is. This is the name often found inscribed in the nimbus (halo) around the head of Jesus in Orthodox icons. The name given to Jesus, then, when pronounced in Greek is merely an exhalation of breath, rather than a name per se. (Is it just a wild flight of fancy in my mind that connects this with the Sanskrit divine name of *Aum* or *Om*?)

So, in the Philippians passage, the name given to Jesus is YHWH, otherwise known as The One Who Is, Being Itself, the Eternal. So while the name "Jesus" is still profoundly precious to Christians, it need not be understood as a name truly beyond all names. Thus we are able to move toward a more universal, inclusive understanding of this text, one that fits more comfortably in interfaith conversations.

In sum, this enigmatic passage from St. Paul's letter to the Philippians is full of surprises. It takes us back to Christ the new Adam, the truly Human One, who, by his humility and self-emptying, is given the name beyond all names. It shows that there is nothing to grasp and everything to receive, that God speaks God's name within us, and we are set free. And Paul wishes that the joy of this discovery, the compassion and sympathy that it evokes, be the ever-present experience of those "who have the mind of Christ."

Nicholas Alan Worssam is a member of the Anglican (Episcopalian) religious community, the Society of Saint Francis; he is based at Glasshampton Monastery in Worcestershire, England.

A Comparison of the Cosmic Being of Hinduism and the Christ of 2:6–8

John Shearer (India)

The Cosmic Being, or the Universal Self (Purusa) as it is called in certain branches of Hinduism, is a concept that is quite difficult to put into words, often evading description and clear understanding. The Spirit of the Cosmic Being is everywhere, but we cannot see it. It is not necessarily meant to be seen, but to be experienced in the heart of our very being. It is a notion that can be found at the deepest core of many religious traditions, assuming the same elusive nature in each one, yet ever present within our very selves and in everything around us. It exists within us all, and can be found only when one relinquishes control of that which is material, and looks inward, wherein lies an in-depth wisdom that rejects the ego and selfishness. Still, we are only human, and to our finite minds this concept of a Cosmic Being is difficult to grasp.

Bede Griffiths (1906–1993) was a Catholic monk who lived in India and adopted the practices of Hindu monastic life; he wrote 12 books on Hindu–Christian dialogue. According to Griffiths, the figure of the Primordial Cosmic Being is an archetype that can be found throughout history among many of the world's traditions, thus linking humanity together in a Universal Spirit. In Christianity this all-encompassing figure is the Cosmic Christ that we see in Philippians 2:6–8 and Colossians 1:15, where Jesus Christ is referred to in His original form as the firstborn of all creation and in whom all of creation in heaven and on earth was brought into existence. While many have understood this to be saying that Jesus is God, for Griffiths this passage was specifically saying that He is the manifestation of God, or the Primordial Man in whom God revealed Himself. Griffiths goes on further to state, "What happened was that He emptied Himself of that heavenly state, and took the form of a (universal) man" (Griffiths *A New Vision of Reality: Western Science, Eastern Mysticism and Christian faith* [Springfield, IL: Templegate, 1990], 122). Here Griffiths is referring specifically to the notion expounded on in Philippians 2:6–8, which says that Christ is, "in the form of God . . . but emptied himself . . . being born in human likeness," as well as that found in Colossians 1:15, which refers to Christ as the image of the invisible God. This implies that the invisible God's image, or reflection that was created in the beginning, and was the preexistent, all-encompassing Christ, was at once the same as, and yet distinct from, God. As Griffiths points out, all things were made through Him and for Him, but they were not made by Him, again distinguishing between God and Christ (Griffiths, *A New Vision of Reality*, 123).

Griffiths also claimed that the Cosmic Christ, in which the fullness of God dwells, is truly at the center of each and every one of us, within our heart, at the depths of our very being. He elaborates further on this idea, saying, "the one Spirit is present in every moment of love . . . The Father gives Himself in love to the Son, who is the very form, expression, of his love . . . This is its [the universe] coming into being, this response to the drawing of Love. At the same time it's [the Cosmic Christ-Universal Soul] being continually drawn to give itself in love . . . and so the rhythm of the universe is created" (*Return to the Center* [Springfield, IL: Templegate, 2002], 60–61). He went on to say that the Cosmic Christ is also within every religious tradition, including Hinduism, Buddhism, and Islam, even though members of various traditions may not know it. He is even present in the hearts and minds of those who claim not to believe in anything at all. This being the case, we are all united in the Cosmic Christ. As Griffiths asserts, "Our ecumenical task is to cooperate with that mystery of grace, seeking to discover that presence of Christ in every religion and in every human soul" (*Christ in India* [Springfield, IL: Templegate, 1984], 177).

In accord with the claim that the Cosmic Christ is present in every religion, Griffiths expounds on the form He takes in other various traditions, one of those being Hinduism. In this tradition the Cosmic Being is known as the Atman (Self), or Purusa. Throughout the epic tale *The Bhagavad-Gita* the god Krishna elaborates on who the Self is. The first reference to the Self is in 2:17–19 where Lord Krishna tells the warrior Arjuna that this great presence, this Universal Soul, is indestructible, pervading all the eye can see and beyond. Krishna continues to elaborate on the essence of this Cosmic Being, claiming that He is enduring, constant, and primordial. Here Krishna is imparting to the much grieved prince Arjuna who is facing a terrible battle that we are all part of the ever-present Self, which endures beyond all that is.

Krishna then goes on to reveal to Arjuna that it is he (Krishna) who is actually the Cosmic Being, referring to himself as the womb of all creatures and the source of the universe. Krishna explains how humans can fully embrace him, and enter into him, the Cosmic Being upon death: "A man who dies remembering me at the time of death enters my being when he is freed from his body; of this there is no doubt."

Akin to the concept of the Atman (Self) or Universal Soul, the Cosmic Christ belongs to the figure of the Son within the Holy Trinity, but it is Christ in His heavenly, universal form, larger than life, and far more profound than the human mind can even begin to fathom. As such, He is the bridge that connects humanity and the world directly to the Divine. In *The Bhagavad-Gita* Krishna reveals himself as the cosmic, all-encompassing spirit, permeating throughout all of creation, and in which all of creation exists. Likewise the Cosmic Christ, this Cosmic Being, is ever present, and to know it one must be silent, listening deep within to that which speaks to the heart.

This Cosmic Being is the Universal Spirit who connects humanity and all of life back to the source, the Godhead. It can only be perceived in spiritual terms, requiring one to think outside of time, space, and that which is material. That this is a universal notion makes sense, for when one looks at the myriad traditions and religions of the world, and the goals therein, they will see many similarities. Griffiths says the primary goal of all religions is "the absolute, transcendent state, the one Reality, the eternal Truth, which cannot be expressed, cannot be conceived. This is the goal not only of all religion, but of all human existence" (Griffiths, *Return to the Center*, 74). He claims that essentially all religions are the same, and all will ultimately end in the same understanding of the Cosmic Being.

John Shearer is a graduate student of Religious Studies at Florida International University, United States.

A Baha'i Perspective on the Humility of Christ

Daniel Grolin (Denmark)

Baha'u'llah is the prophet founder of the Baha'i Faith. There is, I would propose, a certain way in which God sends his chosen ones, such as Baha'u'llah, which is unchanging like the seasons, and which the keen observer can recognize. This is the underlying assumption of Jesus' Parable of the Fig Tree (Luke 21:29–31) and his condemnation of weather-watching hypocrites (12:54–7) and in Baha'u'llah's many allusions and references to the Bible, calling his readers to consider carefully the lessons of the past. One of the most important lessons is the cautionary tale of rejection of God's emissary.

At the heart of the rejection is how God's emissary appears. In Paul's letter to the Philippians he refers to what one might think of as divine humility. In the hymn of Philippians 2 the image of Adam is used to compare and contrast. Adam too was made in the form (*morfe*) of God (2:6; Genesis 1:26). Unlike Adam, Jesus did not seize divinity to become the same as (*isa*) God (in Genesis 3:22 God says that man had become like God), instead he became like a servant (2:7). Unlike Adam who was cast out of Paradise, Jesus was exalted by God (2:9). Yet, until his crucifixion Jesus appeared to most as nothing but a servant.

Nevertheless we must ask why so many of Jesus' contemporaries reject him. Certainly one reason was a sense of complacency about their religious assumptions. John the Baptist castigated "this generation of vipers" for not showing proper repentance, and relying on the assumed safety of the thought, "We have Abraham as our father" (Luke 3:7–8). I once asked a bishop if he would be willing to discuss the merits of the Baha'i Faith and in answer I was told that as far back as one could remember it was Christianity that had carried them through. Such a response has a striking similarity to the kind of reliance on forefathers that John the Baptist condemned. Surely when one venerates the faith of one's forefathers because it is the faith of one's forefathers, it has become a veneration of one's forefathers.

Yet, forefathers made mistakes. Because when prophets come, it is seldom a comfortable thing. It was easier to kill prophets than to heed them. Heeding them meant changing the status quo. Those who were in a position of power (rulers, priests, and learned) were particularly interested in keeping their positions. People not only failed to accept Jesus because of fear of losing their leadership status, or the status granted by wealth, but sometimes they were also simply caught up in their own expectations. Paul addresses this idea several times in his writings. For instance, 1 Corinthians 1:22–23 reads, "Because Jews require a sign and Greeks want wisdom, but we proclaim Christ crucified, an offense to Jews and foolishness to Greeks." Likewise, in Philippians 2, Christians are urged to have the mind of Christ, who made himself into nothing, took the form of a servant, humbled himself, and willingly died a humiliating death on the cross. This is not the type of person that would naturally be recognized as a divine emissary. A dead man on a cross could hardly be God in the flesh.

Jews required signs that would demonstrate that Jesus was who he said he was, but Jesus failed to live up to almost every expectation that most Jews had for the Messiah. To be sure, Christians referred to scripture that they regarded as fulfilled by Jesus, but none of these were what the Jews wished to see fulfilled. They had no need for a humble Messiah, but wanted one who would stand against Rome. Was that not what had been prophesied? Where was Elijah on the chariot of fire which whorled him into heaven (2 Kings 2:11) who was supposed to return on the great and dreadful day of Yahweh (Malachi 4:5)?

Ironically, the Romans expected something akin to it. The idea of a divine man was not incredible: Caesars were clearly and manifestly divine and visibly powerful since they ruled most of the world. What was incredible was that a poor, humble man from an insignificant village, from an unremarkable family, was divine. Who was this Jesus who had been executed embarrassingly like a common criminal? To believe such a one was divine was utter foolishness. For instance, sometime in the second century, in Rome, someone thought to poke fun at some Christian acquaintance by the name Alexamenos, by depicting him worshipping a crucified man with a donkey's head. Like Jews, Christians were widely believed to be worshipers of donkeys. Such foolishness was obviously worthy of the graffitist's derision.

What was more, Christians were superstitious. The same label was also used of Jews, but unlike Jews, Christianity could not, in a society that venerated all things ancient, call upon great age to garner respect. The Greek word *deisideaimonia* applied to Christians (which stands in place of the Latin *superstitio*) literally means "fearful of demons." The label had the sense of people who were immoderately scrupulous in their observance of religious practice. This behavior, which was offensive to the sensibilities of the educated people of the Graeco-Roman world, was regarded as stemming from an ignorance of how deities behaved, and leading to a fretful following of religious cultic minutia. All of this was, of course, utter foolishness, as absurd as trying to imitate the humility of a crucified criminal.

But today, of course, it is clear that those who labeled Christianity as a superstition failed to heed history. The foolishness of the present may turn out to be the established wisdom of the future; the lowly servant who died on a cross might turn out to be the one whom God exalts

(Phil. 2:9). As George Santayana said, "Those who cannot remember the past are condemned to repeat it."

In the opening passage of his *Book of Certitude*, which makes extensive use of the Bible to present its arguments, Baha'u'llah writes that "No man shall attain the shores of the ocean of true understanding except he be detached from all that is in heaven and on earth." He later goes on to state:

> Consider the past. How many, both high and low, have, at all times, yearningly awaited the advent of the Manifestations of God in the sanctified persons of His chosen Ones. How often have they expected His coming, how frequently have they prayed that the breeze of divine mercy might blow, and the promised Beauty step forth from behind the veil of concealment, and be made manifest to all the world. And whensoever the portals of grace did open, and the clouds of divine bounty did rain upon mankind, and the light of the Unseen did shine above the horizon of celestial might, they all denied Him, and turned away from His face—the face of God Himself. Refer ye, to verify this truth, to that which hath been recorded in every sacred Book. (Chapter XIII)

Philippians should remind us that Jesus, despite his divinity, outwardly was only a servant, and that he was crucified on a cross, the final sign of rejection. And yet Jesus was exalted by God. Unfortunately, the same thing has again happened with Baha'u'llah: Too many have rejected God's emissary because he came in an unexpected form. Indeed, Baha'u'llah observed in his own days that many were too taken with their preconceptions to see that Baha'u'llah had come to once more fulfill God's promise of guidance and salvation.

*Daniel Grolin (Masters of Computer Engineering, University of Southern Denmark) is an information technology architect, journal editor (*Baha'i Studies Review*), and author (*Jesus and Early Christianity in the Gospels: A New Dialogue*).*

Jesus' Humility and Selflessness in Opposition to Today's Self-Centeredness

Paula Roberts (United States)

He is obviously maladjusted; the poor soul doesn't think much about himself but focuses on meeting the needs of others regardless of what it costs him personally. He doesn't even demand his rights or what he is entitled to. What a perfect candidate for an "extreme makeover." He needs a good therapist who would reprogram his thinking, shift his values, and teach him to look out for "number one."

Interestingly enough, this individual is joyful, content, fulfilled. His life has meaning and direction. He is at peace, has no worries, and enjoys lasting, loving relationships. So, what's the problem? There is none. He has what we all desire. His example: Jesus Christ.

It begins with the Christmas story—the birth of Jesus, the Son of God. We picture Him sweetly resting in a manger and stand in awe of His miraculous virgin birth. Equally profound and incomprehensible is the fact that this baby boy Jesus was God incarnate, God born in the flesh. In Philippians 2:5–11 the Apostle Paul presents a clear, concise synopsis of this life- and death-changing event. Let's place these verses in context. In verses 1–4 Paul is encouraging the church at Philippi to be one in love, spirit, and purpose. He instructs each believer to do nothing out of selfish ambition or self-glorification, to humbly esteem every person better than himself, and to concentrate more on the welfare of others than his own.

Paul then exhorts the Philippians in verse 5 to adopt the attitude of Christ, which he proceeds to reveal in the subsequent three verses. Although Jesus Christ was in His very essence unalterably God, He did not concern Himself with asserting His right to be equal with God. He did not tenaciously cling to His supreme existence, His omniscience, omnipresence, omnipotence, majesty, glory, privileges, or honor. Instead, in an inconceivably selfless act, Jesus emptied Himself not of His deity, but of all that was rightfully and uniquely His in order to become a man, a mere human being. He abandoned His life in the heavens among the angels, forfeiting his seat at the right hand of His Father God, to take up residence shoulder-to-shoulder with sinful mankind.

It is virtually impossible to grasp the ramifications of Jesus becoming man, clothing Himself with the rags of human nature; it transcends the mind. Reduced to an ordinary life with its mundane routines, countless limitations, and unpleasantries, confined to a physical body susceptible to infirmities, surrounded by flawed man in an imperfect environment is at best an epically inadequate portrayal of what the God–man endured.

Verse 7 captures the depth of Jesus' extraordinary journey on earth. Not only did He condescend to become a man, but also assumed the position of a bondservant, the lowliest of the lowly, a person without status, power, respect, or entitlements of his own—not a role to be coveted or envied.

It would be reasonable and justifiable to expect the Son of God to safeguard His glory by detaching Himself from the masses and joining the upper class with its power, prestige, and comfortable lifestyle. No one would begrudge Him that. In unparalleled contrast, however, He elected to be less than a commoner and to serve rather than be served.

Submission was the hallmark of a servant. The same held true of Jesus with God as His master. In His case, however, perfect obedience ushered Him to death's door. In one stunning final demonstration of love, humility, and obedience, Jesus died on a cross, the most excruciatingly painful and degrading form of execution imposed on a human being. He willingly suffered the punishment for the sins of all mankind, establishing the one and only way to God. Without the sacrifice of Jesus' sinless life, sinful man would forever be alienated from God and condemned to eternity apart from Him.

Paul concludes the passage by recounting in verses 9–11 the exaltation of Jesus. Reflecting on His son's obedience, God bestowed on Him a name which is above every name. That name and all it represents is worthy of worship from every thing and every being, in every place, bowing down and confessing that Jesus is Lord, to the glory of God, the One who willingly relinquished His son to redeem man.

Without a doubt, Jesus Christ in His incarnation epitomized the life Paul outlined for the Philippians to pursue, which could be condensed in two words—"be selfless." Reversing the syllables of *selfless* pinpoints its meaning—less self. Not something we are eager to hear and certainly not an acceptable or popular philosophy in today's world.

Self is a driving factor, a powerful motivator, a relentless priority in our society. Self-actualization, self-esteem, self-worth, self-love—number one sits proudly on the throne. Yet, man remains restless, still searching for meaning, peace, joy, contentment, and love. Perhaps there is another way.

Paula Roberts is a retired English teacher, author, freelance editor, and nonprofit director.

QUESTIONS

1. Assess Worssam's argument that "YHWH" is the name given to Jesus. What implications does this have for an interfaith interpretation beyond those mentioned by Worssam?
2. Is the Cosmic Christ compatible with Philippians 2:6–8? How would Griffiths deal with verses 9–11?
3. How might one who accepts Christ as an emissary of God, but not Baha'u'llah, argue with Grolin?
4. How is the biblical context important for Roberts? Does she offer a compelling reading of verses 5–11 in light of verses 1–4?

CHAPTER 39

REVELATION (PART I)

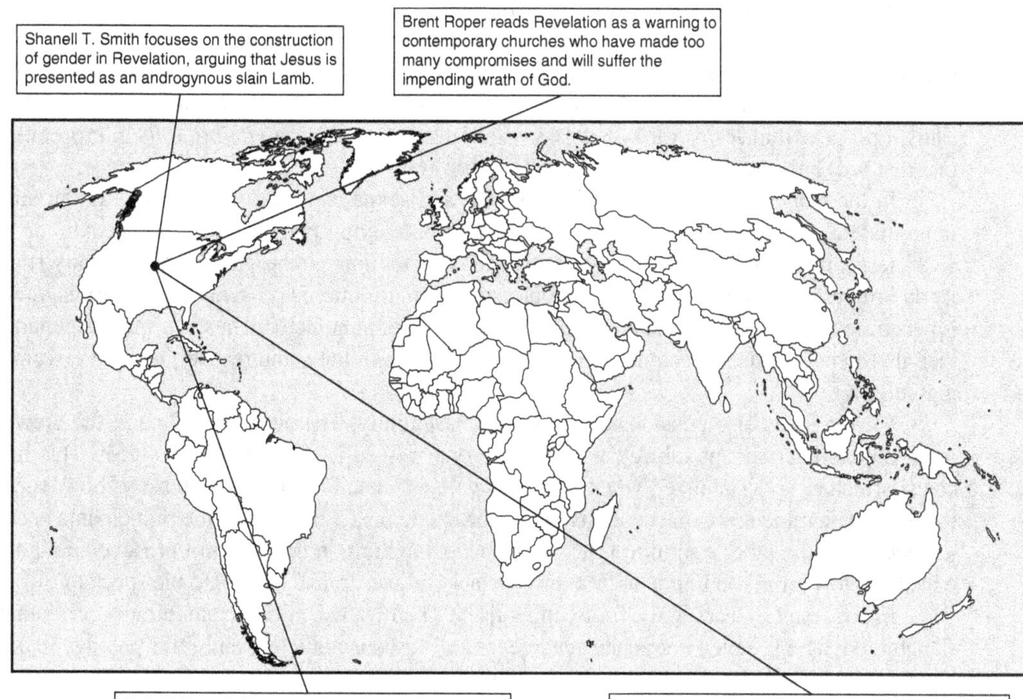

Shanell T. Smith focuses on the construction of gender in Revelation, arguing that Jesus is presented as an androgynous slain Lamb.
Brent Roper reads Revelation as a warning to contemporary churches who have made too many compromises and will suffer the impending wrath of God.
Beth M. Stovell offers a reading of Revelation 19–21 from Goth subculture, which invites readers to question if they have bought the lies of Western culture.
Chris Griffin argues for a literal reading of Revelation and critiques other spiritual or symbolic interpretations as inadequate and misguided.

READINGS

The Construction of Gender in Revelation
Shanell T. Smith

A Goth Reading of Revelation 19–21
Beth M. Stovell

Revelation as a Warning to Contemporary Churches
Brent Roper

A Literal Reading of Revelation
Chris Griffin

The Construction of Gender in Revelation

Shanell T. Smith (United States)

As an African American, Christian, female New Testament scholar (representing myself, and not as a spokeswoman for any of these perceived "groups"), I will focus on the construction of gender in the book of Revelation as it pertains to ancient Roman notions of penetration and viewing. I will argue that Jesus in the figure of the Lamb espouses both genders simultaneously. Initially, I thought that by "preserving" the so-called "feminine" aspect of Jesus throughout Revelation, I had finally done the impossible, that is, made Revelation a liberating text. However, further analysis and challenging conversations with colleagues have opened my eyes to see the possibility that liberation is already and always in tension with the suffering and violence that occur in the text. The borders between liberation and violence are always blurred. Thus, I propose that Jesus, the *androgynous* slain Lamb leads to an *ambiguous* interpretation—one that will have to sit well with me, at least for now.

In the Roman Empire, concepts of gender and sexuality were intertwined. Roman authors (elite males) who wrote about sex often did so by classifying persons as either "active" or "passive," terms that were synonymous for masculine and feminine, respectively. Masculinity is activity and represents one who penetrates; contrastingly, femininity is passivity and signifies one who is penetrated. One's anatomical makeup was not a determining factor. Thus, if a male is penetrated, then that male, for these ancient writers, is effeminized; in the same respect, an active woman is masculinized.

Viewing was also considered a mode of masculinity. The active participant, the viewer, is regarded as the dominant subject; whereas, the one viewed is the submissive object. This hierarchical structure is destabilized when a mutual gaze is shared with equal intensity; however, it is maintained anytime this engagement is disproportionate (i.e., when one of the participants becomes a spectacle of the other's scrutiny). It is this unequal exhibition that we find in Revelation, and to which we now turn. The Lamb, at first the spectacle, is later transformed into the spectator.

In 5:6 Jesus appears in the following guise: "Then I saw...a Lamb standing as if it had been slaughtered, having seven horns and seven eyes..." Jesus is not a human in this passage, but he is also not simply an animal. Although one might consider this small lamb as a beast in its own right, with the presence of its seven horns and seven eyes, which are symbolic of power and wisdom, the fact that the Lamb is slain should not be overlooked. The phrase, "as if slain," reflects the sacrificial markings and scars that Jesus has endured on the cross. Penetration in ancient antiquity is not limited to penile function; it pertains to any form of insertion or any penetration of one's flesh. Thus, according to Roman gender ideologies, the *slain* Lamb would be considered feminine.

The image of the slain Lamb lingers in the recesses of one's mind as we proceed through Revelation. However, when we reach Revelation 14, the vision of this itty-bitty Lamb bearing the markings of torture is replaced with an extraordinary Lamb with a strong stomach for witnessing death and destruction. The Lamb displays strength as he watches and oversees the destruction of those who worship the beast and its image: "Those who worship the beast...will be tormented with fire and sulfur in the presence of the holy angels and in the presence of the Lamb. And the smoke of their torment goes up forever and ever" (14:9–11). Thus, the Lamb, although textually regarded as slain, figuratively emerges as a muscular, robust figure, strong enough to open the seven seals of the scroll (which no one else could do, 5:1–5), and digestively durable enough to withstand the sight of his adversaries being tortured. In essence, the Lamb becomes a man. The Lamb's femininity, as indicated by its slaughtered state, is followed by the emergence of masculinity when the Lamb becomes a powerful celestial warrior.

It has been argued that the Lamb, in the larger narrative of Revelation, makes the move from femininity to masculinity. This argument is problematic to me on two fronts: domination of the masculine gender over the feminine, and its implications for those of us who view Jesus as Christ and a Savior for all. At no time should one gender prevail over another, especially in the figure of Christ (even if depicted as a Lamb). This view, in which the masculine gender is the "last one standing," causes problems for womanists such as myself. The term "womanist" reflects a group of African American women committed to the survival and flourishing of an entire people, both male and female. Furthermore, for some African American women who regard Jesus as the divine cosufferer, that is, a God who supports and empowers them in the struggle to overcome their suffering, reading Jesus as one who overcomes femininity with masculinity would render Jesus as a source of comfort for men only, or suggest that a woman must become manly to persevere, which is clearly problematic. Therefore, I contend that the Lamb maintains both genders simultaneously throughout the narrative, an argument to which we now turn—that is, Jesus as the androgynous Lamb.

Coupling Roman imperial ideology with the two-ness of Jesus' nature suggests that Jesus maintains the supposed "feminine" aspect of his character, what I define as victory and strength masked by the *appearance* of weakness: recall the *slain* Lamb's ability to open the seven scrolls. But it also suggests that he maintains the *supposed* "masculine" qualities to master, conquer, and destroy—qualities he possesses as the celestial warrior. In essence, Revelation imparts a word of caution: looks can be deceiving. Specifically, the appearance of the Lamb is deceiving; that is, his femininity is not to be viewed as fragility.

But what are we to make of the presence of these seemingly conflicting characteristics of Jesus, and what implications does it have for African American female readers of Revelation? Although it can be perceived as problematic, it seems to me that it is a description of God that has the potential to give African American women (including myself) a sense of hope. A victim of tri-fold oppression in terms of race, sex, and class, I need Jesus to be a source of strength and comfort, as well as an avenger, protector, and defender of my well-being. For many African American churches, liberation entails violent images of God (such as in Exodus 14) in which God brings about deliverance and freedom from oppression through violent means.

Thus, in light of the androgyny of the Lamb, I posit that the Apocalypse invites an ambivalent interpretation. The borders of liberation and violence (whether or not justified) are always blurred. Liberation, most often, necessitates violence, and violence most often is a prelude to the need for liberation. Violence and liberation, although seemingly two opposed realities, simultaneously coexist like the two-fold gender of Jesus in Revelation. They both exist in strained relation within the figure of the Lamb. To be sure, this tension does not render the Lamb neutral and ineffective, but rather complex, elusive, and even ambiguous.

In conclusion, we must continue to find ways to reveal inclusive and liberating traditions in the early Christian writings, despite the androcentric nature of biblical texts. John's gaze is exclusionary (elevating the masculine and abandoning the feminine), but my understanding of Jesus problematizes his view by directing our attention to Jesus' gendered complexity. My hope is that reading Jesus as an androgynous Lamb will present a new vision of an all-embracing Jesus, instead of a masculine Jesus who conquers femininity. However, the reality of my reading, despite my dissatisfaction, is that as long as violence and liberation exist in tandem, such as in the text of Revelation via the characterization of Jesus, liberation will always already be and not yet be. This is ambiguity at its best.

Shanell T. Smith is a Ph.D. candidate in New Testament and Early Christianity at Drew University, United States; she is also a Candidate for Minister of Word and Sacrament in the Presbyterian Church (USA).

A Goth Reading of Revelation 19–21

Beth M. Stovell (United States)

Here I will offer a reading of Revelation 19–21 through the eyes of the Goth subculture. Often traced to the sounds and images of the band Bauhaus, Goths emerged in Britain in the early 1980s as punk, glam rock, and new romantic merged with other elements to form a new and distinctive music and fashion style. The music of the Goth scene was often described as dark, macabre, and sinister. While in many ways, Goths define themselves in terms of these similar musical interests and fashion style, Goths will often point to other more internal elements that form the Goth worldview.

First, Goth is a resistance subculture that reacts against "mainstream" culture. What the "mainstream" culture of America (and other parts of North America and Western Europe) tells us to deny, Goths instead openly embrace. One example of this is the Goth goal of putting the darkness on the outside where everyone can see it (making it innocuous), rather than keeping it hidden (thereby letting it smolder and become truly evil). By embracing this awareness of evil, Goths also point to the darkness that is inside everyone. When hidden, this inner evil can extend to the rest of the world, impacting society, religion, and the environment. Goth music and movies often react against the hypocrisy present in the world and its inherent effects of oppression, marginalization, and alienation. In contrast, Goth subculture aims toward inclusion of people whom mainstream society has rejected, often getting rejected themselves in the process. Goths also reject the mainstream notion of hiding the suffering and pain present in life. Goths will often note that mainstream culture unreasonably expects everyone to put on a happy face. In contrast, Goths argue that the willingness to acknowledge the suffering and evil present in the world and within themselves can actually allow for more happiness in their lives.

The growing movement of Goth Christianity accentuates these central tenets of Goth subculture in light of Christian belief. For example, the awareness of inner darkness is often heightened among Goth Christians, who seek to warn others of the dangers of ignoring or denying sin. Further, Christian Goths point to the system of lies sold by the world and seek to replace them with the truth. Goth Christians point to Jesus Christ as the model for the inclusion of the marginalized and oppressed and as one who rejected the world's lies. Goth Christians identify their persecution in the world with Christ's persecution. Their acknowledgment of suffering and darkness often causes them to emphasize the suffering of Christ in his Passion and revel in the gruesome cannibalistic language of the Eucharist. For example, in the Goth Christian video *The Night of the Living Bread* zombies eat Christ's body and are transformed by this cannibalistic Eucharist act.

Each of these tenets impacts the way Goths read the Bible. In their reinterpretation of the Bride, the New Jerusalem, in Revelation 19–21, they often identify themselves with the Bride of Christ figure, the New Jerusalem herself. Yet this identification combines the somber, the macabre, and the sarcastic tendencies within Goth subculture. The Bride of Christ becomes a gothic bride. Whether one pictures Tim Burton's corpse bride or a Goth female dressed in a black wedding dress with a silver cross, black fingernails, lips, and nails, and, most importantly, black veil (as found on one Christian Goth website), this reinterpretation cannot help but cause a change in the way one visually imagines this figure in the Apocalypse.

This identification of the Bride of Christ with Goth Christianity is pressed further as some Goths connect the robes of white drenched in the blood of the Lamb in Revelation 7 with the Bride of Christ adorned in white for her wedding day in 19:7–9 and 21:1–9. Such an interpretation draws upon the natural connections between the removal of suffering and the springs of living water in 7:17 and 21:3,6 and the imagery of the bride within these contexts. One Goth poet (David Dellman, "Why Black?" on gothicchristianity.com) connects his black clothes of mourning with his anticipation of this coming day of redemption: "I wear black because it is the color of mourning./I mourn for the dying world…I mourn for each senseless act of injustice. I mourn for Him and with Him and I know that He and He alone will comfort me./And I will wear black until the day when He adorns me in white…" Here the choice of black is linked to the mourning of the present world and the hope of the future age to come where this Goth shall be God's bride and all mourning shall cease. Others push this combined vision of Revelation 7 and 21 in macabre directions. In this depiction, the bride may only be dressed in white because she is first bathed in blood. Thus, the bride must have a "blood bath" to be cleansed. This use of the horror genre allows for dramatic and surprising new ways of seeing the true macabre nature of Revelation's apocalyptic vision.

This vision of the Gothic Bride of Christ stands in contrast to the Goth reinterpretation of the figure of Babylon in Revelation 18. In many ways, the ancient depiction of Babylon as the Roman imperial power representing social injustice, exploitation, and oppression finds its parallel in the gothic interpretation of the United States of America as Babylon. For many Goths, the tendency to "rage against the machine" and to question the duplicitous nature of Western society goes hand in hand with interpreting Babylon in terms of the misdeeds of America specifically. One such example (though there are quite a few) is the song "American Babylon" by Saviour Machine. In this song, terms like "fascism" and "tyranny," which have become "highly organized" by Satan himself, are placed beside the language of liberty and light, demonstrating the distinction between appearances and reality that have caused the ultimate fall of America, according to Saviour Machine.

The ultimate picture of inclusion comes in the final vision of the wedding of the Lamb. As the Bride of Christ herself is pictured as a Goth, not surprisingly the guests at the dinner party include Goths and all others who have been marginalized, oppressed, and alienated. Those "scary freaks" whom some mainstream Christians feared would mislead their children are in fact found sitting elbow-to-elbow with them at the Lamb's dinner table. This subverts the usual expectations of this metaphor by extending the table in surprising directions.

Goth interpretations of Revelation press their readers toward seeing with squeamish eyes the vivid, even horrific metaphors employed to depict the reversal of mainstream expectations. Using the conventions of horror, Goth readings challenge their readers to question whether they, like the merchants wailing at Babylon's fall, have bought the lies offered by today's society—wealth, empty happiness, and false righteousness so prevalent in much of Western culture. Through parody and irony, Goth readings subvert the expectations of their readers, surprising them and moving them toward deeper questions of inclusion and exclusion, of center and margin. The use of inversion of symbolic frameworks of imperialism and the dualism inherent in apocalyptic literature and within Goth subculture leads to a radical and dangerous choice; for choosing to align oneself with those on the "inside" means standing in solidarity with the oppressed and potentially becoming the oppressed. The value of Goth readings of Revelation is the new configuration of this symbolism as culturally relevant to today's world. If America is truly Babylon, how might one "come out of [her]," while still living in her? Perhaps Goth Christians provide at least one way to reside in this tension.

Beth M. Stovell is Assistant Professor in Biblical Studies in the School of Theology and Ministry at St. Thomas University, Miami Gardens, Florida, United States.

Revelation as a Warning to Contemporary Churches

Brent Roper (United States)

Did you *really* think no one was watching and you collectively could kill hundreds of millions of innocent babies worldwide through "abortion" and get away with it? The standard is "Thou shalt not kill." Did you *really* think you could start wars and murder at will worldwide with no accountability? There were zero weapons of mass destruction in Iraq—remember? Did you *really* think you could slip mass adultery (remarriage after divorce; Mark 10:11), fornication, sodomy, marrying homosexuals, and the like under the radar past God and He wouldn't notice?

When Christ returns to earth it's going to be as the days of Noah and the days of Lot. That is, mass sin and sodomy will flourish, and all the commandments of God will be cast aside. Christ is coming in judgment. That is the basic plotline of the book of Revelation. The Revelation of Jesus Christ is holy payback time! All mankind will cry for the mountains and rocks to fall on them to hide them from Him and His wrath (6:16). He's coming for you; He's gonna find you!

When the effeminate preachers of this evil, adulterous, and sinful generation speak of a limp-wristed, sissy, apologetic, soft-on-sin, hippy Christ, it is laughable. It's the blind leading the blind. Revelation 1 opens with Christ having eyes as a flame of fire and a sharp double-edged sword coming out of His mouth (vv. 14–16). All peoples of the earth will wail when they see Him (v. 7). And for good reason, the sword is to strike down the nations and to rule them with a rod of iron, and to trod them on the winepress of the wrath of God (19:15–16).

Interestingly, though, before Christ unfolds widespread destruction and mayhem on man, beast, and everything on the whole earth, He turns his full attention to His seven churches (Rev. 2–3). If the pusillanimous Christ of the modern churches were on the throne He would look on them lovingly and accept all their filthy sinful behavior as perfect. Not the true Christ of the Bible! He is interested in one thing: the spiritual state of His churches. He gives a failing grade to five of the seven churches and threatens them! Yes, you read right, He threatens them. He tells them that if they don't immediately repent, He will take their candlestick and leave them to die! It's obedience to the commandments or He's out of there. So, what were these five failing churches doing to anger Him? Answer: Having no zeal for God, fornication, idol worship, woman preachers, adultery, being lukewarm, being rich and arrogant.

In other words, nearly 100 percent of the so-called churches in America have some or all of the same characteristics of these five churches that had enraged their God. Here is what He is going to do to these lukewarm, apologetic, disobedient churches: "I will spew thee out of my mouth" (3:15–16). Spewing time cometh!

With the spiritual state of the churches out of the way, Christ ascends to the throne and now judgment is on (Rev. 4)! Christ steps forward as the Redeemer to pay for the sins of His people and to rid the purchased possession (earth) of the dynasties of wickedness, to cast out the rulers of the darkness of the world and prince of the power of the air, to restore the earth to its proper fertility and peace, and to bring the empire of righteousness and salvation into being. A holy eviction notice is being served on nearly all of humanity as Revelation 6 opens. The time of Satan's rule on earth with gross sin, filthiness, and abomination is over! At Christ's coming He sends forth His angels to gather the wicked tares, and casts them into a furnace of fire, and then the righteous shall shine forth as the sun. Christ is taking possession of the earth by force and moving forward His administration and assuming power. The kingdoms of this world become the kingdoms of our Lord, and of his Christ; and He shall reign forever and ever (11:15).

Once Christ ascends to the throne, He immediately starts opening the seals of the book of judgment and, bang, the four horses of the apocalypse are loosed! Christ on the white horse is loosed to conquer; the red horse, great war and all peace from the earth is taken (there will be no regard for life); the black horse, great famine; and the pale green horse, great disease will reign. These horses will devastate the people of the earth. One-fourth of the inhabitants of the world will be slain by these four horses! That means 1.7 billion corpses will litter the landscape—more than can possibly be buried! And, that's just the opener!

Then, great commotions in the fabric of nature take place: earthquakes, the sun becomes black, and so on. Then it's time for the seven angels with seven trumpets to sound. The de-creation of the earth begins to take place. One-third of the trees and grass are incinerated, one-third of the oceans and life in the sea are killed, one-third of the freshwater is poisoned, and one-third of the sun, moon, and stars are darkened. Then it really gets bad!

Creatures from hell are loosed (Rev. 9) to torment men; angels are loosed, and more earthquakes occur, and another one-third of mankind are killed. After all this, do men repent of their murders, sorceries, fornication, and thefts? No! Then seven bowls and plagues are poured into the earth and more de-creation! Satan, the false prophet, and the beast do not go quietly; instead they assemble to fight God. How stupid is that? The end of the book depicts the King of Kings and Lord of Lords on His white horse hunting down His enemies with their blood on his garments in total and complete victory over Satan and the wicked people that inhabit earth (Rev. 19). Who are the wicked? They are clearly identified: "But the fearful, and unbelieving, and the abominable, and murderers, and whoremongers, and sorcerers, and idolaters, and all liars, shall have their part in the lake which burneth with fire and brimstone: which is the second death" (21:8). Are there any who are the righteous? Yes, "Blessed are they that do his commandments, that they may have right to the tree of life, and may enter in through the gates into the city" (22:14).

The Lord is coming in judgment. Destruction is imminent. Fear God and Keep his commandments while you still can!

Brent Roper is a servant of God and member of Westboro Baptist Church, United States.

A Literal Reading of Revelation

Chris Griffin (United States)

The Revelation of John written in exile on Patmos is a fascinating prophetic work that draws the reader into future cataclysmic events that are the judgments of God, the culmination of this age, and the ushering in of the eternal state. Here, I offer a literal reading of Revelation and an identification and explanation of some pitfalls associated with other nonliteral readings.

An investigation of literal interpretation must precede a look at Revelation in particular. A literal approach to Scripture takes the text at face value, understanding that the writers used different writing styles while under the inspiration of the Holy Spirit; yet the entirety of Scripture is to be understood on a literal level—this approach must be practiced for the whole content of the Bible. For example, it is not acceptable to switch gears from a literal view to a symbolic view when focusing on a different genre of writing. In fact, to interpret it in a spiritual sense is dangerous and inconsistent at best. There are several reasons. First, it is inconsistent because other prophetic writings have come to pass in a literal, physical way. One may read the account of God's dealing with the serpent in Genesis 3 as allegorical, but the fact is that both the punishment to the serpent (crawling on his belly) and his ultimate destruction ("He shall bruise your head, and you shall bruise your heel," 3:15b) have been actualized in a literal, physical way. The same must be said about Messianic prophecy. Isaiah 53:5 uses language such as "But He was wounded for our transgressions; He was crushed for our iniquities; upon Him was the chastisement that brought us peace, and with His stripes we are healed." We can very clearly see that this prophecy came true in a literal way with the death of Jesus.

Another pitfall is that a spiritual, nonliteral interpretation allows all kinds of readings. It would be very difficult to verify or prove false any particular interpretation of Scripture. That is, without any standard of truth to measure interpretation, there would be no grounds for arguing any claim made about the meaning of a passage of Scripture.

It must be noted that John did use allegorical language when writing Revelation, as he attempted to describe what he saw; but there is no reason to think that what he saw will not come to pass in a tangible fashion. For example, there is no reason to conclude that the beast in Revelation 13 cannot or will not come to fruition in a literal way. The "beast rising up out of the sea" that John saw is no different from Daniel 7 where the "four beasts" represented real people and actual earthly kingdoms, such as Nebuchadnezzar and the Babylonians. Indeed, the beast of Revelation 13 is a man, as is evident at the end of the chapter, who is most likely the antichrist. Likewise, why is it difficult to conclude that the many types of judgments (natural disaster, etc.) outlined in Revelation will literally take place? If one believes wholeheartedly in a literal worldwide flood as the judgment of God (Genesis 6–8), why would one not read literally the final verdict of the Lord on an unrighteous world in Revelation?

The book of Revelation is often associated with the rapture of the church (1 Thessalonians 4:13–18) in which Christ comes back to take the church to be with Him. We will be translated from here to there. It is a literal event that we hope for and should "comfort one another" with these words. This concept is not foreign. In the Old Testament, we read that the translation of Enoch was a literal event as was that of Elijah. There is no reason to debate then, whether or not God could orchestrate a global translation of the church as He did with these individuals. If a spiritualist holds that the future events are of a spiritual nature, then why the physical, bodily resurrection of Jesus? The answer is simple. The prophecies and promises of God are not spiritual, but literal. The fact is that God is consistent in His purpose and writing of Scripture. It does not make logical sense that in the first 65 books of the Bible all prophecy would come to literal fulfillment (as it did), and then in the Bible's final book, prophecy would suddenly change to a spiritual fulfillment. Thus, the reader of Revelation should come to the conclusion that the events of the book will come to a literal completion in some way, shape, or form, even if the reader does not understand precisely how they will happen.

Finally, there are many spiritual truths contained within the Bible, and the writers use many methods to express those truths, including the use of symbolic, allegorical language. But I believe that even this type of language results, more often than not, in a physical fulfillment. There is no doubt that God used the unique abilities of each writer to accomplish His Word, including different writing styles. But my view is that a literal reading of Scripture should be the norm, and any secondary approach should not precede, but rather follow it.

Chris Griffin (B.A., MRE) is a Second Lieutenant and Chaplain Candidate in the National Guard, United States.

QUESTIONS

1. Why is it important for Smith to argue for the androgyny of the Lamb? Are there unintended negative consequences of this reading?
2. Compare the countercultural aspects of Goths with the countercultural aspects of the biblical text. What is your reaction to the association of the United States with Babylon?
3. Assess Roper's reading approach and rhetoric. What critiques might be offered?
4. How might one challenge Griffin's arguments for a literal reading of Revelation?

CHAPTER 40

REVELATION (PART II)

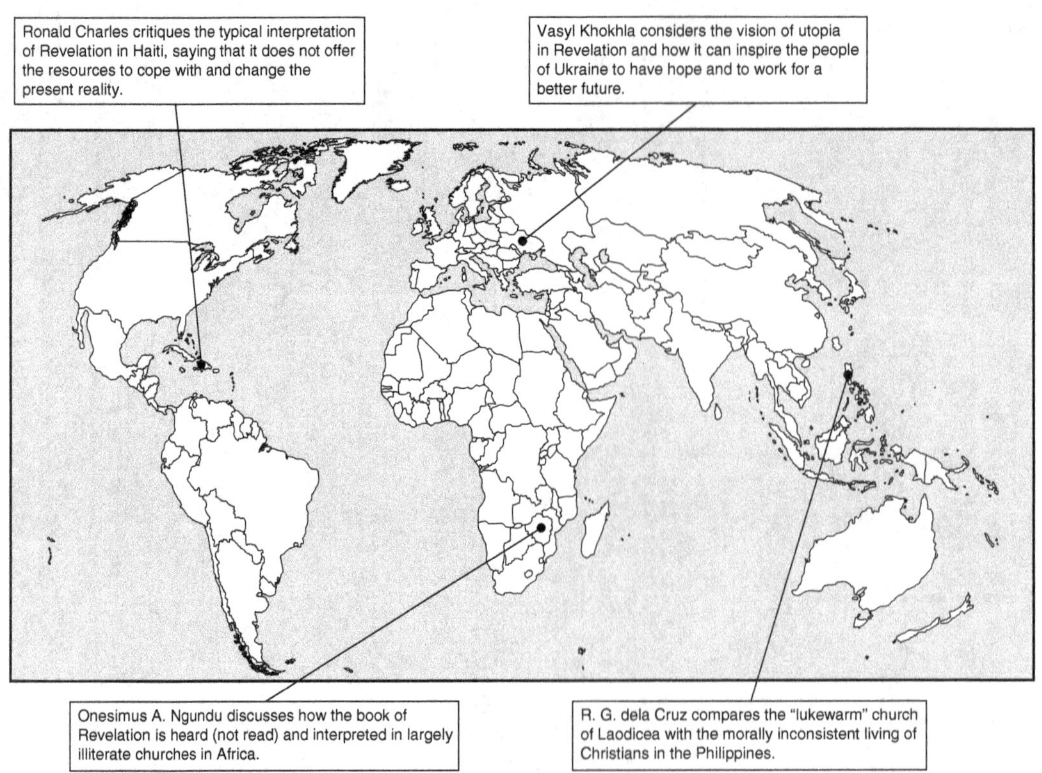

Ronald Charles critiques the typical interpretation of Revelation in Haiti, saying that it does not offer the resources to cope with and change the present reality.
Vasyl Khokhla considers the vision of utopia in Revelation and how it can inspire the people of Ukraine to have hope and to work for a better future.
Onesimus A. Ngundu discusses how the book of Revelation is heard (not read) and interpreted in largely illiterate churches in Africa.
R. G. dela Cruz compares the "lukewarm" church of Laodicea with the morally inconsistent living of Christians in the Philippines.

READINGS

Interpreting Revelation in Largely Illiterate Churches in Africa
Onesimus A. Ngundu

Ukraine and the Vision of Utopia in Revelation
Vasyl Khokhla

A Critique of the Typical Interpretation of Revelation in Haiti
Ronald Charles

The "Lukewarm" Church of Laodicea and Morally Inconsistent Christians in the Philippines
R. G. dela Cruz

Interpreting Revelation in Largely Illiterate Churches in Africa

Onesimus A. Ngundu (Zimbabwe)

Reading and studying the book of Revelation is a privilege that the original audience did not have. They had to take it all in aurally, probably in more than one hearing (1:3). The book of Revelation was designed to be read aloud in a congregational setting since it was sent to seven churches (1:11). *The one who reads* reflects the early form of worship where a reader would read the Scriptures aloud on the Lord's Day. At that time, only the reader had a copy of the letter or of a particular Old Testament book.

Revelation 1:3 declares the blessedness of the one who reads the book or letter of Revelation to a congregation and of those who *hear* it and take its message to heart. We assume that the original recipients understood the message of the book of Revelation that was read to them because they were encouraged to "*keep* what is written in it." Logically, they could only rightly keep or obey what they would have understood read aloud and interpreted to them at their Christian gatherings.

As someone involved in theological education and church ministry in the Majority World (a much more appropriate term than "Third World"), I can testify that most Christians in the Majority World do not possess a Bible, Bible commentaries, or any Bible study tools. They simply cannot afford them. As I was growing up in a Christian home in rural Zimbabwe, the only Bible reading I ever heard and listened to was either at school or at church services on Sundays. Even when I later became a Christian at a mission boarding high school, I could not afford one. Thus, most Africans totally depend on the public reading and preaching of the Bible at places of worship for biblical instruction and spiritual encouragement.

An African Initiated Church (AIC) is one started independently in Africa by Africans and not by missionaries from another continent. There are thousands of such churches (more than 10,000 in South Africa alone) and each one has its own characteristics. At a typical open-air AIC worship service (AICs prefer open-air gatherings instead of church buildings), the designated Scripture reader stands in front of the congregation next to the leader or preacher. After reading each verse, the reader pauses to allow the leader to interpret the text. Ordinary members, most of them illiterate, totally depend on biblical instruction from what they hear at such worship gatherings.

Indeed, illiteracy continues to plague Africa. In sub-Saharan Africa, primary school enrollment has declined from 58 percent to 50 percent because members of the AICs deny their children school education. They also deny them any hospital treatment or immunization. There are two basic reasons for this. First, AICs have always been suspicious of white missionaries, their teachings, and their motives for establishing institutions in Africa. It was Western mission organizations which introduced school education, hospitals, and clinics in the European colonies in Africa. Second, AICs, as "Spirit Churches," believe that the Holy Spirit is the only teacher of all people. They strongly believe that they and their children only need God (or the Holy Spirit) as their teacher. They try to pattern their lifestyle after that of the children of Israel: no schools, no hospitals, and so forth. Men in AICs mostly wear sandals or sometimes walk barefoot. Their religious practices are based on Old Testament laws and practices. Remarkably, they are the fastest growing church group in Africa today.

Members of AICs unquestionably look up to their spiritual leaders as prophets or messengers of God. They believe that just as the children of Israel heard from God through Moses and the prophets, they too can hear from God through their leaders as they listen to them read and interpret the Word of God.

The character of God who initially revealed the message of Revelation to Jesus Christ who communicated that message to the seven churches in Asia Minor through John should lead us to believe that the message was intended to be understood especially by its original recipients who were apparently quite familiar with apocalyptic literature. It is always good to keep in mind that the literary genre of any literature is determined by its intended recipients. In other words, the original recipients, unlike us today, were familiar with the apocalyptic language and symbols that characterize the book of Revelation. The frustration and confusion we all experience in trying to figure out the meaning of Revelation's symbolism and imagery results from the fact that we are far removed from the time and place when the use of apocalyptic genre was a common practice.

Apocalypses typically contain curious visions whose meaning is not clear until they are explained, usually by an angelic personage. Often the whole apocalypse depends on the contribution made by the heavenly guide. It is not unusual to have God himself pictured as contributing to the apocalyptic message. In the book of Revelation this kind of explanation appears occasionally. For example, in 17:7 an angel explains the mystery of the scarlet woman and the beast on which she rides. But the general practice is simply to narrate the vision and to allow the hearer or reader to work out the meaning. This is where the challenge for any modern reader of Revelation lies.

It is here that AICs leaders and preachers would benefit from some form of theological education and sound Bible commentaries if they are to correctly interpret the symbolism that characterizes the book of Revelation and other apocalyptic sections of the bible. Instead, the leaders believe that their insight is instantaneously God-given as they confidently assign some weird meaning to symbols and images of Revelation. Unfortunately, such imaginative interpretation of apocalyptic literature results in wrong views of the end-times (eschatology).

The purpose of Revelation is stated in 22:6–20. It is to encourage Christians to remain faithful until the end, even if it means martyrdom, since they will also be raised from the dead at the second coming of Christ and live with him in the eternal new kingdom. The focus on Jesus Christ's triumph over death through his glorious resurrection means that Revelation is a book that has far more to say about the exercise of power than about the manifestation of divine love. Divine power is demonstrated throughout the book, even in the vindication of the Lamb who was a victim. It is that power of unmasking everything that runs like a thread throughout the vision of the book.

Indeed, although AIC leaders may offer for their (mostly illiterate) congregations interpretations of Revelation that are uninformed, they nonetheless certainly find encouragement in God's ultimate victory over suffering, sickness, and death. It is quite common to hear them sing in their Sunday worship services choruses and hymns that exalt the all-powerful and almighty God as portrayed in the book of Revelation.

Onesimus A. Ngundu (Ph.D., University of Cambridge; Th.D., Dallas Theological Seminary) is currently a Research Assistant at the University of Cambridge, England.

UKRAINE AND THE VISION OF UTOPIA IN REVELATION

Vasyl Khokhla (Ukraine)

Throughout the ages, people have nurtured the hopes for the ideal, for the perfect, for the high and exalted. Concepts such as democracy, rule of law, peace, and prosperity have been considered as worthwhile aims for the evolvement of steady and prosperous societies. The current climate of "globalization" embodies the ideas of universal peace and harmony. Although such concepts and ideals are unattainable in their pure forms, it does not, and should not, stop people from hoping, believing, and aspiring toward these praiseworthy goals.

A similar idea can be found in the apocalyptic book of Revelation, particularly in its final chapters which describe the ultimate victory of God and the coming of God's new kingdom. It is a dramatic vision in which God "will wipe away every tear" where there will be "no more death or mourning or crying or pain" because the "old order of things has passed away" and God is "making all things new" (21:3–5). Life in the "new Jerusalem" will indeed be one where there is no thirst (21:6), no evil (21:8; 22:15), no darkness (21:25; 22:5), and no death (22:5, 17). This is utopia—a perfect place. And isn't this a picture of what people are aspiring to today? Scientists are revolutionizing their methods of study and research to invent the cure for every kind of disease and ailment; ultimately, they desire to reverse the aging process so that we can conquer death. People are weary of war; they want peace and security. They fight crime, corruption, and other forms of evil. The United Nations, for example, has put forth Millennium Development Goals, one of the aims of which is to eradicate abject poverty by 2015.

But yet for many countries, including my native Ukraine, such a vision remains far from reality. One of the declared goals of Ukraine is to join the European Union (EU), which the people believe will help to alleviate the ills of the notorious era of Soviet rule. Yet, Ukraine has been unable to meet these objectives. Numerous problems continue to exist within Ukraine, preventing its acceptance into the EU. Political corruption is rampant. Politicians are dishonest, constantly scheming to increase their own power and wealth at the expense of the people. The legal system is equally bad, with its fraudulent law enforcement and unfair court system. Many social problems are prevalent—including widespread alcoholism as people try to escape the dreary reality. In fact, according to the Corruption Perception Index by the renowned Transparency International, Ukraine is rated 2.4 (on a scale from 1 to 10, with 1 being most corrupt); it shares its place with such countries as Nigeria, Sierra Leone, and Togo.

When we read Revelation, we find that there are certain types of people who are left out of God's kingdom—they must be expelled if the utopian vision is to become a reality. These are the cowards, the immoral, the murders, idolaters, liars, and all those who love and practice falsehood (21:8; 22:15). Might we say that it is these types of people in Ukraine—our corrupt leaders—who are preventing the amelioration of our government, of our nation, who are disabling our move toward a better society?

We can also ask if it's worthwhile for the Ukrainian citizenry to keep on hoping, or should all such goals and aspirations simply be abandoned as unattainable? Though the forces of evil are significant, the book of Revelation offers hope that one day Goodness and Truth will prevail. God wins. God destroys his wicked enemies (Rev. 19–20) and institutes an idyllic world for those who are on God's side. This can inspire and motivate the people of Ukraine not only to maintain hope for the future but to work diligently to "make everything new" (21:5), to follow the Rider on the White Horse (19:11) in the fight for political, economic, and social reforms.

Indeed, human striving for the ideal should not be abandoned since it is that compelling force which inspires people to constant improvement. Plato said that our ideas have the capacity to transcend the outside reality. He also advocated the idea that people can achieve their goals and live up to the high standards if they try to understand the things beyond the limits of the human mind. Even if we cannot achieve the ideal, our aim should be to approach it as closely as possible. In a similar vein, Albert Einstein is reported to have said, "Some people do not believe in miracles. I would rather be the one who does, for otherwise life would be very boring."

From my perspective as a Ukrainian now living in the United States, the United States became the land of opportunity because people did not lose their belief in success. They, we might say, pursued their vision of utopia in which each individual has a favorable opportunity at life, liberty, and happiness. Of course, the United States still faces many social problems, but it has attained a level of success that I hope my native Ukraine can also reach. The biggest difference between the two countries remains governmental structures. The United States has managed to make democracy work. It may not be perfect—as Winston Churchill once said, "Democracy is not the best form of government, but so far nothing better has been invented"—but it has brought a relatively high quality of life. The United States, I suspect, has done so in part because of their religious, specifically Christian, heritage. The United States has perceived themselves to be a place reminiscent of Revelation 21:3: "Now the dwelling of God is with men, and he will live with them. They will be his people, and God himself will be with them and be their God." As it says on American currency, "In God we trust." Perhaps this is at least part of the reason why America is much closer to the utopia of Revelation than Ukraine.

As someone who desires peace and prosperity in Ukraine, we should not abandon the hope we find in Revelation, even if true utopia will never be realized. To believe and pursue the vision of Revelation does not guarantee that it will become a reality, but it can inspire, motivate, and give the hope that is so much needed in Ukraine and many other places around the globe where murderers, liars, idolaters, and those who love and practice falsehood thwart the vision of utopia.

Vasyl Khokhla was born in Kalush in Western Ukraine; he is currently working on a law degree in Ukraine and a finance degree in the United States.

A Critique of the Typical Interpretation of Revelation in Haiti

Ronald Charles (Haiti)

The mention of "Apocalypse" has a certain resonance in people's imagination. For those of us from the Third World it brings disturbing images of dictators, bloodshed, coups d'état, ecological disaster, boat people, and abject poverty. For many in Haiti, the Apocalypse is now. Famine, hurricanes, looting, violence, corruption, rioting, and prostitution characterize the daily nightmare of many poor in this small and impoverished country. Thus the question becomes, As a Haitian and as a Christian how can *I* read the book of Revelation *today*? I grew up in Haiti in a Baptist church and then, in my teenage years, moved to a Pentecostal church until I left the country in my late 20s to undertake graduate work, which I am now doing in biblical studies in Canada. The usual reading of the book of Revelation in Haiti that I am about to describe is what I grew up with, and it is this common, debilitating reading that is still the main—or the sole—reading of the book in the Haitian context.

The book of Revelation is written out of the experience of a minority in the colonized Roman Empire. It speaks of sufferings and of struggles with which people from the Third World are too familiar because their communities share with Revelation's addressees a longing for justice, for peace, and for the well-being of humanity. Although the text of Revelation is close at heart to Third World Christian communities, it is also interpreted in ways that are devastating in some Third World contexts. Haiti is a case in point.

Even as a "son of Haiti" myself, I regard it a strange place. It is difficult to comprehend its realities. Many people there live as if they were in a fantastic world where demons and angels, God and Satan, the living and the dead are not so far apart. This extraordinary existential condition makes the whole Haitian social reality fascinating and puzzling at the same time. The Apocalypse is now, but that does not stop Haitians from partying, laughing, dancing, and living with the reality of the supernatural, and to hope for a *demen miyò* (a tomorrow that is going to be better than today) because *Bondye bon* (God is good).

Reading the book of Revelation is an odd exercise for a Haitian. According to many of them, it's about God and Satan, angels and demons, battles and victories; all of which they have some familiarity with in real life. The typical interpretation of Revelation in Haiti is that we are living at the brink of time, that the end is beginning to dawn on our island of 9 million souls. As Christians we need to live a life pleasing to God and not miss the call of the last trumpets in order to ensure that we are caught up in the rapture of the church. There is usually a certain fancy about the idea of leaving the mess behind, of going to glory to live a life of security and of plenty. The usual thinking is that life is extremely difficult and the best way out is to project oneself into a blissful kind of future. The Lord will come to take his own in a sudden rapture, and the rest who did not live up to the biblical standards will be left behind. For those who did not make it to heaven at the rapture, they are to endure the great tribulation and wait until the battle of Armageddon for the final victory of God. Then, those who resisted the Antichrist during the terrible years will be rescued by God and be saved. Afterwards, a thousand years of worldwide peace and security will be ushered in under the Lordship and authority of Christ before the final release of Satan and the ultimate victory of God.

But there is also a second way in which the book of Revelation intersects with life in Haiti. In Protestant churches certain ambivalence has always existed within the in-groups as they see themselves and as they relate to the society at large. The typical social dynamic of internal class divisions based on income, culture, and race spills over in some large Protestant churches in Haiti that are situated mostly in Port-au-Prince (the capital city) to serve middle-class clienteles. Thus, just as Haitian society is greatly divided by political, economical, and even racial factions, so the church in Haiti is greatly divided by denominational divisions and rivalries.

Unfortunately this kind of "combat myth" mentality and horizontal violence as portrayed in Revelation is not far from the minds of many evangelical Christians in Haiti. The predominant mentality of many Protestant churches is that of *Pa m pi bon* (mine is better). The rejection of Christian groups perceived to be different and the diabolizing of other religions is a common and accepted phenomenon in most Christian churches in Haiti.

Many evangelical pastors have used violent language against the religion of Vodou and its practitioners. Many Vodou priests or *ougan* have been lynched, stoned, or burned alive and those horrible acts were perpetuated with the blessings of the church at large in Haiti. Many Haitian Christians (the so-called evangelicals with whom I am more familiar) take a certain pleasure in pointing to the cataclysmic destruction that will befall unbelievers. They divide the world between good and evil, between those anointed to act as agents of God battling the Antichrist, attacking hypocrites and castigating the corrupt, and those who act as agents of Satan. They have a clear agenda to send to hell all who do not share their readings of some particular texts. Usually, the language they use is one not only of exclusion, hatred, and fear, but also a call for apocalyptic violence, in short, the language of war reminiscent of Revelation.

Unfortunately, this common reading of Revelation in Haiti offers nothing empowering to change the present. This uninformed reading has the potential to keep Haiti in its apocalypse forever, while doing two kinds of damage. First, by insisting on a futuristic rapture, it can pacify a population that is otherwise known for its resistance. Second, the combat myth attitude directed against other groups with different religious sentiments can be fatal in a land that has experienced too much violence in its history. It is unfortunate that many in the Christian church in Haiti are caught up in endless debates about the end-times, and about identifying who the Antichrist might be, and are looking at world events to figure out if the time of the rapture is close or not. What is important in this kind of reading is not to worry about global warming, ecological disaster, or any urgent matter that is menacing our lives today, but to hide in a spiritual cocoon in order not to face the overwhelming present realities.

The overall message of the book of Revelation offers an alternative in terms of imagination and faith for the purpose of facing the practical problems of marginalized groups in the here and now (not the hereafter). By renewing his audience's imagination, the writer of Revelation aims to create a new reality to help his communities cope with the uncertainties of the present. Revelation is, in this sense, a call to resistance, to perseverance in the time of persecution, and to faithfulness to God and to Jesus Christ. Revelation can speak comfort to the people of faith in Haiti so that they can imagine, as the text had aimed to produce for the first recipients, a new reality in opposition to the world of the present in its crisis. Indeed, a different reading offers hope for the apocalyptic situation in Haiti, not just for tomorrow, but for today also. We can take this reading/hearing and be empowered by it for social, political, and economic changes now.

Ronald Charles is a Ph.D. candidate in the Department and Centre for the Study of Religion at University of Toronto, Ontario, Canada; he spent most of his early life in Haiti.

THE "LUKEWARM" CHURCH OF LAODICEA AND MORALLY INCONSISTENT CHRISTIANS IN THE PHILIPPINES

R. G. dela Cruz (Philippines)

The Philippines is a predominately Christian nation, with more than 90 percent of its population belonging to the Christian faith. But there is a fracture between what we say and what we do. The phrase "split-level Christianity" as it applies to Filipino Christian spirituality and values was first articulated by Jesuit priest Jaime Bulatao in the mid-1960s. The "split" is between what is expected and required of Christians and what is commonly accepted in Filipino culture and politics. This so-called "split-level" Christian value of the Filipinos is reminiscent of Revelation 3:14–22 where the Church of Laodicea is judged for being neither hot nor cold. Split-level Christianity results in a country that, like the Laodiceans, is "lukewarm": We do not live like a people who are Christians.

Filipinos have gone through many difficulties as a people. During the Spanish, American, and Japanese colonizations, the Filipinos were oppressed. After gaining independence immediately after World War II, the new state struggled to survive. There was great effort exerted by the people to preserve democracy when the Martial Law was declared. Then the People Power of the EDSA Revolution was successful in a peaceful revolt to bring back democracy. Today, the

Philippines are seen by many as the "ill person" of the region. Many Filipinos see themselves as people in need of healing. The nation is disadvantaged in globalization. The impoverished population struggles to survive daily; there is displacement of various ethnicities. One of the ways to survive is for Filipinos to migrate and become OFWs (Overseas Filipino Workers) in different parts of the world. For many, migration is not a luxury; it is a necessity to survive. Thus, it is common to hear about Filipinos being exploited. To witness suffering is common to Filipino eyes. There is a big gap between the wealthy and the underprivileged.

Filipino religiosity is formed by these national encounters of domination and change. Naturally, religion, culture, and politics are intertwined. But there are far too many problems that exist in the Philippines—problems that could be overcome if Christian principles and ethics were followed, instead of allowing "lukewarm" values and morality to continue. For example, when Filipino politicians claim in their campaigns that they are *makadios*, *makabayan*, *makatao* (godly or pious, patriotic or nationalistic, humane or humanitarian), they are sincere. And yet they do not commonly see graft (abuse of power for personal gain) and corruption as wrong; rather, politicians and voters tend to see graft and corruption as unavoidable ingredients of politics. No administration in the Philippine government has solved this problem. But since we are a Christian nation—again, over 90 percent of the population claims they are Catholic or Protestant—something must be done.

The problem for Filipino Christianity is that their lukewarmness, their inconsistency, has become so ingrained in them that they are no longer conscious of it. They have for so long accepted so much that flies in the face of their Christian ideals and values that they fail to perceive the tension. It's part of the culture. It's taken for granted, accepted as the norm.

In light of this tension, Revelation 3:14–22 can be appropriated and read to challenge Filipinos in general to clear up the split and contribute positively to Filipino values. It is well recognized by Filipinos that confronting the split-level attitude is necessary to bring positive orderliness in the Philippine society. Revelation 3:22 is confrontational: "He who has an ear, let him hear what the Spirit says to the churches." There is no mincing of words. It is a straight rebuke of their lukewarm attitude. There is nothing positive said about the Laodiceans. The heavenly Christ says, "I know your works: you are neither cold nor hot. Would that you were either cold or hot! So, because you are lukewarm, and neither hot nor cold, I will spit you out of my mouth" (3:15–16). Repentance and discipline are necessary to deal with the problem: "Those whom I love, I reprove and discipline, so be zealous and repent" (v. 19).

The split-level value system must be addressed head-on. Filipinos must deal with the issue by separating cultural tradition from religious convictions. Establishing a firm separation is the key step toward a solution. When this happens, there is a deliverance from sickness and corruption in society by allowing the values of the heavenly Christ to take over: "Behold, I stand at the door and knock. If anyone hears my voice and opens the door, I will come in to him and eat with him, and he with me" (v. 20). The supper echoes the idea of the Lord's Supper where the continuing and conscious presence of Christ is both symbolized and remembered. There is a promise of harmony and victory (v. 21) for the Filipino who would dine with the heavenly Christ and allow him to take control based on his principles and values.

R. G. dela Cruz is Lecturer at Asia Pacific Theological Seminary in Baguio City, Philippines; he is an ordained minister of the South Central Cordillera District Council of the Philippines General Council of the Assemblies of God.

QUESTIONS

1. Try listening to a few chapters of Revelation. How is the listening experience different from reading the text?
2. Compare the peace and utopia described in Revelation to that desired by Khokhla for Ukraine.
3. Does the biblical text support the use of violence against practitioners of other religions? Does it offer hope for coping with present realities of suffering and evil?
4. What is the "firm separation" dela Cruz envisions as the solution to "split-level Christianity"?

CREDITS

Chapter 1: p. 2; Fang Li (ed.). *Imperial Readings of the Taiping Era*, 977–983; p. 7; Desmond Tutu. *No Future without Forgiveness* [2000]. Image.

Chapter 2: pp. 11–12; Saint Ambrose. *Hexameron*; p. 14; Ludwig Feuerbach. *The Essence of Christianity* [New York: Harper and Row, 1957], 287.

Chapter 3: p. 21; *The Intrareligious Dialogue* [New York: Mahwah/Paulist Press, 1978], 2.

Chapter 4: p. 21; Abdullah Yusuf Ali. *An English Interpretation of the Holy Quran* [Lushena Books, 2001]; p. 32; Julia Ward Howe's *Mother's Day Proclamation,* 1870.

Chapter 5: p. 40; *New Revised Standard Version Bible*, copyright 1989, Division of Christian Education of the National Council of the Churches of Christ in the United States of America. Used by permission. All rights reserved.

Chapter 7: p. 57; *New Revised Standard Version Bible*, copyright 1989, Division of Christian Education of the National Council of the Churches of Christ in the United States of America. Used by permission. All rights reserved.

Chapter 8: p. 70; "Familism and Ancestor Veneration: A Look at Chinese Funeral Rites," *Missiology* 24 O [1996]: 516.

Chapter 11: p. 96; *New Revised Standard Version Bible*, copyright 1989, Division of Christian Education of the National Council of the Churches of Christ in the United States of America. Used by permission. All rights reserved.

Chapter 12: p. 102; Chris White (ed.). *Nineteenth Century Writings on Homosexuality: A Sourcebook* [London: Routledge, 1999]; pp. 102, 104; *New Revised Standard Version Bible*, copyright 1989, Division of Christian Education of the National Council of the Churches of Christ in the United States of America. Used by permission. All rights reserved.

Chapter 13: p. 113; *New Revised Standard Version Bible*, copyright 1989, Division of Christian Education of the National Council of the Churches of Christ in the United States of America. Used by permission. All rights reserved; p. 114; Jesse Russell and Ronald Cohn. *Vayu Purana* [Books on Demand, 2012]; p. 114; Mahatma Jyatorao Foole, *Gulamgiri*, 1873.

Chapter 14: pp. 118, 123, and 124; *New Revised Standard Version Bible*, copyright 1989, Division of Christian Education of the National Council of the Churches of Christ in the United States of America. Used by permission. All rights reserved; p. 123; *New International Version Bible* [Zondervan, 2011].

Chapter 15: pp. 126, 143; *New Revised Standard Version Bible*, copyright 1989, Division of Christian Education of the National Council of the Churches of Christ in the United States of America. Used by permission. All rights reserved.

Chapter 17: p. 143; *New Revised Standard Version Bible*, copyright 1989, Division of Christian Education of the National Council of the Churches of Christ in the United States of America. Used by permission. All rights reserved.

Chapter 18: pp. 154, 156; *New Revised Standard Version Bible*, copyright 1989, Division of Christian Education of the National Council of the Churches of Christ in the United States of America. Used by permission. All rights reserved.

Chapter 19: p. 162; *A Testimony of Our Inexhaustible Treasure*. American Council of the Ramabai Mukti Mission.

Chapter 20: p. 172; *New Revised Standard Version Bible,* copyright 1989, Division of Christian Education of the National Council of the Churches of Christ in the United States of America. Used by permission. All rights reserved.

Chapter 21: p. 183; *New Revised Standard Version Bible*, copyright 1989, Division of Christian Education of the National Council of the Churches of Christ in the United States of America. Used by permission. All rights reserved.

Chapter 22: pp. 188, 189, 190; *New Revised Standard Version Bible*, copyright 1989, Division of Christian Education of the National Council of the Churches of Christ in the United States of America. Used by permission. All rights reserved.

Chapter 23: pp. 197, 198; *New Revised Standard Version Bible*, copyright 1989, Division of Christian Education of the National Council of the Churches of Christ in the United States of America. Used by permission. All rights reserved.

Chapter 25: p. 212; Translated by Abdullah Yusaf Ali; p. 212; Abdullah Yusuf Ali. *The Koran* [Wordsworth, 2001]; p. 214; Reprinted by permission from The Taoist Experience by Livia Kohn, the State University of New York Press ©1993, State University of New York. All rights reserved; p. 218; Frederick Buechner, *Wishful Thinking*.

Chapter 26: pp. 223, 224; Accra Confession. *World Alliance of Reformed Churches* [2004].

Chapter 27: p. 231; Douglass, "The General Assembly of the Free Church" in *The Frederick Douglass Papers: 1841–46*, ed. J. W. Blassingame, vol. 1 of *The Frederick Douglass Papers;* Series 1: Speeches, Debates and Interviews [New Haven and London: Yale University Press, 1979], 427; quotation marks added to offset biblical quotes, Hebrews 13:3 and Luke 10:32 respectively); p. 232; *The Frederick Douglass Papers*; series 1: Speeches, Debates and Interviews; vol. 2, 1847–54; ed. J. W. Blassingame [New Haven and London: Yale University Press, 1982], 99–100; p. 232; *The Frederick Douglass Papers*, vol. 1, 369.

Chapter 28: p. 241; [Bangalore: TPI, 2007], 488; pp. 244, 245; *New Revised Standard Version Bible*, copyright 1989, Division of Christian Education of the National Council of the Churches of Christ in the United States of America. Used by permission. All rights reserved.

Chapter 29: p. 250; *New Revised Standard Version Bible*, copyright 1989, Division of Christian Education of the National Council of the Churches of Christ in the United States of America. Used by permission. All rights reserved.

Chapter 31: p. 268; Abdullah Yusuf Ali. *The Koran* [Wordsworth, 2001]; p. 270; *New Revised Standard Version Bible*, copyright 1989, Division of Christian Education of the National Council of the Churches of Christ in the United States of America. Used by permission. All rights reserved.

Chapter 32: pp. 274, 280 and, 281; *New Revised Standard Version Bible*, copyright 1989, Division of Christian Education of the National Council of the Churches of Christ in the United States of America. Used by permission. All rights reserved; p. 275; Muhammed Ibn Ismaiel Al-Bukhari. *The Sahih of Imam Bukhari*. Translated by Muhammad M. Khan [Houston: Dar-us-Salam, 1997]; p. 276; *Chinese Proverb*. Translated by the author; p. 281; Edwards, Jonathan. *Sinners in the Hands of an Angry God*, 1741.

Chapter 33: p. 283; Neil Darragh. *At Home in the Earth* [Auckland: Ascent Publications, 2000], 124; pp. 283, 290; *New Revised Standard Version Bible*, copyright 1989, Division of Christian Education of the National Council of the Churches of Christ in the United States of America. Used by permission. All rights reserved; p. 284; *The Cosmic Circle: Jesus and Ecology* [Dublin: Columbia Press, 2004], 125–126; p. 287; *Kitab-i-Iqan: The Book of Certitude*, Translated by Shoghi Effendi [Wilmette, Illinois: USA Baha'i Publishing Trust, 1989].

Chapter 34: p. 300; *The Political Dictionary* [Pyongyang: Social Science Publishing, 1973].

Chapter 35: pp. 308, 309; *New Revised Standard Version Bible*, copyright 1989, Division of Christian Education of the National Council of the Churches of Christ in the United States of America. Used by permission. All rights reserved.

Chapter 36: p. 312; *Re-reading Paul: A Guidelines for Christian Clergy and Teachers.* Edited by Council of Christians and Jews [Victoria, Australia, 1995]. Published by www.jcrelations.net; p. 318; *New Revised Standard Version Bible*, copyright 1989, Division of Christian Education of the National Council of the Churches of Christ in the United States of America. Used by permission. All rights reserved.

Chapter 37: p. 322; The Social Science Publisher, *The Political Dictionary* [Pyongyang: The Social Science Publisher, 1973]; pp. 323, 325; *New Revised Standard Version Bible*, copyright 1989, Division of Christian Education of the National Council of the Churches of Christ in the United States of America. Used by permission. All rights reserved; p. 324; *Theology for the Community of God* [Grand Rapids: Eerdmans, 1994], pp. 233, 324; Eugene Peterson. *The Message Bible*; p. 325; C. S. Lewis. *The Screwtape Letters* [New York: Macmillan, 1961].

Chapter 38: p. 333; *Griffiths A New Vision of Reality: Western Science, Eastern Mysticism and Christian faith* [Springfield, IL: Templegate, 1990], 122; p. 333; *Return to the Center* [Springfield, IL: Templegate, 2002], 60–61; p. 334; *The Bhagavad-Gita*; p. 334; Griffiths, *Return to the Center*, 74; p. 335; *New Revised Standard Version Bible*, copyright 1989, Division of Christian Education of the National Council of the Churches of Christ in the United States of America. Used by permission. All rights reserved.

Chapter 39: pp. 340, 345, and 346; *New Revised Standard Version Bible*, copyright 1989, Division of Christian Education of the National Council of the Churches of Christ in the United States of America. Used by permission. All rights reserved.

Chapter 40: p. 351; Albert Einstein; p. 352; Winston Churchill.